THEORIES OF RELIGION
A READER

Edited by
Seth D. Kunin

with Jonathan Miles-Watson

EDINBURGH UNIVERSITY PRESS

© Selection and editorial material
Seth D. Kunin, 2006. The texts are
reprinted by permission of other publishers;
the acknowledgements on pp. 513–16
constitute an extension of this copyright page.

Edinburgh University Press Ltd
22 George Square, Edinburgh

Typeset in Sabon and Gill Sans
by TechBooks, New Delhi, India, and
printed and bound in Great Britain by
MPG Books Ltd, Bodmin, Cornwall

A CIP record for this book is available from
the British Library

ISBN-10 0 7486 2000 1 (hardback)
ISBN-13 978 0 7486 2000 5 (hardback)
ISBN-10 0 7486 2001 X (paperback)
ISBN-13 978 0 7486 2001 2 (paperback)

The right of the contributors to be
identified as authors of this work
has been asserted in accordance with the
Copyright, Designs and Patents Act 1988.

Published with the support of the Edinburgh University Scholarly Publishing
Initiatives Fund.

CONTENTS

CONTENTS

INTRODUCTION

Although the word 'religion' is used throughout the full range of discourse (popular and academic) in Western society, both about itself and about other societies, the exact definition of the term has provided an ongoing challenge to scholars – with seemingly as many definitions as there are scholars of the subject. The problems associated with defining this term were brought into sharp contrast at the recent meeting of the British Association for the Study of Religion. The keynote speaker set this very question as the primary issue for debate and challenged whether the basis upon which many of the established definitions of religion were set could be defended on academic grounds within either a modern or post-modern discourse. Other speakers raised the question of whether religion actually exists as a separable and identifiable object of study. Whether religion exists and whether it can be adequately defined are the central issues for religious studies and in fact they are questions that go to the very heart of the existence of religious studies as an academic discipline.

The study of religion(s) and more specifically the problems relating to the definition of religion have been found in a wide range of disciplines and approaches. These disciplines have ranged from the specifically theological to the broad humanistic or social-scientific traditions. While the presuppositions underlying these approaches are often specific to the particular discipline and the types of question and issue significant to it, there are several trajectories that are common to many of them. These commonalities are related to the historical traditions out of which modern disciplines have emerged, the movement of ideas among the disciplinary approaches, and the nature of the economic and social conditions that form the foundation of academia today.

These issues go to the heart of how one might organise a reader on the theories of religion. As discussed below, the theories could have a number of different organisational structures. We could organise them based on the type of definition or on a thematic basis. We have chosen on the whole, however, to retain a disciplinary structure. This is primarily due to the fact that while the forms of definition and the themes cross-cut all of the disciplines, there are specific trajectories of argumentation that give the different disciplines a coherence that would be lost if the material was organised on a different basis. The introductory section, however, does not attempt to divide the material on the basis of discipline, which at the time the sources were written would be largely anachronistic. The material chosen for that section is in many senses the common inheritance of all of the subsequent approaches and thus should be understood in that foundational sense. In many cases the material included raises the questions that both form the continuing arguments within the study of religion and in another sense create many of the intellectual problems with which that study continues to struggle.

In considering the organisation and content of this volume one additional issue needs to be highlighted, that is, the comprehensiveness of coverage. This issue is clearly significant both at the level of range of disciplines and equally within those disciplines chosen for inclusion. At the level of discipline we have chosen to focus this volume on disciplines engaging in work related to or emerging from the empirical study of religion or religions – thus the focus is on the broadly social-scientific. This narrowing of focus is due to the attempt to highlight a coherence of issues and arguments – the disciplines chosen largely attempt to analyse the same material and work within similar modes of argumentation. They also address questions related to theories of religion as a whole rather than explaining or justifying the basis or existence of a particular religion. We have therefore chosen not to include theories of religion that are consciously theological (though we do include approaches that have theological implications) as these approaches are established on a different argumentative structure. Some might argue that in doing this we are ignoring the insider's understanding of religion, particularly their own. While this is true we would justify this exclusion on the basis that these theories tend to be based on the understanding of a single tradition and are not seen as being generally applicable (often there is a distinction in approach between how one views one's own tradition and how other traditions are viewed). The second reason is based on the nature of argumentation – the disciplines included all have arguments with ultimately an empirical basis while theological approaches usually base them on non-empirical presuppositions.

FORMS OF DEFINITION

At the most basic level it is possible to categorise most definitions or discussions with implied definitions into three ideal types: essentialist, substantialist and functionalist – with the clear proviso that many of the definitions will have aspects of more than one type. The essentialist mode of definition seeks to determine the essence of the object being studied – it is this essence that gives the object its essential nature. Essentialist definitions tend to focus on religion as arising from some unique and essential aspect of the human being or the human experience. Thus they might point to the experience of some transcendental other as the basis for the origins and existence of religion. In more humanistic approaches they might point to some aspect of human psychology or the biological structure of the brain as the basis for defining religion. Thus, an example of the first type is found in Rudolf Otto (see pages 75–85). He defines religion in relation to experience of the Holy, an essential human faculty that enables the apprehension of the Holy, which is a transcendent other. An example of the second type is found in Sigmund Freud (see pages 53–62). He defines religion as arising due to human psychology – and thus universal to all human beings. In *Totem and Taboo*, for example, he suggests that religion arises in relation to the universal Oedipus complex.

While essentialist definitions are not intrinsically problematic, there are several interrelated problems or issues that are found in many of them. The most basic problem is found in relation to the element being essentialised. In those definitions that focus their attention on objects external to the human being or human society it is often impossible to do more than posit the existence of these objects – they are by (internal) definition beyond the possibility of human study or even understanding. These definitions, while in many cases recapitulating the internal believer's point of view, do not provide the basis for academic definition or comparative analysis by those who stand outside the circle of belief or experience. They move to the realm of theology discourse either in a broad or narrow sense – relating to belief rather than academic analysis. Even where theological approaches attempt to include a wide range of religions within their ambit, they involve a choice or emphasis on the aspect of significance to the particular tradition or approach from which they arise. Thus, unless it was demonstrable that the specific elements essentialised were indeed present, and equally significant to other internal views (why should we privilege one internal view over another?), there would be no reason to accept the definition as presenting anything more than a definition of a particular theological position from a specific time and cultural context. Ultimately this form of definition is problematic because it is not falsifiable, that is, it is based on an essential object whose existence cannot be tested or ascertained.

A different though equally significant problem is associated with approaches that essentialise some aspect of the individual psychology or biology. While these approaches emphasise the psychological/biological unity of humanity, that is, that genetically and therefore biologically and, arguably, psychologically all human beings are almost identical, in some instantiations of the approach the element suggested is arguably not a universal aspect of either biology or psychology. This problem is particularly associated with approaches like that of Freud which attribute the origin and persistence of religion to a specific psychological complex, that is, the Oedipus complex. Ethnographic evidence, however, suggests that the Oedipus complex is not universal and thus cannot be essentialised in the way suggested. If, however, Freud had argued that neurosis in a more general sense was the basis of religion, although not completely unproblematic it would have provided a more defensible essentialist basis for religion.

It is clear from this final point that essentialist definitions can provide an arguable definition for religion. They must, however, provide a biological or psychological basis that can demonstrably be seen to have ethnographic extension. Essentialist elements can be seen, often in relation to other elements, to form significant parts of many recent attempts to define the boundaries of the phenomenon and discipline.

Substantialist definitions are closely related to essentialist definitions, particularly in selecting one aspect of the phenomenon as significant or definitional. The fundamental difference, however, is that the element selected is not seen as deriving from a unique and essential aspect of humanity or human experience; rather it is chosen because it is seen as providing the basis for commonality of the elements under study. Substantialist approaches often suggest that the definitional element is selected due to its prevalence in the empirical data (this of course begs the question of how that data is selected, and suggests that the definition must precede the data). At other times this choice is argued on the basis of 'common sense' in others because the element is seen as the primary definitional aspect in the phenomenon in either our own or some other ethnographic example.

The most common form of substantialist definition focuses on the presence of either gods or the supernatural as the defining feature of religion. This feature is found within Spiro's highly influential definition in which 'culturally postulated superhuman beings' are the significant defining feature of religion. Spiro justifies this inclusion on the basis of 'intra-cultural intuitivity' (Spiro 1966: 91): 'intra-cultural intuitivity' is another way of saying common sense. Common sense, however, is a culturally constructed object that is merely the naturalised product of a particular group's understanding of the world; thus it would seem to be ethnocentric, and clearly unreflexive, to adopt one group's common sense as a significant aspect of defining a cross-cultural phenomenon. This is particularly true in Spiro's case, as the unstated reason for selecting this definition is actually an essentialist element, that is, Spiro accepts Freud's argument relating to neurosis, and neuroses analogous to the Oedipus complex as the basis of religion.

The selection of particular elements can be ethnocentric in a more significant way, that is, as a way of privileging or deprivileging the object of study within a cultural system. Thus, the emphasis on gods or the supernatural is a way of supporting the dichotomy between religion and science. The selection of this element, one which is scientifically unverifiable, potentially places religion in the realm of the irrational or at best non-rational. This process of definition is often related to aspects of authority within an ideological structure. When this definition is applied to other cultures it has implications that can be related to imperialism or neo-colonialism; it has the effect of defining the other societies' modelling of the world as religion as opposed to Western society's modelling as science.

While the argument relating to ethnocentrism is a significant challenge to substantialist approaches, there are theorists who have attempted to move beyond both this problem and the problems relating to the narrowness of many substantialist definitions by broadening out the definitions to include a set of characteristics or elements from a set of characteristics. If, however, these elements are selected because of a descriptive bias, that is, they happen to be found in some or many chosen examples that are deemed to be religion, there still appears to be an artificiality or arbitrariness in the process of establishing the definition – the definitions cannot answer the question of why these elements and not others – what makes this set of elements, however many or few, significant while others are not?

The problems associated with substantialist definitions are particularly highlighted in discussions relating to civil religion.[1] The concept of civil religion suggests either that there is a similarity in substance between civil and non-civil religion, or that civil practices are considered to be religion because they are seen to function in the same way, that is, they serve the same social purposes as normative religion. In the first case we would remain within a substantialist argument, in the second the argument and its theoretical basis would be functionalist. The problems associated with determining a common substantialist basis are particularly highlighted by Thrower (1992). His discussion suggests two aspects that unite civil religion and normative religion: a totalising framework of system of legitimisation and a mythological basis (Thrower 1992: 13). While the first of these elements is based on a functionalist perspective, the second might be seen as substantialist. In Thrower's discussion, however, even this second element, in order to encompass the narratives of a structure that works within a civil frame, is ultimately defined from a functionalist perspective. At each of the levels of the argument the substantialist aspects of the discussion have to be removed as they limit the application and use of the term.

Functionalist definitions focus on the role that the object under study plays for either society (Radcliffe-Brown, pages 253–64) or the individual (Malinowski, pages 229–52). These types of definition, depending on the nature of the functions selected, tend to be much broader than either essentialist or substantialist definitions. Functionalist definitions of religion range from seeing religions as legitimising the social order to providing a basis for understanding and constructing cosmos. It is apparent that both of these examples will include social phenomena that are not normally considered to be religion; thus, the first might include civil religion and nationalism while the second might include science or other modes of modelling human existence and being in the world/universe.

Functionalist definitions and functionalism have been challenged on a number of levels. Specifically regarding definitions of religion, Spiro, for example, has highlighted the fact that functionalist definitions often include phenomena that would not normally be seen to fit into the same category.[2] His argument ultimately rests on the above-mentioned 'intra-cultural intuitivity', which as we have suggested has ethnocentric implications. In our view the fact that these definitions bring together data that may be intra-culturally counter-intuitive is a strength rather than a weakness, as they may force us to look at social institutions from new perspectives.

Functionalism has also been seen to present a static view of society. In its early formulations (e.g. Durkheim and Radcliffe-Brown) functionalism tended to present a static historical view of society based on an organic analogy in which each organ or social institution tended to remain essentially the same in order to provide for the survival of the society as a whole. Many more recent theorists, for instance Gluckman, have utilised functionalist analysis in a more nuanced way, seeing it within a more historical and potentially transformative context.

The most significant critique of functionalism is that of circular reasoning. The functions that an institution is said to have are also said to be the reasons for its existence. This critique suggests that while functionalism may not be able to explain the origin of a particular social phenomenon, it may explain or partially explain the persistence and present-day role of that object in society. If, however, functionalist and essentialist arguments are brought together, for example, positing a need based in human psychology and therefore universal, then it is possible to explain both the origins of a phenomenon and its persistence in society – it also would suggest that given the basis of the need all societies would find some method to deal with that need.

Each one of these modes of definition implies a theoretical stance – in relation to the nature either of the object being studied or of society in general. Essentialist and functionalist definitions are explicitly theoretical. Essentialist definitions are based on either a theory about the nature of human beings, in terms of fundamental faculties (Kant or Schleiermacher), psychological structuring (Freud) or biological structuring (Lévi-Strauss), or about the nature of human experience of the transcendent. Thus these approaches presuppose a theoretical stance about the nature of human beings or the world in which they live.

Functionalist definitions also are based on a theoretical stance in relation to human beings or society – thus Malinowski focuses on individual needs and the roles institutions play in fulfilling them while Radcliffe-Brown emphasises societal needs. Other theorists, for example Peter Berger (pages 317–29), focus on the interface between the individual and society in fulfilling the need for cosmos, that is, totalising structures of meaning.

Some scholars suggest that substantialist definitions are different from other forms of definition in not being implicated by theory. This view in part relates to the strong association of this form of definition with the school of phenomenology of religion – one of the planks of this approach is the rejection of explicit theorizing – and is suggested by Thrower's discussion of definitions of religion, in which he prefers substantialist definitions over functionalist due to the fact that 'functionalist definitions . . . are not definitions at all, but really theories of religion' (Thrower 1999: 5). While we clearly agree that functionalist approaches are explicit theories of religion, we would also argue that substantialist approaches are minimally implicit theories. Many of the issues relating to this question have been explored above. Thus, the fact of selection of a particular item as definitional has clear theoretical implications. Such a selection may as in Thrower's discussion of civil religion actually rest on a functionalist basis. When such foundations are absent, however, the implicit theorising can be much more problematic, particularly as it is often unstated or unrecognised. Thus the basis of selection often presupposes patterns of authority, with the definition privileging or deprivileging some aspect of society or other societies as a whole. While this process is clearly implicated in theory when privileging Western scientific discourse over non-Western forms of discourse, each mode of discrimination is implicated in a theory of human discourse and/or theory relating to institutions, humanity or the world. In many cases the substantialist definitions are based on unstated evolutionary views (discussed below) which have clear theoretical implications regarding the nature of society or societies. This last aspect is particularly evident in Thrower's later work (1999), in which he pairs a substantialist bias with an evolutionary view encapsulated in the concept of primal religion (we will explore the evolutionary issues below).

Issues and Arguments in the Study of Religion

Alongside the issues relating to form of definition, the study of religion has been shaped by a number of broadly theoretical or methodological dichotomies: transcendent/human, essentialist/reductionalist, inside/outside (emic/etic), unilinear evolutionist/multilinear or relativist, religion/religions and individual/society. While in some cases one side of a dichotomy is associated with a particular form of definition or a particular disciplinary approach, in many cases these issues cut across the range of definitions and disciplines and form the foundation for many of the ongoing arguments within the study of religion as a whole.

Transcendent/human

The dichotomy of transcendent/human raises the issue of the origin and basis of religion. One side of the dichotomy suggests that religion has its basis in a transcendent aspect of reality, however defined; the other side suggests that religion arises from some aspect either of human nature or of society without reference to a transcendent source. While the transcendent side of this distinction clearly demarcates the domain of theology, which sees religion as having a transcendent source (this of course does not deny that aspects of it may arise from the individual or society) and thus falls outside the scope of this volume, there are theorists within other academic traditions that have included this element within their discussions. This is most often seen in, albeit not exclusive to, the discussions of phenomenologists of religion. In their attempt to take seriously internal approaches or indeed their own religious understandings many phenomenologists' discussions include some form of the transcendent as the fundamental and common basis for religion and religions. This form of argumentation is most clearly seen in the work of Otto (pages 78–85) and Eliade (pages 127–33). It is argued below (see the introduction to Chapter 2) that this form of theological essentialisation is required by the phenomenological approach in order to provide an argumentative basis for its typological approach, which seeks to isolate the essence of religious phenomena and more broadly in order to provide a theoretical basis for the view that religion has a teleology, that is, a history of religion rather than a history of religions.

Most of the academic disciplines studying religion have, due to their empirical stance, focused on the human side of this dichotomy. Thus, they tend to define religion in human terms, often as serving or resolving some problem inherent in the human condition or society. The human element is central to disciplines in two primary ways, individual and societal. Thus psychological approaches tend to focus on how religion relates to the individual psyche while sociological approaches broadly focus on what religion does for society as a whole (the dichotomy of individual and societal is discussed below).

Essentialism/reductionism

One of the most significant critiques of the humanist approaches, whether individual or societal, is encapsulated in the argument about reductionism, that is, whether the phenomena of religion can or should be reducible to serving a particular social or individual function (this argument is encapsulated in the dichotomy of essentialism/reductionism). This argument is often made in regard to functionalism but is also extended to any attempt to explain the origin or persistence of religion on the basis of theoretical positions developed in relation to other social phenomena. One version of this discussion is found in two terms suggested by Paul Ricoeur – hermeneutics of recollection and of suspicion, with the second, utilising an essentially negative term, being equivalent to reductionism. Both Ricoeur's terms and arguments employed by opponents of reductionism suggest insensitivity to the insider's point of view and a denial of any possibility that religion might, in accordance with that internal point of view, be a product of divine origin.

The primary opponents of reductionism can be characterised as essentialist in several different respects. The nature of their arguments suggests that religion must have some essential and unique character that distinguishes it from other social phenomena such that it cannot be explained in similar terms. It is suggested that just as psychology and physics are different domains, related though perhaps not reducible one to the other, so religion is a different disciplinary domain from those studied by sociology or anthropology. If a non-essentialist argument is made about the nature of religion, there seems little argumentative basis for supporting this distinction – religion would be a social phenomenon similar to other social phenomena and arguably analysed in similar terms on the basis of similar theories. In order to defend the distinction of religion as unique some form of essentialist argumentation is required. If the essential aspect is rooted in the human being, either biological or psychological, this would still entail, from the perspective of the opponents of reductionism, a form of reductionism, analysing religion as a secondary phenomenon. Thus, the only form of reductionism that would not reduce religion to a secondary phenomenon in relation to other human phenomena would be transcendent essentialism; in this sense the essentialists are also practising a form of reductionism, for example reducing religion to experience of the Holy, but nonetheless it would provide religion with a unique and distinctive basis that would conform to the views of believers. While this form of *deus ex machina* certainly preserves religion from other forms of reductionism, it does so at the expense of turning the methods of study that accept it into theological arguments either in their own terms or as mere replicators parasitical on the religious phenomena which they describe. While theological approaches are significant in and of themselves as statements of particular forms of believing, they cannot serve as definitions of religion(s) usable beyond those particular traditions (either in relation to other traditions or to a non-theological understanding of religion).

One of the primary motivators for the arguments against reductionism, or more broadly the application of models other than those developed specifically for religion, seems to rest on the issue of disciplinary distinctiveness. If theories related to, for example, other social or psychological phenomena can be used to explain the origins or persistence of religion, does the study of religion merit being a separable and distinct disciplinary structure, the underlying assumption being that if a unique basis is not found then there would be no reason for the discipline of religious studies? This argument, however, assumes that disciplines have some essential existence that stands out in any cultural or historical context. If disciplines are seen as historical constructs, with increasingly permeable boundaries (and this is indeed found in the self-perception of many academic disciplines and in the rise of inter- and multi-disciplinary approaches) then there is no reason to expect or argue for an essentialist basis for any of them. This is particularly true with respect to religion, which in many aspects of its social construction is an artefact of modern Western thought.

Theorists who argue in favour of reductionism also point to several positive aspects of such approaches. They particularly highlight the process undergone in a reductionist analysis. Such analyses, they suggest, do not presuppose that religion (or any object being studied) has a particular basis or meaning (as does the theological essentialist model). The reductionist explanation is the result of the analysis rather than the start of the analysis. A materialist/empirical reductionist analysis analyses the data that is available, and does not seek to explain the phenomena on the basis of unfalsifiable hypotheses – on this basis reductionist analyses fall within the realm of scientific argumentation, being both empirically verifiable and falsifiable. Strenski (1994: 97) also suggests that if religions are only understandable via an insider point of view then there is no possible development of conceptual frameworks; reductionism allows for the test and challenging of frameworks of understanding.

There are, however, two challenges to a purely reductionist approach to religion, that is, purely privileging the outside perspective over that of the insider. Reductionist approaches often suggest that they can both test the validity of religious propositions and that they can exhaust their meaning. The first of these propositions is problematic from two respects. First, even if a reductionist analysis explains the origin and persistence of a religious institution or belief, this does not necessarily disprove the transcendent aspect. Thus for example, analyses of how religious experiences are culturally constructed or contextualised while explaining how and in what ways religious experiences occur cannot disprove whether or not there may also be a transcendent aspect – that aspect is not testable through empirical means. Thus, the analysis can suggest that the transcendent element is not necessary to explain the event; it cannot determine its presence or absence. The privileging of reductionist forms of explanation can also be seen as a form of neo-colonialism – giving authority to the Western modes of thought over the non-Western (or non-dominant). If a relativist stance is taken there seems no reason to privilege either approach, and thus both the reductionist and non-reductionist explanations can be seen as alternative and perhaps incommensurable modes of explanation.

The issue of whether a reductionist analysis exhausts the meaning of religion or a religious practice is similarly problematic. Thus a materialist explanation might suggest that religion is solely superstructure, and serves as an ideological support for the dominant structures of economic power. Although this might explain many features of religious practice and its role within society, it seems likely that social practices are much more complex than this simplistic model would suggest. Even Marxist materialism recognises that religion is a complex phenomenon, serving as false consciousness, ideological indoctrination and a cry of the oppressed. The reductionist argument also overlooks the fact that while it may uncover latent functions or explanations of the practice, the manifest functions are also of meaning and significance to the insider.

Insider/outsider

The dichotomy of insider/outsider is closely related to those already discussed. The debates associated with this dichotomy are found on a cross-disciplinary level in relation to the phenomenological approach, which claims to privilege the insider approach, and other approaches, which are seen as privileging the outsider point of view. It is also found within anthropology, in which the terms 'emic' (inside) and 'etic' (outside) have been used as the expression of this debate. Aspects of the debate within anthropology will be touched upon before moving the discussion to the meta-theoretical level.

The debate in anthropology was highlighted by the work of Kenneth Pike, who coined the terms 'emic' and 'etic' to describe the two approaches to the study of cultures. The term 'emic' was seen as describing a process of discovery, that is, distinguishing a pre-existent internal understanding that was then presented by the anthropologist. The etic approach was seen as akin to creation, that is creating the explanation rather than discovering an explanation that pre-existed the study (these terms are closely related to a more general question about science: does the scientist discover the models that explain the universe, that is, laws that are built into the universe, or does he create models of the universe, with the laws being the product of analysis rather than the object of analysis?). Pike describes etic analysis as an alien view imposed on the object being studied (1999: 29). Pike considers the emic approach as being a more accurate portrayal of cultures as it arises from an internal understanding immanent in the object being studied. The alternative emphasis is forcefully presented by Marvin Harris (1968: 568–92). Harris suggests that although emic analyses are important anthropological data, only etic analyses are properly scientific, that is, they are predictable and subject to falsification. He argues that individuals within a social system may know what they believe but they may not be able to determine with scientific rigour why they believe it; etic analysis provides the proper scientific analytical framework that can assess the reasons for belief in a testable fashion. A second problem with the reliance on the emic is that it prevents proper comparative analysis – if the explanation of each religion can only be examined in terms of its internal explanations then it would be impossible to compare it to another religion, as the emic terms of reference would be incommensurable.

There are, however, broader questions about the emic approach that encompass the practices both of anthropology and of the phenomenology of religion. There are serious questions as to whether the emic point of view, particularly as espoused by phenomenologists, is possible, that is, is it possible for the phenomenologist to actually present the emic point of view of a religion other than his or her own? The internal perspective as used in analysis contains two elements, the actual view of an insider, and the view of an insider as replicated by an outsider. The internal view of an insider, that is, in the case of religion, a believer, is ultimately a theological view based on theological presuppositions, and as such it is not a theory of religion(s). If the goal of the discussion (to call it an analysis would be inappropriate) is to present this perspective, then translation or recapitulation of internal theological statements or beliefs would be sufficient without significant mediation (except perhaps elucidation) by either the anthropologist or the phenomenologist. While the collection of such data is important, its incommensurable status in relation to other data renders it relatively useless in understanding broader human or social phenomena and even the attempt would be moving from the emic to the etic.

The second form of internal perspective is that presented by the anthropologist or phenomenologist. If they are merely, as the approach claims, parroting the internal point of view, with no significant external mediation, then, as some phenomenologists suggest, their work is parasitical, and ultimately in no way distinct from an internal theological statement. While this form of internal perspective at best has the same problems associated with it as the first form, it also potentially has an even more problematic status – can it even be said to be what it claims, that is, an emic perspective? If the scholar is presenting material from one context to another context with different presuppositions and modes of thinking as well as a different language, can the emic position so transposed still be considered to be emic? The material would have to be mediated in at least two respects: it would have to be translated into a new language with all of the issues that translation entails (there is no such thing as a direct translation – translation involves selection and interpretation by the translator whether they are from within the community or without), and it would have to be presented in terms of concepts that were understandable within its new cultural context; concepts such as 'natural' or 'supernatural' are not cross-culturally transposable, for they have different conceptual ranges with different cultural contexts. On this basis even a description that claims to be emic would have undergone a significant level of interpretation and transformation, both of which involve the imposition of an etic frame of reference.

This argument is not suggesting that there is no value in attempting to understand or present a mediated emic perspective. Indeed mediated emic perspectives are a necessary source of data which should be the basis of all theorising and analysis. The discussion, however, suggests that scholars and students must be aware of the limitations inherent in both these perspectives and their status. The discussion thus far also suggests that merely replicating even a mediated form of the etic point of view is not a form of analysis or a substitute for analysis. Etic perspectives are also necessary in moving the data onto a level which allows both comparison and the possibility of abstraction.

If the scholar is not serving as a direct conduit, then the claim to be able to present an emic perspective is even more problematic – in this case the observer, like the scientist, is trying to determine pre-existing laws which are not explicitly available. Any form of observation involves an etic perspective. Observations depend on a process of selection, that is, a determination on the point of view of the observer of what is significant and what is not – the selection process is both conscious (based on the questions addressed) and unconscious (based on implicit presupposition and the nature of our own conceptual framework). In order to study religion in a society, the observer must have some view (stated or unstated) of the parameters of the phenomenon, thus the observations will always be implicated by an external point of view. If, as many so-called emic analyses suggest, the etic theorizing is unstated and unreflexive, then it is also unchallengeable. Awareness of our own positioning in relation to the observational process is necessary in order to question and challenge that positioning.

Although this discussion suggests that a truly emic description is probably impossible (even an insider would need to translate his or her religion from one culture to the other), relative emic descriptions are an essential part of the understanding of a religious or cultural tradition. If the etic view is privileged to the exclusion of the emic, then, while it might be possible to understand and apply the data on a broad cross-cultural basis, such an analysis would lose significant features of the religious system under study. These elements, found in the emic interpretations, are significant data. Theologies speak to the ideas that motivate and move individuals and communities, elements which are necessary in a useful understanding of a religious system – if we ignore what motivates people to follow a system, for example revelation or religious experience, we cannot fully understand that system.

Unilinear evolutionist/multilinear or relativist
Our discussion of issues relating to the study of religion now moves from issues of methodology to those relating to how we theorise both society and

religion, one of its constituent parts (at least if one does not view religion as a unique and separable element). Although the debate between evolutionism and relativism had its roots in the nineteenth century, many aspects of the debate continue to be found in discussions of religion. Thus, for example, evolutionist assumptions underlie conceptualisations of primal religion and, even more significantly, discussion of the process of secularisation. Due to the persistence of evolutionism within a framework that generally has challenged its role within the development of culture, it is important to trace some of the presuppositions and implications of both evolutionism and its dichotomous pair, relativism.

The nineteenth century saw the birth of Darwin's theory of evolution and hence the proliferation of applications of evolutionary theory to the development of culture. These models usually depicted culture as developing according to a fixed unilinear model that moved from simple 'primitive' forms of society to culminate in the most complex form, which in some formulations (particularly those of British origin) was seen as exemplified by Victorian Britain. The distinctions between the different levels were based on a variety of different measures including complexity and technology. These theories, represented below by the work of Tylor (pages 99–108), saw religion as developing along an analogous path, usually culminating in Christianity with particular associations with the Protestant forms dominant in Britain or the United States. Many of the other approaches emerging in the nineteenth or early twentieth century, even if not focusing on evolutionary theory, are heavily influenced by this theoretical model; this is seen in the work of Frazer (pages 44–52), Marx (pages 68–9) and to some extent Freud (pages 53–62). Most of the evolutionary models or those influenced by them share a number of additional presuppositions: progress, analogy of modern-day 'pre-modern' societies with earlier forms of societal development and the related notion of recapitulation, that is, that individuals and more specifically children undergo in their individual development stages analogous to those of societal evolution – this final theme is particularly emphasised in the psychological theory of Freud (pages 53–62).

The models of unilinear cultural and religious evolution share a number of inherent problems. Key problems are highlighted by their false analogy with biological evolution. Unlike the fixed unilinear model proposed for culture, in which change occurs due to the passing down by cultural means of acquired traits, biological evolution is precisely not fixed nor is it unilinear. There are many paths of evolutionary development, none of which are fixed, nor is there any built-in direction or necessary progress – it is just as likely to become less complex as more complex. Biological evolution's motor is based on chance mutation and the passing down of inherited traits rather than acquired traits. If the analogy between cultural evolution and biological evolution is unsupportable, then the logic behind cultural evolution, which relied on biological evolution as its foundation, is also untenable.

Without the support of evolutionary theory unilinear cultural evolution relies on some form of teleology. Only a teleological impetus, either internal or external, could provide a logical basis for the fixed path of development suggested by the theory; without this type of force it seems likely that there will be many different paths of development, perhaps as many as there are cultures, a view that would represent the historical relativist position established by Boas. An alternative view that gained some credence in the twentieth century is that of multilinear evolution; this approach suggests that while there is no single path of evolution there are a limited number of paths or trajectories that describe the historical development of most societies – these models often draw on external factors, particularly materialist, as a basis for the limitation of paths. Lacking any single fixed path of development (change has no specific directionality), the concept of progress becomes meaningless as does the analogy between modern-day societies and those existing in the historical past.

Three final critiques need to be mentioned respecting unilinear evolutionary theories. The theories as applied by theorists (and in all likelihood intrinsically) are ethnocentric. Western society, either Britain or the USA, is chosen as the point from which other societies are judged – to the extent that they are different they are judged inferior, that is, lower down the evolutionary scale. Secondly, the evolutionary theories respecting culture as a whole or specifically religion did not receive support from ethnographic studies. The empirical data suggested that there was no single path of development, nor are particular forms of religion clearly associated with any form of technology or social structure. The final and most significant critique is that of ideology. Both the collection of data and the theorists were complicit in colonial or imperialist systems. The theory thus serves as an ideological justification for the domination or even eradication of societies seen as evolutionarily inferior.

While explicit versions of unilinear cultural evolution are no longer found within the mainstream of the academic disciplines associated with the study of religion, the influence of these models is still implicitly found in many theories. One of the clearest expressions of this influence is found in those theories that espouse the concept of 'primal' religion (Thrower, 1999: 11). While these approaches ostensibly reject evolutionary argumentation, stating that the term 'primal' is used in place of 'primitive', the evolutionary implications are retained. Thus, for example, Thrower suggests that societies characterised as having 'primal' religion existing in the world today are seen as sharing a 'primal worldview' with historical societies that preceded the development of modern cultures. His discussion clearly harks back to the analogy between currently existing societies identified as 'primitive' and those societies of the past that were earlier stages of historical development. If, however, there is no single path of development then there is no argumentative basis for a single 'primal world-view'.

The second area implicitly influenced by evolutionary models is secularisation theory. Secularisation theory suggests that with the processes associated with modernisation, the role and power of religion within society will progressively diminish, hence society will become increasingly secular. While on its own this model can be seen as descriptive of processes occurring within some parts of Western society, for example, arguably the United Kingdom, and as a descriptive model would have necessary evolutionary implications, the theory, however, tends to be seen as a predictive model for how society changes, and is often presented as a model applicable to any society that has reached the process of modernisation. In this form of presentation the unilinear evolutionary aspects are evident, as indeed are the ethnocentric aspects as the decline of religion is associated with the rise of rationality – a process clearly seen as positive by many of the exponents of this position.

Religion/religions

This dichotomy brings together a number of theoretical issues about the nature (and teleology) of religion as well as methodological issues relating to the status of the object being studied. Within the study of religion, particularly the related schools of phenomenology and history of religion, there has been a tendency to view religion (in the senses of both history and essence) as in some way separable from particular religions. Some phenomenologists, for example, would argue that there is some essence of religion that can be separated from the particular religions, thus the goal of analysis is to understand this universal essence. Other scholars, historians of religion, take this argument a step further, seeing religion (as opposed to religions) as having a single history or historic trajectory. Both of these approaches clearly rely on an essentialist theoretical stance – only an essentialist basis (either internal or external) would provide an argumentative base for religion having a single universal essence. If this argument is taken in association with the view that religion is irreducible, as argued by many scholars from these approaches, then the essentialist basis must be external and therefore outside of the realm of social-scientific academic argumentation. The view that religion has a single history argument is equally implicated by an implicit evolutionary presupposition.

From a different perspective it is also important to ask whether religion can be viewed as a singular object. If some of the critiques of theorising about religion are taken seriously, then the question arises as to whether the concept of religion (as opposed to religions) is an artefact of Western culture and its imposition an act of neo-colonialism. This view is specifically articulated by Asad (pages 178–95). If there is a need to move from one definition of religion to many dialectically related definitions then the view that there is one object called religion is untenable.

The dichotomy of religion/religions also relates to a second level of analysis, that is, of particular religious traditions. Many discussions of religion tend to present essentialised monolithic views of various religions, thus they speak of Judaism or Islam. This form of essentialisation can be sustained if the focus is on a dominant literary tradition or system of authority; if, however, the religions are examined in terms of practice within and among communities the essentialised view tends to break down. One attempt to resolve the apparent paradox is to speak of two different levels of tradition – hence distinctions like great tradition/small tradition. Different approaches have tended to focus on one side or the other; thus, phenomenologists have tended to emphasise the great tradition (thus supporting a more essentialist view) while anthropologists have emphasised (often to the exclusion of the great tradition) the local small traditions encountered in ethnographic fieldwork. To a degree these different foci are due to the practices of the two approaches – phenomenologists have often focused on the literary traditions while anthropologists have studied the small ethnographic example.

While a balance between the two approaches is desirable, religion as a social institution exists within particular contexts – historically, geographically and culturally. It therefore seems imperative that discussions move from the idealised to the actualised. The specific ethnographic examples are products of an interaction with the idealised form; analysis of this interaction in its lived reality would bring out the processes of authorisation and power that seek to maintain or create a unitary model, as well as the countervailing forces that militate against this.

Individual/society

The dichotomy of the individual and society has been touched upon above in relation to functionalist definitions of religion; it is also found in relation to the other forms of definition and in relation to most of the disciplinary approaches. The essential issue relating to this dichotomy is the location of the basis of religion in terms both of its origins and of its persistence. This dichotomy addresses issues in relation both to the function that religion plays and to the source from which religion emerges. In relation to the first aspect we have highlighted above the debate within functionalist theory of whether function relates to the individual or society – this debate is seen in the work of Malinowski, who sees religion as primarily serving individual functions, for example dealing with the problem of death, and that of Radcliffe-Brown, who emphasises the functions at the level of society, for example religion serving as a means of maintaining social order.

The second issue, which is also implied in the first, relates to the question of whether religion emerges as a result of some aspect of individual experience or need or in relation to society. Focus on the individual side of the dichotomy is specifically characteristic of many essentialist approaches to religion. Many of the psychological arguments provide good examples of the emphasis on the individual rather than society. This is particularly true of the work of Freud (pages 53–62). These approaches see religion as emerging from or relating to some aspect of the individual psyche – the unconscious in the case of Freud. The work of Otto (pages 78–85) provides a good example of a theological essentialist argument in which individual experience of the Holy becomes the basis for religion.

One of the issues that arises in relation to the focus on the individual side of the dichotomy is how the individual basis of religion relates to the observable fact that religion is a social phenomenon – how does religion move from the individual to the social? In some cases, particularly on the theological side, the move is seen as negative, with the organised aspects of religion often standing in the way of the authentic individual experience which remains at the heart of religion. In others, particularly the psychological, the move from the individual to the social raises more questions – if religion arises in relation to individual neuroses, why and how are these issues extended to society? One form of explanation rested on an aspect of evolutionary theory, recapitulation. Recapitulation suggested that the social/psychological development of individuals recapitulates that of society – thus the individual Oedipus complex, which underlies religion, recapitulates an event in human history that instantiated the Oedipus complex at the societal level. The theory thus suggests that religion arises in relation to both society and the individual, and that the ongoing existence of the individual Oedipus complex allows religion to continue to persist at the societal level. It should be noted that there is no mechanism that would allow for this type of recapitulation from the societal to the individual, nor is there evidence that it occurs. Recapitulation, as used for example by Freud, is also problematic due to its ethnocentric implications. It suggests that there is a threefold analogy: early humanity = 'primitive' today = child = neurotic. Religion within this concept arises in early humanity, it is perpetuated in 'primitive' society as they are seen to be at the same level of development, it reoccurs in children due to recapitulation and it is found in modern adults only to the extent that they are neurotic.

Examples of theories that emphasise the social side of the dichotomy are particularly found in the work of sociologists and many anthropologists. These approaches tend to have a functionalist basis, seeing religion as primarily serving a social rather than an individual function. Examples of this approach can be seen in Durkheim (pages 26–38). This emphasis is also characteristic of many twentieth century functionalists within sociology. Durkheim's approach provides a good example of the approach – indeed it provides the foundation of many of the subsequent analyses emphasising the society rather than the individual. Durkheim suggests that religion arises in relation to the beginnings of society – God is seen as the projected embodiment of society, and thus religion functions as a means of creating and strengthening the social solidarity.

While the theories emphasising society provide good explanations for why religion as observed is a group phenomenon, they tend to overlook the place and significance of the individual in religion. While this issue could be illustrated in many ways by the theorists mentioned thus far, it is particularly evident in some modern sociological discussions of religion. This is specifically seen in some aspects of Bruce's work (pages 330–47). These analyses examine the prevalence and persistence of religion in modern society and tend to argue that if there is a decline in institutional participation in religion, that is the group/social aspect, then this is equivalent to the decline of religion as a whole, even if individual patterns of practice and belief continue or are even strengthened.

Many scholars have recognised the limitations of focusing too strongly on either side of this dichotomy. Thus, even Malinowski (pages 229–52), who emphasises individual function, also discusses the institutional functions of religion. The mixture of both aspects is also picked up in the highly influential work of the American sociologist Talcott Parsons (pages 365–77). The examination of the creative interaction between the individual and the social is increasingly prominent in recent theories of religion.

DEFINITIONS

Thus far we have examined the basic forms of definition and some of the thematic or methodological trajectories that have shaped the study of religion. In recent years academics from many traditions have begun to question many of these presuppositions, and even the possibility of establishing any form of definition. Our discussion will touch on some of the issues raised by these theorists.

Due to many of the issues raised above many theorists have questioned whether it is possible to define religion in simple terms, therefore in many cases they have begun to explore different types of open-ended definition. Two examples of this are found within the phenomenological approach and that of history of religions. Smart (pages 154–61) presents a form of definition that includes a range of different dimensions – the number of dimensions ranges from six to eight. While all of the dimensions need to be present for the institution to be considered religion, the definition provides a high degree of flexibility by emphasising that different traditions would be characterised by different degrees of interrelation between the elements. His definition also expands the traditional phenomenological preoccupation with the internal point of view and rejection of theory, by suggesting that both the internal point of view and external theorizing are necessary means of understanding religion. Bianchi (pages 111–26) suggests an even more open-ended form of definition. He suggests that the term 'religion' is meaningful only in a contextual sense, thus when using it in different contexts it can only be used analogically – allowing us to use the term based on similarity rather than identity. He suggests further that the term 'religion' should be used provisionally, as the basis for discussion rather than assuming that it reflects a common phenomenology.

Other thinkers have brought these two approaches together. Thus, some thinkers have drawn on Wittgenstein's concept of family resemblance – in which, while members of the category (family) share different characteristics, none of the characteristics is necessary to be part of the category. The polythetic definition suggested by Southwold (pages 277–89) is a useful example of this form of analysis. The most comprehensive example of the family resemblance approach is found in the work of Saler (pages 265–76). The key aspect of these developments is the move away from the concept of definition in the strict sense of the term.

CONCLUSIONS AND SUGGESTIONS

The goal of this introduction has been to introduce both the forms of definition and the significant issues found in the academic disciplines that have attempted to understand religion. It should be clear from the discussions presented here that there is little agreement either between or within disciplines as to how religion can be defined, understood or explained or indeed whether it should be defined, understood or explained. While it would be impossible to bring real coherence to this diverse picture, it is possible to suggest some directions that have been suggested by some of the recent discussions of the subject:

- There is a need to challenge the very basis of definition – all definitions of whatever form have an intrinsic problem of being culturally constructed within a particular system of authority and based on specific disciplinary practices.
- One possible direction is to move to a form of definition that focuses on family resemblances rather than setting specific and limited boundaries. This approach would view the definition as having an analogical sense that allows for difference and particularity.
- A second direction would move to a more dialectical stance. A definition or characterisation established on the basis of one set of cultural data would be set in a dialectical relation with a new set of data – this dialectical relation would allow for both a transformation of the characterisation and an interpretation of the data.

- Whatever method of characterisation is used, there needs to be an awareness of the systems of power and legitimisation both within the cultural practices associated with the observer and within those of the society being studied.

NOTES

1. See for example Thrower (1992).
2. See Spiro (1966). Elements from Spiro's arguments are found in Chapter 3 (pages 290–6).

I

THE ANCESTORS

Introduction

In this chapter we have included a very diverse selection of texts ranging from theology and philosophy to the early roots of psychology and anthropology. Perhaps the only element that unites the material included (other than their subject matter, that is) is that they form the argumentative foundations for many of the theoretical approaches developed in the twentieth century. While in terms of date or disciplinary approach some of the texts could have been included in the chapters that have a disciplinary focus, due to the centrality or influence of the approach we have chosen to include them here. Thus, for example, Durkheim, while arguably being a founder of modern sociology, has also had significant influence on anthropological theory as well as more general influence on Western thought. Similarly Freud's analysis of both the psyche and specifically religion has had immense influence on almost every disciplinary discussion of religion.

One of the main criteria for selection of material for inclusion or exclusion, both in this chapter and in the volume as a whole, relates to the approach to the subject matter. We include only material that is interested in the question of religions or the nature of religion separate from any particular instantiation. Thus we have excluded most theological material as it tends to have as its primary focus the religious perspective and tradition out of which it emerges. We have, however, included two specifically theological approaches in this chapter, that of Schleiermacher (pages 86–98) and Otto (pages 78–85). In both of these cases the issues raised in respect of religion relate directly to significant questions in a more general debate

23

about the nature of religion – this debate can best be seen by examining the texts from Schleiermacher and Otto (who both look back to the work by Kant in respect of *a priori* faculties) on the one hand, and that specifically of James (pages 63–7) on the other. To a great extent these texts illustrate some attempts to understand possible essentialist understandings of religion. Due to the empirical element of the material included in this volume we have also excluded much of the material on the philosophy of religion. We have, however, included Feuerbach (pages 39–43) due to his relation to the trajectory initiated by Marx.

One debate that is found throughout this chapter, either implicitly or explicitly, relates to evolution. As mentioned in the introduction to this volume, Darwin's theory of evolution was taken by his adherents and extended to almost every disciplinary area. Thus in some discussions it was generalised to the developmental processes of the universe and, of particular significance to our discussions here, extended to every aspect of culture including religion. We have included among the texts in this chapter a text on animism by Tylor (pages 99–107) that is explicitly evolutionary; indeed Tylor was one of the foremost exponents of unilinear evolutionism in early anthropology. We also include sections of Frazer's *Golden Bough* (pages 44–52) that develop an evolutionary theory, tracing the developments from magic to religion to science. While the work of Marx included here is not explicitly evolutionary, Marx's views on the development of economic forms is closely related to the works of the anthropological evolutionists. Unilinear evolutionary models also clearly underlie the works of Freud and Jung; this is specifically seen in the concept of recapitulation that provides a basis for some of the analogies used. Jung, following Lévi-Bruhl (not included in this volume), sees an evolutionary development in the move from 'primitive' to 'modern' ways of thinking. Although we have not included works of Boas, his introduction of cultural relativism and fieldwork to anthropological theory and method posed a significant challenge to these unilinear models, and ultimately rendered them obsolete in relation to both culture and religion.

The majority of the texts included here tend to emphasise the external etic as opposed to the internal emic perspective. In part this can be associated with a general positivist trend in Western thought. It can also be associated with the relative position of the theorists and the people being studied. The emphasis of the etic almost to the exclusion of the emic can be historically mapped in relation to neo-colonialism or indeed various forms of Western imperialism. Perhaps the only text that may be seen as reflecting an aspect of the emic is that of Otto. Even this text, however, can only be seen as presenting an insider's point of view in relation to particular forms of Christianity; in its view of other religions it must be considered an external theoretical analysis. It is only with the decline of positivism (with the rise of post-modernism) and the loss of confidence by Western intellectuals that the insider view begins to be taken seriously; this change only happens in those approaches that move away from a strong view of themselves as scientific.

The texts included here also relate to the debate of the role of religion in relation to either the individual or society. The early anthropological and sociological models, for example, Durkheim (pages 26–38), tend to emphasise the social over the individual; Durkheim sees religion as relating to social solidarity. Freud and James, as well as Otto and Schleiermacher, place a stronger emphasis on the relationship between religion and the individual; these approaches (with the possible or partial exception of James) are all characterised by an essentialist view of religion while Durkheim utilises various forms of functionalist argumentation.

As indicated at the start of this discussion all of these theorists provide the argumentative bases for the study of religion. While some of these approaches are clearly dead ends, particularly the unilinear evolutionary approach and the distinction between 'primitive' and 'modern' thought of Jung (as derived from Lévi-Bruhl), even these theories continue to insinuate themselves into more recent discussions (as in the discussions relating to primal religion that have echoes of both of the forementioned theories). Many of the other theories, while in some respects superseded or transformed, continue to play a significant part in the understanding of religion.

EMILE DURKHEIM
'DEFINITION OF RELIGIOUS PHENOMENA AND OF RELIGION'[1]

Emile Durkheim was born in the Lorraine region of France in 1859. He was born into a Jewish family and his father was the last in a great line of family rabbis. Durkheim, however, distanced himself from his faith without ever becoming a member of another movement. Durkheim was educated at a top Parisian lycée, where he was inspired to go on and train to become a lycée teacher himself, an ambition that was realised in 1882. By 1887 Durkheim had managed to secure his first academic post at Bordeaux University, where he lectured in social science and pedagogy. Whilst in this position Durkheim began publishing, through which he hoped to expand the popularity and status of the social sciences. However, it soon became clear that in order to fulfil this role he must have a grip on the academic world of Paris and this ambition was realised with the establishment of the Parisian periodical L'Année Sociologique. Durkheim died in 1917, at the age of fifty-nine.

Durkheim can be considered one of the founding fathers of both anthropology and sociology. His theoretical model of functionalism is still influential in some quarters of both of these disciplines. We have included material that presents his definition of religion and its close association with society. Durkheim's view that god(s) was an expression of society is the basis of many of the theories that view religion as a social construction.

If we are going to look for the most primitive and simple religion which we can observe, it is necessary to begin by defining what is meant by a religion; for without this, we would run the risk of giving the name to a system of ideas and practices which has nothing at all religious about it, or else of leaving to one side many religious facts, without perceiving their true nature. That this is not an imaginary danger, and that nothing is thus sacrificed to a vain formalism of method, is well shown by the fact that owing to his not having taken this precaution, a certain scholar to whom the science of comparative religions owes a great deal, Professor Frazer, has not been able to recognize the profoundly religious character of the beliefs and rites which will be studied below, where, according to our view, the initial germ of the religious life of humanity is to be found. So this is a prejudicial question, which must be treated before all others. It is not that we dream of arriving at once at the profound characteristics which really explain religion: these can be determined only at the end of our study. But that which is necessary and possible, is to indicate a certain number of

Emile Durkheim ([1915] 1954), *The Elementary Forms of the Religious Life*, London: Allen and Unwin.

external and easily recognizable signs, which will enable us to recognize religious phenomena wherever they are met with, and which will deter us from confounding them with others. We shall proceed to this preliminary operation at once.

But to attain the desired results, it is necessary to begin by freeing the mind of every preconceived idea. Men have been obliged to make for themselves a notion of what religion is, long before the science of religions started its methodical comparisons. The necessities of existence force all of us, believers and non-believers, to represent in some way these things in the midst of which we live, upon which we must pass judgment constantly, and which we must take into account in all our conduct. However, since these preconceived ideas are formed without any method, according to the circumstances and chances of life, they have no right to any credit whatsoever, and must be rigorously set aside in the examination which is to follow. It is not from our prejudices, passions or habits that we should demand the elements of the definition which we must have; it is from the reality itself which we are going to define.

Let us set ourselves before this reality. Leaving aside all conceptions of religion in general, let us consider the various religions in their concrete reality, and attempt to disengage that which they have in common; for religion cannot be defined except by the characteristics which are found wherever religion itself is found. In this comparison, then, we shall make use of all the religious systems which we can know, those of the present and those of the past, the most primitive and simple as well as the most recent and refined; for we have neither the right nor the logical means of excluding some and retaining others. For those who regard religion as only a natural manifestation of human activity, all religions, without any exception whatsoever, are instructive; for all, after their manner, express man, and thus can aid us in better understanding this aspect of our nature. Also, we have seen how far it is from being the best way of studying religion to consider by preference the forms which it presents among the most civilized peoples.[2]

But to aid the mind in freeing itself from these usual conceptions which, owing to their prestige, might prevent it from seeing things as they really are, it is fitting to examine some of the most current of the definitions in which these prejudices are commonly expressed, before taking up the question on our own account.

[...]

III

[...] Let us set ourselves before the problem.

First of all, let us remark that in all these formulæ it is the nature of religion as a whole that they seek to express. They proceed as if it were a sort of indivisible entity, while, as a matter of fact, it is made up of parts; it is a more or less complex system of myths, dogmas, rites and ceremonies. Now a whole cannot be defined except in relation to its parts. It will be more methodical, then, to try to characterize the various elementary phenomena of which all religions are made up, before we attack the system produced by their union. This method is imposed still more forcibly by the fact that there are religious phenomena which belong to no determined religion. Such are those phenomena which constitute the matter of folk-lore. In general, they are the debris of passed religions, in-organized survivals; but there are some which have been formed spontaneously under the influence of local causes. In our European countries Christianity has forced itself to absorb and as-similate them; it has given them a Christian colouring. Nevertheless, there are many which have persisted up until a recent date, or which still exist with a relative autonomy: celebrations of May Day, the summer solstice or the carnival, beliefs relative to genii, local demons, etc., are cases in point. If the religious character of these facts is now diminishing, their religious importance is nevertheless so great that they have enabled Mannhardt and his school to revive the science of religions. A definition which did not take account of them would not cover all that is religious.

Religious phenomena are naturally arranged in two fundamental cat-egories: beliefs and rites. The first are states of opinion, and consist in representations; the second are determined modes of action. Between these two classes of facts there is all the difference which separates thought from action.

The rites can be defined and distinguished from other human practices, moral practices, for example, only by the special nature of their object. A moral rule prescribes certain manners of acting to us, just as a rite does, but which are addressed to a different class of objects. So it is the object of the rite which must be characterized, if we are to characterize the rite itself. Now it is in the beliefs that the special nature of this object is expressed. It is possible to define the rite only after we have defined the belief.

All known religious beliefs, whether simple or complex, present one com-mon characteristic; they presuppose a classification of all the things, real and ideal, of which men think, into two classes or opposed groups, gener-ally designated by two distinct terms which are translated well enough by the words *profane* and *sacred* (*profane, sacré*). This division of the world into two domains, the one containing all that is sacred, the other all that is profane, is the distinctive trait of religious thought; the beliefs, myths, dog-mas and legends are either representations or systems of representations which express the nature of sacred things, the virtues and powers which are attributed to them, or their relations with each other and with profane things. But by sacred things one must not understand simply those personal beings which are called gods or spirits; a rock, a tree, a spring, a pebble, a piece of wood, a house, in a word, anything can be sacred. A rite can have this character; in fact, the rite does not exist which does not have it to a certain degree. There are words, expressions and formulæ which can be pronounced only by the mouths of consecrated persons; there are gestures and movements which everybody cannot perform. If the Vedic sacrifice has had such an efficacy that, according to mythology, it was the creator of the gods, and not merely a means of winning their favour, it is because it possessed a virtue comparable to that of the most sacred beings. The circle of sacred objects cannot be determined, then, once for all. Its extent varies infinitely, according to the different religions. That is how Buddhism is a religion: in default of gods, it admits the existence of sacred things, namely, the four noble truths and the practices derived from them.[3]

Up to the present we have confined ourselves to enumerating a certain number of sacred things as examples: we must now show by what general characteristics they are to be distinguished from profane things.

One might be tempted, first of all, to define them by the place they are generally assigned in the hierarchy of things. They are naturally considered superior in dignity and power to profane things, and particularly to man, when he is only a man and has nothing sacred about him. One thinks of himself as occupying an inferior and dependent position in relation to them; and surely this conception is not without some truth. Only there is nothing in it which is really characteristic of the sacred. It is not enough that one thing be subordinated to another for the second to be sacred in regard to the first. Slaves are inferior to their masters, subjects to their king, soldiers to their leaders, the miser to his gold, the man ambitious for power to the hands which keep it from him; but if it is sometimes said of a man that he makes a religion of those beings or things whose eminent value and superiority to himself he thus recognizes, it is clear that in any case the word is taken in a metaphorical sense, and that there is nothing in these relations which is really religious.[4]

On the other hand, it must not be lost to view that there are sacred things of every degree, and that there are some in relation to which a man feels himself relatively at his ease. An amulet has a sacred character, yet the respect which it inspires is nothing exceptional. Even before his gods, a man is not always in such a marked state of inferiority; for it very frequently happens that he exercises a veritable physical constraint upon them to obtain what he desires. He beats the fetich with which he is not contented, but only to reconcile himself with it again, if in the end it shows itself more docile to the wishes of its adorer.[5] To have rain, he throws stones into the spring or sacred lake where the god of rain is thought to reside; he believes that by this means he forces him to come out and show himself.[6] Moreover, if it is true that man depends upon his gods, this dependence is reciprocal. The gods also have need of man; without offerings and sacrifices they would die. We shall even have occasion to show that this dependence of the gods upon their worshippers is maintained even in the most idealistic religions.

But if a purely hierarchic distinction is a criterion at once too general and too imprecise, there is nothing left with which to characterize the sacred in its relation to the profane except their heterogeneity. However, this heterogeneity is sufficient to characterize this classification of things and to distinguish it from all others, because it is very particular: *it is absolute*. In all the history of human thought there exists no other example of two categories of things so profoundly differentiated or so radically opposed to one another. The traditional opposition of good and bad is nothing beside this; for the good and the bad are only two opposed species of the same class, namely morals, just as sickness and health are two different aspects of the same order of facts, life, while the sacred and the profane have always and everywhere been conceived by the human mind as two distinct classes, as two worlds between which there is nothing in common. The forces which play in one are not simply those which are met with in the other, but a little stronger; they are of a different sort. In different religions, this opposition has been conceived in different ways. Here, to separate these two sorts of things, it has seemed sufficient to localize them in different parts of the physical universe; there, the first have been put into an ideal and transcendental world, while the material world is left in full possession of the others. But howsoever much the forms of the contrast may vary,[7] the fact of the contrast is universal.

This is not equivalent to saying that a being can never pass from one of these worlds into the other: but the manner in which this passage is effected, when it does take place, puts into relief the essential duality of the two kingdoms. In fact, it implies a veritable metamorphosis. This is notably demonstrated by the initiation rites, such as they are practised by a multitude of peoples. This initiation is a long series of ceremonies with the object of introducing the young man into the religious life: for the first time, he leaves the purely profane world where he passed his first infancy, and enters into the world of sacred things. Now this change of state is thought of, not as a simple and regular development of pre-existent germs, but as a transformation *totius substantiae* – of the whole being. It is said that at this moment the young man dies, that the person that he was ceases to exist, and that another is instantly substituted for it. He is re-born under a new form. Appropriate ceremonies are felt to bring about this death and re-birth, which are not understood in a merely symbolic sense, but are taken literally.[8] Does this not prove that between the profane being which he was and the religious being which he becomes, there is a break of continuity?

This heterogeneity is even so complete that it frequently degenerates into a veritable antagonism. The two worlds are not only conceived of as separate, but as even hostile and jealous rivals of each other. Since men cannot fully belong to one except on condition of leaving the other completely, they are exhorted to withdraw themselves completely from the profane world, in order to lead an exclusively religious life. Hence comes the monasticism which is artificially organized outside of and apart from the natural environment in which the ordinary man leads the life of this world, in a different one, closed to the first, and nearly its contrary. Hence comes the mystic asceticism whose object is to root out from man all the attachment for the profane world that remains in him. From that come all the forms of religious suicide, the logical working-out of this asceticism; for the only manner of fully escaping the profane life is, after all, to forsake all life.

The opposition of these two classes manifests itself outwardly with a visible sign by which we can easily recognize this very special classification, wherever it exists. Since the idea of the sacred is always and everywhere separated from the idea of the profane in the thought of men, and since we picture a sort of logical chasm between the two, the mind irresistibly refuses to allow the two corresponding things to be confounded, or even to be merely put in contact with each other; for such a promiscuity, or even too direct a contiguity, would contradict too violently the dissociation of these ideas in the mind. The sacred thing is *par excellence* that which the profane should not touch, and cannot touch with impunity. To be sure, this interdiction cannot go so far as to make all communication between the two worlds impossible; for if the profane could in no way enter into relations with the sacred, this latter could be good for nothing. But, in addition to the fact that this establishment of relations is always a delicate operation in itself, demanding great precautions and a more or less complicated initiation,[9] it is quite impossible, unless the profane is to lose its specific characteristics and become sacred after a fashion and to a certain degree itself. The two classes cannot even approach each other and keep their own nature at the same time.

Thus we arrive at the first criterion of religious beliefs. Undoubtedly there are secondary species within these two fundamental classes which, in their turn, are more or less incompatible with each other.[10] But the real characteristic of religious phenomena is that they always suppose a bipartite division of the whole universe, known and knowable, into two classes which embrace all that exists, but which radically exclude each other. Sacred things are those which the interdictions protect and isolate; profane things, those to which these interdictions are applied and which must remain at a distance from the first. Religious beliefs are the representations which express the nature of sacred things and the relations which they sustain, either with each other or with profane things. Finally, rites are the rules of conduct which prescribe how a man should comport himself in the presence of these sacred objects.

When a certain number of sacred things sustain relations of co-ordination or subordination with each other in such a way as to form a system having a certain unity, but which is not comprised within any other system of the same sort, the totality of these beliefs and their corresponding rites constitutes a religion. From this definition it is seen that a religion is not necessarily contained within one sole and single idea, and does not proceed from one unique principle which, though varying according to the circumstances under which it is applied, is nevertheless at bottom always the same: it is rather a whole made up of distinct and relatively individualized parts. Each homogeneous group of sacred things, or even each sacred thing of some importance, constitutes a centre of organization about which gravitate a group of beliefs and rites, or a particular cult; there is no religion, howsoever unified it may be, which does not recognize a plurality of sacred things. Even Christianity, at least in its Catholic form, admits, in addition to the divine personality which, incidentally, is triple as well as one, the Virgin, angels, saints, souls of the dead, etc. Thus a religion cannot be reduced to one single cult generally, but rather consists in a system of cults, each endowed with a certain autonomy. Also, this autonomy is variable. Sometimes they are arranged in a hierarchy, and subordinated to some predominating cult, into which they are finally absorbed; but sometimes, also, they are merely rearranged and united. The religion which we are going to study will furnish us with an example of just this latter sort of organization.

At the same time we find the explanation of how there can be groups of religious phenomena which do not belong to any special religion; it is because they have not been, or are no longer, a part of any religious system. If, for some special reason, one of the cults of which we just spoke happens to be maintained while the group of which it was a part disappears, it survives only in a disintegrated condition. That is what has happened to many agrarian cults which have survived themselves as folk-lore. In certain cases, it is not even a cult, but a simple ceremony or particular rite which persists in this way.[11]

Although this definition is only preliminary, it permits us to see in what terms the problem which necessarily dominates the science of religions should be stated. When we believed that sacred beings could be distinguished from others merely by the greater intensity of the powers attributed to them, the question of how men came to imagine them was sufficiently simple: it was enough to demand which forces had, because of their exceptional energy, been able to strike the human imagination forcefully enough to inspire religious sentiments. But if, as we have sought to establish, sacred things differ in nature from profane things, if they have a wholly different essence, then the problem is more complex. For we must first of all ask what has been able to lead men to see in the world two heterogeneous and incompatible worlds, though nothing in sensible experience seems able to suggest the idea of so radical a duality to them.

IV

However, this definition is not yet complete, for it is equally applicable to two sorts of facts which, while being related to each other, must be distinguished nevertheless: these are magic and religion.

Magic, too, is made up of beliefs and rites. Like religion, it has its myths and its dogmas; only they are more elementary, undoubtedly because, seeking technical and utilitarian ends, it does not waste its time in pure speculation. It has its ceremonies, sacrifices, lustrations, prayers, chants and dances as well. The beings which the magician invokes and the forces which he throws in play are not merely of the same nature as the forces and beings to which religion addresses itself; very frequently, they are identically the same. Thus, even with the most inferior societies, the souls of the dead are essentially sacred things, and the object of religious rites. But at the same time, they play a considerable rôle in magic. In Australia[12] as well as in Melanesia,[13] in Greece as well as among the Christian peoples,[14] the souls of the dead, their bones and their hair, are among the intermediaries used the most frequently by the magician. Demons are also a common instrument for magic action. Now these demons are also beings surrounded with interdictions; they too are separated and live in a world apart, so that it is frequently difficult to distinguish them from the gods properly so-called.[15] Moreover, in Christianity itself, is not the devil a fallen god, or even leaving aside all question of his origin, does he not have a religious character from the mere fact that the hell of which he has charge is something indispensable to the Christian religion? There are even some regular and official deities who are invoked by the magician. Sometimes these are the gods of a foreign people; for example, Greek magicians called upon Egyptian, Assyrian or Jewish gods. Sometimes, they are even national gods; Hecate and Diana were the object of a magic cult; the Virgin, Christ and the saints have been utilized in the same way by Christian magicians.[16]

Then will it be necessary to say that magic is hardly distinguishable from religion; that magic is full of religion just as religion is full of magic, and consequently that it is impossible to separate them and to define the one without the other? It is difficult to sustain this thesis, because of the marked repugnance of religion for magic, and in return, the hostility of the second towards the first. Magic takes a sort of professional pleasure in profaning holy things;[17] in its rites, it performs the contrary of the religious ceremony.[18] On its side, religion, when it has not condemned and prohibited magic rites, has always looked upon them with disfavour. As Hubert and Mauss have remarked, there is something thoroughly anti-religious in the doings of the magician.[19] Whatever relations there may be between these two sorts of institutions, it is difficult to imagine their not being opposed somewhere; and it is still more necessary for us to find where they are differentiated, as we plan to limit our researches to religion, and to stop at the point where magic commences.

Here is how a line of demarcation can be traced between these two domains.

The really religious beliefs are always common to a determined group, which makes profession of adhering to them and of practising the rites connected with them. They are not merely received individually by all the members of this group; they are something belonging to the group, and they make its unity. The individuals which compose it feel themselves united to each other by the simple fact that they have a common faith. A society whose members are united by the fact that they think in the same way in regard to the sacred world and its relations with the profane world, and by the fact that they translate these common ideas into common practices, is what is called a Church. In all history, we do not find a single religion without a Church. Sometimes the Church is strictly national, sometimes it passes the frontiers; sometimes it embraces an entire people (Rome, Athens, the Hebrews), sometimes it embraces only a part of them (the Christian societies since the advent of Protestantism); sometimes it is directed by a corps of priests, sometimes it is almost completely devoid of any official directing body.[20] But wherever we observe the religious life, we find that it has a definite group as its foundation. Even the so-called private cults, such as the domestic cult or the cult of a corporation, satisfy this condition; for they are always celebrated by a group, the family or the corporation. Moreover, even these particular religions are ordinarily only special forms of a more general religion which embraces all;[21] these restricted Churches are in reality only chapels of a vaster Church which, by reason of this very extent, merits this name still more.[22]

It is quite another matter with magic. To be sure, the belief in magic is always more or less general; it is very frequently diffused in large masses of the population, and there are even peoples where it has as many adherents as the real religion. But it does not result in binding together those who adhere to it, nor in uniting them into a group leading a common life. *There is no Church of magic.* Between the magician and the individuals who consult him, as between these individuals themselves, there are no lasting bonds which make them members of the same moral community, comparable to that formed by the believers in the same god or the observers of the same cult. The magician has a clientele and not a Church, and it is very possible that his clients have no other relations between each other, or even do not know each other; even the relations which they have with him are generally accidental and transient; they are just like those of a sick man with his physician. The official and public character with which he is sometimes invested changes nothing in this situation; the fact that he works openly does not unite him more regularly or more durably to those who have recourse to his services.

It is true that in certain cases, magicians form societies among themselves; it happens that they assemble more or less periodically to celebrate certain rites in common; it is well known what a place these assemblies of witches hold in European folk-lore. But it is to be remarked that these associations are in no way indispensable to the working of the magic; they are even rare and rather exceptional. The magician has no need of uniting himself to his fellows to practise his art. More frequently, he is a recluse; in general, far from seeking society, he flees it. 'Even in regard to his colleagues, he always keeps his personal independence.'[23] Religion, on the other hand, is inseparable from the idea of a Church. From this point of view, there is an essential difference between magic and religion. But what is especially important is that when these societies of magic are formed, they do not include all the adherents to magic, but only the magicians; the laymen, if they may be so called, that is to say, those for whose profit the rites are celebrated, in fine, those who represent the worshippers in the regular cults, are excluded. Now the magician is for magic what the priest is for religion, but a college of priests is not a Church, any more than a religious congregation which should devote itself to some particular saint in the shadow of a cloister, would be a particular cult. A Church is not a fraternity of priests; it is a moral community formed by all the believers in a single faith, laymen as well as priests. But magic lacks any such community.[24]

But if the idea of a Church is made to enter into the definition of religion, does that not exclude the private religions which the individual establishes for himself and celebrates by himself? There is scarcely a society where these are not found. Every Ojibway, [. . .] has his own personal *manitou*, which he chooses himself and to which he renders special religious services; the Melanesian of the Banks Islands has his *tamaniu*;[25] the Roman, his *genius*;[26] the Christian, his patron saint and guardian angel, etc. By definition all these cults seem to be independent of all idea of the group. Not only are these individual religions very frequent in history, but nowadays many are asking if they are not destined to be the pre-eminent form of the religious life, and if the day will not come when there will be no other cult than that which each man will freely perform within himself.[27]

But if we leave these speculations in regard to the future aside for the moment, and confine ourselves to religions such as they are at present or have been in the past, it becomes clearly evident that these individual cults are not distinct and autonomous religious systems, but merely aspects of the common religion of the whole Church, of which the individuals are members. The patron saint of the Christian is chosen from the official list of saints recognized by the Catholic Church; there are even canonical rules prescribing how each Catholic should perform this private cult. In the same way, the idea that each man necessarily has a protecting genius is found, under different forms, at the basis of a great number of American religions, as well as of the Roman religion (to cite only these two examples); for, as will be seen later, it is very closely connected with the idea of the soul, and this idea of the soul is not one of those which can be left entirely to individual choice. In a word, it is the Church of which he is a member which teaches the individual what these personal gods are, what their function is, how he should enter into relations with them and how he should honour them. When a methodical analysis is made of the doctrines of any Church whatsoever, sooner or later we come upon those concerning private cults. So these are not two religions of different types, and turned in opposite directions; both are made up of the same ideas and the same principles, here applied to circumstances which are of interest to the group as a whole, there to the life of the individual. This solidarity is even so close that among certain peoples,[28] the ceremonies by which the faithful first enter into communication with their protecting geniuses are mixed with rites whose public character is incontestable, namely the rites of initiation.[29]

There still remain those contemporary aspirations towards a religion which would consist entirely in internal and subjective states, and which would be constructed freely by each of us. But howsoever real these aspirations may be, they cannot affect our definition, for this is to be applied only to facts already realized, and not to uncertain possibilities. One can define religions such as they are, or such as they have been, but not such as they more or less vaguely tend to become. It is possible that this religious individualism is destined to be realized in facts; but before we can say just how far this may be the case, we must first know what religion is, of what elements it is made up, from what causes it results, and what function it fulfils – all questions whose solution cannot be foreseen before the threshold of our study has been passed. It is only at the close of this study that we can attempt to anticipate the future.

Thus we arrive at the following definition: *A religion is a unified system of beliefs and practices relative to sacred things, that is to say, things set apart and forbidden – beliefs and practices which unite into one single moral community called a Church, all those who adhere to them.* The second element which thus finds a place in our definition is no less essential than the first; for by showing that the idea of religion is inseparable from that of the Church, it makes it clear that religion should be an eminently collective thing.[30]

NOTES

1. We have already attempted to define religious phenomena in a paper which was published in the *Année Sociologique* (Vol. II, pp. 1 ff.). The definition then given differs, as will be seen, from the one we give to-day.
2. See *Elementary Forms of the Religious Life*, p. 3. We shall say nothing more upon the necessity of these preliminary definitions nor upon the method to be followed to attain them. That is exposed in our *Règles de la Méthode sociologique*, pp. 43 ff. Cf. *Le Suicide*, pp. 1 ff. (Paris, F. Alcan).
3. Not to mention the sage and the saint who practise these truths and who for that reason are sacred.
4. This is not saying that these relations cannot take a religious character. But they do not do so necessarily.
5. Schultze, *Fetichismus*, p. 129.
6. Examples of these usages will be found in Frazer, *Golden Bough*, 2 edit., I, pp. 81 ff.

7. The conception according to which the profane is opposed to the sacred, just as the irrational is to the rational, or the intelligible is to the mysterious, is only one of the forms under which this opposition is expressed. Science being once constituted, it has taken a profane character, especially in the eyes of the Christian religions; from that it appears as though it could not be applied to sacred things.

8. See Frazer, 'On Some Ceremonies of the Central Australian Tribes' in *Australian Association for the Advancement of Science*, 1901, pp. 313 ff. This conception is also of an extreme generality. In India, the simple participation in the sacrificial act has the same effects; the sacrificer, by the mere act of entering within the circle of sacred things, changes his personality. (See Hubert and Mauss, 'Essai sur le Sacrifice' in the *Année Sociologique*, II, p. 101).

9. See what was said of the initiation above.

10. For example, certain species of sacred things exist, between which there is an incompatibility as all-exclusive as that between the sacred and the profane (Bk. III, ch. v, § 4).

11. This is the case with certain marriage and funeral rites, for example.

12. See Spencer and Gillen, *Native Tribes of Central Australia*, pp. 534 ff.; *Northern Tribes of Central Australia*, p. 463; Howitt, *Native Tribes of S.E. Australia*, pp. 359–361.

13. See Codrington, *The Melanesians*, ch. xii.

14. See Hubert, art. 'Magia' in *Dictionnaire des Antiquités*.

15. For example, in Melanesia, the *tindalo* is a spirit, now religious, now magic (Codrington, pp. 125 ff., 194 ff.).

16. See Hubert and Mauss, 'Théorie Générale de la Magie', in *Année Sociologique*, vol. VII, pp. 83–84.

17. For example, the host is profaned in the black mass.

18. One turns his back to the altar, or goes around the altar commencing by the left instead of by the right.

19. *Loc. cit.*, p. 19.

20. Undoubtedly it is rare that a ceremony does not have some director at the moment when it is celebrated; even in the most crudely organized societies, there are generally certain men whom the importance of their social position points out to exercise a directing influence over the religious life (for example, the chiefs of the local groups of certain Australian societies). But this attribution of functions is still very uncertain.

21. At Athens, the gods to whom the domestic cult was addressed were only specialized forms of the gods of the city (Ζεύς κτήσιος, Ζεὺς ἑρκεῖος). In the same way, in the Middle Ages, the patrons of the guilds were saints of the calendar.

22. For the name Church is ordinarily applied only to a group whose common beliefs refer to a circle of more special affairs.

23. Hubert and Mauss, *loc. cit.*, p. 18.

24. Robertson Smith has already pointed out that magic is opposed to religion, as the individual to the social (*The Religion of the Semites*, 2 edit., pp. 264–265). Also, in thus distinguishing magic from religion, we do not mean to establish a break of continuity between them. The frontiers between the two domains are frequently uncertain.

25. Codrington, *Trans. and Proc. Roy. Soc. of Victoria*, XVI, p. 136.

26. Negrioli, *Dei Genii presso i Romani*.

27. This is the conclusion reached by Spencer in his *Ecclesiastical Institutions* (ch. xvi), and by Sabatier in his *Outlines of a Philosophy of Religion, based on Psychology and History* (tr. by Seed), and by all the school to which he belongs.

28. Notably among numerous Indian tribes of North America.

29. This statement of fact does not touch the question whether exterior and public religion is not merely the development of an interior and personal religion which

was the primitive fact, or whether, on the contrary, the second is not the projection of the first into individual consciences. [...] For the moment, we confine ourselves to remarking that the individual cult is presented to the observer as an element of, and something dependent upon, the collective cult.

30. It is by this that our present definition is connected to the one we have already proposed in the *Année Sociologique*. In this other work, we defined religious beliefs exclusively by their obligatory character; but [...] this obligation evidently comes from the fact that these beliefs are the possession of a group which imposes them upon its members. The two definitions are thus in a large part the same. If we have thought it best to propose a new one, it is because the first was too formal, and neglected the contents of the religious representations too much. It will be seen, in the discussions which follow, how important it is to put this characteristic into evidence at once. Moreover, if their imperative character is really a distinctive trait of religious beliefs, it allows of an infinite number of degrees; consequently there are even cases where it is not easily perceptible. Hence come difficulties and embarrassments which are avoided by substituting for this criterion the one we now employ.

LUDWIG FEUERBACH
'THE ESSENCE OF RELIGION CONSIDERED GENERALLY'

Ludwig Feuerbach was born in 1804 in Bavaria. His father was a lawyer of some repute and his family of general good standing. By the age of sixteen Ludwig was showing a talent for theology and he pursued this first at Heidelberg and later at Berlin. In Berlin he quickly fell under the spell of Hegel and abandoned theological studies, throwing himself wholly into the study of philosophy. However, in 1826 his stipend was cut and Feuerbach was forced to complete his studies at the more moderately priced Erlangen University. In 1829 he moved from being a student in Erlangen to being a lecturer. His radical theological convictions ensured that he struggled to find promotion, nor could he secure a superior post in any other university. In protest at being denied promotion Feuerbach refused to teach, yet remained active in research, producing a string of increasingly less well-received publications. Feuerbach died at the age of 68.

Feuerbach developed three different approaches to religion. Each of these approaches attempted to reduce religion to another sphere: the essence of human nature, the essence of nature, and ultimately to the essence of human desire. We have included material that develops the first of these approaches, that is, God is reduced to expressing the essence of human nature.

What we have hitherto been maintaining generally, even with regard to sensational impressions, of the relation between subject and object, applies especially to the relation between the subject and the religious object.

In the perceptions of the senses consciousness of the object is distinguishable from consciousness of self; but in religion, consciousness of the object and self-consciousness coincide. The object of the senses is out of man, the religious object is within him, and therefore as little forsakes him as his self-consciousness or his conscience; it is the intimate, the closest object. 'God,' says Augustine, for example, 'is nearer, more related to us, and therefore more easily known by us, than sensible, corporeal things.'[1] The object of the senses is in itself indifferent – independent of the disposition or of the judgment; but the object of religion is a selected object; the most excellent, the first, the supreme being; it essentially presupposes a critical judgment, a discrimination between the divine and the non-divine, between that which is worthy of adoration and that which is not worthy.[2] And here may be applied, without any limitation, the proposition: the object of any subject is nothing else than the subject's own nature taken objectively. Such as are a man's thoughts and dispositions, such is his God; so much worth

---

Ludwig Feuerbach ([1855], 1957), *The Essence of Christianity*, tr. George Eliot, New York: Harper and Row.

as a man has, so much and no more has his God. Consciousness of God is self-consciousness, knowledge of God is self-knowledge. By his God thou knowest the man, and by the man his God; the two are identical. Whatever is God to a man, that is his heart and soul; and conversely, God is the manifested inward nature, the expressed self of a man – religion the solemn unveiling of a man's hidden treasures, the revelation of his intimate thoughts, the open confession of his love-secrets.

But when religion – consciousness of God – is designated as the self-consciousness of man, this is not to be understood as affirming that the religious man is directly aware of this identity; for, on the contrary, ignorance of it is fundamental to the peculiar nature of religion. To preclude this misconception, it is better to say, religion is man's earliest and also indirect form of self-knowledge. Hence, religion everywhere precedes philosophy, as in the history of the race, so also in that of the individual. Man first of all sees his nature as if *out of* himself, before he finds it in himself. His own nature is in the first instance contemplated by him as that of another being. Religion is the childlike condition of humanity; but the child sees his nature – man – out of himself; in childhood a man is an object to himself, under the form of another man. Hence the historical progress of religion consists in this: that what by an earlier religion was regarded as objective, is now recognised as subjective; that is, what was formerly contemplated and worshipped as God is now perceived to be something *human*. What was at first religion becomes at a later period idolatry; man is seen to have adored his own nature. Man has given objectivity to himself, but has not recognised the object as his own nature: a later religion takes this forward step; every advance in religion is therefore a deeper self-knowledge. But every particular religion, while it pronounces its predecessors idolatrous, excepts itself – and necessarily so, otherwise it would no longer be religion – from the fate, the common nature of all religions: it imputes only to other religions what is the fault, if fault it be, of religion in general. Because it has a different object, a different tenour, because it has transcended the ideas of preceding religions, it erroneously supposes itself exalted above the necessary eternal laws which constitute the essence of religion – it fancies its object, its ideas, to be superhuman. But the essence of religion, thus hidden from the religious, is evident to the thinker, by whom religion is viewed objectively, which it cannot be by its votaries. And it is our task to show that the antithesis of divine and human is altogether illusory, that it is nothing else than the antithesis between the human nature in general, and the human individual: that, consequently, the object and contents of the Christian religion are altogether human.

Religion, at least the Christian, is the relation of man to himself, or more correctly to his own nature (*i.e.*, his subjective nature);[3] but a relation to it, viewed as a nature apart from his own. The divine being is nothing else than the human being, or, rather the human nature purified, freed from the limits of the individual man, made objective – *i.e.*, contemplated and revered as another, a distinct being. All the attributes of the divine nature are, therefore, attributes of the human nature.[4]

In relation to the attributes, the predicates, of the Divine Being, this is admitted without hesitation, but by no means in relation to the subject of these predicates. The negation of the subject is held to be irreligion, nay, atheism; though not so the negation of the predicates. But that which has no predicates or qualities, has no effect upon me; that which has no effect upon me, has no existence for me. To deny all the qualities of a being is equivalent to denying the being himself. A being without qualities is one which cannot become an object to the mind; and such a being is virtually non-existent. Where man deprives God of all qualities, God is no longer anything more to him than a negative being. To the truly religious man, God is not a being without qualities, because to him he is a positive, real being. The theory that God cannot be defined, and consequently cannot be known by man, is therefore the offspring of recent times, a product of modern unbelief.

[...]

But he who defines God as an active being, and not only so, but as morally active and morally critical, – as a being who loves, works, and rewards good, punishes, rejects, and condemns evil, – he who thus defines God, only in appearance denies human activity, in fact making it the highest, the most real activity. He who makes God act humanly, declares human activity to be divine; he says: a god who is not active, and not morally or humanly active, is no god; and thus he makes the idea of the Godhead dependent on the idea of activity, that is, of human activity, for a higher he knows not.

Man – this is the mystery of religion – projects his being into objectivity,[5] and then again makes himself an object to this projected image of himself thus converted into a subject; he thinks of himself, is an object to himself, but as the object of an object, of another being than himself. Thus here. Man is an object to God. That man is good or evil is not indifferent to God; no! He has a lively, profound interest in man's being good; he wills that man should be good, happy – for without goodness there is no happiness. Thus the religious man virtually retracts the nothingness of human activity, by making his dispositions and actions an object to God, by making man the end of God – for that which is an object to the mind is an end in action; by making the divine activity a means of human salvation. God acts, that man may be good and happy. Thus man, while he is apparently humiliated to the lowest degree, is in truth exalted to the highest. Thus, in and through God, man has in view himself alone. It is true that man places the aim of his action in God, but God has no other aim of action than the moral and eternal salvation of man: thus man has in fact no other aim than himself. The divine activity is not distinct from the human.

How could the divine activity work on me as its object, nay, work in me, if it were essentially different from me; how could it have a human aim, the aim of ameliorating and blessing man, if it were not itself human? Does not the purpose determine the nature of the act? When man makes his moral improvement an aim to himself, he has divine resolutions, divine projects; but also, when God seeks the salvation of man, He has human ends and a human mode of activity, corresponding to these ends. Thus in God man has only his own activity as an object. But, for the very reason that he regards his own activity as objective, goodness only as an object, he necessarily receives the impulse, the motive, not from himself, but from this object. He contemplates his nature as external to himself, and this nature as goodness; thus it is self-evident, it is mere tautology to say, that the impulse to good comes only from thence where he places the good.

God is the highest subjectivity of man abstracted from himself; hence man can do nothing of himself, all goodness comes from God. The more subjective God is, the more completely does man divest himself of his subjectivity, because God is, *per se*, his relinquished self, the possession of which he however again vindicates to himself. As the action of the arteries drives the blood into the extremities, and the action of the veins brings it back again, as life in general consists in a perpetual systole and diastole; so is it in religion. In the religious systole man propels his own nature from himself, he throws himself outward; in the religious diastole he receives the rejected nature into his heart again. God alone is the being who acts of himself, – this is the force of repulsion in religion; God is the being who acts in me, with me, through me, upon me, for me, is the principle of my salvation, of my good dispositions and actions, consequently my own good principle and nature, – this is the force of attraction in religion.

The course of religious development which has been generally indicated, consists specifically in this, that man abstracts more and more from God, and attributes more and more to himself. This is especially apparent in the belief in revelation. That which to a later age or a cultured people is given by nature or reason, is to an earlier age, or to a yet uncultured people, given by God. Every tendency of man, however natural – even the impulse to cleanliness, was conceived by the Israelites as a positive divine ordinance. From this example we again see that God is lowered, is conceived more entirely on the type of ordinary humanity, in proportion as man detracts from himself. How can the self-humiliation of man go further than when he disclaims the capability of fulfilling spontaneously the requirements of common decency?[6] The Christian religion, on the other hand, distinguished the impulses and passions of man according to their quality, their character; it represented only good emotions, good dispositions, good thoughts, as revelations, operations – that is, as dispositions, feelings, thoughts, – of

God; for what God reveals is a quality of God himself: that of which the heart is full, overflows the lips, as is the effect such is the cause, as the revelation, such the being who reveals himself. A God who reveals himself in good dispositions is a God whose essential attribute is only moral perfection. The Christian religion distinguishes inward moral purity from external physical purity; the Israelites identified the two.[7] In relation to the Israelitish religion, the Christian religion is one of criticism and freedom. The Israelite trusted himself to do nothing except what was commanded by God; he was without will even in external things; the authority of religion extended itself even to his food. The Christian religion, on the other hand, in all these external things, made man dependent on himself, *i.e.*, placed in man what the Israelite placed out of himself, in God. Israel is the most complete presentation of positivism in religion. In relation to the Israelite, the Christian is an *esprit fort*, a free-thinker. Thus do things change. What yesterday was still religion, is no longer such to-day; and what to-day is atheism, to-morrow will be religion.

NOTES

1. De Genesi ad litteram, 1. v. c. 16.
2. Unusquisque vestrum non cogitat, *prius* se debere Deum *nosse*, quam *colere*. – M. Minucii Felicis Octavianus, c. 24.
3. The meaning of this parenthetic limitation will be clear in the sequel.
4. Les perfections de Dieu sont celles de nos âmes, mais il les possède sans bornes – il y a en nous quelque puissance, quelque connaissance, quelque bonté, mais elles sont toutes entières en Dieu. – Leibnitz, (Théod. Preface.) Nihil in anima esse putemus eximium, quod non etiam divinæ naturæ proprium sit – Quidquid a Deo alienum extra definitionem animæ. – S. Gregorius Nyss. Est ergo, ut videtur, disciplinarum omnium pulcherrima et maxima se ipsum nosse; si quis enim se ipsum norit, Deum cognoscet. – Clemens Alex. (Pæd. 1. iii. c. 1.)
5. The religious, the original mode in which man becomes objective to himself, is (as is clearly enough explained in this work) to be distinguished from the mode in which this occurs in reflection and speculation; the latter is voluntary, the former involuntary, necessary – as necessary as art, as speech. With the progress of time, it is true, theology coincides with religion.
6. Deut. xxiii. 12, 13.
7. See, for example, Gen. xxxv. 2; Levit. xi. 44; xx. 26; and the Commentary of Le Clerc on these passages.

JAMES FRAZER
'MAGIC AND RELIGION'

James Frazer was born into a middle-class, Christian Glaswegian family in 1854. He excelled at school and graduated from Glasgow University whilst still a teenager. At Glasgow Frazer had been particularly impressed by Ramsay and this was no doubt the inspiration for Frazer's lifelong obsession with classics. Although he had developed a general dislike of modern science he became interested in the burgeoning discipline of anthropology. This fascination with anthropology developed during his time at Trinity College, Cambridge, where he was first a student and later a fellow. It was at Cambridge that Frazer came into contact with Robertson Smith, who took a post there in 1884. Six years later the first edition of Frazer's most famous work, The Golden Bough, *was published.*

While James Frazer was highly influential in the early part of the twentieth century, anthropologists largely ignore his analyses today. The Golden Bough *highlights many of the problems with his approach. It brings together wide ranges of unrelated data, which often arise from unreliable or problematic sources (for example missionaries). It is also problematic due to its strongly evolutionary basis. The material chosen here illustrates many of these issues.*

The fatal flaw of magic lies not in its general assumption of a sequence of events determined by law, but in its total misconception of the nature of the particular laws which govern that sequence. If we analyse the various cases of sympathetic magic which have been passed in review in the preceding pages, and which may be taken as fair samples of the bulk, we shall find, as I have already indicated, that they are all mistaken applications of one or other of two great fundamental laws of thought, namely, the association of ideas by similarity and the association of ideas by contiguity in space or time. A mistaken association of similar ideas produces homoeopathic or imitative magic: a mistaken association of contiguous ideas produces contagious magic. The principles of association are excellent in themselves, and indeed absolutely essential to the working of the human mind. Legitimately applied they yield science; illegitimately applied they yield magic, the bastard sister of science. It is therefore a truism, almost a tautology, to say that all magic is necessarily false and barren; for were it ever to become true and fruitful, it would no longer be magic but science. From the earliest times man has been engaged in a search for general rules whereby to turn the order of natural phenomena to his own advantage, and in the long search he has scraped together a great hoard of such maxims, some of them golden and some of them mere dross. The true or golden rules constitute the body of applied science which we call the arts; the false are magic.

James Frazer (1923), *The Golden Bough*, London: Macmillan.

If magic is thus next of kin to science, we have still to enquire how it stands related to religion. But the view we take of that relation will necessarily be coloured by the idea which we have formed of the nature of religion itself; hence a writer may reasonably be expected to define his conception of religion before he proceeds to investigate its relation to magic. There is probably no subject in the world about which opinions differ so much as the nature of religion, and to frame a definition of it which would satisfy every one must obviously be impossible. All that a writer can do is, first, to say clearly what he means by religion, and afterwards to employ the word consistently in that sense throughout his work. By religion, then, I understand a propitiation or conciliation of powers superior to man which are believed to direct and control the course of nature and of human life. Thus defined, religion consists of two elements, a theoretical and a practical, namely, a belief in powers higher than man and an attempt to propitiate or please them. Of the two, belief clearly comes first, since we must believe in the existence of a divine being before we can attempt to please him. But unless the belief leads to a corresponding practice, it is not a religion but merely a theology; in the language of St. James, 'faith, if it hath not works, is dead, being alone.' In other words, no man is religious who does not govern his conduct in some measure by the fear or love of God. On the other hand, mere practice, divested of all religious belief, is also not religion. Two men may behave in exactly the same way, and yet one of them may be religious and the other not. If the one acts from the love or fear of God, he is religious; if the other acts from the love or fear of man, he is moral or immoral according as his behaviour comports or conflicts with the general good. Hence belief and practice or, in theological language, faith and works are equally essential to religion, which cannot exist without both of them. But it is not necessary that religious practice should always take the form of a ritual; that is, it need not consist in the offering of sacrifice, the recitation of prayers, and other outward ceremonies. Its aim is to please the deity, and if the deity is one who delights in charity and mercy and purity more than in oblations of blood, the chanting of hymns, and the fumes of incense, his worshippers will best please him, not by prostrating themselves before him, by intoning his praises, and by filling his temples with costly gifts, but by being pure and merciful and charitable towards men, for in so doing they will imitate, so far as human infirmity allows, the perfections of the divine nature. It was this ethical side of religion which the Hebrew prophets, inspired with a noble ideal of God's goodness and holiness, were never weary of inculcating. Thus Micah says: 'He hath shewed thee, O man, what is good; and what doth the Lord require of thee, but to do justly, and to love mercy, and to walk humbly with thy God?' And at a later time much of the force by which Christianity conquered the world was drawn from the same high conception of God's moral nature and the duty laid on men of conforming themselves to it. 'Pure religion and undefiled,' says St. James, 'before God and the Father is this, To visit the fatherless and widows in their affliction, and to keep himself unspotted from the world.'

But if religion involves, first, a belief in superhuman beings who rule the world, and, second, an attempt to win their favour, it clearly assumes that the course of nature is to some extent elastic or variable, and that we can persuade or induce the mighty beings who control it to deflect, for our benefit, the current of events from the channel in which they would otherwise flow. Now this implied elasticity or variability of nature is directly opposed to the principles of magic as well as of science, both of which assume that the processes of nature are rigid and invariable in their operation, and that they can as little be turned from their course by persuasion and entreaty as by threats and intimidation. The distinction between the two conflicting views of the universe turns on their answer to the crucial question, Are the forces which govern the world conscious and personal, or unconscious and impersonal? Religion, as a conciliation of the superhuman powers, assumes the former member of the alternative. For all conciliation implies that the being conciliated is a conscious or personal agent, that his conduct is in some measure uncertain, and that he can be prevailed upon to vary it in the desired direction by a judicious appeal to his interests, his appetites, or his emotions. Conciliation is never employed towards things which are regarded as inanimate, nor towards persons whose behaviour in the particular circumstances is known to be determined with absolute certainty. Thus in so far as religion assumes the world to be directed by conscious agents who may be turned from their purpose by persuasion, it stands in fundamental antagonism to magic as well as to science, both of which take for granted that the course of nature is determined, not by the passions or caprice of personal beings, but by the operation of immutable laws acting mechanically. In magic, indeed, the assumption is only implicit, but in science it is explicit. It is true that magic often deals with spirits, which are personal agents of the kind assumed by religion; but whenever it does so in its proper form, it treats them exactly in the same fashion as it treats inanimate agents, that is, it constrains or coerces instead of conciliating or propitiating them as religion would do. Thus it assumes that all personal beings, whether human or divine, are in the last resort subject to those impersonal forces which control all things, but which nevertheless can be turned to account by any one who knows how to manipulate them by the appropriate ceremonies and spells. In ancient Egypt, for example, the magicians claimed the power of compelling even the highest gods to do their bidding, and actually threatened them with destruction in case of disobedience. Sometimes, without going quite so far as that, the wizard declared that he would scatter the bones of Osiris or reveal his sacred legend, if the god proved contumacious. Similarly in India at the present day the great Hindoo trinity itself of Brahma, Vishnu, and Siva is subject to the sorcerers, who, by means of their spells, exercise such an ascendancy over the mightiest deities, that these are bound submissively to execute on earth below, or in heaven above, whatever commands their masters the magicians may please to issue. There is a saying everywhere current in India: 'The whole universe is subject to the gods; the gods are subject to the spells (*mantras*); the spells to the Brahmans; therefore the Brahmans are our gods.'

This radical conflict of principle between magic and religion sufficiently explains the relentless hostility with which in history the priest has often pursued the magician. The haughty self-sufficiency of the magician, his arrogant demeanour towards the higher powers, and his unabashed claim to exercise a sway like theirs could not but revolt the priest, to whom, with his awful sense of the divine majesty, and his humble prostration in presence of it, such claims and such a demeanour must have appeared an impious and blasphemous usurpation of prerogatives that belong to God alone. And sometimes, we may suspect, lower motives concurred to whet the edge of the priest's hostility. He professed to be the proper medium, the true intercessor between God and man, and no doubt his interests as well as his feelings were often injured by a rival practitioner, who preached a surer and smoother road to fortune than the rugged and slippery path of divine favour.

Yet this antagonism, familiar as it is to us, seems to have made its appearance comparatively late in the history of religion. At an earlier stage the functions of priest and sorcerer were often combined or, to speak perhaps more correctly, were not yet differentiated from each other. To serve his purpose man wooed the good-will of gods or spirits by prayer and sacrifice, while at the same time he had recourse to ceremonies and forms of words which he hoped would of themselves bring about the desired result without the help of god or devil. In short, he performed religious and magical rites simultaneously; he uttered prayers and incantations almost in the same breath, knowing or recking little of the theoretical inconsistency of his behaviour, so long as by hook or crook he contrived to get what he wanted. Instances of this fusion or confusion of magic with religion have already met us in the practices of Melanesians and of other peoples.

[. . .]

Yet though magic is thus found to fuse and amalgamate with religion in many ages and in many lands, there are some grounds for thinking that this fusion is not primitive, and that there was a time when man trusted to magic alone for the satisfaction of such wants as transcended his immediate animal cravings. In the first place a consideration of the fundamental notions of magic and religion may incline us to surmise that magic is older than religion in the history of humanity. We have seen that on the one hand magic is nothing but a mistaken application of the very simplest and most elementary processes of the mind, namely the association of ideas by virtue of resemblance or contiguity; and that on the other hand religion assumes the operation of conscious or personal agents, superior to man, behind the visible screen of nature. Obviously the conception of personal agents is more complex than a simple recognition of the similarity or contiguity of ideas; and a theory which assumes that the course of nature is determined by conscious agents is more abstruse and recondite, and requires for its apprehension a far higher degree of intelligence and reflection, than the view that things succeed each other simply by reason of their contiguity or resemblance. The very beasts associate the ideas of things that are like each other or that have been found together in their experience; and they could hardly survive for a day if they ceased to do so. But who attributes to the animals a belief that the phenomena of nature are worked by a multitude of invisible animals or by one enormous and prodigiously strong animal behind the scenes? It is probably no injustice to the brutes to assume that the honour of devising a theory of this latter sort must be reserved for human reason. Thus, if magic be deduced immediately from elementary processes of reasoning, and be, in fact, an error into which the mind falls almost spontaneously, while religion rests on conceptions which the merely animal intelligence can hardly be supposed to have yet attained to, it becomes probable that magic arose before religion in the evolution of our race, and that man essayed to bend nature to his wishes by the sheer force of spells and enchantments before he strove to coax and mollify a coy, capricious, or irascible deity by the soft insinuation of prayer and sacrifice.

The conclusion which we have thus reached deductively from a consideration of the fundamental ideas of magic and religion is confirmed inductively by the observation that among the aborigines of Australia, the rudest savages as to whom we possess accurate information, magic is universally practised, whereas religion in the sense of a propitiation or conciliation of the higher powers seems to be nearly unknown. Roughly speaking, all men in Australia are magicians, but not one is a priest; everybody fancies he can influence his fellows or the course of nature by sympathetic magic, but nobody dreams of propitiating gods by prayer and sacrifice.

But if in the most backward state of human society now known to us we find magic thus conspicuously present and religion conspicuously absent, may we not reasonably conjecture that the civilised races of the world have also at some period of their history passed through a similar intellectual phase, that they attempted to force the great powers of nature to do their pleasure before they thought of courting their favour by offerings and prayer – in short that, just as on the material side of human culture there has everywhere been an Age of Stone, so on the intellectual side there has everywhere been an Age of Magic? There are reasons for answering this question in the affirmative. When we survey the existing races of mankind from Greenland to Tierra del Fuego, or from Scotland to Singapore, we observe that they are distinguished one from the other by a great variety of religions, and that these distinctions are not, so to speak, merely coterminous with the broad distinctions of race, but descend into the minuter sub-divisions of states and commonwealths, nay, that they honeycomb the town, the village, and even the family, so that the surface of society all over the world is cracked and seamed, sapped and mined with rents and fissures and yawning crevasses opened up by the disintegrating influence of religious dissension. Yet when we have penetrated through these differences, which affect mainly the intelligent and thoughtful part of the community, we shall find underlying them all a solid stratum of intellectual agreement among the dull, the weak, the ignorant, and the superstitious, who constitute, unfortunately, the vast majority of mankind. One of the great achievements of the nineteenth century was to run shafts down into this low mental stratum in many parts of the world, and thus to discover its substantial identity everywhere. It is beneath our feet – and not very far beneath them – here in Europe at the present day, and it crops up on the surface in the heart of the Australian wilderness and wherever the advent of a higher civilisation has not crushed it underground. This universal faith, this truly Catholic creed, is a belief in the efficacy of magic. While religious systems differ not only in different countries, but in the same country in different ages, the system of sympathetic magic remains everywhere and at all times substantially alike in its principles and practice. Among the ignorant and superstitious classes of modern Europe it is very much what it was thousands of years ago in Egypt and India, and what it now is among the lowest savages surviving in the remotest corners of the world. If the test of truth lay in a show of hands or a counting of heads, the system of magic might appeal, with far more reason than the Catholic Church, to the proud motto, 'Quod semper, quod ubique, quod ab omnibus,' as the sure and certain credential of its own infallibility.

It is not our business here to consider what bearing the permanent existence of such a solid layer of savagery beneath the surface of society, and unaffected by the superficial changes of religion and culture, has upon the future of humanity. The dispassionate observer, whose studies have led him to plumb its depths, can hardly regard it otherwise than as a standing menace to civilisation. We seem to move on a thin crust which may at any moment be rent by the subterranean forces slumbering below. From time to time a hollow murmur underground or a sudden spirt of flame into the air tells of what is going on beneath our feet. Now and then the polite world is startled by a paragraph in a newspaper which tells how in Scotland an image has been found stuck full of pins for the purpose of killing an obnoxious laird or minister, how a woman has been slowly roasted to death as a witch in Ireland, or how a girl has been murdered and chopped up in Russia to make those candles of human tallow by whose light thieves hope to pursue their midnight trade unseen. But whether the influences that make for further progress, or those that threaten to undo what has already been accomplished, will ultimately prevail; whether the impulsive energy of the minority or the dead weight of the majority of mankind will prove the stronger force to carry us up to higher heights or to sink us into lower depths, are questions rather for the sage, the moralist, and the statesman, whose eagle vision scans the future, than for the humble student of the present and the past. Here we are only concerned to ask how far the uniformity, the universality, and the permanence of a belief in magic, compared with the endless variety and the shifting character of religious creeds, raises a presumption that the former represents a ruder and earlier phase of the human mind, through which all the races of mankind have passed or are passing on their way to religion and science.

If an Age of Religion has thus everywhere, as I venture to surmise, been preceded by an Age of Magic, it is natural that we should enquire what causes have led mankind, or rather a portion of them, to abandon magic as a principle of faith and practice and to betake themselves to religion instead. When we reflect upon the multitude, the variety, and the complexity of the facts to be explained, and the scantiness of our information regarding them, we shall be ready to acknowledge that a full and satisfactory solution of so profound a problem is hardly to be hoped for and that the most we can do in the present state of our knowledge is to hazard a more or less plausible conjecture. With all due diffidence, then, I would suggest that a tardy recognition of the inherent falsehood and barrenness of magic set the more thoughtful part of mankind to cast about for a truer theory of nature and a more fruitful method of turning her resources to account. The shrewder intelligences must in time have come to perceive that magical ceremonies and incantations did not really effect the results which they were designed to produce, and which the majority of their simpler fellows still believed that they did actually produce. This great discovery of the inefficacy of magic must have wrought a radical though probably slow revolution in the minds of those who had the sagacity to make it. The discovery amounted to this, that men for the first time recognised their inability to manipulate at pleasure certain natural forces which hitherto they had believed to be completely within their control. It was a confession of human ignorance and weakness. Man saw that he had taken for causes what were no causes, and that all his efforts to work by means of these imaginary causes had been vain. His painful toil had been wasted, his curious ingenuity had been squandered to no purpose. He had been pulling at strings to which nothing was attached; he had been marching, as he thought, straight to the goal, while in reality he had only been treading in a narrow circle. Not that the effects which he had striven so hard to produce did not continue to manifest themselves. They were still produced, but not by him. The rain still fell on the thirsty ground: the sun still pursued his daily, and the moon her nightly journey across the sky: the silent procession of the seasons still moved in light and shadow, in cloud and sunshine across the earth: men were still born to labour and sorrow, and still, after a brief sojourn here, were gathered to their fathers in the long home hereafter. All things indeed went on as before, yet all seemed different to him from whose eyes the old scales had fallen. For he could no longer cherish the pleasing illusion that it was he who guided the earth and the heaven in their courses, and that they would cease to perform their great revolutions were he to take his feeble hand from the wheel. In the death of his enemies and his friends he no longer saw a proof of the resistless potency of his own or of hostile enchantments; he now knew that friends and foes alike had succumbed to a force stronger than any that he could wield, and in obedience to a destiny which he was powerless to control.

Thus cut adrift from his ancient moorings and left to toss on a troubled sea of doubt and uncertainty, his old happy confidence in himself and his powers rudely shaken, our primitive philosopher must have been sadly perplexed and agitated till he came to rest, as in a quiet haven after a tempestuous voyage, in a new system of faith and practice, which seemed to offer a solution of his harassing doubts and a substitute, however precarious, for that sovereignty over nature which he had reluctantly abdicated. If the great world went on its way without the help of him or his fellows, it must surely be because there were other beings, like himself, but far stronger, who, unseen themselves, directed its course and brought about all the varied series of events which he had hitherto believed to be dependent on his own magic. It was they, as he now believed, and not he himself, who made the stormy wind to blow, the lightning to flash, and the thunder to roll; who had laid the foundations of the solid earth and set bounds to the restless sea that it might not pass; who caused all the glorious lights of heaven to shine; who gave the fowls of the air their meat and the wild beasts of the desert their prey; who bade the fruitful land to bring forth in abundance, the high hills to be clothed with forests, the bubbling springs to rise under the rocks in the valleys, and green pastures to grow by still waters; who breathed into man's nostrils and made him live, or turned him to destruction by famine and pestilence and war. To these mighty beings, whose handiwork he traced in all the gorgeous and varied pageantry of nature, man now addressed himself, humbly confessing his dependence on their invisible power, and beseeching them of their mercy to furnish him with all good things, to defend him from the perils and dangers by which our mortal life is compassed about on every hand, and finally to bring his immortal spirit, freed from the burden of the body, to some happier world, beyond the reach of pain and sorrow, where he might rest with them and with the spirits of good men in joy and felicity for ever.

In this, or some such way as this, the deeper minds may be conceived to have made the great transition from magic to religion. But even in them the change can hardly ever have been sudden; probably it proceeded very slowly, and required long ages for its more or less perfect accomplishment.

For the recognition of man's powerlessness to influence the course of nature on a grand scale must have been gradual; he cannot have been shorn of the whole of his fancied dominion at a blow. Step by step he must have been driven back from his proud position; foot by foot he must have yielded, with a sigh, the ground which he had once viewed as his own. Now it would be the wind, now the rain, now the sunshine, now the thunder, that he confessed himself unable to wield at will; and as province after province of nature thus fell from his grasp, till what had once seemed a kingdom threatened to shrink into a prison, man must have been more and more profoundly impressed with a sense of his own helplessness and the might of the invisible beings by whom he believed himself to be surrounded. Thus religion, beginning as a slight and partial acknowledgment of powers superior to man, tends with the growth of knowledge to deepen into a confession of man's entire and absolute dependence on the divine; his old free bearing is exchanged for an attitude of lowliest prostration before the mysterious powers of the unseen, and his highest virtue is to submit his will to theirs: *In la sua volontade è nostra pace.* But this deepening sense of religion, this more perfect submission to the divine will in all things, affects only those higher intelligences who have breadth of view enough to comprehend the vastness of the universe and the littleness of man. Small minds cannot grasp great ideas; to their narrow comprehension, their purblind vision, nothing seems really great and important but themselves. Such minds hardly rise into religion at all. They are, indeed, drilled by their betters into an outward conformity with its precepts and a verbal profession of its tenets; but at heart they cling to their old magical superstitions, which may be discountenanced and forbidden, but cannot be eradicated by religion, so long as they have their roots deep down in the mental framework and constitution of the great majority of mankind.

SIGMUND FREUD
'THE RETURN OF TOTEMISM IN CHILDHOOD'

Sigmund Freud was born in Freiberg in Moravia (now Příbor, Czech Republic) in 1856. He was educated at the local Gymnasium and later at the University of Vienna, where he enrolled to study biology and medicine in 1873. He qualified in medicine in 1881 and began specialist studies in neurology. His work resulted in him receiving a lectureship in neuropathology in 1885 and a travelling fellowship, which he used to go to Paris, to study under Charcot. On his return to Vienna Freud set about putting into practice the techniques of treatment he had learned in Paris; although he was sceptically received at first, by the turn of the century he was well established with a burgeoning international reputation. The First World War caused his patients for psychoanalysis to dwindle and Freud believed that it was time to move into a new sphere of research and he began to pursue more metaphysical deliberations. In 1938 the Nazis invaded Austria and the 82-year-old Freud was forced to flee Vienna. He settled in London, where he lived out the rest of his life, dying as a result of morphine-induced coma in 1939.

Freud develops two interrelated theories of religion, the first in Totem and Taboo *and the second in* The Future of an Illusion. *While* Totem and Taboo *(included here) focuses on the Oedipus complex as the basis of religion,* The Future of an Illusion, *which is more concerned with the persistence and future of religion, relates religion to the child's projection of the father and the development of the superego.*

5

Let us call up the spectacle of a totem meal of the kind we have been discussing, amplified by a few probable features which we have not yet been able to consider. The clan is celebrating the ceremonial occasion by the cruel slaughter of its totem animal and is devouring it raw – blood, flesh and bones. The clansmen are there, dressed in the likeness of the totem and imitating it in sound and movement, as though they are seeking to stress their identity with it. Each man is conscious that he is performing an act forbidden to the individual and justifiable only through the participation of the whole clan; nor may anyone absent himself from the killing and the meal. When the deed is done, the slaughtered animal is lamented and bewailed. The mourning is obligatory, imposed by dread of a threatened retribution. As Robertson Smith (1894: 412) remarks of an analogous occasion, its chief purpose is to disclaim responsibility for the killing.

But the mourning is followed by demonstrations of festive rejoicing: every instinct is unfettered and there is licence for every kind of gratification. Here

---

Sigmund Freud (1950), *Totem and Taboo*, London: Routledge and Kegan Paul.

we have easy access to an understanding of the nature of festivals in general. A festival is a permitted, or rather an obligatory, excess, a solemn breach of a prohibition. It is not that men commit the excesses because they are feeling happy as a result of some injunction they have received. It is rather that excess is of the essence of a festival; the festive feeling is produced by the liberty to do what is as a rule prohibited.

What are we to make, though, of the prelude to this festive joy – the mourning over the death of the animal? If the clansmen rejoice over the killing of the totem – a normally forbidden act – why do they mourn over it as well?

As we have seen, the clansmen acquire sanctity by consuming the totem: they reinforce their identification with it and with one another. Their festive feelings and all that follows from them might well be explained by the fact that they have taken into themselves the sacred life of which the substance of the totem is the vehicle.

Psycho-analysis has revealed that the totem animal is in reality a substitute for the father; and this tallies with the contradictory fact that, though the killing of the animal is as a rule forbidden, yet its killing becomes a festive occasion – the fact that it is killed and yet mourned. The ambivalent emotional attitude, which to this day characterizes the father-complex in our children and which often persists into adult life, seems to extend to the totem animal in its capacity as substitute for the father.

If, now, we bring together the psycho-analytic translation of the totem with the fact of the totem meal and with Darwin's theories of the earliest state of human society, the possibility of a deeper understanding emerges – a glimpse of a hypothesis which may seem fantastic but which offers the advantage of establishing an unsuspected correlation between groups of phenomena that have hitherto been disconnected.

There is, of course, no place for the beginnings of totemism in Darwin's primal horde. All that we find there is a violent and jealous father who keeps all the females for himself and drives away his sons as they grow up. This earliest state of society has never been an object of observation. The most primitive kind of organization that we actually come across – and one that is in force to this day in certain tribes – consists of bands of males; these bands are composed of members with equal rights and are subject to the restrictions of the totemic system, including inheritance through the mother. Can this form of organization have developed out of the other one? and if so along what lines?

If we call the celebration of the totem meal to our help, we shall be able to find an answer. One day[1] the brothers who had been driven out came together, killed and devoured their father and so made an end of the patriarchal horde. United, they had the courage to do and succeeded in doing what would have been impossible for them individually. (Some cultural advance, perhaps, command over some new weapon, had given them a sense of superior strength.) Cannibal savages as they were, it goes without saying that they devoured their victim as well as killing him. The violent primal father had doubtless been the feared and envied model of each one of the company of brothers: and in the act of devouring him they accomplished their identification with him, and each one of them acquired a portion of his strength. The totem meal, which is perhaps mankind's earliest festival, would thus be a repetition and a commemoration of this memorable and criminal deed, which was the beginning of so many things – of social organization, of moral restrictions and of religion.[2]

In order that these latter consequences may seem plausible, leaving their premises on one side, we need only suppose that the tumultuous mob of brothers were filled with the same contradictory feelings which we can see at work in the ambivalent father-complexes of our children and of our neurotic patients. They hated their father, who presented such a formidable obstacle to their craving for power and their sexual desires; but they loved and admired him too. After they had got rid of him, had satisfied their hatred and had put into effect their wish to identify themselves with him, the affection which had all this time been pushed under was bound to make itself felt.[3] It did so in the form of remorse. A sense of guilt made its appearance, which in this instance coincided with the remorse felt by the whole group. The dead father became stronger than the living one had been – for events took the course we so often see them follow in human affairs to this day. What had up to then been prevented by his actual existence was thenceforward prohibited by the sons themselves, in accordance with the psychological procedure so familiar to us in psycho-analyses under the name of 'deferred obedience'. They revoked their deed by forbidding the killing of the totem, the substitute for their father; and they renounced its fruits by resigning their claim to the women who had now been set free. They thus created out of their filial sense of guilt the two fundamental taboos of totemism, which for that very reason inevitably corresponded to the two repressed wishes of the Œdipus complex. Whoever contravened those taboos became guilty of the only two crimes with which primitive society concerned itself.[4]

The two taboos of totemism with which human morality has its beginning, are not on a par psychologically. The first of them, the law protecting the totem animal, is founded wholly on emotional motives: the father had actually been eliminated, and in no real sense could the deed be undone. But the second rule, the prohibition of incest, has a powerful practical basis as well. Sexual desires do not unite men but divide them. Though the brothers had banded together in order to overcome their father, they were all one another's rivals in regard to the women. Each of them would have wished, like his father, to have all the women to himself. The new organization would have collapsed in a struggle of all against all, for none of them was of such over-mastering strength as to be able to take on his father's part with success. Thus the brothers had no alternative, if they were to live together, but – not, perhaps, until they had passed through many dangerous crises – to institute the law against incest, by which they all alike renounced the women whom they desired and who had been their chief motive for despatching their father. In this way they rescued the organization which had made them strong – and which may have been based on homosexual feelings and acts, originating perhaps during the period of their expulsion from the horde. Here, too, may perhaps have been the germ of the institution of matriarchy, described by Bachofen (1861), which was in turn replaced by the patriarchal organization of the family.

On the other hand, the claim of totemism to be regarded as a first attempt at a religion is based on the first of these two taboos – that upon taking the life of the totem animal. The animal struck the sons as a natural and obvious substitute for their father; but the treatment of it which they found imposed on themselves expressed more than the need to exhibit their remorse. They could attempt, in their relation to this surrogate father, to allay their burning sense of guilt, to bring about a kind of reconciliation with their father. The totemic system was, as it were, a covenant with their father, in which he promised them everything that a childish imagination may expect from a father – protection, care and indulgence – while on their side they undertook to respect his life, that is to say, not to repeat the deed which had brought destruction on their real father. Totemism, moreover, contained an attempt at self-justification: 'If our father had treated us in the way the totem does, we should never have felt tempted to kill him.' In this fashion totemism helped to smooth things over and to make it possible to forget the event to which it owed its origin.

Features were thus brought into existence which continued thenceforward to have a determining influence on the nature of religion. Totemic religion arose from the filial sense of guilt, in an attempt to allay that feeling and to appease the father by deferred obedience to him. All later religions are seen to be attempts at solving the same problem. They vary according to the stage of civilization at which they arise and according to the methods which they adopt; but all have the same end in view and are reactions to the same great event with which civilization began and which, since it occurred, has not allowed mankind a moment's rest.

There is another feature which was already present in totemism and which has been preserved unaltered in religion. The tension of ambivalence was evidently too great for any contrivance to be able to counteract it; or it is possible that psychological conditions in general are unfavourable to getting rid of these antithetical emotions. However that may be, we find that the ambivalence implicit in the father-complex persists in totemism and in religions generally. Totemic religion not only comprised expressions of remorse and attempts at atonement, it also served as a remembrance of the triumph over the father. Satisfaction over that triumph led to the institution of the memorial festival of the totem meal, in which the restrictions of deferred obedience no longer held. Thus it became a duty to repeat the crime of parricide again and again in the sacrifice of the totem animal, whenever, as a result of the changing conditions of life, the cherished fruit of the crime – appropriation of the paternal attributes – threatened to disappear. We shall not be surprised to find that the element of filial rebelliousness also emerges, in the *later* products of religion, often in the strangest disguises and transformations.

Hitherto we have followed the developments of the *affectionate* current of feeling towards the father, transformed into remorse, as we find them in religion and in moral ordinances (which are not sharply distinguished in totemism). But we must not overlook the fact that it was in the main with the impulses that led to parricide that the victory lay. For a long time afterwards, the social fraternal feelings, which were the basis of the whole transformation, continued to exercise a profound influence on the development of society. They found expression in the sanctification of the blood tie, in the emphasis upon the solidarity of all life within the same clan. In thus guaranteeing one another's lives, the brothers were declaring that no one of them must be treated by another as their father was treated by them all jointly. They were precluding the possibility of a repetition of their father's fate. To the religiously based prohibition against killing the totem was now added the socially based prohibition against fratricide. It was not until long afterwards that the prohibition ceased to be limited to members of the clan and assumed the simple form: 'Thou shalt do no murder.' The patriarchal horde was replaced in the first instance by the fraternal clan, whose existence was assured by the blood tie. Society was now based on complicity in the common crime; religion was based on the sense of guilt and the remorse attaching to it; while morality was based partly on the exigencies of this society and partly on the penance demanded by the sense of guilt.

Thus psycho-analysis, in contradiction to the more recent views of the totemic system but in agreement with the earlier ones, requires us to assume that totemism and exogamy were intimately connected and had a simultaneous origin.

6

A great number of powerful motives restrain me from any attempt at picturing the further development of religions from their origin in totemism to their condition to-day. I will only follow two threads whose course I can trace with especial clarity as they run through the pattern: the theme of the totemic sacrifice and the relation of son to father.[5]

Robertson Smith has shown us that the ancient totem meal recurs in the original form of sacrifice. The meaning of the act is the same: sanctification through participation in a common meal. The sense of guilt, which can only be allayed by the solidarity of all the participants, also persists. What is new is the clan deity, in whose supposed presence the sacrifice is performed, who participates in the meal as though he were a clansman, and with whom those who consume the meal become identified. How does the god come to be in a situation to which he was originally a stranger?

The answer might be that in the meantime the concept of God had emerged – from some unknown source – and had taken control of the whole of religious life; and that, like everything else that was to survive, the totem meal had been obliged to find a point of contact with the new system. The psycho-analysis of individual human beings, however, teaches us with quite special insistence that the god of each of them is formed in the likeness of his father, that his personal relation to God depends on his relation to his father in the flesh and oscillates and changes along with that relation, and that at bottom God is nothing other than an exalted father. As in the case of totemism, psycho-analysis recommends us to have faith in the believers who call God their father, just as the totem was called the tribal ancestor. If psycho-analysis deserves any attention, then – without prejudice to any other sources or meanings of the concept of God, upon which psycho-analysis can throw no light – the paternal element in that concept must be a most important one. But in that case the father is represented twice over in the situation of primitive sacrifice: once as God and once as the totemic animal victim. And, even granting the restricted number of explanations open to psycho-analysis, one must ask whether this is possible and what sense it can have.

We know that there are a multiplicity of relations between the god and the sacred animal (the totem or the sacrificial victim). (1) Each god usually has an animal (and quite often several animals) sacred to him. (2) In the case of certain specially sacred sacrifices – 'mystic' sacrifices – the victim was precisely the animal sacred to the god (Smith 1894: 290). (3) The god was often worshipped in the shape of an animal (or, to look at it in another way, animals were worshipped as gods) long after the age of totemism. (4) In myths the god often transforms himself into an animal, and frequently into the animal that is sacred to him.

It therefore seems plausible to suppose that the god himself was the totem animal, and that he developed out of it at a later stage of religious feeling. But we are relieved from the necessity for further discussion by the consideration that the totem is nothing other than a surrogate of the father. Thus, while the totem may be the *first* form of father-surrogate, the god will be a later one, in which the father has regained his human shape. A new creation such as this, derived from what constitutes the root of every form of religion – a longing for the father – might occur if in the process of time some fundamental change had taken place in man's relation to the father, and perhaps, too, in his relation to animals.

Signs of the occurrence of changes of this kind may easily be seen, even if we leave on one side the beginning of a mental estrangement from animals and the disrupting of totemism owing to domestication. [...] There was one factor in the state of affairs produced by the elimination of the father which was bound in the course of time to cause an enormous increase in the longing felt for him. Each single one of the brothers who had banded together for the purpose of killing their father was inspired by a wish to become like him and had given expression to it by incorporating parts of their father's surrogate in the totem meal. But, in consequence of the pressure exercised upon each participant by the fraternal clan as a whole, that wish could not be fulfilled. For the future no one could or might ever again attain the father's supreme power, even though that was what all of them had striven for. Thus after a long lapse of time their bitterness against their father, which had driven them to their deed, grew less, and their longing for him increased; and it became possible for an ideal to emerge which embodied the unlimited power of the primal father against whom they had once fought as well as their readiness to submit to him. As a result of decisive cultural changes, the original democratic equality that had prevailed among all the individual clansmen became untenable; and there developed at the same time an inclination, based on veneration felt for particular human individuals, to revive the ancient paternal ideal by creating gods. The notion of a man becoming a god or of a god dying strikes us to-day as shockingly presumptuous; but even in classical antiquity there was nothing revolting in it.[6] The elevation of the father who had once been murdered into a god from whom the clan claimed descent was a far more serious attempt at atonement than had been the ancient covenant with the totem.

I cannot suggest at what point in this process of development a place is to be found for the great mother-goddesses, who may perhaps in general have preceded the father-gods. It seems certain, however, that the change in attitude to the father was not restricted to the sphere of religion but that it extended in a consistent manner to that other side of human life which had been affected by the father's removal – to social organization. With the introduction of father-deities a fatherless society gradually changed into one organized on a patriarchal basis. The family was a restoration of the former primal horde and it gave back to fathers a large portion of their former rights. There were once more fathers, but the social achievements of the fraternal clan had not been abandoned; and the gulf between the new fathers of a family and the unrestricted primal father of the horde was wide enough to guarantee the continuance of the religious craving, the persistence of an unappeased longing for the father.

We see, then, that in the scene of sacrifice before the god of the clan the father *is* in fact represented twice over – as the god and as the totemic animal victim. But in our attempts at understanding this situation we must beware of interpretations which seek to translate it in a two-dimensional fashion as though it were an allegory, and which in so doing forget its historical stratification. The two-fold presence of the father corresponds to the two chronologically successive meanings of the scene. The ambivalent attitude towards the father has found a plastic expression in it, and so, too, has the victory of the son's affectionate emotions over his hostile ones. The scene of the father's vanquishment, of his greatest defeat, has become the stuff for the representation of his supreme triumph. The importance which is everywhere, without exception, ascribed to sacrifice lies in the fact that it offers satisfaction to the father for the outrage inflicted on him in the same act in which that deed is commemorated.

As time went on, the animal lost its sacred character and the sacrifice lost its connection with the totem feast; it became a simple offering to the deity, an act of renunciation in favour of the god. God Himself had become so far exalted above mankind that He could only be approached through an intermediary – the priest. At the same time divine kings made their appearance in the social structure and introduced the patriarchal system into the state. It must be confessed that the revenge taken by the deposed and restored father was a harsh one: the dominance of authority was at its climax. The subjugated sons made use of the new situation in order to unburden themselves still further of their sense of guilt. They were no longer in any way responsible for the sacrifice as it now was. It was God Himself who demanded it and regulated it. This is the phase in which we find myths showing the god himself killing the animal which is sacred to him and which is in fact himself. Here we have the most extreme denial of the great crime which was the beginning of society and of the sense of guilt. But there is a second meaning to this last picture of sacrifice which is unmistakable. It expresses satisfaction at the earlier father-surrogate having been abandoned in favour of the superior concept of God. At this point the psycho-analytic interpretation of the scene coincides approximately with the allegorical, surface translation of it, which represents the god as overcoming the animal side of his own nature.[7]

Nevertheless it would be a mistake to suppose that the hostile impulses inherent in the father-complex were completely silenced during this period of revived paternal authority. On the contrary, the first phases of the dominance of the two new father-surrogates – gods and kings – show the most energetic signs of the ambivalence that remains a characteristic of religion.

In his great work, *The Golden Bough*, Frazer (1911: 2, Chap. XVIII) puts forward the view that the earliest kings of the Latin tribes were foreigners who played the part of a god and were solemnly executed at a particular festival. The annual sacrifice (or, as a variant, self-sacrifice) of a god seems to have been an essential element in the Semitic religions. The ceremonials of human sacrifice, performed in the most different parts of the inhabited globe, leave very little doubt that the victims met their end as representatives of the deity; and these sacrificial rites can be traced into late times, with an inanimate effigy or puppet taking the place of the living human being. The theanthropic sacrifice of the god, into which it is unfortunately impossible for me to enter here as fully as into animal sacrifice, throws a searching retrospective light upon the meaning of the older forms of sacrifice. (Smith 1894: 410 f.) It confesses, with a frankness that could hardly be excelled, to the fact that the object of the act of sacrifice has always been the same – namely what is now worshipped as God, that is to say, the father. The problem of the relation between animal and human sacrifice thus admits of a simple solution. The original animal sacrifice was already a substitute for a human sacrifice – for the ceremonial killing of the father; so that, when the father-surrogate once more resumed its human shape, the animal sacrifice too could be changed back into a human sacrifice.

NOTES

1. To avoid possible misunderstanding, I must ask the reader to take into account the final sentences of the following footnote as a corrective to this description.
2. This hypothesis, which has such a monstrous air, of the tyrannical father being over-whelmed and killed by a combination of his exiled sons was also arrived at by Atkinson (1903: 220 f.) as a direct implication of the state of affairs in Darwin's primal horde: 'The patriarch had only one enemy whom he should dread . . . a youth-ful band of brothers living together in forced celibacy, or at most in polyandrous relation with some single female captive. A horde as yet weak in their impubescence they are, but they would, when strength was gained with time, inevitably wrench by combined attacks, renewed again and again, both wife and life from the paternal tyrant.' Atkinson, who incidentally passed his whole life in New Caledonia and had unusual opportunities for studying the natives, also pointed out that the conditions which Darwin assumed to prevail in the primal horde may easily be observed in herds of wild oxen and horses and regularly lead to the killing of the father of the herd, (Ibid., 222 f.) He further supposed that, after the father had been disposed of, the horde would be disintegrated by a bitter struggle between the victorious sons. Thus any new organization of society would be precluded: there would be 'an ever-recurring violent succession to the solitary paternal tyrant, by sons whose parricidal hands were so soon again clenched in fratricidal strife.' (Ibid., 228.) Atkinson, who had no psycho-analytic hints to help him and who was ignorant of Robertson Smith's studies, found a less violent transition from the primal horde to the next social stage, at which numbers of males live together in a peaceable community. He believed that through the intervention of maternal love the sons – to begin with only the youngest, but later others as well – were allowed to remain with the horde, and that in return for this toleration the sons acknowledged their father's sexual privilege by renouncing all claim to their mother and sisters. (Ibid., 231 ff.)

    Such is the highly remarkable theory put forward by Atkinson. In its essential feature it is in agreement with my own; but its divergence results in its failing to effect a correlation with many other issues.

    The lack of precision in what I have written in the text above, its abbreviation of the time factor and its compression of the whole subject-matter, may be attributed to the reserve necessitated by the nature of the topic. It would be as foolish to aim at exactitude in such questions as it would be unfair to insist upon certainty.
3. This fresh emotional attitude must also have been assisted by the fact that the deed cannot have given complete satisfaction to those who did it. From one point of view it had been done in vain. Not one of the sons had in fact been able to put his original wish – of taking his father's place – into effect. And, as we know, failure is far more propitious for a moral reaction than satisfaction.

4. 'Murder and incest, or offences of a like kind against the sacred laws of blood, are in primitive society the only crimes of which the community as such takes cognizance.' (Smith 1894: 419.)
5. Cf. the discussion by C. G. Jung (1912), which is governed by views differing in certain respects from mine.
6. 'To us moderns, for whom the breach which divides the human and the divine has deepened into an impassable gulf, such mimicry may appear impious, but it was otherwise with the ancients. To their thinking gods and men were akin, for many families traced their descent from a divinity, and the deification of a man probably seemed as little extraordinary to them as the canonization of a saint seems to a modern Catholic.' (Frazer 1911: 2, 177 f.)
7. It is generally agreed that when, in mythologies, one generation of gods is overcome by another, what is denoted is the historical replacement of one religious system by a new one, whether as a result of foreign conquest or of psychological development. In the latter case myth approximates to what Silberer (1909) has described as 'functional phenomena'. (Cf. Freud 1900, English translation 1932, 464 ff.) The view maintained by Jung (1912) that the god who kills the animal is a libidinal symbol implies a concept of libido other than that which has hitherto been employed and seems to me questionable from every point of view.

WILLIAM JAMES
'CIRCUMSCRIPTION OF THE TOPIC'

William James was born in 1842 in New York. His father was a theologian and his family were affluent. In 1861 he enrolled in Harvard's Scientific School, transferring to the Medical School in 1864. James graduated from Harvard with an MD in 1869; however, medicine had failed to satisfy his intellectual needs and he never became a medical practitioner. In 1872 James secured a post lecturing in comparative psychology at Harvard. He was promoted to full professor in 1885. In 1907 James retired from his chair at Harvard; however, he still remained active in research, publishing his last work in 1910, the same year that he died of heart failure.

William James provides a distinctive approach to the psychology of religion. Unlike Freud, who focused on the relationship of religion to neurosis, James focuses on the nature of religious experience often in a manner that is reminiscent of Otto. Unlike Otto, however, James sees religious experience as arising from the human rather than from a transcendent other. Ultimately James takes a pragmatic view stressing the positive regenerative role of religion – James's pragmatism shares some similarities with the individualistic form of functionalism developed by Malinowski.

Most books on the philosophy of religion try to begin with a precise definition of what its essence consists of. Some of these would-be definitions may possibly come before us in later portions of this course, and I shall not be pedantic enough to enumerate any of them to you now. Meanwhile the very fact that they are so many and so different from one another is enough to prove that the word 'religion' cannot stand for any single principle or essence, but is rather a collective name. The theorizing mind tends always to the over-simplification of its materials. This is the root of all that absolutism and one-sided dogmatism by which both philosophy and religion have been infested. Let us not fall immediately into a one-sided view of our subject, but let us rather admit freely at the outset that we may very likely find no one essence, but many characters which may alternately be equally important in religion. If we should inquire for the essence of 'government', for example, one man might tell us it was authority, another submission, another police, another an army, another an assembly, another a system, of laws; yet all the while it would be true that no concrete government can exist without all these things, one of which is more important at one moment and others at another. The man who knows governments most completely

William James ([1902] 1985), *The Varieties of Religious Experience*, Cambridge, MA: Harvard University Press.

is he who troubles himself least about a definition which shall give their essence. Enjoying an intimate acquaintance with all their particularities in turn, he would naturally regard an abstract conception in which these were unified as a thing more misleading than enlightening. And why may not religion be a conception equally complex?[1]

Consider also the 'religious sentiment' which we see referred to in so many books, as if it were a single sort of mental entity.

In the psychologies and in the philosophies of religion, we find the authors attempting to specify just what entity it is. One man allies it to the feeling of dependence; one makes it a derivative from fear; others connect it with the sexual life; others still identify it with the feeling of the infinite; and so on. Such different ways of conceiving it ought of themselves to arouse doubt as to whether it possibly can be one specific thing; and the moment we are willing to treat the term 'religious sentiment' as a collective name for the many sentiments which religious objects may arouse in alternation, we see that it probably contains nothing whatever of a psychologically specific nature. There is religious fear, religious love, religious awe, religious joy, and so forth. But religious love is only man's natural emotion of love directed to a religious object; religious fear is only the ordinary fear of commerce, so to speak, the common quaking of the human breast, in so far as the notion of divine retribution may arouse it; religious awe is the same organic thrill which we feel in a forest at twilight, or in a mountain gorge; only this time it comes over us at the thought of our supernatural relations; and similarly of all the various sentiments which may be called into play in the lives of religious persons. As concrete states of mind, made up of a feeling *plus* a specific sort of object, religious emotions of course are psychic entities distinguishable from other concrete emotions; but there is no ground for assuming a simple abstract 'religious emotion' to exist as a distinct elementary mental affection by itself, present in every religious experience without exception.

As there thus seems to be no one elementary religious emotion, but only a common storehouse of emotions upon which religious objects may draw, so there might conceivably also prove to be no one specific and essential kind of religious object, and no one specific and essential kind of religious act.

The field of religion being as wide as this, it is manifestly impossible that I should pretend to cover it. My lectures must be limited to a fraction of the subject. And, although it would indeed be foolish to set up an abstract definition of religion's essence, and then proceed to defend that definition against all comers, yet this need not prevent me from taking my own narrow view of what religion shall consist in *for the purpose of these lectures*, or, out of the many meanings of the word, from choosing the one meaning in which I wish to interest you particularly, and proclaiming arbitrarily that when I say 'religion' I mean *that*. This, in fact, is what I must do, and I will now preliminarily seek to mark out the field I choose.

One way to mark it out easily is to say what aspects of the subject we leave out. At the outset we are struck by one great partition which divides the religious field. On the one side of it lies institutional, on the other personal religion. As M. P. Sabatier says, one branch of religion keeps the divinity, another keeps man most in view. Worship and sacrifice, procedures for working on the dispositions of the deity, theology and ceremony and ecclesiastical organization, are the essentials of religion in the institutional branch. Were we to limit our view to it, we should have to define religion as an external art, the art of winning the favor of the gods. In the more personal branch of religion it is on the contrary the inner dispositions of man himself which form the centre of interest, his conscience, his deserts, his helplessness, his incompleteness. And although the favor of the God, as forfeited or gained, is still an essential feature of the story, and theology plays a vital part therein, yet the acts to which this sort of religion prompts are personal not ritual acts, the individual transacts the business by himself alone, and the ecclesiastical organization, with its priests and sacraments and other go-betweens, sinks to an altogether secondary place. The relation goes direct from heart to heart, from soul to soul, between man and his maker.

Now in these lectures I propose to ignore the institutional branch entirely, to say nothing of the ecclesiastical organization, to consider as little as possible the systematic theology and the ideas about the gods themselves, and to confine myself as far as I can to personal religion pure and simple. To some of you personal religion, thus nakedly considered, will no doubt seem too incomplete a thing to wear the general name. 'It is a part of religion,' you will say, 'but only its unorganized rudiment; if we are to name it by itself, we had better call it man's conscience or morality than his religion. The name "religion" should be reserved for the fully organized system of feeling, thought, and institution, for the Church, in short, of which this personal religion, so called, is but a fractional element.'

But if you say this, it will only show the more plainly how much the question of definition tends to become a dispute about names. Rather than prolong such a dispute, I am willing to accept almost any name for the personal religion of which I propose to treat. Call it conscience or morality, if you yourselves prefer, and not religion – under either name it will be equally worthy of our study. As for myself, I think it will prove to contain some elements which morality pure and simple does not contain, and these elements I shall soon seek to point out; so I will myself continue to apply the word 'religion' to it; and in the last lecture of all, I will bring in the theologies and the ecclesiasticisms, and say something of its relation to them.

In one sense at least the personal religion will prove itself more fundamental than either theology or ecclesiasticism. Churches, when once established, live at second-hand upon tradition; but the *founders* of every church owed their power originally to the fact of their direct personal communion with the divine. Not only the superhuman founders, the Christ, the Buddha, Mahomet, but all the originators of Christian sects have been in this case; – so personal religion should still seem the primordial thing, even to those who continue to esteem it incomplete.

There are, it is true, other things in religion chronologically more primordial than personal devoutness in the moral sense. Fetishism and magic seem to have preceded inward piety historically – at least our records of inward piety do not reach back so far. And if fetishism and magic be regarded as stages of religion, one may say that personal religion in the inward sense and the genuinely spiritual ecclesiasticisms which it founds are phenomena of secondary or even tertiary order. But, quite apart from the fact that many anthropologists – for instance, Jevons and Frazer – expressly oppose 'religion' and 'magic' to each other, it is certain that the whole system of thought which leads to magic, fetishism, and the lower superstitions may just as well be called primitive science as called primitive religion. The question thus becomes a verbal one again; and our knowledge of all these early stages of thought and feeling is in any case so conjectural and imperfect that farther discussion would not be worth while.

Religion, therefore, as I now ask you arbitrarily to take it, shall mean for us *the feelings, acts, and experiences of individual men in their solitude, so far as they apprehend themselves to stand in relation to whatever they may consider the divine.* Since the relation may be either moral, physical, or ritual, it is evident that out of religion in the sense in which we take it, theologies, philosophies, and ecclesiastical organizations may secondarily grow. In these lectures, however, as I have already said, the immediate personal experiences will amply fill our time, and we shall hardly consider theology or ecclesiasticism at all.

[. . .]

The sort of appeal that Emersonian optimism, on the one hand, and Buddhistic pessimism, on the other, make to the individual and the sort of response which he makes to them in his life are in fact indistinguishable from, and in many respects identical with, the best Christian appeal and response. We must therefore, from the experiential point of view, call these godless or quasi-godless creeds 'religions'; and accordingly when in our definition of religion we speak of the individual's relation to 'what he considers the divine', we must interpret the term 'divine' very broadly, as denoting any object that is god*like*, whether it be a concrete deity or not.

But the term 'godlike', if thus treated as a floating general quality, becomes exceedingly vague, for many gods have flourished in religious history, and their attributes have been discrepant enough. What then is that essentially godlike quality – be it embodied in a concrete deity or not – our relation to which determines our character as religious men? It will repay us to seek some answer to this question before we proceed farther.

For one thing, gods are conceived to be first things in the way of being and power. They overarch and envelop, and from them there is no escape. What relates to them is the first and last word in the way of truth. Whatever then were most primal and enveloping and deeply true might at this rate be treated as godlike, and a man's religion might thus be identified with his attitude, whatever it might be, towards what he felt to be the primal truth.

Such a definition as this would in a way be defensible. Religion, whatever it is, is a man's total reaction upon life, so why not say that any total reaction upon life is a religion? Total reactions are different from casual reactions, and total attitudes are different from usual or professional attitudes. To get at them you must go behind the foreground of existence and reach down to that curious sense of the whole residual cosmos as an everlasting presence, intimate or alien, terrible or amusing, lovable or odious, which in some degree everyone possesses. This sense of the world's presence, appealing as it does to our peculiar individual temperament, makes us either strenuous or careless, devout or blasphemous, gloomy or exultant, about life at large; and our reaction, involuntary and inarticulate and often half unconscious as it is, is the completest of all our answers to the question, 'What is the character of this universe in which we dwell?' It expresses our individual sense of it in the most definite way. Why then not call these reactions our religion, no matter what specific character they may have? Non-religious as some of these reactions may be, in one sense of the word 'religious', they yet belong to *the general sphere of the religious life*, and so should generically be classed as religious reactions. 'He believes in No-God, and he worships him,' said a colleague of mine of a student who was manifesting a fine atheistic ardor; and the more fervent opponents of Christian doctrine have often enough shown a temper which, psychologically considered, is indistinguishable from religious zeal.

NOTE

1. I can do no better here than refer my readers to the extended and admirable remarks on the futility of all these definitions of religion, in an article by Professor LEUBA, published in the *Monist* for January, 1901, after my own text was written.

KARL MARX
'CRITIQUE OF HEGEL'S PHILOSOPHY OF RIGHT'

Karl Marx was born in the Prussian Rhineland (now in Germany) on 5 May 1818. His parents were from professional families and had a Jewish background, but due to the events of the period his whole family converted to Christianity. In 1836 Marx cut himself off from his childhood home and his parents and began the study of law in Bonn; however, while at Bonn he took several liberal arts electives, which led him to realise that his passion and aptitude lay in the field of philosophy. Therefore, the following year Marx transferred to Berlin, where he enrolled on a course of philosophy. Berlin University at that time was still in the grip of Hegel, who had lectured there until his death five years earlier. It is therefore not surprising that Marx's early philosophical influence was the work of Hegel and in particular the thinking of the young Hegelians: his earliest work was published in their journal Anekadata. *However, Marx was sceptical of the ideas of Hegel, a scepticism that was increased when he began to have contact with French socialist ideology during his time working for the* Rheinische Zeitung. *Marx's contact with French ideals was furthered when he moved to Paris in 1843; here he met Engels and together they began to develop a system of thought which went beyond Marx's German training. However, Marx could not stay in Paris and was forced to flee to England, where he lived out the remainder of his days in poverty.*

Perhaps the most famous one-liner about religion is taken from Karl Marx. While the material here includes this statement, that is, 'religion is the opium of the people', it places it into the context of a much more complex understanding of religion. On the one hand Marx sees religion as both the source and expression of false consciousness; on the other hand he sees it as an expression of alienation. Thus, unlike the usual understanding of Marx that sees religion as entirely negative, this more nuanced reading sees it as both positive and negative.

For Germany, the *criticism of religion* has been essentially completed, and the criticism of religion is the prerequisite of all criticism.

The *profane* existence of error is compromised as soon as its *heavenly oratio pro aris et focis* [plea on behalf of hearth and home] has been refuted. Man, who has found only the *reflection* of himself in the fantastic reality of heaven, where he sought a superman, will no longer feel disposed to find the mere *appearance* of himself, the non-man, where he seeks and must seek his true reality.

The foundation of irreligious criticism is: *Man makes religion*, religion does not make man. Religion is indeed the self-consciousness and

Karl Marx and Friedrich Engels (1964), *On Religion*, New York: Schocken.

self-esteem of man who has either not yet won through to himself or has already lost himself again. But *man* is no abstract being squatting outside the world. Man is *the world of man*, state, society. This state and this society produce religion, which is an *inverted consciousness of the world*, because they are an *inverted world*. Religion is the general theory of this world, its encyclopedic compendium, its logic in popular form, its spiritual *point d'honneur*, its enthusiasm, its moral sanction, its solemn complement, and its universal basis of consolation and justification. It is the *fantastic realization* of the human essence since the human essence has not acquired any true reality. The struggle against religion is therefore indirectly the struggle against *that world* whose spiritual *aroma* is religion.

Religious suffering is at one and the same time the *expression* of real suffering and a protest against real suffering. Religion is the sigh of the oppressed creature, the heart of a heartless world and the soul of soulless conditions. It is the *opium* of the people.

The abolition of religion as the *illusory* happiness of the people is the demand for their *real* happiness. To call on them to give up their illusions about their condition is to *call on them to give up a condition that requires illusions*. The criticism of religion is therefore in *embryo* the *criticism of that vale of tears* of which religion is the *halo*.

Criticism has plucked the imaginary flowers on the chain not in order that man shall continue to bear that chain without fantasy or consolation but so that he shall throw off the chain and pluck the living flower. The criticism of religion disillusions man, so that he will think, act, and fashion his reality like a man who has discarded his illusions and regained his senses, so that he will move around himself as his own true sun. Religion is only the illusory sun which revolves around man as long as he does not revolve around himself.

It is therefore the *task of history*, once the *other-world of truth* has vanished, to establish the *truth of this world*. It is the immediate *task of philosophy*, which is in the service of history, to unmask self-estrangement in its *unholy forms* once the *holy form* of human self-estrangement has been unmasked. Thus the criticism of heaven turns into the criticism of earth, the *criticism of religion* into the *criticism of law* and the *criticism of theology* into the *criticism of politics*.

MAX MÜLLER
'SUMMARY OF THE RESULTS OF PHYSICAL RELIGION'

Friedrich Max Müller was born in the small German town of Dessau in 1823; his father, Wilhelm, was a renowned poet, who tragically died when Max was only four years old. Max Müller was educated in Leipzig, first at the Nicolai school and later at the university, where he studied philology and philosophy, specialising in Sanskrit. After completing his studies in Germany he moved to Paris, where he collected together manuscripts of the Rig Veda, eventually synthesising them into the first scholarly edition, which he completed in 1845. In 1850 he was rewarded with the post of Deputy Taylorian Professor of Modern European Languages at Oxford, becoming a full professor in 1854. In 1868 a new Chair of Comparative Philology was created for him. In 1899 he became seriously ill and he died in 1900.

Müller's work provides one of the early attempts to associate the origins of religion with natural phenomena. This trajectory of approach is taken up in different ways by those theorists who see religion and myth as defective science, or those who see religious experience as arising from a sense of awe in response to the wonder of the universe. This approach and that of Tylor (in relation to animism) is strongly and decisively challenged in Durkheim's The Elementary Forms of the Religious Life.

OUTCOME OF PHYSICAL RELIGION

Before we proceed to an analysis of what is meant by Anthropological Religion, it will be useful to look back to see what has been the outcome of our last course of lectures. To put it as briefly as possible, it was this, that man, as soon as he began to observe, to name, and to know the movements and changes in the world around him, suspected that there was something behind what he saw, that there must be an agent for every action, a mover for every movement. Instead of saying and thinking, as we do at present, *the rain, the thunder, the moon,* he said, *the rainer, the thunderer, the measurer.* Instead of saying and thinking, as we do at present, *It rains, It thunders,* he said, *He rains, He thunders,* without caring as yet who that He might be.

Man could not help this. He was driven, as we saw, to speak in this way by a necessity inherent in language, that is, in thought. This necessity arose from the fact that his earliest concepts consisted in the consciousness of his own repeated acts, and that the only elements of conceptual speech which were at his disposal, the so-called roots, were all, or nearly all, expressive of his own actions. If this is true, and I do not know of any one who has

Max Müller (1892), *Anthropological Religion*, London: Longmans, Green and Co.

seriously controverted it, it is clear that man in speaking of a rainer, a thunderer, a measurer, was unconsciously, or at least unintentionally, speaking and thinking in what Kant would call the category of causality. The rainer was not only a name for the rain, but a name for a rainer, the agent of the rain, whoever or whatever that agent might be. This category of causality which most philosophers consider as the *sine quâ non* of all rational thought, and as an indefeasible necessity of our understanding, thus manifests itself in the historical growth of the human mind as the *sine quâ non* of all rational speech, as an indefeasible necessity of our very language.

This is an unexpected coincidence, and therefore, if properly understood, all the more valuable and significant.

[. . .]

FIRST CONSCIOUSNESS OF OUR ACTS

Psychologists tell us that the first manifestation of self-consciousness in man consists, not only as a fact, but by necessity, in the consciousness of our own acts. Even of our suffering, we are told, we become conscious only when we act, or react, against it, when we resist or try to escape from it. Mere sensuous impressions may come and go, unobserved, unnamed, unrecorded, but our own acts must always be accompanied by a consciousness that they are the acts of ourselves, the acts of a self different from other selves. I do not speak of purely mechanical or involuntary acts; they would *ipso facto* cease to be what can properly be called acts.

If then we can well understand how our true consciousness begins with the consciousness of our own acts, whatever the impulse of these acts may have been, it would seem to follow that our true language also, as distinct from mere cries of joy or pain, should begin with signs of our own acts. And this, as we shall see, which at first was a mere postulate of the psychologist, has now received the most complete confirmation from the Science of Language.

Some philosophers try to go back even further. They observe that breathing of a certain sort is crying, and that children have no language but a cry. As the muscles of a child increase in strength, he begins to gesticulate, and his cries diminish in proportion to the increase of his gestures. His cries become also more differentiated, and they accompany certain of his acts and wishes with such regularity that a nurse can often understand the different meanings of these cries.[1] All this is true, and may throw some light on certain phases in the growth of the human mind and of human language. It may show the close connection between certain acts and certain sounds, but it does not touch the real problem, the historical origin and growth of language and thought, which must be studied first of all *a posteriori*, that is, by an analysis of language, such as we actually find it, not by a mere synthesis of possibilities.

POSTULATE OF PSYCHOLOGY FULFILLED BY LANGUAGE

Now an analysis of language, and more particularly of the Aryan and Semitic languages, carried on without any preconceived psychological theories, has clearly shown that what we call roots, that is, the real elements of speech which defy further analysis, are all, with a few insignificant exceptions, expressive of the acts of man. They signify to go, to run, to strike, to push, to find, to bend, to join, to rub, to smoothe, and a number of similar acts of a more or less special character, such as would be most familiar to the members of an incipient society. Much may lie even beyond this stage when the acts of men received their simple expression. But these earlier stages concern the biologist, possibly the geologist. They do not concern the student of language and thought.

With a small number of radicals, such as we find at the end of our analysis of speech, more particularly of Aryan and Semitic speech, it was found possible to express all that was wanted in an early state of society; while looks, gestures, cries, accents would, no doubt, have helped to supply what in more developed languages is supplied by grammar.

How these radicals arose, why they had one sound and not another, we cannot tell. Not even the most careful observations of children in their cradles can help us here. What Bopp said in 1833 is quite as true to-day. We shall never know why the act of going was signified by the sound g â, the act of standing by the sound s t h â. We can only accept the fact that they were felt to be natural expressions for the acts which they signified, or that they remained out of a number of cognate sounds which might have answered the same purpose. If I call, for instance, such a root as MAR, the *clamor concomitans* of the act of pounding or rubbing, I do not mean to say that this was the only possible sound that could have accompanied this special act, but simply that it was one out of many that did accompany that act, and that it survived in the struggle for existence in the Aryan family of speech.

I tried to explain how with such a root as MAR man might convey a command, asking his friends to pound or strike. He might also inform them that he was himself in the act of pounding and striking. Nay, he might point to a stone with which he pounded as a pounder, and to the pounded stones as the result of his pounding, as pounded or powder.

In this way the whole world of his experience would be divided into two spheres, what we call an active and a passive sphere. The result of an act, the pounded stones, for instance, would be passive, while whatever produces such results would be active. First of all, the man himself who pounded, then also his fellow-workers, would all be active. Even the instruments they used, whether of stone, or wood, or metal, would have to be named as active, as pounders, as borers, or cutters.

Naming of Objects

It has been urged with an air of triumph that it might be quite possible with a given number of active roots to express all that is active, but that this theory would break down, when we try to account for the names of objects, such as a stone, or a tree, or a knife.[2] This, no doubt, is a difficulty, but when that difficulty has been fully discussed both by Professor Noiré and by myself, it is rather hard that we should be supposed never to have thought of it. It is true that we do not quite take the same view of the psychological process that led to the naming of objects. But we do not differ as to the facts, and these facts are there to speak for themselves.

First of all, with regard to the naming of instruments, we find that even in our modern languages we still speak of scrapers, pincers, squeezers, borers, holders, etc., all conceived originally as active, though we are hardly conscious of it now. It was the same in Latin, Greek, and Sanskrit. Thus *vomer*, a plough-share, was really he who threw up; *securis*, an axe, was really she who cut; $\zeta\omega\sigma\tau\eta\rho$ was a girder, before it became a mere girdle. Even such words as $\dot{\epsilon}\nu\delta\upsilon\tau\eta\rho$, a cloak, was at first he who helped to clothe, just as in German, *ein Überzieher*, an overcoat, was originally he who drew over or covered. All this may seem strange to us, but it is still perfectly intelligible to popular poets. There is a famous German Volkslied, in which a soldier addresses his old cloak, and says:

> Thou art thirty years old
> And hast weathered many a storm –
> Thou hast guarded me, like a brother,
> And when the cannons thundered,
> We two have never trembled.

In all these words, the masculine came first, then the feminine, and lastly the neuter.

But how were mere objects named, it is asked. Noiré has laboured very hard to show that, at first, they too could only have been named and conceived as our acts; that a cave, for instance, could only have become objective to us as our subjective act, viz. as our excavating. This may sound very unlikely, but here also language has still preserved a few faint vestiges of its former ways. Even now, how do people in a primitive state of society call a newly-opened mine? Our diggings, they say. The French *maison*, house, meant originally a remaining, Lat. *mansio*, a mansion. The *venison* which we eat was called *venatio*, our chase, our sport, and all such words as *oration, invention, pension, picture*, were names of acts, before they became the names of objects. After a time, no doubt, the human mind accustomed itself to look upon the actions as independent of the agents, the *cutter* became a ship, the *cutting* a slice, the *writing* a book. But the chain from the active root to the passive nouns was never broken, and every link is there to attest the continuous progress of human language and human thought.

THE AGENTS IN NATURE

If then we ask ourselves how, with such materials at their disposal as have been discovered by students in the lowest stratum of human speech, the ancient dwellers on earth could think and speak of the great phenomena of nature, say the storm-wind, the fire, the sun, the sky, we shall see that, at first, they could name and conceive them in no other way but as active or as agents, and not yet as mere causes. What we now call the category of causality is no doubt at the bottom of all this, but historically it manifested itself, first of all, not in a search for something like a cause, but in the assertion of something like an agent. The storm-wind, if it was to be singled out at all, if it was to be named with the materials supplied by the radical dictionary of that early period of thought, could be called in one way only, as the pounder, the striker, the smasher. And so it was as a matter of fact. From the root MAR, to smash, we found that the Âryas had formed the name Mar‑ut, the smashers, the name of what we now call the gods of the storm-wind, while to them it was no more at first than a name of the agents of the storm-wind.

We saw that the same process of naming the most prominent phenomena of nature led in the end to the creation of a complete physical pantheon. Not only trees, mountains, and rivers were named as agents, but the sea and the earth, the fire and the wind, the sky, the stars, the sun, the dawn, the moon, day and night, all were represented under different names as agents.

TRANSITION TO HUMAN AGENTS

It might be said that with all this we had only explained why every object of experience had to be named and conceived at first as an agent, and that we have not explained why it should ever have been conceived as a human agent. This is quite true. But if we consider that all roots were originally the expressions of human actions, and that they were predicated at first of human agents, it becomes perfectly intelligible how, when nothing but human agents were known as yet, other agents, having the same names as human agents, should have been conceived as something *like* human agents. Suppose that a strong man had been called a *striker*, and that he had spoken of himself as *I strike*, of others as *thou strikest*, and *he strikes*, was it not almost inevitable that, if the lightning was called *a striker*, he should likewise be spoken of as something like a man who strikes, and that people should say of that lightning striker, *he strikes*, and not as yet, *it strikes*.

DIFFERENCE BETWEEN HUMAN AND SUPER-HUMAN AGENTS

No doubt a difference was soon perceived between the ordinary human strikers, and that terrible and irresistible striker, the lightning. And what would be the inevitable result of this? The striker in the lightning would by necessity be called a non-human striker, and from a non-human striker to a super-human striker the steps are small and few.

So far, I hope, all is clear, for the process is really extremely simple. Whatever in nature had to be named, could at first be named as an agent only. Why? Because the roots of language were at first expressive of agency. Having been named as agents, and no other agents being known but human agents, the agents in nature were, if not necessarily, yet very naturally, spoken of as like human agents, then as more than human agents – and, at last, as super-human agents.

THE TRUE MEANING OF ANIMISM

Consider now how different this is from what is generally understood by Animism and Anthropomorphism. The facts are no doubt the same, but the explanation is totally different, theoretical in the one case, historical in the other; nay, irrational in the one case, rational in the other. I cannot help calling it irrational when we are asked to believe that at any time in the history of the world a human being could have been so dull as not to be able to distinguish between inanimate and animate beings, a distinction in which even the higher animals hardly ever go wrong; or again that man was pleased to ascribe life or a soul to the sun and the moon, to trees and rivers, though he was perfectly aware that they possessed neither one nor the other. Even Mr. Herbert Spencer protests against this insult to the human intellect.

A knowledge of the nature of language explains everything, not only as possible, but as necessary. Human language, being what we found it to be, could not help itself. If it wished to name sun or moon, tree or river, it could only name them as agents, simply as agents, without ascribing as yet life or soul to them.

Here, it seems to me, we often do great injustice to the ancients, when we translate their language literally, but after all not truly, into our own. Thus Epicharmos, no mean philosopher, who lived in the fifth century B.C., is often quoted as having declared that the gods of the Greeks were the winds, water, the earth, the sun, fire, and the stars.[3] The question is, were the winds and the water and the earth, the sun, fire, and the stars, to his mind mere things, dead material objects, or were they conceived, if not as masculine or feminine, at all events as active powers, possibly as something like what the so-called positivist philosophers would accept even now, when they speak of act and agent being one.

The transition from animate to man-like beings is much less violent, if we account for it not so much by the poetry, as by the poverty of language, which knew at first of no agents except human agents, and therefore had often to use the same word for natural agents and human agents, without thereby committing the speaker to the startling assertion that the sun and moon, the tree and river were, in the true sense of the word, anthropomorphous, or man-like. Later religious and mythological fancy, particularly when assisted by sculpture and painting, achieved this also, but that stage of thought was reached slowly and gradually, and not by the sudden impulses of what is vaguely called Animism and Anthropomorphism.

GENERAL NAMES OF THE AGENTS IN NATURE

There was one more step that had to be explained, namely, how these different agents, in or behind nature, came to be classed together and called by names which we, very glibly, translate by gods.

We saw how they came to be distinguished from merely human agents, as non-human, and super-human. And we also saw how from certain important features which all these super-human agents shared in common, they were emphatically called d e v a, bright, v a s u, brilliant, a s u r a, breathing or living, and many other names. We saw how this word d e v a, meaning originally bright, was gradually divested of its purely physical meaning, and, instead of meaning brilliant agents, came to mean in the end great and good, or what we now mean by divine agents. The history of that one word d e v a in Sanskrit, and *deus* in Latin, disclosed, in fact, better than anything else, one of the most important channels of the historical evolution of the concept of deity, at least among our own Aryan ancestors.

HIGHEST GENERALISATION OR MONOTHEISM

When that concept of d e v a had been realised, it was at first a generic concept. It applied, not to one power, but to many. Even when the human mind tried to combine the idea of supremacy and therefore of oneness with that of deity, this was done at first by predicating supremacy of single d e v a s or gods only, each supreme in his own domain. After this stage in which we find a number of single gods, neither co-ordinate nor subordinate, there follows the next in which all the single gods were combined into a kind of organic whole, one god being supreme, the others subject to him, but to him only, and standing among themselves on a certain level of equality. After these two stages, which I called *Henotheism* and *Polytheism*, follows in the end that of real *Monotheism*, a belief in one god, as excluding the very possibility of any other gods. We saw that this highest stage was not only reached by the most thoughtful and religious poets in Greece and Rome, but even by some of the Vedic poets in India.

These stages in the development of the idea of the godhead are not therefore merely theoretical postulates. They are historical realities which we may watch in many religions, if only we are enabled to follow their history in literary documents. Nowhere, however, can this be done more effectually than in India, where some fortunate accident has preserved to us in the Vedic hymns relics of the henotheistic stage in wonderful completeness. Only we must not imagine, as some scholars seem to do, that the whole of the Veda belongs to the worship of single gods. On the contrary, and this is what renders the Veda so valuable, we see in it all the three stages together, the henotheistic, the polytheistic, and the monotheistic, representing the different levels of religious thought that had been reached at that early time by different classes of the same society.

NOTES

1. See an able article by Dr. J. M. Buckley, The Philosophy of Gesture, in Werner's *Voice Magazine*, Nov. 1890.
2. *Athenœum*, Dec. 6, 1890.
3. Stobaeus, *Florilegium*, xci. 29: Ὁ μὲν Ἐπίχαρμος τοὺς θεοὺς εἶναι λέγει Ἀνέμους, ὕδωρ, γῆν, ἥλιον, πῦρ, ἀστέρα.

RUDOLF OTTO
'THE IDEA OF THE HOLY'

Rudolf Otto was born in 1869, in Peine, Prussia (now in Germany). In 1888 Otto joined the University of Erlangen, to study theology. After his graduation in 1895 he taught at the University of Gottigen for eight years before being promoted to assistant professor in 1906. In 1915 he secured promotion to a full professorship in systematic theology at Breslau. However, two years later he was to leave Breslau in order to accept a chair at Marburg. Otto died in 1937.

While Rudolf Otto takes up many of the presuppositions found in Kant and Schleiermacher about basic human faculties, he adds to the list of rational, ethical and aesthetic the additional faculty of the 'Holy'. It is this faculty in relation with the transcendent that forms the basis of religion. In The Idea of the Holy *Otto outlines the nature of this faculty, and in much greater detail discusses the nature of the experience of the Holy and the understanding of the transcendent that emerges from it.*

THE RATIONAL AND THE NON-RATIONAL

It is essential to every theistic conception of God, and most of all to the Christian, that it designates and precisely characterizes deity by the attributes spirit, reason, purpose, good will, supreme power, unity, selfhood. The nature of God is thus thought of by analogy with our human nature of reason and personality; only, whereas in ourselves we are aware of this as qualified by restriction and limitation, as applied to God the attributes we use are 'completed', i.e. thought as absolute and unqualified. Now all these attributes constitute clear and definite *concepts*: they can be grasped by the intellect; they can be analysed by thought; they even admit of definition. An object that can thus be thought conceptually may be termed *rational*. The nature of deity described in the attributes above mentioned is, then, a rational nature; and a religion which recognizes and maintains such a view of God is in so far a 'rational' religion. Only on such terms is *belief* possible in contrast to mere *feeling*. And of Christianity at least it is false that 'feeling is all, the name but sound and smoke';[1] – where 'name' stands for conception or thought. Rather we count this the very mark and criterion of a religion's high rank and superior value – that it should have no lack of *conceptions* about God; that it should admit knowledge – the knowledge that comes by faith – of the transcendent in terms of conceptual thought, whether those already mentioned or others which continue and develop them. Christianity not only possesses such conceptions but possesses them in unique clarity

---

Rudolf Otto (1950), *The Idea of the Holy*, 2nd edn, tr. John W. Harvey, Oxford: Oxford University Press.

and abundance, and this is, though not the sole or even the chief, yet a very real sign of its superiority over religions of other forms and at other levels. This must be asserted at the outset and with the most positive emphasis.

But, when this is granted, we have to be on our guard against an error which would lead to a wrong and one-sided interpretation of religion. This is the view that the essence of deity can be given completely and exhaustively in such 'rational' attributions as have been referred to above and in others like them. It is not an unnatural misconception. We are prompted to it by the traditional language of edification, with its characteristic phraseology and ideas; by the learned treatment of religious themes in sermon and theological instruction; and further even by our Holy Scriptures themselves. In all these cases the 'rational' element occupies the foreground, and often nothing else seems to be present at all. But this is after all to be expected. All language, in so far as it consists of words, purports to convey ideas or concepts; – that is what language means; – and the more clearly and unequivocally it does so, the better the language. And hence expositions of religious truth in language inevitably tend to stress the 'rational' attributes of God.

But though the above mistake is thus a natural one enough, it is none the less seriously misleading. For so far are these 'rational' attributes from exhausting the idea of deity, that they in fact imply a non-rational or suprarational Subject of which they are predicates. They are 'essential' (and not merely 'accidental') attributes of that subject, but they are also, it is important to notice, *synthetic* essential attributes. That is to say, we have to predicate them of a subject which they qualify, but which in its deeper essence is not, nor indeed can be, comprehended in them; which rather requires comprehension of a quite different kind. Yet, though it eludes the conceptual way of understanding, it must be in some way or other within our grasp, else absolutely nothing could be asserted of it. And even mysticism, in speaking of it as τὸ ἄρρητον, the ineffable, does not really mean to imply that absolutely nothing can be asserted of the object of the religious consciousness; otherwise, mysticism could exist only in unbroken silence, whereas what has generally been a characteristic of the mystics is their copious eloquence.

Here for the first time we come up against the contrast between rationalism and profounder religion, and with this contrast and its signs we shall be repeatedly concerned in what follows. We have here in fact the first and most distinctive mark of rationalism, with which all the rest are bound up. It is not that which is commonly asserted, that rationalism is the denial, and its opposite the affirmation, of the miraculous. That is manifestly a wrong or at least a very superficial distinction. For the traditional theory of the miraculous as the occasional breach in the causal nexus in nature by a Being who himself instituted and must therefore be master of it – this theory is itself as massively 'rational' as it is possible to be. Rationalists have often enough acquiesced in the possibility of the miraculous in this sense; they have even themselves contributed to frame a theory of it; – whereas anti-rationalists have been often indifferent to the whole controversy about miracles. The difference between rationalism and its opposite is to be found elsewhere. It resolves itself rather into a peculiar difference of *quality* in the mental attitude and emotional content of the religious life itself. All depends upon this: in our idea of God is the non-rational overborne, even perhaps wholly excluded, by the rational? Or conversely, does the non-rational itself preponderate over the rational? Looking at the matter thus, we see that the common dictum, that orthodoxy itself has been the mother of rationalism, is in some measure well founded. It is not simply that orthodoxy was preoccupied with doctrine and the framing of dogma, for these have been no less a concern of the wildest mystics. It is rather that orthodoxy found in the construction of dogma and doctrine no way to do justice to the non-rational aspect of its subject. So far from keeping the non-rational element in religion alive in the heart of the religious experience, orthodox Christianity manifestly failed to recognize its value, and by this failure gave to the idea of God a one-sidedly intellectualistic and rationalistic interpretation.

This bias to rationalization still prevails, not only in theology but in the science of comparative religion in general, and from top to bottom of it. The modern students of mythology, and those who pursue research into the religion of 'primitive man' and attempt to reconstruct the 'bases' or 'sources' of religion, are all victims to it. Men do not, of course, in these cases employ those lofty 'rational' concepts which we took as our point of departure; but they tend to take these concepts and their gradual 'evolution' as setting the main problem of their inquiry, and fashion ideas and notions of lower value, which they regard as paving the way for them. It is always in terms of concepts and ideas that the subject is pursued, 'natural' ones, moreover, such as have a place in the general sphere of man's ideational life, and are not specifically 'religious'. And then with a resolution and cunning which one can hardly help admiring, men shut their eyes to that which is quite unique in the religious experience, even in its most primitive manifestations. But it is rather a matter for astonishment than for admiration! For if there be any single domain of human experience that presents us with something unmistakably specific and unique, peculiar to itself, assuredly it is that of the religious life. In truth the enemy has often a keener vision in this matter than either the champion of religion or the neutral and professedly impartial theorist. For the adversaries on their side know very well that the entire 'pother about mysticism' has nothing to do with 'reason' and 'rationality'.

And so it is salutary that we should be incited to notice that religion is not exclusively contained and exhaustively comprised in any series of 'rational' assertions; and it is well worth while to attempt to bring the relation of the different 'moments' of religion to one another clearly before the mind, so that its nature may become more manifest.

This attempt we are now to make with respect to the quite distinctive category of the holy or sacred.

'NUMEN' AND THE 'NUMINOUS'

'Holiness' – 'the holy' – is a category of interpretation and valuation peculiar to the sphere of religion. It is, indeed, applied by transference to another sphere – that of ethics – but it is not itself derived from this. While it is complex, it contains a quite specific element or 'moment', which sets it apart from 'the rational' in the meaning we gave to that word above, and which remains inexpressible – an ἄρρητον or *ineffabile* – in the sense that it completely eludes apprehension in terms of concepts. The same thing is true (to take a quite different region of experience) of the category of the beautiful.

Now these statements would be untrue from the outset if 'the holy' were merely what is meant by the word, not only in common parlance, but in philosophical, and generally even in theological usage. The fact is we have come to use the words 'holy', 'sacred' (*heilig*) in an entirely derivative sense, quite different from that which they originally bore. We generally take 'holy' as meaning 'completely good'; it is the absolute moral attribute, denoting the consummation of moral goodness. In this sense Kant calls the will which remains unwaveringly obedient to the moral law from the motive of duty a 'holy' will; here clearly we have simply the *perfectly moral* will. In the same way we may speak of the holiness or sanctity of duty or law, meaning merely that they are imperative upon conduct and universally obligatory.

But this common usage of the term is inaccurate. It is true that all this moral significance is contained in the word 'holy', but it includes in addition – as even we cannot but feel – a clear overplus of meaning, and this it is now our task to isolate. Nor is this merely a later or acquired meaning; rather, 'holy', or at least the equivalent words in Latin and Greek, in Semitic and other ancient languages, denoted first and foremost *only* this overplus: if the ethical element was present at all, at any rate it was not original and never constituted the whole meaning of the word. Any one who uses it to-day does undoubtedly always feel 'the morally good' to be implied in 'holy'; and accordingly in our inquiry into that element which is separate and peculiar to the idea of the holy it will be useful, at least for the temporary purpose of the investigation, to invent a special term to stand for 'the holy' *minus* its moral factor or 'moment', and, as we can now add, minus its 'rational' aspect altogether.

It will be our endeavour to suggest this unnamed Something to the reader as far as we may, so that he may himself feel it. There is no religion in which it does not live as the real innermost core, and without it no religion would be worthy of the name. It is pre-eminently a living force in the Semitic religions, and of these again in none has it such vigour as in that of the

Bible. Here, too, it has a name of its own, viz. the Hebrew *qādôsh*, to which the Greek ἅγιος and the Latin *sanctus*, and, more accurately still, *sacer*, are the corresponding terms. It is not, of course, disputed that these terms in all three languages connote, as part of their meaning, *good, absolute goodness*, when, that is, the notion has ripened and reached the highest stage in its development. And we then use the word 'holy' to translate them. But this 'holy' then represents the gradual shaping and filling in with ethical meaning, or what we shall call the 'schematization', of what was a unique original feeling-response, which can be in itself ethically neutral and claims consideration in its own right. And when this moment or element first emerges and begins its long development, all those expressions (*qādôsh*, ἅγιος, *sacer*, &c.) mean beyond all question something quite other than 'the good'. This is universally agreed by contemporary criticism, which rightly explains the rendering of *qādôsh* by 'good' as a mistranslation and unwarranted 'rationalization' or 'moralization' of the term.

Accordingly, it is worth while, as we have said, to find a word to stand for this element in isolation, this 'extra' in the meaning of 'holy' above and beyond the meaning of goodness. By means of a special term we shall the better be able, first, to keep the meaning clearly apart and distinct, and second, to apprehend and classify connectedly whatever subordinate forms or stages of development it may show. For this purpose I adopt a word coined from the Latin *numen*. *Omen* has given us 'ominous', and there is no reason why from *numen* we should not similarly form a word 'numinous'. I shall speak, then, of a unique 'numinous' category of value and of a definitely 'numinous' state of mind, which is always found wherever the category is applied. This mental state is perfectly *sui generis* and irreducible to any other; and therefore, like every absolutely primary and elementary datum, while it admits of being discussed, it cannot be strictly defined. There is only one way to help another to an understanding of it. He must be guided and led on by consideration and discussion of the matter through the ways of his own mind, until he reach the point at which 'the numinous' in him perforce begins to stir, to start into life and into consciousness. We can co-operate in this process by bringing before his notice all that can be found in other regions of the mind, already known and familiar, to resemble, or again to afford some special contrast to, the particular experience we wish to elucidate. Then we must add: 'This X of ours is not precisely *this* experience, but akin to this one and the opposite of that other. Cannot you now realize for yourself what it is?' In other words our X cannot, strictly speaking, be taught, it can only be evoked, awakened in the mind; as everything that comes 'of the spirit' must be awakened.

[. . .]

History and the *a Priori* in Religion:
Summary and Conclusion

We have considered 'the holy' on the one hand as an *a priori* category of mind, and on the other as manifesting itself in outward appearance. The contrast here intended is exactly the same as the common contrast of inner and outer, general and special revelation. And if we take 'reason' (*ratio*) as an inclusive term for all cognition which arises in the mind from principles native to it, in contrast to those based upon facts of history, then we may say that the distinction between holiness as an *a priori* category and holiness as revealed in outward appearance is much the same as that between 'reason' (in this wide sense) and history.

Every religion which, so far from being a mere faith in traditional authority, springs from personal assurance and inward convincement (i.e. from an inward first-hand cognition of its truth) – as Christianity does in a unique degree – must presuppose principles in the mind enabling it to be independently recognized as true.[2] But these principles must be *a priori* ones, not to be derived from 'experience' or 'history'. It has little meaning, however edifying it may sound, to say that they are inscribed upon the heart by the pencil of the Holy Spirit 'in history'. For whence comes the assurance that it was the pencil of the 'Holy Spirit' that wrote, and not that of a deceiving spirit of imposture, or of the 'tribal fantasy' of anthropology? Such an assertion is itself a presumption that it is possible to distinguish the signature of the Spirit from others, and thus that we have an *a priori* notion of what is of the Spirit independently of history.

And there is a further consideration. There is something presupposed by history as such – not only the history of mind or spirit, with which we are here concerned – which alone makes it history, and that is the existence of a *quale*, something with a potentiality of its own, capable of *becoming*, in the special sense of coming to be that to which it was predisposed and predetermined. An oak-tree can *become*, and thus have a sort of 'history'; whereas a heap of stones cannot. The random addition and subtraction, displacement and re-arrangement, of elements in a mere aggregation can certainly be followed in narrative form, but this is not in the deeper sense an historical narrative. We only have the history of a people in proportion as it enters upon its course equipped with an endowment of talents and tendencies; it must already *be something* if it is really to *become* anything. And biography is a lamentable and unreal business in the case of a man who has no real unique potentiality of his own, no special idiosyncrasy, and is therefore a mere point of intersection for various fortuitous causal series, acted upon, as it were, from without. Biography is only a real narration of a real life where, by the interplay of stimulus and experience on the one side and predisposition and natural endowment on the other, something individual and unique comes into being, which is therefore neither the result of a 'mere self-unfolding' nor yet the sum of mere traces and impressions, written from without from moment to moment upon a *tabula rasa*. In short, to propose a history of mind is to presuppose a mind or spirit determinately qualified; to profess to give a history of religion is to presuppose a spirit specifically qualified for religion.

There are, then, three factors in the process by which religion comes into being in history. First, the interplay of predisposition and stimulus, which in the historical development of man's mind actualizes the potentiality in the former, and at the same time helps to determine its form. Second, the groping recognition, by virtue of this very disposition, of specific portions of history as the manifestation of 'the holy', with consequent modification of the religious experience already attained both in its quality and degree. And third, on the basis of the other two, the achieved fellowship with 'the holy' in knowing, feeling, and willing. Plainly, then, religion is only the offspring of history in so far as history on the one hand develops our disposition for knowing the holy, and on the other is itself repeatedly the manifestation of the holy. 'Natural' religion, in contrast to historical, does not exist, and still less does 'innate' religion.[3]

A priori cognitions are not such as every one does have – such would be *innate* cognitions – but such as every one is *capable* of having. The loftier *a priori* cognitions are such as – while every one is indeed capable of having them – do not, as experience teaches us, occur spontaneously, but rather are 'awakened' through the instrumentality of other more highly endowed natures. In relation to these the universal 'predisposition' is merely a faculty of *receptivity* and a *principle of judgement and acknowledgement*, not a capacity to produce the cognitions in question for oneself independently. This latter capacity is confined to those specially 'endowed'. And this 'endowment' is the universal disposition on a higher level and at a higher power, differing from it in quality as well as in degree. The same thing is very evident in the sphere of art: what appears in the multitude as mere receptiveness, the capacity of response and judgement by trained aesthetic taste, reappears at the level of the *artist* as invention, creation, composition, the original production of genius. This difference of level and power, e.g. in musical composition, seen in the contrast between what is a mere capacity for musical experience and the actual production and revelation of music, is obviously something more than a difference of degree. It is very similar in the domain of the religious consciousness, religious production, and revelation. Here, too, most men have only the 'predisposition', in the sense of a receptiveness and susceptibility to religion and a capacity for freely recognizing and judging religious truth at first hand. The 'Spirit' is only 'universal' in the form of the '*testimonium Spiritus internum*' (and this again only '*ubi ipsi visum fuit*'). The higher stage, not to be derived from the first stage of mere receptivity, is in the sphere of religion *the prophet*. The prophet corresponds in the religious sphere to the creative artist in that of

art: he is the man in whom the Spirit shows itself alike as the power to hear the 'voice within' and the power of divination, and in each case appears as a creative force. Yet the prophet does not represent the highest stage. We can think of a third, yet higher, beyond him, a stage of revelation as underivable from that of the prophet as was his from that of common men. We can look, beyond the prophet, to one in whom is found the Spirit in all its plenitude, and who at the same time in His person and in His performance is become most completely the object of divination, in whom Holiness is recognized apparent.

Such a one is more than Prophet. He is the Son.

NOTES

1. Goethe, *Faust*.
2. The attestation of such principles is the '*testimonium Spiritus Sancti internum*' of which we have already spoken. And this must clearly be itself immediate and self-warranted, else there would be need of another 'witness of the Holy Spirit' to attest the truth of the first, and so on *ad infinitum*.
3. For the distinction between 'innate' and *a priori* cf. R. Otto, *Religionsphilosophie*, p. 42.

FRIEDRICH SCHLEIERMACHER
'THE ESSENCE OF RELIGION'[1]

Friedrich Daniel Ernst Schleiermacher was born in the Prussian city of Breslau (now Wrocław, Poland) in 1768. His father was an army chaplain and his mother's side of the family also had members of the clergy. He was educated first at a pietistic boarding school and later at Barby seminary; however, in search of more liberal ideals he moved from Barby in 1787 and completed his studies at the University of Halle. In 1790 he became a house tutor in the household of Count Dohna. After a brief spell as a school teacher (in 1793), he took a post as an assistant pastor at Landsberg, which commenced in 1794. In 1796 the chance for promotion arose and Schleiermacher became chaplain of a reform church in Berlin. In 1804 he was rewarded with a chair at the University of Halle, where he also served as the university's chaplain. However, the Napoleonic war was to interfere with his academic career and in 1806 Halle was plundered. Schleiermacher himself was relieved of his valuable possessions and this experience spurred him to become a member of the German resistance. In 1807 he moved to Berlin, where he was a political activist, joining the civil service in 1808. In 1809 a chance to combine his politics with his theology arose when he was offered the pulpit of the reformed church Trinity. In 1810 Schleiermacher returned to academia, accepting a chair in theology at the newly constituted University of Berlin. From this period forth he was an active academic until his death in the winter of 1834.

While Schleiermacher and Otto are essentially theologians and thus in a different category from most of the other thinkers included in this volume, both developed ways of approaching religion that were influential on subsequent theorists. Some aspects of Schleiermacher's approach are related to arguments set forth by Kant; thus, he accepts the threefold division of human faculties into the rational, ethical and aesthetic. Unlike Kant, however, he argues that religion arises from the aesthetic faculty rather than the rational. Ultimately Schleiermacher argues that religion arises from within the human being in the 'feeling of utter dependence'.

INITIAL CLARIFICATIONS

Basic concepts

For you religion is a way of thinking, a faith, a special way of looking at the world and of organizing what confronts us in the world.[1] Or it is a way of acting, a special love or pleasure, a particular kind of motivation and conduct. Apparently, without this separation of a 'theoretical' and a 'practical' side you could hardly think at all. Since you are accustomed to

---

Friedrich Schleiermacher (1969), *On Religion*, tr. Terrence N. Tice, Richmond, VA: John Knox Press.

stressing only one at any given time, even though both sides are thought to belong to religion, we shall want to take a close look at religion from each of the sides in turn.

Life and art

We begin with activity, of which you generally posit two kinds: 'life' and 'art'. With the poet[2] you might ascribe earnestness to life and lightheartedness to art. You could contrast these two things in some other way, but separate them you certainly will. Looking at life, you take 'duty' to be the key word; your 'moral law' is to order it; 'virtue' is to prove the ruling power within it. In this way the individual is to be harmonized with, and kept from ruffling, the general 'orders' of the world. A man can make a go of this, you think, without betraying a trace of art, because he attains his goal by adhering to strict rules, which have nothing whatsoever to do with the freewheeling prescriptions of art. In fact, you come close to making it a rule that when people manifest such adherence to order in a most thoroughgoing way, art becomes subsidiary and dispensable in their lives. On the other hand, you expect imagination to animate the artist. You expect inventiveness to hold sway in him. And to your mind these activities are quite separate from virtue and morality. In large part imagination and inventiveness can be sustained with very little support from them, you think. Indeed, aren't you inclined to release the artist from the strict demands of life somewhat, because the flaming sword of art often forces prudence out of bounds anyway?[3]

Now where do you place what you would call 'piety'? Is it a particular form of conduct? Does it belong within the sphere of life? If so, is it something distinctive, and is it therefore something good and praiseworthy on its own account, though different from morality? You certainly will not consider piety and morality to be the same thing. If they are not, then morality is not alone within the domain it was supposed to rule; another force is active alongside it, one both entitled to be there and able to remain there. Correct? Or will you perhaps retreat to the position that piety is a particular virtue and religion a particular duty or division of duties, so that piety is incorporated into morality and subordinate to it, as part to whole? Is religion then, as some contend, the fulfillment of a set of 'special duties' before God and in this way a part of morality, on the assumption that morality as a totality consists in the performance of all duties?[4] But you wouldn't agree to this connection, if I understand your views correctly and am accurately reproducing what I have been hearing you say. For your pitch is that there is something thoroughly peculiar in what the pious person does or leaves undone. Accordingly, you think that a person can be entirely and completely moral without being pious.

And how are religion and art related? You would hardly claim they are wholly unallied, since from ancient times the greatest examples of art have borne an obviously religious character. When you speak of someone as a 'religious artist', then, are you still exempting him from the strict demands of virtue? Not likely, because in that circumstance he is as subject to the demands of virtue as anyone else. But then you would also want to counsel life-oriented persons against remaining wholly without art, if they are really to be pious, wouldn't you? Otherwise I don't see how a significant parallel can be drawn. Such persons must accordingly take something from the domain of art into their life. Perhaps it is from this that the particular form their pious life attains emerges. The following alternative, then, seems to be the only one that really arises from your view: religion as a form of conduct is thought to be a mixture of life and art, however clouded such mixtures may usually turn out to be. As they mix, the two elements attack and neutralize each other. This, however, only accounts for your displeasure, not for your point of view. For how can you wish to draw something new out of such an accidental conjunction of two elements? How can you want to do this, even if the most uniform solution is achieved, as long as the two remain unaltered side by side? Suppose this is not the case. Suppose piety is a truly internal, mutual penetration of both life and art. Then you can very well see that the comparison I set up will not apply. That is, piety cannot arise as a result of life and art conjoining; it must be an original unity of the two. Only I warn you, take care not to give me this point! For if my thesis holds true, then in isolation morality and inventiveness are simply the distorted remains of religion, what is left over once religion has died! Religion would then in fact be supreme over both, the truly divine life itself. In exchange for this warning, however – if you accept it and have found no other solution meanwhile – would you mind informing me how your opinion on religion can help but appear nonsensical? Until you do, I have no other recourse than to suppose that you have not yet looked into the matter well enough to get a clear position about this so-called practical side of religion. Perhaps we shall have better luck with the other side – what is known as a particular way of thinking, or 'faith'.

Science and morality

You will grant me, I take it, that your views on things, however variegated they may appear, may all nevertheless be classified under two distinct types of knowledge. I won't stop to discuss how you might further subdivide and categorize these. That is a matter of argument between your various schools of thought, and I have nothing to do with such controversy here. Please don't quibble over my terminology, therefore, even though it may come from different sources. Let's call the one 'physics' or 'metaphysics', using either as a class name or the two as subdivisions of the same class. And let's call the other 'ethics' or 'theory of obligation' or 'practical philosophy'.[5] We will surely agree to the contrast I have in mind. That is, the one science may be taken to describe the nature of things. Or if that strikes you as an overambitious or impossible task, then it at least describes man's representation of things, what the world is to him as a totality of things, and how the world must impinge upon him.[6] In contrast, the other science would be about what effect man is to have upon the world and what he is to do within it. Now insofar as religion is a way of thinking about something and insofar as a knowledge of something accordingly arises within that process, hasn't religion an object in common with those two types of knowledge? What else does faith know than the relationship of man to God and to the world: God's purpose in making him, and the world's capacity to help or to hinder him? But further, it is not only in the worldly domain that man knows or posits things. He also does so in the domain of God, for in his fashion he also distinguishes between good and bad conduct. What, then? Is religion all of one piece with natural science and ethics? Clearly you would not agree, because you would never admit that our faith is so securely founded or that it stands on the same plane of certainty as your scientific knowledge.[7] No, you would contend that our faith does not know how to distinguish between the demonstrable and the probable. You would immediately go on to point out that the most astounding shall's and shall-not's have frequently issued from religion. And you may be quite right! Only do not forget that the same has been the case with what you call 'science'. Do not forget that in both natural science and ethics you believe you have made improvements in many respects, doing better at each than your fathers did.

What, then, are we to say that religion is? Shall we say, as before, that it is a mixture, only this time a mixture of theoretical and practical knowledge? But this is even less admissible in the sphere of knowledge. The difficulty even intensifies to the degree that each of the two branches has a distinctive procedure for constructing its knowledge; and this certainly appears to be the case. Only in the most arbitrary fashion could such a mixture be contrived. Either its two elements would be forced to swirl confusedly against each other, or they would naturally separate out again. Scarcely anything could be gained by this procedure except to add one more object lesson for introducing beginners to the results of science and for arousing in them the desire for inquiry. But if that is all you mean to do, why fight religion? As long as there are beginners around, you can leave religion to them, while you yourselves remain at peace, secure from attack. If we took it upon ourselves to win you over, you could reasonably laugh at our fantastic self-deception. Knowing only too well that you have left religion far behind you and that our use of it is actually prepared for by you more knowledgeable people, you would be wasting your time to devote any serious attention to the subject. But I don't think this is how matters stand. If I am not mistaken, you have labored long and hard to equip the masses with just such a brief abstract of your knowledge. Whether you call it religion or enlightenment or whatnot is of no consequence in this context. But there is one intruder which you would want to exclude or expel, as the case may be. The culprit is faith. Clearly faith is the object of our controversy. And it is not an item you would care to put in the hopper, is it?

Already we can see that faith must be something quite different from a mishmash of opinions about God and the world or a collocation of commands for one life or two. Piety must be something more than the craving after this hodgepodge of metaphysical and moral crumbs, something more than a way of stirring them up. Otherwise you would hardly bother to oppose it. Otherwise it would not occur to you to speak of religion as something differentiable from your much-vaunted knowledge, however distant. On that suggestion you would have to consider the struggle of the learned and cultured against the pious as simply the struggle of depth and thoroughness against superficiality, of the teacher against pupils who want to be dismissed from school before they are ready.

Suppose you should want to hold this view nonetheless. I should be obliged to plague you with all sorts of Socratic questions, in that case. I would do so until a good number of you were compelled to give an unreserved answer to one great question. I mean the question of whether it is in any way possible for an individual to be wise and pious at the same time. To all of you I would put the further question of whether you lack knowledge of the principles by which things similar are placed together and the particular is subordinated to the general in other familiar things as well. Or perhaps by neglecting to apply the relevant principles here you intend to play a joke on the world despite the seriousness of the matter. If neither is the case, then what is one to think? How does it come about that what you separate into two domains in science are in religious faith so intertwined and indissolubly bound together that the one cannot be thought of without the other? For the pious person does not believe that one can discern the right course of action only insofar as one knows something of the relationship of man to God at the same time. Nor does he believe the other way around. Suppose the binding principle presumably involved lies on the theoretical side. Why, then, do you still set a practical philosophy over against the theoretical, rather than seeing it as only a part of this? The same sort of question arises if the principle is thought to lie on the practical side. Now perhaps this mutual relation really does hold. Or the two factors which you are used to separating may be one in a still higher, original knowledge. But you could not believe that religion would be this higher unity of knowledge now restored – not you, who have both detected and fought religion most among people most removed from science. I will certainly not hold you to such a conclusion, for I would not take up a position I could not truly affirm. But you might well agree that you must take some time to discover the proper meaning of this side of religion too.

Sacred writings: ethics and metaphysics?
Let's be completely open with each other.[8] You do not care for religion –
we have just now been assuming that. But in carrying on an honest war
against it, which after all is not entirely without cost, surely you would not
want to expend your strength striking out at a mere shadow, like the one we
have been wrangling over thus far. Your object must be something special,
something that can be formed within the human heart so as to be special.
You want something thinkable, something the essence of which can be dealt
with in its own right and thus spoken of and argued about. And so I find it
quite improper for you to patch together an untenable something-or-other
out of such disparate cloth as modes of knowing and modes of acting are,
to call it religion, and then to be so needlessly ceremonious over it.

You would deny that you have gone to work with any such cunning. You
would demand that since I have already thrown all systems, commentaries,
and apologies aside I must now refer back to all the 'original sources' of
religion, from the fine poetry of the Greeks to the sacred Scriptures of the
Christians. Then wouldn't I find the nature of the gods and the will of
the gods there? And wouldn't I regard a man holy and blessed who knew
the nature of the gods and did their will? But this is precisely what I have told
you: religion never appears unalloyed. Its outer form is always determined
by something else. Thus our task, as I have said, is to exhibit its essence
from the inside out, not to take its outer form for its essence as you seem
to do so quickly and summarily. Even the corporeal world does not hand
on its elements to you in their pristine form, presented as a spontaneous
product of nature. You would not take very large things for simple in the
physical sphere, would you, as you have done in matters of the mind?
No, it is the unending goal of the analytic art to be able to exhibit such a
thing accurately. But this is the way it will be with spiritual as well as with
physical things: you cannot produce the original without refashioning it in
yourself through a second artful creation like the first, and even then only
for the moment in which you are fashioning it. I beg of you, please get this
point clear, because you will have cause to be reminded of it over and over
again.

As for the various sources and scriptures of religion, it is their unavoidable fate to be attached to your sciences of being and of conduct, or to your
sciences of nature and of spirit, since they can only draw their language
from these areas. It is an essential requirement, inseparable from their own
purpose. This is the case because in order to make headway the sources and
scriptures of religion must make contact with what has been more or less
scientifically thought on these broad subjects, so as to release men's consciousness to deal with their own still higher subject. For what appears to be
the first and last word in a work does not always comprise its most special
and sublime elements. If you only knew how to read between the lines you

could see this! All sacred writings are like those unassuming books which were formerly current in our unassuming fatherland. Such books discussed very weighty matters despite their paltry titles. Offering few elucidations, they sought to plummet into the profoundest depths.[9] Admittedly, the sacred writings also appropriate metaphysical and moral concepts – where they do not suddenly arise as it were in an immediately poetic fashion, which however is for you ordinarily the least satisfactory way. They seem, in fact, to be almost completely occupied within this circle of concepts. But you can be expected to see through this phenomenon and to recognize the real intent behind it. Nature also yields precious metals blended in ore, yet we learn how to mine them and to restore their brightness. The sacred writings were not intended for the maturely faithful alone. They were especially intended for those who are still children in their faith: for the newly initiated, for persons who stand at the threshold waiting to be invited in. How could they operate any differently than I am doing even now with you? If they wish to arouse a new sensitivity out of the dim presentiments in which it slumbers, they have to use what is at hand. There is no other source for inciting the intense concentration and heightened disposition of mind that is needed.

When you look closely at the manner in which these metaphysical and moral concepts are dealt with, and when you observe the drive to create within them – even if it is often expressed in a poor uncommon speech – what do you see? Don't you already recognize in these efforts an endeavor to break through from a lower into a higher domain? Such efforts to communicate, as you can readily see, could only be poetical or rhetorical in form. And what is more nearly akin to rhetorical speech than dialectic? What has been more masterfully and effectively used for opening up the higher nature of men – not only our capacity for knowledge but our inner feelings as well? Naturally this aim is only achieved if one passes beyond the merely formal investiture of language. Therefore, since it has become so widespread a practice to seek chiefly metaphysics and morals in the sacred writings and to appraise them accordingly, it seems high time to approach the subject for once from the other end. It seems appropriate to begin, for once, with the clear-cut opposition in which our faith finds itself over against your morals and metaphysics, to see what our piety looks like in distinction from what you call morality. This is what I have intended by digressing here: to throw some light on the conception of religion that is dominant among you. Having done so, I return to the matter at hand.

Contemplation, not knowledge or science
At the very outset, religion waives all claims to anything belonging to the two domains of science and morality. It would now return all that has been either loaned or pressed upon it from those sources. I hope that in this way you can be shown what the original and distinctive province of religion is.

First let's look at your 'science of being', your 'natural science', in which your 'theoretical philosophy' claims it must combine everything pertaining to the real world. What is its aim? I suppose it is this: to know things in their distinctive essence; to display the particular relations through which each thing is what it is; to determine the place of each thing within the whole and to distinguish it correctly from all else; finally, to present all the aspects of reality in their necessary interconnections and to demonstrate the correspondence of all phenomena with the eternal laws that lie behind them. This aim is truly excellent. I wouldn't want to disparage it at all. Even more, if my sketchy description does not suffice, I would be willing to grant you the highest, most exhaustive account of knowledge and science you are able to provide. Yet, however much further you take me – even if you take natural science beyond the eternal laws to the supreme Lawgiver of the universe, who embraces and unites all things, and even if you acknowledge that nature cannot be apprehended without God[10] – I would still contend that religion has nothing to do even with this knowledge. I would also contend that its essence may be perceived without incorporating this knowledge.

The measure of piety is different from the measure of knowledge. Piety can be gloriously revealed, quite originally and distinctively, even in a person who does not really possess this sort of knowledge himself but only as others do, as bits of information gathered in other contexts. Indeed, the pious man will readily grant you – even if you are somewhat haughtily looking down at him! – that as such he does not have knowledge at his fingertips as you do. This is true even though he must also be a man of wisdom. And so I would explain to you in clear words something most pious men only dimly perceive but do not know enough about to express. I mean, should you place God at the apex of your science, taking God to be the ground of all knowing or even of all knowledge as well, they would of course honor and praise this position. But this is not the same thing as their way of experiencing and knowing God. Actually, their way, as they would gladly admit and as can easily enough be seen in their behavior, does not directly produce knowledge or science.

Religion is essentially contemplative, to be sure. You would never call a person pious who goes about in a state of impervious stupidity, whose senses are not open to the life of the world. But religious contemplation, unlike your knowledge of nature, is never concerned with the essence of a finite object in its connection and contrast with other finite objects. Unlike your knowledge of God, religious contemplation is not concerned with the essence of 'the first cause' either (if I may use an older terminology for a moment) – not in itself or in its relationship to all else along the cause-and-effect continuum.[11] The contemplation of pious men is only the immediate consciousness[12] of the universal being of all finite things in and through the infinite, of all temporal things in and through the eternal. To seek and to find this infinite and eternal factor in all that lives and moves, in all growth and change, in all action and passion, and to have and to know life itself only in immediate feeling – that is religion. Where this awareness is found, religion is satisfied; where this awareness is hidden, religion experiences frustration and anguish, emptiness and death. And so religion is, indeed, a life in the infinite nature of the whole, in the one and all, in God – a having and possessing[13] of all in God and of God in all. Knowledge and knowing, however, it is not, either of the world or of God; it only acknowledges these things without being either. For religion, science is also a movement and revelation of the infinite in the finite. But religion further sees this movement and revelation in God, and God sees it in religion.

Not ethics or morality
On the other side, then, what is your 'ethics', your 'science of conduct', supposed to accomplish? Manifestly it too seeks to make a clear distinction between the various particulars of human conduct and achievement, to construct all this into one whole, and to order this whole on its own grounds. But the pious man confesses to you that, strictly speaking, he knows nothing of this. He contemplates human conduct, to be sure, but his contemplation is not at all the sort from which an ethical system arises. In all this material he expects to find only what I mentioned before: only that action or conduct which derives from God – specifically, the activity of God among men. Certainly, if your ethics is correct and his piety is correct too, he would acknowledge no other action as divine than that which is also embraced in your system. But you are the learned men. To know and to construct the actual system is your affair, not his. If you are not disposed to agree, consider the women. You yourselves do not ascribe religion to them simply as an adornment. You also expect it of them as the finest sort of feeling for distinguishing divine action from other kinds. Do you require them to have a scientific understanding of your ethics as well?

The same situation, I hasten to add, applies to conduct itself. The artist fashions what is given him to fashion, by virtue of his special talent. Human talents are so diverse that the one he possesses another lacks – unless someone would dream, in defiance of heaven, of possessing all. Moreover, when someone is acclaimed as a pious man, you do not ask which of these many gifts he possesses by virtue of his piety. The citizen – a term I use in the old sense, not in the meager sense of 'bourgeois' used today – orders his life, conducts his affairs, and bears influence by virtue of his morality. But this morality is something quite different from his piety, which has its passive side as well. Piety also comes on the scene as surrender, whereby a person allows himself to be affected by the whole of that which confronts man. Morality, however, always manifests itself as an invasion of this whole, as self-assertion. Accordingly, morality depends entirely upon the consciousness of freedom. All that it produces falls within that sphere. Piety, on the other hand, is not bound to this side of life. Piety is just as much at home in the opposite sphere of necessity, where there is no strictly individual and unique action. Therefore the two are quite different from each other. Although piety dwells with pleasure upon every activity by which the infinite is revealed in the finite, it is nevertheless not itself identical with this activity. It maintains its own domain and character only by steering clear of science[14] and praxis, as such. Only insofar as piety takes its place beside them both, moreover, will the field they hold in common be completely filled out and this aspect of human nature be fulfilled. Piety presents itself to you as the necessary and indispensable third to science and morality, as their natural counterpart, one no less endowed with that dignity and excellence which you attribute to them.

Piety not divorced from knowing and doing

Please don't misunderstand me here. Don't read me as if I had taken the odd position that one of these could exist without the other, so that a person could be immoral, for example, by virtue of having religion or being pious. This is assuredly impossible. But it is just as impossible, in my opinion, for a person to be moral or scientific without religion. Now you might want to recall something I have said earlier, and not without some justice. Didn't I claim that one could have religion without science? Didn't this mean introducing a separation between them myself? But remember, I am still supposing that the measure of piety and the measure of science is not the same. We have noted that the pious man can be ignorant but never falsely knowledgeable. It is just as true, however, that one cannot be truly scientific without piety. You see, the being of the pious man is not of that inferior kind which, following the old adage that like is only known to like, attaches pseudo-knowledge to the delusive semblance of reality. His being is real. He knows true being, and he does not believe he sees something where reality does not confront him. You can already tell what a precious jewel of science I regard ignorance to be for a man if he is still held captive to false appearances. If you have not yet seen the point for yourselves, go learn it from your Socrates. You will at least admit that I am not inconsistent. I trust you will also agree that the proper opposite of knowledge is not ignorance but a vague presumption of knowledge, because you are aware that knowledge always has ignorance mixed up in it. Perhaps you will also agree that vague presumption of knowledge is most surely overcome by piety in its own context, for piety cannot stand to live with it long.

Do not accuse me of divorcing knowledge and conduct from piety, therefore. You cannot do this without ascribing to me your own viewpoint, undeserved. But it is the very confusion contained in your viewpoint – a very common one, and very difficult to avoid – that I would expose through this discussion. In the first place, you do not recognize religion to be the third basic element along with knowledge and conduct. This is precisely why the other two part so widely from each other that you cannot discern their unity but suppose that people could have right knowledge without right conduct and vice versa. In the second place, you disdain that separation in the one place where I regard it to be necessary, namely, for purposes of reflection; and you carry that separation over into life, as if the things we are speaking of present themselves already separated and independent from each other in life. This is precisely why you possess no vital perspective on these activities. For you each one is an isolated fragment. In the last analysis, your conception of these activities is thoroughly wanting, nonsensical, because it does not fasten onto life in any vital way.

True science is perspective fully achieved; true praxis is art and culture created of oneself; true religion is sense and taste for the infinite. To wish to have true science or praxis without true religion, or to suppose one has them under this condition, is wanton delusion, insolent distortion. It is like sneaking up to something one could safely claim and expect to receive in quiet and quickly snatching it away, except that here one ends up with a mere show of possession anyway.[15] But what can man accomplish worth talking about, in life or in art, than what has been stimulated within him by this sense for the infinite I speak of? Without this inner sense, how can one hope to comprehend the world scientifically? How can one hope even to exercise such knowledgeability as may be thrust upon him through some particular talent? For what else is science than the existence of things within you, within your reason? What else is art and culture than your existence in things on which you bestow measure, form, and order? And how can either science or art and culture spring to life for you except insofar as the eternal unity of reason and nature, the universal being of all finite things in the infinite, thrives within you?

[. . .]

The essence of the matter

Here, then, you have these three things, about which my discussion has revolved thus far: knowing, feeling, and conduct. And now you understand what I mean by asserting that they are not identical and are yet inseparable. If you will simply gather all that belongs to each grouping together and consider each one by itself, you will discover that all those moments in which you exercise power over things and place your stamp upon them make up what you call the practical life – or in a narrower sense, the moral life. In contrast, you will no doubt call those more or less frequent moments of observation, in which things generate their existence within you through perspectivity, your scientific life. Now can either of these two categories of activity form a human life alone, without the other? Wouldn't the self-destruction of each activity result if it were not stimulated and renewed through the other? And wouldn't this be death? Are they both identical, then, or must you differentiate them if you are to understand your life and to speak intelligently about it? Now the same sort of relation these two groupings have to each other must also hold between the third one mentioned and these two. And what name will you give to this third category having to do with feeling? What sort of life is this to form in relation to knowing and conduct? The religious life, in my view. And probably you wouldn't be able to put it otherwise yourselves once you gave closer attention to the matter.

The chief point in this address has now been stated. This is the distinctive domain which I would assign to religion, alone and in its entirety. This is the domain which you would no doubt mark out and concede to religion, too. If not, then either you must prefer the old confusion to clear explanation or you must bring forth I know not what new and marvelous scheme in its place. Your feeling is your piety, with two qualifications: first, insofar as that feeling expresses the being and life common to you and to the universe[16] in the way described and, second, insofar as the particular moments of that feeling come to you as an operation of God within you mediated through the operation of the world upon you. The details that make up this category consist neither of your knowledge nor of its objects, neither of your works and deeds nor of the various spheres of conduct. They consist simply of your experiences of receptivity[17] and the influences upon you of all that lives and moves around you accompanying and conditioning those experiences. These and only these are the exclusive elements of religion – all of them. There is no sensing, no experience of receptivity, which is not pious, unless this sensing indicates a diseased, impaired situation in life, which, however, could not help but spread to the other areas of life as well. It naturally follows, then, that in themselves all concepts and principles are alien to religion, in every respect. And this brings us back to a point that has come up before. That is, if concepts and principles are to be anything at all, they must belong to the category of knowledge; but whatever is subsumed under the category of knowledge lies in a domain of life altogether different from that of religion.

Notes

1. As indicated in each place, numerous alterations and additions were made to this address in 1806; some were extensive, amounting to a complete rewriting of about half the original text. Considerable editing was also done in 1821, though only one change was of paragraph length – the ending. In Pünjer (1879) there are some 254 changes in II, many from several lines to several pages in length, and some 653 in III. Nevertheless the detailed outline, basic theses, and use of major terms remained largely the same. The first edition was simpler than the later ones. It was occasionally somewhat more forthright in address, less guarded in attack. But it was also far less precise and clear.

    In I, the discussion here centered on metaphysics and morals, both of which have the same intended object: 'the *Universum* and the relationship of man to it'. Both they and religion, said Schleiermacher, should be differentiated from each other, so that they must 'treat the same material in quite a different way, express or deal with a different relationship of man to that material, and have a different aim or mode of procedure'. By metaphysics he then especially meant 'transcendental philosophy', which 'breaks the universe into classes ... and spins the reality of the world and its laws out of itself'. By morals he meant that which 'develops a system of duties out of man's nature and circumstances in the universe' (Pünjer 1879: 35–37).

2. The poet is Friedrich von Schiller (1759–1805). The reference is to the last line of the Prologue to his dramatic trilogy *Wallenstein* recited at the reopening of the theater in Weimar on October 12, 1798: '*Ernst ist das Leben, heiter ist die Kunst*'. This was the first performance of the first part, *Wallensteins Lager (Schillers sämmtliche Schriften*, 12. Teil, Stuttgart 1872, p. 10).

3. Compare the sole biblical reference to a 'flaming sword', in Gen. 3:24. When God had driven man out of the garden, he put to the east of Eden the cherubim and 'a flaming sword which turned every way, to guard the way to the tree of life'.

4. Sentence added in III.

5. The discussion in I was of 'metaphysics' and 'morals' only, but with the same scope of inclusion. The two were not called 'sciences' in I.

6. II: 'Or if that will not do, then it describes the nature of man and of his relations to the universe as determined by the nature of things'.

7. II: 'your philosophy'.

8. For the most part, the next two paragraphs are retained from I. No paragraph in this second address has remained unrevised.

9. Until the final pages of this address, from here on II takes over almost entirely perhaps three times the earlier text in length.

10. Parenthetical statement added in III.

11. Sentence added in III.

12. II: 'perception' (*Wahrnehmung*); III: 'consciousness' (*Bewusstsein*).

13. II: 'a seeing'.

14. I: 'speculation'. In all this section, only the rest of this paragraph remains from I, where he had already stated: 'The essence of religion is neither thinking nor conduct, but perspectivity and feeling' (*Anschauung und Gefühl*; Pünjer 1879: 46).

15. In I, reference is made here to the legend of Prometheus.

16. II: *Universum*; III: *All*.

17. *Empfindungen*. [In an earlier section of *On Religion*, not included in this extract] this key term is used in an even broader sense, referring to 'the capacity for sentience' – sensing, of both the more empirical and the more cognitive kinds. In the succeeding paragraph there, 'conception' translates *Empfängnis* (as in 'the immaculate conception'), which reflects the same basic sense of receptivity in Schleiermacher's usage. Thus in other works he sometimes interchanged *Receptivität* with *Empfänglichkeit*, in contrast with *Spontaneität* and *Selbsttätigkeit* respectively.

EDWARD TYLOR
'ANIMISM'

Edward Burnett Tylor was born in London in 1832. His parents were members of the Society of Friends and his father owned a brass company. At the age of sixteen he left education and entered the family business; however, after seven years of service his constant ill health allowed him to be excused from these duties and in 1855 he began a period of travelling. In 1856 he was in South America and here he met with the ethnologist Henry Christy, who served to awaken Tylor's interest in anthropology, and the two proceeded together on a survey of Mexico. In 1858 Tylor returned to England. He, however, maintained an armchair interest in Mexican culture and published in 1861, 1865 and 1871. This last publication coincided with him being elected a Fellow of the Royal Society. Four years after his election he was presented with an honorary doctorate from Oxford University, where he was to take up employment as keeper of the museum in 1883. A year later he was elected to a readership in anthropology at Oxford and in the same year he was the first to preside over the newly formed Anthropological Section of the British Association. In 1888 he came to Aberdeen University to deliver the first Gifford lecture. Tylor was promoted to a chair of anthropology in 1896, which he maintained until his retirement in 1909. He died in the winter of 1917 at his home in Wellington, Somerset.

Tylor's work provides a good example of the most influential theories of the nineteenth century, that is, unilinear evolution. As indicated in the text Tylor sees animism as the earliest form out of which all religions emerged. While the form of unilinear evolution found in Tylor and his contemporaries has been superseded, more flexible evolutionary models, particularly multilinear, continued to be developed well into the twentieth century.

Religious ideas generally appear among low races of Mankind – Negative statements on this subject frequently misleading and mistaken: many cases uncertain – Minimum definition of Religion – Doctrine of Spiritual Beings, here termed Animism – Animism treated as belonging to Natural Religion – Animism divided into two sections, the philosophy of Souls, and of other Spirits – Doctrine of Souls, its prevalence and definition among the lower races – Definition of Apparitional Soul or Ghost-Soul – It is a theoretical conception of primitive Philosophy, designed to account for phenomena now classed under Biology, especially Life and Death, Health and Disease, Sleep and Dreams, Trance and Visions – Relation of Soul in name and nature to Shadow, Blood, Breath – Division or Plurality of Souls – Soul cause

---

Edward Tylor (1891), *Primitive Culture*, 3rd edn, London: John Murray.

of Life; its restoration to body when supposed absent – Exit of Soul in Trances – Dreams and Visions: theory of exit of dreamer's or seer's own soul; theory of visits received by them from other souls – Ghost-Soul seen in Apparitions – Wraiths and Doubles – Soul has form of body; suffers mutilation with it – Voice of Ghost – Soul treated and defined as of Material Substance; this appears to be the original doctrine – Transmission of Souls to service in future life by Funeral Sacrifice of wives, attendants, &c. – Souls of Animals – Their transmission by Funeral Sacrifice – Souls of Plants – Souls of Objects – Their transmission by Funeral Sacrifice – Relation of doctrine of Object-Souls to Epicurean theory of Ideas – Historical development of Doctrine of Souls, from the Ethereal Soul of primitive Biology to the Immaterial Soul of modern Theology.

Are there, or have there been, tribes of men so low in culture as to have no religious conceptions whatever? This is practically the question of the universality of religion, which for so many centuries has been affirmed and denied, with a confidence in striking contrast to the imperfect evidence on which both affirmation and denial have been based. Ethnographers, if looking to a theory of development to explain civilization, and regarding its successive stages as arising one from another, would receive with peculiar interest accounts of tribes devoid of all religion. Here, they would naturally say, are men who have no religion because their forefathers had none, men who represent a præ-religious condition of the human race, out of which in the course of time religious conditions have arisen. It does not, however, seem advisable to start from this ground in an investigation of religious development. Though the theoretical niche is ready and convenient, the actual statue to fill it is not forthcoming. The case is in some degree similar to that of the tribes asserted to exist without language or without the use of fire; nothing in the nature of things seems to forbid the possibility of such existence, but as a matter of fact the tribes are not found. Thus the assertion that rude non-religious tribes have been known in actual existence, though in theory possible, and perhaps in fact true, does not at present rest on that sufficient proof which, for an exceptional state of things, we are entitled to demand.

It is not unusual for the very writer who declares in general terms the absence of religious phenomena among some savage people, himself to give evidence that shows his expressions to be misleading. Thus Dr. Lang not only declares that the aborigines of Australia have no idea of a supreme divinity, creator, and judge, no object of worship, no idol, temple, or sacrifice, but that 'in short, they have nothing whatever of the character of religion, or of religious observance, to distinguish them from the beasts that perish'. More than one writer has since made use of this telling statement, but without referring to certain details which occur in the very same book. From these it appears that a disease like small-pox, which sometimes attacks the natives, is ascribed by them 'to the influence of Budyah, an evil spirit who delights in mischief'; that when the natives rob a wild bees' hive, they generally leave a little of the honey for Buddai; that at certain biennial gatherings of the Queensland tribes, young girls are slain in sacrifice to propitiate some evil divinity; and that, lastly, according to the evidence of the Rev. W. Ridley,

> whenever he has conversed with the aborigines, he found them to have definite traditions concerning supernatural beings – Baiame, whose voice they hear in thunder, and who made all things, Turramullun the chief of demons, who is the author of disease, mischief, and wisdom, and appears in the form of a serpent at their great assemblies, &c.[1]

By the concurring testimony of a crowd of observers, it is known that the natives of Australia were at their discovery, and have since remained, a race with minds saturated with the most vivid belief in souls, demons, and deities. In Africa, Mr. Moffat's declaration as to the Bechuanas is scarcely less surprising – that 'man's immortality was never heard of among that people', he having remarked in the sentence next before, that the word for the shades or manes of the dead is 'liriti'.[2] In South America, again, Don Felix de Azara comments on the positive falsity of the ecclesiastics' assertion that the native tribes have a religion. He simply declares that they have none; nevertheless in the course of his work he mentions such facts as that the Payaguas bury arms and clothing with their dead and have some notions of a future life, and that the Guanas believe in a Being who rewards good and punishes evil. In fact, this author's reckless denial of religion and law to the lower races of this region justifies D'Orbigny's sharp criticism, that 'this is indeed what he says of all the nations he describes, while actually proving the contrary of his thesis by the very facts he alleges in its support'.[3]

Such cases show how deceptive are judgments to which breadth and generality are given by the use of wide words in narrow senses. Lang, Moffat, and Azara are authors to whom ethnography owes much valuable knowledge of the tribes they visited, but they seem hardly to have recognized anything short of the organized and established theology of the higher races as being religion at all. They attribute irreligion to tribes whose doctrines are unlike theirs, in much the same manner as theologians have so often attributed atheism to those whose deities differed from their own, from the time when the ancient invading Aryans described the aboriginal tribes of India as *adeva*, i. e. 'godless', and the Greeks fixed the corresponding term ἄθεοι on the early Christians as unbelievers in the classic gods, to the comparatively modern ages when disbelievers in witchcraft and apostolical succession were denounced as atheists; and down to our own day, when controversialists are apt to infer, as in past centuries, that naturalists who support a theory of development of species therefore necessarily hold atheistic opinions.[4] These are in fact but examples of a general perversion of judgment in theological matters, among the results of which is a popular misconception of the religions of the lower races, simply amazing to students who have reached a higher point of view. Some missionaries, no doubt, thoroughly understand the minds of the savages they have to deal with, and indeed it is from men like Cranz, Dobrizhoffer, Charlevoix, Ellis, Hardy, Callaway, J. L. Wilson, T. Williams, that we have obtained our best knowledge of the lower phases of religious belief. But for the most part the 'religious world' is so occupied in hating and despising the beliefs of the heathen whose vast regions of the globe are painted black on the missionary maps, that they have little time or capacity left to understand them. It cannot be so with those who fairly seek to comprehend the nature and meaning of the lower phases of religion. These, while fully alive to the absurdities believed and the horrors perpetrated in its name, will yet regard with kindly interest all record of men's earnest seeking after truth with such light as they could find. Such students will look for meaning, however crude and childish, at the root of doctrines often most dark to the believers who accept them most zealously; they will search for the reasonable thought which once gave life to observances now become in seeming or reality the most abject and superstitious folly. The reward of these enquirers will be a more rational comprehension of the faiths in whose midst they dwell, for no more can he who understands but one religion understand even that religion than the man who knows but one language can understand that language. No religion of mankind lies in utter isolation from the rest, and the thoughts and principles of modern Christianity are attached to intellectual clues which run back through far præ-Christian ages to the very origin of human civilization, perhaps even of human existence.

While observers who have had fair opportunities of studying the religions of savages have thus sometimes done scant justice to the facts before their eyes, the hasty denials of others who have judged without even facts can carry no great weight. A 16th-century traveller gave an account of the natives of Florida which is typical of such:

> Touching the religion of this people, which wee have found, for want of their language wee could not understand neither by signs nor gesture that they had any religion or lawe at all . . . We suppose that they have no religion at all, and that they live at their own libertie.[5]

Better knowledge of these Floridans nevertheless showed that they had a religion, and better knowledge has reversed many another hasty assertion to the same effect; as when writers used to declare that the natives of Madagascar had no idea of a future state, and no word for soul or spirit;[6] or when Dampier enquired after the religion of the natives of Timor, and was told that they had none;[7] or when Sir Thomas Roe landed in Saldanha Bay on his way to the court of the Great Mogul, and remarked of the Hottentots that 'they have left off their custom of stealing, but know no God or religion'.[8] Among the numerous accounts collected by Sir John Lubbock as evidence bearing on the absence or low development of religion among low races,[9] some may be selected as lying open to criticism from this point of view. Thus the statement that the Samoan Islanders had no religion cannot stand, in face of the elaborate description by the Rev. G. Turner of the Samoan religion itself; and the assertion that the Tupinambas of Brazil had no religion is one not to be received on merely negative evidence, for the religious doctrines and practices of the Tupi race have been recorded by Lery, De Laet, and other writers. Even with much time and care and knowledge of language, it is not always easy to elicit from savages the details of their theology. They try to hide from the prying and contemptuous foreigner their worship of gods who seem to shrink, like their worshippers, before the white man and his mightier Deity. Mr. Sproat's experience in Vancouver's Island is an apt example of this state of things. He says:

> I was two years among the Ahts, with my mind constantly directed to-
> wards the subject of their religious beliefs, before I could discover that
> they possessed any ideas as to an overruling power or a future state of
> existence. The traders on the coast, and other persons well acquainted
> with the people, told me that they had no such ideas, and this opin-
> ion was confirmed by conversation with many of the less intelligent
> savages; but at last I succeeded in getting a satisfactory clue.[10]

It then appeared that the Ahts had all the time been hiding a whole characteristic system of religious doctrines as to souls and their migrations, the spirits who do good and ill to men, and the great gods above all. Thus, even where no positive proof of religious ideas among any particular tribe has reached us, we should distrust its denial by observers whose acquaintance with the tribe in question has not been intimate as well as kindly. It is said of the Andaman Islanders that they have not the rudest elements of a religious faith; yet it appears that the natives did not even display to the foreigners the rude music which they actually possessed, so that they could scarcely have been expected to be communicative as to their theology, if they had any.[11] In our time the most striking negation of the religion of savage tribes is that published by Sir Samuel Baker, in a paper read in 1866 before the Ethnological Society of London, as follows:

> The most northern tribes of the White Nile are the Dinkas, Shillooks,
> Nuehr, Kytch, Bohr, Aliab, and Shir. A general description will suffice
> for the whole, excepting the Kytch. Without any exception, they are
> without a belief in a Supreme Being, neither have they any form of
> worship or idolatry; nor is the darkness of their minds enlightened by
> even a ray of superstition.

Had this distinguished explorer spoken only of the Latukas, or of other tribes hardly known to ethnographers except through his own intercourse with them, his denial of any religious consciousness to them would have been at least entitled to stand as the best procurable account, until more intimate communication should prove or disprove it. But in speaking thus of comparatively well known tribes such as the Dinkas, Shilluks, and Nuehr, Sir S. Baker ignores the existence of published evidence, such as describes the sacrifices of the Dinkas, their belief in good and evil spirits (adjok and djyok), their good deity and heaven-dwelling creator, Dendid, as likewise Néar the deity of the Nuehr, and the Shilluks' creator, who is described as visiting, like other spirits, a sacred wood or tree. Kaufmann, Brun-Rollet, Lejean, and other observers, had thus placed on record details of the religion of these White Nile tribes, years before Sir S. Baker's rash denial that they had any religion at all.[12]

The first requisite in a systematic study of the religions of the lower races, is to lay down a rudimentary definition of religion. By requiring in this definition the belief in a supreme deity or of judgment after death, the adoration of idols or the practice of sacrifice, or other partially-diffused doctrines or rites, no doubt many tribes may be excluded from the category of religious. But such narrow definition has the fault of identifying religion rather with particular developments than with the deeper motive which underlies them. It seems best to fall back at once on this essential source, and simply to claim, as a minimum definition of Religion, the belief in Spiritual Beings. If this standard be applied to the descriptions of low races as to religion, the following results will appear. It cannot be positively asserted that every existing tribe recognizes the belief in spiritual beings, for the native condition of a considerable number is obscure in this respect, and from the rapid change or extinction they are undergoing, may ever remain so. It would be yet more unwarranted to set down every tribe mentioned in history, or known to us by the discovery of antiquarian relics, as necessarily having possessed the defined minimum of religion. Greater still would be the unwisdom of declaring such a rudimentary belief natural or instinctive in all human tribes of all times; for no evidence justifies the opinion that man, known to be capable of so vast an intellectual development, cannot have emerged from a non-religious condition, previous to that religious condition in which he happens at present to come with sufficient clearness within our range of knowledge. It is desirable, however, to take our basis of enquiry in observation rather than from speculation. Here, so far as I can judge from the immense mass of accessible evidence, we have to admit that the belief in spiritual beings appears among all low races with whom we have attained to thoroughly intimate acquaintance; whereas the assertion of absence of such belief must apply either to ancient tribes, or to more or less imperfectly described modern ones. The exact bearing of this state of things on the problem of the origin of religion may be thus briefly stated. Were it distinctly proved that non-religious savages exist or have existed, these might be at least plausibly claimed as representatives of the condition of Man before he arrived at the religious stage of culture. It is not desirable, however, that this argument should be put forward, for the asserted existence of the non-religious tribes in question rests, as we have seen, on evidence often mistaken and never conclusive. The argument for the natural evolution of religious ideas among mankind is not invalidated by the rejection of an ally too weak at present to give effectual help. Non-religious tribes may not exist in our day, but the fact bears no more decisively on the development of religion, than the impossibility of finding a modern English village without scissors or books or lucifer-matches bears on the fact that there was a time when no such things existed in the land.

I purpose here, under the name of Animism, to investigate the deep-lying doctrine of Spiritual Beings, which embodies the very essence of Spiritualistic as opposed to Materialistic philosophy. Animism is not a new technical term, though now seldom used.[13] From its special relation to the doctrine of the soul, it will be seen to have a peculiar appropriateness to the view here taken of the mode in which theological ideas have been developed among mankind. The word Spiritualism, though it may be, and sometimes is, used in a general sense, has this obvious defect to us, that it has become the designation of a particular modern sect, who indeed hold extreme spiritualistic views, but cannot be taken as typical representatives of these views in the world at large. The sense of Spiritualism in its wider acceptation, the general belief in spiritual beings, is here given to Animism.

Animism characterizes tribes very low in the scale of humanity, and thence ascends, deeply modified in its transmission, but from first to last preserving an unbroken continuity, into the midst of high modern culture. Doctrines adverse to it, so largely held by individuals or schools, are usually due not to early lowness of civilization, but to later changes in the intellectual course, to divergence from, or rejection of, ancestral faiths; and such newer developments do not affect the present enquiry as to the fundamental religious condition of mankind. Animism is, in fact, the groundwork of the Philosophy of Religion, from that of savages up to that of civilized men. And although it may at first sight seem to afford but a bare and meagre definition of a minimum of religion, it will be found practically sufficient; for where the root is, the branches will generally be produced. It is habitually found that the theory of Animism divides into two great dogmas, forming parts of one consistent doctrine; first, concerning souls of individual creatures, capable of continued existence after the death or destruction of the body; second, concerning other spirits, upward to the rank of powerful deities. Spiritual beings are held to affect or control the events of the material world, and man's life here and hereafter; and it being considered that they hold intercourse with men, and receive pleasure or displeasure from human actions, the belief in their existence leads naturally, and it might almost be said inevitably, sooner or later to active reverence and propiti-ation. Thus Animism, in its full development, includes the belief in souls and in a future state, in controlling deities and subordinate spirits, these doctrines practically resulting in some kind of active worship. One great element of religion, that moral element which among the higher nations forms its most vital part, is indeed little represented in the religion of the lower races. It is not that these races have no moral sense or no moral standard, for both are strongly marked among them, if not in formal pre-cept, at least in that traditional consensus of society which we call public opinion, according to which certain actions are held to be good or bad, right or wrong. It is that the conjunction of ethics and Animistic philoso-phy, so intimate and powerful in the higher culture, seems scarcely yet to have begun in the lower. I propose here hardly to touch upon the purely moral aspects of religion, but rather to study the animism of the world so far as it constitutes, as unquestionably it does constitute, an ancient and world-wide philosophy, of which belief is the theory and worship is the practice. Endeavouring to shape the materials for an enquiry hitherto strangely undervalued and neglected, it will now be my task to bring as clearly as may be into view the fundamental animism of the lower races, and in some slight and broken outline to trace its course into higher regions of civilization. Here let me state once for all two principal conditions under which the present research is carried on. First, as to the religious doctrines and practices examined, these are treated as belonging to theological sys-tems devised by human reason, without supernatural aid or revelation; in other words, as being developments of Natural Religion. Second, as to the connexion between similar ideas and rites in the religions of the savage and the civilized world. While dwelling at some length on doctrines and ceremonies of the lower races, and sometimes particularizing for special reasons the related doctrines and ceremonies of the higher nations, it has not seemed my proper task to work out in detail the problems thus suggested among the philosophies and creeds of Christendom. Such applications, ex-tending farthest from the direct scope of a work on primitive culture, are briefly stated in general terms, or touched in slight allusion, or taken for granted without remark. Educated readers possess the information required to work out their general bearing on theology, while more technical discus-sion is left to philosophers and theologians specially occupied with such arguments.

NOTES

1. J. D. Lang, *Queensland*, pp. 340, 374, 380, 388, 444 (Buddai appears, p. 379, as causing a deluge; he is probably identical with Budyah).
2. Moffat, *South Africa*, p. 261.
3. Azara, *Voy. dans l'Amérique Méridionale*, vol. ii. pp. 3, 14, 25, 51, 60, 91, 119, &c.; D'Orbigny, *L'Homme Américain*, vol. ii. p. 318.

4. Muir, *Sanskrit Texts*, part ii. p. 435; Euseb. *Hist. Eccl.*, iv. 15; Bingham, book i. ch. ii.; Vanini, *De Admirandis Naturae Arcanis*, dial. 37; Lecky, *Hist. of Rationalism*, vol. i. p. 126; Encyclop. Brit. (5th ed.) s. v. 'Superstition'.
5. J. de Verrazano in Hakluyt, vol. iii. p. 300.
6. See Ellis, *Madagascar*, vol. i. p. 429; Flacourt, *Hist. de Madagascar*, p. 59.
7. Dampier, *Voyages*, vol. ii. part ii. p. 76.
8. Roe in Pinkerton, vol. viii. p. 2.
9. Lubbock, *Prehistoric Times*, p. 564 : see also *Origin of Civilization*, p. 138.
10. Sproat, *Scenes and Studies of Savage Life*, p. 205.
11. Mouat, *Andaman Islanders*, pp. 2, 279, 303. Since the above was written, the remarkable Andaman religion has been described by Mr. E. H. Man, in *Journ. Anthrop. Inst.* vol. xii. (1883) p. 156. [Note to 3rd. ed.]
12. Baker, 'Races of the Nile Basin,' in *Tr. Eth. Soc.* vol. v. p. 231; *The Albert Nyanza*, vol. i. p. 246. See Kaufmann, *Schilderungen aus Centralafrika*, p. 123; Brun-Rollet, *Le Nil Blanc et le Soudan*, pp. 100, 222, also pp. 164, 200, 234; G. Lejean in *Rev. des Deux M.* April 1, 1862, p. 760; Waitz, *Anthropologie*, vol. ii. pp. 72–5; Bastian, *Mensch*, vol. iii. p. 208. Other recorded cases of denial of religion of savage tribes on narrow definition or inadequate evidence may be found in Meiners, *Gesch. der Rel.* vol. i. pp. 11–15 (Australians and Californians); Waitz, *Anthropologie*, vol. i. p. 323 (Aru Islanders, &c.); Farrar in *Anthrop. Rev.* Aug. 1864, p. ccxvii. (Kafirs, &c.); Martius, *Ethnog. Amer.* vol. i. p. 583 (Manaos); J. G. Palfrey, *Hist. of New England*, vol. i. p. 46 (New England tribes).
13. The term has been especially used to denote the doctrine of Stahl, the promulgator also of the phlogiston-theory. The Animism of Stahl is a revival and development in modern scientific shape of the classic theory identifying vital principle and soul. See his *Theoria Medica Vera*, Halle, 1737; and the critical dissertation on his views, Lemoine, *Le Vitalisme et l' Animisme de Stahl*, Paris, 1864.

2

PHENOMENOLOGY AND HISTORY
OF RELIGIONS

INTRODUCTION

The material included in this chapter comes from the interrelated schools of phenomenology of religion and history of religion(s). While these two approaches have a slightly different focus, the first tending to be synchronic and the second focusing on the diachronic, nonetheless many of their adherents see the approaches as two aspects of a broader academic enterprise, one which ultimately seeks to determine the essence of religion in an almost ideal sense. The search for essences is illustrated in the two approaches in different ways. Phenomenology, as discussed below, includes typology or morphology as a key part of its method. These typologies, which include data from a wide range of ethnographic contexts, are often seen as providing insight into the essential characteristics of the phenomena included. Within history of religions, the search for essences is seen in the argumentative move from the history of a religion to a history of religion – this move assumes that religion as an essence has a history that is separable from the histories of particular religions.

Phenomenology of religion draws its inspiration from the philosophical school of phenomenology, particularly via the work of Husserl. It attempts or claims to describe and understand the religious consciousness of the believers who practise the particular religion being studied. Most phenomenological studies share three methodological approaches inspired by philosophical phenomenology: *epochē, einfühlung* and the eidetic vision.

The first two of these elements provide a methodological basis for the presentation and discussion of the insider point of view. *Epochē* is defined as the bracketing out of the observer's belief system. It therefore claims to separate the two horizons and thus present the insider's point of view in its own terms. The process of bracketing also involves the suspension or abandoning of any external theoretical perspective. *Einfühlung* is a closely related methodological presupposition. It suggests that the observer must empathise with the internal understanding – in a sense it suggests that the internal understanding should be privileged in relation to any external points of view. The final element, the eidetic vision, refers to the typological or occasionally morphological element that is characteristic of phenomenological analyses. It suggests that religions cannot be compared as wholes; rather, the key building blocks, for example power or sacrifice, can be abstracted and analysed in relation to similar components from a wide range of religions. This analysis is often seen as leading to the discovery of some essence that transcends any particular religion. One of the problems with phenomenological approaches is the inherent internal contradiction between these three presuppositions – the first two deny the possibility of external theorising while the third demands it.

The readings included here within both phenomenology and history of religion(s) reveal a common trajectory in relation to the issue of definition. Both disciplines initially place a strong emphasis on essentialised aspects of religion – with phenomenology seeking the common essences that arise from its process of typology and history of religion(s) seeking the history of religion (an essentialised concept) rather than of religions. With both Smart (pages 154–61) and Bianchi (pages 111–26) we see attempts to think about religion in a less essentialised and more nuanced sense – their works suggest an attempt to find more open-ended forms of discussion that move away from the simple classical notions of definition.

In addition to the readings from the schools of phenomenology and history of religion(s) we also include a set of texts relating to the issue of reductionism. As indicated both here and in the main introduction, phenomenological approaches have assumed that theories emerging from other disciplines are not applicable to religion, and that since such theoretical approaches tend to focus on some other aspect as being the motivating factor, for example the psyche or the material component of society, these approaches are reductionist (that is, they reduce all motivation and explanation to a single element). While this characterisation is arguably the case, it is not clear why this should be a problem. The readings included take up this argument and highlight many of the key issues.

UGO BIANCHI
'THE HISTORY OF RELIGIONS'

Ugo Bianchi was born in 1922 and died in 1995. He was Professor of the History of Religion at the University of Rome and the University of Messina. He served as president of the International Association for the History of Religions from 1990 to 1995.

Bianchi's work took definitions of religion in new directions. He suggests that definitions need to be both analogical and dialectical. In many respects his ideas foreshadow some of the directions taken by Smart, Southwold and Saler.

OBJECT AND METHODOLOGY OF THE HISTORY OF RELIGIONS

Questions of definition

The history of religions, as the term suggests, is a science which has as its object the manifestations in universal time and space of that human attitude which we call 'religious': an attitude which is hard to define or describe, even before we begin to discuss its nature, origin and development. Generally speaking, the historian of religions, faithful to the positive and inductive character of his investigation, will describe as 'religious', using this adjective as a hypothetical term for purposes of research, all those phenomena which he has encountered in civilizations similar or dissimilar to those in which he has received his *Bildung* and scientific training, and which show an analogy, even if with a marked contrast of principles and forms, with what in his own cultural circle (for example, European civilization with its classical and Near East antecedents) signifies 'religion'. And in this he will not be led into an ethnocentric deviation, that is, an anti-humanist and anti-scientific deformation and diminution of perspective. On the contrary, the very fact that he is aware of the historical cultural background of the concepts of 'religion' and 'religious' with which he begins his work will enable him, once he has established the philological foundations of a research that extends beyond the above mentioned cultural boundaries, to present concretely and historically, that is, in a positive inductive manner, the scientific problems concerning cultures which he found at first to be extraneous to him. And this will be true also of the student who has another ethnical and cultural background: he also must begin the work of understanding civilizations very different from his own.

It is true that there is one initial requirement in all this effort of scientific approach:[1] the research which aims at studying civilizations and religions

Ugo Bianchi (1975), *The History of Religions*, Leiden: E. J. Brill.

of all kinds, and irrespectively of the particular cultural territory to which the student belongs, must have recourse to historical methodology. This means that the history of religions is based upon philological documentary research, with great attention paid to the chronological, geographical and historical-cultural localization of the phenomena, personages, texts and historical processes which form the object of its enquiry.

In other words, the 'when', 'who', 'where' and 'how' are problems which arise before and apart from any vague formulations, before any generalizations or intuitive judgments, however brilliant these may be, and in opposition to any reduction to 'today's' terms, or to merely presupposed and possibly anachronistic or undocumented 'origins'.

Genesis and development are problems and perspectives which respond to authentic research into the history of religions. This suffices to show that, in spite of any eventual inadequacy, the history of religions owes much to the scientific methodology of European historians and philologists. Today students of non-European religious history rightly protest against the great harm done to the history of religions, especially in the 19th century, by presuppositions of an ethnocentric, positivist and abstractly progressivist nature (with the consequent reduction of the primitive and exotic to the status of inferior forms, or forms less worthy of mankind). But one must also admit that certain intuitive judgments, found in many studies by Asiatic, African or, in other circumstances, American or European students, which represent certain currents of thought which are too generically 'phenomenological', are in reality quite extraneous to the history of religions. This is seen in the propensity of many of these students to reduce the history of religions to ethnology or anthropology, or, on the contrary, to interest themselves exclusively in the 'great living religions', with a particular predilection for those of India, and without paying sufficient attention to historical questions concerning their genesis, development, historical and cultural circumstances.

One may therefore say that an *a priori* approach, typical of European ethnocentric positivism, which claimed to reduce all religion, or at least its most essential aspects, to embryonic forms which were to be sought in the religions of the 'primitive peoples', summarily interpreted, is today opposed, in certain writers on religious phenomenology, by a generalization which is itself harmful, at least from the point of view of practical research, because it is subtle and spiritually attractive. For example, a positivism which refuses to recognise religion as a living and complex element in factual history is sometimes opposed by a 'religionistic' approach which is almost purely intuitional, applied to primitive religions or to the mystiques of the living religions of the East, and which discusses at length, but generically and unhistorically, the so-called 'holy', understood as a common denominator of all religion.[2]

The history of religions as a comparative-historical science

Like all historical sciences, the history of religions approaches its subject by studying historical facts and details: what really existed and was manifest. It is not, therefore, *at least primarily*, interested in generic questions about religion, or even about this or that great religion as a whole, but in an enquiry into facts, with a view to the identification of historical processes, bound by links of space, time, objects and individual human beings. It is true, as we shall point out, that the history of religions is not to be confused with a religious historiography which deliberately confines itself to one religion, or to certain aspects of this, to the exclusion of the study of more universal historical and phenomenological problems. These problems are always essential to the purpose of the history of religions which some still define (superfluously but, if the adjective is properly understood, justifiably) as the 'comparative' history of religions. In reality the history of religions is not only a historical, but a comparative-historical study. It certainly investigates individual historical processes which are in their own way unique, although even here one cannot exclude a certain historical typology or even some of its immanent 'laws' or 'possibilities'. But it tries to see these processes as they actually developed, in their own *milieux*, and it tries to take into consideration all the problems of historical influence, of convergence or divergence in relation to other processes or *milieux*.

The comparative-historical method, then, presents the history of religions as something very different from a factual classification of particular religious histories, as they can be listed and compared in a text-book. What we must now point out is that, on the basis of what we have already said, it is clear that the history of religions has not as its primary, and still less as its only, object or as a presupposition, a too immediate and exclusive study of the characteristics of a generic religious *quality* which might emerge too easily from the context of the facts investigated. Certainly, this also may emerge from historical-comparative research, that is, from a phenomenology firmly based on historical-positive enquiry.[3] In other words, there may result, even with all its complexities and analogies, a form, or rather an aspect (among other variants) common to all civilizations and to all men which we call 'religious'. This common 'religious' quality is of course analogically (see further on) and historically conditioned, that is, it is always open (as to its adequacy) to conceptual verification on the basis of progressive historical positive research. Nevertheless, between phenomenological generalities on the one hand and concrete individualization on the other, the philological and historical, or rather comparative-historical method will be a necessary mediator and guarantor. This method implies the investigation of cultural processes and *milieux* in which the religious facts are concrete and, as such, objects of history. And this will be true not only for all that concerns the study of those religions which are called 'ethnical', that is, religions which, like the Etruscan or the original Roman religions, or the Sumerian or Egyptian, are an integrating part of a civilization or of a culture, with which they rise and with which, or before which, they decline, but is also true in the case of 'founded' religions, that is, religions which develop through the operation of a clearly individuated Founder, although always of course, at least in their origin and early development, in the context of a culture and a history. Thus even the individual 'religious' man who is the Founder of a religion is historically localised in a context from which it is impossible to isolate him until this context has been the object of all the historical study which it deserves.

Of course the intimate and personal aspects of religion will not be sacrificed or diminished by a legitimate historical investigation which therefore will not descend to sociological over-simplifications or preconceptions. In fact, just because of his concentration on actual fact, on detail, on the individual, on what is unique, and unrepeatable, the historian of religions must be willing to appreciate the personalities of those who have in their own persons incarnated, actively and passively, the religious history of mankind. This means, among other things, that the historian of religions must beware of the 'reductionist' temptation, and of the tendency to give facile explanations; he must not consider that all the facts and personalities he comes across can be 'explained' merely on the basis of an over mechanical application of a historical-cultural criterion (or, still less, of merely sociological, geographical, psychological-social or ethno-psychological criteria). He will find difficulty in studying in depth the personalities of the Founders, reformers and prophets – but this does not mean that he must have recourse too frequently to intuitive judgments or, worse still, to the exaggerated intuitionistic method of which we have already spoken, especially if by so doing he intends to isolate these personages from the whole complex historical, sociological and psychological problem. But to avoid these dangers and to build on a sound foundation the study of the personalities which are at the source of so great a part of this problem, the historian of religions will indeed have to appeal to the resources of his methodology, which is historical-positive, and avoid having recourse to generic preconceptions or to various eventual alternatives to historical research [...]. Religion and religiosity as general concepts will certainly remain as much a problem of phenomenology and religious psychology as they are of comparative history. But one will be able to say more about this, on historical and phenomenological grounds, only at the end of an investigation, which is always undertaken from a positive-inductive angle, and never in the early stages of research and its extension.

The meaning of historical-religious comparison. The
analogous meaning of 'religion' and 'religious'

The history of religions is therefore a historical science which has as its object those phenomena which, in universal time and space, we call 'religious'. Every one of these phenomena has its own peculiar individuality and character, and therefore exercises more or less a power of attraction or repulsion, or both together, with regard to other 'religious' phenomena in its vicinity. Religions present themselves for investigation as historical processes, as closely woven complexes of belief and practice, as more or less compact systems even if more or less inter-communicative. These systems correspond on the one hand to a human attitude, the 'religious' attitude (and in this they betray more or less obvious analogies) but, on the other hand, they seem to vary so much that a large section of the history and phenomenology of religions must be devoted to questions of historical-typological categorization.

Here the problem arises as to whether a given phenomenon or a given system (for example, the Buddhism of the 'Small Vehicle') deserves the term 'religion' or 'religious', not in relation to the concept of 'true' religion and the 'truly' religious in the philosophical and theological sense (as opposed to 'false' religion and 'false' religiosity) but in relation to that historical-phenomenological 'analogy' to which we have already referred, which is the special object of the history of religions.

The problem is more common than is generally thought, because it is not only the objects which are so diverse but also the spirit, intention and perspective of 'religions' and the 'religious'. In extreme cases the comparative-historical method will be put to a hard test but will show all its powers of discrimination when it discovers those characteristics which nevertheless justify from the scientific point of view the intuitions of the common man who so frequently, while remaining faithful to his creed (which sometimes renders him even more sensitive) has been able and willing to call 'religions' even those beliefs which at first (but not always and not necessarily) appeared to him strange, unacceptable or superstitious. Even here, between a genuinely fertile intuition, which must however always be verified from the historical point of view, and an improper use of ready made conceptual categories, the mediator will be the comparative-historical method proper to the history of religions. This is seen for example in the case of a Buddhist monk of the 'Small Vehicle' who might be called 'religious', but might also be denied that description because of his indifference to the essential problems of all the other religions. The comparative-historical method will draw upon all its resources in order to single out those aspects under which, concretely and positively, that form of Buddhism, or rather Buddhism as lived in that *milieu*, is 'analogous' to other more usual religious forms – an analogy which may be true when, for example, Buddhist 'atheism', or the Buddhist doctrine of the impermanence of the soul, operates concretely and historically as the radicalization of an obviously religious problem, such as that of Vedantic speculation about the illusory nature of the world of the living, in the perspective of a final liberation in the Absolute.[4]

From what we have already said it is clear that the comparison implicit in the history of religions – a comparison which does not mean to identify things different but on the contrary to distinguish elements otherwise left in confusion, will be above all a comparison between religions, between religious systems and complexes, and not mainly a comparison of detached elements or individual phenomena. In fact these latter, separated from their context, would be misunderstood and arbitrarily identified or contrasted. Here one sees the inevitable limitations of a phenomenology which would break up history and historical processes into so many elements of belief or practice especially if the student reserved for himself the supreme privilege of putting them together again, or interpreting them on the basis of arbitrarily erected structures, in homage to religions or philosophies taken *de facto* as models. If he were to do this explicitly his method would be more legitimate but would then become a philosophy or a theology. Even then he would misunderstand the facts, or fail to render them full justice, in so far as he neglected the results of historical and positive research. Hence the danger of studies and publications, undertaken from the phenomenological point of view (on pre-established religious items: God, sacrifice, soul, salvation, religion), which do not take into account the exigencies of historical method and research.

Another danger inherent in a mistaken application of the comparative method (apart from the old claim to compare only what is linguistically comparable, a claim which however at least indicates praiseworthy scruples proper to a philological-positive approach) would be that of wishing to make comparisons in an unorganic and arbitrary manner which may even be fortuitous or capricious, and unjustifiable even from the point of view of phenomenology. This occurs in certain 'comparisons' between, say, the religion of Israel and the Chinese religions, without the necessary historical framework which would explain the contexts and, wherever possible, the geographical, chronological and historical-cultural links which might make a more positive contribution to the comparisons between one *milieu* and another. Comparative arguments have been used also in connection with the famous 'questions of rites', which would often be easier to resolve by means of some practical initiative, that is, by a concrete cultural contact, than in a mere theoretical enquiry which be abstracted from such a contact.[5]

The historical-comparative method has still less in common with that comparative method which calls itself historical but is in reality far from being such, for it admits (as did Goblet d'Alviella) the possibility of supplying the lack of true or supposed documentary elements in the history of a cultural *milieu* or of a period by substituting elements and events taken from the history of other historical periods or *milieux*, on the basis of hypothetical evolutionary laws of universal validity [...].

Our attempt to clear up this point will then be justified, if, not withstanding, we attach a certain importance [...] to a presentation of general religious phenomena which will however always imply, and sometimes explicitly contain, concrete historical-cultural references to the respective *milieux* in which they existed and still exist, and in which they have significance.

The 'structures' of religion and the historical
typology of religions

Several objections have been made to the history of religions being considered as a subject in itself. Some of these objections derive from purely practical reasons. For example, its scope is said to be too vast to be explored scientifically by a single student. There is implicit in this objection the just requirement that any discussion on facts and texts must presuppose a philological (and of course linguistic) competence adequate for the purpose.

Certainly one must from the beginning concede that the historian of religions, besides having considerably enriched his own interest in comparative studies with practical experience and knowledge, must have a philological competence in some special field, a competence which can direct his enquiry and enable him to profit also by the philological achievements of others. However, it is also true that the history of religions, in coping with its own problems, cannot reduce itself to a mere summary of particular religious chronicles, each of which has to be entrusted to experts in the respective cultures and philologies. In fact, whoever has any experience of inter-cultural problems, concerning the contacts and reciprocal influences between different civilizations and cultural *milieux*, must know that even in the field of religious concepts and practice, although this is often the field in which peoples are most jealous of their spiritual inheritance and most anxious to conserve it, nevertheless the phenomena of the influence of other systems, active or passive, were and still are of great importance. The cosmopolitic and universalist religions show that barriers of race, culture and language may easily and significantly be overcome in the religious field.

Moreover, even apart from the question of diffusion, which in the ethnological field is indeed much more widespread than is generally thought (forms of culture and religion studied by ethnologists sometimes show that they have migrated across cultural areas and continents, oceans and deserts formerly considered impassable) there remains the fact of the vast extension of certain well defined types of culture and religion, and of certain elements of religious belief and practice, which hold out no possibility of their lines of diffusion being traced. For example, one finds concepts like that of a Supreme Being, of an ancestor who has become the object of worship, of a fertility rite, of 'spirit' in the animist sense, and there are institutions such as the 'passage rites', initiations, oracles and other 'structures', even if this term is inadequate and dangerous because too constrictive. There is the element of sacrifice, a factor in worship which is present in most varied forms and always relative to the type of religion to which it belongs, and prayer and the priesthood, and the tendency to create formulae, symbolism and myth. But one must remember especially that very 'analogical' form or 'structure' which is 'religion' itself, whatever may be, as we have already said, the historical value of this very generic term.

One may object that these 'structures' concern religious phenomenology, with all the dangers of abstract conceptualism and arbitrary judgments involved in this, more than they concern historical research, such as is implied in the history of religions; thus – the same person could object – the comparison which verifies these structures and forms is more a question of phenomenology than of historical research. So it would be vain to hope for a truly comparative-historical method capable of studying religious phenomena throughout the whole civilised world. This is also the objection raised by Italian 'historicism' (B. Croce and others) against the history of religions, which was accused of being a typically positivist study, without any real significance for true historical research, because of its claims to be universalist and comparative. In fact, comparative research, especially on a vast scale, was accused of having at most resulted in catalogues and collections of mere heuristic interest.

Now all these objections derive from an insufficient appreciation of the comparative-historical method proper to the history of religions, and from an inadequate sense of the urgency with which, in spite of any theoretical contestation, certain problems present themselves. These demand a reply, and one which is scientifically sound. In fact, whoever studies human phenomenology will see that certain aspects of the religious element – in fact, more precisely, certain facts such as concepts, rites and institutions, are present at least 'analogously'[6] in various civilizations and function in these, because of cross-cultural influences which may still be traced, or because of circumstances (diffusion? parallel development? convergence?) which are none the less real for being indefinable in our present state of knowledge.

Hence the necessity to study these facts and processes or 'structures'[7] with first hand documentation, and with the help of a scientific hypothesis (which must be prudent and aware of its limitations) in various regions, peoples, civilizations and continents and in various types of culture. But here also is the opportunity to attempt to establish, as it were, a 'historical phenomenology' or 'historical typology' of religious facts, that is, a typology no longer merely composed of individual religious elements (specific creeds, rites, institutions, etc.) which would make it too sectional, 'horizontal' and abstract, but also a typology of historical-cultural processes, that is of 'religious histories': by this we mean an enquiry into the historical meaning of 'analogous' developments in various religions, or the development of 'analogous' religions or religious forms in different localities and periods.

A typical example of this requirement is the study of historical circumstances (which may be reproduced in various localities but are apparently almost always accompanied by influences and stimuli which can be traced historically) in which can be seen, in differing civilizations, that typical form of religious complex called 'polytheism'. This implies a religious concept and practice which do not arise spontaneously, and certainly not as the result of a 'naturalistic' necessity, but in relation to a clearly defined historical development, that is, in connection with the rise of the 'high civilizations' of the ancient world, characterised by the building of cities, with specific shrines and specific deities, and with the parallel development of political and religious institutions which are peculiarly apt for the organisation of a polytheistic cult.[8]

Similar problems and similar historical solutions or hypotheses arise also in the case of other types of cultures and religious forms which may be reconstructed by students of cultural history. Such are, for example, the very ancient civilizations of the primitive hunters, with certain fairly constant forms of religious belief and practice (hunting rites, tribal initiation rites, etc.).

Apart from the 'ethnological' civilizations it will be even more useful for the historian of religions who is alive to comparative-historical problems to make use of written sources or of those other elements for investigation in which the 'literary' civilizations abound. The enquiry will be all the more meticulous, the more specific the type of historical problem to which it leads, revealing eventual links much more closely circumscribed in space and time. But here also appear historical problems of an amplitude which it would be difficult for a historian to perceive if he were insensitive to questions of comparison. One must try to imagine what the investigation into a phenomenon like gnosticism or, even more, dualism (in the sense in which this term is used in the history of religions) [...] would be like if the comparative-historical problem were neglected, even in its concretely typological aspects. This is all the more obvious if one reflects that other branches of study would immediately invade the field destined for historical-phenomenological comparison, and we should see philologists and historians interested in a given civilization or historical period basing their enquiries, with regard to the more general localization and comparative interpretation of the facts and structures they are studying, on theses borrowed from phenomenologists, philosophers, sociologists and theologians, all of which theses are legitimate in their own field but not the product of that comparative-historical method which is typical for religious-historical research.

Finally, the judges of these conflicting claims will be, in this case, the facts themselves. If the historians of religions, with their comparative-historical studies, have encouraged philologists to pursue new knowledge, or if they have revealed the existence of relationships, not previously noted, between various phenomena, or even if they have merely raised new problems, they will have given proof of the scientific legitimacy of their field of studies, and certainly they have done this many times already even if – on other occasions – they have strayed from the right path. And it would be wrong to object that they have achieved these ends merely through their individual philological competence or their skill in related fields – for those problems and those results often have a much wider range than that of any system of enquiry relating to a single ethnical group or a single cultural *milieu*.

[. . .]

RELIGION AND THE VARIOUS RELIGIONS

Universality and the meaning of religion

The reason for the student's interest in the historical study of religions is at once obvious when we consider the universality of the religious element in all civilizations, from the most ancient to the most modern, from those most remote in space to our own. It is clear also when we consider the determining influence religions had and still have in these civilizations which, as R. Pettazzoni observes, can only be understood when their religions are understood. Finally, it is obvious when we consider the profundity of the existential and spiritual interests involved in religions, not only in the context of their external institutions but also in that of the inner life of individuals – an inner life to which, no less than to social and historical-cultural structures, however important these may be, is entrusted the essential dynamism of the religious phenomenon in history, in spite of the theories of sociologists who follow Durkheim.

The universality of the religious element in the history of human civilizations, although not considered as an *a priori* factor in the history of religions, an inductive science which therefore may not assert anything which is beyond the reach of its investigations, is well attested objectively if we bear in mind what we have already said about the 'analogous' meaning of terms such as 'religion' and 'religious' (see above). Every attempt to discern or, even more, to presuppose in an evolutionary and historical system the existence of peoples entirely without 'religious' notions is regularly frustrated by the progress of ethnological studies. This hypothesis of an a-religious phase of primitive mankind, put forward by Lubbock in the last century, cannot be proved. What is more, the undoubtedly archaic nature of beliefs of a theistic type which, according to these evolutionists, must have been the most recent to appear (because most similar to our present day beliefs) has been made quite clear. Ethnologists also refute the suggestion that ethical notions come at a later date, or that in archaic civilizations they had no connection with religious ideas.

Apart from the question of individual atheism – which in various forms, commensurate with the respective concepts of religion, was present long before the modern age and, as we know, is possibly not always true atheism but is sometimes caused by particular reactions, variously motivated, expressing itself in arbitrary and generalizing formulae – one must consider, especially today, the question of mass atheism, which seems to prevail in certain highly politicized societies, as for example in the 'aristocracies' of Nazism or, more explicitly, in those societies which are more intent on the 'scientific' diffusion of Communist materialism. In both cases, moreover, we are faced with a political-cultural phenomenon (in some cases similar, though more radical and more widely diffused, to certain illuminist-deist, positivist-materialist and historical-idealist episodes in the history of liberalism) that cannot abolish the 'religious' connotation of the relative civilizations and peoples. These therefore cannot be described – at least for the present – as a-religious civilizations or peoples, whether with regard to their commonly shared convictions or to the more or less conscious motivations of their behaviour and civil institutions. This is shown by the introduction, in these latter, of 'ritual' forms which, although purely secular, seem to retain something of the religious forms they have superseded, as for example in the solemnization of weddings in the U.S.S.R.

But the universal presence of the religious element is interesting not only as an expression of historical-geographical diffusion but also as an expression of the variety of spiritual manifestations. The study of the fundamental elements of religion excludes the possibility of this latter being a product of one or other spiritual faculty with exclusion of the others, or of this or that psychical or social structure. No religious form is reducible to the mere expression of a feeling, un-anchored to conceptual determinants. Nor can it be reduced to mere agnostic voluntarism, or to a frigid philosophizing rationalism. In no historical religious forms do we find an absence of the elements of personal religiosity, able to animate and actively embody traditional norms and beliefs. No religious doctrine or institution denies the existence of mysterious and transcendent truths, or of a destiny incompatible with mere worldly interests. In fact, the irrefutable presence of existential interests and needs in religious manifestations is itself, in religions, elevated to a typical hierophany, that is, a manifestation of the presence and fundamentality of the divine, understood as the source of life, of daily life, but also as a sure indication of a loftier purpose, without which man is something less than man.

The 'holy' is thus understood as the source, the foundation, the purpose of existence, but not necessarily in the sense, implicit in M. Eliade's research and developed by him in many ways, that religious civilization finds its essence in a 'return to the origins', fearing and denying the course of history or the visible world or even, as E. De Martino asserts, that religion has a de-historicizing function, intended to save man from the terror he would feel when faced with the 'risk' of existence and of historical creation. On the contrary, the existence of religions which include the concept of the 'history of salvation' throughout the course of human history implies, as even these authors at least partially admit, a different outlook, although still orientated towards transcendence. The autonomy of the temporal and the secular, and even certain aspects of secularization[9] itself, have shown themselves to be not incompatible with Christian experience and even to be, to some extent, postulated or encouraged by this. It is nevertheless true that religion, in the great universalist as well as in primitive religions, in which the religious-social texture – at least as far as 'externals' are concerned – is undoubtedly more difficult to disentangle, presents itself as the total meaning of life, even in man's most intimate self, his conscience. And the great landmark of death (like that of birth or of any very significant existential event) is always present to urge every man, and every human society, to extend the panorama of life beyond what is merely visible. This is the 'dialogue' with the transcendent, and this is what we call 'religion'.

Moreover, to define this it is insufficient to draw up preconceived schemes which do not take facts into account – not only external, institutional facts but also the phenomena of the inner life which are not only the effect but also the main cause of these. Nor will any definitions of religion suffice which, in order to ensure their general applicability, are based on preconceived lowest common denominators, as for example in the case of the theory of 'primitive animism' elaborated by Tylor in the nineteenth century. Animism, understood as a belief in 'separate' souls, revealed in dreams or other similar experiences, and expressing itself frequently in concepts like the worship of the dead, or of supernatural 'presences' in this or that natural entity, is by no means the lowest common denominator or even, as Tylor asserted, the most ancient and embryonic form of religion.

It is certainly not easy to formulate a positive-historical definition of religion. It must be sufficiently elastic for a historical approximation and, at the same time, it must bear in mind the documentary possibilities, often diverse, offered by the various special sciences (ethnology with its studies of the living world of primitive peoples, prehistory, which works on fragments only, and can, therefore, lead to inductions which are not always trustworthy, and philology with its analysis of texts, etc.). In any case, *at the very basis of religion, we usually find belief in one or more powers, conceived as superior persons older than human beings and independent of them. Man, and the human collectivities, adopt an attitude of dependence on these beings, and this is reflected in their conduct, ethical or ritual, and in a belief in the possibility of communicating with these higher powers.* Nevertheless, every interpretation of life which admits of an other-worldly life has an essential connection with religious thought. *In other words, religion implies a 'breakthrough',*[10] *in the sense that one of the first characteristics of the religious element may be discerned in the establishment of a relationship with a super-human power which is understood to condition the life of the world and life in the world.*

How to begin the study of religions

As we have already said, in approaching the historical study of religions the student must adopt the most methodologically comprehensive attitude, in the sense that he must take into consideration not only those elements which seem most appropriate for any exemplary definition of religion, but also those elements which, though more or less similar to the preceding, may nevertheless, according to the religious standards of his own time and *milieu*, appear less adequate to the needs of an awakened religious conscience. The history of religions, as a historical science, must start with the facts, classifying them according to their apparent homogeneity or resemblance and also, contextually, differentiating between them, since the task of comparison is to point out not only similarities, but also differences, analyzing and interpreting them in their development, their historical associations and, within certain limits, their nature.

In other words, two dangers, already referred to, must be avoided. The first is that of using a method which, like the positivist-evolutionist method adopted by Tylor, the founder of the theory of 'animism', claims to start from a religious *minimum* found in all religions, and identical *in nuce* with the beliefs of primitive societies ('primitive' understood evolutionistically) in which the most embryonic, shadowy and 'savage' forms are considered the most ancient and so influence the interpretation of all religious evolution. This would lead to the error, for which the French sociological school and other interpretative trends have been reproached, of studying religion merely on the basis of 'primitive' documents or rather of certain primitive elements chosen from among those which seem most elementary (e.g. 'animism', 'totemism'), thus precluding any serious interest and research in the whole field of the study of religions, whether of the primitive or, more particularly, of the most advanced cults.

One might also fall into the error, rightly condemned when found in irrationalistic, modernist schools, etc. of studying only a certain *animus* or religious inspiration, the so-called 'feeling for the holy', which is found even among primitive peoples, and neglecting the study of the content of the various religions in question. But it is this content which is essential for an understanding of the religions themselves and of the history of the religious phenomenon in its concrete and historical reality as well as in its true significance.

The second danger, instead, is that of proceeding, in historical questions, with a certain intellectualist rigidity of principles which, because it presumes to define or to presuppose too much on a theoretical basis, runs the risk of misunderstanding the phenomena in question, comparing them too arbitrarily with 'patterns' or systematic formulae which are not always appropriate. This danger is found, for example, in certain studies of the Viennese cultural-historical school which have tried too glibly to reconstruct perfect monotheistic forms among primitive peoples studied by ethnologists, and also in a certain philosophical phenomenology of religion. This science, while it claims to determine the characteristics of religion on a positive-historical basis, without, however, subjecting them to a judgment based on criteria of value and truth (this being reserved for a later stage) seems at times to postulate, in the choice and description of an 'exemplary' phenomenology and of a pattern of interpretation, that very judgment, however correct and legitimate it may be in its own sphere, which it claims to have excluded [. . .].[11]

For these reasons also the historical-comparative method, which we have dealt with at length in the preceding chapter, is most valuable. The first advantage to be gained from this method is that the student does not examine merely the details, which may sometimes appear analogous and yet are in reality of a very different portent, but must approach the whole complex of phenomena, that is, consider not only themes, motives, details of creeds and cults, but the whole system of which these form an integral part, and judge the details in the light of this whole. He must, that is, consider religious systems or (as phenomenologists of religion say) 'structures' (i.e. religions) and not merely ideological and ritual fragments. This approach would free the comparative method of much of that arbitrariness from which it would inevitably suffer if it concentrated only on the fragmentary and the particular, and would at the same time create the most solid basis for research, the philological-historical basis; this so more, when those systems to which we referred were once in contact with each other, spatially and chronologically. Tradition or revolution, slow evolution or sudden forward leap, syncretism or originality: historical research, applied to detail but attentive also to holistic and comparative study, may pronounce judgment on all these cases, without assuming preconceived attitudes of an individualistic type (such as seeing new and original elements on every hand) or of an evolutionistic type (claiming to indicate a pre-existent and determining cause for everything) or even of a dialectic type because this dialectic would adopt the conclusions of this or that 'philosophy of history' or 'theology of history' – conclusions which must be judged in their own sphere of study, which is not that of the history of religions.[12]

Religion and religions. Forms and structures of religion

When he comes to the question of the variety of religious forms, the first thing the historian has to do, therefore, is to study them objectively and examine the problem of their first manifestations and their development. In doing so he must make use of terms and concepts appropriate to the religions in question. For example, he must be particularly chary in his use of the terms 'god' and 'deity'. The content of these terms differs notably (even when it is to some extent analogous), as does the content of other terms which more or less correspond to these in the various religions, for example, in the classical Greek religion and in the monotheistic religions of the Old Testament and of Christianity. The terms 'god' or 'deity' are not always appropriate for superhuman beings, either in the polytheistic or the monotheistic sense of those terms. There are beings, like the angels and devils of the monotheistic religions, which are in no sense divine and can, therefore, be included in a monotheistic system. And in certain religions there are also primordial entities, of a more or less pantheistic nature, that are quite different from a polytheistic god like Apollo, or a Creator like the God of the Bible: for example, the Indian Brahman or the Chinese Tao. Moreover, primordial beings of an animist and naturist type (the sun as a primordial 'spirit', the sky as the progenitor, the *dema* deities which, slain at the beginning of the world, were transformed into vegetable foods etc.) cannot be described as 'deities' in the same sense as the others we have mentioned.

Notes

1. Or, as is usually said today, of 'mutual understanding', but the expression is a little dangerous because it does not help us to distinguish between scientific and ecumenical understanding.
2. Lehmann, in a study on *mana* (1922), protested against the too facile recourse to ethnology to support R. Otto's theory of the 'holy'. This criticism is repeated with references also to other religions, by the Leipzig followers of Lehmann, W. Baetke and K. Rudolph.
3. See further on, for the concept of 'historical typology of religions'.
4. It is useless to observe in this connection, as H. Clavier does in *Numen*, XV, 2 (1968) p. 105, that Buddhism is a philosophy which 'wherever it becomes religious in fact [devient religieuse en fait], even in its most rigid tradition, that of the Hīnayāna, created its own divine personages'. In fact, except in the case of Amidism, it is not these personages which characterize it, or constitute its essence or final significance, and it would be strange if a non-religious doctrine and practice were to become religious merely through the accretion of elements which are to it accessory and secondary.
5. For example, it is incorrect or at least dangerous, to ask whether or when the traditional God of the Chinese is the true God of Christian theodicy or theology. This is not because the philosopher or theologian cannot accept a supreme concept of God and compare with it other concepts of Supreme Beings or Deities, etc., but because it may happen, and indeed often happens, that the Chinese concrete idea of God, in one or other period of their history, is on such occasions made the object of selection in an arbitrary way or in any case subjected to an hermeneutic which does not take account of the specific and complex character of its ideological and historical-cultural associations. As for the problem of Deity in that cultural milieu see now J. Shih, '*The Notions of God in the Chinese Religions*' in *Numen*, XVI (2), 1969, pp. 99–138.
6. As we have said, the definition of the historical-phenomenological sense of this 'analogy', which is valid also as regards the concept of 'religion', is the principal aim of the history of religions.
7. This term also presents a historical problem, unless one is prepared to accept over facile 'psychologistic' solutions, that is, to see in the 'structures' timeless 'archetypes' of the human psyche, individual or collective [...].
8. As we see, this is very different from research founded on the positivist dogma of the 'laws' of historical evolution, and is also a very different concept from that of the 'analogous developments in different religions, under the influence of similar factors', of which Clavier speaks, *op. cit.*, p. 108.
    Even if this may sometimes be true in other cases, this type of analogy is too extraneous to the interior dynamism of history, common, by hypothesis, to religious

processes which historical typology finds similar. This is proved by the type of example which Clavier adduces (evil influence of prosperity or privilege over the religious life of a community), examples which clearly imply the application of criteria not necessarily valid for every type of religion [...].

9. See e.g. the monograph, 'Problemi universalistici del cristianesimo', in G. Castellani (ed.), Storia delle religioni, 6th edit., Turin 1971, vol. IV.

10. For closer study see U. Bianchi, Problemi di Storia delle religioni (Series Universale Studium, No. 56) Rome 1958, pp. 116–19 and 132 et seqq. (= Probleme der Religionsgeschichte, Göttingen, Vandenhoeck & Ruprecht, 1964, pp. 79–81 and 88 et seqq.).

11. Concerning the 'judgement of value' see also our observations in Problemi di Storia delle religioni, Rome, 1958 (Series Universale Studium, No. 56) pp. 20–24 (= Probleme der Religionsgeschichte, Göttingen, Vandenhoeck & Ruprecht, 1964, pp. 15 et seqq.) [...].

12. This does not mean that the history of religions is reduced to a descriptive study: the historical enquiry always includes interpretation, but this is always based on a specific method, the comparative-historical method on a positive-inductive basis.

MIRCEA ELIADE
'APPROXIMATIONS: THE STRUCTURE AND MORPHOLOGY OF THE SACRED'

Mircea Eliade was born into a relatively prosperous military family in Romania in 1907. He enrolled at the University of Bucharest in 1925, from where he graduated (with an MA specialising in Italian philosophy) three years later. Eliade accepted a scholarship to study Sanskrit and Indian philosophy under Professor Surendranath Dasgupta at the University of Calcutta between 1928 and 1932. However, this period ended traumatically due to the uncovering of his affair with the daughter of his host family and he spent his last six months in India living in the Himalayan ashram of Rishikesh.

In 1933 he returned to a much-changed Romania, where he took an assistant lectureship at the University of Bucharest while completing his PhD, entitled 'Yoga, Immortality and Freedom'. Eliade took a professorship at the University of Paris, where he began to develop his thesis on the methodology of religion. Here he met with and was influenced by Dumezeil but a greater influence was the constant political turmoil of Romania, which led him to develop a terror of history. In 1956 he began a career lecturing in religious studies at the University of Chicago, where he enjoyed a long and prosperous career; he died in 1986 having published over 1,500 items.

Eliade develops many of the key elements of the phenomenological school, in many cases, particularly regarding morphology, taking them to their logical extreme. Eliade's works often range widely in time and space, with elements from the Neolithic vying for space with those of modern India or Mesoamerica. Unlike many other phenomenologists he focuses on the basis of the experience, arguing for a unifying transcendent experience.

'SACRED' AND 'PROFANE'

All the definitions given up till now of the religious phenomenon have one thing in common: each has its own way of showing that the sacred and the religious life are the opposite of the profane and the secular life. But as soon as you start to fix limits to the notion of the sacred you come upon difficulties – difficulties both theoretical and practical. For, before you attempt any definition of the phenomenon of religion, you must know where to look for the evidence, and, first and foremost, for those expressions of religion that can be seen in the 'pure state' – that is, those which are 'simple' and as close as possible to their origins. Unfortunately, evidence of this sort is nowhere to be found ; neither in any society whose history we know, nor among the

---

Mircea Eliade (1958), *Patterns in Comparative Religion*, tr. Rosemary Sheed, London: Sheed and Ward.

'primitives', the uncivilized peoples of to-day. Almost everywhere the religious phenomena we see are complex, suggesting a long historical evolution.

Then, too, assembling one's material presents certain important practical difficulties. Even if one were satisfied with studying only one religion, a lifetime would scarcely be long enough to complete the research, while, if one proposed to compare religions, several lifetimes would not suffice to attain the end in view. Yet it is just such a comparative study that we want, for only thus can we discover both the changing morphology of the sacred, and its historical development. In embarking, therefore, on this study, we must choose a few among the many religions which have been discovered by history, or ethnology, and then only some of their aspects or phases.

This choice, even if confined to the major manifestations, is a delicate matter. If we want to limit and define the sacred, we shall have to have at our disposal a manageable number of expressions of religion. If it starts by being difficult, the diversity of those expressions becomes gradually paralysing. We are faced with rites, myths, divine forms, sacred and venerated objects, symbols, cosmologies, theologoumena, consecrated men, animals and plants, sacred places, and more. And each category has its own morphology – of a branching and luxuriant richness. We have to deal with a vast and ill-assorted mass of material, with a Melanesian cosmogony myth or Brahman sacrifice having as much right to our consideration as the mystical writings of a St. Teresa or a Nichiren, an Australian totem, a primitive initiation rite, the symbolism of the Borobudur temple, the ceremonial costumes and dances of a Siberian shaman, the sacred stones to be found in so many places, agricultural ceremonies, the myths and rites of the Great Goddesses, the enthroning of an ancient king or the superstitions attaching to precious stones. Each must be considered as a hierophany in as much as it expresses in some way some modality of the sacred and some moment in its history; that is to say, some one of the many kinds of experience of the sacred man has had. Each is valuable for two things it tells us: because it is a hierophany, it reveals some modality of the sacred; because it is a historical incident, it reveals some attitude man has had towards the sacred. For instance, the following Vedic text addressing a dead man: 'Crawl to your Mother, Earth! May she save you from the void!'[1] This text shows the nature of earth worship; the earth is looked upon as the Mother, *Tellus Mater*; but it also shows one given stage in the history of Indian religions, the moment when Mother Earth was valued – at least by one group – as a protectress against the void, a valuation which was to be done away with by the reform of the Upaniṣads and the preaching of Buddha.

To return to where we began, each category of evidence (myths, rites, gods, superstitions, and so on) is really equally important to us if we are to understand the religious phenomenon. And this understanding will always come about in relation to history. Every hierophany we look at is also an historical fact. Every manifestation of the sacred takes place in some historical situation. Even the most personal and transcendent mystical experiences are affected by the age in which they occur. The Jewish prophets owed a debt to the events of history, which justified them and confirmed their message; and also to the religious history of Israel, which made it possible for them to explain what they had experienced. As a historical phenomenon – though not as personal experience – the nihilism and ontologism of some of the Mahāyāna mystics would not have been possible without the Upaniṣad speculations, the evolution of Sanskrit and other things. I do not mean that every hierophany and every religious experience whatsoever is a unique and never-to-be-repeated incident in the working of the spirit. The greatest experiences are not only alike in content, but often also alike in their expression. Rudolf Otto discovered some astonishing similarities between the vocabulary and formulæ of Meister Eckhardt and those of Śaṅkara.

The fact that a hierophany is always a historical event (that is to say, always occurs in some definite situation) does not lessen its universal quality. Some hierophanies have a purely local purpose; others have, or attain, world-wide significance. The Indians, for instance, venerate a certain tree called *aśvattha*; the manifestation of the sacred in that particular plant species has meaning only for them, for only to them is the *aśvattha* anything more than just a tree. Consequently, that hierophany is not only of a certain time (as every hierophany must be), but also of a certain place. However, the Indians also have the symbol of a cosmic tree (*Axis Mundi*), and this mythico-symbolic hierophany is universal, for we find Cosmic Trees everywhere among ancient civilizations. But note that the *aśvattha* is venerated because it embodies the sacred significance of the universe in constant renewal of life; it is venerated, in fact, because it embodies, is part of, or symbolizes the universe as represented by all the Cosmic Trees in all mythologies. But although the *aśvattha* is explained by the same symbolism that we find in the Cosmic Tree, the hierophany which turns a particular plant-form into a sacred tree has a meaning only in the eyes of that particular Indian society.

To give a further example – in this case a hierophany which was left behind by the actual history of the people concerned: the Semites at one time in their history adored the divine couple made up of Ba'al, the god of hurricane and fecundity, and Belit, the goddess of fertility (particularly the fertility of the earth). The Jewish prophets held these cults to be sacrilegious. From their standpoint – from the standpoint, that is, of those Semites who had, as a result of the Mosaic reforms, reached a higher, purer and more complete conception of the Deity – such a criticism was perfectly justified. And yet the old Semitic cult of Ba'al and Belit *was* a hierophany: it showed (though in unhealthy and monstrous forms) the religious value of organic life, the elementary forces of blood, sexuality and fecundity.

This revelation maintained its importance, if not for thousands, at least for hundreds of years. As a hierophany it held sway till the time when it was replaced by another, which – completed in the religious experience of an élite – proved itself more satisfying and of greater perfection. The 'divine form' of Yahweh prevailed over the 'divine form' of Ba'al; it manifested a more perfect holiness, it sanctified life without in any way allowing to run wild the elementary forces concentrated in the cult of Ba'al, it revealed a spiritual economy in which man's life and destiny gained a totally new value; at the same time it made possible a richer religious experience, a communion with God at once purer and more complete. This hierophany of Yahweh had the final victory; because it represented a universal modality of the sacred, it was by its very nature open to other cultures; it became, by means of Christianity, of world-wide religious value. It can be seen, then that some hierophanies are, or can in this way become, of universal value and significance, whereas others may remain local or of one period – they are not open to other cultures, and fall eventually into oblivion even in the society which produced them.

[. . .]

THE COMPLEXITY OF 'PRIMITIVE' RELIGION

The examples I have so far quoted help, I think, to establish certain guiding principles:

1. The sacred is qualitatively different from the profane, yet it may manifest itself no matter how or where in the profane world because of its power of turning any natural object into a paradox by means of a hierophany (it ceases to be itself, *as* a natural object, though in appearance it remains unchanged);

2. This dialectic of the sacred belongs to all religions, not only to the supposedly 'primitive' forms. It is expressed as much in the worship of stones and trees, as in the theology of Indian avatars, or the supreme mystery of the Incarnation;

3. Nowhere do you find *only* elementary hierophanies (the kratophanies of the unusual, the extraordinary, the novel, *mana*, etc.), but also traces of religious forms which evolutionist thought would call superior (Supreme Beings, moral laws, mythologies, and so on);

4. We find everywhere, even apart from these traces of higher religious forms, a system into which the elementary hierophanies fit. The 'system' is always greater than they are: it is made up of all the religious *experiences* of the tribe (*mana*, kratophanies of the unusual, etc., totemism, ancestor worship, and much more), but also contains a corpus of traditional *theories* which cannot be reduced to elementary hierophanies: for instance, myths about the origin of the world and the human race, myths explaining present

human conditions, the theories underlying various rites, moral notions, and so on. It is important to stress this last point.

One has only to glance through a few ethnological writings (Spencer and Gillen or Strehlow on the Australians, for instance, Schebesta or Trilles on the African Pygmies, Gusinde on the Fuegians) to note first, that the religious life of the 'primitive' spreads beyond the sphere one normally allots to religious experience and theory, and second, that that religious life is always complex – the simple and one-dimensional presentation so often to be found in works of synthesis and popularization depends entirely on the author's more or less arbitrary selectiveness. Certainly some forms will be found to dominate the religious picture (totemism in Australia for example, *mana* in Melanesia, ancestor-worship in Africa, and so on), but they are never the whole of it. We find as well a mass of symbols, cosmic, biological or social occurrences, ideograms and ideas, which are of great importance on the religious plane, though their connection with actual religious experience may not always be clear to us moderns. We can understand, for instance, how the phases of the moon, the seasons, sexual or social initiation, or space symbolism, might have come to have religious value for early mankind, might have become hierophanies; but it is much harder to see how the same would apply to physiological actions such as nutrition or sexual intercourse, or ideograms like 'the year'. We face in fact a double difficulty: first that of accepting that there is something sacred about all physiological life and, secondly, that of looking at certain patterns of thought (ideograms, mythograms, natural or moral laws and so forth) as hierophanies.

Indeed one of the major differences separating the people of the early cultures from people to-day is precisely the utter incapacity of the latter to live their organic life (particularly as regards sex and nutrition) as a sacrament. Psychoanalysis and historical materialism have taken as surest confirmation of their theses the important part played by sexuality and nutrition among peoples still at the ethnological stage. What they have missed, however, is how utterly different from their modern meaning are the value and even the function of eroticism and of nutrition among those peoples. For the modern they are simply physiological acts, whereas for primitive man they were sacraments, ceremonies by means of which he communicated with the *force* which stood for Life itself. [...] This force and this life are simply expressions of ultimate reality, and such elementary actions for the primitive become a rite which will assist man to approach reality, to, as it were, wedge himself into Being, by setting himself free from merely automatic actions (without sense or meaning), from change, from the profane, from nothingness.

[...] As the rite always consists in the repetition of an archetypal action performed *in illo tempore* (before 'history' began) by ancestors or by gods, man is trying, by means of the hierophany, to give 'being' to even his most ordinary and insignificant acts. By its repetition, the act coincides with its archetype, and time is abolished. We are witnessing, so to speak, the same act that was performed *in illo tempore*, at the dawn of the universe. Thus, by transforming all his physiological acts into ceremonies, primitive man strove to 'pass beyond', to thrust himself out of time (and change) into eternity. I do not want to stress here the function fulfilled by ritual, but we must note at once that it is the normal tendency of the primitive to transform his physiological acts into rites, thus investing them with spiritual value. When he is eating or making love, he is putting himself on a plane which is not simply that of eating or sexuality. This is true both of initiatory experiences (first-fruits, first sexual act), and also of the whole of erotic or nutritional activity. One might say that here you have an indistinct religious experience, different in form from the distinct experiences represented by the hierophanies of the unusual, the extraordinary, *mana*, etc. But the part this experience plays in the life of primitive man is none the less for that, though it is, by its very nature, liable to escape the eye of the observer. This explains my earlier statement that the religious life of primitive peoples goes beyond the categories of *mana*, hierophanies and startling kratophanies. A real religious experience, indistinct in form, results from this effort man makes to enter the real, the sacred, by way of the most fundamental physiological acts transformed into ceremonies.

Then, too, the religious life of any human group at the ethnological stage will always include certain elements of theory (symbols, ideograms, nature- and genealogy-myths, and so on). [...] Such 'truths' are held to be hiero-phanies by primitive peoples – not only because they reveal modalities of the sacred, but because these 'truths' help man to protect himself against the meaningless, nothingness; to escape, in fact, from the profane sphere. Much has been said of the backwardness of primitives in regard to theory. Even if this were the case (and a great many observers think otherwise), it is too often forgotten that the workings of primitive thought were not ex-pressed only in concepts or conceptual elements, but also, and primarily, in symbols. [...] The 'handling' of symbols works according to its own sym-bolic logic. It follows from this that the apparent conceptual poverty of the primitive cultures does not imply an inability to construct theory, but im-plies rather that they belong to a style of thinking totally different from our modern style, with its roots in the speculation of the Greeks. Indeed we can identify, even among the groups least developed ethnologically, a collection of truths fitting coherently into a system or theory (among, for instance, the Australians, Pygmies and Fuegians). That collection of truths does not simply constitute a *Weltanschauung*, but a pragmatic ontology (I would even say soteriology) in the sense that with the help of these 'truths' man is trying to gain salvation by uniting himself with reality.

To quote only one example, [...] the greater part of primitive man's actions were, so he thought, simply the repetition of a primeval action accomplished at the beginning of time by a divine being, or mythical figure.

An act only had meaning in so far as it repeated a transcendent model, an archetype. The object of that repetition was also to ensure the *normality* of the act, to legalize it by giving it an ontological status; it only became real in so far as it repeated an archetype. Now, every action performed by the primitive supposes a transcendent model – his actions are effective only in so far as they are real, as they follow the pattern. The action is both a ceremony (in that it makes man part of a sacred zone) and a thrusting into reality.

NOTE

1. *RV*, x, 18, 10.

GERARDUS VAN DER LEEUW
'RELIGION IN ESSENCE AND MANIFESTATION'

Gerardus van der Leeuw lived in the period of European unrest, from 1863 to 1950. He enrolled in studies at Leiden, Göttingen and Berlin, majoring in ancient Egyptian religion. In 1913 he graduated and began pursuing postgraduate studies, which were to result in the award of a doctorate in 1916. The same year as he received his doctorate he married and began work as a minister of the Dutch Reformed Church. In 1918 he was elected Professor of History of Religion at Groningen. After the war he became Minister for Education.

Leeuw's work is a good example of the phenomenological school. The material chosen reflects the typological emphasis that is perhaps the most characteristic element of the phenomenologists' analyses of religion. Unlike some others, however, Leeuw's work is more consciously theological.

RELIGION

1. We can try to understand religion from a flat plain, from ourselves as the centre; and we can also understand how the essence of religion is to be grasped only from above, beginning with God. In other words: we can – in the manner already indicated – observe religion as intelligible experience; or we can concede to it the status of incomprehensible revelation. For in its 'reconstruction', experience is a phenomenon. Revelation is not; but man's reply to revelation, his assertion about what has been revealed, is also a phenomenon from which, indirectly, conclusions concerning the revelation itself can be derived (*per viam negationis*).

Considered in the light of both of these methods, religion implies that man does not simply accept the life that is given to him. In life he seeks *power*; and if she does not find this, or not to an extent that satisfies him, then he attempts to draw the power, in which he believes, into his own life. He tries to elevate life, to enhance its value, to gain for it some deeper and wider meaning. In this way, however, we find ourselves on the horizontal line: religion is the extension of life to it uttermost limit. The religious man desires richer, deeper, wider life: he desires power for himself.[1] In other terms: in and about his own life man seeks something that is superior, whether he wishes merely to make use of this or to worship it.

He who does not merely accept life, then, but demands something from it – that is, power – endeavours to find some meaning in life. He arranges life into a significant whole: and thus culture arises. Over the variety of the given he throws his systematically fashioned net, on which various designs

---

Gerardus van der Leeuw (1938), *Religion in Essence and Manifestation*, tr. J. E. Turner, London: George Allen and Unwin.

appear: a work of art, a custom, an economy. From the stone he makes himself an image, from the instinct a commandment, from the wilderness a tilled field; and thus he develops power. But he never halts; he seeks ever further for constantly deeper and wider *meaning*. When he realizes that a flower is beautiful and bears fruit, he enquires for its ampler, ultimate significance; when he knows that his wife is beautiful, that she can work and bear children, when he perceives that he must respect another man's wife, just as he would have his own respected, he seeks still further and asks for her final meaning. Thus he finds the secret of the flower and of woman; and so he discovers their religious significance.

The religious significance of things, therefore, is that on which no wider nor deeper meaning whatever can follow. It is the meaning of the whole: it is the last word. But this meaning is never understood, this last word is never spoken; always they remain superior, the ultimate meaning being a secret which reveals itself repeatedly, only nevertheless to remain eternally concealed. It implies an advance to the farthest boundary, where only one sole fact is understood:– that all comprehension is 'beyond'; and thus the ultimate meaning is at the same moment the limit of meaning.[2]

Homo religiosus thus betakes himself to the road to omnipotence, to complete understanding, to ultimate meaning. He would fain comprehend life, in order to dominate it. As he understands soil so as to make it fruitful, as he learns how to follow animals' ways, so as to subject them to himself – so too he resolves to understand the world, in order to subjugate it to himself. Therefore he perpetually seeks new superiorities: until at last he stands at the very frontier and perceives that the ultimate superiority he will never attain, but that it reaches him in an incomprehensible and mysterious way. Thus the horizontal line of religion resembles the way of St. Christopher, who seeks his master and at last finds him too.

2. But there is also a vertical way: from below upwards, and from above downwards. This way however is not, like the former, an experience that is passed through before a frontier. It is a revelation, coming from beyond that frontier. The horizontal path, again, is an experience which certainly has an inkling or presage[3] of revelation, but which cannot attain to it. The vertical way, on the other hand, is a revelation, which never becomes completely experienced, though it participates in experience. The first road is certainly not a tangible, but is all the more an intelligible, phenomenon. The second is not a phenomenon at all, and is neither attainable nor understandable; what we obtain from it phenomenologically, therefore, is merely its reflection in experience. We can never understand God's utterance by means of any purely intellectual capacity: what we can understand is only our own answer; and in this sense, too, it is true that we have the treasure only in an earthen vessel.

Man, seeking power in life, does not reach the frontier; but he realizes that he has been removed to some foreign region. Thus he not only reaches the place from which a prospect of infinite distance is disclosed to him, but he knows too that, while he is still on the way, he is at every moment surrounded by marvellous and far-off things. He has not only a firm awareness (*Ahnung*) of the superior, but is also directly seized by it. He has not merely descried the throne of the Lord *from afar*, and fain would have sent on his heart in advance, but he realizes too that *this* place itself is dreadful, because it is a 'house of God' and a 'gate of heaven'. Perhaps angels descend to his resting-place: perhaps demons press upon his path. But he knows quite definitely that *something meets him on the road*. It may be the angel who goes before him and will lead him safely: it may be the angel with the flashing sword who forbids him the road. But it is quite certain that something foreign has traversed the way of his own powerfulness.

And just because it is not to be found in the prolongation of man's own path, this strange element has no name whatever. Otto has suggested 'the numinous', probably because this expression says nothing at all! This foreign element, again, can be approached only *per viam negationis*; and here again it is Otto who has found the correct term in his designation 'the Wholly Other'. For this, however, religions themselves have coined the word 'holy'.[4] The German term is derived from *Heil*, 'powerfulness'; the Semitic and Latin, קדוש, *sanctus*, and the primitive expression, *tabu*, have the fundamental meaning of 'separated', 'set aside by itself'. Taken all together, they provide the description of what occurs in all religious experience: *a strange, 'Wholly Other', Power obtrudes into life*. Man's attitude to it is first of all *astonishment*,[5] and ultimately *faith*.

3. The limit of human powerfulness, in conclusion, and the commencement of the divine, together constitute the goal which has been sought and found in the religion of all time:– *salvation*. It may be the enhancing of life, improvement, beautifying, widening, deepening; but by 'salvation' there may also be meant completely new life, a devaluation of all that has preceded, a new creation of the life that has been received 'from elsewhere'. But in any case, religion is always directed towards salvation, never towards life itself as it is given; and in this respect all religion, with no exception, is the religion of deliverance.[6]

The Phenomenology of Religion

1. Phenomenology is the systematic discussion of what appears. Religion, however, is an ultimate experience that evades our observation, a revelation which in its very essence is, and remains, concealed. But how shall I deal with what is thus ever elusive and hidden? How can I pursue phenomenology when there is no phenomenon? How can I refer to 'phenomenology of religion' at all?

Here there clearly exists an antinomy that is certainly essential to all religions, but also to all understanding; it is indeed precisely because it holds good for *both*, for religion and understanding alike, that our own science becomes possible. It is unquestionably quite correct to say that faith and intellectual suspense (the *epoche*) do not exclude each other. It may further be urged that the Catholic Church, too, recognizes a *duplex ordo* of contemplation, on the one hand purely rational, and on the other wholly in accord with faith; while such a Catholic as Przywara also wishes to exclude every apologetic subsidiary aim from philosophy, and strenuously maintains the *epoche*.[7] But at the same time one cannot but recognize that all these reflections are the result of embarrassment. For it is at bottom utterly impossible contemplatively to confront an event which, on the one hand, is an ultimate experience, and on the other manifests itself in profound emotional agitation, in the attitude of such pure intellectual restraint. Apart from the existential attitude that is concerned with reality, we could never know anything of either religion or faith. It may certainly be advisable and useful methodically to presuppose this intellectual suspense; it is also expedient, since crude prejudice can so readily force its way into situations where only such an existential attitude would be justifiable. But, once again, how shall we comprehend the life of religion merely by contemplative observation from a distance? How indeed can we understand what, in principle, wholly eludes our understanding?

Now [...] not the understanding of religion alone, but *all* understanding without exception, ultimately reaches the limit where it loses its own proper name and can only be called 'becoming understood'. In other words: the more deeply comprehension penetrates any event, and the better it 'understands' it, the clearer it becomes to the understanding mind that the ultimate ground of understanding lies not within itself, but in some 'other' by which it is comprehended from beyond the frontier. Without this absolutely valid and decisive understanding, indeed, there would be no understanding whatever. For all understanding that extends 'to the ground' ceases to be understanding before it reaches the ground, and recognizes itself as a 'becoming understood'. In other terms: all understanding, irrespective of whatever object it refers to, is ultimately religious: all significance sooner or later leads to ultimate significance. As Spranger states this: 'in so far as it always refers to the whole man, and actually finds its final completion in the totality of world conditions, all understanding has a religious factor ... we understand each other in God.'[8]

What has previously been said with reference to the horizontal line in religion can also be translated into the language of the vertical line. And that ultimately all understanding is 'becoming understood' then means that, ultimately, all love is 'becoming loved'; that all human love is only the response to the love that was bestowed upon us. 'Herein is love, not that we loved God, but that he loved us ... we love him, because he first loved us.'[9]

Understanding, in fact, itself presupposes intellectual restraint. But this is never the attitude of the cold-blooded spectator: it is, on the contrary, the loving gaze of the lover on the beloved object. For all understanding rests upon self-surrendering love. Were that not the case, then not only all discussion of what appears in religion, but all discussion of appearance in general, would be quite impossible; since to him who does not love, nothing whatever is manifested; this is the Platonic, as well as the Christian, experience.

I shall therefore not anticipate fruitlessly, and convert phenomenology into theology. Nor do I wish to assert that the faith upon which all comprehension is grounded, and religion as itself faith, are without further ado identical. But 'it is plainly insufficient to permit theology to follow on philosophy [for my purpose, read 'phenomenology'] purely in virtue of its content, since the fundamental problem is one of method, and concerns the claim of philosophy [again, here, phenomenology] to justification in view of the obvious data, and also the impossibility of referring back faith, as the methodical basis of theology, to these data. In other terms: the problem becomes that of what is obviously evidence.'[10] And I am prepared, with Przywara, to seek the intimate relationship that nevertheless exists between faith and the obvious data, in the fact that the evidence they provide is essentially a 'preparedness for revelation'.[11]

2. The use of the expressions: history of religion, science of religion, comparative history of religion, psychology of religion, philosophy of religion: and others similar to these, is still very loose and inexact; and this is not merely a formal defect, but is practical also.[12] It is true that the different subdivisions of the sciences concerned with religion (the expression is here employed in its widest possible sense), cannot subsist independently of each other; they require, indeed, incessant mutual assistance. But much that is essential is forfeited as soon as the limits of the investigation are lost to sight. The history of religion, the philosophy and psychology of religion, and alas! theology also, are each and all harsh mistresses, who would fain compel their servants to pass beneath the yoke which they hold ready for them; and the phenomenology of religion desires not only to distinguish itself from them, but also, if possible, to teach them to restrain themselves! I shall therefore first of all indicate what the phenomenology of religion is not, and what fails to correspond to its own essential character in the character or usage of the other disciplines.

The phenomenology of religion, then, is not the poetry of religion; and to say this is not at all superfluous, since I have myself expressly referred to the poetic character of the structural experience of ideal types. In this sense, too, we may understand Aristotle's assertion that the historian relates what has happened, while the poet recounts what might have occurred under any given circumstances; and that poetry is therefore a philosophical affair and of more serious import than history;[13] as against all bare historicism and all mere chronicle, this should always be remembered. Nor should it be forgotten that 'art is just as much investigation as is science, while science is just as much the creation of form as is art'.[14] But in any case there is a clear distinction between poetry and science, which forces itself into notice in the procedure of both from beginning to end: in his own work, then, the phenomenologist is bound up with the object; he cannot proceed without repeatedly confronting the chaos of the given, and without submitting again and again to correction by the facts; while although the artist certainly sets out from the object, he is not inseparably linked with this. In other words: the poet need know no particular language, nor study the history of the times; even the poet of the so-called historical novel need not do this. In order to interpret a myth he may completely remodel it, as for example Wagner treated the German and Celtic heroic sagas. Here the phenomenologist experiences his own limit, since his path lies always between the unformed chaos of the historical world and its structural endowment with form. All his life he oscillates hither and thither. But the poet advances.

Secondly, the phenomenology of religion is not the history of religion. History, certainly, cannot utter one word without adopting some phenomenological viewpoint; even a translation, or the editing of a Text, cannot be completed without hermeneutics. On the other hand, the phenomenologist can work only with historical material, since he must know what documents are available and what their character is, before he can undertake their interpretation. The historian and the phenomenologist, therefore, work in the closest possible association; they are indeed in the majority of cases combined in the person of a *single* investigator. Nevertheless the historian's task is essentially different from the phenomenologist's, and pursues other aims.[15] For the historian, everything is directed first of all to establishing what has actually happened; and in this he can never succeed unless he understands. But also, when he fails to understand, he must describe what he has found, even if he remains at the stage of mere cataloguing. But when the phenomenologist ceases to comprehend, he can have no more to say. He strides here and there; the historian of course does the same, but more frequently he stands still, and often he does not stir at all. If he is a poor historian, this will be due only to idleness or incapacity; but if he is a sound historian, then his halts imply a very necessary and admirable resignation.

Thirdly, the phenomenology of religion is not a psychology of religion. Modern psychology, certainly, appears in so many forms that it becomes difficult to define its limits with respect to other subjects.[16] But that phenomenology is not identical with experimental psychology should be sufficiently obvious, though it is harder to separate it from the psychology of form and structure. Nevertheless it is probably the common feature of all psychologies that they are concerned only with the psychical. The psychology of religion, accordingly, attempts to comprehend the psychical aspects of religion. In so far therefore as the psychical is expressed and involved in all that is religious, phenomenology and psychology have a common task. But in religion far more appears than the merely psychical: the whole man participates in it, is active within it and is affected by it. In this sphere, then, psychology would enjoy competence only if it rose to the level of the science of Spirit – of course in its philosophic sense – in general which, it must be said, is not seldom the case. But if we are to restrict psychology to its own proper object, it may be said that the phenomenologist of religion strides backwards and forwards over the whole field of religious life, but the psychologist of religion over only a part of this.[17]

Fourthly, the phenomenology of religion is not a philosophy of religion, although it may be regarded as a preparation therefor. For it is systematic, and constitutes the bridge between the special sciences concerned with the history of religion and philosophical contemplation.[18] Of course phenomenology leads to problems of a philosophic and metaphysical character, 'which it is itself not empowered to submit';[19] and the philosophy of religion can never dispense with its phenomenology. Too often already has that philosophy of religion been elaborated which naïvely set out from 'Christianity' – that is, from the Western European standpoint of the nineteenth century, or even from the humanistic deism of the close of the eighteenth century. But whoever wishes to philosophize about religion must know what it is concerned with; he should not presuppose this as self-evident. Nevertheless the aim of the philosopher of religion is quite different; and while he must certainly know what the religious issues are, still he has something other in view; he wishes to move what he has discovered by means of the dialectical motion of Spirit. His progress, too, is hither and thither: only not in the sense of phenomenology; rather is it immanent in the Spirit. Every philosopher, indeed, has somewhat of God within him: it is quite seemly that he should stir the world in his inner life. But the phenomenologist should not become merely frightened by the idea of any similarity to God: he must shun it as the sin against the very spirit of his science.

Finally, phenomenology of religion is not theology. For theology shares with philosophy the claim to search for truth, while phenomenology, in this respect, exercises the intellectual suspense of the *epoche*. But the contrast lies deeper even than this. Theology discusses not merely a horizontal line leading, it may be, to God, nor only a vertical, descending from God and ascending to Him. Theology speaks about God Himself. For phenomenology, however, God is neither subject nor object; to be either of these He would have to be a phenomenon – that is, He would have to appear. But He does not appear: at least not so that we can comprehend and speak about Him. If He does appear He does so in a totally different manner, which results not in intelligible utterance, but in proclamation; and it is with this that theology has to deal. It too has a path 'hither and thither'; but the 'hither' and the 'thither' are not the given and its interpretation, but concealment and revelation, heaven and earth, perhaps heaven, earth and hell. Of heaven and hell, however, phenomenology knows nothing at all; it is at home on earth, although it is at the same time sustained by love of the beyond.

3. [...] The phenomenology of religion must in the first place assign names:– sacrifice, prayer, saviour, myth, *etc.* In this way it appeals to appearances. Secondly, it must interpolate these appearances within its own life and experience them systematically. And in the third place, it must withdraw to one side, and endeavour to observe what appears while adopting the attitude of intellectual suspense. Fourthly, it attempts to clarify what it has seen, and again (combining all its previous activities) try to comprehend what has appeared. Finally, it must confront chaotic 'reality', and its still uninterpreted signs, and ultimately testify to what it has understood. Nevertheless all sorts of problems that may be highly interesting in themselves must thereby be excluded. Thus phenomenology knows nothing of any historical 'development' of religion,[20] still less of an 'origin' of religion.[21] Its perpetual task is to free itself from every non-phenomenological standpoint and to retain its own liberty, while it conserves the inestimable value of this position always anew.[22]

Kierkegaard's impressive description of the psychological observer, therefore, may serve not as a rule, and not even as an ideal, but as a permanent reproach: 'Just as the psychological investigator must possess a greater suppleness than a tight-rope walker, so that he can install himself within men's minds and imitate their dispositions: just as his taciturnity during periods of intimacy must be to some degree seductive and passionate, so that reserve can enjoy stealing forth, in this artificially achieved atmosphere of being quietly unnoticed, in order to feel relief, as it were in monologue: so he must have a poetic originality within his soul, so as to be able to construct totality and orderliness from what is presented by the *individuum* only in a condition of dismemberment and irregularity.'[23]

NOTES

1. Herein consists the essential unity between religion and culture. Ultimately, all culture is religious; and, on the horizontal line, all religion is culture.
2. E. Spranger, *Lebensformen*, 1925, *passim.*
3. *Ahmung.*
4. *Cf.* R. Otto, *The Idea of the Holy, passim.*
5. Otto.
6. P. Hofmann, *Das religiöse Erlebnis*, 1925, 12*ff.*
7. 'Die Problematik der Neuscholastik', Kantstudien 33, 1928.
8. *Lebensformen*, 418.
9. 1 *John* iv. 10, 19.
10. Przywara, *ibid.*, 92.
11. *ibid.*, 95.
12. Wach, Religionswissenschaft, 12.
13. *Poetics*, Chap. 9.
14. E. Utitz, *Ästhetik*, 1923, 18.
15. Wach, *ibid.*, 56.
16. *cf*, Spranger, *Einheit der Psychologie.*
17. That psychology is concerned purely with actual, and not with historical, experiences, and that consequently a limit subsists here also, obviously cannot be admitted

for one moment; without psychology we should be unable to deal with history; *cf*, Spranger, *Einheit der Psychologie*, 184.

18. Wach, Verstehen I, 12.
19. Wach, Rel. wiss. 131.
20. Wach, Rel. wiss. 82.
21. Th. de Laguna, 'The Sociological Method of Durkheim', *Phil. Rev.* 29, 1920, 224. E. Troeltsch, *Gesammelte Schriften*, II, 1913, 490.
22. Jaspers, *Allgemeine Psychopathologie*, 36.
23. *Begrebet Angest (The Concept of Dread), Saml. Vaerker*, IV^2, 1923, 360; *cf*, the entire fine passage.

ROBERT SEGAL
'REDUCTIONISM IN THE STUDY OF RELIGION'

Robert Segal is Professor of Religious Studies at Lancaster University. His research centres on methodological approaches to the study of religion and various aspects of gnosticism. He has recently published several books on mythology, including a text for the Very Short Introduction series.

Robert Segal is one of the protagonists in the debate about whether reductionism is appropriate in relation to the study of religion. His work on this issue has sparked this debate into life. Ultimately the issue behind the debate is whether religion can be analysed using theories developed in other social domains, and thus whether the study of religion should or should not be seen as a bounded disciplinary unit. Segal's arguments suggest that religion is not so bounded and must be analysed as part of culture rather than separate from it.

As the term gets used in religious studies, 'reductionism' refers to an analysis of religion in secular rather than religious terms. The origin, function, meaning, and even truth of religion are subject to reduction. Scholars within religious studies, though by no means all of those outside it, rail against reductionism. Four assumptions underlie their anathema. First, it is assumed that the true nature of religion is distinctively religious – wholly so for some 'religionists', as I call scholars within religious studies; primarily so for others. Second, it is consequently assumed that reductionism, in reducing religion to something nonreligious, transforms it into something other than what it is. Third, it is assumed that reductionism is avoidable. Fourth, it is assumed that religious studies, as a discipline, approaches religion nonreductively and that the social sciences – the disciplines of psychology, anthropology, and sociology – approach religion reductively. It is on the last two of these four assumptions that I will focus.

Religionists employ two main strategies for fending off threats from the reductive social sciences. One is to neutralize the social sciences. The other is to embrace them. Both strategies presuppose that the social sciences threaten religion to whatever extent they are reductive. They differ over the extent.

The first strategy, at once the more defiant and the more defensive, argues that the social sciences run askew to the nature of religion and therefore pose no threat to the religionists domain. At the least, it is argued, the social sciences can give only certain kinds of answers to the fundamental questions about religion: the questions of origin, function, meaning, and truth. The answers the social sciences give are uniformly reductive or, even

Robert Segal (1994), 'Reductionism in the study of religion', in Thomas A. Idinopulos and Edward A. Yonan (eds), *Religion and Reductionism*, Leiden: E. J. Brill.

more specifically, materialist. Worse, it is often said, the social sciences can answer only the questions of origin and function, which themselves the social sciences can still answer only reductively or just materially. Worst, it is said, the social sciences cannot answer any questions about religion because the social sciences study psychology, anthropology, or sociology *rather than* religion. The grandest exemplar of the first strategy is Mircea Eliade, who declares that

> a religious phenomenon will only be recognized as such if it is grasped at its own level, that is to say, if it is studied *as* something religious. To try to grasp the essence of such a phenomenon by means of physiology, psychology, sociology, economics, linguistics, art or any other is false.[1]

The second strategy, at once more irenic yet more insidious than the first, argues that the social scientific threat, while once real, happily exists no more. Religionists and social scientists now analyze religion the same way. It is not that religionists have come round to analyzing religion the way social scientists do. It is that social scientists have belatedly come round to analyzing religion the way religionists do. In contrast to classical social scientists, contemporary ones analyze religion as religion rather than as psychology, anthropology, or sociology. They analyze religion nonreductively rather than reductively. This second strategy is by far the more fashionable today. It is, however, only rarely employed by Eliade, who typically lumps contemporary social scientists with classical ones.[2]

NEUTRALIZING THE SOCIAL SCIENCES

I contend that neither strategy works and that social scientific analyses of religion continue to challenge religionist ones. The limits imposed on the social sciences by the first strategy are fallacious. To take the most severe limit first: to assert *a priori* that the social sciences study the mind, culture, or society *rather than* religion is conspicuously to beg the question: what is the nature of religion? The capacity of the social sciences to analyze religion ought to be an open rather than a closed issue. It ought to be decided not by *ex cathedra* proclamations but by testing – by the capacity or incapacity of social scientists to analyze religion psychologically, anthropologically, or sociologically.[3]

To say in response, as Eliade and others do, that religion is religion the way literature is literature is doubly to miss the point: not only is the nature of literature moot, but the final answer, if final answer there is, likewise depends on the outcome of research. Literary critics *debate*, not *assume*, the literariness of literature, and they do so by appealing to their capacity or incapacity to analyze it nonliterarily. If literature seems self-evidently literary, even in part, the reason is that what is provisionally called 'literature' has been *demonstrated* to be irreducibly literary in nature. After all, the *Iliad* does not come labeled as literature rather than history – or as literature as well as history.[4]

Nor does the Bible come prepackaged as religion rather than as literature, history, or sociology. Even if one argues that the Bible, with all its references to 'God', is obviously religious in nature, those references can be taken as projections of aspects of humans, society, or even the physical world, the way the gods in Homer have often been taken. The issue is not whether *at first-glance* the Bible or Homer seems to be at heart religious but whether it really is. The issue is whether the Bible really is a religious document rather than a literary, historical, or sociological one.

The issue is not whether the *manifest* nature of the Bible, or of 'religion' generally, is religious. Of course it is. Who would demur? Who would deny that references to 'god' are *apparent* references to religious entities? Who would deny that self-professed believers offer prayers and sacrifices *because* they believe in god? The issue is whether religious texts and practices are most deeply, much less *solely*, irreducibly religious. They are so only to the extent that the efforts of social scientists, literary critics, and others to categorize them otherwise fail. To declare in advance that the social sciences cannot 'touch' 'religion' because it is irreducibly religious in nature is, again, to beg, not settle, the key question.

Religionists who grant that the social sciences cannot be barred altogether from analyzing 'religion' often argue instead that the social sciences can treat only certain aspects of religion: only the origin and function, not the meaning and truth, of it. This argument is tamer than the prior one insofar as it allows the social sciences some place in the study of religion. But it is bolder insofar as it claims that the social sciences cannot deal at all with the issues of meaning and truth, not just that it misses the correct answers when it does.

Whether, to take the topics of meaning and truth in turn, the social sciences have any bearing on the 'meaning' of religion depends, not coincidentally, on the definition of this notoriously elusive term. 'Meaning' gets associated with 'interpretation' and gets contrasted to 'cause', which gets associated with 'explanation', One *interprets* the *meaning* and *explains* the *cause* of religion. But what defines interpretation and explanation?

There are at least four ways in which interpretation and explanation get distinguished.[5] By one distinction an explanation alone says what accounts for, or causes, religion, and an interpretation says what the content, or meaning, of religion is. Human behavior here is often compared with a text. Just as most literary critics still distinguish rigidly between the question why an author wrote a work and the question of what the theme of the work is, so many 'interpretivists' distinguish between the question why persons become religious and the question of what ideas religious beliefs and practices contain.

By this first distinction the social sciences are hardly barred from interpreting as well as explaining religion. Certainly social scientists find psychological, anthropological, and sociological content in religion. The richest social scientific interpretations – Freud's, Jung's and Marx's – provide whole glossaries for translating 'religious' terms into secular ones. Furthermore, it is Clifford Geertz and other social scientists who, together with philosophers like Paul Ricoeur, propose this first distinction. They scarcely do so to exclude the social sciences from the interpretation of religion. Rather, they seek to distinguish interpretive from explanatory social science.

Even if by this first distinction one *were* somehow able to confine the social sciences to explaining religion, explaining and interpreting religion would not be incompatible activities. Religionists would be able to keep the social sciences from the meaning of religion but not from the origin and function of it.

By a second, more technical distinction an interpretation as well as an explanation is an account of religion, and the two accounts are incompatible. The difference now between interpretation and explanation is the difference between one way of characterizing why persons become religious and another. In explanation the 'why' is separated from the behavior it brings about, in which case that behavior is the effect and what brings it about is the cause. In interpretation the 'why' is logically inseparable from what it brings about, in which case that behavior is the expression rather than the effect and what brings it about is the meaning rather than the cause. Taken as an explanation, the claim that humans strive to make sense of their lives says that striving *causes* them to engage in sense-making activities like religion. Taken as an interpretation, the same claim says simply *that* humans engage in religion and other sense-making activities, which *evince* rather than *result from* the sense-making character of humans.

Social scientists are no more barred from interpreting religion by this second distinction than by the first. Since the distinction is not over why there is religion but only over the way to characterize the relationship between the 'why' and religion, a psychological, anthropological, or sociological 'why' is categorizable as either a meaning or a cause. Likewise an irreducibly religious 'why' like Eliade's is categorized as either a cause or a meaning. Where the first distinction between interpretation and explanation is over the kind of question asked of religion, the second is not even over the kind of answer given to the same question. It is over the way to characterize the same answer. The distinction is not between religionists and social scientists but between one way of characterizing social science and another. Furthermore, it is again social scientists as well as philosophers who propose it. In fact, some of them propose it as a way of characterizing not just one branch but all of social science.

If by this second distinction one *were* somehow able to restrict the social sciences to explaining religion, the analyses of social sciences and of religionists would be incompatible, as they *would* not by the first. By the first distinction religionists could not keep social scientists from accounting for religion. By the second set they could – if, of course, they could justify their account as the correct one.

By the third distinction an interpretation, whether an account or a content, is always mental, and an explanation, which remains an account, always material. When taken as an account in the second, technical sense, an interpretation *is* always mental: the 'why' of behavior is always an intent – be the intent a motive, reason, or purpose. Likewise an explanation is always material. If, then, one *adds* this third distinction to the second, explanations do prove material and interpretations mental. But otherwise they do not. Certainly they do not by the first distinction. The content, or 'what', provided by an interpretation can be material or mental, and the account, or 'why', can be either mental or material.

Social scientists are as free to interpret religion by this third distinction as by the prior two distinctions. Whether or not religionist accounts of religion are necessarily mentalistic, as Eliade's happens to be, social scientific ones are by no means necessarily materialistic. Indeed, many practicing social scientists, like many natural scientists, account for human behavior in mental as well as material terms. Some social scientists, like some natural ones, may *hope* that mental states will one day be reduced to material ones to form a unified science, but they do not thereby consider mental states less scientific than material ones. For the mental states not only exist but also cause behavior. As anthropologist Melford Spiro puts it, 'But the contention that the scientific conception of cause is restricted to material conditions is hardly self-evident ... For by the most rigorous conception of cause – any antecedent condition in the absence of which some stipulated consequent condition would not occur – purposes, motives, intentions, and the like, for all their being non-material, are no less causal than hormonal secretions and subsistence techniques.'[6] By no means are most social scientists either materials or behaviorists.

Moreover, few social scientific materialists deny the *existence* of culture and other forms of mental life. Even as extreme a materialist as Marvin Harris is seeming merely to *account* for culture materially. Similarly, few classical, let alone contemporary, social scientific behaviorists deny the *existence* of the mind. Only philosophical behaviorists like Gilbert Ryle reduce mental states to simply a tendency to behave a certain way.

Where the first distinction between interpretation and explanation is over the kind of question asked of religion and the second over ways to characterize the same answer to the same question, the third is over the answer to the same question. An 'interpretivist' answers the question why there is religion in mental terms; an 'explainer' answers it in material terms. This third distinction is not between religionists and social scientists but between some social scientists and others – with religionists allied on one side or perhaps even on both sides.

If by this third distinction one *were* somehow able to restrict the social sciences to explaining religion, the analyses of social scientists and of religionists *would* be incompatible. Religionists could keep social scientists from accounting for religion – but only if, again, they could justify their account as the correct one.

By a fourth and final distinction an interpretation is necessarily reductive and an explanation necessarily nonreductive. This distinction is the one assumed by Eliade himself. While one can assess this distinction when an interpretation is taken as either an account or a content, for convenience sake assume an interpretation to be the content of religion and an explanation an account of it. So Eliade does. By this fourth distinction to explain religion is to account for it nonreligiously. To interpret religion is to characterize its contents as religious. Here a would-be translation of religion into psychological, anthropological, or sociological terms would be no interpretation at all.

But on what grounds can one bar a nonreligious interpretation of religion? The only plausible grounds would be that a nonreligious interpretation misses the religious content of religion. But those grounds continue to beg the question: what is the content of 'religion'? Certainly nothing inherent in interpretation as content or in explanation as origin and function entails a specific kind of content, origin, or function. While an interpretation must match the object of interpretation – *religion* must be interpreted *religiously* – 'religion' is only the putative, not necessarily the underlying, object of interpretation. A Freudian interpretation of religion does not *miss* the subject of interpretation. Rather, it *transforms* that subject from religion to psychology and thereby retains the parallel between interpretation and subject.

The same symmetry holds between explanation and *explanandum*. But because the subject of explanation, like that of interpretation, may really *be* religious, a religious explanation of religion is hardly impossible. Certainly Eliade, despite his equation of explanation with reductionism, himself explains religion religiously: as a yearning for contact with the sacred. For Eliade, that yearning is a necessary, perhaps even sufficient, condition for the existence of religion. Religion originates as a way of satisfying that yearning and functions to satisfy it. Since this final distinction between explanation and interpretation appeals to the differing *concepts* of the approaches, it fails to bar reductive interpretations and nonreductive explanations.

There are yet another means of distinguishing interpretation from explanation, and so meaning from cause, they, too, fail to exclude the social sciences. In short, the argument that the social sciences cannot deal with the meaning of religion, which is therefore left to religionists to analyze, is unwarranted.

As for truth, the standard religionist ploy is the invocation of the genetic fallacy or its functionalist equivalent. But in the first place few social scientists who assess the truth of religion do so on the basis of their social scientific findings. Certainly none of the classical social scientists who dare to pronounce religion false – for example, Marx, Freud, Edward Tylor, James Frazer – does so. Rather, they do the reverse: they argue for a secular origin and function and, even more, for the harmfulness or futility of the function on the grounds of the falsity of religion. For them, religion is false on philosophical, not social scientific, grounds.

For Marx, for example, religion is dysfunctional – not because it fails to accomplish its intended function but because the escapist and justificatory functions it accomplishes are more harmful than helpful. Religion would not, however, be escapist if Marx believed in the place of escape: heaven. Marx, then, deems religion dysfunctional because he deems it false, but he does not deem religion false because he deems it dysfunctional. Someone else might invoke economic harm as an argument against the existence of a fair or powerful god, in which case the dysfunctional effect of religion would argue for the falsity of religion. But Marx himself disbelieves in a god of any kind – and does so on philosophical, not social scientific, grounds.

Religionists can disagree with Marx's premise that religion is false, but they cannot charge him with exceeding his professional ken. For it is not *as* a social scientist that he pronounces religion false. He is not, then, guilty of the genetic fallacy. The same is true of Freud, Tylor, and Frazer.[7]

In the second place it is not clear that religionists operate any differently from social scientists. Religionists assume the truth of religion and on that basis determine the origin and function, if not also meaning, of it. When, for example, Eliade praises religion of serving to link humans to the sacred, his praise presupposes the existence of the sacred: he can scarcely be praising religion for opening persons to the sacred unless the sacred exists – the determination of which must surely be on metaphysical grounds.[8] If Eliade can apply his metaphysical views to the determination of the origin and function of religion, so can social scientists.

In the third place it is not self-evident that the social sciences commit the genetic fallacy when they assess the truth of religion. The fallacy is the claim that the origin of religion *necessarily* bears on the truth of it, not that it has no bearing at all. The bearing must simply be *shown*.

I contend that one possible bearing *has* been shown. In *The Future of an Illusion* Freud argues that the origin of religion in a wish renders religion likely false:

> We shall tell ourselves that it would be very nice if there were a God who created the world and was a benevolent Providence, and if there were a moral order in the universe and an afterlife; but it is a very striking fact that all this is exactly as we are bound to wish it to be.'[9]

Freud is saying that it would be an extraordinary coincidence if our wishes about the world, constituting as they do 'the oldest, strongest, and most urgent wishes of mankind,'[10] matched the world. The challenge to religion stems not from its origin in wishes – to say otherwise *would* be to commit the genetic fallacy – but from the rarity with which our mildest, let along fondest, wishes are fulfilled. A wish to believe that god exists does not *preclude* the existence of god, but it does make the existence of god improbable.

Extending Freud's point, I have argued that the origin of religion in not only a wish but also projection lessens the probability of its truth. While the object of a projection can still exist on its own, projection itself nevertheless constitutes error. Whoever projects god onto the world does not discover god in the world but rather imposes god on it. Should god exist after all, the projection would represent no insight on the believer's part. It would represent mere coincidence. The extraordinariness that such a coincidence would represent challenges the truth of religion. Projection challenges the truth of religion not because projection fails to establish the truth of religion but because a belief originating in projection is statistically unlikely to be true.

Not every social scientific explanation of religion involves either projection or wish fulfillment, but every social scientific explanation does involve a naturalistic rather than divine origin. Where a divine origin automatically justifies as well as explains belief in the existence of god, a naturalistic origin, if accepted, automatically challenges the justification as well as the explanation of the belief. A naturalistic cause reduces the effect to error, which lies not in the postulation of a being who does not exist but in the postulation of a being on a basis that does not warrant the postulation. Should that being exist, the postulation would again represent a remarkable coincidence, the unlikelihood of which constitutes the challenge.[11] In sum, the religionist claim that the social sciences can no more deal with the truth than with the meaning of religion is unjustified.

EMBRACING THE SOCIAL SCIENCES

Where the first strategy for fending off the social scientific threat is to deny the relevance of the social sciences to the study of religion, the second strategy is the opp: it is to declare them kindred souls. Where the first strategy blanketly consigns *all* social scientists to intellectual Siberia, the second recalls *present-day* social scientists from exile. Religionists here rigidly demarcate contemporary from classical social scientists. Classical ones mean above all Marx, Freud, Tylor, Frazer, Emile Durkheim, Bronisław Malinowski, and sometimes Carl Jung. Contemporary ones mean above all Peter Berger, Robert Bellah, Mary Douglas, Victor Turner, Clifford Geertz, and Erik Erikson. 'Poststructuralist' social scientists are only beginning to be assimilated, though it is certain that religionists will welcome these newest social scientists as comrades in arms.

What, however, is the decisive difference between classical and contemporary social scientists? The difference cannot be over the importance of religion. Classical social scientists considered religion at least as significant as any of their contemporary counterparts do.

Nor can the difference be over the truth of religion. Classical social scientists who judged religion false did so, as noted, on philosophical rather than social scientific grounds. Contemporary social scientists typically shun the issue of truth *as* philosophical rather than social scientific. True, Turner does berate his fellow social scientists for automatically assuming the falsity of religion. Berger, at least in his later writings, does say that the social sciences can affirm the truth of religion. But it is only her relativism that commits Douglas to the truth of all religions. When Bellah says that religion is true, he means that it is true to human experience of the world, not thereby true of the world itself. Geertz and Erikson skirt the issue of truth altogether.[12]

The difference between 'classicals' and 'contemporaries' must be over the origin and especially the function of religion. Yet the difference even here cannot be over the utility of the function religion serves. While Marx, Freud, and perhaps Frazer consider religion harmful, Tylor, Durkheim, Malinowski, and Jung do not. For them, religion is one of the best, if not the best, means of serving the beneficial functions they attribute to it. 'Contemporaries' grant religion no greater due.

The difference between 'classicals' and 'contemporaries' must be over the reducibility of the function religion serves. In contrast to 'classicals', who account for religion nonreligiously, 'contemporaries' purportedly account for it religiously, the way religionists do. Religion arises and serves to link humans to the sacred.

In actuality, 'contemporaries' account for religion as reductively as 'classicals'. Where religionists attribute religion to a yearning for the sacred itself, 'contemporaries' attribute it to a yearning for, most often, a meaningful life. Religion may be one of the best means of providing meaningfulness, but even if it were the only means, it would still be a mere means to a nonreligious end: meaningfulness. For Berger, Bellah, Turner, Geertz, and Erikson, humans need 'existential' meaningfulness: they need to be able to explain, endure, or justify their experiences. For Douglas, humans need cognitive meaningfulness, or orderliness: they need to be able to organize their experiences. In short, contemporary, not classical, social scientists stand far apart from religionists.[13] The second strategy for fending off the threat of the social sciences therefore fails. Reductionism has been neither refuted nor tamed.

SUMMARY

In sum, I have made two points. On the one hand I have contended that the social sciences have more to contribute to the study of religion than religionists recognize. On the other hand I have maintained that social scientific analyses of religion differ in kind from religionist ones. If religionists cannot neutralize the social sciences, they cannot embrace them either. Religionists are wrong not only in dismissing social scientific analyses as, among other characteristics, necessarily reductive but also in taking contemporary social scientific analyses as *non*reductive. Both insofar as social scientists can interpret as well as explain religion and insofar as explanations as well as interpretations of religion can be nonreductive, social scientific analyses need to be reductive. At the same time present as well as past ones *are* reductive.

Put another way, the difference between religionists and social scientists is not that the two groups answer different questions about the nature of religion. The difference is not that social scientists deal with only the origin and function of religion and religionists with only the meaning and truth of religion. The difference is that social scientists and religionists give contrary answers to the same four questions: meaning and truth as well as origin and function. And it is not just classical but also contemporary social scientists who do so. The difference between religionists and social scientists is not that social scientists explain religion and religionists interpret it. The difference is that social scientists interpret as well as explain religion differently from the way religionists explain as well as interpret it. And again, it is not just classical but also contemporary social scientists who do so. Contemporary and classical social scientists may differ sharply from each other, but both differ even more severely from religionists.

NOTES

1. Mircea Eliade, *Patterns in Comparative Religion*. tr. Rosemary Sheed (Cleveland: Meridian Books, 1963), xiii.
2. See esp. Eliade, 'On Understanding Primitive Religion', in *Glaube/Geist/Geschichte*, eds. Gerhard Muller and Wintried Zeller (Leiden: Brill, 1967), 502–3.
3. See my *Religion and the Social Sciences: Essays on the Confrontation* (Atlanta: Scholars Press, 1989), Chapter 1.
4. On the analogy between religion and literature see Segal and Donald Wiebe, 'On Axioms and Dogmas in the Study of Religion', *Journal of the American Academy of Religion*, 57 (Fall 1987), esp. 600–2.
5. On these distinctions see my *Religion and the Social Sciences*, Chapter 6; 'Meanings and Causes', *Journal for the Scientific Study of Religion*, 27 (December 1988), 637–44; 'Interpreting and Explaining Religion: Geertz and Durkheim', *Soundings* 71 (Spring 1988), esp. 40–6; 'Religionist and Social Scientific Strategies', *Religion*, 19 (October 1989), esp. 311–14; review essay on J. Samuel Preus' *Explaining Religion*, *Religious Studies Review*, 15 (October 1989), esp. 334–6; and 'Religion as Interpreted Rather Than Explained' (*Soundings*) (Forthcoming).
6. Melford E. Spiro, 'Cultural Relativism and the Future of Anthropology', *Cultural Anthropology*, 1 (August 1986), 272–3.
7. See my *Religion and the Social Sciences*. 89–91; 'Misconceptions of the Social Sciences', *Zygon*, 25 (September 1990), 273–5.
8. See my *Religion and the Social Sciences*, Chapter 2.

9. Sigmund Freud, *The Future of an Illusion*. tr. W.D. Robson-Scott, rev. James Strachey (Garden City, NY: Doubleday Anchor Books, 1964), 52–3.
10. Ibid. 47.
11. See my *Religion and the Social Sciences*, Chapter 7.
12. See my 'Misconceptions of the Social Sciences', 272–3.
13. See my *Religion and the Social Sciences*, Chapter 4.

NINIAN SMART
'THE NATURE OF A RELIGION'

Roderick Ninian Smart was born in 1927 in Cambridge. His father was an academic and his two brothers were also to become academics. After receiving an education at Oxford University he served at the end of the Second World War in Army Intelligence. This was to prove to be a life-altering experience for him as it brought him into contact with Chinese and Sri Lankan philosophy and culture. After the war he returned to Britain, where he taught first at the University College of Wales, then the University of London and the University of Birmingham, before finally joining the University of Lancaster faculty in 1967. At Lancaster he founded Britain's first Department of Religious Studies, which still flourishes today. In 1982 Smart left Lancaster for the University of California, Santa Barbara, where he had been teaching for some years prior to the move. He retired from his chair at Santa Barbara in 1998; however, he continued to live in his West Campus home up until 2001, when, a month before his death, he returned to Britain.

Ninian Smart has been one of the most influential figures in the study of religion in the United Kingdom. Although he emerged from the school of phenomenology his approach to defining religion is closer to trends in other related disciplines, for example anthropology. He moves away from a single essentialist form of definition, and offers a more dynamic dimensional definition. In his early discussions he suggests six different dimensions and culminates with seven. Although this approach is indeed more open ended than more classical forms of definition, the fact that all seven dimensions need to be present does not enable it to encompass some data – thus for example Marxism as practised by the Soviet Union falls outside his definition.

In thinking about religion, it is easy to be confused about what it is. Is there some essence which is common to all religions? And cannot a person be religious without belonging to any of the religions? The search for an essence ends up in vagueness – for instance in the statement that a religion is some system of worship or other practice recognizing a transcendent Being or goal. Our problems break out again in trying to define the key term 'transcendent'. And in answer to the second question, why yes: there are plenty of people with deep spiritual concerns who do not ally themselves to any formal religious movement, and who may not themselves recognize anything as transcendent. They may see ultimate spiritual meaning in unity with nature or in relationships to other persons.

It is more practical to come to terms first of all not with what religion is in general but with what *a* religion is. Can we find some scheme of

---

Ninian Smart (1989), *The World's Religions*, Cambridge: Cambridge University Press.

ideas which will help us to think about and to appreciate the nature of the religions?

Before I describe such a scheme, let me first point to something which we need to bear in mind in looking at religious traditions such as Christianity, Buddhism or Islam. Though we use the singular label 'Christianity', in fact there is a great number of varieties of Christianity, and there are some movements about which we may have doubts as to whether they count as Christian. The same is true of all traditions: they manifest themselves as a loosely held-together family of subtraditions. Consider: a Baptist chapel in Georgia is a very different structure from an Eastern Orthodox church in Romania, with its blazing candles and rich ikons; and the two house very diverse services – the one plain, with hymns and Bible-reading, prayers and impassioned preaching; the other much more ritually anchored, with processions and chanting, and mysterious ceremonies in the light behind the screen where the ikons hang, concealing most of the priestly activities. Ask either of the religious specialists, the Baptist preacher or the Orthodox priest, and he will tell you that his own form of faith corresponds to original Christianity. To list some of the denominations of Christianity is to show something of its diverse practice – Orthodox, Catholic, Coptic, Nestorian, Armenian, Mar Thoma, Lutheran, Calvinist, Methodist, Baptist, Unitarian, Mennonite, Congregationalist, Disciples of Christ – and we have not reached some of the newer, more problematic forms: Latter-Day Saints, Christian Scientists, Unificationists, Zulu Zionists, and so forth.

Moreover, each faith is found in many countries, and takes color from each region. German Lutheranism differs from American; Ukrainian Catholicism from Irish; Greek Orthodoxy from Russian. Every religion has permeated and been permeated by a variety of diverse cultures. This adds to the richness of human experience, but it makes our tasks of thinking and feeling about the variety of faiths more complicated than we might at first suppose. We are dealing with not just traditions but many subtraditions.

It may happen, by the way, that a person within one family of subtraditions may be drawn closer to some subtradition of another family than to one or two subtraditions in her own family (as with human families; this is how marriage occurs). I happen to have had a lot to do with Buddhists in Sri Lanka and in some ways feel much closer to them than I do to some groups within my own family of Christianity.

The fact of pluralism inside religious traditions is enhanced by what goes on between them. The meeting of different cultures and traditions often produces new religious movements, such as the many black independent churches in Africa, combining classical African motifs and Christianities. All around us in Western countries are to be seen new movements and combinations.

Despite all this, it is possible to make sense of the variety and to discern some patterns in the luxurious vegetation of the world's religions and subtraditions. One approach is to look at the different aspects or dimensions of religion.

THE PRACTICAL AND RITUAL DIMENSION

Every tradition has some practices to which it adheres – for instance regular worship, preaching, prayers, and so on. They are often known as rituals (though they may well be more informal than this word implies). This *practical* and *ritual* dimension is especially important with faiths of a strongly sacramental kind, such as Eastern Orthodox Christianity with its long and elaborate service known as the Liturgy. The ancient Jewish tradition of the Temple, before it was destroyed in 70 C.E., was preoccupied with the rituals of sacrifice, and thereafter with the study of such rites seen itself as equivalent to their performance, so that study itself becomes almost a ritual activity. Again, sacrificial rituals are important among Brahmin forms of the Hindu tradition.

Also important are other patterns of behavior which, while they may not strictly count as rituals, fulfill a function in developing spiritual awareness or ethical insight: practices such as yoga in the Buddhist and Hindu traditions, methods of stilling the self in Eastern Orthodox mysticism, meditations which can help to increase compassion and love, and so on. Such practices can be combined with rituals of worship, where meditation is directed towards union with God. They can count as a form of prayer. In such ways they overlap with the more formal or explicit rites of religion.

THE EXPERIENTIAL AND EMOTIONAL DIMENSION

We only have to glance at religious history to see the enormous vitality and significance of experience in the formation and development of religious traditions. Consider the visions of the Prophet Muhammad, the conversion of Paul, the enlightenment of the Buddha. These were seminal events in human history. And it is obvious that the *emotions* and *experiences* of men and women are the food on which the other dimensions of religion feed; ritual without feeling is cold, doctrines without awe or compassion are dry, and myths which do not move hearers are feeble. So it is important in understanding a tradition to try to enter into the feelings which it generates – to feel the sacred awe, the calm peace, the rousing inner dynamism, the perception of a brilliant emptiness within, the outpouring of love, the sensations of hope, the gratitude for favors which have been received. One of the main reasons why music is so potent in religion is that it has mysterious powers to express and engender emotions.

Writers on religion have singled out differing experiences as being central. For instance, Rudolf Otto (1869–1937) coined the word 'numinous'. For the ancient Romans there were *numina* or spirits all around them, present in brooks and streams, and in mysterious copses, in mountains and in dwelling-places; they were to be treated with awe and a kind of fear. From the word, Otto built up his adjective, to refer to the feeling aroused by a *mysterium tremendum et fascinans*, a mysterious something which draws you to it but at the same time brings an awe-permeated fear. It is a good characterization of many religious experiences and visions of God as Other. It captures the impact of the prophetic experiences of Isaiah and Jeremiah, the theophany through which God appeared to Job, the conversion of Paul, the overwhelming vision given to Arjuna in the Hindu Song of the Lord (*Bhagavadgītā*). At a gentler level it delineates too the spirit of loving devotion, in that the devotee sees God as merciful and loving, yet Other, and to be worshiped and adored.

But the numinous is rather different in character from those other experiences which are often called 'mystical'. Mysticism is the inner or contemplative quest for what lies within – variously thought of as the Divine Being within, or the eternal soul, or the Cloud of Unknowing, emptiness, a dazzling darkness. There are those, such as Aldous Huxley (1894–1963), who have thought that the imageless, insight-giving inner mystical experience lies at the heart of all the major religions.

There are other related experiences, such as the dramas of conversion, being 'born again', turning around from worldly to otherworldly existence. There is also the shamanistic type of experience, where a person goes upon a vision quest and acquires powers to heal, often through suffering himself and vividly traveling to the netherworld to rescue the dying and bring them to life again. Shamans are common to many small-scale societies and peoples that make their living by hunting, but many of the marks of the shamanistic quest have been left upon larger religions.

The Narrative or Mythic Dimension

Often experience is channeled and expressed not only by ritual but also by sacred narrative or myth. This is the third dimension – the *mythic* or *narrative*. It is the story side of religion. It is typical of all faiths to hand down vital stories: some historical; some about that mysterious primordial time when the world was in its timeless dawn; some about things to come at the end of time; some about great heroes and saints; some about great founders, such as Moses, the Buddha, Jesus, and Muhammad; some about assaults by the Evil One; some parables and edifying tales; some about the adventures of the gods; and so on. These stories often are called myths. The term may be a bit misleading, for in the context of modern study of religion there is no implication that a myth is false.

The seminal stories of a religion may be rooted in history or they may not. Stories of creation are before history, as are myths which indicate how death and suffering came into the world. Others are about historical events – for instance the life of the Prophet Muhammad, or the execution of Jesus, and the enlightenment of the Buddha. Historians have sometimes cast doubt on some aspects of these historical stories, but from the standpoint of the student of religion this question is secondary to the meaning and function of the myth; and to the believer, very often, these narratives *are* history.

This belief is strengthened by the fact that many faiths look upon certain documents, originally maybe based upon long oral traditions, as true scriptures. They are canonical or recognized by the relevant body of the faithful (the Church, the community, Brahmins and others in India, the Buddhist Sangha or Order). They are often treated as inspired directly by God or as records of the very words of the Founder. They have authority, and they contain many stories and myths which are taken to be divinely or otherwise guaranteed. But other documents and oral traditions may also be important – the lives of the saints, the chronicles of Ceylon as a Buddhist nation, the stories of famous holy men of Eastern Europe in the Hasidic tradition, traditions concerning the life of the Prophet (*hadīth*), and so forth. These stories may have lesser authority but they can still be inspiring to the followers.

Stories in religion are often tightly integrated into the ritual dimension. The Christian Mass or communion service, for instance, commemorates and presents the story of the Last Supper, when Jesus celebrated with his disciples his forthcoming fate, by which (according to Christians) he saved humankind and brought us back into harmony with the Divine Being. The Jewish Passover ceremonies commemorate and make real to us the events of the Exodus from Egypt, the sufferings of the people, and their relationship to the Lord who led them out of servitude in ancient Egypt. As Jews share the meal, so they retrace the story. Ritual and story are bound together.

The Doctrinal and Philosophical Dimension

Underpinning the narrative dimension is the *doctrinal* dimension. Thus, in the Christian tradition, the story of Jesus' life and the ritual of the communion service led to attempts to provide an analysis of the nature of the Divine Being which would preserve both the idea of the Incarnation (Jesus as God) and the belief in one God. The result was the doctrine of the Trinity, which sees God as three persons in one substance. Similarly, with the meeting between early Christianity and the great Graeco-Roman philosophical and intellectual heritage it became necessary to face questions about the ultimate meaning of creation, the inner nature of God, the notion of grace, the analysis of how Christ could be both God and human being, and so on. These concerns led to the elaboration of Christian doctrine. In the case of Buddhism, to take another example, doctrinal ideas were more crucial right from the start, for the Buddha himself presented a philosophical vision of the world which itself was an aid to salvation.

In any event, doctrines come to play a significant part in all the major religions, partly because sooner or later a faith has to adapt to social reality and so to the fact that much of the leadership is well educated and seeks some kind of intellectual statement of the basis of the faith.

It happens that histories of religion have tended to exaggerate the importance of scriptures and doctrines; and this is not too surprising since so much of our knowledge of past religions must come from the documents which have been passed on by the scholarly elite. Also, and especially in the case of Christianity, doctrinal disputes have often been the overt expression of splits within the fabric of the community at large, so that frequently histories of a faith concentrate upon these hot issues. This is clearly unbalanced; but I would not want us to go to the other extreme. There are scholars today who have been much impressed with the symbolic and psychological force of myth, and have tended to neglect the essential intellectual component of religion.

THE ETHICAL AND LEGAL DIMENSION

Both narrative and doctrine affect the values of a tradition by laying out the shape of a worldview and addressing the question of ultimate liberation or salvation. The law which a tradition or subtradition incorporates into its fabric can be called the *ethical* dimension of religion. In Buddhism for instance there are certain universally binding precepts, known as the five precepts or virtues, together with a set of further regulations controlling the lives of monks and nuns and monastic communities. In Judaism we have not merely the ten commandments but a complex of over six hundred rules imposed upon the community by the Divine Being. All this Law or Torah is a framework for living for the Orthodox Jew. It also is part of the ritual dimension, because, for instance, the injunction to keep the Sabbath as a day of rest is also the injunction to perform certain sacred practices and rituals, such as attending the synagogue and maintaining purity.

Similarly, Islamic life has traditionally been controlled by the Law or *Sharīa*, which shapes society both as a religious and a political society, as well as the moral life of the individual – prescribing that he should pray daily, give alms to the poor, and so on, and that society should have various institutions, such as marriage, modes of banking, etc.

Other traditions can be less tied to a system of law, but still display an ethic which is influenced and indeed controlled by the myth and doctrine of the faith. For instance, the central ethical attitude in the Christian faith is love. This springs not just from Jesus' injunction to his followers to love God and their neighbors: it also flows from the story of Christ himself who gave his life out of love for his fellow human beings. It also is rooted in the very idea of the Trinity, for God from all eternity is a society of three persons. Father, Son and Holy Spirit, kept together by the bond of love. The Christian joins a community which reflects, it is hoped at any rate, the life of the Divine Being, both as Trinity and as suffering servant of the human race and indeed of all creation.

THE SOCIAL AND INSTITUTIONAL DIMENSION

The dimensions outlined so far – the experiential, the ritual, the mythic, the doctrinal, and the ethical – can be considered in abstract terms, without being embodied in external form. The last two dimensions have to do with the incarnation of religion. First, every religious movement is embodied in a group of people, and that is very often rather formally organized – as Church, or Sangha, or *umma*. The sixth dimension therefore is what may be called the *social* or *institutional* aspect of religion. To understand a faith we need to see how it works among people. This is one reason why such an important tool of the investigator of religion is that subdiscipline which is known as the sociology of religion. Sometimes the social aspect of a worldview is simply identical with society itself, as in small-scale groups such as tribes. But there is a variety of relations between organized religions and society at large: a faith may be the official religion, or it may be just one denomination among many, or it may be somewhat cut off from social life, as a sect. Within the organization of one religion, moreover, there are many models – from the relative democratic governance of a radical Protestant congregation to the hierarchical and monarchical system of the Church of Rome.

It is not however the formal officials of a religion who may in the long run turn out to be the most important persons in a tradition. For there are charismatic or sacred personages, whose spiritual power glows through their demeanor and actions, and who vivify the faith of more ordinary folk – saintly people, gurus, mystics and prophets, whose words and example stir up the spiritual enthusiasm of the masses, and who lend depth and meaning to the rituals and values of a tradition. They can also be revolutionaries and set religion on new courses. They can, like John Wesley, become leaders of a new denomination, almost against their will; or they can be founders of new groups which may in due course emerge as separate religions – an example is Joseph Smith II, Prophet of the new faith of Mormonism. In short, the social dimension of religion includes not only the mass of persons but also the outstanding individuals through whose features glimmer old and new thoughts of the heaven towards which they aspire.

THE MATERIAL DIMENSION

This social or institutional dimension of religion almost inevitably becomes incarnate in a different way, in *material* form, as buildings, works of art, and other creations. Some movements – such as Calvinist Christianity, especially in the time before the present century – eschew external symbols as being potentially idolatrous; their buildings are often beautiful in their simplicity, but their intention is to be without artistic or other images which might seduce people from the thought that God is a spirit who transcends all representations. However, the material expressions of religion are more often elaborate, moving, and highly important for believers in their approach to the divine. How indeed could we understand Eastern Orthodox Christianity without seeing what ikons are like and knowing that they are regarded as windows onto heaven? How could we get inside the feel of Hinduism without attending to the varied statues of God and the gods?

Also important material expressions of a religion are those natural features of the world which are singled out as being of special sacredness and meaning – the river Ganges, the Jordan, the sacred mountains of China, Mount Fuji in Japan, Ayers Rock in Australia, the Mount of Olives, Mount Sinai, and so forth. Sometimes of course these sacred landmarks combine with more direct human creations, such as the holy city of Jerusalem, the sacred shrines of Banaras, or the temple at Bodh Gaya which commemorates the Buddha's Enlightenment.

USES OF THE SEVEN DIMENSIONS

To sum up: we have surveyed briefly the seven dimensions of religion which help to characterize religions as they exist in the world. The point of the list is so that we can give a balanced description of the movements which have animated the human spirit and taken a place in the shaping of society, without neglecting either ideas or practices.

Naturally, there are religious movements or manifestations where one or other of the dimensions is so weak as to be virtually absent: nonliterate small-scale societies do not have much means of expressing the doctrinal dimension; Buddhist modernists, concentrating on meditation, ethics and philosophy, pay scant regard to the narrative dimension of Buddhism; some newly formed groups may not have evolved anything much in the way of the material dimension. Also there are so many people who are not formally part of any social religious grouping, but have their own particular worldviews and practices, that we can observe in society atoms of religion which do not possess any well-formed social dimension. But of course in forming a phenomenon within society they reflect certain trends which in a sense form a shadow of the social dimension (just as those who have not yet got themselves a material dimension are nevertheless implicitly storing one up, for with success come buildings and with rituals ikons, most likely).

IVAN STRENSKI
'REDUCTION WITHOUT TEARS'

Ivan Strenski is Professor and Holstein Endowed Chairholder of Religious Studies at the University of California, Riverside. He carried out undergraduate studies at the University of Toronto before moving to the University of Birmingham, where he was awarded a doctorate. He then proceeded to work at Connecticut College and the University of California, Santa Barbara before moving in 1995 to Riverside. At Riverside his research has focused on the work of Emile Durkheim, which has led to him being involved in the formation of an international group of scholars which concentrates on the implications of the work of Durkheim for contemporary scholars. Strenski has also recently been involved in founding a research team made to explore the topic 'LA: Religion in the World City'. In recognition of his work he was awarded the Templeton Prize in the Science of Religion in 1998.

The material by Strenski included here is part of the ongoing debate about reductionism. As indicated by the title of his contribution Strenski is an advocate of reductionism. His work particularly emphasises the positive role that reductionism plays in challenging established positions and paradigms.

AVOIDING THE TRUTH-TRAP

'Reduction' and 'reductionism' are terms originating in the sober field of philosophy of science. These terms apply to theories about theories and conceptual change, and thus have to do with a theory about explanation.[1] But quite another mood prevails in the study of religion, where 'reduction' is an all-purpose pejorative and boo-word. Thus, in characteristic style, Eliade lashes out at 'the audacious and irrelevant interpretations [sic] of religious realities made by psychologists, sociologists, or devotees [sic] of various reductionist ideologies.'[2] More recently, Robert N. Minor, for example, claims that students of religion 'are suspicious of any possibility of reductionism that may reduce the religious person's understanding to other categories.'[3] Reeking of fideism, these views declare that religious faith must be kept sacrosanct, must be protected from being 'reduced', and thus diminished, in any way.

Such apologetic attacks on reduction invite attack themselves. What is fortunate, however, is that otherwise thoughtful critics of anti-reductionism, like Robert Segal, fall into the theological trap of the anti-reductionists, and perpetuate their wrongheaded intellectual agendas. This Segal does by assuming, along with the anti-reductionists, that the central issue in the reduction debate is (or should be) the question of the *truth* of religious claims,

Ivan Strenski (1994), 'Reduction without tears', in Thomas A. Idinopulos and Edward A. Yonan (eds), *Religion and Reductionism*, Leiden: E. J. Brill.

or that this discussion should turn on the question of the epistemological status of the native's (believer's) point of view.[4] To wit, this leads Segal into, what I take to be well-formed, but misguided, discussions about the possibility or impossibility of a believer being a reductionist or a sceptic being an anti-reductionist. (In Segal's view, both are impossibilities.[5]) What it means to be a believer means to take religion as real in all relevant respects, for example, function, origin and source, as Segal tells us. What kind of believer would see religion as an illusion!? Similarly, to be a non-believer means that one assumes the opposite. Thus how could a non-believer remain so, if they felt that religion were real in the relevant senses?

But before tackling the principal mistake of taking this line in the first place, let me show how Segal's way of putting the problem leads him into intellectual deadends.

Both Segal's believer/anti-reductionism and skeptic/reductionist linkages are faulty. First, believers may very well be reductionists; indeed some actually need to be! Barthians routinely reject 'religion' in favor of the 'Word', and are perfectly content to 'reduce' it to whatever one would like. The more religion is humiliated, in fact, the better, since for Barthians 'religion' is the human attempt to grasp deity, to promote salvation by human doing. The same might also be said of Advaitin Hindus for whom 'religion' (each particular *darshana*) is mâyâ, and thus subject to relativizing comparison with 'true' non-dual experience. Then what of theological liberals who look on ('reduce') 'religion' to morality? They are certainly still believers, but ones who have cheerfully made of 'religious' belief what many would call a 'reduced' form. Second, as for skeptical anti-reductionists, their number is equally great. Anyone who uses the term 'religion' to stand for something discernible in culture is in a way an anti-reductionist, since they accept that there is something substantial enough in this phenomenon to permit talking about an 'it'. All that is required for being so is the conviction that we live in a world where social forms get reified. Thus Louis Dumont admits as much in accepting that the social world in the modern period in the West is divided into realms such as politics, religion, art, economy, etc.[6]

But Segal's biggest mistake is to have taken up with the agenda dictated by the anti-reductionists in the first place. Segal gets led down this road because he has unwittingly perhaps taken for granted the terms of the argument about reduction from the anti-reductionist apologists. Where Segal goes wrong is in accepting that questions of the truth of religion or believer's point of view are or ought to be *paramount* in discussions of reduction. Segal accepts their use of reduction as normative, then simply inverts their priorities.

But, given the collapse of the believer/anti-reductionist etc. dichotomy, I want to ask why should we play this theological game at all? Why fall into the truth-trap – the 'trap' of considering questions about reduction in religious studies because they are questions about ultimate truth? Why not simply dump the entire agenda of theological discussion of reduction? I say this not because I think the truth of religious claims is never an issue here, but rather because it is not an issue of *paramount* concern to the scientific study of religion, any more than the 'ultimate reality' of politics itself or the truth of liberalism or fascism are paramount concerns of political scientists. We should instead lay out an agenda about reduction which speaks to the concerns of the scientific and humanistic *study* of religion, rather than to the concerns of its theological propagation or dismissal. This paper is devoted to showing what such a new agenda for discussing the notion of reduction would look like.

REDUCTION IS ABOUT CONCEPTUAL CHANGE

In its home context in the natural sciences and philosophy of science, 'reduction' names a process by which concepts and theories from one domain change by being logically and/or conceptually subsumed by – 'reduced to' – those of another. While it is true that all academic disciplines are to an extent jealous about intrusions onto their 'turf',[7] theoretical and conceptual change are taken more in stride than in the perhaps more fragile domain of the humanities. In the sciences, where in part a belief in the unity of nature prevails, conceptual changes come and go like the weather. Indeed part of the progress of knowledge amounts to being able to see the same 'thing' or 'nature' in a variety of different 'ways', under different conceptualization. 'Reductionism' is thus the obverse of the view that theories are *a priori* 'autonomous' and immune to the subsumption by other theories. 'Reductionism' thus rejects the claim that phenomena can forever and always be *explained* in their own terms alone (whatever that means) in favor of the view that they can (and, sometimes, ought to) be explained in terms which are not [at] first sight proper to them (as we conceive 'them'). Thus when biological phenomena are *reduced* to chemical phenomena, some part, at least, of biological theory has been reduced to chemical theory, some biological explanations have been *reduced* to chemical ones. In general, this is seen as marking real progress because a single theory is now seen capable of including more data under its explanatory umbrella. Like riding a well-planned subway system, we do not, as it were, need constantly to change 'trains' and transfer to different 'lines' to complete our journey successfully. One line will take us there directly.

Reductions: 'kinds' and 'directions'

Yet in speaking of reductionism *en bloc*, I risk underplaying the variety in 'reductionism' itself. Let me correct this. There are, in fact, several classes of reduction, many with surprising characteristics, and further many subclasses of the primary classes. The primary classes can be organized under the following scheme: these are the 'kinds', 'directions' and 'interpretations' of reductions. Of 'kinds' there are two. One speaks, first either of 'homogeneous' *kinds* of reductions, as between theories *within* the same domain of knowledge, such as between different systems of theories of astronomy, or say between Durkheim's two theories of religion.[8] Second, one may speak of 'inhomogeneous' *kinds* of reductions, such as between theories *across* presumed different domains of knowledge. These reductions are those which not only produce the conceptual change of homogeneous reductions, but they also reduce theories previously thought to cover qualitatively *different* domains. The inhomogeneous reduction of biology to chemistry, for instance, connects theories with domains thought to be radically different up to that moment. So also might Durkheim's so-called sociological reduction of religion qualify as 'inhomogenous'.

Then, one may consider the two *directions* of reduction. In 'micro-reduction', wholes are explained in terms of parts, e.g. if biochemistry explains cell division, microbiology is reduced to biochemistry; in 'macro-reduction' wholes explain parts, e.g. if general systems theory explains human behavior without remainder, it 'reduces' psychology to itself. Here also all theories of religion which try to ground the essence of religion in religious experience, say, over against religious institutions, would qualify as cases of micro-reduction. Done in reverse, theories of religious institutions which promised to be able to subsume religious experience would qualify as cases of macro-reduction. Finally, reductions may be 'interpreted' in at least three ways, although we will only treat two here.

'Interpretations' of reductions: by deduction

First, reduction by 'deduction' or 'derivation' names a logical operation by which the theorems of one theory are *logically* subsumed by those of another, such as in attempts to derive mathematics from logic. Thus Kenneth Schaffner, presenting Ernest Nagel's views, argues that in reduction by deduction 'the basic terms and entities of one theory are related to the basic terms and entities of the other theory . . . And the axioms and laws of the reduced theory are derivable from the reducing theory'.[9] The reduced theory thus becomes a special case of the reducing theory, which in turn provides a logically broader and more powerful etiological vantage point. Consider Nagel's example of the reduction of thermodynamics to statistical mechanics. Here the concept and phenomena of 'temperature' are explained in terms of the energy of large numbers of discrete particles, rather [than] in terms of the concept of 'heat'. This signals that the laws of thermodynamics can be deduced from the laws of statistical mechanics – from the laws governing the motion of large numbers of discrete molecular particles, if one can also go further and identify 'temperature' with 'mean kinetic energy of molecules'. I see no instances of this 'interpretation' of reduction in religious studies, simply because theories in the social or psychological sciences have not achieved the degree of formalism allowing them rigorously to 'reduce' or 'derive' anything at all!

'Interpretations' of reductions: by replacement[10]

The second 'interpretation' of reduction – 'reduction by replacement' – contrasts sharply with this. Here we have the wholesale dismissal of one theory and the substitution of another. Such reductions are assumed, for instance, by attempts to replace mentalist psychology with brain-state materialism. Transition from one theory to another produces a 'complete replacement' of the ontology and, perhaps, of the formalisms of the old theory by the new. Knowledge grows discontinuously, in leaps, not cumulatively by accretions. Paul Feyerabend argues in this vein that one cannot strictly derive thermodynamics from statistical mechanics. Derivation or deduction requires linking key terms like 'temperature' with 'the mean kinetic energy of molecules'. But this cannot be sanctioned because, as it is argued, the two concepts belong to incommensurable fields of discourse. Feyerabend notes that in the case of the succession of statistical mechanics over thermodynamics 'replacement rather than incorporation ... or derivation ... is seen to be the process that characterizes the transition from a less general theory to a more general one'.[11]

So different is [this] from reduction by deduction, that reduction by replacement might be considered a rejection of reduction itself. This is partly so because Nagel's reduction by deduction is a feature specific to a positivist view of theories.[12] If, as Eliade and others do, one rejects positivism, it is only natural that one would reject one of its key operations, namely reduction. Reduction by deduction is how one would expect to interpret theory change, given a positivist interpretation of theories – if we looked on theories primarily as sets of sentences arranged in deductive order. Such a view of theories is held by Nagel. But if we supported a view like that of the Oxford philosopher of science, Rom Harré, we would contend that theories are essentially pictures of [the] inner nature of things 'and that the existence of a deductive system among the conditional propositions which describe the possibilities of change for that structure is not essential'.[13] One would expect this theory of theories to reflect the fact that *theorems* are less important than theoretical *ideas* or *models*. Like Feyerabend, one would conceive theoretical change – reduction – as getting a new picture of things. With Feyerabend, our attention would focus on the paradigm, the central concept of a theory.

MIRCEA ELIADE, REDUCTIONIST ... (BY REPLACEMENT)

One unanticipated benefit of this scheme is [that we can] locate and thus better understand Mircea Eliade's situation in the reductionism quarrel. Straightaway we can see that the sort of reduction stirring his rage is reduction by replacement. This is so because it has, as Feyerabend notes, ontological implications.

Eliade's way of protesting reduction is to assert that 'our documents ... constitute ... so many creations of the human mind .... We do not have the right to reduce them to something other than what they are, namely spiritual creations'.[14] Eliade of course blatantly begs the question here, since it is the very *identity* of so-called religious phenomena which is in question. If I am right about the intellectual history of the notion of religion, it has shifted several times in the last hundred years already. Reduction has been a way of life for all serious thinkers about religion, as each one in turn has pushed an older conception of religion aside for their own. But, as much a part of this moving history of the concept of religion as Eliade himself is, Eliade slams the door shut on possible competitors to his own 'spiritualist' position. Instead, he just insists on the identity of religious phenomena by appeal to 'what they are....' But 'what they are' is or should be an open question; Eliade's anti-reductionist (by replacement) stance rejects alternatives out of hand. This is so even if the alternatives are 'homogeneous' ones, since for Eliade the concept of religion is fixed once and for all. He thus assumes that what it means to 'reduce' 'spiritual creations' is to replace their spiritual nature with something else – to treat 'them as other than what they are' [sic]. And, he will have none of it!

Putting his case positively, Eliade tells us he wants a study of religion in which religion is 'looked at . . . *in itself, in that which belongs to it alone and can be explained in no other terms*'.[15] Thus, in Eliade's view, to take a 'reductive' approach to religion, changes the way we classify reality, since we don't 'look at' religion 'in itself' [sic]; furthermore, doing so makes claims to explain the nature of that reality in some 'other' than religious 'terms'. Thus what Eliade fears is the 'replacement' of 'the' [sic] religious view of the world, a wholesale profanation and desacralization. He fears religion may be shown to be false. But what he fears is the replacement of the particular religious picture to which he is devoted by some other non-religious 'picture'.

Ironically enough we can also see that Eliade is himself a major offender to his own announced anti-reductionism. He is equally reductionist (by replacement) – as at least one writer has noted with perhaps a differently nuanced meaning than my own.[16] First, against so-called scientific theories of religion, Eliade rejects all explanations of religion which do not reflect their 'spiritual nature' (whatever that means), as he states above. This is, on its other side, a substitution or *replacement* of them by an approach which he believes is truer to their 'spiritual nature'. Recall Eliade's earlier words about 'the audacious and irrelevant interpretations of religious realities made by psychologists, sociologists, or devotees of various reductionist ideologies'.[17] If an interpretation is charged with being 'irrelevant', we are invited to replace it with one which is assumed to be 'relevant'.

Second, against other academic explanations of religion, Eliade tries to replace all other definitions and theories of religion by his well-known interpretation of data in terms of their reflection of transcendental archetypes. Archetypal analysis replaces all others; archetypal analysis (micro-)reduces (by replacement) individual, historically specific data to the status of epiphenomena of the divine archetypes. Creative hermeneutics is after all a 'total hermeneutics', 'the royal road' for the study of religion.[18]

Third, although many commentators take Eliade at his word (in places) and assume that he speaks from the native's point of view,[19] his general theoretical ambitions are quite opposed to making the native's (*religious*) point of view normative. He cannot accommodate the range of diversity among religious 'natives', nor is he finally willing so to do. 'It does not matter in the least', says Eliade beginning his dismissal of any Dilthey-like advocacy of the native's point of view, 'whether or not the "primitives" of today realize that immersion in water is the equivalent both of the deluge and of the submerging of a continent in the sea . . . .' What matters for Eliade is to replace all others. To wit what matters is that both 'immersion' and 'deluge'

> symbolize the disappearance of an 'outworn form' in order that a 'new form' may appear. Only one thing matters in the history of religions; and that is the fact that the immersion of a man or a continent, together with the cosmic and eschatological meaning of such immersions are present in myth and ritual – the fact that all these myths and rituals fit together or . . . make up a symbolic system which in a sense pre-existed them all. We are therefore . . . quite justified in speaking of . . . the symbolism expressed in the subconscious and transconscious activity of man.[20]

Instead, Eliade proposes nothing less than a total theory of religion, and thus one which *replaces* old meanings with (his) new ones. 'Creative hermeneutics' – the 'royal road of the history of religions',[21] the crowning level of Eliade's method – is a *'total hermeneutics'*. At the very minimum this involves 'being called to decipher and explicate every kind of encounter of man with the sacred, from prehistory to our day'.[22] This 'totalizing' ambition explains why in the end, Eliade does not care what the 'natives' say or think: he cares about *replacing* previous views with his own.[23]

Thus when we put Eliade's talk against reduction into the context of conceptual change by way of reduction by replacement ironically, we see Eliade really does not oppose reductionism in itself. He is quite prepared to replace non-religious *and* religious accounts of things by his *own* religious one, like any good anti-positivist might. Eliade just objects to those reductions which threaten the protective cocoon he wants to throw round his 'history of religions'!

REDUCTION: NO BUSINESS OF CRY BABIES

From this survey of what real reductionism means, we can see how nuanced and sophisticated a matter it is, how rich in logical possibilities for relating theories to one another it is. The issue of 'diminishment' or humiliation never comes into it. Students of religion have not even begun to explore these. Thus they have not understood the many shifts we have seen in our basic understanding and conceptualization of religion. What do these shifts amount to, in terms of their being changes in theories of religion? Are they all 'homogeneous' – all really changes within the same broad category? Or are they 'heterogeneous', and thus imply that some real break has occurred in the way religion has been conceived and lived? Are they reductions to be interpreted as 'deductions'? For instance, in the recent history of the West, religion as having to do with beliefs and rituals, gave way in part to religion as morality (nineteenth century liberalism). Then again religion as morality gave way to something having to do with the sacred, in the wake of the First World War. These all have to do with fundamental conceptual shifts, with changes that can well be called reductions.

I propose that instead of using the term 'reduction' as a pejorative, nor even with Segal, instead of using it as having to do with the truth of religious claims, we simply conform our usage to that which has been formed by the philosophy of science. In this way, we can put changes in scientific theories, and thus learn something in the process about conceptual and theoretical change. Such a set of reductions by replacement can be charted in Durkheim's changing conceptualizations of religion. Beginning perhaps from his own Jewish background of religious life where ritual and belief were central, Durkheim moved to a position he shared with the liberal Jews of his day in 'Continuing the Definition of Religious Phenomena' (1899).[24] There religion was reduced to 'morality'. Finally in *The Elementary Forms of the Religious Life* (1912), Durkheim defines religion in terms of the 'sacred', thus reducing morality 'by replacement' with the 'sacred'.

Further, for example, if I am right in characterizing the threatened reduction in religious studies as a 'reduction by replacement', do we find similar fears among, say, biologists facing reduction to chemistry as students of religion have felt over against the social sciences? If entire paradigms or conceptualizations are replaced, so also is the pertinence of certain perspectives, such as, say, a religious one – whatever that might be. This may or may not involve an impoverishment of things, but it certainly changes them and how they are identified. Is the situation in all cases parallel between such threatened reductions by replacement in religious studies as in other disciplines?

Thus despite the real risks of reconceptualization, we must resist looking on reduction like our cry-baby colleagues in the study of religion. Reconceptualization also promises renewal and revival – as past conceptual changes in the study of religion already have, for example, the shift from morality to the sacred as a key element in defining religion. Discussions of 'reductionism' need to become more than wails of woe. 'Reductionism' must thus become more than a vague pejorative and emotive term, reflecting anxiety about academic 'turf' and the adequacy of a discipline's ability to account for a range of phenomena in its own precious, particular and unique way. We have to begin accepting conceptual change as a normal part of trading in the world of knowledge. An added bonus of this view is that if 'religion' can be reduced (by replacement) to something else, so also can those other 'things' be reduced to religion. It is now commonplace to read in works of political science references to religious notions such as 'myth' and 'ritual'. With the fall of Communism in the Soviet Union, somehow its cultic, dogmatic and numinous dimensions stand out even more clearly than before.[25] Even in economics, books with titles such Spencer Pack's *Capitalism as a Moral System* are now appearing.[26]

WHERE THERE'S 'SMOKE', THERE'S POLITICS

It is critical to understand that beneath the imprecision and heat of such attacks on 'reductionism' by students of religion there are real conflicts about how things should be explained. Left to themselves, disciplines like academic departments often ignore each other. But once the desire to establish conceptual order in favor of one theory over another is set into motion, the issue of reduction arises. For instance, psychologists might wish to establish the power of their methods of explanation over non-psychological religious explanations of mystic trance. Religious (whatever that means here) accounts of mystic trance would then be subsumed to more general psychological ones by first showing that religious explanations were either special cases of more inclusive psychological ones 'inhomogeneously replaced' *en bloc* by psychological ones. This brings us to the practical and political value of the rhetoric of reduction, which is the same issue as the assertion of autonomy.

The uses of autonomy

I do not think that autonomy is some *a priori* absolute truth about the disciplines or their subject-matters. Academic disciplines change, as do their subject matters. But we should not be so naive as to imagine that autonomy is invoked or reductionism resisted innocent of crass considerations of academic politics. In these days of financial crises in the university, it is not cynical to conclude that whenever someone trumpets the special status of their particular academic field, we can be pretty sure that budget allocations and FTE are at stake. But there is nonetheless some good news for antireductionists – news which merits raising a cheer now and then for the resistance of religious studies to reduction by competing disciplines.

Although autonomy is asserted for the political reason of fighting the 'turf war', its assertion also has certain strategic purposes in the world of ideas. Aside from considerations about protecting FTE, claiming that a discipline, subject or phenomenon is autonomous, helps both define and focus attention. Consider Robert N. Minor's concluding remarks into a collection of essays on interpretations of the Bhagavad Gîtâ. Although Minor begs the question of what religion is (and therefore is guilty of 'reducing' someons's notion of religion to his own), he does usefully exemplify the utility of focusing attention in certain ways arguably called religious. Thus Minor expresses at one and the same time a concern for demarcating a particular academic discipline's 'turf' as well as a decision to focus intellectual attention in a certain way:

> The authors of these essays are from departments of religious studies who are interested in studying religion as religion, as the study of the ultimate concerns of human beings. They are suspicious of any possibility of reductionism that may reduce the religious person's understanding to other categories.[27]

In this sense, consider how impoverished our understanding of modern Iran would be had Shi'a religiosity not been appreciated at least partly in religious terms. How much richer is our understanding [of] Shi'a martyrdom, for example, when we locate it within the context of the particular history of Shi'a Islamic *religion* in Iran, and further within the broader set of martyrdom provided by the comparative history of *religions*. Such understanding comes only when we forget about the issue of truth, and instead we focus on religion as some special category of thought and culture, as some sort of thing – in effect insist on its autonomy. When we insist that there is some real enough *thing* called 'religion', we are at least insisting that it has a history and structure as 'real' as *things* such as 'politics', 'art', 'the economy', 'sexuality' and so on. Now, none of these may *really* be autonomous, either; but that casts them and 'religion' adrift in the same lifeboat, so to speak. So, insisting on the autonomy of religion at least lets us define and focus on domains of life that might get missed otherwise. We must of course not insist on *a priori* absolute autonomy. We could use a relative autonomy – one which recognizes that *all* disciplinary divisions are somewhat provisional and strategic, that the lines drawn between phenomena are done primarily for the sake of convenience. And, best of all, this helps us avoid the 'truth-trap', and all those interminable arguments about the transcendental reality of religion. The cultural reality of religion has made work enough for us all. When we have finished with that, perhaps the transcendental will have its day.

While raising a cheer for autonomy, it is equally well to bear in mind that the kind of autonomy propagated by the Eliade school has only made matters worse for an *effective* assertion of autonomy for the study of religion. Eliade misstated the case for autonomy by exaggerating religion's purity and independence from the secular domain, as for instance when he says that in the history of religions, religion is 'looked at . . . *in itself, in that which belongs to it alone and can be explained in no other terms*'.[28] Further by locating essential religiousness in a transcendental world unassailable ahistorical and acultural archetypes, he guaranteed that many students of religion would ignore history and culture insofar as politics, economics, culture, and any other non-religious domain was concerned. What other effect would Eliade's reference to 'the audacious and irrelevant interpretations [sic] of religious realities made by psychologists, sociologists, or devotees [sic] of various reductionist ideologies',[29] be likely [to] produce? The sacred quest for these absolutely autonomous Eliadean archetypal patterns in religious data led to a kind of symbolic analysis of religious materials as if the symbols arose from and trafficked in a world beyond the human realm. No small wonder then that news about the *religious* dimension of the Iranian revolution was delivered by scholars from departments of political science or history, when students of religion should have been in the forefront. Thus, in exaggerating claims of autonomy, Eliade ironically caused the study of religion to miss a unique opportunity to assert itself.

NOTES

1. See Lorne L. Dawson's useful discussion of kinds of reduction in his *Reason, Freedom, and Religion* (New York: Peter Lang, 1988), 161–79.
2. Mircea Eliade, 'Crisis and Renewal', *The Quest: History and Meaning of Religion* (Chicago: University of Chicago, 1969), 70.
3. Robert N. Minor, 'Conclusion', *Modern Indian Interpreters of the 'Bhagavadgita'*, Robert N. Minor, ed. (Albany: SUNY Press, 1986), 226.
4. Robert Segal, 'In Defense of Reductionism', *Religion and the Social Sciences: Essays on the Confrontation* (Atlanta: Scholars Press, 1989), 6–8.
5. Robert Segal, 'In Defense of Reductionism', *Religion and the Social Sciences: Essays on the Confrontation* (Atlanta: Scholars Press, 1989), 20–6.
6. Louis Dumont, 'Religion, Politics, and Society in the Individualistic Universe', *Proceedings of the Royal Anthropological Institute for 1970* (London: Royal Anthropological Institute, 1971): 31–41. 'Preface', (to the French Edition of Evans-Pritchard, *The Nuer*) *Studies in Social Anthropology*, John Beattie and R. Godfrey Lienhardt, eds. (Oxford: Oxford University, 1975), 328–42.
7. Here we would do well to recall that the attack upon the validity of claims about Cold Fusion was led by physicists. Whatever else their failings, Fleischer and Pons had the misfortune of being chemists, and thus appearing as intruders into the domain of physics.
8. W. S. F. Pickering, *Durkheim's Sociology of Religion* (London: Routledge and Kegan Paul, 1984), Chapters 3–5.
9. Kenneth Schaffner, 'Approaches to Reduction', *Philosophy of Science* 34 (1967), 138.
10. We can also identify a third and final interpretatin of reduction – 'reduction by approximate deduction' – which is in a way a compromise between the first two interpretations of reduction (Kenneth Schaffner, 'Approaches to Reduction', *Philosophy of Science* 34 (1967): 138.) But for our purposes, we can ignore this class, and proceed directly to the matter of the bearing of these distinctions upon our central discussion. Thus, *three* 'interpretations' can, in theory, be instantiated across *two* 'kinds' and two 'directions' of reduction. In all, therefore, twelve logically possible combinations of reductions can be generated.
11. Paul Feyerabend, 'Explanation, Reduction and Empiricism', *Minnesota Studies in the Philosophy of Science* Vol III, H. Feigl and G. Maxwell, eds. (Minneapolis: University of Minnesota, 1962), 78.

12. Ivan Strenski, 'Reductionism and Structural Anthropology', *Inquiry* 19 (1976), 78–80.
13. Rom Harré, *The Philosophies of Science* (Oxford: Oxford University Press, 1970), 15.
14. Mircea Eliade, 'Prolegomenon to Religious Dualism: Dyads and Polarities', *The Quest: History and Meaning in Religion* (Chicago: University of Chicago, 1969), 132–3.
15. Mircea Eliade, *Patterns in Comparative Religion* [1949], Rosemary Sheed, trans. (London: Sheed and Ward, 1958), xi.
16. Adrian Marino, 'Mircea Eliade's Hermeneutics', *Imagination and Meaning*, Norman Girardot and MacLinscott Ricketts, eds. (New York: Seabury, 1982), 44.
17. Mircea Eliade, 'Crisis and Renewal', *The Quest: History and Meaning in Religion* (Chicago: University of Chicago, 1969), 70.
18. Mircea Eliade, 'Crisis and Renewal', *The Quest: History and Meaning in Religion* (Chicago: University of Chicago, 1969), 57, 62.
19. Robert Segal, 'In Defense of Reductionism', *Religion and the Social Sciences: Essays on the Confrontation* (Atlanta: Scholars Press, 1989), 11 and passim.
20. Mircea Eliade, *Patterns in Comparative Religion* [1949], Rosemary Sheed, trans. (London: Sheed and Ward, 1958), 450.
21. Mircea Eliade, 'Crisis and Renewal', *The Quest: History and Meaning in Religion* (Chicago: University of Chicago, 1969), 62.
22. Mircea Eliade, 'Crisis and Renewal', *The Quest: History and Meaning in Religion* (Chicago: University of Chicago, 1969), 57.
23. For a detailed discussion of this program see Ivan Strenski, *Four Theories of Myth in Twentieth-Century History* (London and Iowa City: Macmillan and Iowa University Press, 1987), 118–22.
24. See the discussion of Durkheimian scholarship in relation to liberal Judaism in France in my [...] *The Time of 'Sacrifice'* (Chicago: University of Chicago, 1992).
25. William Pfaff, 'Workers of the World...Forgiveness', *Los Angeles Times* 28 August 1991: B7.
26. Spencer J. Pack, *Capitalism as a Moral System* (Brookfield, VT: Edward Elgar, 1991).
27. Robert N. Minor, 'Conclusion', *Modern Indian Interpreters of the 'Bhagavadgita'*, Robert N. Minor, ed. (Albany: SUNY Press, 1986), 226.
28. Mircea Eliade, *Patterns in Comparative Religion* [1949], Rosemary Sheed, trans. (London: Sheed and Ward, 1958), xi.
29. Mircea Eliade, 'Crisis and Renewal', *The Quest: History and Meaning in Religion* (Chicago: University of Chicago, 1969), 70.

3

ANTHROPOLOGY

INTRODUCTION

While the anthropological material included in this chapter is theoretically
diverse, due to certain aspects of the disciplinary approach, many of which
arise from the practice of ethnographic fieldwork, there are certain commonalities or presuppositions. Perhaps the most significant of these is the
focus on the local as opposed to the general. Most anthropological research
on religion has been concerned with religion as practised by particular communities as distinct from the idealised form of a religion as depicted in some
theological or phenomenological approaches. The aspect has also perforce
led many anthropologists to focus on the multiplicity within religious traditions. Most anthropological theories of religion thus arise at least initially
from engagement with the practice of religion rather than religion as an
ideal and abstract concept. The ethnographic focus also leads anthropologists to appreciate the connection between religion and culture – in many of
the societies that they study, religion appears to be inextricably associated
and shaped by its particular cultural context. This is as true of the particular
instantiations of the so-called world religions as it is of religions specifically
associated with a specific ethnographic context, for example Hopi religion.

Anthropological approaches to religion have been shaped by many of
the trends associated with the wider development of thought about religion
and culture. Thus, in the nineteenth century, evolutionary models were the
dominant theoretical frameworks. This is illustrated in Chapter 1 in the
work of Tylor (pages 99–107) and in that of Frazer (pages 44–52). While
the particular emphasis on unilinear cultural evolution was associated with

the 'armchair' anthropologists of the nineteenth and early twentieth centuries, and by the start of the twentieth century, based on attacks from an increasingly professional and fieldwork-based discipline, was largely discredited, the work of some evolutionists, particularly Frazer, continued to be taken seriously by some, especially outside the discipline, well into the mid-twentieth century. Within the evolutionist school unilinear evolution was generally replaced by multilinear evolutionary models – as many of these models relied on a materialist perspective they often had little specifically to say about the development of religion or to offer to original theories of religion. As in a traditional Marxist critique, religion is seen as ideology arising in relation to the material component of society with additional significant influences from functionalist approaches.

For much of the twentieth century functionalism was the dominant theoretical approach, particularly in relation to anthropologists based or trained in the United Kingdom. Functionalist analyses move in increasingly subtle directions, taking for example into their ambit the role of violence and the possibility of ritual serving as a means of challenging dominant structures, but meanwhile we find continued influence of the trends established by Malinowski (pages 229–52) and Radcliffe-Brown (pages 253–66), the first of these focusing on individual functions and the second on societal functions. While the work of anthropological functionalists had close and fruitful interrelationships with the functionalist theories developed in sociology, particularly by Talcott Parsons (Chapter 4, pages 365–77), functionalism's dominance was increasingly challenged. While many modern theories are influenced by functionalism, and may have functionalist presuppositions, a wider range of theoretical approaches have been dominant. The selections from Geertz and Spiro, for example, although based on very different theoretical presuppositions, include a significant element of functionalism: seeing religion as fulfilling a number of individual needs in respect of both meaning and the problem of evil. The approach taken by Geertz has affinities with the sociological view of religion as a means of constructing the cosmos, developed by Berger (Berger, pages 317–29).

A number of more recent trajectories are evident in the last group of sections included in this chapter. Asad's material, while specifically challenging Geertz's approach, raises the issues inherent in a definition that arises from a Western theoretical perspective. His views force us to introduce into the discussion issues relating both to power and structures of dominance, and perhaps even more significantly to the need for more culturally situated forms of definition. This can be associated with other trends in anthropology which seek to deconstruct Western theoretical perspectives by dialectically relating them to perspectives and understandings situated in the communities being studied. This approach can be seen as part of the inside/outside or emic/etic dichotomy. This dichotomy has been a constant feature of debate within the discipline even if the theoretical perspectives have tended to privilege the etic side of the dichotomy. The sections from Southwold (pages 277–89) and Saler (pages 267–76) draw their inspiration from phenomenology and philosophy (though both also can be directly linked to suggestions in Needham relating to definitions). Both of these theorists are challenging the process of definition and to a greater or lesser extent are moving towards analogical characterisations as opposed to formal definitions. It seems likely that the process of deprivileging formal definition as indicated in the works of Asad, Southwold and Saler is likely to be the most fruitful trajectory in the continuing attempts to understand religion within anthropological theoretical discussions.

TALAL ASAD
'THE CONSTRUCTION OF RELIGION AS AN ANTHROPOLOGICAL
CATEGORY'

Talal Asad was born in Saudi Arabia, but spent his formative years in India and Pakistan. His father was a Jewish convert to Islam who changed his name from Leopold Weiss to Muhammad Asad after his conversion in 1926. Throughout Talal's childhood his father was heavily involved with the new government in Pakistan: first serving as Director of the Department of Islamic Reconstruction, West Punjab, then becoming Under-Secretary of State for Near Eastern Affairs, before finally becoming Pakistan's permanent representative to the United Nations in 1952. Talal was educated in England and was awarded a PhD from the University of Oxford in 1968. In 1989 he emigrated to America and currently lives in New York. He is currently Distinguished Professor of Anthropology at the City University of New York Graduate Center.

While Asad's work, particularly in Genealogies of Religion, makes original contributions to the theorising of religion, the material included here relates directly to a critique of Geertz's definition and discussion of religion. Asad challenges the anthropologist to have a more culturally contextualised approach, aware of authorising systems of power and authority.

In much nineteenth-century evolutionary thought, religion was considered to be an early human condition from which modern law, science, and politics emerged and became detached.[1] In this century most anthropologists have abandoned Victorian evolutionary ideas, and many have challenged the rationalist notion that religion is simply a primitive and therefore outmoded form of the institutions we now encounter in truer form (law, politics, science) in modern life. For these twentieth-century anthropologists, religion is not an archaic mode of scientific thinking, nor of any other secular endeavor we value today; it is, on the contrary, a distinctive space of human practice and belief which cannot be reduced to any other. From this it seems to follow that the essence of religion is not to be confused with, say, the essence of politics, although in many societies the two may overlap and be intertwined.

In a characteristically subtle passage, Louis Dumont has told us that medieval Christendom was one such composite society:

> I shall take it for granted that a change in relations entails a change in whatever is related. If throughout our history religion has developed (to a large extent, with some other influences at play) a revolution in

Talal Asad (1993), *Genealogies of Religion*, Baltimore: Johns Hopkins University Press.

social values and has given birth by scissiparity, as it were, to an autonomous world of political institutions and speculations, then surely religion itself will have changed in the process. Of some important and visible changes we are all aware, but, I submit, we are not aware of the change in the very nature of religion as lived by any given individual, say a Catholic. Everyone knows that religion was formerly a matter of the group and has become a matter of the individual (in principle, and in practice at least in many environments and situations). But if we go on to assert that this change is correlated with the birth of the modern State, the proposition is not such a commonplace as the previous one. Let us go a little further: medieval religion was a great cloak – I am thinking of the Mantle of Our Lady of Mercy. Once it became an individual affair, it lost its all-embracing capacity and became one among other apparently equal considerations, of which the political was the first born. Each individual may, of course, and perhaps even will, recognise religion (or philosophy), as the same all-embracing consideration as it used to be *socially*. Yet on the level of social consensus or ideology, the same person will switch to a different configuration of values in which autonomous values (religious, political, etc.) are seemingly juxtaposed, much as individuals are juxtaposed in society. (1971: 32; emphasis in original)

According to this view, medieval religion, pervading or encompassing other categories, is nevertheless *analytically* identifiable. It is this fact that makes it possible to say that religion has the same essence today as it had in the Middle Ages, although its social extension and function were different in the two epochs. Yet the insistence that religion has an autonomous essence – not to be confused with the essence of science, or of politics, or of common sense – invites us to define religion (like any essence) as a transhistorical and transcultural phenomenon. It may be a happy accident that this effort of defining religion converges with the liberal demand in our time that it be kept quite separate from politics, law, and science – spaces in which varieties of power and reason articulate our distinctively modern life. This definition is at once part of a strategy (for secular liberals) of the confinement, and (for liberal Christians) of the defense of religion.

Yet this separation of religion from power is a modern Western norm, the product of a unique post-Reformation history. The attempt to understand Muslim traditions by insisting that in them religion and politics (two essences modern society tries to keep conceptually and practically apart) are coupled must, in my view, lead to failure. At its most dubious, such attempts encourage us to take up an *a priori* position in which religious discourse in the political arena is seen as a disguise for political power.

In what follows I want to examine the ways in which the theoretical search for an essence of religion invites us to separate it conceptually from the domain of power. I shall do this by exploring a universalist definition of religion offered by an eminent anthropologist: Clifford Geertz's 'Religion as a Cultural System.'[2] I stress that this is not primarily a critical review of Geertz's ideas on religion – if that had been my aim I would have addressed myself to the entire corpus of his writings on religion in Indonesia and Morocco. My intention in this chapter is to try to identify some of the historical shifts that have produced our concept of religion as the concept of a transhistorical essence – and Geertz's article is merely my starting point.

It is part of my basic argument that socially identifiable forms, preconditions, and effects of what was regarded as religion in the medieval Christian epoch were quite different from those so considered in modern society. I want to get at this well-known fact while trying to avoid a simple nominalism. What we call religious power was differently distributed and had a different thrust. There were different ways in which it created and worked through legal institutions, different selves that it shaped and responded to, and different categories of knowledge which it authorized and made available. Nevertheless, what the anthropologist is confronted with, as a consequence, is not merely an arbitrary collection of elements and processes that we happen to call 'religion'. For the entire phenomenon is to be seen in large measure in the context of Christian attempts to achieve a coherence in doctrines and practices, rules and regulations, even if that was a state never fully attained. My argument is that there cannot be a universal definition of religion, not only because its constituent elements and relationships are historically specific, but because that definition is itself the historical product of discursive processes.

A universal (i.e., anthropological) definition is, however, precisely what Geertz aims at: a *religion*, he proposes, is

> (1) a system of symbols which act to (2) establish powerful, pervasive, and long-lasting moods and motivations in men by (3) formulating conceptions of a general order of existence and (4) clothing these conceptions with such an aura of factuality that (5) the moods and motivations seem uniquely realistic. (1973: 90)

In what follows I shall examine this definition, not only in order to test its interlinked assertions, but also to flesh out the counterclaim that a transhistorical definition of religion is not viable.

THE CONCEPT OF SYMBOL AS A CLUE TO THE ESSENCE OF RELIGION

Geertz sees his first task as the definition of symbol: 'any object, act, event, quality, or relation which serves as a vehicle for a conception – the conception is the symbol's "meaning"' (1973: 91). But this simple, clear statement – in which *symbol* (any object, etc.) is differentiated from but linked to *conception* (its meaning) – is later supplemented by others not entirely consistent with it, for it turns out that the symbol is not an object that serves as a vehicle for a conception, *it is itself the conception.* Thus, in the statement 'the number 6, written, imagined, laid out as a row of stones, or even punched into the program tapes of a computer, is a symbol' (Geertz 1973: 91), what constitutes all these diverse representations as versions of the same symbol ('the number 6') is of course *a conception.* Furthermore, Geertz sometimes seems to suggest that even as a conception a symbol has an intrinsic connection with empirical events from which it is merely 'theoretically' separable: 'The symbolic dimension of social events is, like the psychological, itself theoretically abstractable from these events as empirical totalities' (1973: 91). At other times, however, he stresses the importance of keeping symbols and empirical objects quite separate: 'There is something to be said for not confusing our traffic with symbols with our traffic with objects or human beings, for these latter are not in themselves symbols, however often they may function as such' (1973: 92). Thus, 'symbol' is sometimes an aspect of reality, sometimes of its representation.[3]

These divergencies are symptoms of the fact that cognitive questions are mixed up in this account with communicative ones, and this makes it difficult to inquire into the ways in which discourse and understanding are connected in social practice.[. . .] What is being argued is that the authoritative status of representations/discourses is dependent on the appropriate production of other representations/discourses; the two are intrinsically and not just temporally connected.

Systems of symbols, says Geertz, are also *culture patterns*, and they constitute 'extrinsic sources of information' (1973: 92). Extrinsic, because 'they lie outside the boundaries of the individual organism as such in that intersubjective world of common understandings into which all human individuals are born' (Geertz 1973: 92). And sources of information in the sense that 'they provide a blueprint or template in terms of which processes external to themselves can be given a definite form' (Ibid.: 92). Thus, culture patterns, we are told, may be thought of as 'models *for* reality' as well as 'models *of* reality.'[4]

This part of the discussion does open up possibilities by speaking of modeling: that is, it allows for the possibility of conceptualizing discourses in the process of elaboration, modification, testing, and so forth. Unfortunately, Geertz quickly regresses to his earlier position: 'Culture patterns have an intrinsic double aspect,' he writes; 'they give meaning, that is objective conceptual form, to social and psychological reality both by shaping themselves to it and by shaping it to themselves' (1973: 93). This alleged dialectical tendency toward isomorphism, incidentally, makes it difficult to understand how social change can ever occur. The basic problem, however, is not with the idea of mirror images as such but with the assumption that there are two separate levels – the cultural, on the one side (consisting of symbols) and the social and psychological, on the other – which interact. This resort to Parsonian theory creates a logical space for defining the essence of religion. By adopting it, Geertz moves away from a notion of symbols that are intrinsic to signifying and organizing practices, and back to a notion of symbols as meaning-carrying objects external to social conditions and states of the self ('social and psychological reality').

This is not to say that Geertz doesn't think of symbols as 'doing' something. In a way that recalls older anthropological approaches to ritual,[5] he states that religious symbols act 'by inducing in the worshipper a certain distinctive set of dispositions (tendencies, capacities, propensities, skills, habits, liabilities, proneness) which lend a chronic character to the flow of his activity and the quality of his experience' (1973: 95). And here again, symbols are set apart from mental states. But how plausible are these propositions? Can we, for example, predict the 'distinctive' set of dispositions for a Christian worshiper in modern, industrial society? Alternatively, can we say of someone with a 'distinctive' set of dispositions that he is or is not a Christian?[6] The answer to both questions must surely be no. The reason, of course, is that it is not simply worship but social, political, and economic institutions in general,[7] within which individual biographies are lived out, that lend a stable character to the flow of a Christian's activity and to the quality of her experience.

Religious symbols, Geertz elaborates, produce two kinds of dispositions, *moods* and *motivations*: 'motivations are "made meaningful" with reference to the ends towards which they are conceived to conduce, whereas moods are "made meaningful" with reference to the conditions from which they are conceived to spring' (1973: 97). Now, a Christian might say that this is not their essence, because religious symbols, even when failing to produce moods and motivations, are still religious (i.e., true) symbols – that religious symbols possess a truth independent of their effectiveness. Yet surely even a committed Christian cannot be unconcerned at the existence of truthful symbols that appear to be largely powerless in modern society. He will rightly want to ask: What are the conditions in which religious symbols can actually produce religious dispositions? Or, as a nonbeliever would put it: How does (religious) power create (religious) truth?

[. . .]

It was not the mind that moved spontaneously to religious truth, but power that created the conditions for experiencing that truth.[8] Particular discourses and practices were to be systematically excluded, forbidden, denounced – made as much as possible unthinkable; others were to be included, allowed, praised, and drawn into the narrative of sacred truth. The configurations of power in this sense have, of course, varied profoundly in Christendom from one epoch to another – from Augustine's time, through the Middle Ages, to the industrial capitalist West of today. The patterns of religious moods and motivations, the possibilities for religious knowledge and truth, have all varied with them and been conditioned by them. Even Augustine held that although religious truth was eternal, the means for securing human access to it were not.

FROM READING SYMBOLS TO ANALYZING PRACTICES

One consequence of assuming a symbolic system separate from practices is that important distinctions are sometimes obscured, or even explicitly denied. 'That the symbols or symbol systems which induce and define dispositions we set off as religious and those which place these dispositions in a cosmic framework are the same symbols ought to occasion no surprise' (Geertz 1973: 98). But it does surprise! Let us grant that religious dispositions are crucially dependent on certain religious symbols, that such symbols operate in a way integral to religious motivation and religious mood. Even so, the symbolic process by which the concepts of religious motivation and mood are placed within 'a cosmic framework' is surely quite a different operation, and therefore the signs involved are quite different. Put another way, theological discourse is not identical with either moral attitudes or liturgical discourses – of which, among other things, theology speaks.[9] Thoughtful Christians will concede that, although theology has an essential function, theological discourse does not necessarily induce religious dispositions, and that, conversely, having religious dispositions does not necessarily depend on a clear-cut conception of the cosmic framework on the part of a religious actor. Discourse involved in practice is not the same as that involved in speaking about practice. It is a modern idea that a practitioner cannot know how to live religiously without being able to articulate that knowledge.

Geertz's reason for merging the two kinds of discursive process seems to spring from a wish to distinguish in general between religious and secular dispositions. The statement quoted above is elaborated as follows:

> For what else do we mean by saying that a particular mood of awe is religious and not secular, except that it springs from entertaining a conception of all-pervading vitality like mana and not from a visit to the Grand Canyon? Or that a particular case of asceticism is an example of a religious motivation except that it is directed toward the achievement of an unconditioned end like nirvana and not a conditioned one like weight-reduction? If sacred symbols did not at one and the same time induce dispositions in human beings and

formulate . . . general ideas of order, then the empirical differentia of religious activity or religious experience would not exist. (Ibid.: 98).

The argument that a particular disposition is religious partly because it occupies a conceptual place within a cosmic framework appears plausible, but only because it presupposes a question that must be made explicit: how do authorizing processes represent practices, utterances, or dispositions so that they can be discursively related to general (cosmic) ideas of order? In short, the question pertains to the authorizing process by which 'religion' is created.

[. . .]

What appears to anthropologists today to be self-evident, namely that religion is essentially a matter of symbolic meanings linked to ideas of general order (expressed through either or both rite and doctrine), that it has generic functions/features, and that it must not be confused with any of its particular historical or cultural forms, is in fact a view that has a specific Christian history. From being a concrete set of practical rules attached to specific processes of power and knowledge, religion has come to be abstracted and universalized.[10] In this movement we have not merely an increase in religious toleration, certainly not merely a new scientific discovery, but the mutation of a concept and a range of social practices which is itself part of a wider change in the modern landscape of power and knowledge. That change included a new kind of state, a new kind of science, a new kind of legal and moral subject. To understand this mutation it is essential to keep clearly distinct that which theology tends to obscure: the occurrence of events (utterances, practices, dispositions) and the authorizing processes that give those events meaning and embody that meaning in concrete institutions.

RELIGION AS MEANING AND RELIGIOUS MEANINGS

The equation between two levels of discourse (symbols that induce dispositions and those that place the idea of those dispositions discursively in a cosmic framework) is not the only problematic thing in this part of Geertz's discussion. He also appears, inadvertently, to be taking up the standpoint of theology. This happens when he insists on the primacy of meaning without regard to the processes by which meanings are constructed. 'What any particular religion affirms about the fundamental nature of reality may be obscure, shallow, or, all too often, perverse,' he writes, 'but it must, if it is not to consist of the mere collection of received practices and conventional sentiments we usually refer to as moralism, affirm something' (1973: 98–9).

The requirement of affirmation is apparently innocent and logical, but through it the entire field of evangelism was historically opened up, in particular the work of European missionaries in Asia, Africa, and Latin America. The demand that the received practices must *affirm something about the fundamental nature of reality*, that it should therefore always be possible to state meanings for them which are not plain nonsense, is the first condition for determining whether they belong to 'religion'. The un-evangelized come to be seen typically either as those who have practices but affirm nothing, in which case meaning can be attributed to their practices (thus making them vulnerable), or as those who do affirm something (probably 'obscure, shallow, or perverse'), an affirmation that can therefore be dismissed. In the one case, religious theory becomes necessary for a correct reading of the mute ritual hieroglyphics of others, for reducing their practices to texts; in the other, it is essential for judging the validity of their cosmological utterances. But always, there must be something that exists beyond the observed practices, the heard utterances, the written words, and it is the function of religious theory to reach into, and to bring out, that background by giving them meaning.[11]

Geertz is thus right to make a connection between religious theory and practice, but wrong to see it as essentially cognitive, as a means by which a disembodied mind can identify religion from an Archimedean point. The connection between religious theory and practice is fundamentally a matter of intervention – of constructing religion in the world (not in the mind) through definitional discourses, interpreting true meanings, excluding some utterances and practices and including others. Hence my repeated question: how does theoretical discourse actually define religion? What are the historical conditions in which it can act effectively as a demand for the imitation, or the prohibition, or the authentication of truthful utterances and practices? How does power create religion?

What kinds of affirmation, of meaning, must be identified with practice in order for it to qualify as religion? According to Geertz, it is because all human beings have a profound need for a general order of existence that religious symbols function to fulfill that need. It follows that human beings have a deep dread of disorder.

> There are at least three points where chaos – a tumult of events which lack not just interpretations but *interpretability* – threatens to break in upon man: at the limits of his analytic capabilities, at the limits of his power of endurance, and at the limits of his moral insight. (Geertz 1973: 100)

It is the function of religious symbols to meet perceived threats to order at each of these points (intellectual, physical, and moral):

> The Problem of Meaning in each of its intergrading aspects...is a matter of affirming, or at least recognizing, the inescapability of

ignorance, pain, and injustice on the human plane while simultaneously denying that these irrationalities are characteristic of the world
as a whole. And it is in terms of religious symbolism, a symbolism
relating man's sphere of existence to a wider sphere within which it is
conceived to rest, that both the affirmation and the denial are made.
(Ibid.:108)

Notice how the reasoning seems now to have shifted its ground from
the claim that religion must affirm something specific about the nature of
reality (however obscure, shallow, or perverse) to the bland suggestion that
religion is ultimately a matter of having a positive attitude toward the problem of disorder, of affirming simply that in some sense or other the world
as a whole is explicable, justifiable, bearable.[12] This modest view of religion (which would have horrified the early Christian Fathers or medieval
churchmen)[13] is a product of the only legitimate space allowed to Christianity by post-Enlightenment society, the right to individual *belief*: the human
condition is full of ignorance, pain, and injustice, and religious symbols
are a means of coming positively to terms with that condition. One consequence is that this view would in principle render any philosophy that
performs such a function into religion (to the annoyance of the nineteenth-
century rationalist), or alternatively, make it possible to think of religion
as a more primitive, a less adult mode of coming to terms with the human
condition (to the annoyance of the modern Christian). In either case, the
suggestion that religion has a universal function in belief is one indication
of how marginal religion has become in modern industrial society as the
site for producing disciplined knowledge and personal discipline. As such it
comes to resemble the conception Marx had of religion as ideology – that
is, as a mode of consciousness which is other than consciousness of reality, external to the relations of production, producing no knowledge, but
expressing at once the anguish of the oppressed and a spurious consolation.

Geertz has much more to say, however, on the elusive question of religious
meaning: not only do religious symbols formulate conceptions of a general
order of existence, they also clothe those conceptions with an aura of factuality. This, we are told, is 'the problem of belief'. *Religious belief* always
involves 'the prior acceptance of authority', which transforms experience:

> The existence of bafflement, pain, and moral paradox – of the Prob-
> lem of Meaning – is one of the things that drives men toward belief in
> gods, devils, spirits, totemic principles, or the spiritual efficacy of can-
> nibalism, . . . but it is not the basis upon which those beliefs rest, but
> rather their most important field of application. (Geertz 1973: 109)

This seems to imply that religious belief stands independently of the
worldly conditions that produce bafflement, pain, and moral paradox,

although that belief is primarily a way of coming to terms with them. But surely this is mistaken, on logical grounds as well as historical, for changes in the object of belief change that belief; and as the world changes, so do the objects of belief and the specific forms of bafflement and moral paradox that are a part of that world. What the Christian believes today about God, life after death, the universe, is not what he believed a millennium ago – nor is the way he responds to ignorance, pain, and injustice the same now as it was then. The medieval valorization of pain as the mode of participating in Christ's suffering contrasts sharply with the modern Catholic perception of pain as an evil to be fought against and overcome as Christ the Healer did. That difference is clearly related to the post-Enlightenment secularization of Western society and to the moral language which that society now authorizes.[14]

Geertz's treatment of religious belief, which lies at the core of his conception of religion, is a modern, privatized Christian one because and to the extent that it emphasizes the priority of belief as a state of mind rather than as constituting activity in the world: 'The basic axiom underlying what we may perhaps call "the religious perspective" is everywhere the same: he who would know must first believe' (1973: 110). In modern society, where knowledge is rooted either in an a-Christian everyday life or in an a-religious science, the Christian apologist tends not to regard belief as the conclusion to a knowledge process but as its precondition. However, the knowledge that he promises will not pass (nor, in fairness, does he claim that it will pass) for knowledge of social life, still less for the systematic knowledge of objects that natural science provides. Her claim is to a particular state of mind, a sense of conviction, not to a corpus of practical knowledge. But the reversal of belief and knowledge she demands was not a basic axiom to, say, pious learned Christians of the twelfth century, for whom knowledge and belief were not so clearly at odds. On the contrary, Christian belief would then have been built on knowledge – knowledge of theological doctrine, of canon law and Church courts, of the details of clerical liberties, of the powers of ecclesiastical office (over souls, bodies, properties), of the preconditions and effects of confession, of the rules of religious orders, of the locations and virtues of shrines, of the lives of the saints, and so forth. Familiarity with all such (religious) knowledge was a precondition for normal social life, and belief (embodied in practice and discourse) an orientation for effective activity in it – whether on the part of the religious clergy, the secular clergy, or the laity. Because of this, the form and texture and function of their beliefs would have been different from the form and texture and function of contemporary belief – and so too of their doubts and their disbelief.

The assumption that belief is a distinctive mental state characteristic of all religions has been the subject of discussion by contemporary scholars. Thus, Needham (1972) has interestingly argued that belief is nowhere a distinct mode of consciousness, nor a necessary institution for the conduct of social life. Southwold (1979) takes an almost diametrically opposed view, asserting that questions of belief do relate to distinctive mental states and that they are relevant in any and every society, since 'to believe' always designates a relation between a believer and a proposition and through it to reality. Harré (1981: 82), in a criticism of Needham, makes the more persuasive case that 'belief is a mental state, a grounded disposition, but it is confined to people who have certain social institutions and practices'.

At any rate, I think it is not too unreasonable to maintain that 'the basic axiom' underlying what Geertz calls 'the religious perspective' is *not* everywhere the same. It is preeminently the Christian church that has occupied itself with identifying, cultivating, and testing belief as a verbalizable inner condition of true religion.[15]

RELIGION AS A PERSPECTIVE

The phenomenological vocabulary that Geertz employs raises two interesting questions, one regarding its coherence and the other concerning its adequacy to a modern cognitivist notion of religion. I want to suggest that although this vocabulary is theoretically incoherent, it is socially quite compatible with the privatized idea of religion in modern society.

Thus, 'the religious perspective', we are told, is one among several – common-sense, scientific, aesthetic – and it differs from these as follows. It differs from the *common-sense* perspective, because it 'moves beyond the realities of everyday life to wider ones which correct and complete them, and [because] its defining concern is not action upon those wider realities but acceptance of them, faith in them'. It is unlike the *scientific* perspective, because 'it questions the realities of everyday life not out of an institutionalized scepticism which dissolves the world's givenness into a swirl of probabilistic hypotheses, but in terms of what it takes to be wider, nonhypothetical truths'. And it is distinguished from the *aesthetic* perspective, because 'instead of effecting a disengagement from the whole question of factuality, deliberately manufacturing an air of semblance and illusion, it deepens the concern with fact and seeks to create an aura of utter actuality' (Geertz 1973: 112). In other words, although the religious perspective is not exactly rational, it is not irrational either.

It would not be difficult to state one's disagreement with this summary of what common sense, science, and aesthetics are about.[16] But my point is that the optional flavor conveyed by the term *perspective* is surely misleading when it is applied equally to science and to religion in modern society: religion is indeed now optional in a way that science is not. Scientific practices, techniques, knowledges, permeate and create the very fibers of social life in ways that religion no longer does.[17] In that sense, religion today *is* a perspective (or an 'attitude', as Geertz sometimes calls it), but science is not. In that sense, too, science is not to be found in every society, past and present. We shall see in a moment the difficulties that Geertz's perspectivism gets him into, but before that I need to examine his analysis of the mechanics of reality maintenance at work in religion.

Consistent with previous arguments about the functions of religious symbols is Geertz's remark that 'it is in ritual – that is, consecrated behavior – that this conviction that religious conceptions are veridical and that religious directives are sound is somehow generated' (1973: 112). The long passage from which this is taken swings back and forth between arbitrary speculations about what goes on in the consciousness of officiants and unfounded assertions about ritual as imprinting. At first sight, this seems a curious combination of introspectionist psychology with a behaviorist one – but as Vygotsky (1978: 58–9) argued long ago, the two are by no means inconsistent, insofar as both assume that psychological phenomena consist essentially in the consequence of various stimulating environments.

Geertz postulates the function of rituals in generating religious conviction ('In these plastic dramas men attain their faith as they portray it' [1973: 114]), but how or why this happens is nowhere explained. Indeed, he concedes that such a religious state is not always achieved in religious ritual:

> Of course, all cultural performances are not religious performances, and the line between those that are, and artistic, or even political, ones is often not so easy to draw in practice, for, like social forms, symbolic forms can serve multiple purposes. (1973: 113)

But the question remains: What is it that ensures the participant's taking the symbolic forms in the way that leads to faith if the line between religious and nonreligious perspectives is not so easy to draw? Mustn't the ability and the will to adopt a religious standpoint be present prior to the ritual performance? That is precisely why a simple stimulus–response model of how ritual works will not do. And if that is the case, then ritual in the sense of a sacred performance cannot be the place where religious faith is attained, but the manner in which it is (literally) played out. If we are to understand how this happens, we must examine not only the sacred performance itself but also the entire range of available disciplinary activities, of institutional forms of knowledge and practice, within which dispositions are formed and sustained and through which the possibilities of attaining the truth are marked out – as Augustine clearly saw.

I have noted more than once Geertz's concern to define religious symbols according to universal, cognitive criteria, to distinguish the religious perspective clearly from nonreligious ones. The separation of religion from science, common sense, aesthetics, politics, and so on, allows him to defend it against charges of irrationality. If religion has a distinctive perspective (its own truth, as Durkheim would have said) and performs an indispensable function, it does not in essence compete with others and cannot, therefore, be accused of generating false consciousness. Yet in a way this defense is equivocal. Religious symbols create dispositions, Geertz observes, which seem uniquely realistic. Is this the point of view of a reasonably confident agent (who must always operate within the denseness of historically given probabilities) or that of a skeptical observer (who can see through the representations of reality to the reality itself)? It is never clear. And it is never clear because this kind of phenomenological approach doesn't make it easy to examine whether, and if so to what extent and in what ways, religious experience relates to something in the real world that believers inhabit. This is partly because religious symbols are treated, in circular fashion, as the precondition for religious experience (which, like any experience, must, by definition, be genuine), rather than as one condition for engaging with life.

Toward the end of his essay, Geertz attempts to connect, instead of separating, the religious perspective and the common-sense one – and the result reveals an ambiguity basic to his entire approach. First, invoking Schutz, Geertz states that the everyday world of common-sense objects and practical acts is common to all human beings because their survival depends on it: 'A man, even large groups of men, may be aesthetically insensitive, religiously unconcerned, and unequipped to pursue formal scientific analysis, but he cannot be completely lacking in common sense and survive' (1973: 119). Next, he informs us that individuals move 'back and forth between the religious perspective and the common-sense perspective' (1973: 119). These perspectives are so utterly different, he declares, that only 'Kierkegaardian leaps' (1973: 120) can cover the cultural gaps that separate them. Then, the phenomenological conclusion: 'Having ritually "leapt" ... into the framework of meaning which religious conceptions define, and the ritual ended, returned again to the common-sense world, a man is – unless, as sometimes happens, the experience fails to register – changed. *And as he is changed, so also is the common-sense world*, for it is now seen as but the partial form of a wider reality which corrects and completes it' (Geertz 1973: 122; emphasis added).

This curious account of shifting perspectives and changing worlds is puzzling – as indeed it is in Schutz himself. It is not clear, for example, whether the religious framework and the common-sense world, between which the individual moves, are independent of him or not. Most of what Geertz has said at the beginning of his essay would imply that they are independent (cf. 1973: 92), and his remark about common sense being vital to every man's survival also enforces this reading. Yet it is also suggested that as the believer changes his perspective, so he himself changes; and that as he changes, so too is his common-sense world changed and corrected. So the latter, at any rate, is not independent of his moves. But it would appear from the account that the religious world *is* independent, since it is the source of distinctive experience for the believer, and through that experience, a source of change in the common-sense world: there is no suggestion any-where that the religious world (or perspective) is ever affected by experience in the common-sense world.

This last point is consistent with the phenomenological approach in which religious symbols are *sui generis*, marking out an independent religious domain. But in the present context it presents the reader with a paradox: the world of common sense is always common to all human beings, and quite distinct from the religious world, which in turn differs from one group to another, as one culture differs from another; but experience of the religious world affects the common-sense world, and so the distinctiveness of the two kinds of world is modified, and the common-sense world comes to differ, from one group to another, as one culture differs from another. The paradox results from an ambiguous phenomenology in which reality is at once the distance of an agent's social perspective from the truth, measurable only by the privileged observer, and also the substantive knowledge of a socially constructed world available to both agent and observer, but to the latter only through the former.[18]

CONCLUSION

Perhaps we can learn something from this paradox which will help us eval-uate Geertz's confident conclusion:

> The anthropological study of religion is therefore a two-stage oper-ation: first, an analysis of the system of meanings embodied in the symbols which make up *the religion proper*, and, second, the relat-ing of these systems to social-structural and psychological processes. (1973: 125; emphasis added)

How sensible this sounds, yet how mistaken, surely, it is. If religious symbols are understood, on the analogy with words, as vehicles for meaning, can such meanings be established independently of the form of life in which they are used? If religious symbols are to be taken as the signatures of a sacred text, can we know what they mean without regard to the social disciplines by which their correct reading is secured? If religious symbols are to be thought of as the concepts by which experiences are organized, can we say much about them without considering how they come to be authorized? Even if it be claimed that what is experienced through religious symbols is not, in essence, the social world but the spiritual,[19] is it possible to assert that conditions in the social world have nothing to do with making that kind of experience accessible? Is the concept of religious training entirely vacuous?

The two stages that Geertz proposes are, I would suggest, one. Religious symbols – whether one thinks of them in terms of communication or of cog-nition, of guiding action or of expressing emotion – cannot be understood independently of their historical relations with nonreligious symbols or of their articulations in and of social life, in which work and power are always crucial. My argument, I must stress, is not just that religious symbols are intimately linked to social life (and so change with it), or that they usually support dominant political power (and occasionally oppose it). It is that different kinds of practice and discourse are intrinsic to the field in which religious representations (like any representation) acquire their identity and their truthfulness. From this it does not follow that the meanings of religious practices and utterances are to be sought in social phenomena, but only that their possibility and their authoritative status are to be explained as products of historically distinctive disciplines and forces. The anthropological student of *particular* religions should therefore begin from this point, in a sense unpacking the comprehensive concept which he or she translates as 'religion' into heterogeneous elements according to its historical character.

A final word of caution. Hasty readers might conclude that my discussion of the Christian religion is skewed towards an authoritarian, centralized, elite perspective, and that consequently it fails to take into account the religions of heterodox believers, of resistant peasantries, of all those who cannot be completely controlled by the orthodox church. Or, worse still, that my discussion has no bearing on nondisciplinarian, voluntaristic, localized cults of noncentralized religions such as Hinduism. But that conclusion would be a misunderstanding of this chapter, seeing in it an attempt to advocate a better anthropological definition of religion than Geertz has done. Nothing could be farther from my intention. If my effort reads in large part like a brief sketch of transmutations in Christianity from the Middle Ages until today, then that is not because I have arbitrarily confined my ethnographic examples to one religion. My aim has been to problematize the idea of an anthropological definition of religion by assigning that endeavor to a particular history of knowledge and power (including a particular understanding of our legitimate past and future) out of which the modern world has been constructed.[20]

NOTES

1. Thus, Fustel de Coulanges(1873). Originally published in French in 1864, this was an influential work in the history of several overlapping disciplines – anthropology, biblical studies, and classics.
2. Originally published in 1966, it was reprinted in his widely acclaimed *The Interpretation of Cultures* (1973).
3. Compare Peirce's more rigorous account of *representations*. 'A representation is an object which stands for another so that an experience of the former affords us a knowledge of the latter. There must be three essential conditions to which every representation must conform. It must in the first place like any other object have qualities independent of its meaning .... In the 2nd place a representation must have a real causal connection with its object .... In the third place, every representation addresses itself to a mind. It is only in so far as it does this that it is a representation' (Peirce 1986: 62).

4. Or, as Kroeber and Kluckhohn (1952: 181) put it much earlier, 'Culture consists of patterns, explicit and implicit, of and for behaviour acquired and transmitted by symbols.'

5. If we set aside Radcliffe-Brown's well-known preoccupation with social cohesion, we may recall that he too was concerned to specify certain kinds of psychological states said to be induced by religious symbols: 'Rites can be seen to be the regulated symbolic expressions of certain sentiments (which control the behaviour of the individual in his relation to others). Rites can therefore be shown to have a specific social function when, and to the extent that, they have for their effect to regulate, maintain and transmit from one generation to another sentiments on which the constitution of society depends' (1952: 157).

6. Some ways in which symbolization (discourse) can *disguise lack of distinctiveness* are well brought out in MacIntyre's trenchant critique of contemporary Christian writers, where he argues that 'Christians behave like everyone else but use a different vocabulary in characterising their behaviour, and also to conceal their lack of distinctiveness' (1971: 24).

7. The phenomenon of declining church attendance in modern industrial society and its progressive marginalization (in Europe, at least) to those sectors of the population not directly involved in the industrial work process illustrates the argument that if we must look for causal explanations in this area, then socioeconomic conditions in general will appear to be the independent variable and formal worship the dependent. See the interesting discussion in Luckmann (1967: chap. 2).

8. This was why Augustine eventually came around to the view that insincere conversion was not a problem (Chadwick 1967: 222–4.).

9. A modern theologian puts it: 'The difference between the professing, proclaiming and orienting way of speaking on the one hand, and descriptive speech on the other is sometimes formulated as the difference between "speaking about" and "speaking to". As soon as these two ways of speaking are confused, the original and unique character of religious speech, so it is said, is corrupted so that reality-for-the-believer can no longer "appear" to him as it appears in professing speech' (Luijpen 1973: 90–1).

10. Phases in the gradual evacuation of specificity from public religious discourse in the eighteenth century are described in some detail in Gay (1973).

11. The way in which representations of occurrences were transformed into meanings by Christian theology is analyzed by Auerbach in his classic study of representations of reality in Western literature and briefly summed up in this passage: 'The total content of the sacred writings was placed in an exegetic context which often removed the thing told very far away from its sensory base, in that the reader or listener was forced to turn his attention away from the sensory occurrence and toward its meaning. This implied the danger that the visual element of the occurrences might succumb under the dense texture of meanings. Let one example stand for many: it is a visually dramatic occurrence that God made Eve, the first woman, from Adam's rib while Adam lay asleep; so too is it that a soldier pierced Jesus' side, as he hung dead on the cross, so that blood and water flowed out. But when these two occurrences are exegetically interrelated in the doctrine that Adam's sleep is a figure of Christ's death-sleep; that, as from the wound in Adam's side mankind's primordial mother after the flesh, Eve, was born, so from the wound in Christ's side was born the mother of all men after the spirit, the Church (blood and water are sacramental symbols) – then the sensory occurrence pales before the power of the figural meaning. What is perceived by the hearer or reader ... is weak as a sensory impression, and all one's interest is directed toward the context of meanings. In comparison, the Greco-Roman specimens of realistic presentation are, though less serious and fraught with problems and far more limited in their conception of historical movement, nevertheless perfectly

integrated in their sensory substance. They do not know the antagonism between sensory appearance and meaning, an antagonism which permeates the early, and indeed the whole, Christian view of reality' (1953: 48–9). As Auerbach goes on to demonstrate, Christian theory in the later Middle Ages invested representations of everyday life with characteristic figural meanings, and so with the possibilities for distinctive kinds of religious experience. Figural interpretation, in Auerbach's usage, is not synonymous with symbolism. The latter is close to allegory, in which the symbol is substituted for the object symbolized. In figural interpretation the representation of an event (Adam's sleep) is made explicit by the representation of another event (Christ's death) that is its meaning. The latter representation fulfills the former (the technical term, Auerbach tells us, was *figuram implire*) – it is *implicit* in it.

12. Cf. Douglas (1975: 76): 'The person without religion would be the person content to do without explanations of certain kinds, or content to behave in society without a single unifying principle validating the social order.'

13. When the fifth-century bishop of Javols spread Christianity into the Auvergne, he found the peasants 'celebrating a three-day festival with offerings on the edge of a marsh.... "Nulla est religio in stagno," he said: there can be no religion in a swamp' (Brown 1981: 125). For medieval Christians, religion was not a universal phenomenon: religion was a site on which universal truth was produced, and it was clear to them that truth was not produced universally.

14. As a contemporary Catholic theologian puts it: 'The secularistic challenge, even though separating many aspects of life from the religious field, brings with it a more sound, interpretative equilibrium: the natural phenomena, even though sometimes difficult to understand, have their cause and roots in processes that can and must be recognized. It is man's job, therefore, to enter into this cognitive analysis of the meaning of suffering, in order to be able to affront and conquer it. The contemporary condition of man, of the believer on the threshold of the third millennium, is undoubtedly more adult and more mature and allows a new approach to the problem of human suffering' (Autiero 1987: 124).

15. I have attempted a description of one aspect of this process in Asad (1986b).

16. Philosophical attempts to define science have not reached a firm consensus. In the Anglo-Saxon world, recent arguments have been formulated in and around the works of Popper, Kuhn, Lakatos, Feyerabend, Hacking, and others; in France, those of Bachelard and Canguilhem. One important tendency has been to abandon the attempt at solving what is known in the literature as the demarcation problem, which is based on the assumption that there must be a single, essential, scientific method. The idea that the scientist 'dissolves the world's givenness into a swirl of probabilistic hypotheses' is as questionable as the complementary suggestion that in religion there is no scope for experimentation. On this latter point, there is massive evidence of experiment, even if we went no farther than the history of Christian asceticism. Equally, the suggestion that art is a matter of 'effecting a disengagement from the whole question of factuality, deliberately manufacturing an air of semblance and illusion' would not be taken as self-evident by all writers and artists. For example, when the art critic John Berger argues, in his brilliant essay 'The Moment of Cubism', that cubism 'changed the nature of the relationship between the painted image and reality, and by so doing expressed a new relationship between man and reality' (1972: 145), we learn something about cubism's concern to redefine visual factuality.

17. In case some readers are tempted to think that what I am talking about is not science (theory) but technology (practical application), whereas Geertz is concerned only with the former, I would stress that any attempt to make a sharp distinction between the two is based on an oversimplified view of the historical practice of both (cf. Musson and Robinson 1969). My point is that science and technology *together* are

basic to the structure of modern lives, individual and collective, and that religion, in any but the most vacuous sense, is not.

18. In the introduction to his 1983 collection of essays, Geertz seems to want to abandon this perspectival approach: 'The debate over whether [art] is an applicable category in "non-Western" or "pre-Modern" contexts has, even when compared to similar debates concerning "religion", "science", "ideology", or "law", been peculiarly unrelenting. It has also been peculiarly unproductive. Whatever you want to call a cave wall crowded with overlapping images of transfixed animals, a temple tower shaped to a phallus, a feathered shield, a calligraphic scroll, or a tattooed face, you still have *the phenomenon* to deal with, as well as perhaps the sense that to add kula exchange or the Doomsday Book would be to spoil the series. The question is not whether art (or anything else) is universal; it is whether one can talk about West African carving, New Guinea palm-leaf painting, quattrocento picture making, and Moroccan versifying in such a way as to cause them to shed some sort of light on one another' (1983: 11; emphasis added). The answer to this question must surely be: yes, of course one should try to talk about disparate things in relation to one another, but what exactly is the purpose of constructing a series whose items can all easily be recognized by cultivated Westerners as instances of *the phenomenon* of art? Of course, any one thing may shed light on another. But is it not precisely when one abandons conventional perspectives, or pre-established series, for opportunistic comparison that illumination (as opposed to recognition) *may* be achieved? Think of Hofstadter's splendid *Gödel, Escher, Bach* (1979), for instance.

19. Cf. the final chapter in Evans-Pritchard (1956), and also the conclusion to Evans-Pritchard (1965).

20. Such endeavors are unceasing. As a recent, engaging study by Tambiah (1990: 6) puts it in the first chapter: 'In our discussion hereafter I shall try to argue that from a general anthropological standpoint the distinctive feature of religion as a generic concept lies not in the domain of belief and its "rational accounting" of the workings of the universe, but in a special awareness of the transcendent, and the acts of symbolic communication that attempt to realize that awareness and live by its promptings.'

EDWARD EVANS-PRITCHARD
'THEORIES OF PRIMITIVE RELIGION'

Edward Evans-Pritchard was born in Sussex in 1902; his father was an Anglican clergyman. He first studied history at Exeter College, Oxford before moving to the LSE, where he was awarded a PhD for his studies in anthropology. His first period of fieldwork stretched from 1926 to 1932, when he lived amongst the Azande. He engaged in further fieldwork in 1935, the year that he was appointed lecturer at the University of Oxford. This second period of fieldwork focused on the Nuer and other Nilotic peoples of southern Sudan. In 1946 he was appointed to a chair at Oxford, which he held until 1970. During this time he established himself as one of the leading figures of British anthropology.

We include here material from Theories of Primitive Religion; *this volume provides an excellent critique of many of the prevalent theories of religion. The conclusion of the book provides an insight both into the theoretical problems associated with theories of religion and into Evans-Pritchard's own approach, which brings together aspects of functionalism and structuralism.*

CONCLUSION

I have given you an account, with some illustrations, of various types of theory which have been put forward to explain the religious beliefs and practices of primitive man. For the most part the theories we have been discussing are, for anthropologists at least, as dead as mutton, and today are chiefly of interest as specimens of the thought of their time. Some of the books – those, for example, of Tylor, Frazer, and Durkheim – will doubtless continue to be read as classics, but they are no longer much of a stimulus for the student. Others – for example, Lang, King, Crawley, and Marett – have more or less passed into oblivion. That these theories no longer make much appeal is due to a number of factors, a few of which I shall mention.

One reason is, I believe, that religion has ceased to occupy men's minds in the way it did at the end of last, and at the beginning of this, century. Anthropological writers then felt that they were living at a momentous crisis in the history of thought, and that they had their part to play in it. Max Müller remarked in 1878 that

> Every day, every week, every month, every quarter, the most widely read journals seem just now to vie with each other in telling us that the time for religion is past, that faith is a hallucination or an infantile disease, that the gods have at last been found out and exploded... [1]

E. E. Evans-Pritchard (1965). *Theories of Primitive Religion*, Oxford: Clarendon Press.

Crawley wrote, twenty-seven years later, in 1905, that the enemies of religion 'have developed the opposition of science and religion into a deadly struggle, and the opinion is everywhere gaining ground that religion is a mere survival from a primitive and mythopoeic age, and its extinction only a matter of time'.[2] I have discussed elsewhere[3] the part played by anthropologists in this struggle, so I do not pursue the matter any further. I mention it here only because I think that the crisis of conscience to some extent accounts for the efflorescence of books on primitive religion during this period, and also that the passing of the crisis may account in some degree for the absence among later generations of anthropologists of the passionate interest their predecessors had in the subject. The last book in which one senses a feeling of urgency and conflict is S. A. Cook's *The Study of Religion*, finished and published when the calamity of 1914 had already fallen.

There were other reasons why the debate abated. Anthropology was becoming an experimental subject, and as field research developed, both in quality and in quantity, what appeared to be more in the nature of philosophical speculation on the part of scholars who had never seen a primitive people was at a discount. It was not merely that facts revealed by modern research only too often cast doubt on earlier theories, but that the theories came to be seen to have faulty construction. When anthropologists attempted to make use of them in their field studies, they found that they had little experimental value, because they were formulated in terms which seldom permitted their being broken down into problems which observation could solve, so they could not be proved either true or false. What use as a guide to field research are Tylor's and Müller's and Durkheim's theories of the genesis of religion?

It is the word genesis on which emphasis is placed. It was because explanations of religion were offered in terms of origins that these theoretical debates, once so full of life and fire, eventually subsided. To my mind, it is extraordinary that anyone could have thought it worth while to speculate about what might have been the origin of some custom or belief, when there is absolutely no means of discovering, in the absence of historical evidence, what was its origin. And yet this is what almost all our authors explicitly or implicitly did, whether their theses were psychological or sociological; even those most hostile to what they dubbed pseudo-history were not immune from putting forward similar explanations themselves. A long essay might be written about the appalling confusion in these discussions with regard to the ideas of evolution, development, history, progress, primitive, origin, genesis, and cause, and I do not propose to unravel it. It must suffice to say that there is little or nothing one can do with such theories.

[...]

In these theories it was assumed, taken for granted, that we were at one end of the scale of human progress and the so-called savages were at the other end, and that, because primitive men were on a rather low technological level, their thought and custom must in all respects be the antithesis of ours. We are rational, [they are] primitive peoples prelogical, living in a world of dreams and make-believe, of mystery and awe; we are capitalists, they communists; we are monogamous, they promiscuous; we are monotheists, they fetishists, animists, pre-animists or what have you, and so on.

Primitive man was thus represented as childish, crude, prodigal, and comparable to animals and imbeciles. This is no exaggeration. Herbert Spencer tells us that the mind of primitive man is 'unspeculative, uncritical, incapable of generalizing, and with scarcely any notions save those yielded by the perceptions'.[4] Then, again, he says that in the undeveloped vocabularies and grammatical structures of primitives only the simplest thoughts can be conveyed, so, according to an unnamed authority whom he quotes, the Zuni Indians 'require much facial contortion and bodily gesticulation to make their sentences perfectly intelligible'; and that the language of the Bushmen needs, according to another source, so many signs to eke it out that 'they are unintelligible in the dark', while the Arapahos, says a third authority, 'can hardly converse with one another in the dark'.[5] Max Müller quotes Sir Emerson Tennent to the effect that the Veddahs of Ceylon have no language: 'They mutually make themselves understood by signs, grimaces, and guttural sounds, which have little resemblance to definite words or language in general'.[6] In fact they speak Sinhalese (an Indo-European tongue). Then, does not Darwin, in a most unscientific passage, describe the people of Tierra del Fuego, a rather pleasant people according to better observers, as practically sub-human beasts,[7] and does not Galton, in an even more unscientific spirit, claim that his dog had more intelligence than the Damara (Herero) whom he met?[8] Many other examples could be cited. A superb collection of foolish, if not outrageous, observations of this sort may be found in the paper 'Aptitudes of Races'[9] by the Reverend Frederic W. Farrar, the author of *Eric, or Little by Little* and *The Life of Christ*. His dislike of, and hostility to, Negroes equals that of Kingsley. Fifty years of research have shown that such denigrations (the word in this context is etymologically ironical) were ill-informed misconceptions, or in other words so much rubbish.

All this fitted in very well with colonialist and other interests, and some were prepared to admit that some of the discredit must go to the American ethnologists who wanted an excuse for slavery, and some also to those who desired to find a missing link between men and monkeys.

Needless to say, it was held that primitive peoples must have the crudest religious conceptions, and we have had occasion to observe the various ways in which they are supposed to have reached them. This may further be illustrated in the condescending argument, once it was ascertained beyond doubt that primitive peoples, even the hunters and collectors, have gods with high moral attributes, that they must have borrowed the idea, or just the word without comprehension of its meaning, from a higher culture, from missionaries, traders, and others.

[. . .]

Such views as I have outlined would not be acceptable today. On whether they were justified by the information available at the time I will pronounce no judgement, not having carried out the laborious literary research that would be required to form one. My task is expository, but I have also to put before you what seems to me to be the fundamental weakness of the interpretations of primitive religion which at one time appeared to carry conviction. The first error was the basing of them on evolutionary assumptions for which no evidence was, or could be, adduced. The second was that, besides being theories of chronological origins, they were also theories of psychological origins; and even those we have labelled sociological could be said to rest ultimately on psychological suppositions of the 'if I were a horse' sort. They could scarcely have been otherwise so far as the armchair anthropologists were concerned, those whose experience was restricted to their own culture and society, within that society to a small class, and within that class to a yet smaller group of intellectuals. I am sure that men like Avebury, Frazer, and Marett had little idea of how the ordinary English working man felt and thought, and it is not surprising that they had even less idea of how primitives, whom they had never seen, feel and think. As we have seen, their explanations of primitive religion derived from introspection. If the scholar himself believed what primitives believe, or practised what they practise, he would have been guided by a certain line of reasoning, or impelled by some emotional state, or immersed in crowd psychology, or entangled in a network of collective and mystical representations.

How often have we been warned not to try to interpret the thought of ancient or primitive peoples in terms of our own psychology, which has been moulded by a set of institutions very different from theirs – by Adam Ferguson, Sir Henry Maine, and others, including Lévy-Bruhl, who in this respect might be said to be the most objective of all the writers about primitive mentality whose works we have reviewed? 'German scholars' Bachofen wrote to Morgan, 'propose to make antiquity intelligible by measuring it according to the popular ideas of the present day. They only see themselves in the creation of the past. To penetrate to the structure of a mind different from our own, is hardy work.'[10] It is indeed hardy work, especially when we are dealing with such difficult subjects as primitive magic and religion, in which it is all too easy, when translating the conceptions of the simpler peoples into our own, to transplant our thought into theirs. If it be true, as the Seligmans have said, that in the matter of magic black and white peoples regard each other with total lack of understanding,[11] primitive man's ideas about it are liable to be gravely distorted, especially by those who have never seen a primitive people and who also regard magic as a futile superstition. The phenomenon then tends to be analysed by the process of imagining ourselves in the same conditions as primitive man.

As I indicated in my first lecture, I regard this problem of translation as being central to our discipline. I give one more example. We use the word 'supernatural' when speaking of some native belief, because that is what it would mean for us, but far from increasing our understanding of it, we are likely by the use of this word to misunderstand it. We have the concept of natural law, and the word 'supernatural' conveys to us something outside the ordinary operation of cause and effect, but it may not at all have that sense for primitive man. For instance, many peoples are convinced that deaths are caused by witchcraft. To speak of witchcraft being for these peoples a supernatural agency hardly reflects their own view of the matter, since from their point of view nothing could be more natural. They experience it through the senses in deaths and other misfortunes, and the witches are their neighbours. Indeed, for them, if a person did not die from witchcraft, it might be better said, at least in a certain sense, that he did not die a natural death, and that to die from witchcraft is to die from natural causes. We might here consider further the dichotomy between sacred and profane, also the meaning of *mana* and similar ideas, the differences between magic and religion, and other topics which appear to me to be still in a very confused state, largely on account of failure to realize that very fundamental semantic problems confront us – or, if we prefer to say so, problems of translation: but this would require a lengthy discussion, to which I hope to give attention at another time and in another place.

[. . .]

Here and now I have a different task to perform: to suggest what should be the procedure in investigations of primitive religions. I do not deny that peoples have reasons for their beliefs – that they are rational; I do not deny that religious rites may be accompanied by emotional experiences, that feeling may even be an important element in their performance; and I certainly do not deny that religious ideas and practices are directly associated with social groups – that religion, whatever else it may be, is a social phenomenon. What I do deny is that it is explained by any of these facts, or all of them together, and I hold that it is not sound scientific method to seek for origins, especially when they cannot be found. Science deals with relations, not with origins and essences. In so far as it can be said that the facts of primitive religions can be sociologically explained at all, it must be in relation to other facts, both those with which it forms a system of ideas and practices and other social phenomena associated with it. As an example of the first kind of partial explanation, I would instance magic. To try to understand magic as an idea in itself, what is the essence of it, as it were, is a hopeless task. It becomes more intelligible when it is viewed not only in relation to empirical activities but also in relation to other beliefs, as part of a system of thought; for it is certainly often the case that it is primarily not so much a means of controlling nature as of preventing witchcraft and other mystical forces operating against human endeavour by interfering with the empirical measures taken to attain an end. As an example of explanation in terms of the relation of religion to other social, and in themselves non-religious, facts, we might instance ancestor cults, which clearly can only be understood when they are viewed as part of a whole set of family and kin relationships. The ghosts have power over their descendants, among whom they act as sanction for conduct, seeing that they carry out their obligations to one another and punishing them if they fail to do so. Or again, in some societies God is conceived of as both the one and the many, the one as thought of in relation to all men or a total society, and the many as thought of, in the form of a variety of spirits, in relation to one or other segment of society. A knowledge of the social structure is here obviously required for the understanding of some features of religious thought. Then again, religious ritual is performed on ceremonial occasions in which the relative status of individuals and groups is affirmed or confirmed, as at birth, initiation, marriage, and death. Clearly, to understand the role of religion on these occasions one must here again have a knowledge of the social structure. I have given some very simple examples. A relational analysis of the kind suggested can be made at any point where religion is in a functional relation to any other social facts – moral, ethical, economic, juridical, aesthetic, and scientific – and when it has been made at all points, we have as full a sociological understanding of the phenomenon as we are ever likely to have.

All this amounts to saying that we have to account for religious facts in terms of the totality of the culture and society in which they are found, to try to understand them in terms of what the *Gestalt* psychologists called the *Kulturganze*, or of what Mauss called *fait total*. They must be seen as a relation of parts to one another within a coherent system, each part making sense only in relation to the others, and the system itself making sense only in relation to other institutional systems, as part of a wider set of relations.

[. . .]

Now, sooner or later, if we are to have a general sociological theory of religion, we shall have to take into consideration all religions and not just primitive religions; and only by so doing can we understand some of its essential features. For as the advances of science and technology have rendered magic redundant, religion has persisted, and its social role has become ever more embracing, involving persons more and more remote and no longer, as in primitive societies, bound by ties of family and kin and participating in corporate activities.

If we do not have some general statements to make about religion, we do not go beyond innumerable particular studies of the religions of particular peoples. During last century such general statements were indeed attempted, as we have seen, in the form of evolutionary and psychological and sociological hypotheses, but since these attempts at general formulations seem to have been abandoned by anthropologists, our subject has suffered from loss of common aim and method. The so-called functional method was too vague and too slick to persist, and also too much coloured by pragmatism and teleology. It rested too much on a rather flimsy biological analogy; and little was done by comparative research to support conclusions reached in particular studies – indeed, comparative studies were becoming almost obsolete.

[...]

The German social historian Max Weber[12] [...] touches on the same problem, though not so explicitly; and his 'rational' as against the 'traditional' and 'charismatic' to some degree corresponds to the opposed terms of the other writers. He distinguishes these three ideal or 'pure' types of social activity. The rational is the most intelligible type, best observed in the capitalist economics of the West, though evident in all activities subject to bureaucratic control, routinization, and their product, almost complete depersonalization. The traditional is characterized by piety for what has always existed, typical of conservative and relatively changeless societies in which affective, or affectual, sentiments predominate. Primitive societies belong to this type, though he appears to have read little about them. The charismatic, until it becomes routinized by banausic officialdom, as it inevitably does if it is successful, is the free, individual, emergence of the spirit: it is represented by the prophet, the heroic warrior, the revolutionary, &c., who appear as leaders in times of distress, and are credited with extraordinary and supernatural gifts. Such leaders may appear in any society.

Like Bergson, Max Weber distinguishes between what he calls magical religiosity, the religions of primitive and barbarous peoples, and the universalist religions of the prophets who shattered the mystical (in his sense of the word) ties of the closed society, of the exclusive groups and associations of community life; though both alike are mostly concerned with this-worldly values: health, long life, and wealth. In one sense of the word, religion is not in itself non-rational. Puritanism and apologetics and casuistry are highly rational. This being so, it follows that doctrines may create an ethos conducive to secular developments: the Protestant sects and the rise of Western capitalism are an example. But it is nevertheless in tension with secular rationality, which slowly ousts it from one sphere after another – law, politics, economics, and science – and so this leads, in Friedrich Schiller's phrase, to the 'disenchantment of the world'. In another sense, therefore, religion is non-rational, even in its rationalized forms; and although Max Weber saw it as a refuge from the complete destruction of the personality by the inevitable trends of modern life, he could not himself take shelter in it: one must rather accept imprisonment in a terrible society and be prepared to be a cog in a machine, depriving oneself of all that it means to be an individual who has personal relations with other individuals. But, though things are moving in that direction, religion still plays an important part in social life, and it is the role of the sociologist to show what that part is, not only in the rationalized societies of Western Europe but also in earlier periods of history and in other parts of the world, demonstrating how, in different types of society, different types of religion both shaped, and were shaped by, other areas of social life. In brief, we have to ask what is the role of the non-rational in social life and what parts are, and have been, played in that life by the rational, the traditional, and the charismatic. He is asking much the same questions as Pareto and Bergson.

Such are the questions – I give no more examples. Are the answers to them any more satisfactory than those we have considered in earlier lectures? I think not. They are too vague, too general, a bit too easy, and they smell strongly of pragmatist special pleading. Religion helps to preserve social cohesion, it gives men confidence, and so on. But do such explanations take us very far, and if they are true, which has to be proved, how does one set about determining in what way and in what degree does religion have these effects?

My answer to the question I have asked must be that I think that while the problem posed is, wide though it may be, a real one, the answers are not impressive. I would propose instead that we do some research into the matter. Comparative religion is a subject hardly represented in our universities, and the data of what claims to be such are derived almost entirely from books – sacred texts, theological writings, exegetics, mystical writings, and all the rest of it. But for the anthropologist or sociologist, I would suggest, this is perhaps the least significant part of religion, especially as it is very evident that the scholars who write books on the historical religions are sometimes uncertain what even key words meant to the authors of the original texts. The philological reconstructions and interpretations of these key words are only too often uncertain, contradictory, and unconvincing, e.g. in the case of the word 'god'. The student of an ancient religion or of a religion in its early phases has no other means of examining it than in texts, for the people contemporaneous with the texts are no more and cannot therefore be consulted. Serious distortions may result, as when it is said that Buddhism and Jainism are atheistic religions. No doubt they may have been regarded as systems of philosophy and psychology by the authors of the systems but we may well ask whether they were by ordinary people; and it is ordinary people the anthropologist is chiefly interested in. To him what is most important is how religious beliefs and practices affect in any society the minds, the feelings, the lives, and the interrelations of its members. There are few books which describe and analyse in any adequate manner the role of religion in any Hindu, Buddhist, Moslem, or Christian community. For the social anthropologist, religion is what religion does. I must add that such studies among primitive peoples have been few and far between. In both civilized and primitive societies herein lies an enormous and almost untilled field for research.

Furthermore, comparative religion must be comparative in a relational manner if much that is worth while is to come out of the exercise. If comparison is to stop at mere description – Christians believe this, Moslems that, and Hindus the other – or even if it goes a step further and classifies – Zoroastrianism, Judaism, and Islam are prophetic religions, Hinduism and Buddhism are mystical religions (or, certain religions are world-accepting while others are world-denying) – we are not taken very far towards an understanding of either similarities or differences. The Indian monists, the Buddhists, and the Manichees may all be alike in desiring release from the body and detachment from the world of sense, but the question we would ask is whether this common element is related to any other social facts. An attempt was made in this direction by Weber and Tawney[13] in relating certain Protestant teachings to certain economic changes. Indeed, far be it from me to belittle students of comparative religion on this score, for, as I hope I have shown in earlier lectures, we anthropologists have not made much progress in the sort of relational studies which I believe to be those required and the only ones which are likely to lead us to a vigorous sociology of religion.

Indeed, I have to conclude that I do not feel that on the whole the different theories we have reviewed, either singly or taken together, give us much more than common-sense guesses, which for the most part miss the mark. If we ask ourselves, as we naturally do, whether they have any bearing on our own religious experience – whether, shall we say, they make any more significant for us 'Peace I leave you, my peace I give unto you...' – I suppose that the answer must be that they have little, and this may make us sceptical about their value as explanations of the religions of primitives, who cannot apply the same test. The reason for this is, I believe, partly one I have already given, that the writers were seeking for explanations in terms of origins and essences instead of relations; and I would further suggest that this followed from their assumptions that the souls and spirits and gods of religion have no reality. For if they are regarded as complete illusions, then some biological, psychological, or sociological theory of how everywhere and at all times men have been stupid enough to believe in them seems to be called for. He who accepts the reality of spiritual being does not feel the same need for such explanations, for, inadequate though the conceptions of soul and God may be among primitive peoples, they are not just an illusion for him. As far as a study of religion as a factor in social life is concerned, it may make little difference whether the anthropologist is a theist or an atheist, since in either case he can only take into account what he can observe. But if either attempts to go further than this, each must pursue a different path. The non-believer seeks for some theory – biological, psychological, or sociological – which will explain the illusion; the believer seeks rather to understand the manner in which a people conceives of a reality and their relations to it. For both, religion is part of social life, but for the believer it has also another dimension. On this point I find myself in agreement with Schmidt in his confutation of Renan:

> If religion is essentially of the inner life, it follows that it can be truly grasped only from within. But beyond a doubt, this can be better done by one in whose inward consciousness an experience of religion plays a part. There is but too much danger that the other [the non-believer] will talk of religion as a blind man might of colours, or one totally devoid of ear, of a beautiful musical composition.[14]

In these lectures I have given you an account of some of the main past attempts at explaining primitive religions, and I have asked you to accept that none of them is wholly satisfactory. We seem always to have come out by the same door as we went in. But I would not wish to have you believe that so much labour has been to no purpose. If we are now able to see the errors in these theories purporting to account for primitive religions, it is partly because they were set forth, thereby inviting logical analysis of their contents and the testing of them against recorded ethnological fact and in field research. The advance in this department of social anthropology in the last forty or so years may be measured by the fact that, in the light of the knowledge we now have, we can point to the inadequacies of theories which at one time carried conviction, but we might never have obtained this knowledge had it not been for the pioneers whose writings we have reviewed.

NOTES

1. *Lectures on the Origin and Growth of Religion*, 1878, p. 218.
2. Crawley, *The Tree of Life*, 1905, p. 8.
3. Evans-Pritchard, 'Religion and the Anthropologists', *Blackfriars*, Apr. 1960, pp. 104–18.
4. H. Spencer, *The Principles of Sociology*, 1882, i. 344.
5. Op. cit. i. 149.
6. *Selected Essays on Language, Mythology and Religion*, ii. 27.

7. C. Darwin, *Voyage of the Beagle, 1831–36*, 1906 edit., chap. x.
8. F. Galton, *Narrative of an Explorer in Tropical South Africa*, 1889 edit., p. 82.
9. *Transactions of the Ethnological Society of London*, N.S., v (1867), pp. 115–26.
10. C. Resek, *Lewis Henry Morgan: American Scholar*, 1960, p. 136.
11. C. G. and B. Z. Seligman, *Pagan Tribes of the Nilotic Sudan*, 1932, p. 25.
12. *From Max Weber: Essays in Sociology*, 1947.
13. M. Weber, *The Protestant Ethic and the Spirit of Capitalism*, 1930; R. H. Tawney, *Religion and the Rise of Capitalism*, 1944 edit.
14. W. Schmidt, *The Origin and Growth of Religion*, 1931, p. 6.

CLIFFORD GEERTZ
'RELIGION AS A CULTURAL SYSTEM'

Clifford James Geertz was born in San Francisco in 1926. At the age of 17 he joined the navy to serve his country during the Second World War. However, his service was characterised not by the hectic action of war but by the desolate calm of the empty ocean, which provided ample opportunity for him to read. As part of a post-war naval scheme he received a free college education at Antioch, Ohio, where he read literature. He subsequently studied anthropology at Harvard, from which he received a PhD in 1956. During his PhD Geertz undertook fieldwork in Java, where he came to focus on religion. From 1960 to 1970 Geertz lectured at the University of Chicago, where his theoretical focus was symbolic anthropology, and his fieldwork broadened from Java, to Bali, to Indonesia, before finally seeing him relocate to the more tranquil realm of a Moroccan oasis. In 1970 Geertz took the post of Professor of Anthropology at Princeton, where he still holds an emeritus role.

Geertz's definition of religion has been highly influential both within and without the discipline of anthropology. As indicated by the material by Asad (pages 178– 95) it is not without its problems. These problems highlighted by Asad, which focus on Geertz's symbolic emphasis, however, are also part of the strength and originality of Geertz's approach. Geertz's model focuses on the role of religion in creating and sustaining a worldview, that is, the construction of a coherent system of meaning. It is also sufficiently open-ended to be able to embrace a wide range of data and institutions.

As we are to deal with meaning, let us begin with a paradigm: viz. that sacred symbols function to synthesize a people's ethos – the tone, character, and quality of their life, its moral and aesthetic style and mood – and their world-view – the picture they have of the way things in sheer actuality are, their most comprehensive ideas of order (Geertz 1958). In religious belief and practice a group's ethos is rendered intellectually reasonable by being shown to represent a way of life ideally adapted to the actual state of affairs the world-view describes, while the world-view is rendered emotionally convincing by being presented as an image of an actual state of affairs peculiarly well arranged to accommodate such a way of life. This confrontation and mutual confirmation has two fundamental effects. On the one hand, it objectivizes moral and aesthetic preferences by depicting them as the imposed conditions of life implicit in a world with a particular structure, as mere common sense given the unalterable shape of reality. On

Clifford Geertz (1966), 'Religion as a cultural system', in Michael Banton (ed.), *Anthropological Approaches to the Study of Religion*, London: Tavistock.

the other, it supports these received beliefs about the world's body by invoking deeply felt moral and aesthetic sentiments as experiential evidence for their truth. Religious symbols formulate a basic congruence between a particular style of life and a specific (if, most often, implicit) metaphysic, and in so doing sustain each with the borrowed authority of the other.

Phrasing aside, this much may perhaps be granted. The notion that religion tunes human actions to an envisaged cosmic order and projects images of cosmic order onto the plane of human experience is hardly novel. But it is hardly investigated either, so that we have very little idea of how, in empirical terms, this particular miracle is accomplished. We just know that it is done, annually, weekly, daily, for some people almost hourly; and we have an enormous ethnographic literature to demonstrate it. But the theoretical framework which would enable us to provide an analytic account of it, an account of the sort we can provide for lineage segmentation, political succession, labor exchange, or the socialization of the child, does not exist.

Let us, therefore, reduce our paradigm to a definition, for, although it is notorious that definitions establish nothing, in themselves they do, if they are carefully enough constructed, provide a useful orientation, or reorientation, of thought, such that an extended unpacking of them can be an effective way of developing and controlling a novel line of inquiry. They have the useful virtue of explicitness: they commit themselves in a way discursive prose, which, in this field especially, is always liable to substitute rhetoric for argument, does not. Without further ado, then, a *religion* is:

> (1) a system of symbols which acts to (2) establish powerful, pervasive, and long-lasting moods and motivations in men by (3) formulating conceptions of a general order of existence and (4) clothing these conceptions with such an aura of factuality that (5) the moods and motivations seem uniquely realistic.

I. A system of symbols which acts to . . .

Such a tremendous weight is being put on the term 'symbol' here that our first move must be to decide with some precision what we are going to mean by it. This is no easy task, for, rather like 'culture', 'symbol' has been used to refer to a great variety of things, often a number of them at the same time. In some hands it is used for anything which signifies something else to someone: dark clouds are the symbolic precursors of an oncoming rain. In others it is used only for explicitly conventional signs of one sort or another: a red flag is a symbol of danger, a white of surrender. In others it is confined to something which expresses in an oblique and figurative manner that which cannot be stated in a direct and literal one, so that there are symbols in poetry but not in science, and symbolic logic is misnamed. In yet others, however (Langer 1953, 1960, 1962), it is used for any object, act, event, quality, or relation which serves as a vehicle for a conception – the conception is the symbol's 'meaning' – and that is the approach I shall follow here. The number 6, written, imagined, laid out as a row of stones, or even punched into the program tapes of a computer is a symbol. But so also is the Cross, talked about, visualized, shaped worriedly in air or fondly fingered at the neck, the expanse of painted canvas called *Guernica* or the bit of painted stone called a churinga, the word 'reality', or even the morpheme '-ing'. They are all symbols, or at least symbolic elements, because they are tangible formulations of notions, abstractions from experience fixed in perceptible forms, concrete embodiments of ideas, attitudes, judgements, longings, or beliefs. To undertake the study of cultural activity – activity in which symbolism forms the positive content – is thus not to abandon social analysis for a Platonic cave of shadows, to enter into a mentalistic world of introspective psychology or, worse, speculative philosophy, and wander there forever in a haze of 'Cognitions', 'Affections', 'Conations', and other elusive entities. Cultural acts, the construction, apprehension, and utilization of symbolic forms, are social events like any other; they are as public as marriage and as observable as agriculture.

They are not, however, exactly the same thing; or, more precisely, the symbolic dimension of social events is, like the psychological, itself theoretically abstractable from those events as empirical totalities. There is still, to paraphrase a remark of Kenneth Burke's (1941: 9), a difference between building a house and drawing up a plan for building a house, and reading a poem about having children by marriage is not quite the same thing as having children by marriage. Even though the building of the house may proceed under the guidance of the plan or – a less likely occurrence – the having of children may be motivated by a reading of the poem, there is something to be said for not confusing our traffic with symbols with our traffic with objects or human beings, for these latter are not in themselves symbols, however often they may function as such.[1] No matter how deeply interfused the cultural, the social, and the psychological may be in the everyday life of houses, farms, poems, and marriages, it is useful to distinguish them in analysis, and, so doing, to isolate the generic traits of each against the normalized background of the other two (Parsons and Shils 1951).

So far as culture patterns, i.e. systems or complexes of symbols, are concerned, the generic trait which is of first importance for us here is that they are extrinsic sources of information (Geertz 1964a). By 'extrinsic', I mean only that – unlike genes, for example – they lie outside the boundaries of the individual organism as such in that intersubjective world of common understandings into which all human individuals are born, in which they pursue their separate careers, and which they leave persisting behind them after they die (Schutz 1962). By 'sources of information', I mean only that – like genes – they provide a blueprint or template in terms of which processes external to themselves can be given a definite form (Horowitz 1956).

As the order of bases in a strand of DNA forms a coded program, a set of instructions, or a recipe, for the synthesization of the structurally complex proteins which shape organic functioning, so culture patterns provide such programs for the institution of the social and psychological processes which shape public behavior. Though the sort of information and the mode of its transmission are vastly different in the two cases, this comparison of gene and symbol is more than a strained analogy of the familiar 'social heredity' sort. It is actually a substantial relationship, for it is precisely the fact that genetically programmed processes are so highly generalized in men, as compared with lower animals, that culturally programmed ones are so important, only because human behavior is so loosely determined by intrinsic sources of information that extrinsic sources are so vital (Geertz 1962). To build a dam a beaver needs only an appropriate site and the proper materials – his mode of procedure is shaped by his physiology. But man, whose genes are silent on the building trades, needs also a conception of what it is to build a dam, a conception he can get only from some symbolic source – a blueprint, a textbook, or a string of speech by someone who already knows how dams are built, or, of course, from manipulating graphic or linguistic elements in such a way as to attain for himself a conception of what dams are and how they are built.

This point is sometimes put in the form of an argument that cultural patterns are 'models', that they are sets of symbols whose relations to one another 'model' relations among entities, processes or what-have-you in physical, organic, social, or psychological systems by 'paralleling', 'imitating', or 'simulating' them (Craik 1952). The term 'model' has, however, two senses – an 'of' sense and a 'for' sense – and though these are but aspects of the same basic concept they are very much worth distinguishing for analytic purposes. In the first, what is stressed is the manipulation of symbol structures so as to bring them, more or less closely, into parallel with the pre-established non-symbolic system, as when we grasp how dams work by developing a theory of hydraulics or constructing a flow chart. The theory or chart models physical relationships in such a way – i.e. by expressing their structure in synoptic form – as to render them apprehensible: it is a model *of* 'reality'. In the second, what is stressed is the manipulation of the non-symbolic systems in terms of the relationships expressed in the symbolic, as when we construct a dam according to the specifications implied in an hydraulic theory or the conclusions drawn from a flow chart. Here, the theory is a model under whose guidance physical relationships are organized: it is a model *for* 'reality'. For psychological and social systems, and for cultural models that we would not ordinarily refer to as 'theories', but rather as 'doctrines', 'melodies', or 'rites', the case is in no way different. Unlike genes, and other non-symbolic information sources, which are only models *for*, not models *of*, culture patterns have an intrinsic double aspect: they give meaning, i.e. objective conceptual form, to social and psychological reality both by shaping themselves to it and by shaping it to themselves.

It is, in fact, this double aspect which sets true symbols off from other sorts of significative forms. Models *for* are found, as the gene example suggests, through the whole order of nature, for wherever there is a communication of pattern such programs are, in simple logic, required. Among animals, imprint learning is perhaps the most striking example, because what such learning involves is the automatic presentation of an appropriate sequence of behavior by a model animal in the presence of a learning animal which serves, equally automatically, to call out and stabilize a certain set of responses genetically built into the learning animal (Lorenz 1952). The communicative dance of two bees, one of which has found nectar and the other of which seeks it, is another, somewhat different, more complexly coded, example (von Frisch 1962). Craik (1952) has even suggested that the thin trickle of water which first finds its way down from a mountain spring to the sea and smooths a little channel for the greater volume of water that follows after it plays a sort of model *for* function. But models *of* – linguistic, graphic, mechanical, natural, etc. processes which function not to provide sources of information in terms of which other processes can be patterned, but to represent those patterned processes as such, to express their structure in an alternative medium – are much rarer and may perhaps be confined, among living animals, to man. The perception of the structural congruence between one set of processes, activities, relations, entities, etc. and another set for which it acts as a program, so that the program can be taken as a representation, or conception – a symbol – of the programmed, is the essence of human thought. The inter-transposability of models *for* and models *of* which symbolic formulation makes possible is the distinctive characteristic of our mentality.

2. ... to establish powerful, pervasive, and long-lasting moods and motivations in men by ...

So far as religious symbols and symbol systems are concerned this inter-transposability is clear. The endurance, courage, independence, perseverance, and passionate willfulness in the vision quest practices of the Plains Indian are the same flamboyant virtues by which he attempts to live: while achieving a sense of revelation he stabilizes a sense of direction (Lowie 1924). The consciousness of defaulted obligation, secreted guilt, and, when a confession is obtained, public shame in which Manus' seance rehearses him are the same sentiments that underlie the sort of duty ethic by which his property-conscious society is maintained: the gaining of an absolution involves the forging of a conscience (Fortune 1935). And the same self-discipline which rewards a Javanese mystic staring fixedly into the flame of a lamp with what he takes to be an intimation of divinity drills him in that rigorous control of emotional expression which is necessary to a man who would follow a quietistic style of life (Geertz 1960). Whether one sees the conception of a personal guardian spirit, a family tutelary or an immanent God as synoptic formulations of the character of reality or as templates for producing reality with such a character seems largely arbitrary, a matter of which aspect, the model *of* or model *for*, one wants for the moment to bring into focus. The concrete symbols involved – one or another mythological figure materializing in the wilderness, the skull of the deceased household head hanging censoriously in the rafters, or a disembodied 'voice in the stillness' soundlessly chanting enigmatic classical poetry – point in either direction. They both express the world's climate and shape it.

They shape it by inducing in the worshipper a certain distinctive set of dispositions (tendencies, capacities, propensities, skills, habits, liabilities, pronenesses) which lend a chronic character to the flow of his activity and the quality of his experience. A disposition describes not an activity or an occurrence but a probability of an activity being performed or an occurrence occurring in certain circumstances:

> When a cow is said to be a ruminant, or a man is said to be a cigarette-smoker, it is not being said that the cow is ruminating now or that the man is smoking a cigarette now. To be a ruminant is to tend to ruminate from time to time, and to be a cigarette-smoker is to be in the habit of smoking cigarettes. (Ryle 1949: 117)

Similarly, to be pious is not to be performing something we would call an act of piety, but to be liable to perform such acts. So, too, with the Plains Indian's bravura, the Manus' compunctiousness, or the Javanese's quietism which, in their contexts, form the substance of piety. The virtue of this sort of view of what are usually called 'mental traits' or, if the Cartesianism is unavowed, 'psychological forces' (both unobjectionable enough terms in themselves) is that it gets them out of any dim and inaccessible realm of private sensation into that same well-lit world of observables in which reside the brittleness of glass, the inflammability of paper, and, to return to the metaphor, the dampness of England.

So far as religious activities are concerned (and learning a myth by heart is as much a religious activity as detaching one's finger at the knuckle), two somewhat different sorts of disposition are induced by them: moods and motivations.

A motivation is a persisting tendency, a chronic inclination to perform certain sorts of act and experience certain sorts of feeling in certain sorts of situation, the 'sorts' being commonly very heterogenous and rather ill-defined classes in all three cases:

> ... on hearing that a man is vain [i.e. motivated by vanity] we expect him to behave in certain ways, namely to talk a lot about himself, to cleave to the society of the eminent, to reject criticisms, to seek the footlights and to disengage himself from conversations about the merits of others. We expect him to indulge in roseate daydreams about his own successes, to avoid recalling past failures and to plan for his own advancement. To be vain is to tend to act in these and innumerable other kindred ways. Certainly we also expect the vain man to feel certain pangs and flutters in certain situations; we expect him to have an acute sinking feeling when an eminent person forgets his name, and to feel buoyant of heart and light of toe on hearing of the misfortunes of his rivals. But feelings of pique and buoyancy are not more directly indicative of vanity than are public acts of boasting or private acts of daydreaming... (Ryle 1949: 86)

Similarly for any motivations. As a motive, 'flamboyant courage' consists in such enduring propensities as to fast in the wilderness, to conduct solitary raids on enemy camps, and to thrill to the thought of counting coup. 'Moral circumspection' consists in such ingrained tendencies as to honor onerous promises, to confess secret sins in the face of severe public disapproval, and to feel guilty when vague and generalized accusations are made at seances. And 'dispassionate tranquillity' consists in such persistent inclinations as to maintain one's poise come hell or high water, to experience distaste in the presence of even moderate emotional displays, and to indulge in contentless contemplations of featureless objects. Motives are thus neither acts (i.e. intentional behaviors) nor feelings, but liabilities to perform particular classes of act or have particular classes of feeling. And when we say that a man is religious, i.e. motivated by religion, this is at least part – though only part – of what we mean.

Another part of what we mean is that he has, when properly stimulated, a susceptibility to fall into certain moods, moods we sometimes lump together under such covering terms as 'reverential', 'solemn', or 'worshipful'. Such generalized rubrics actually conceal, however, the enormous empirical variousness of the dispositions involved, and, in fact, tend to assimilate them to the unusually grave tone of most of our own religious life. The moods that sacred symbols induce, at different times and in different places, range from exultation to melancholy, from self-confidence to self-pity, from an incorrigible playfulness to a bland listlessness – to say nothing of the erogenous power of so many of the world's myths and rituals. No more than there is a single sort of motivation one can call piety is there a single sort of mood one can call worshipful.

The major difference between moods and motivations is that where the latter are, so to speak, vectorial qualities, the former are merely scalar. Motives have a directional cast, they describe a certain overall course, gravitate toward certain, usually temporary, consummations. But moods vary only as to intensity: they go nowhere. They spring from certain circumstances but they are responsive to no ends. Like fogs, they just settle and lift; like scents, suffuse and evaporate. When present they are totalistic: if one is sad everything and everybody seems dreary; if one is gay, everything and everybody seems splendid. Thus, though a man can be vain, brave, willful and independent at the same time, he can't very well be playful and listless, or exultant and melancholy, at the same time (Ryle 1949: 99). Further, where motives persist for more or less extended periods of time, moods merely recur with greater or lesser frequency, coming and going for what are often quite unfathomable reasons. But perhaps the most important difference, so far as we are concerned, between moods and motivations is that motivations are 'made meaningful' with reference to the ends toward which they are conceived to conduce, whereas moods are 'made meaningful' with reference to the conditions from which they are conceived to spring. We interpret motives in terms of their consummations, but we interpret moods in terms of their sources. We say that a person is industrious because he wishes to succeed, we say that a person is worried because he is conscious of the hanging threat of nuclear holocaust. And this is no less the case when the interpretations invoked are ultimate. Charity becomes Christian charity when it is enclosed in a conception of God's purposes; optimism is Christian optimism when it is grounded in a particular conception of God's nature. The assiduity of the Navaho finds its rationale in a belief that, since 'reality' operates mechanically, it is coercible; their chronic fearfulness finds its rationale in a conviction that, however 'reality' operates, it is both enormously powerful and terribly dangerous (Kluckhohn 1949).

3. . . . by formulating conceptions of a general order of existence and . . .

That the symbols or symbol systems which induce and define dispositions we set off as religious and those which place those dispositions in a cosmic framework are the same symbols ought to occasion no surprise. For what else do we mean by saying that a particular mood of awe is religious and not secular except that it springs from entertaining a conception of all-pervading vitality like mana and not from a visit to the Grand Canyon? Or that a particular case of asceticism is an example of a religious motivation except that it is directed toward the achievement of an unconditioned end like nirvana and not a conditioned one like weight-reduction? If sacred symbols did not at one and the same time induce dispositions in human beings and formulate, however obliquely, inarticulately, or unsystematically, general ideas of order, then the empirical differentia of religious activity or religious experience would not exist. A man can indeed be said to be 'religious' about golf, but not merely if he pursues it with passion and plays it on Sundays: he must also see it as symbolic of some transcendent truths. And the pubescent boy gazing soulfully into the eyes of the pubescent girl in a William Steig cartoon and murmuring, 'There is something about you, Ethel, which gives me a sort of religious feeling', is, like most adolescents, confused. What any particular religion affirms about the fundamental nature of reality may be obscure, shallow, or, all too often, perverse, but it must, if it is not to consist of the mere collection of received practices and conventional sentiments we usually refer to as moralism, affirm something. If one were to essay a minimal definition of religion today it would perhaps not be Tylor's famous 'belief in spiritual beings', to which Goody (1961), wearied of theoretical subtleties, has lately urged us to return, but rather what Salvador de Madariaga has called 'the relatively modest dogma that God is not mad'.

Usually, of course, religions affirm very much more than this: we believe, as James (1904: vol. 2, 299) remarked, all that we can and would believe everything if we only could. The thing we seem least able to tolerate is a threat to our powers of conception, a suggestion that our ability to create, grasp, and use symbols may fail us, for were this to happen we would be more helpless, as I have already pointed out, than the beavers. The extreme generality, diffuseness, and variability of man's innate (i.e. genetically programmed) response capacities means that without the assistance of cultural patterns he would be functionally incomplete, not merely a talented ape who had, like some under-privileged child, unfortunately been prevented from realizing his full potentialities, but a kind of formless monster with neither sense of direction nor power of self-control, a chaos of spasmodic impulses and vague emotions (Geertz 1962). Man depends upon symbols and symbol systems with a dependence so great as to be decisive for his creatural viability and, as a result, his sensitivity to even the remotest indication that they may prove unable to cope with one or another aspect of experience raises within him the gravest sort of anxiety:

> [Man] can adapt himself somehow to anything his imagination can cope with; but he cannot deal with Chaos. Because his characteristic function and highest asset is conception, his greatest fright is to meet what he cannot construe – the 'uncanny', as it is popularly called. It need not be a new object; we do meet new things, and 'understand' them promptly, if tentatively, by the nearest analogy, when our minds are functioning freely; but under mental stress even perfectly familiar things may become suddenly disorganized and give us the horrors. Therefore our most important assets are always the symbols of our general *orientation* in nature, on the earth, in society, and in what we are doing: the symbols of our *Weltanschauung* and

Lebensanschauung. Consequently, in a primitive society, a daily ritual is incorporated in common activities, in eating, washing, fire-making, etc., as well as in pure ceremonial; because the need of reasserting the tribal morale and recognizing its cosmic conditions is constantly felt. In Christian Europe the Church brought men daily (in some orders even hourly) to their knees, to enact if not to contemplate their assent to the ultimate concepts. (Langer 1960: 287, italics original)

There are at least three points where chaos – a tumult of events which lack not just interpretations but *interpretability* – threatens to break in upon man: at the limits of his analytic capacities, at the limits of his powers of endurance, and at the limits of his moral insight. Bafflement, suffering, and a sense of intractable ethical paradox are all, if they become intense enough or are sustained long enough, radical challenges to the proposition that life is comprehensible and that we can, by taking thought, orient ourselves effectively within it – challenges with which any religion, however 'primitive', which hopes to persist must attempt somehow to cope.

Of the three issues, it is the first which has been least investigated by modern social anthropologists (though Evans-Pritchard's (1937) classic discussion of why granaries fall on some Azande and not on others, is a notable exception). Even to consider people's religious beliefs as attempts to bring anomalous events or experiences – death, dreams, mental fugues, volcanic eruptions, or marital infidelity – within the circle of the at least potentially explicable seems to smack of Tyloreanism or worse. But it does appear to be a fact that at least some men – in all probability, most men – are unable to leave unclarified problems of analysis merely unclarified, just to look at the stranger features of the world's landscape in dumb astonishment or bland apathy without trying to develop, however fantastic, inconsistent, or simple-minded, some notions as to how such features might be reconciled with the more ordinary deliverances of experience. Any chronic failure of one's explanatory apparatus, the complex of received culture patterns (common sense, science, philosophical speculation, myth) one has for mapping the empirical world, to explain things which cry out for explanation tends to lead to a deep disquiet – a tendency rather more widespread and a disquiet rather deeper than we have sometimes supposed since the pseudo-science view of religious belief was, quite rightfully, deposed. After all, even that high priest of heroic atheism, Lord Russell, once remarked that although the problem of the existence of God had never bothered him, the ambiguity of certain mathematical axioms had threatened to unhinge his mind. And Einstein's profound dissatisfaction with quantum mechanics was based on a – surely religious – inability to believe that, as he put it, God plays dice with the universe.

[. . .]

The second experiential challenge in whose face the meaningfulness of a particular pattern of life threatens to dissolve into a chaos of thingless names and nameless things – the problem of suffering – has been rather more investigated, or at least described, mainly because of the great amount of attention given in works on tribal religion to what are perhaps its two main loci: illness and mourning. Yet for all the fascinated interest in the emotional aura that surrounds these extreme situations, there has been, with a few exceptions such as Lienhardt's recent (1961: 151ff.) discussion of Dinka divining, little conceptual advance over the sort of crude confidence-type theory set forth by Malinowski: viz. that religion helps one to endure 'situations of emotional stress' by 'open[ing] up escapes from such situations and such impasses as offer no empirical way out except by ritual and belief into the domain of the supernatural' (1948: 67). The inadequacy of this 'theology of optimism', as Nadel (1957) rather drily called it, is, of course, radical. Over its career religion has probably disturbed men as much as it has cheered them; forced them into a head-on, unblinking confrontation of the fact that they are born to trouble as often as it has enabled them to avoid such a confrontation by projecting them into [a] sort of infantile fairy-tale world where – Malinowski again (1948: 67) – 'hope cannot fail nor desire deceive'. With the possible exception of Christian Science, there are few if any religious traditions, 'great' or 'little', in which the proposition that life hurts is not strenuously affirmed and in some it is virtually glorified:

> She was an old [Ba-Ila] woman of a family with a long genealogy. Leza, 'the Besetting-One', stretched out his hand against the family. He slew her mother and father while she was yet a child, and in the course of years all connected with her perished. She said to herself, 'Surely I shall keep those who sit on my thighs.' But no, even they, the children of her children, were taken from her. . . . Then came into her heart a desperate resolution to find God and to ask the meaning of it all. . . . So she began to travel, going through country after country, always with the thought in her mind: 'I shall come to where the earth ends and there I shall find a road to God and I shall ask him: "What have I done to thee that thou afflictist me in this manner?"' She never found where the earth ends, but though disappointed she did not give up her search, and as she passed through the different countries they asked her, 'What have you come for, old woman?' And the answer would be, 'I am seeking Leza.' 'Seeking Leza! For what?' 'My brothers, you ask me! Here in the nations is there one who suffers as I have suffered?' And they would ask again, 'How have you suffered?' 'In this way. I am alone. As you see me, a solitary old woman; that is how I am!' And they answered, 'Yes, we see. That is how you are! Bereaved of friends and husband? In what do you differ from others? The Besetting-One

sits on the back of every one of us and we cannot shake him off.' She never obtained her desire: she died of a broken heart. (Smith and Dale 1920: II, 197ff; quoted in Radin 1957: 100–1)

As a religious problem, the problem of suffering is, paradoxically, not how to avoid suffering but how to suffer, how to make of physical pain, personal loss, worldly defeat, or the helpless contemplation of others' agony something bearable, supportable – something, as we say, sufferable. It was in this effort that the Ba-Ila woman – perhaps necessarily, perhaps not – failed and, literally not knowing how to feel about what had happened to her, how to suffer, perished in confusion and despair. Where the more intellective aspects of what Weber called the Problem of Meaning are a matter affirming the ultimate explicability of experience, the more affective aspects are a matter of affirming its ultimate sufferableness. As religion on one side anchors the power of our symbolic resources for formulating analytic ideas in an authoritative conception of the overall shape of reality, so on another side it anchors the power of our, also symbolic, resources for expressing emotions – moods, sentiments, passions, affections, feelings – in a similar conception of its pervasive tenor, its inherent tone and temper. For those able to embrace them, and for so long as they are able to embrace them, religious symbols provide a cosmic guarantee not only for their ability to comprehend the world, but also, comprehending it, to give a precision to their feeling, a definition to their emotions which enables them, morosely or joyfully, grimly or cavalierly, to endure it.

[. . .]

The problem of suffering passes easily into the problem of evil, for if suffering is severe enough it usually, though not always, seems morally undeserved as well, at least to the sufferer. But they are not, however, exactly the same thing – a fact I think Weber, too influenced by the biases of a monotheistic tradition in which, as the various aspects of human experience must be conceived to proceed from a single, voluntaristic source, man's pain reflects directly on God's goodness, did not fully recognize in his generalization of the dilemmas of Christian theodicy Eastward. For where the problem of suffering is concerned with threats to our ability to put our 'undisciplined squads of emotion' into some sort of soldierly order, the problem of evil is concerned with threats to our ability to make sound moral judgements. What is involved in the problem of evil is not the adequacy of our symbolic resources to govern our affective life, but the adequacy of those resources to provide a workable set of ethical criteria, normative guides to govern our action. The vexation here is the gap between things as they are and as they ought to be if our conceptions of right and wrong make sense, the gap between what we deem various individuals deserve and what we see that they get – a phenomenon summed up in that profound quatrain:

> The rain falls on the just
> And on the unjust fella;
> But mainly upon the just,
> Because the unjust has the just's umbrella.

[. . .]

Thus the problem of evil, or perhaps one should say the problem *about* evil, is in essence the same sort of problem of or about bafflement and the problem of or about suffering. The strange opacity of certain empirical events, the dumb senselessness of intense or inexorable pain, and the enigmatic unaccountability of gross iniquity all raise the uncomfortable suspicion that perhaps the world, and hence man's life in the world, has no genuine order at all – no empirical regularity, no emotional form, no moral coherence. And the religious response to this suspicion is in each case the same: the formulation, by means of symbols, of an image of such a genuine order of the world which will account for, and even celebrate, the perceived ambiguities, puzzles, and paradoxes in human experience. The effort is not to deny the undeniable – that there are unexplained events, that life hurts, or that rain falls upon the just – but to deny that there are inexplicable events, that life is unendurable, and that justice is a mirage. The principles which constitute the moral order may indeed often elude men, as Lienhardt puts it, in the same way as fully satisfactory explanations of anomalous events or effective forms for the expression of feeling often elude them. What is important, to a religious man at least, is that this elusiveness be accounted for, that it be not the result of the fact that there are no such principles, explanations, or forms, that life is absurd and the attempt to make moral, intellectual or emotional sense out of experience is bootless. The Dinka can admit, in fact insist upon, the moral ambiguities and contradictions of life as they live it because these ambiguities and contradictions are seen not as ultimate, but as the 'rational', 'natural', 'logical' (one may choose one's own adjective here, for none of them is truly adequate) outcome of the moral structure of reality which the myth of the withdrawn 'Divinity' depicts, or as Lienhardt says, 'images'.

The Problem of Meaning in each of its intergrading aspects (how these aspects in fact intergrade in each particular case, what sort of interplay there is between the sense of analytic, emotional, and moral impotence, seems to me one of the outstanding, and except for Weber untouched, problems for comparative research in this whole field) is a matter of affirming, or at least recognizing, the inescapability of ignorance, pain, and injustice on the human plane while simultaneously denying that these irrationalities are characteristic of the world as a whole. And it is in terms of religious symbolism, a symbolism relating man's sphere of existence to a wider sphere within which it is conceived to rest, that both the affirmation and the denial are made.[2]

4. ... and clothing those conceptions with such an aura of factuality that ...

There arises here, however, a profounder question: how is it that this denial comes to be believed? how is it that the religious man moves from a troubled perception of experienced disorder to a more or less settled conviction of fundamental order? just what does 'belief' mean in a religious context? Of all the problems surrounding attempts to conduct anthropological analysis of religion this is the one that has perhaps been most troublesome and therefore the most often avoided, usually by relegating it to psychology, that raffish outcast discipline to which social anthropologists are forever consigning phenomena they are unable to deal with within the framework of a denatured Durkheimianism. But the problem will not go away, it is not 'merely' psychological (nothing social is), and no anthropological theory of religion which fails to attack it is worthy of the name. We have been trying to stage Hamlet without the Prince quite long enough.

It seems to me that it is best to begin any approach to this issue with frank recognition that religious belief involves not a Baconian induction from everyday experience – for then we should all be agnostics – but rather a prior acceptance of authority which transforms that experience. The existence of bafflement, pain, and moral paradox – of The Problem of Meaning – is one of the things that drive men toward belief in gods, devils, spirits, totemic principles, or the spiritual efficacy of cannibalism (an enfolding sense of beauty or a dazzling perception of power are others), but it is not the basis upon which those beliefs rest, but rather their most important field of application:

> We point to the state of the world as illustrative of doctrine, but never as evidence for it. So Belsen illustrates a world of original sin, but original sin is not an hypothesis to account for happenings like Belsen. We justify a particular religious belief by showing its place in the total religious conception; we justify a religious belief as a whole by referring to authority. We accept authority because we discover it at some point in the world at which we worship, at which we accept the lordship of something not ourselves. We do not worship authority, but we accept authority as defining the worshipful. So someone may discover the possibility of worship in the life of the Reformed Churches and accept the Bible as authoritative; or in the Roman Church and accept papal authority. (MacIntyre 1957: 201–2)

This is, of course, a Christian statement of the matter; but it is not to be despised on that account. In tribal religions authority lies in the persuasive power of traditional imagery; in mystical ones in the apodictic force of supersensible experience; in charismatic ones in the hypnotic attraction of an extraordinary personality. But the priority of the acceptance of an authoritative criterion in religious matters over the revelation which is conceived to flow from that acceptance is not less complete than in scriptural or hieratic ones. The basic axiom underlying what we may perhaps call 'the religious perspective' is everywhere the same: he who would know must first believe.

But to speak of 'the religious perspective' is, by implication, to speak of one perspective among others. A perspective is a mode of seeing, in that extended sense of 'see' in which it means 'discern', 'apprehend', 'understand', or 'grasp'. It is a particular way of looking at life, a particular manner of construing the world, as when we speak of an historical perspective, a scientific perspective, an aesthetic perspective, a common-sense perspective, or even the bizarre perspective embodied in dreams and in hallucinations.[3] The question then comes down to, first, what is 'the religious perspective' generically considered, as differentiated from other perspectives; and second, how do men come to adopt it.

If we place the religious perspective against the background of three of the other major perspectives in terms of which men construe the world – the common-sensical, the scientific, and the aesthetic – its special character emerges more sharply. What distinguishes common sense as a mode of 'seeing' is, as Schutz (1962) has pointed out, a simple acceptance of the world, its objects, and its processes as being just what they seem to be – what is sometimes called naïve realism – and the pragmatic motive, the wish to act upon that world so as to bend it to one's practical purposes, to master it, or so far as that proves impossible, to adjust to it. The world of everyday life, itself, of course, a cultural product, for it is framed in terms of the symbolic conceptions of 'stubborn fact' handed down from generation to generation, is the established scene and given object of our actions. Like Mt. Everest it is just there and the thing to do with it, if one feels the need to do anything with it at all, is to climb it. In the scientific perspective it is precisely this givenness which disappears (Schutz 1962). Deliberate doubt and systematic inquiry, the suspension of the pragmatic motive in favor of disinterested observation, the attempt to analyze the world in terms of formal concepts whose relationship to the informal conceptions of common sense become increasingly problematic – these are the hallmarks of the attempt to grasp the world scientifically. And as for the aesthetic perspective, which under the rubric of 'the aesthetic attitude' has been perhaps most exquisitely examined, it involves a different sort of suspension of naïve realism and practical interest, in that instead of questioning the credentials of everyday experience that experience is merely ignored in favor of an eager dwelling upon appearances, an engrossment in surfaces, an absorption in things, as we say, 'in themselves':

> The function of artistic illusion is not "make-believe" ... but the very
> opposite, disengagement from belief – the contemplation of sensory
> qualities without their usual meanings of "here's that chair", "That's
> my telephone" ... etc. The knowledge that what is before us has no
> practical significance in the world is what enables us to give attention
> to its appearance as such. (Langer 1953: 49)

And like the common-sensical and the scientific (or the historical, the
philosophical, and the autistic), this perspective, this 'way of seeing' is not
the product of some mysterious Cartesian chemistry, but is induced, mediated, and in fact created by means of symbols. It is the artist's skill which
can produce those curious quasi-objects – poems, dramas, sculptures, sym-
phonies – which, dissociating themselves from the solid world of common
sense, take on the special sort of eloquence only sheer appearances can
achieve.

The religious perspective differs from the common-sensical in that, as
already pointed out, it moves beyond the realities of everyday life to wider
ones which correct and complete them, and its defining concern is not action upon those wider realities but acceptance of them, faith in them. It
differs from the scientific perspective in that it questions the realities of everyday life not out of an institutionalized scepticism which dissolves the
world's givenness into a swirl of probabilistic hypotheses, but in terms of
what it takes to be wider, non-hypothetical truths. Rather than detachment,
its watchword is commitment; rather than analysis, encounter. And it differs from art in that instead of effecting a disengagement from the whole
question of factuality, deliberately manufacturing an air of semblance and
illusion, it deepens the concern with fact and seeks to create an aura of utter
actuality. It is this sense of the 'really real' upon which the religious perspective rests and which the symbolic activities of religion as a cultural system
are devoted to producing, intensifying, and, so far as possible, rendering in-
violable by the discordant revelations of secular experience. It is, again, the
imbuing of a certain specific complex of symbols – of the metaphysic they
formulate and the style of life they recommend – with a persuasive authority
which, from an analytic point of view is the essence of religious action.

Which brings us, at length, to ritual. For it is in ritual – i.e. consecrated
behavior – that this conviction that religious conceptions are veridical and
that religious directives are sound is somehow generated. It is in some sort
of ceremonial form – even if that form be hardly more than the recitation
of a myth, the consultation of an oracle, or the decoration of a grave – that
the moods and motivations which sacred symbols induce in men and the
general conceptions of the order of existence which they formulate for men
meet and reinforce one another. In a ritual, the world as lived and the world

as imagined, fused under the agency of a single set of symbolic forms, turn out to be the same world, producing thus that idiosyncratic transformation in one's sense of reality to which Santayana refers in my epigraph. Whatever role divine intervention may or may not play in the creation of faith – and it is not the business of the scientist to pronounce upon such matters one way or the other – it is, primarily at least, out of the context of concrete acts of religious observance that religious conviction emerges on the human plane.

However, though any religious ritual, no matter how apparently automatic or conventional (if it is truly automatic or merely conventional it is not religious), involves this symbolic fusion of ethos and world-view, it is mainly certain more elaborate and usually more public ones, ones in which a broad range of moods and motivations on the one hand and of metaphysical conceptions on the other are caught up, which shape the spiritual consciousness of a people. Employing a useful term introduced by Singer (1955), we may call these full-blown ceremonies 'cultural performances' and note that they represent not only the point at which the dispositional and conceptual aspects of religious life converge for the believer, but also the point at which the interaction between them can be most readily examined by the detached observer:

> Whenever Madrasi Brahmans (and non-Brahmans, too, for that matter) wished to exhibit to me some feature of Hinduism, they always referred to, or invited me to see, a particular rite or ceremony in the life cycle, in a temple festival, or in the general sphere of religious and cultural performances. Reflecting on this in the course of my interviews and observations I found that the more abstract generalizations about Hinduism (my own as well as those I heard) could generally be checked, directly or indirectly, against these observable performances. (Singer 1958)

Of course, all cultural performances are not religious performances, and the line between those that are and artistic, or even political ones is often not so easy to draw in practice, for, like social forms, symbolic forms can serve multiple purposes. But the point is that, paraphrasing slightly, Indians – 'and perhaps all peoples' – seem to think of their religion 'as encapsulated in these discrete performances which they [can] exhibit to visitors and to themselves' (Singer 1955). The mode of exhibition is however radically different for the two sorts of witness, a fact seemingly overlooked by those who would argue that 'religion is a form of human art' (Firth 1951: 250). Where for 'visitors' religious performances can, in the nature of the case, only be presentations of a particular religious perspective, and thus aesthetically appreciated or scientifically dissected, for participants they are in addition enactments, materializations, realizations of it – not only models *of* what they believe, but also models *for* the believing of it. In these plastic dramas men attain their faith as they portray it.

[. . .]

5. . . . *that the moods and motivations seem uniquely realistic*

But no one, not even a saint, lives in the world religious symbols formulate all of the time, and the majority of men live in it only at moments. The everyday world of common-sense objects and practical acts is, as Schutz (1962: 226ff.) says, the paramount reality in human experience – paramount in the sense that it is the world in which we are most solidly rooted, whose inherent actuality we can hardly question (however much we may question certain portions of it), and from whose pressures and requirements we can least escape. A man, even large groups of men, may be aesthetically insensitive, religiously unconcerned, and unequipped to pursue formal scientific analysis, but he cannot be completely lacking in common sense and survive. The dispositions which religious rituals induce thus have their most important impact – from a human point of view – outside the boundaries of the ritual itself as they reflect back to color the individual's conception of the established world of bare fact. The peculiar tone that marks the Plains vision quest, the Manus confession, or the Javanese mystical exercise pervades areas of the life of these peoples far beyond the immediately religious, impressing upon them a distinctive style in the sense both of a dominant mood and a characteristic movement. [. . .] Religion is sociologically interesting not because, as vulgar positivism would have it (Leach 1954; 10ff.), it describes the social order (which, in so far as it does, it does not only very obliquely but very incompletely), but because, like environment, political power, wealth, jural obligation, personal affection, and a sense of beauty, it shapes it.

The movement back and forth between the religious perspective and the common-sense perspective is actually one of the more obvious empirical occurrences on the social scene, though, again, one of the most neglected by social anthropologists, virtually all of whom have seen it happen countless times. Religious belief has usually been presented as an homogeneous characteristic of an individual, like his place of residence, his occupational role, his kinship position, and so on. But religious belief in the midst of ritual, where it engulfs the total person, transporting him, so far as he is concerned, into another mode of existence, and religious belief as the pale, remembered reflection of that experience in the midst of everyday life are not precisely the same thing, and the failure to realize this has led to some confusion, most especially in connection with the so-called 'primitive mentality' problem. Much of the difficulty between Lévy-Bruhl (1926) and Malinowski (1948) on the nature of 'native thought', for example, arises from a lack of full recognition of this distinction; for where the French philosopher was concerned with the view of reality savages adopted when taking a specifically religious perspective, the Polish-English ethnographer was concerned with that which they adopted when taking a strictly common-sense one. Both perhaps vaguely sensed that they were not talking about exactly the same thing, but where they went astray was in failing to give a specific accounting of the way in which these two forms of 'thought' – or, as I would rather say, these two modes of symbolic formulation – interacted, so that where Lévy-Bruhl's savages tended to live, despite his postludial disclaimers, in a world composed entirely of mystical encounters, Malinowski's tended to live, despite his stress on the functional importance of religion, in a world composed entirely of practical actions. They became reductionists (an idealist is as much of a reductionist as a materialist) in spite of themselves because they failed to see man as moving more or less easily, and very frequently, between radically contrasting ways of looking at the world, ways which are not continuous with one another but separated by cultural gaps across which Kierkegaardian leaps must be made in both directions:

> There are as many innumerable kinds of different shock experiences as there are different finite provinces of meaning upon which I may bestow the accent of reality. Some instances are: the shock of falling asleep as the leap into the world of dreams; the inner transformation we endure if the curtain in the theatre rises as the transition to the world of the stageplay; the radical change in our attitude if, before a painting, we permit our visual field to be limited by what is within the frame as the passage into the pictorial world; our quandary relaxing into laughter, if, in listening to a joke, we are for a short time ready to accept the fictitious world of the jest as a reality in relation to which the world of our daily life takes on the character of foolishness; the child's turning toward his toy as the transition into the play-world; and so on. But also the religious experiences in all their varieties – for instance, Kierkegaard's experience of the 'instant' as the leap into the religious sphere – are examples of such a shock, as well as the decision of the scientist to replace all passionate participation in the affairs of 'this world' by a disinterested [analytical] attitude. (Schutz 1962: 231)

The recognition and exploration of the qualitative difference – an empirical, not a transcendental difference – between religion pure and religion applied, between an encounter with the supposedly 'really real' and a viewing of ordinary experience in light of what that encounter seems to reveal, will, therefore, take us further toward an understanding of what a Bororo means when he says 'I am a parakeet', or a Christian when he says 'I am a sinner', than either a theory of primitive mysticism in which the commonplace world disappears into a cloud of curious ideas or of a primitive pragmatism in which religion disintegrates into a collection of useful fictions. The parakeet example, which I take from Percy (1961), is a good one. For, as he points out, it is unsatisfactory to say either that the Bororo thinks he is literally a parakeet (for he does not try to mate with other parakeets), that his statement is false or nonsense (for, clearly, he is not offering – or at least not only offering – the sort of class-membership argument which can be confirmed or refuted as, say, 'I am a Bororo' can be confirmed or refuted), or yet again that it is false scientifically but true mythically (because that leads immediately to the pragmatic fiction notion which, as it denies the accolade of truth to 'myth' in the very act of bestowing it, is internally self-contradictory). More coherently it would seem to be necessary to see the sentence as having a different sense in the context of the 'finite province of meaning' which makes up the religious perspective and of that which makes up the common-sensical. In the religious, our Bororo is 'really' a 'parakeet', and given the proper ritual context might well 'mate' with other 'parakeets' – with metaphysical ones like himself not commonplace ones such as those which fly bodily about in ordinary trees. In the common-sensical perspective he is a parakeet in the sense – I assume – that he belongs to a clan whose members regard the parakeet as their totem, a membership from which, given the fundamental nature of reality as the religious perspective reveals it, certain moral and practical consequences flow. A man who says he is a parakeet is, if he says it in normal conversation, saying that, as myth and ritual demonstrate, he is shot through with parakeetness and that this religious fact has some crucial social implications – we parakeets must stick together, not marry one another, not eat mundane parakeets, and so on, for to do otherwise is to act against the grain of the whole universe. It is this placing of proximate acts in ultimate contexts that makes religion, frequently at least, socially so powerful. It alters, often radically, the whole landscape presented to common sense, alters it in such a way that the moods and motivations induced by religious practice seem themselves supremely practical, the only sensible ones to adopt given the way things 'really' are.

Having ritually 'leapt' (the image is perhaps a bit too athletic for the actual facts – 'slipped' might be more accurate) into the framework of meaning which religious conceptions define and, the ritual ended, returned again to the common-sense world, a man is – unless, as sometimes happens, the experience fails to register – changed. And as he is changed so also is the common-sense world, for it is now seen as but the partial form of a wider reality which corrects and completes it. But this correction and completion is not, as some students of 'comparative religion' (e.g. Campbell 1949: 236–7) would have it, everywhere the same in content. The nature of the bias religion gives to ordinary life varies with the religion involved, with the particular dispositions induced in the believer by the specific conceptions of cosmic order he has come to accept. On the level of the 'great' religions, organic distinctiveness is usually recognized, at times insisted upon to the point of zealotry. But even at its simplest folk and tribal levels – where the individuality of religious traditions has so often been dissolved into such desiccated types as 'animism', 'animatism', 'totemism', 'shamanism', 'ancestor worship', and all the other insipid categories by means of which ethnographers of religion devitalize their data – the idiosyncratic character of how various groups of men behave because of what they believe they have experienced is clear. A tranquil Javanese would be no more at home in guilt-ridden Manus than an activist Crow would be in passionless Java. And for all the witches and ritual clowns in the world, Rangda and Barong are not generalized but thoroughly singular figurations of fear and gaiety. What men believe is as various as what they are – a proposition that holds with equal force when it is inverted.

It is this particularity of the impact of religious systems upon social systems (and upon personality systems) which renders general assessments of the value of religion in either moral or functional terms impossible. The sorts of moods and motivations which characterize a man who has just come from an Aztec human sacrifice are rather different from those of one who has just put off his Kachina mask. Even within the same society, what one 'learns' about the essential pattern of life from a sorcery rite and from a commensual meal will have rather diverse effects on social and psychological functioning. One of the main methodological problems in writing about religion scientifically is to put aside at once the tone of the village atheist and that of the village preacher, as well as their more sophisticated equivalents, so that the social and psychological implications of particular religious beliefs can emerge in a clear and neutral light. And when that is done, overall questions about whether religion is 'good' or 'bad', 'functional' or 'dysfunctional', 'ego strengthening' or 'anxiety producing' disappear like the chimeras they are, and one is left with particular evaluations, assessments, and diagnoses in particular cases. There remain, of course, the hardly unimportant questions of whether this or that religious assertion is true, this or that religious experience genuine, or whether true religious assertions and genuine religious experiences are possible at all. But such questions cannot even be asked, much less answered, within the self-imposed limitations of the scientific perspective.

NOTES

1. The reverse mistake, especially common among neo-Kantians such as Cassirer (1953–57), of taking symbols to be identical with, or 'constitutive of', their referents is equally pernicious. 'One can point to the moon with one's finger,' some, probably well-invented, Zen Master is supposed to have said, 'but to take one's finger for the moon is to be a fool.'
2. This is *not*, however, to say that everyone in every society does this; for as the immortal Don Marquis once remarked, you don't have to have a soul unless you really want one. The oft-heard generalization (e.g. Kluckhohn 1953) that religion is a

human universal embodies a confusion between the probably true (though on present evidence unprovable) proposition that there is no human society in which cultural patterns that we can, under the present definition or one like it, call religious are totally lacking, and the surely untrue proposition that all men in all societies are, in any meaningful sense of the term, religious. But if the anthropological study of religious commitment is underdeveloped, the anthropological study of religious non-commitment is non-existent. The anthropology of religion will have come of age when some more subtle Malinowski writes a book called 'Belief and Unbelief (or even "Faith and Hypocrisy") in a Savage Society'.

3. The term 'attitude' as in 'aesthetic attitude' (Bell 1914) or 'natural attitude' (Schutz 1962; the phrase is originally Husserl's) is another, perhaps more common term for what I have here called 'perspective'. But I have avoided it because of its strong subjectivist connotations, its tendency to place the stress upon a supposed inner state of an actor rather than on a certain sort of relation – a symbolically mediated one – between an actor and a situation. This is not to say, of course, that a phenomenological analysis of religious experience, if cast in inter-subjective, non-transcendental, genuinely scientific terms (see Percy 1958) is not essential to a full understanding of religious belief, but merely that that is not the focus of my concern here. 'Outlook', 'frame of reference', 'frame of mind', 'orientation', 'stance', 'mental set', etc. are other terms sometimes employed, depending upon whether the analyst wishes to stress the social, psychological, or cultural aspects of the matter.

Bronisław Malinowski
'Magic, science and religion'

Bronisław Kaspar Malinowski was born in Krakow in 1884. His parents were from a rich aristocratic family and he was educated at the local public school before going on to study physics and mathematics at Krakow University. However, his reading of The Golden Bough *inspired him to study anthropology and in 1910 he began studies in anthropology at the LSE. During the course of his studies he was fortunate enough to receive a large fieldwork grant, which enabled him to travel to the Trobriand Islands and it was while undertaking this journey that he met with Radcliffe-Brown. In 1916 he graduated from the LSE with a doctorate in anthropology and began work there as an occasional lecturer in ethnology. In 1923 Malinowski was promoted to the position of a full-time lecturer, a year later he was made a reader and three years after that he was made the school's first Professor of Anthropology. In 1939 he took the position of associate professor at Yale. A year later he was made a visiting professor and two years after that would have made full professor had it not been for his untimely death.*

Malinowski is perhaps better known for his ethnographic fieldwork than his theorising. Nonetheless he did develop a particular take on functionalism, emphasising the functions for the individual rather than society. His analysis of religion, with its focus on death, reflects this theoretical perspective. Malinowski's ethnographic fieldwork also led him to challenge the theories of both Frazer and Lévy-Bruhl. He argues that all societies think in fundamentally the same ways and that magic, religion and science are not part of an evolutionary cycle but are found in all societies.

Primitive Man and his Religion

There are no peoples however primitive without religion and magic. Nor are there, it must be added at once, any savage races lacking either in the scientific attitude or in science, though this lack has been frequently attributed to them. In every primitive community, studied by trustworthy and competent observers, there have been found two clearly distinguishable domains, the Sacred and the Profane; in other words, the domain of Magic and Religion and that of Science.

On the one hand there are the traditional acts and observances, regarded by the natives as sacred, carried out with reverence and awe, hedged around with prohibitions and special rules of behavior. Such acts and observances are always associated with beliefs in supernatural forces, especially those of magic, or with ideas about beings, spirits, ghosts, dead ancestors, or

Bronisław Malinowski (1954), *'Magic, Science and Religion' and Other Essays*, Garden City, NY: Doubleday.

gods. On the other hand, a moment's reflection is sufficient to show that no art or craft however primitive could have been invented or maintained, no organized form of hunting, fishing, tilling, or search for food could be carried out without the careful observation of natural process and a firm belief in its regularity, without the power of reasoning and without confidence in the power of reason; that is, without the rudiments of science.

The credit of having laid the foundations of an anthropological study of religion belongs to Edward B. Tylor. In his well-known theory he maintains that the essence of primitive religion is animism, the belief in spiritual beings, and he shows how this belief has originated in a mistaken but consistent interpretation of dreams, visions, hallucinations, cataleptic states, and similar phenomena. Reflecting on these, the savage philosopher or theologian was led to distinguish the human soul from the body. Now the soul obviously continues to lead an existence after death, for it appears in dreams, haunts the survivors in memories and in visions and apparently influences human destinies. Thus originated the belief in ghosts and the spirits of the dead, in immortality and in a nether world. But man in general, and primitive man in particular, has a tendency to imagine the outer world in his own image. And since animals, plants, and objects move, act, behave, help man or hinder him, they must also be endowed with souls or spirits. Thus animism, the philosophy and the religion of primitive man, has been built up from observations and by inferences, mistaken but comprehensible in a crude and untutored mind.

Tylor's view of primitive religion, important as it was, was based on too narrow a range of facts, and it made early man too contemplative and rational. Recent field work, done by specialists, shows us the savage interested rather in his fishing and gardens, in tribal events and festivities than brooding over dreams and visions, or explaining 'doubles' and cataleptic fits, and it reveals also a great many aspects of early religion which cannot be possibly placed in Tylor's scheme of animism.

The extended and deepened outlook of modern anthropology finds its most adequate expression in the learned and inspiring writings of Sir James Frazer. In these he has set forth the three main problems of primitive religion with which present-day anthropology is busy: magic and its relation to religion and science; totemism and the sociological aspect of early faith; the cults of fertility and vegetation. It will be best to discuss these subjects in turn.

Frazer's *Golden Bough*, the great codex of primitive magic, shows clearly that animism is not the only, nor even the dominating belief in primitive culture. Early man seeks above all to control the course of nature for practical ends, and he does it directly, by rite and spell, compelling wind and weather, animals and crops to obey his will. Only much later, finding the limitations of his magical might, does he in fear or hope, in supplication or defiance, appeal to higher beings; that is, to demons, ancestor-spirits or gods. It is in this distinction between direct control on the one hand and propitiation of superior powers on the other that Sir James Frazer sees the difference between religion and magic. Magic, based on man's confidence that he can dominate nature directly, if only he knows the laws which govern it magically, is in this akin to science. Religion, the confession of human impotence in certain matters, lifts man above the magical level, and later on maintains its independence side by side with science, to which magic has to succumb.

This theory of magic and religion has been the starting point of most modern studies of the twin subjects. Professor Preuss in Germany, Dr. Marett in England, and MM. Hubert and Mauss in France have independently set forth certain views, partly in criticism of Frazer, partly following up the lines of his inquiry. These writers point out that similar as they appear, science and magic differ yet radically. Science is born of experience, magic made by tradition. Science is guided by reason and corrected by observation, magic, impervious to both, lives in an atmosphere of mysticism. Science is open to all, a common good of the whole community, magic is occult, taught through mysterious initiations, handed on in hereditary or at least in very exclusive filiation. While science is based on the conception of natural forces, magic springs from the idea of a certain mystic, impersonal power, which is believed in by most primitive peoples. This power, called *mana* by some Melanesians, *arungquiltha* by certain Australian tribes, *wakan, orenda, manitu* by various American Indians, and nameless elsewhere, is stated to be a well-nigh universal idea found wherever magic flourishes. According to the writers just mentioned we can find among the most primitive peoples and throughout the lower savagery a belief in a supernatural, impersonal force, moving all those agencies which are relevant to the savage and causing all the really important events in the domain of the sacred. Thus *mana*, not animism, is the essence of 'pre-animistic religion', and it is also the essence of magic, which is thus radically different from science.

There remains the question, however, what is *mana*, this impersonal force of magic supposed to dominate all forms of early belief? Is it a fundamental idea, an innate category of the primitive mind, or can it be explained by still simpler and more fundamental elements of human psychology or of the reality in which primitive man lives? The most original and important contribution to these problems is given by the late Professor Durkheim, and it touches the other subject, opened up by Sir James Frazer: that of totemism and of the sociological aspect of religion.

Totemism, to quote Frazer's classical definition, 'is an intimate relation which is supposed to exist between a group of kindred people on the one side and a species of natural or artificial objects on the other side, which objects are called the totems of the human group'. Totemism thus has two sides: it is a mode of social grouping and a religious system of beliefs and practices.

As religion, it expresses primitive man's interest in his surroundings, the desire to claim an affinity and to control the most important objects: above all, animal or vegetable species, more rarely useful inanimate objects, very seldom man-made things. As a rule species of animals and plants used for staple food or at any rate edible or useful or ornamental animals are held in a special form of 'totemic reverence' and are tabooed to the members of the clan which is associated with the species and which sometimes performs rites and ceremonies for its multiplication. The social aspect of totemism consists in the subdivision of the tribe into minor units, called in anthropology *clans, gentes, sibs,* or *phratries.*

In totemism we see therefore not the result of early man's speculations about mysterious phenomena, but a blend of a utilitarian anxiety about the most necessary objects of his surroundings, with some preoccupation in those which strike his imagination and attract his attention, such as beautiful birds, reptiles and dangerous animals. With our knowledge of what could be called the totemic attitude of mind, primitive religion is seen to be nearer to reality and to the immediate practical life interests of the savage, than it appeared in its 'animistic' aspect emphasized by Tylor and the earlier anthropologists.

By its apparently strange association with a problematic form of social division, I mean the clan system; totemism has taught anthropology yet another lesson: it has revealed the importance of the sociological aspect in all the early forms of cult. The savage depends upon the group with whom he is in direct contact both for practical co-operation and mental solidarity to a far larger extent than does civilized man. Since – as can be seen in totemism, magic, and many other practices – early cult and ritual are closely associated with practical concerns as well as with mental needs, there must exist an intimate connection between social organization and religious belief. This was understood already by that pioneer of religious anthropology, Robertson Smith, whose principle that primitive religion 'was essentially an affair of the community rather than of individuals' has become a *Leitmotiv* of modern research. According to Professor Durkheim, who has put these views most forcibly, 'the religious' is identical with 'the social'. For 'in a general way ... a society has all that is necessary to arouse the sensation of the Divine in minds, merely by the power that it has over them; for to its members it is what a God is to its worshippers'.[1] Professor Durkheim arrives at this conclusion by the study of totemism, which he believes to be the most primitive form of religion. In this the 'totemic principle' which is identical with *mana* and with 'the God of the clan...can be nothing else than the clan itself'.[2]

These strange and somewhat obscure conclusions will be criticized later, and it will be shown in what consists the grain of truth they undoubtedly contain and how fruitful it can be. It has borne fruit, in fact, in influencing some of the most important writing of mixed classical schol-arship and anthropology, to mention only the works of Miss Jane Harrison and Mr. Cornford.

The third great subject introduced into the Science of Religion by Sir James Frazer is that of the cults of vegetation and fertility. In *The Golden Bough*, starting from the awful and mysterious ritual of the wood divinities at Nemi, we are led through an amazing variety of magical and religious cults, devised by man to stimulate and control the fertilizing work of skies and earth and of sun and rain, and we are left with the impression that early religion is teeming with the forces of savage life, with its young beauty and crudity, with its exuberance and strength so violent that it leads now and again to suicidal acts of self-immolation. The study of *The Golden Bough* shows us that for primitive man death has meaning mainly as a step to resurrection, decay as a stage of rebirth, the plenty of autumn and the decline of winter as preludes to the revival of spring. Inspired by these passages of *The Golden Bough* a number of writers have developed, often with greater precision and with a fuller analysis than by Frazer himself, what could be called the *vitalistic* view of religion. Thus Mr. Crawley in his *Tree of Life*, M. van Gennep in his *Rites de Passage*, and Miss Jane Harrison in several works, have given evidence that faith and cult spring from the crises of human existence, 'the great events of life, birth, adolescence, marriage, death . . . it is about these events that religion largely focuses'.[3] The tension of instinctive need, strong emotional experiences, leads in some way or other to cult and belief. 'Art and Religion alike spring from unsatisfied desire'.[4] How much truth there is in this somewhat vague statement and how much exaggeration we shall be able to assess later on.

There are two important contributions to the theory of primitive religion which I mention here only, for they have somehow remained outside the main current of anthropological interest. They treat of the primitive idea of one God and of the place of morals in primitive religion respectively. It is remarkable that they have been and still are neglected, for are not these two questions first and foremost in the mind of anyone who studies religion, however crude and rudimentary it may be? Perhaps the explanation is in the preconceived idea that 'origins' must be very crude and simple and different from the 'developed forms', or else in the notion that the 'savage' or 'primitive' is really savage and primitive!

The late Andrew Lang indicated the existence among some Australian na-tives of the belief in a tribal All-Father, and the Rev. Pater Wilhelm Schmidt has adduced much evidence proving that this belief is universal among all the peoples of the simplest cultures and that it cannot be discarded as an irrelevant fragment of mythology, still less as an echo of missionary teach-ing. It looks, according to Pater Schmidt, very much like an indication of a simple and pure form of early monotheism.

The problem of morals as an early religious function was also left on one side, until it received an exhaustive treatment, not only in the writings of Pater Schmidt but also and notably in two works of outstanding importance: the *Origin and Development of Moral Ideas* of Professor E. Westermarck, and *Morals in Evolution* of Professor L. T. Hobhouse.

It is not easy to summarize concisely the trend of anthropological studies in our subject. On the whole it has been towards an increasingly elastic and comprehensive view of religion. Tylor had still to refute the fallacy that there are primitive peoples without religion. Today we are somewhat perplexed by the discovery that to a savage all is religion, that he perpetually lives in a world of mysticism and ritualism. If religion is co-extensive with 'life' and with 'death' into the bargain, if it arises from all 'collective' acts and from all 'crises in the individual's existence', if it comprises all savage 'theory' and covers all his 'practical concerns' – we are led to ask, not without dismay: What remains outside it, what is the world of the 'profane' in primitive life? Here is a first problem into which modern anthropology, by the number of contradictory views, has thrown some confusion, as can be seen even from the above short sketch. [...] Primitive religion, as fashioned by modern anthropology, has been made to harbor all sorts of heterogeneous things. At first reserved in animism for the solemn figures of ancestral spirits, ghosts and souls, besides a few fetishes, it had gradually to admit the thin, fluid, ubiquitous *mana* ; then, like Noah's Ark, it was with the introduction of totemism loaded with beasts, not in pairs but in shoals and species, joined by plants, objects, and even manufactured articles; then came human activities and concerns and the gigantic ghost of the Collective Soul, Society Divinized. Can there be any order or system put into this medley of apparently unrelated objects and principles? This question will occupy us in the third section.

One achievement of modern anthropology we shall not question: the recognition that magic and religion are not merely a doctrine or a philosophy, not merely an intellectual body of opinion, but a special mode of behavior, a pragmatic attitude built up of reason, feeling, and will alike. It is a mode of action as well as a system of belief, and a sociological phenomenon as well as a personal experience. But with all this, the exact relation between the social and the individual contributions to religion is not clear, as we have seen from the exaggerations committed on either side. Nor is it clear what are the respective shares of emotion and reason. All these questions will have to be dealt with by future anthropology, and it will be possible only to suggest solutions and indicate lines of argument in this short essay.

[...]

LIFE, DEATH, AND DESTINY IN EARLY FAITH AND CULT

We pass now to the domain of the *sacred*, to religious and magical creeds and rites. Our historical survey of theories has left us somewhat bewildered with the chaos of opinions and with the jumble of phenomena. While it was difficult not to admit into the enclosure of religion one after the other, spirits and ghosts, totems and social events, death and life, yet in the process religion seemed to become a thing more and more confused, both an all and a nothing. It certainly cannot be defined by its subject matter in a narrow sense, as 'spirit worship', or as 'ancestor cult', or as the 'cult of nature'. It includes animism, animalism, totemism, and fetishism, but it is not any one of them exclusively. The *ism* definition of religion in its origins must be given up, for religion does not cling to any one object or class of objects, though incidentally it can touch and hallow all. Nor, as we have seen, is religion identical with Society or the Social, nor can we remain satisfied by a vague hint that it clings to life only, for death opens perhaps the vastest view on to the other world. As an 'appeal to higher powers,' religion can only be distinguished from magic and not defined in general, but even this view will have to be slightly modified and supplemented.

The problem before us is, then, to try to put some order into the facts. This will allow us to determine somewhat more precisely the character of the domain of the *Sacred* and mark it off from that of the *Profane*. It will also give us an opportunity to state the relation between magic and religion.

The creative acts of religion

It will be best to face the facts first and, in order not to narrow down the scope of the survey, to take as our watchword the vaguest and most general of indices: 'Life'. As a matter of fact, even a slight acquaintance with ethnological literature is enough to convince anyone that in reality the physiological phases of human life, and, above all, its crises, such as conception, pregnancy, birth, puberty, marriage, and death, form the nuclei of numerous rites and beliefs. Thus beliefs about conception, such as that in reincarnation, spirit-entry, magical impregnation, exist in one form or another in almost every tribe, and they are often associated with rites and observances. During pregnancy the expectant mother has to keep certain taboos and undergo ceremonies, and her husband shares at times in both. At birth, before and after, there are various magical rites to prevent dangers and undo sorcery, ceremonies of purification, communal rejoicings and acts of presentation of the newborn to higher powers or to the community. Later on in life the boys and, much less frequently, the girls have to undergo the often protracted rites of initiation, as a rule shrouded in mystery and marred by cruel and obscene ordeals.

Without going any further, we can see that even the very beginnings of human life are surrounded by an inextricably mixed-up medley of beliefs and rites. They seem to be strongly attracted by any important event in life, to crystallize around it, surround it with a rigid crust of formalism and ritualism – but to what purpose? Since we cannot define cult and creed by their objects, perhaps it will be possible to perceive their function.

A closer scrutiny of the facts allows us to make from the outset a preliminary classification into two main groups. Compare a rite carried out to prevent death in childbirth with another typical custom, a ceremony in celebration of a birth. The first rite is carried out as a means to an end, it has a definite practical purpose which is known to all who practice it and can be easily elicited from any native informant. The post-natal ceremony, say a presentation of a newborn or a feast of rejoicing in the event, has no purpose: it is not a means to an end but an end in itself. It expresses the feelings of the mother, the father, the relatives, the whole community, but there is no future event which this ceremony foreshadows, which it is meant to bring about or to prevent. This difference will serve us as a *prima facie* distinction between magic and religion. While in the magical act the underlying idea and aim is always clear, straight-forward, and definite, in the religious ceremony there is no purpose directed toward a subsequent event. It is only possible for the sociologist to establish the function, the sociological *raison d'être* of the act. The native can always state the end of the magical rite, but he will say of a religious ceremony that it is done because such is the usage, or because it has been ordained, or he will narrate an explanatory myth.

In order to grasp better the nature of primitive religious ceremonies and their function, let us analyze the ceremonies of initiation. They present right through the vast range of their occurrence certain striking similarities. Thus the novices have to undergo a more or less protracted period of seclusion and preparation. Then comes initiation proper, in which the youth, passing through a series of ordeals, is finally submitted to an act of bodily mutilation: at the mildest, a slight incision or the knocking out of a tooth; or, more severe, circumcision; or, really cruel and dangerous, an operation such as the subincision practiced in some Australian tribes. The ordeal is usually associated with the idea of the death and rebirth of the initiated one, which is sometimes enacted in a mimetic performance. But besides the ordeal, less conspicuous and dramatic, but in reality more important, is the second main aspect of initiation: the systematic instruction of the youth in sacred myth and tradition, the gradual unveiling of tribal mysteries and the exhibition of sacred objects.

The ordeal and the unveiling of tribal mysteries are usually believed to have been instituted by one or more legendary ancestors or culture heroes, or by a Superior Being of superhuman character. Sometimes he is said to swallow the youths, or to kill them, and then to restore them again as fully initiated men. His voice is imitated by the hum of the bull-roarer to inspire awe in the uninitiated women and children. Through these ideas initiation brings the novice into relationship with higher powers and personalities, such as the Guardian Spirits and Tutelary Divinities of the North American Indians, the Tribal All-Father of some Australian Aborigines, the Mythological Heroes of Melanesia and other parts of the world. This is the third fundamental element, besides ordeal and the teaching of tradition, in the rites of passing into manhood.

Now what is the sociological function of these customs, what part do they play in the maintenance and development of civilization? As we have seen, the youth is taught in them the sacred traditions under most impressive conditions of preparation and ordeal and under the sanction of Supernatural Beings – the light of tribal revelation bursts upon him from out of the shadows of fear, privation, and bodily pain.

Let us realize that in primitive conditions tradition is of supreme value for the community and nothing matters as much as the conformity and conservatism of its members. Order and civilization can be maintained only by strict adhesion to the lore and knowledge received from previous generations. Any laxity in this weakens the cohesion of the group and imperils its cultural outfit to the point of threatening its very existence. Man has not yet devised the extremely complex apparatus of modern science which enables him nowadays to fix the results of experience into imperishable molds, to test it ever anew, gradually to shape it into more adequate forms and enrich it constantly by new additions. The primitive man's share of knowledge, his social fabric, his customs and beliefs, are the invaluable yield of devious experience of his forefathers, bought at an extravagant price and to be maintained at any cost. Thus, of all his qualities, truth to tradition is the most important, and a society which makes its tradition sacred has gained by it an inestimable advantage of power and permanence. Such beliefs and practices, therefore, which put a halo of sanctity round tradition and a supernatural stamp upon it, will have a 'survival value' for the type of civilization in which they have been evolved.

We may, therefore, lay down the main function of initiation ceremonies: they are a ritual and dramatic expression of the supreme power and value of tradition in primitive societies; they also serve to impress this power and value upon the minds of each generation, and they are at the same time an extremely efficient means of transmitting tribal lore, of insuring continuity in tradition and of maintaining tribal cohesion.

We still have to ask: What is the relation between the purely physiological fact of bodily maturity which these ceremonies mark, and their social and religious aspect? We see at once that religion does something more, infinitely more, than the mere 'sacralizing of a crisis of life'. From a natural event it makes a social transition, to the fact of bodily maturity it adds the vast conception of entry into manhood with its duties, privileges, responsibilities, above all with its knowledge of tradition and the communion with sacred things and beings. There is thus a creative element in the rites of religious nature. The act establishes not only a social event in the life of the individual but also a spiritual metamorphosis, both associated with the biological event but transcending it in importance and significance.

Initiation is a typically religious act, and we can see clearly here how the ceremony and its purpose are one, how the end is realized in the very consummation of the act. At the same time we can see the function of such acts in society in that they create mental habits and social usages of inestimable value to the group and its civilization.

Another type of religious ceremony, the rite of marriage, is also an end in itself in that it creates a supernaturally sanctioned bond, superadded to the primarily biological fact: the union of man and woman for lifelong partnership in affection, economic community, the procreation and rearing of children. This union, monogamous marriage, has always existed in human societies – so modern anthropology teaches in the face of the older fantastic hypotheses of 'promiscuity' and 'group marriage'. By giving monogamous marriage an imprint of value and sanctity, religion offers another gift to human culture. And that brings us to the consideration of the two great human needs of propagation and nutrition.

Providence in primitive life

Propagation and nutrition stand first and foremost among the vital concerns of man. Their relation to religious belief and practice has been often recognized and even overemphasized. Especially sex has been, from some older writers up to the psychoanalytic school, frequently regarded as the main source of religion. In fact, however, it plays an astonishingly insignificant part in religion, considering its force and insidiousness in human life in general. Besides love magic and the use of sex in certain magical performances – phenomena not belonging to the domain of religion – there remain to be mentioned here only acts of licence at harvest festivities or other public gatherings, the facts of temple prostitution and, at the level of barbarism and lower civilization, the worship of phallic divinities. Contrary to what one would expect, in savagery sexual cults play an insignificant role. It must also be remembered that acts of ceremonial licence are not mere indulgence, but that they express a reverent attitude towards the forces of generation and fertility in man and nature, forces on which the very existence of society and culture depends. Religion, the permanent source of moral control, which changes its incidence but remains eternally vigilant, has to turn its attention to these forces, at first drawing them merely into its sphere, later on submitting them to repression, finally establishing the ideal of chastity and the sanctification of askesis.

When we pass to nutrition, the first thing to be noted is that eating is for primitive man an act surrounded by etiquette, special prescriptions and prohibitions, and a general emotional tension to a degree unknown to us. Besides the magic of food, designed to make it go a long way, or to prevent its scarcity in general – and we do not speak here at all of the innumerable forms of magic associated with the procuring of food – food has also a conspicuous role in ceremonies of a distinctly religious character. First-fruit offerings of a ritual nature, harvest ceremonies, big seasonal feasts in which crops are accumulated, displayed, and, in one way or another, sacralized, play an important part among agricultural people. Hunters, again, or fishers celebrate a big catch or the opening of the season of their pursuit by feasts and ceremonies at which food is ritually handled, the animals propitiated or worshipped. All such acts express the joy of the community, their sense of the great value of food, and religion through them consecrates the reverent attitude of man towards his daily bread.

To primitive man, never, even under the best conditions, quite free from the threat of starvation, abundance of food is a primary condition of normal life. It means the possibility of looking beyond the daily worries, of paying more attention to the remoter, spiritual aspects of civilization. If we thus consider that food is the main link between man and his surroundings, that by receiving it he feels the forces of destiny and providence, we can see the cultural, nay, biological importance of primitive religion in the sacralization of food. We can see in it the germs of what in higher types of religion will develop into the feeling of dependence upon Providence, of gratitude, and of confidence in it.

Sacrifice and communion, the two main forms in which food is ritually ministered, can now be held in a new light against the background of man's early attitude of religious reverence towards the providential abundance of food. That the idea of giving, the importance of the exchange of gifts in all phases of social contact, plays a great role in sacrifice seems – in spite of the unpopularity of this theory nowadays – unquestionable in view of the new knowledge of primitive economic psychology.[5] Since the giving of gifts is the normal accompaniment of all social intercourse among primitives, the spirits who visit the village or the demons who haunt some hallowed spot, or divinities when approached are given their due, their share sacrificed from the general plenty, as any other visitors or persons visited would be. But underlying this custom there is a still deeper religious element. Since food is to the savage the token of the beneficence of the world, since plenty gives him the first, the most elementary, inkling of Providence, by sharing in food sacrificially with his spirits or divinities the savage shares with them in the beneficial powers of his Providence already felt by him but not yet comprehended. Thus in primitive societies the roots of sacrificial offerings are to be found in the psychology of gift, which is to the communion in beneficent abundance.

The sacramental meal is only another expression of the same mental attitude, carried out in the most appropriate manner by the act by which life is retained and renewed – the act of eating. But this ritual seems to be extremely rare among lower savages, and the sacrament of communion, prevalent at a level of culture when the primitive psychology of eating is no more, has by then acquired a different symbolic and mystical meaning. Perhaps the only case of sacramental eating, well attested and known with some detail, is the so-called 'totemic sacrament' of Central Australian tribes, and this seems to require a somewhat more special interpretation.

Man's selective interest in nature

This brings us to the subject of totemism, briefly defined in the first section. As may have been seen, the following questions have to be asked about totemism. First, why does a primitive tribe select for its totems a limited number of species, primarily animals and plants; and on what principles is this selection made? Secondly, why is this selective attitude expressed in beliefs of affinity, in cults of multiplication, above all in the negative injunctions of totemic taboos, and again in injunctions of ritual eating, as in the Australian 'totemic sacrament'? Thirdly and finally, why with the subdivision of nature into a limited number of selected species does there run parallel a subdivision of the tribe into clans correlated with the species?

The above outlined psychology of the primitive attitude towards food and its abundance and our principle of man's practical and pragmatic outlook lead us directly to an answer. We have seen that food is the primary link between the primitive and providence. And the need of it and the desire for its abundance have led man to economic pursuits, collecting, hunting, fishing, and they endow these pursuits with varied and tense emotions. A number of animal and vegetable species, those which form the staple food of the tribe, dominate the interests of the tribesmen. To primitive man nature is his living larder, to which – especially at the lowest stages of culture – he has to repair directly in order to gather, cook, and eat when hungry. The road from the wilderness to the savage's belly and consequently to his mind is very short, and for him the world is an indiscriminate background against which there stand out the useful, primarily the edible, species of animals or plants. Those who have lived in the jungle with savages, taking part in collecting or hunting expeditions, or who have sailed with them over the lagoons, or spent moonlit nights on sandbanks waiting for the shoals of fish or for the appearance of turtle, know how keen and selective is the savage's interest, how it clings to the indications, trails, and to the habits and peculiarities of his quarry, while it yet remains quite indifferent to any other stimuli. Every such species which is habitually pursued forms a nucleus round which all the interests, the impulses, the emotions of a tribe tend to crystallize. A sentiment of social nature is built round each species, a sentiment which naturally finds its expression in folklore, belief, and ritual.

It must also be remembered that the same type of impulse which makes small children delight in birds, take a keen interest in animals, and shrink from reptiles, places animals in the front rank of nature for primitive man. By their general affinity with man – they move, utter sounds, manifest emotions, have bodies and faces like him – and by their superior powers – the birds fly in the open, the fishes swim under water, reptiles renew their skins and their life and can disappear in the earth – by all this the animal, the intermediate link between man and nature, often his superior in strength, agility, and cunning, usually his indispensable quarry, assumes an exceptional place in the savage's view of the world.

The primitive is deeply interested in the appearance and properties of beasts; he desires to have them and, therefore, to control them as useful and edible things; sometimes he admires and fears them. All these interests meet and, strengthening each other, produce the same effect: the selection, in man's principal preoccupations, of a limited number of species, animal first, vegetable in the second place, while inanimate or man-made things are unquestionably but a secondary formation, an introduction by analogy, of objects which have nothing to do with the substance of totemism.

The nature of man's interest in the totemic species indicates also clearly the type of belief and cult to be there expected. Since it is the desire to control the species, dangerous, useful, or edible, this desire must lead to a belief in special power over the species, affinity with it, a common essence between man and beast or plant. Such a belief implies, on the one hand, certain considerations and restraints – the most obvious being a prohibition to kill and to eat; on the other hand, it endows man with the supernatural faculty of contributing ritually to the abundance of the species, to its increase and vitality.

This ritual leads to acts of magical nature, by which plenty is brought about. Magic [...] tends in all its manifestations to become specialized, exclusive and departmental and hereditary within a family or clan. In totemism the magical multiplication of each species would naturally become the duty and privilege of a specialist, assisted by his family. The families in course of time become clans, each having its headman as the chief magician of its totem. Totemism in its most elementary forms, as found in Central Australia, is a system of magical co-operation, a number of practical cults, each with its own social basis but all having one common end: the supply of the tribe with abundance. Thus totemism in its sociological aspect can be explained by the principles of primitive magical sociology in general. The existence of totemic clans and their correlation with cult and belief is but an instance of departmental magic and of the tendency to inheritance of magical ritual by one family. This explanation, somewhat condensed as it is, attempts to show that, in its social organization, belief, and cult, totemism is not a freakish outgrowth, not a fortuitous result of some special accident or constellation, but the natural outcome of natural conditions.

Thus we find our questions answered: man's selective interest in a limited number of animals and plants and the way in which this interest is ritually expressed and socially conditioned appear as the natural result of primitive existence, of the savage's spontaneous attitudes towards natural objects and of his prevalent occupations. From the survival point of view, it is vital that man's interest in the practically indispensable species should never abate, that his belief in his capacity to control them should give him strength and endurance in his pursuits and stimulate his observation and knowledge of the habits and natures of animals and plants. Totemism appears thus as a blessing bestowed by religion on primitive man's efforts in dealing with his useful surroundings, upon his 'struggle for existence'. At the same time it develops his reverence for those animals and plants on which he depends, to which he feels in a way grateful, and yet the destruction of which is a necessity to him. And all this springs from the belief of man's affinity with those forces of nature upon which he mainly depends. Thus we find a moral value and a biological significance in totemism, in a system of beliefs, practices, and social arrangements which at first sight appears but a childish, irrelevant, and degrading fancy of the savage.

Death and the reintegration of the group

Of all sources of religion, the supreme and final crisis of life – death – is of the greatest importance. Death is the gateway to the other world in more than the literal sense. According to most theories of early religion, a great deal, if not all, of religious inspiration has been derived from it – and in this orthodox views are on the whole correct. Man has to live his life in the shadow of death, and he who clings to life and enjoys its fullness must dread the menace of its end. And he who is faced by death turns to the promise of life. Death and its denial – Immortality – have always formed, as they form today, the most poignant theme of man's forebodings. The extreme complexity of man's emotional reactions to life finds necessarily its counterpart in his attitude to death. Only what in life has been spread over a long space and manifested in a succession of experiences and events is here at its end condensed into one crisis which provokes a violent and complex outburst of religious manifestations.

Even among the most primitive peoples, the attitude towards death is infinitely more complex and, I may add, more akin to our own, than is usually assumed. It is often stated by anthropologists that the dominant feeling of the survivors is that of horror at the corpse and of fear of the ghost. This twin attitude is even made by no less an authority than Wilhelm Wundt the very nucleus of all religious belief and practice. Yet this assertion is only a half-truth, which means no truth at all. The emotions are extremely complex and even contradictory; the dominant elements, love of the dead and loathing of the corpse, passionate attachment to the personality still lingering about the body and a shattering fear of the gruesome thing that has been left over, these two elements seem to mingle and play into each other. This is reflected in the spontaneous behavior and in the ritual proceedings at death. In the tending of the corpse, in the modes of its disposal, in the post-funerary and commemorative ceremonies, the nearest relatives, the mother mourning for her son, the widow for her husband, the child for the parent, always show some horror and fear mingled with pious love, but never do the negative elements appear alone or even dominant.

The mortuary proceedings show a striking similarity throughout the world. As death approaches, the nearest relatives in any case, sometimes the whole community, forgather by the dying man, and dying, the most private act which a man can perform, is transformed into a public, tribal event. As a rule, a certain differentiation takes place at once, some of the relatives watching near the corpse, others making preparations for the pending end and its consequences, others again performing perhaps some religious acts at a sacred spot. Thus in certain parts of Melanesia the real kinsmen must keep at a distance and only relatives by marriage perform the mortuary services, while in some tribes of Australia the reverse order is observed.

As soon as death has occurred, the body is washed, anointed and adorned, sometimes the bodily apertures are filled, the arms and legs tied together. Then it is exposed to the view of all, and the most important phase, the immediate mourning begins. Those who have witnessed death and its sequel among savages and who can compare these events with their counterpart among other uncivilized peoples must be struck by the fundamental similarity of the proceedings. There is always a more or less conventionalized and dramatized outburst of grief and wailing in sorrow, which often passes among savages into bodily lacerations and the tearing of hair. This is always done in a public display and is associated with visible signs of mourning, such as black or white daubs on the body, shaven or disheveled hair, strange or torn garments.

The immediate mourning goes on round the corpse. This, far from being shunned or dreaded, is usually the center of pious attention. Often there are ritual forms of fondling or attestations of reverence. The body is sometimes kept on the knees of seated persons, stroked and embraced. At the same time these acts are usually considered both dangerous and repugnant, duties to be fulfilled at some cost to the performer. After a time the corpse has to be disposed of. Inhumation with an open or closed grave; exposure in caves or on platforms, in hollow trees or on the ground in some wild desert place; burning or setting adrift in canoes – these are the usual forms of disposal.

This brings us to perhaps the most important point, the two-fold contradictory tendency, on the one hand to preserve the body, to keep its form intact, or to retain parts of it; on the other hand the desire to be done with it, to put it out of the way, to annihilate it completely. Mummification and burning are the two extreme expressions of this two-fold tendency. It is impossible to regard mummification or burning or any intermediate form as determined by mere accident of belief, as a historical feature of some culture or other which has gained its universality by the mechanism of spread and contact only. For in these customs is clearly expressed the fundamental attitude of mind of the surviving relative, friend or lover, the longing for all that remains of the dead person and the disgust and fear of the dreadful transformation wrought by death.

One extreme and interesting variety in which this double-edged attitude is expressed in a gruesome manner is sarco-cannibalism, a custom of partaking in piety of the flesh of the dead person. It is done with extreme repugnance and dread and usually followed by a violent vomiting fit. At the same time it is felt to be a supreme act of reverence, love, and devotion. In fact it is considered such a sacred duty that among the Melanesians of New Guinea, where I have studied and witnessed it, it is still performed in secret, although severely penalized by the white Government. The smearing of the body with the fat of the dead, prevalent in Australia and Papuasia is, perhaps, but a variety of this custom.

In all such rites, there is a desire to maintain the tie and the parallel tendency to break the bond. Thus the funerary rites are considered as unclean and soiling, the contact with the corpse as defiling and dangerous, and the performers have to wash, cleanse their body, remove all traces of contact, and perform ritual lustrations. Yet the mortuary ritual compels man to overcome the repugnance, to conquer his fears, to make piety and attachment triumphant, and with it the belief in a future life, in the survival of the spirit.

And here we touch on one of the most important functions of religious cult. In the foregoing analysis I have laid stress on the direct emotional forces created by contact with death and with the corpse, for they primarily and most powerfully determine the behavior of the survivors. But connected with these emotions and born out of them, there is the idea of the spirit, the belief in the new life into which the departed has entered. And here we return to the problem of animism with which we began our survey of primitive religious facts. What is the substance of a spirit, and what is the psychological origin of this belief?

The savage is intensely afraid of death, probably as the result of some deep-seated instincts common to man and animals. He does not want to realize it as an end, he cannot face the idea of complete cessation, of annihilation. The idea of spirit and of spiritual existence is near at hand, furnished by such experiences as are discovered and described by Tylor. Grasping at it, man reaches the comforting belief in spiritual continuity and in the life after death. Yet this belief does not remain unchallenged in the complex, double-edged play of hope and fear which sets in always in the face of death. To the comforting voice of hope, to the intense desire of immortality, to the difficulty, in one's own case, almost the impossibility, of facing annihilation there are opposed powerful and terrible forebodings. The testimony of the senses, the gruesome decomposition of the corpse, the visible disappearance of the personality – certain apparently instinctive suggestions of fear and horror seem to threaten man at all stages of culture with some idea of annihilation, with some hidden fears and forebodings. And here into this play of emotional forces, into this supreme dilemma of life and final death, religion steps in, selecting the positive creed, the comforting view, the culturally valuable belief in immortality, in the spirit independent of the body, and in the continuance of life after death. In the various ceremonies at death, in commemoration and communion with the departed, and worship of ancestral ghosts, religion gives body and form to the saving beliefs.

Thus the belief in immortality is the result of a deep emotional revelation, standardized by religion, rather than a primitive philosophic doctrine. Man's conviction of continued life is one of the supreme gifts of religion, which judges and selects the better of the two alternatives suggested by self-preservation – the hope of continued life and the fear of annihilation. The belief in spirits is the result of the belief in immortality. The substance of which the spirits are made is the full-blooded passion and desire for life, rather than the shadowy stuff which haunts his dreams and illusions. Religion saves man from a surrender to death and destruction, and in doing this it merely makes use of the observations of dreams, shadows, and visions. The real nucleus of animism lies in the deepest emotional fact of human nature, the desire for life.

Thus the rites of mourning, the ritual behavior immediately after death, can be taken as pattern of the religious act, while the belief in immortality, in the continuity of life and in the nether world, can be taken as the prototype of an act of faith. Here, as in the religious ceremonies previously described, we find self-contained acts, the aim of which is achieved in their very performance. The ritual despair, the obsequies, the acts of mourning, express the emotion of the bereaved and the loss of the whole group. They endorse and they duplicate the natural feelings of the survivors; they create a social event out of a natural fact. Yet, though in the acts of mourning, in the mimic despair of wailing, in the treatment of the corpse and in its disposal, nothing ulterior is achieved, these acts fulfill an important function and possess a considerable value for primitive culture.

What is this function? The initiation ceremonies we have found fulfill theirs in sacralizing tradition; the food cults, sacrament and sacrifice bring man into communion with providence, with the beneficent forces of plenty; totemism standardizes man's practical, useful attitude of selective interest towards his surroundings. If the view here taken of the biological function of religion is true, some such similar role must also be played by the whole mortuary ritual.

The death of a man or woman in a primitive group, consisting of a limited number of individuals, is an event of no mean importance. The nearest relatives and friends are disturbed to the depth of their emotional life. A small community bereft of a member, especially if he be important, is severely mutilated. The whole event breaks the normal course of life and shakes the moral foundations of society. The strong tendency on which we have insisted in the above description: to give way to fear and horror, to abandon the corpse, to run away from the village, to destroy all the belongings of the dead one – all these impulses exist, and if given way to would be extremely dangerous, disintegrating the group, destroying the material foundations of primitive culture. Death in a primitive society is, therefore, much more than the removal of a member. By setting in motion one part of the deep forces of the instinct of self-preservation, it threatens the very cohesion and solidarity of the group, and upon this depends the organization of that society, its tradition, and finally the whole culture. For if primitive man yielded always to the disintegrating impulses of his reaction to death, the continuity of tradition and the existence of material civilization would be made impossible.

We have seen already how religion, by sacralizing and thus standardizing the other set of impulses, bestows on man the gift of mental integrity. Exactly the same function it fulfills also with regard to the whole group. The ceremonial of death which ties the survivors to the body and rivets them to the place of death, the beliefs in the existence of the spirit, in its beneficent influences or malevolent intentions, in the duties of a series of commemorative or sacrificial ceremonies – in all this religion counteracts the centrifugal forces of fear, dismay, demoralization, and provides the most powerful means of reintegration of the group's shaken solidarity and of the re-establishment of its morale.

In short, religion here assures the victory of tradition and culture over the mere negative response of thwarted instinct.

With the rites of death we have finished the survey of the main types of religious acts. We have followed the crises of life as the main guiding thread of our account, but as they presented themselves we also treated the side issues, such as totemism, the cults of food and of propagation, sacrifice and sacrament, the commemorative cults of ancestors and the cults of the spirits. To one type already mentioned we still have to return – I mean, the seasonal feasts and ceremonies of communal or tribal character – and to the discussion of this subject we proceed now.

THE PUBLIC AND TRIBAL CHARACTER OF PRIMITIVE CULTS

The festive and public character of the ceremonies of cult is a conspicuous feature of religion in general. Most sacred acts happen in a congregation; indeed, the solemn conclave of the faithful united in prayer, sacrifice, supplication, or thanksgiving is the very prototype of a religious ceremony. Religion needs the community as a whole so that its members may worship in common its sacred things and its divinities, and society needs religion for the maintenance of moral law and order.

In primitive societies the public character of worship, the give-and-take between religious faith and social organization, is at least as pronounced as in higher cultures. It is sufficient to glance over our previous inventory of religious phenomena to see that ceremonies at birth, rites of initiation, mortuary attentions to the dead, burial, the acts of mourning and commemoration, sacrifice and totemic ritual, are one and all public and collective, frequently affecting the tribe as a whole and absorbing all its energies for the time being. This public character, the gathering together of big numbers, is especially pronounced in the annual or periodical feasts held at times of plenty, at harvest or at the height of the hunting or fishing season. Such feasts allow the people to indulge in their gay mood, to enjoy the abundance of crops and quarry, to meet their friends and relatives, to muster the whole community in full force, and to do all this in a mood of happiness and harmony. At times during such festivals visits of the departed take place: the spirits of ancestors and dead relatives return and receive offerings and sacrificial libations, mingle with the survivors in the acts of cult and in the rejoicings of the feast. Or the dead, even if they do not actually revisit the survivors, are commemorated by them, usually in the form of ancestor cult. Again, such festivities being frequently held, embody the ritual of garnered crops and other cults of vegetation. But whatever the other issues of such festivities, there can be no doubt that religion demands the existence of seasonal, periodical feasts with a big concourse of people, with rejoicings and festive apparel, with an abundance of food, and with relaxation of rules and taboos. The members of the tribe come together, and they relax the usual restrictions, especially the barriers of conventional reserve in social and in sexual intercourse. The appetites are provided for, indeed pandered to, and there is a common participation in the pleasures, a display to everyone of all that is good, the sharing of it in a universal mood of generosity. To the interest in plenty of material goods there is joined the interest in the multitude of people, in the congregation, in the tribe as a body.

With these facts of periodical festive gathering a number of other distinctly social elements must be ranged: the tribal character of almost all religious ceremonies, the social universality of moral rules, the contagion of sin, the importance of sheer convention and tradition in primitive religion and morals, above all the identification of the whole tribe as a social unit with its religion; that is, the absence of any religious sectarianism, dissention, or heterodoxy in primitive creed.

[. . .]

To sum up, the views of Durkheim and his school cannot be accepted. First of all, in primitive societies religion arises to a great extent from purely individual sources. Secondly, society as a crowd is by no means always given to the production of religious beliefs or even to religious states of mind, while collective effervescence is often of an entirely secular nature. Thirdly, tradition, the sum total of certain rules and cultural achievements, embraces, and in primitive societies keeps in a tight grip, both Profane and

Sacred. Finally, the personification of society, the conception of a 'Collective Soul', is without any foundation in fact, and is against the sound methods of social science.

The moral efficiency of savage beliefs

With all this, in order to do justice to Robertson Smith, Durkheim, and their school, we have to admit that they have brought out a number of relevant features of primitive religion. Above all, by the very exaggeration of the sociological aspect of primitive faith they have set forth a number of most important questions: Why are most religious acts in primitive societies performed collectively and in public? What is the part of society in the establishment of the rules of moral conduct? Why are not only morality but also belief, mythology, and all sacred tradition compulsory to all the members of a primitive tribe? In other words, why is there only one body of religious beliefs in each tribe, and why is no difference of opinion ever tolerated?

To give an answer to these questions we have to go back to our survey of religious phenomena, to recall some of our conclusions there arrived at, and especially to fix our attention upon the technique by which belief is expressed and morals established in primitive religion.

Let us start with the religious act par excellence, the ceremonial of death. Here the call to religion arises out of an individual crisis, the death which threatens man or woman. Never does an individual need the comfort of belief and ritual so much as in the sacrament of the viaticum, in the last comforts given to him at the final stage of his life's journey – acts which are well-nigh universal in all primitive religions. These acts are directed against the overwhelming fear, against the corroding doubt, from which the savage is no more free than the civilized man. These acts confirm his hope that there is a hereafter, that it is not worse than present life; indeed, better. All the ritual expresses that belief, that emotional attitude which the dying man requires, which is the greatest comfort he can have in his supreme conflict. And this affirmation has behind it weight of numbers and the pomp of solemn ritual. For in all savage societies, death, as we have seen, compels the whole community to forgather, to attend to the dying, and to carry out the duties towards him. These duties do not, of course, develop any emotional sympathy with the dying – this would lead merely to a disintegrating panic. On the contrary, the line of ritual conduct opposes and contradicts some of the strongest emotions to which the dying man might become a prey. The whole conduct of the group, in fact, expresses the hope of salvation and immortality; that is, it expresses only one among the conflicting emotions of the individual.

After death, though the main actor has made his exit, the tragedy is not at an end. There are the bereaved ones, and these, savage or civilized, suffer alike, and are thrown into a dangerous mental chaos. We have given an analysis of this already, and found that, torn between fear and piety, reverence and horror, love and disgust, they are in a state of mind which might lead to mental disintegration. Out of this, religion lifts the individual by what could be called spiritual co-operation in the sacred mortuary rites. We have seen that in these rites there is expressed the dogma of continuity after death, as well as the moral attitude towards the departed. The corpse, and with it the person of the dead one, is a potential object of horror as well as of tender love. Religion confirms the second part of this double attitude by making the dead body into an object of sacred duties. The bond of union between the recently dead and the survivors is maintained, a fact of immense importance for the continuity of culture and for the safe keeping of tradition. In all this we see that the whole community carries out the biddings of religious tradition, but that these are again enacted for the benefit of a few individuals only, the bereaved ones, that they arise from a personal conflict and are a solution of this conflict. It must also be remembered that what the survivor goes through on such an occasion prepares him for his own death. The belief in immortality, which he has lived through and practised in the case of his mother or father, makes him realize more clearly his own future life.

In all this we have to make a clear distinction between the belief and the ethics of the ritual on the one hand, and on the other the means of enforcing them, the technique by which the individual is made to receive his religious comfort. The saving belief in spiritual continuity after death is already contained in the individual mind; it is not created by society. The sum total of innate tendencies, known usually as 'the instinct of self-preservation', is at the root of this belief. The faith in immortality is, as we have seen, closely connected with the difficulty of facing one's own annihilation or that of a near and beloved person. This tendency makes the idea of the final disappearance of human personality odious, intolerable, socially destructive. Yet this idea and the fear of it always lurk in individual experience, and religion can remove it only by its negation in ritual.

Whether this is achieved by a Providence directly guiding human history, or by a process of natural selection in which a culture which evolves a belief and a ritual of immortality will survive and spread – this is a problem of theology or metaphysics. The anthropologist has done enough when he has shown the value of a certain phenomenon for social integrity and for the continuity of culture. In any case we see that what religion does in this matter is to select one out of the two alternatives suggested to man by his instinctive endowment.

This selection once made, however, society is indispensable for its enactment. The bereaved member of the group, himself overwhelmed by sorrow and fear, is incapable of relying on his own forces. He would be unable by his single effort to apply the dogma to his own case. Here the group steps in. The other members, untouched by the calamity, not torn mentally by the metaphysical dilemma, can respond to the crisis along the lines dictated by the religious order. Thus they bring consolation to the stricken one and lead him through the comforting experiences of religious ceremony. It is always easy to bear the misfortunes – of others, and the whole group, in which the majority are untouched by the pangs of fear and horror, can thus help the afflicted minority. Going through the religious ceremonies, the bereaved emerges changed by the revelation of immortality, communion with the beloved, the order of the next world. Religion commands in acts of cult, the group executes the command.

But, as we have seen, the comfort of ritual is not artificial, not manufactured for the occasion. It is but the result of the two conflicting tendencies which exist in man's innate emotional reaction to death: the religious attitude consists merely in the selection and ritual affirmation of one of these alternatives – the hope in a future life. And here the public concourse gives the emphasis, the powerful testimony to the belief. Public pomp and ceremony take effect through the contagiousness of faith, through the dignity of unanimous consent, the impressiveness of collective behavior. A multitude enacting as one an earnest and dignified ceremony invariably carries away even the disinterested observer, still more the affected participant.

But the distinction between social collaboration as the only technique necessary for the enactment of a belief on the one hand, and the creation of the belief or self-revelation of society on the other, must be emphatically pointed out. The community proclaims a number of definite truths and gives moral comfort to its members, but it does not give them the vague and empty assertion of its own divinity.

In another type of religious ritual, in the ceremonies of initiation, we found that the ritual establishes the existence of some power or personality from which tribal law is derived, and which is responsible for the moral rules imparted to the novice. To make the belief impressive, strong, and grandiose, there is the pomp of the ceremony and the hardships of preparation and ordeal. An unforgettable experience, unique in the life of the individual, is created, and by this he learns the doctrines of tribal tradition and the rules of its morality. The whole tribe is mobilized and all its authority set in motion to bear witness to the power and reality of the things revealed.

Here again, as at the death, we have to do with a crisis in the individual life, and a mental conflict associated with it. At puberty, the youth has to test his physical power, to cope with his sexual maturity, to take up his place in the tribe. This brings him promises, prerogatives, and temptations, and at the same time imposes burdens upon him. The right solution of the conflict lies in his compliance with tradition, in his submission to the sexual morality of his tribe and to the burdens of manhood, and that is accomplished in the ceremonies of initiation.

The public character of these ceremonies avails both to establish the greatness of the ultimate lawgiver and to achieve homogeneity and uniformity in the teaching of morals. Thus they become a form of condensed education of a religious character. As in all schooling, the principles imparted are merely selected, fixed, emphasized out of what there is in the individual endowment. Here again publicity is a matter of technique, while the contents of what is taught are not invented by society but exist in the individual.

In other cults again, such as harvest festivals, totemic gatherings, first-fruit offerings and ceremonial display of food, we find religion sacralizing abundance and security and establishing the attitude of reverence towards the beneficent forces without. Here again the publicity of the cult is necessary as the only technique suitable for the establishment of the value of food, accumulation and abundance. The display to all, the admiration of all, the rivalry between any two producers, are the means by which value is created. For every value, religious and economic, must possess universal currency. But here again we find only the selection and emphasis of one of the two possible individual reactions. Accumulated food can either be squandered or preserved. It can either be an incentive to immediate heedless consumption and light-hearted carelessness about the future, or else it can stimulate man to devising means of hoarding the treasure and of using it for culturally higher purposes. Religion sets its stamp on the culturally valuable attitude and enforces it by public enactment.

The public character of such feasts subserves another sociologically important function. The members of every group which forms a cultural unit must come in contact with each other from time to time, but besides its beneficent possibility of strengthening social ties, such contact is also fraught with the danger of friction. The danger is greater when people meet in times of stress, dearth, and hunger, when their appetite is unsatisfied and their sexual desires ready to flare up. A festive tribal gathering at times of plenty, when everyone is in a mood of harmony with nature and consequently with each other, takes on, therefore, the character of a meeting in a moral atmosphere. I mean an atmosphere of general harmony and benevolence. The occurrence of occasional licence at such gatherings and the relaxation of the rules of sex and of certain strictures of etiquette are probably due to the same course. All motives for quarrel and disagreement must be eliminated or else a big tribal gathering could not peacefully come to an end. The moral value of harmony and good will is thus shown to be higher than the mere negative taboos which curb the principal human instincts. There is no virtue higher than charity, and in primitive religions as well as in higher it covers a multitude of sins; nay, it outweighs them.

It is, perhaps, unnecessary to go in detail over all the other types of religious acts. Totemism, the religion of the clan, which affirms the common descent from or affinity with the totemic animal, and claims the clan's collective power to control its supply and impresses upon all the clan members a joint totemic taboo and a reverential attitude towards the totemic species, must obviously culminate in public ceremonies and have a distinctly social character. Ancestor cult, the aim of which is to unite into one band of worshippers the family, the sib or the tribe, must bring them together in public ceremonies by its very nature, or else it would fail to fulfill its function. Tutelary spirits of local groups, tribes, or cities; departmental gods; professional or local divinities must one and all – by their very definition – be worshipped by village, tribe, town, profession, or body politic.

In cults which stand on the borderline between magic and religion, such as the Intichuma ceremonies, public garden rites, ceremonies of fishing and hunting, the necessity of performance in public is obvious, for these ceremonies, clearly distinguishable from any practical activities which they inaugurate or accompany, are yet their counterpart. To the co-operation in practical enterprise there corresponds the ceremony in common. Only by uniting the group of workers in an act of worship do they fulfill their cultural function.

In fact, instead of going concretely into all the types of religious ceremony, we might have established our thesis by an abstract argument: since religion centers round vital acts, and since all these command public interest of joint co-operative groups, every religious ceremony must be public and carried out by groups. All crises of life, all important enterprises, arouse the public interest of primitive communities, and they all have their ceremonies, magical or religious. The same social body of men which unites for the enterprise or is brought together by the critical event performs also the ceremonial act. Such an abstract argument, however, correct though it be, would not have allowed us to get a real insight into the mechanism of public enactment of religious acts such as we have gained by our concrete description.

NOTES

1. *The Elementary Forms of the Religious Life*, p. 206.
2. Ibid.
3. J. Harrison, *Themis*, p. 42.
4. J. Harrison, op. cit. p. 44.
5. *Cf.* the writer's *Argonauts of the Western Pacific*, 1923, and the article on 'Primitive Economics' in the *Economic Journal*, 1921; as well as Professor Rich. Thurnwald's memoir on 'Die Gestaltung der Wirtschaftsentwicklung aus ihren Anfangen heraus' in *Erinnerungsgabe für Max Weber*, 1923.

A. R. RADCLIFFE-BROWN
'RELIGION AND SOCIETY'[1]

Alfred Reginald Radcliffe-Brown was born in 1881 in Sparkbrook, Birmingham. He read the moral sciences Tripos at Trinity College, Cambridge. In 1908 Radcliffe-Brown was awarded a junior research fellowship at Trinity and it was while enjoying this position that he was converted to a Durkheimian view of sociology. In 1910 he began his first period of fieldwork in the Andaman Islands. This was something of a disaster and indeed Radcliffe-Brown never really came to terms with anthropological fieldwork, his strength lying more in analysis of ethnography. In 1920 General Smuts invited Radcliffe-Brown to establish anthropology at the University of Cape Town, and six years later he took up a newly established Chair of Anthropology at Sydney. However, his tenure of the Sydney chair was disastrous and he left the department on the point of collapse in 1931. Radcliffe-Brown fled the administrative duties of Sydney to a chair at Chicago; in 1937 he returned to Britain to take up the newly established Chair in Social Anthropology at Oxford. He died in London in 1955.

Radcliffe-Brown is one of the primary early advocates of functionalism in anthropological theory. His form of functionalism, however, differed from that of Malinowski in its focus on society rather than the individual. This aspect is particularly evident in his analysis of religion and religious ritual, which he defined as serving the function of social regulation. In addition to his functionalist analysis Radcliffe-Brown's work also develops a trajectory that would culminate in French structuralism.

The Royal Anthropological Institute has honoured me with an invitation to deliver the Henry Myers Lecture on the rôle of religion in the development of human society. That is an important and complex subject, about which it is not possible to say very much in a single lecture, but as it is hoped that this may be only the first of a continuing series of lectures, in which different lecturers will each offer some contribution, I think that the most useful thing I can do is to indicate certain lines along which I believe that an enquiry into this problem can be profitably pursued.

The usual way of looking at religions is to regard all of them, or all except one, as bodies of erroneous beliefs and illusory practices. There is no doubt that the history of religions has been in great part a history of error and illusion. In all ages men have hoped that by the proper performance of religious actions or observances they would obtain some specific benefit: health and long life, children to carry on their line, material well-being,

A. R. Radcliffe-Brown (1952), *Structure and Function in Primitive Society*, London: Cohen & West.

success in hunting, rain, the growth of crops and the multiplication of cattle, victory in war, admission of their souls after death to a paradise, or inversely, release by the extinction of personality from the round of reincarnation. We do not believe that the rain-making rites of savage tribes really produce rain. Nor do we believe that the initiates of the ancient mysteries did actually attain through their initiation an immortality denied to other men.

When we regard the religions of other peoples, or at least those of what are called primitive peoples, as systems of erroneous and illusory beliefs, we are confronted with the problem of how these beliefs came to be formulated and accepted. It is to this problem that anthropologists have given most attention. My personal opinion is that this method of approach, even though it may seem the most direct, is not the one most likely to lead to a real understanding of the nature of religions.

There is another way in which we may approach the study of religions. We may entertain as at least a possibility the theory that any religion is an important or even essential part of the social machinery, as are morality and law, part of the complex system by which human beings are enabled to live together in an orderly arrangement of social relations. From this point of view we deal not with the origins but with the social functions of religions, i.e. the contribution that they make to the formation and maintenance of a social order. There are many persons who would say that it is only *true* religion (i.e. one's own) that can provide the foundation of an orderly social life. The hypothesis we are considering is that the social function of a religion is independent of its truth or falsity, that religions which we think to be erroneous or even absurd and repulsive, such as those of some savage tribes, may be important and effective parts of the social machinery, and that without these 'false' religions social evolution and the development of modern civilisation would have been impossible.

The hypothesis, therefore, is that in what we regard as false religions, though the performance of religious rites does not actually produce the effects that are expected or hoped for by those who perform or take part in them, they have other effects, some at least of which may be socially valuable.

How are we to set to work to test this hypothesis? It is of no use thinking in terms of religion in general, in the abstract, and society in the abstract. Nor is it adequate to consider some one religion, particularly if it is the one in which we have been brought up and about which we are likely to be prejudiced one way or another. The only method is the experimental method of social anthropology, and that means that we must study in the light of our hypothesis a sufficient number of diverse particular religions or religious cults in their relation to the particular societies in which they are found. This is a task not for one person but for a number.

Anthropologists and others have discussed at length the question of the proper definition of religion. I do not intend to deal with that controversial subject on this occasion. But there are some points that must be considered. I shall assume that any religion or any religious cult normally involves certain ideas or beliefs on the one hand, and on the other certain observances. These observances, positive and negative, i.e. actions and abstentions, I shall speak of as rites.

In European countries, and more particularly since the Reformation, religion has come to be considered as primarily a matter of belief. This is itself a phenomenon which needs to be explained, I think, in terms of social development. We are concerned here only with its effects on the thinking of anthropologists. Among many of them there is a tendency to treat belief as primary: rites are considered as the results of beliefs. They therefore concentrate their attention on trying to explain the beliefs by hypotheses as to how they may have been formed and adopted.

To my mind this is the product of false psychology. For example, it is sometimes held that funeral and mourning rites are the result of a belief in a soul surviving death. If we must talk in terms of cause and effect, I would rather hold the view that the belief in a surviving soul is not the cause but the effect of the rites. Actually the cause–effect analysis is misleading. What really happens is that the rites and the justifying or rationalising beliefs develop together as parts of a coherent whole. But in this development it is action or the need of action that controls or determines belief rather than the other way about. The actions themselves are symbolic expressions of sentiments.

My suggestion is that in attempting to understand a religion it is on the rites rather than on the beliefs that we should first concentrate our attention. Much the same view is taken by Loisy, who justifies his selection of sacrificial rites as the subject of his analysis of religion by saying that rites are in all religions the most stable and lasting element, and consequently that in which we can best discover the spirit of ancient cults.[2]

[. . .]

The relative stability of rites and the variability of doctrines can be illustrated from the Christian religions. The two essential rites of all Christian religions are baptism and the eucharist, and we know that the latter solemn sacrament is interpreted differently in the Orthodox Church, the Roman Church and the Anglican Church. The modern emphasis on the exact formulation of beliefs connected with the rites rather than on the rites themselves is demonstrated in the way in which Christians have fought with and killed one another over differences of doctrine.

Thirty-seven years ago (1908), in a fellowship thesis on the Andaman Islanders (which did not appear in print till 1922), I formulated briefly a general theory of the social function of rites and ceremonies. It is the same theory that underlies the remarks I shall offer on this occasion. Stated in the simplest possible terms the theory is that an orderly social life amongst human beings depends upon the presence in the minds of the members of a society of certain sentiments, which control the behaviour of the individual in his relation to others. Rites can be seen to be the regulated symbolic expressions of certain sentiments. Rites can therefore be shown to have a specific social function when, and to the extent that, they have for their effect to regulate, maintain and transmit from one generation to another sentiments on which the constitution of the society depends. I ventured to suggest as a general formula that religion is everywhere an expression in one form or another of a sense of dependence on a power outside ourselves, a power which we may speak of as a spiritual or moral power.

[. . .]

It is this theory that I propose for your consideration. Applied, not to a single society such as ancient China, but to all human societies, it points to the correlation and co-variation of different characteristics or elements of social systems. Societies differ from one another in their structure and constitution and therefore in the customary rules of behaviour of persons one to another. The system of sentiments on which the social constitution depends must therefore vary in correspondence with the difference of constitution. In so far as religion has the kind of social function that the theory suggests, religion must also vary in correspondence with the manner in which the society is constituted. In a social system constituted on the basis of nations which make war on one another, or stand ready to do so, a well-developed sentiment of patriotism in its members is essential to maintain a strong nation. In such circumstances patriotism or national feeling may be given support by religion. Thus the Children of Israel, when they invaded the land of Canaan under the leadership of Joshua, were inspired by the religion that had been taught to them by Moses and was centred upon the Holy Tabernacle and its rites.

War or the envisaged possibility of war is an essential element in the constitution of great numbers of human societies, though the warlike spirit varies very much from one to another. It is thus in accordance with our theory that one of the social functions of religion is in connection with war. It can give men faith and confidence and devotion when they go out to do battle, whether they are the aggressors or are resisting aggression. In the recent conflict the German people seem to have prayed to God for victory no less fervently than the people of the allied nations.

It will be evident that to test our theory we must examine many societies to see if there is a demonstrable correspondence of the religion or religions of any one of them and the manner in which that society is constituted. If such a correspondence can be made out, we must then try to discover and as far as possible define the major sentiments that find their expression in the religion and at the same time contribute to the maintenance of stability in the society as constituted.

[. . .]

I have dwelt, if only cursorily, with two types of religion: In both [ancestor-worship and Australian totemism] it is possible to demonstrate the close correspondence of the form of religion and the form of the social structure. In both it is possible to see how the religious rites reaffirm and strengthen the sentiments on which the social order depends. Here then are results of some significance for our problem. They point to a certain line of investigation. We can and should examine other religions in the light of the results already reached. But to do this we must study religions *in action*; we must try to discover the effects of active participation in a particular cult, first the direct effects on the individual and then the further effects on the society of which these individuals are members. When we have a sufficient number of such studies, it will be possible to establish a general theory of the nature of religions and their rôle in social development.

In elaborating such a general theory it will be necessary to determine by means of comparative studies the relations between religion and morality. There is only time to refer very briefly here to the question of religion and morality. As representing a theory that seems to be widely held, I quote the following passages from Tylor:

> One great element of religion, that moral element which among the higher nations forms its most vital part, is indeed little represented in the religion of the lower races.[3]
>
> The comparison of savage and civilised religions brings into view, by the side of a deep-lying resemblance in their philosophy, a deep-lying contrast in their practical action on human life. So far as savage religion can stand as representing natural religion, the popular idea that the moral government of the universe is an essential tenet of natural religion simply falls to the ground. Savage animism is almost devoid of that ethical element which to the educated modern mind is the very mainspring of practical religion. Not, as I have said, that morality is absent from the life of the lower races. Without a code of morals, the very existence of the rudest tribe would be impossible; and indeed the moral standards of even savage races are to no small extent well-defined and praiseworthy. But these ethical laws stand on their own ground of tradition and public opinion, comparatively independent of the animistic beliefs and rites which exist beside them. The lower animism is not immoral, it is unmoral. . . . The general problem of the relation of morality to religion is difficult, intricate, and requiring immense array of evidence.[4]

I agree with Tylor that the problem of the relation of morality to religion is difficult and intricate. But I wish to question the validity of the distinction he makes between the religions of savages and those of civilised peoples, and of his statement that the moral element 'is little represented in the religion of the lower races'. I suspect that when this view is held it often means only that in the 'lower races' the religion is not associated with the kind of morality which exists in contemporary Western societies. But societies differ in their systems of morals as in other aspects of the social system, and what we have to examine in any given society is the relation of the religion or religions of that society to their particular system of morality.

Dr. R. F. Fortune, in his book on Manus religion, has challenged the dictum of Tylor.[5] The religion of Manus is what may be called a kind of spiritualism, but it is not ancestor-worship in the sense in which I have used the term in this lecture. The Manus code of morals rigidly forbids sexual intercourse except between husband and wife, condemns dishonesty and insists on the conscientious fulfilment of obligations, including economic obligations, towards one's relatives and others. Offences against the moral code bring down on the offender, or on his household, punishment from the spirits, and the remedy is to be found in confession and reparation for wrong.

Let us now reconsider the case of ancestor-worship. In the societies which practise it, the most important part of the moral code is that which concerns the conduct of the individual in relation to his lineage and clan and the individual members thereof. In the more usual form of ancestor-worship, infractions of this code fall under religious or supernatural sanctions, for they are offences against the ancestors, who are believed to send punishment.

Again we may take as an example of the lower races the aborigines of Australia. Since the fundamental social structure is a complex system of widely extended recognition of relations of kinship, the most important part of the moral code consists of the rules of behaviour towards kin of different categories. One of the most immoral actions of which a man can be guilty is having sexual relations with any woman who does not belong to that category of his kinsfolk into which he may legally marry.

The moral law of the tribe is taught to young men in the very sacred ceremonies known as initiation ceremonies. I will deal only with the Bora ceremonies, as they are called, of some of the tribes of New South Wales. These ceremonies were instituted in the time of the World-Dawn by Baiame, who killed his own son Daramulun (sometimes identified with the sacred bull-roarer) and on the third day brought him back to life. As the ceremony is conducted, the initiates all 'die' and are brought back to life on the third day.[6]

On the sacred ceremonial ground where these initiations take place there is usually an image of Baiame made of earth, and sometimes one of Baiame's wife. Beside these images sacred rites are shown to the initiates, and sacred myths about Baiame are recounted.

Now Baiame instituted not only the initiation ceremonies, which are, amongst other things, schools of morals for young men, but also the kinship system with its rules about marriage and behaviour towards different categories of kin. To the question, 'Why do you observe these complex rules about marriage?' the usual answer is, 'Because Baiame established them'. Thus Baiame is the divine law-giver, or, by an alternative mode of expression, he is the personification of the tribal laws of morality.

I agree with Andrew Lang and Father Schmidt that Baiame thus closely resembles one aspect of the God of the Hebrews. But Baiame gives no assistance in war as Jehovah did for the children of Israel, nor is Baiame the ruler or controller of nature, of storms and seasons. That position is held by another deity, the Rainbow-Serpent, whose image in earth also appears on the sacred ceremonial ground. The position held by Baiame is that of the Divine Being who established the most important rules of morality and the sacred ceremonies of initiation.

These few examples will perhaps suffice to show that the idea that it is only the higher religions that are specially concerned with morality, and that the moral element is little represented in the religions of the lower races, is decidedly open to question. If there were time I could provide instances from other parts of the world.

What makes these problems complex is the fact that law, morality and religion are three ways of controlling human conduct which in different types of society supplement one another, and are combined, in different ways. For the law there are legal sanctions, for morality there are the sanctions of public opinion and of conscience, for religion there are religious sanctions. A single wrongful deed may fall under two or three sanctions. Blasphemy and sacrilege are sins and so subject to religious sanctions; but they may also sometimes be punished by law as crimes. In our own society murder is immoral; it is also a crime punishable by death; and it is also a sin against God, so that the murderer, after his sudden exit from this life at the hands of the executioner, must face an eternity of torment in the fires of Hell.

Legal sanctions may be brought into action in instances where there is no question of morality or immorality, and the same is true of religious sanctions. It is held by some of the Fathers or doctors of the Christian churches that an upright and virtuous life devoted to good works will not save a man from Hell unless he has attained grace by accepting as true the specific doctrines taught by a church.

There are different kinds of religious sanctions. The penalty for sin may be conceived simply as alienation from God. Or there may be a belief in rewards and punishments in an after-life. But the most widespread form of the religious sanction is the belief that certain actions produce in an individual or in a community a condition of ritual pollution, or uncleanness, from which it is necessary to be purified. Pollution may result from things done unintentionally and unwittingly, as you may see from the fifth chapter of the Book of Leviticus. One who unwittingly has touched any unclean thing, such as the carcase of an unclean beast, is guilty and has sinned and must bear his iniquity. He must make a sacrifice, a trespass offering, by which he may be cleansed from his sin.

Ritual uncleanness does not in itself involve moral condemnation. We read in the twelfth chapter of the same Book of Leviticus that the Lord instructed Moses that a woman who has borne a male child shall be unclean for seven days and her purification must continue for a further three and thirty days, during which she shall touch no hallowed thing, nor come into the sanctuary. If the child she bears is female, the first period of uncleanness is to be two weeks and the period of purification threescore-and-six days. Thus, it is polluting, but no one can suppose that it is immoral, to bear a child, and more polluting if the child is female than if it is male.

The opposite of pollution or sinfulness is holiness. But holiness comes not from leading an honest and upright life, but from religious exercises, prayer and fasting, the performance of penance, meditation and the reading of sacred books. In Hinduism the son of a Brahmin is born holy; the son of a leather-worker is born unclean.

The field covered by morality and that covered by religion are different; but either in primitive or in civilised societies there may be a region in which they overlap.

To return to our main topic, a writer who has dealt with the social function of religions on the basis of a comparative study is Loisy, who devotes to the subject a few pages of the concluding chapter of his valuable *Essai historique sur le Sacrifice*.[7] Although he differs from Durkheim in some matters, his fundamental theory is, if not identical, at any rate very similar to that of the earlier writer. Speaking of what he calls the sacred action (*l'action sacrée*), of which the most characteristic form is the rite of sacrifice, he writes:

> We have seen its rôle in human societies, of which it has maintained and strengthened the social bonds, if indeed it has not contributed in a large measure to creating them. It was, in certain respects, the expression of them; but man is so made that he becomes more firmly fixed in his sentiments by expressing them. The sacred action was the expression of social life, of social aspirations, it has necessarily been a factor of society. . . .
>
> Before we condemn out of hand the mirage of religion and the apparatus of sacrifice as a simple waste of social resources and forces, it is proper to observe that, religion having been the form of social conscience, and sacrifice the expression of this conscience, the loss was compensated by a gain, and that, so far as purely material losses

are concerned, there is really no occasion to dwell on them. Moreover the kind of sacred contribution that was required, without real utility as to the effect that was expected from it, was an intrinsic part of the system of renunciations, of contributions which, in every human society, are the condition of its equilibrium and its conservation.[8]

But besides this definition of the social function in terms of social cohesion and continuity, Loisy seeks for what he calls a general formula (*formule générale*) in which to sum up the part that religion has played in human life. Such a formula is useful so long as we remember that it is only a formula. The one that Loisy offers is that magic and religion have served to give men confidence.

In the most primitive societies it is magic that gives man confidence in face of the difficulties and uncertainties, the real and imaginary dangers with which he is surrounded.

> A la merci des éléments, des saisons, de ce que la terre lui donne ou lui refuse, des bonnes ou des mauvaises chances de sa chasse ou de sa pêche, aussi du hasard de ses combats avec ses semblables, il croit trouver le moyen de régulariser par des simulacres d'action ces chances plus ou moins incertaines. Ce qu'il fait ne sert à rien par rapport au but qu'il se propose, mais il prend confiance en ses entreprises et en lui-même, il ose, et c'est en osant que réellement il obtient plus ou moins ce qu'il veut. Confiance rudimentaire, et pour une humble vie; mais c'est le commencement du courage moral.[9]

This is the same theory that was later developed by Malinowski in reference to the magical practices of the Trobriand Islanders.

At a somewhat higher stage of development, 'when the social organism has been perfected, when the tribe has become a people, and this people has its gods, its religion, it is by this religion itself that the strength of the national conscience is measured, and it is in the service of national gods that men find a pledge of security in the present, of prosperity in the future. The gods are as it were the expression of the confidence that the people has in itself; but it is in the cult of the gods that this confidence is nourished'.[10]

At a still higher stage of social development, the religions which give men a promise of immortality give him thereby an assurance which permits him to bear courageously the burdens of his present life and face the most onerous obligations. 'It is a higher and more moral form of confidence in life'.[11]

To me this formula seems unsatisfactory in that it lays stress on what is only one side of the religious (or magical) attitude. I offer as an alternative the formula that religion develops in mankind what may be called a sense of dependence. What I mean by this can best be explained by an example. In an ancestor-worshipping tribe of South Africa, a man feels that he is dependent on his ancestors. From them he has received his life and the cattle that are his inheritance. To them he looks to send him children and to multiply his cattle and in other ways to care for his well-being. This is one side of the matter; on his ancestors he *can* depend. The other side is the belief that the ancestors watch over his conduct, and that if he fails in his duties they will not only cease to send him blessings, but will visit him with sickness or some other misfortune. He cannot stand alone and depend only on his own efforts; on his ancestors he *must* depend.

We may say that the beliefs of the African ancestor-worshipper are illusory and his offerings to his gods really useless; that the dead of his lineage do not really send him either blessings or punishments. But the Confucians have shown us that a religion like ancestor-worship can be rationalised and freed from those illusory beliefs that we call superstition. For in the rites of commemoration of the ancestors it is sufficient that the participants should express their reverential gratitude to those from whom they have received their life, and their sense of duty towards those not yet born, to whom they in due course will stand in the position of revered ancestors. There still remains the sense of dependence. The living depend on those of the past; they have duties to those living in the present and to those of the future who will depend on them.

I suggest to you that what makes and keeps a man a social animal is not some herd instinct, but the sense of dependence in the innumerable forms that it takes. The process of socialisation begins on the first day of an infant's life and it has to learn that it both *can* and *must* depend on its parents. From them it has comfort and succour; but it must submit also to their control. What I am calling the sense of dependence always has these two sides. We can face life and its chances and difficulties with confidence when we know that there are powers, forces and events on which we can rely, but we must submit to the control of our conduct by rules which are imposed. The entirely asocial individual would be one who thought that he could be completely independent, relying only on himself, asking for no help and recognising no duties.

I have tried to present to you a theory of the social function of religion. This theory has been developed by the work of such men as Robertson Smith, Fustel de Coulanges, Durkheim, Loisy. It is the theory that has guided my own studies for nearly forty years.

[. . .]

Like any other scientific theory it is provisional, subject to revision and modification in the light of future research. It is offered as providing what seems likely to be a profitable method of investigation. What is needed to test and further elaborate the theory is a number of systematic studies of various types of religion in relation to social systems in which they occur.

I will summarise the suggestions I have made:

1. To understand a particular religion we must study its effects. The religion must therefore be studied *in action*.
2. Since human conduct is in large part controlled or directed by what have been called sentiments, conceived as mental dispositions, it is necessary to discover as far as possible what are the sentiments that are developed in the individual as the result of his participation in a particular religious cult.
3. In the study of any religion we must first of all examine the specifically religious actions, the ceremonies and the collective or individual rites.
4. The emphasis on belief in specific doctrines which characterises some modern religions seems to be the result of certain social developments in societies of complex structure.
5. In some societies there is a direct and immediate relation between the religion and the social structure. This has been illustrated by ancestor-worship and Australian totemism. It is also true of what we may call national religions, such as that of the Hebrews or those of the city states of Greece and Rome.[12] But where there comes into existence a separate independent religious structure by the formation of different churches or sects or cult-groups within a people, the relation of religion to the total social structure is in many respects indirect and not always easy to trace.
6. As a general formula (for whatever such a formula may be worth) it is suggested that what is expressed in all religions is what I have called the sense of dependence in its double aspect, and that it is by constantly maintaining this sense of dependence that religions perform their social function.

Notes

1. The Henry Myers Lecture, 1945.
2. 'Les rites étant dans toutes les religions l'élément le plus consistant et le plus durable, celui, par conséquent, où se découvre le mieux l'esprit des cultes anciens.' – *Essai historique sur le Sacrifice*, Paris, 1920, p. 1.
3. Tylor, *Primitive Culture*, 3rd ed., 1891, vol. I, p. 427.
4. op cit., vol. II, p. 360.
5. R. F. Fortune, *Manus Religion*, Philadelphia, 1935, pp. 5 and 356. Dr. Fortune's book is a useful contribution to the study of the social function of religion and deals with a religion of a very unusual type.
6. The suggestion has been made that we have here the influence of Christianity, but that opinion can be dismissed. The idea of ritual death and rebirth is very widespread

in religion, and the three-day period is exemplified every month in every part of the world by the death and resurrection of the moon.

7. 1920, pp. 531–40.
8. op cit., pp. 535–7.
9. op cit., p. 533.
10. loc cit.
11. op cit., p. 534.
12. '... among the ancients what formed the bond of every society was a worship. Just as a domestic altar held the members of a family grouped about it, so the city was the collective group of those who had the same protecting deities, and who performed the religious ceremony at the same altar.' Fustel de Coulanges, *The Ancient City* (trans. Willard Small) p. 193.

BENSON SALER
'A PROTOTYPE APPROACH'

Benson Saler is an American anthropologist whose work focuses on 'epistemological issues relating to the study of religions and beliefs'. He was educated first at Princeton and later at the University of Pennsylvania, which awarded him a PhD in 1960. His doctoral ethnographic fieldwork was conducted among a Maya-Quiché population in the Pacific piedmont of Guatemala; however, his later fieldwork came to centre on the Guajiro Indians of northern Colombia and Venezuela. After his graduation he accepted a post at the University of Connecticut, which gave him the Award for Distinguished Teaching in 1963. In 1978 he spent a year as the Sir Isaac Wolfson Visiting Professor at the Hebrew University of Jerusalem. Saler finished his career at Brandeis University, Massachusetts. Since his retirement he has remained research active and holds an Emeritus Chair in the Department of Anthropology at Brandeis.

In Conceptualizing Religion *Saler presents an important critique of theorising about religion. In the material included here we present Saler's outline of his own approach. He suggests that a definition of religion should be based on family resemblance (or analogy) rather than a specific definition. This type of definition would be more open ended and sensitive to the differences found in varying ethnographic contexts.*

CONCEPTUALIZING RELIGION

I first present my viewpoint in relatively compacted form and then elaborate on some of its elements in the pages that follow.

Religion is an abstraction. It is an abstraction promulgated in our culture and supported by our experiences, including our experiences in reading. While many of us illumine our thinking about religion through recollections and a diversity of mental images – the smell of incense, perhaps, or snatches of hymns, or whatever – , religion is an intellectual abstraction, a concept, and not a concrete particular.

Numbers of Westerners, I suspect, if asked to describe at length what they understand by the word religion, might do so in terms of a pool of elements. Faced with analytical questions, they might reply with analytical answers. On other occasions, however, many of them might cognize religion metonymically (in terms, that is, of beliefs in God or Gods).

In any case, I recommend that academic students of religion explicitly conceptualize religion for analytical purposes in terms of a pool of elements

Benson Saler (1993), *Conceptualizing Religion*, Leiden: E. J. Brill.

that often cluster together but that may do so in greater or lesser degrees. Further, elements that we so associate with religion may be said to be in association with other things that are not deemed religions.

Our pool of elements includes belief in and communion with God, Gods, and 'spiritual beings' as variously conceived; a moral code to which religious persons attribute an extra-human reference or warrant; ideas about the possibilities of transcending human suffering; rituals with extra-human and/or eschatological references; and all of the other things in the lists drawn up by Alston and Southwold, along with some of the suggestions made by persons cited in the first four chapters of this work.

Different religions relate to that pool differently. We predicate many religion-constituting elements of 'religion in general', but not all of them are predicable of all religions. This logic also applies to denominated families of religions. While, for instance, some branches or members of the family 'Buddhism' may be deemed 'atheistic', as Durkheim, Southwold, and others claim, others are not. Hence, as Hudson (1977: 238) argues, theism is among the family resemblances of Buddhism and can be predicated of Buddhism even if it cannot be predicated of all Buddhisms. To supply another and more particularized example, the doctrine of the dual nature of Christ, the doctrine that Jesus Christ is both fully human and fully divine, is specifically predicable of Christianity even though it is rejected by many members of monophysite Christian churches and by numbers of other Christians who are members of non-monophysite churches.

The best exemplars of what I mean by religion are the Western monotheisms. They are the most prototypical examples of the category, for they clearly include all of the elements cited by Alston and Southwold in the lists that I quoted in Chapter 5. While we ought not to say that by religion we mean Judaism, Christianity, and Islam – we ought not to say it because by religion we mean a conceptual model that can be described analytically in terms of abstracted elements that we more or less relate together – , those religions are, for most Westerners, the clearest examples of what is normally meant by religion. They can be used as such for reference and for comparative purposes.

My proposal, then, is that we self-consciously conceptualize 'religion' as an analytical category with reference to, but not in actual terms of, our personal and changeable understandings of Judaism, Christianity, and Islam – that we regard our understandings of those familial cases as foregrounding what is notably prototypical of the category *without attempting to draw sharp boundaries around that category*. In doing so, we recognize, of course, that those families of religions, as comparatively understood by knowledgeable persons, differ in various important respects from each other as well as from other religions, and that the members of each family differ in interesting respects from one another.

Some religions will express most of the elements that we utilize in conceptualizing religion. Others will express less. And any element expressed in different religions is likely to be elaborated on differently in those religions.

We may often opine that phenomena that we are reluctant to call religions contain elements that we elsewhere deem to be religious elements. We are reluctant to call these cases religions largely for one or both of two reasons. First, they strike us as containing too few of the elements that we associate with religion. Second, the contexts in which the elements occur, and the ways the elements are elaborated within those contexts, do not remind us strongly enough of other phenomena that we have no hesitation in calling religions. In such cases, then, we identify religious elements that pertain to instantiations of what we regard as other categories – and such cases are legion! So identifying religious elements facilitates going beyond religion and attending to 'the religious dimension' of much of human life. It is important to note in that regard that religious elements are not bounded by the category religion because I conceptualize that category without reference to boundaries.

[. . .]

THE EXEMPLAR VIEW

Conceptualizing and explicating a concept with reference to examples, it must be noted, is not the same thing as actually representing a category in the mind in terms of its best example(s). Lakoff (1987: 136–52) argues against a view of prototype theory that (1) regards a prototype as a representation of a category's structure (with the membership of other entities computed on the basis of similarity to the properties of the prototype) and that (2) holds that prototype effects directly reflect degree of membership in a category.

As for (2), membership in groups comprehended by categories may or may not be scalar, and Lakoff, I think, is right to argue against the generalization that goodness of example is (always) a direct reflection of degree of membership. In the case that concerns us, however, Western analysts and comparativists might safely and productively follow their biases and conceptualize religion as a category that comprehends a group with graded membership.

Various biases do suggest the possibility of graded membership. Thus, for example, Paul Tillich writes of 'quasi-religions', religions that are religions according to his experiential criteria but that are based on concerns that are falsely ultimate. Jill Dubisch conceptualizes the health food movement as religion-like and she deems it productive to analyze it in religious terms. And while Ward Goodenough and B. K. Smith treat communism or Marxism as fully fitting their respective monothetic definitions of religion, some of us are likely to maintain that although communism and Marxism resemble religions in certain important respects (even though many of their adherents claim to be anti-religious), they are not 'full' religions, or they are less of a religion than something else. For certain analytical purposes, however, it can make sense to treat them as religions.

As to point (1) above: Considerations that relate to our analytical and comparative interests in religion can be foregrounded by looking at certain aspects of that point as treated by Smith and Medin (1981: 143–61) in their discussion of what they call "the exemplar view."

According to Smith and Medin (1981: 144), 'there is probably only one assumption that all proponents of the exemplar view would accept: the representation of a concept consists of separate descriptions of some of its exemplars (either instances or subsets)'. This has been criticized as, among other things, leaving little or no room for abstractions.

Smith and Medin (1981: 143) attempt to counter that criticism by arguing that we can use a subset of a concept as exemplification rather than a specific instance (e.g., for the category clothing, a subset corresponding to blue jeans in general rather than some specific pair of blue jeans). The exemplar view in such cases, Smith and Medin (*ibid.*) argue, permits abstractions. In the case that concerns us, however, representation of the concept of religion by a separate description of some exemplar – 'Christianity', say – would require (for anyone who knows a fair amount about the Christian family of confessions, past and present) mind-boggling complexities and subtleties that go well beyond any that I can imagine for blue jeans as an exemplar of clothing – and I do not suppose 'blue jeans in general' to be unproblematical.

A second and even more arresting problem has to do with the disjunction of exemplars associated with a conceptual category. As Smith and Medin (1981: 157) put it, on the view that 'exemplars tend to be represented separately, . . . how can we represent something that pertains to all exemplars?' A possible solution, they suppose, might be that 'knowledge about a correlation between properties is *computed* from an exemplar-based representation when needed, rather than *prestored* in the representation' (1981: 157). They go on to say that

> for the best-examples model, . . . there may be a need to specify some necessary features, or some sufficient ones, for each exemplar represented in a concept; otherwise we are left with problems such as the exemplar permitting too great a degree of disjunctiveness. (1981: 158)

A different – and, I think, better – solution with respect to the case that concerns us specifically is one that seeks to make statements about religion as an analytical category rather than attempting (and failing!) to specify necessary or sufficient conditions for what we deem our most prototypical examples of that category. I have two major reasons for preferring that solution.

First, I don't think that it is productive to posit necessary and/or sufficient conditions of exemplars when dealing with an analytical category such as religion. While biological pheneticists may often hold that there are monothetic cores in polythetic taxa, anthropologists and other students of religion ought not to suppose something analogous for religions and for 'religion' as an analytical instrument. Our most prototypical exemplars of religion are themselves richly polythetic.

Second, my preferred solution – one that calls attention to the importance of contingency-sensitive predicates – has much to recommend it in its own right.

I deal with both of these reasons below.

NECESSITY, SUFFICIENCY, AND BOUNDARIES

It is not enough to point to 'Judaism', 'Christianity', and 'Islam' as being, for persons brought up in Western societies, our clearest examples of religion. We must also come to terms with the understanding that Judaism, Christianity, and Islam must themselves be approached with reference to prototypicality. Each of those families exhibits considerable synchronic as well as diachronic variety. While knowledgeable proponents of one or another may tell us what they suppose to be the distinguishing features of their faith, such talk is valuable not as decisive insider authority – especially if we reject essentialist distinguishing features! – but as data that requires evaluation in our efforts to determine degrees of prototypicality.

A fair amount of information has been gathered by the compilers of textbooks in comparative religion. We can turn to them, but not for statements of what properties are necessary and sufficient for each family of religions. Rather, we find in such compilations descriptions of elements that canonical texts and various respected commentators have emphasized as being most important in constituting prototypes that we respectively identify with the rubrics Judaism, Christianity, and Islam.

Explicitly conceiving of a category 'religion' with reference to (but not in concrete terms of) what we individually and variously take to be some of its clearest (though not unproblematical) exemplars, the Western monotheisms, does not by any means exclude less clear-cut cases from our analytical purview. We need initial orientation, and our most clear-cut examples of religion provide it. They allow us initially to organize our analytical efforts with reference to type cases, comparing the elements of other cases to their elements and rendering judgments with regard to the respective degrees of typicality of those other cases. It is worth reiterating in that connection that, as Rosch (1978: 40) puts it, 'to speak of a *prototype* at all is simply a convenient grammatical fiction; what is really referred to are judgements of degree of prototypicality'.

But where, then, essentialist diehards may nevertheless ask, does the category give out? Where is the line that separates religion from non-religion?

There is no hard and fast line. This admission, however, prompts me to raise and attempt to answer two questions. First, is there no test of 'sufficiency' that will enable us to include and exclude candidates with some facility, to deal expeditiously with, say, 'civil religion' (Bellah 1967, Bellah and Hammond 1980) or Goodenough's claim that 'communism' is 'one of the great religions of modern times' (1989: 6)? And, second, if there is not, does that not pose serious practical problems for our research and teaching?

The prototype approach sketched here can be construed as a variant of the 'multi-factorial' approaches discussed in Chapter 5. Advocates of 'family resemblance' and 'polythetic' conceptualizations of religion, it may be recalled, propose a list of 'attributes' (Southwold 1978a: 370) or 'religion-making characteristics' (Alston 1967: 141), where no single one of them is necessary to establish the existence of religion. Authors who compile such lists, however, generally suppose that some combination of attributes, variable from case to case, is sufficient to do so, although no precise formula specifying what might constitute a sufficient conjunction is usually supplied.

Rem Edwards, who attempts a family resemblance approach to religion, remarks that 'there are many sufficient but no necessary conditions for calling something religion' (1972: 38). Jonathan Z. Smith, who advocates 'polythetic classification', applauds Edwards's remark (1982: 136–7, n. 15). And, as noted earlier, Alston (1967: 142) states that when 'enough' of his nine 'religion-making characteristics' are 'present to a sufficient degree, we have a religion', and that 'given the actual use of the term "religion", this is as precise as we can be'.

All of the authors cited above appear to operate with a notion of sufficiency that requires very few factors. Doing so, however, is not mandated by a strict application of either Wittgenstein's concept of family resemblance or the biologists' numerical phenetics. With respect to the latter, it may be recalled, Sokal and Sneath remark that 'no single feature is either essential to group membership or is sufficient to make an organism a member of the group' (1963: 14), and they advocate using at least forty characters, each with its own character states, in classificatory procedures. And Wittgenstein is concerned with meaning as use rather than analytical criteria of sufficiency.

The student of religion, however, generally operates with a smaller number of characters and character states than does the numerical pheneticist in biology. Scholars of religion, moreover, are less likely than biologists to agree empirically on character states, for the establishment of some of them (as in the study of 'belief systems') requires relatively high order interpretations. And the higher the order of interpretation, the less widespread agreement may tend to be. Nor can the comparatively oriented student rest content with the analysis of natural language usages; cross-cultural studies demand analytical categories developed within the framework of a carefully thought out – indeed, teleological – 'language-game'.

But Alston, Edwards, and J. Z. Smith, in addition to allowing for sufficiency, exhibit slippage between religion as a folk category and religion as an analytical category. Their conceptual structures appear to be weighted by considerations bearing on what Alston describes as 'the actual use of the term "religion"'. Those authors, in effect, supply us with prescriptions about conceptualizing religion that are connected to an appreciation of natural language usages, the prescriptions consisting, fundamentally, in the rejection of a demand for necessity and an allowance for sufficiency. The approach that I recommend, however, differs with respect to the matter of sufficiency and in its self-consciousness about analytical categories.

It is worth noting that prototype semantics as construed by Coleman and Kay for the analysis of natural language categories dispenses with sufficiency as well as necessity. In their gradient framework, they write, 'the bivalent concepts of the "necessity" and "sufficiency" of properties do not apply' (1981: 28). If we commit ourselves to prototype semantics, then, a *descriptive* approach to the category religion, an approach constituted by the investigation and analysis of *how people actually use* the category label, can presumably be accomplished without invoking sufficiency. But does that mean that we might do without it in *prescriptive* statements about religion – in statements, that is, that stipulate what anthropologists *should* mean by religion as an *analytical* category?

Operating without the concepts of necessity and sufficiency would seem to pose practical problems for our research and teaching. The researcher may understandably desire explicit criteria that would serve to govern admission to, and exclusion from, some collectivity of phenomena that are to be assembled for cross-cultural exploration. Similarly, the teacher would find it useful to enunciate clear standards that mark off the field of religious scholarship.

Yet the approach recommended here does operate without universal criteria for inclusion and exclusion in conceptualizing religion as an analytical category. The best that I can do – some will find it unsettling! – is to trace diminishing degrees of typicality, and to offer arguments as cogent as I can make them for my decisions in assigning or failing to assign specific candidates to the group comprehended by the category. In stipulating a research category explicated with reference to the clearest examples, I commit myself to the rendering and defending of analytical judgments respecting less clear cases.

CONTINGENCY-SENSITIVE PREDICATES

In an exposition of polythesis that accommodates prototype theory, Poole writes that

> following Campbell (1965), Needham (1975) has argued that a poly-
> thetic category formed on the basis of the similarities of family

resemblance must have a list of 'basic predicates'. Rather than circum-scribing the boundary of a category on the basis of shared characteristics in the manner of monothetic classification, a polythetic categorization directs attention to the interpretation of basic predi-cates as the principles that enable the connection of phenomena in family resemblance chains. Such predicates, therefore, are not empir-ical properties of the phenomena, but are formal aspects of the model of classification. The use of formal predicates of analytic models rather than empirical properties of phenomena as the basis of categories is largely inimical to any single-factor similarity definitions of a class. (1986: 427)

Assimilating this to a prototype approach to conceptualizing the category religion, I would add that individual predicates associated with the model of classification are contingency-sensitive respecting *particular instantiations* of the category. That is, they may or they may not apply in particular cases. I choose predicates about 'theism' as an example, both because they illustrate this point nicely and because they are important in related ways.

THEISM

Martin Southwold [...] treats theism (which we may broadly identify as the postulation of Gods) as a contingent but not necessary element in religion. In my opinion, he is right to do so. Yet theism, I believe, not only fascinates many anthropologists, but it also constitutes a set of default values for them in their conventional conceptualizations of religion. I explore each of these points in turn.

While I cannot cite much in the way of supporting data, it is my im-pression that many anthropologists who study religion are not themselves conventionally religious. Although some may occasionally attend religious services in their own societies, sizeable numbers of them, or so it seems to me, do not personally endorse theism or the mythic and soteriological understandings that are distinctly associated with religion in their cultures. Distanced from religion, many are intrigued by (if sometimes critical of) religious persons. What is it about religious persons that fascinates them the most? Probably, I suspect, the several sorts of investments that religious persons in Western and in many other societies make in what anthropolo-gists conventionally label Gods.

While numbers of non-religious anthropologists accept the reality of be-liefs in deities, they tend to suppose that deity as such is unreal. Yet many religious persons (numerous Theravada Buddhists included) not only af-firm the existence of Gods, but they often describe them as being invisible or otherwise unobservable much of the time (in many traditions, however, it is affirmed that the Gods may become sensible to their worshippers in certain ways). Further, they generally maintain that the Gods are powerful enough to affect human life in several important respects and that they are inclined to enter into communion with humans. Many religious persons, moreover, expend valued resources on the Gods. Often enough in human history, indeed, they have sincerely and fatally pledged their lives, their fortunes, and their sacred honors in the service or propitiation of beings that, in the opinion of many anthropologists, have no reality independent of the imaginations and assertions of human beings and the cultural traditions that those human beings have created.

Should the non-theist analyst reflect on the apparent proclivity for theism suggested by human history, he or she may feel a certain estrangement from humanity's teeming theistic multitudes. The analyst's sense of his/her own 'otherness' may itself become a factor inspiring and coloring research, rendering theism a scholarly problem deemed 'tremendous and fascinating' – a mystery that we do not embrace but probe.

Theism, of course, is not a simple matter. There are various problems relating to what might be meant by 'God' and the comparability or incomparability of postulations made in different societies respecting the wide range of beings that we conventionally gloss as 'Gods'. Furthermore, while what we call theism occurs within the compass of many cultural traditions that we conventionally term religions, it also occurs outside of that compass.

Theism, most of us would agree, is an element or complex of elements typically encountered in 'religions'. Yet we can also discern it among what we regard as instantiations of other categories. It occurs sometimes, for example, in association with the category 'science', a category that numbers of Western authors have opposed or contrasted to religion. We could argue, of course, that when scientists such as Newton, Kepler, and Boyle invoked God in their scientific theories, they did so because they were themselves religious. But to say that and no more is to miss much of interest. While it is true that Newton, Kepler, and Boyle were socialized and enculturated to be religious, it is also the case that their styles of science required God for theoretical reasons, and that they persisted in being theists partially because they were scientists of a certain sort.

In analyzing religions in the way recommended here, theism, as already pointed out, is to be considered contingent. It can be highly visible and important in some cases, absent in others, and in still others discernable though perhaps neither salient nor, on analysis, crucially important. Yet for numbers of participants in Western cultures, most anthropologists included, theism is quite probably more important for pattern recognition and the study of religion than any other elements. This occasions no problems in principle for prototype theory for, as Coleman and Kay note, 'properties may be of differential importance in constituting the prototype' (1981: 27).

But while employing theism for pattern recognition and subsequent thinking about religion is not a problem in principle, it may well prove to be a problem in practice. For many contemporary Westerners, theism may constitute a metonym for religion. For some persons, indeed, the identification of theism is tantamount to the discovery of religion.

In the analytical approach recommended here, the conventionally determined 'part', theism, is neither necessary nor sufficient for the identification of all cases of religion, regardless of any folk metonymic cognitive models to the contrary and their celebration in academic monothetic definitions. Theism can and should be predicated of religion as a category. We should have no trouble in regarding it as an aspect of our analytical model. It may not, however, be predicable of various cases that, on other (i.e., non-theistic) grounds, some analysts deem religions (e.g., 'communism'). Or it may be predicable in certain cases in troubling, problematic ways. Aristotle's Unmoved Mover, for example, takes no notice of humankind and any sort of communion with it is entirely out of the question. Does Aristotle's God suggest religion?

In my opinion, which is weighted significantly by considerations of communion, Aristotle's Unmoved Mover does not point to religion; rather, it forms part of a theistic metaphysical system. But those analysts who emphasize religion's roles in posing and answering questions about 'ultimate reality' may wish to include Aristotle's God under the rubric religion. Disagreements of this sort should be expected. One hopes, however, that analysts make serious efforts to state explicitly the reasons for their respective positions.

Predications of theism, in short, are contingency-sensitive. For most Westerners, however, certain cases that prominently include theism (e.g., 'Judaism', 'Christianity') are very likely to seem significantly better exemplars of the category religion than those that do not (e.g., 'communism') or that do not accord it crucial cosmogenic and soteriological significance (e.g., 'canonical Theravada Buddhism').

DEFAULT VALUES

Frequently encountered presumptions and expectations about the association of theism and religion suggest that for numbers of Westerners, some anthropologists included, theism often functions as a 'default assignment' in the schematization of religion.

Many readers are probably familiar with the expression default assignment as utilized with respect to computers and software programs. A word processing program, for example, is likely to have various prefigured – 'default' – values for such things as the sizes of right and left page margins, the number of lines that will be accepted on a page of a certain size, and so forth. If the operator does nothing, those are the values that s/he must operate with. Typically, however, those preset values can be overriden by the operator: changed, that is, within a restricted range of possibilities.

In natural language use, default assignments tend to be associated with 'unmarkedness'. Numbers of language terms may be marked or unmarked.

Thus, for example, in English 'dog' as a generalized animal is unmarked, but 'dog' in the sense of male dog is marked, as is 'bitch', a female dog. Default assignments are usually the unmarked elements of categories. Lakoff (1987: 60–1) remarks that the marked/unmarked distinction is employed by linguists for describing a sort of 'prototype effect', an asymmetry, where one element or subcategory pertaining to a category is taken to be 'somehow more basic' than any other.

In the contemporary cognitive sciences, a default assignment is broadly characterized as an attribution not directly and fully specified by knowledge of the situation at hand. In the absence of specific knowledge of actual situational values, assignment is made on the basis of a knowledge of, and expectations derived from, other cases that are apperceived to resemble the one at hand.

So, too, do anthropologists sometimes invoke default values on first apperceiving what appear to be theistic variables in the field. The most widely invoked default values are probably those of the Judeo-Christian God conceived of as a supernatural creator, sustainer, law-giver, judge, and savior. Those values, however, may not always serve us well.

In practice, close attention to specific situations may require the detachment of various default values from our interpretive structures. Critical attitudes and a high capacity for critical thought are of crucial significance for doing so. As Minsky points out, '"Schematic" thinking, based on matching complicated situations against stereotyped frame structures, must be inadequate for some aspects of mental activity. Obviously,' he continues, 'mature people can to some extent think about, as well as use their own representations' (1975: 230).

Critical thought about religion can be advanced by fashioning an explicit analytical approach that both allows for our conventional Western schemata and their default assignments and at the same time prepares us to detach (override) whatever values we may need to discard or supplant in our particularized attentions to the world. I argue in the next (and concluding) chapter that this would contribute to the development of our interpretive approximations to alter understandings by facilitating progressive, self-conscious distanciation from our conventional exemplars while preserving and utilizing them as points of comparison. In short, we might profit from our prototypical biases by critically recognizing and employing them as such, and probing them in the process.

In Summary

My suggestion for conceptualizing religion is this: religion is an abstraction. For analytical purposes we may conceptualize it in terms of a pool of elements that more or less tend to occur together in the best exemplars of the category. While all of the elements that we deem to pertain to the category religion are predicable of that category, not all of them are predicable of all the phenomena that various scholars regard as instantiations of religion. Those instantiations, called religions, include the Western monotheisms, our most prototypical cases of religion. They also include whatever else we deem to participate in the pool of elements to the extent of resembling the Western monotheisms in significant respects. And how do we establish what is significant? By cogent analytical arguments about elements that we deem analogous to those that we associate with our reference religions, the Western monotheisms.

We decide by reasoned arguments the question of whether or not to include under the rubric religion candidates that strike us as representing lesser degrees of prototypicality. We do so in the absence of certitude about, and firm commitments to, boundaries. Ideally, moreover, our reasoned arguments will include some statement of what we hope to accomplish by designating phenomena 'religions' or by pointing out that they contain elements that we identify as 'religious'. Our procedures can be most cogently explicated when they are related to an open consideration of our purposes (cf. Watanabe 1969: 388).

Each candidate must be examined as thoroughly as possible when considered with reference to our analytical model and when compared and contrasted to our clearest cases. While this approach is not entirely open-ended, it is relatively so in comparison to typical monothetic approaches.

The reader may object that the approach recommended here does not actually resolve the problem of identifying religions other than the Western monotheisms but only defers it. That complaint is justified. Case by case analysis must still be accomplished and accompanying arguments constructed about candidates, arguments perhaps in some cases (e.g., 'civil religion' or 'communism') relevant to the construction of a gradient framework by means of which we hope to order them. I have suggested the general direction that the analyst should take, but genuine progress depends on detailed, imaginative analysis.

In the approach recommended here, there are no clear boundaries drawn about religion. Rather, elements that we may apperceive as 'religious' are found in phenomena that numbers of us, for a variety of reasons, may not be prepared to dub religions. But if our ultimate purpose as scholars is to say interesting things about human beings rather than about religions and religion, appreciation of the pervasiveness of religious elements in human life is far more important than any contrivance for bounding religion.

MARTIN SOUTHWOLD
'BUDDHISM AND THE DEFINITION OF RELIGION'

Martin Southwold was a member of the Department of Social Anthropology at the University of Manchester when in 1983 he published his most famous monograph, 'Buddhism in Life'.

Southwold's contribution to theorising about religion is found in a journal article that critiques the definition offered by Spiro (pages 290–6). Southwold's discussion is particularly scathing regarding Spiro's understanding of Buddhism, and whether Buddhism can fit into a proper definition of religion. We have included the sections of the article that develop Southwold's own definition of religion. This definition seeks to be more flexible and open ended, offering a range of different elements out of which religions may be constructed. While this definition is similar to that of Smart (pages 154–61), it offers greater potential flexibility and thus cross-cultural applicability.

V

We have [...] shown that practical Buddhism does not manifest a central concern with godlike beings. Hence, *either* the theistic definitions and conception of religion are wrong *or* Buddhism is not a religion. But the latter proposition is not a viable option. In virtually every other respect Buddhism markedly resembles religions, and especially the religion prototypical for our conception, i.e. Christianity. If we declare that Buddhism is not a religion, we take on the daunting task of explaining how a non-religion can come so uncannily to resemble religions. Moreover, since the comparison of Buddhism with religions is so interesting and important, we should have to form a super-class, called say 'religion-plus', containing all religions plus Buddhism; and this may well seem a scientifically more valuable category than that of religion simply. We should have preserved the purity of our conception of religion at the expense of demoting it in the conceptual hierarchy. In any case the basic conceptual problem and challenge remain, however we shuffle labels: what, confronted with the facts about Buddhism, are we to make of our conception, or prejudice, that central concern with godlike beings is fundamental to phenomena of this kind?

Hence theistic definitions of religion are shown by Buddhism to be wrong, as Durkheim argued. Formally, a definition to be valid must apply to every instance of the phenomena to be defined; hence even one exception is sufficient to refute the definition. It might be countered, with good sense, that exceptions are so rare that theistic definitions, though not perfect, are good enough for practical purposes. This defence, however, fails against a

Martin Southwold (1978), 'Buddhism and the definition of religion', *Man* 13(3).

more substantial objection which applies not only to formal definitions but also more generally to theistic conceptions of religion. We have in Buddhism (which in fact is not wholly unique) a well-authenticated instance of a system of religious behaviour without a central concern with godlike beings. This suggests that such a concern is not fundamental to religious behaviour, and invites us to look again for other features which may be more fundamental. It may be – and I believe that it is – that the near-universality in religions of a central concern with godlike beings has stalled enquiry, leading us to mistake as fundamental what is actually only a secondary or derivative characteristic. The serious objection to theistic definitions and conceptions of religion is not that they fail to be universal but rather that they are too superficial. The theoretical importance of Buddhism is not that it enables us to score points off this or that definition of religion, but that it challenges us to formulate a more adequate conception of religion.

VI

Durkheim's argument follows a similar course: he refutes widely accepted definitions of religion not for the sake of merely negative criticism, but in order to clear the way for presenting a more adequate definition. It seems natural to follow him in this. But in fact by taking this further step Durkheim committed a grievous error.

It is notorious that Durkheim's definition of religion, in terms of the opposition of sacred and profane, fails, both because it does not fit many of the data and because it is incoherent (see especially Stanner 1967 (summarised in Lukes 1973: 26–7), and Evans-Pritchard 1965: 64–5). What is less widely appreciated is the positive harm that has resulted from this failure.

1. Some kind of contrast or polarity between the sacred and the everyday is a significant feature of many religious systems; where it does apply, a concept of a sacred/profane dichotomy is clearly valuable. But by proposing the concept as the definition of religion, Durkheim claimed too much; the refutation of the definition has caused the concept itself to appear discredited.
2. Durkheim sought to impose his definition by what is basically a mere rhetorical device. He outlined, and brilliantly refuted, two familiar definitions: and then suggested that no alternative was left but his own (1912: 33–50 sq.; 1915: 24–37 sq.). The first of the refuted definitions is that which defines religion in terms of mystery and the supernatural – which no anthropologist, for the very reasons Durkheim so ably expounds, is likely to accept. His 'argument' thus reduced to the presentation of a dilemma: *either* theistic definitions *or* Durkheim's own. Oddly, this thoroughly tendentious formulation has been widely accepted: but with just the opposite

result to the one Durkheim intended. Sophistically, he claimed that the objections to theistic definitions recommended his own; just as sophistically, readers seem to have decided that the still greater objections to his definition recommended the alternative. 'Tis the sport to have the engineer hoist with his own petard; but it is unfortunate that his quite valid objections to theistic definitions have thus come to be discounted.

3. By deliberately refuting two respected definitions of religion, and unwillingly exposing the inadequacy of a third, Durkheim lends weight to the supposition that it is impossible to get a satisfactory definition of religion – and therefore we might as well make do with a demonstrably unsatisfactory one. And, since attempts to provide definitions of like kind for other basic terms lead to equally lugubrious results, he lends weight to the widespread view that all definitions are futile, and any concern with them a sheer waste of time. Though this view is very plausible, it is actually false and harmful. In the first place there are some kinds of definition which can be carried through successfully, and which make a genuine if limited contribution to scientific work: these should not be discarded. In the second place, and far more seriously, although definitions of the kind that Durkheim attempted are necessarily futile, they are also misguided attempts to do something very important: that is to reconceptualise phenomena in a way which will enhance our understanding of them. The great danger is that in rejecting as futile attempts at definition, which are the traditional method of attempting this task, we shall reject all attempts.

VII

We should agree with Durkheim that the facts of Buddhism (and some other non-theistic religious phenomena) reveal the inadequacy of theistic conceptions of religion, and the need to seek for better concepts for the phenomena. But concept formation must not be attempted by way of definition, since definitions of this kind almost invariably and inevitably fail. To understand why this is so suggests a more fruitful way to proceed.

Definitions may be divided into two major categories, known traditionally as Nominal Definitions and Real Definitions. A Nominal Definition is described in the *Shorter Oxford English Dictionary* as 'a declaration of the signification of a word or phrase', while a Real Definition is there described as 'a precise statement of the essential nature of a thing'.[1]

Durkheim's definition of religion – like most definitions which promise much but achieve nothing – is a Real Definition. The dictionary's description of Real Definition is not clear; indeed it is very muddled. But what is aimed at by Real Definition, in so far as it has any relevance to scientific purposes, can be more plausibly formulated. I shall say, then, that Real Definitions seek to determine those attributes of the members of a class of phenomena which are most important for yielding an enhanced understanding of the phenomena.

In order to explain why the search for Real Definitions, even in this improved sense, is nearly always abortive, it is useful to draw upon Needham's invaluable distinction between monothetic and polythetic classes (see Needham 1975). A monothetic class is a set of phenomena such that there is some set (or 'bundle') of attributes which is common to all of them – which is possessed by each and every member of the class. With a polythetic class there is again an associated bundle of attributes; but in this case it is not necessary that *all* the attributes in the bundle be possessed by a member of the class. A phenomenon may be treated as a member of the class if it possesses only *some* of the attributes. Since different members of the class may possess different selections from the bundle of attributes, there is no guarantee that any one of these attributes is common to all the members. Indeed a class must be regarded as polythetic when there is no attribute which is both common to all the members and important for understanding them.

Now Real Definition presupposes that the class in question is monothetic: for if the attributes singled out in the definition prove not to be common to all the members of the class, the definition fails. That Durkheim assumed that religion is a monothetic class is shown by his writing 'Since all religions are species of the same class, there are necessarily essential elements which are common to them' (1912: 6; 1915: 4 – my revised translation). His definition is generally rejected because it is evident that the 'essential elements' to which he pointed are *not* common to all religions.

But the classes with which we classify phenomena are mostly polythetic. This is because they are by-products of usage in natural languages: such a class is merely the totality of things to which people have applied a particular word. Such a class is formed piecemeal, and not for strictly scientific purposes. We allow a phenomenon to be a member if it significantly resembles at least one acknowledged member; it is no-one's business to ensure that each member resembles every other member by sharing the same common bundle of attributes. It is not impossible that a class so constituted should turn out to be monothetic; but it is highly improbable.

Thus Real Definition is almost always futile because it amounts to the search for the significant common attributes of a class which has none. Hence Real Definition ought not to be attempted. How then should we try to reconceptualise phenomena which are presented to us as a polythetic class – such as those termed 'religion'?

The simplest and most familiar approach is to let go of the polythetic class, and to form one or more new monothetic classes: by determining attributes which seem scientifically significant, and focusing attention on those phenomena which do in fact possess them. The new monothetic class had better be called by a label: it does not matter greatly what label is used, provided it does not have an established usage to designate a class with different membership. If Durkheim had contented himself with discussing that class of phenomena which actually do manifest a radical opposition between sacred and profane, he would have advanced understanding. It was by making the unwarranted, and superfluous, claim that this class is identical with the class called 'religion' that he sowed confusion.

VIII

An alternative approach, which I shall pursue here, seeks to take positive advantage of the fact that the concepts we actually have are polythetic classes. I shall expound it by exploring how it may be pursued with regard to religion.

With every polythetic class there is associated a bundle of attributes, some of which are possessed by any member of the class. I cannot say precisely what are all the attributes associated with religion, as this would require much more analysis than has been undertaken. But the method can be illustrated by a quite tentative and incomplete list of crudely specified attributes[2]. Roughly, then, anything which we would call a religion must have at least some of the following attributes:

1. A central concern with godlike beings and men's relations with them.
2. A dichotomisation of elements of the world into sacred and profane, and a central concern with the sacred.
3. An orientation towards salvation from the ordinary conditions of worldly existence.
4. Ritual practices.
5. Beliefs which are neither logically nor empirically demonstrable or highly probable, but must be held on the basis of faith (i.e. Evans-Pritchard's (1937: 12) 'mystical notions' but without the requirement that they be false – see below).
6. An ethical code, supported by such beliefs.
7. Supernatural sanctions on infringements of that code.
8. A mythology.
9. A body of scriptures, or similarly exalted oral traditions.
10. A priesthood, or similar specialist religious elite.
11. Association with a moral community, a church (in Durkheim's sense – 1912: 60; 1915: 43–4).
12. Association with an ethnic or similar group.

The word 'religion' designates cultural systems which have at least some of these attributes; this is a polythetic class since some religions lack some of these attributes. Nevertheless, for a long time we have found our concept, called 'religion', serviceable, for much of the time when we have assumed it to be a monothetic class. This indicates that these attributes are very strongly associated with one another, not just in one culture but in human societies throughout the world. On the other hand we can be sure that these associations are not necessary, either logically or empirically, since we do find cultural systems where some of the attributes are dissociated from the others. Buddhism shows us that the first attribute is not necessarily associated with the others; various tribal religions that the second, the third, the sixth, and the tenth, at least, are not. It follows then that the observed strong associations between the attributes must be due to contingent factors, empirical characteristics of human nature and the nature of cultural and social systems. Thus this view of the phenomena indicates a programme of research and analysis to determine how and why these attributes are so frequently found in combination: how and why it is that in almost every human society we encounter a cultural system which plainly, if not perfectly, corresponds to our notion of a religion.

The recognition that religion is a polythetic class which approaches, but does not reach, monotheticity, has a number of advantages:

1. It shows clearly that we need not waste our time searching for a Real Definition.
2. It allows us to point to certain attributes as having especial explanatory value without having to assert that they hold true of all religions.
3. It enables us to perceive certain crucial facts – e.g. the near-universality in religions of concern with godlike beings, or the widespread tendency to contrast the sacred and the everyday – in a more fruitful way. When these are taken – mistaken – as definitive of the class of phenomena, they tend to be taken for granted;[3] when they are seen as contingent facts they pose scientific problems. Why is it, for example, that nearly all religions focus on godlike beings though this is plainly not necessary for the religious life?
4. It is consistent with, and suggests, the view that a religion is not a homogeneous system responding to any single need or inclination. Rather, a religion is compounded of a variety of forms of behaviour which tend to be produced in response to diverse individual and social requirements; but these forms of behaviour, though they have in this sense diverse origins, have marked affinities one with another which tend to lead to their coalescence into a moderately coherent system. Religion is polythetic because of the diverse origins of the forms of behaviour which constitute it; it approaches monotheticity because of these affinities between them.
5. This view in turn suggests a new way of singling out those attributes of religion which may contribute most to understanding

it: we should attend especially to those which contribute crucially to the linking up into one system of basically independent modes of behaviour: that is to those which contribute crucially to the connectivity of the network of attributes that we call 'religion'. For example, it may be noted not only that both central concern with godlike beings, and ritual practices, are among the most nearly universal attributes of religious systems, but also that there are determinative relations between them. On the one hand, once godlike beings are postulated, and regarded as important, it is almost inevitable (though compare Quakerism) that ritual means must be employed to communicate with them. On the other hand, once rites become established, it is very natural (though compare Buddhism) that godlike beings should be postulated as their objects, in order to rationalise the behaviour. More speculatively, I suggest that the exceptions indicated may actually confirm the posited connections. The Quaker concept of God seems to me less godlike than most. I have a little evidence which suggests that Buddhists who are more ritualistic than most are more inclined to suppose that Lord Buddha exists – while yet knowing that he does not; which indeed shows that Gombrich's interpretation corresponds to some of the facts.

IX

This approach seems to be fertile in suggesting new ways of analysing known facts about human religious behaviour. I cannot here explore these further. Instead, I pursue one line of analysis which emerges from my observations of practical Buddhism.

When I asked my informants, as I regularly did, 'Why are you a Buddhist?', the usual reply was 'Because it is what I am accustomed to' or 'Because I was brought up as a Buddhist'. Naive as they may appear, these are very adequate explanations at the individual level. But we may press the enquiry further; if my friends are Buddhists because they were born into and live in a Buddhist culture, why is the culture of the Sinhalese Buddhist? The answer[4] is very plain – though I did not elicit it from my informants. In the third century B.C. virtually the whole of the Indian sub-continent was under the sway of the Emperor Asoka; the principal exception was an area at the Southern tip of India. This is the area adjacent to Sri Lanka; and it is the area from which, in subsequent history at least, there came repeated invasions and a continual threat to the political and cultural integrity of the Sinhalese. Asoka was a devout Buddhist, and sent out missions to proselytise neighbouring domains. When such a mission came to the Sinhalese court (in about 243 B.C.), what could have been more natural than to return a favourable response, thereby securing the alliance of the most powerful empire known, and the enemy of one's own principal enemies? I do not mean to exclude other factors which may have, and probably did, also determine the response. For example, if a king is to establish any national religion, Buddhism offers some distinctive political advantages, as Tambiah has recently made clear (1976).

But why did the Sinhalese continue with Buddhism after the dissolution of the Asokan empire? We might remark that a civilised people, having once adopted and practised so noble a religion as Buddhism, are not likely lightly to abandon it. More important, I think, is the fact that the Sinhalese lived under constant threat and attack from the kingdoms of South India, mainly Tamil, and all 'Hindu' by religion, until the period after A.D. 1500 when the Sinhalese were attacked, and partly subdued, by European, and Christian, colonial powers. Throughout these millennia, Buddhism was the principal symbol of Sinhalese identity, and rallying point and inspiration for its defence.

In modern times the Sinhalese nation does not face any comparable military threat; though the Sinhalese do, and not without reason, feel that their cultural identity is threatened by the Tamils, who have a bridgehead in the vigorous Tamil minority in Sri Lanka. What is also important is the fact that by most criteria the Sinhalese are not leading actors on the world stage; but they can and do take a justified pride in being the principal bearers, preservers, and potential teachers of the Buddhist religion.

X

Now this analysis assumes, what the history of many other areas also shows, that a religion is peculiarly apt to serve as a symbol and rallying point for cultural and ethnic identities, and the societies which realise them. Why should this be so? I perceive two factors, one fairly obvious, and one less so.

In the first place the ethical code which is commonly associated with religion – very prominently in the case of Buddhism – serves both to unite people as an effectively co-operating unit, and to give them a sense of moral coherence and solidarity.

As to the second factor: many of my informants, both villagers and middle-class, insisted, and none denied, that to be a Buddhist one must believe in Rebirth. By this they referred to a combination of what strictly are two separate doctrines: (1) that every living being, animal, human, or godlike, not having attained Nirvana, after death is inevitably reborn into another worldly existence; and (2) that the conditions of this reborn existence are determined by *karma* – which is commonly, if crudely, interpreted as the sums of Merit and Demerit that have been accumulated. I found this surprising, since many Buddhists, even some village Buddhists, often claim that Buddhism is the most rational and scientific of religions, as it does not require a belief in gods: yet here was an equally compulsory and preposterous belief. I also found it disconcerting, since I had accepted the claim. It seemed clear to me that I could never believe in Rebirth: however much I might allow its plausibility and even desirability, it would always seem to me fanciful and without facticity. After some months of living among the Sinhalese I observed that I virtually was believing the doctrine: that is, not only in my speech but also in my private thoughts, to assume the reality of Rebirth had become natural, extremely attractive, and increasingly axiomatic. This was partly because I was constantly engaged in conversations in which, for my partners at least, the reality of Rebirth was assumed. Still more it was because I experienced great affection and respect for the people I was living with and for their culture.

The doctrine of Rebirth has a quality that I would call 'empirical indeterminacy'. There is much to be said, logically and empirically, in support of its truth; there is much to be said, logically and empirically, in support of its falsity; objectively, it seems quite impossible to show that one case is significantly stronger than the other; the evidence, and other relevant considerations, seem to be quite neutral as between its truth and falsity. (Such doctrines can of course be ruled out by Occam's Razor; but Occam's Razor is not often employed outside the field of scientific thinking, and seems to me of questionable validity even within it.) Now once such a doctrine comes to be accepted within a culture, its elements and implications will pervade all manner of modes of speech and behaviour; and anyone who participates in these will be led unwittingly to accept, or at least allow, these assumptions. But once one begins to accept the truth of the assumptions, one selectively perceives and favours the considerations tending to the truth of the doctrine, rather than those suggesting its falsity. This is a self-augmenting process which must rapidly lead to a sense of certainty of the truth of the doctrine. On the other hand, for those who are not immersed in the culture, such a doctrine is likely to appear fanciful and alien, more or less preposterous and perverse. The apparent truth or falsity of such doctrines seems to depend wholly on social factors.

This is why religions, as cultural systems in which empirically indeterminate doctrines are crucial, are so effective in identifying and distinguishing, unifying and separating, cultural communities. A doctrine which is important and indubitably true to members of a cultural community, and more or less preposterous and perverse to outsiders and enemies, must establish a gulf around that cultural community, and powerfully strengthen, for its members, the sense of communal identity, solidarity, and worth. I must add that the doctrine of Rebirth itself would hardly have served this function in confrontations between Buddhists and Hindu enemies, who would not have found it strange. There are other Buddhist doctrines – e.g. the unique efficacy of the Buddha's way to salvation, and the irrelevance of gods thereto – which would have served in that context. I have chosen to enlarge on the Rebirth doctrine because to persons of Western culture, including myself, its empirically indeterminate character seems particularly evident.

Empirically indeterminate doctrines also have a bearing on my first factor, the social importance of the ethical codes which so often form an element of religions. As it seems to me, it is impossible to produce an objective rational argument, which will be convincing to many, for preferring the welfare of others to one's own, provided only that one is sufficiently strategic in one's pursuit of self-interest. This is why, in all societies, a large part of ethics is embedded in kinship, that is the direct and indirect appeal to biologically rooted dispositions. Where this is insufficient, since a worthy ethical code cannot be convincingly derived from determinate truths, it must be founded on indeterminate [doctrines].[5]

Empirically indeterminate doctrines seem to be important for some of the major social functions of religion. This is partly because, since their apparent truth or falsity seems to depend wholly on social factors, they tend to segregate cultural communities; and partly because of their basic contribution to ethical codes. If they most often take the form of belief in godlike beings, this is probably because such beliefs have other notable functions. The example of Buddhism shows that a doctrine of similar character, but quite different content, can also serve.

XI

My concept of empirically indeterminate doctrines is obviously similar to the more familiar concept of mystical notions. Evans-Pritchard (1937: 12), in defining mystical notions, says that they 'attribute to phenomena supra-sensible qualities . . . which they do not possess': and this is to say that they are false. But this is unsound; for many mystical notions, including I think Zande witchcraft beliefs, cannot be known to be false, nor true either: they are empirically indeterminate. Indeed this seems to be a necessary consequence of Evans-Pritchard's definition. As is evident from his definition of 'commonsense notions' (1937: 12), the attribution of *supra-sensible* qualities is crucial, since this alone serves to distinguish mystical from merely mistaken notions. Though Evans-Pritchard fails to define the crucial term 'supra-sensible', its meaning becomes fairly evident from his text: especially the passage (1937: 81) where he says of the action of witchcraft, 'It is not an evident notion but transcends sensory experience'. What transcends sensory experience is *ipso facto* placed beyond the reach of empirical falsification or decisive corroboration.

On the face of it, there do appear to be some mystical notions which are demonstrably false: for example some doctrines proclaimed in Cargo cults. It might be said that these are falsifiable not because they are mystical but because they are insufficiently mystical. Distinctions of this kind seem to me unhelpful in classifying empirical data; I propose instead to reword Evans-Pritchard's definition of mystical notions as follows:

> These are patterns of thought that attribute to phenomena supra-sensible qualities which, or part of which, they cannot objectively be confirmed to possess. Predications of them are either empirically indeterminate or false.

Unless I am mistaken in supposing that some mystical notions are demonstrably false, it follows from these definitions that the concept of mystical notions is more widely applicable than is that of empirically indeterminate doctrines. On the other hand, it has less explanatory power. I have argued that their dependence on empirically indeterminate doctrines helps to explain how some religions serve to segregate cultural communities. It is unlikely that mystical notions which are demonstrably false could serve such a function for long: for the situation of confrontation between persons of different cultures is likely to lead to their falsification and replacement by empirically indeterminate formulations – as has evidently occurred in Christianity in recent centuries.

In other respects both varieties of mystical notions may function in similar ways. Both can provide a basis – a necessary basis, as I have suggested – for an ethical code. Both share another important characteristic. Since mystical notions, of either kind, transcend sensory experience, their supposed truth-value cannot be uniquely identified with any particular kind of experience: they are perceived as equally meaningful in relation to a variety of experiences. Because they are empirically vacuous, they are empirically permeable and elastic.[6] Hence, like ritual acts and symbols, which are equally open to many interpretations, they can be commonly meaningful to people whose actual experiences are quite various. They seem to speak equally to the condition of persons whose actual conditions are quite diverse. This helps to explain why religions are peculiarly able to symbolise the common interest, the sought-for community and harmony of society and the world.

XII

The concept of mystical notions is as applicable to Buddhism as it is to all religions which have a central concern with godlike beings [...]; it appears to apply to all religions. Does this not show that my central contention that religion is a polythetic class is mistaken, since we have now shown that it actually is monothetic? I think not: the issue is not what kind of a class religion 'really' is, but in what way it is most scientifically fruitful to regard the phenomena. Dependence on mystical notions is an attribute which does help to explain some features of religion; but, as I have argued, it explains less than does dependence on empirically indeterminate doctrines, which is less widely distributed. We should do well to employ a Real Definition of religion in terms of dependence on mystical notions if this led us to see what religion is fundamentally about. In my judgement it does not have this power: mystical notions appear to be rather a necessary by-product of religious behaviour than a source thereof.

It may also be objected that for all my scorn for definitions, I have made somewhat free with them myself; I have for example ventured to redefine [...] 'mystical notions', as well as 'Real Definitions'. But these are not Real Definitions. Similarly, it may be conceded that my analysis does imply a definition – though not a Real Definition – of 'religion': it implies that we ought to use the world 'religion' just as we do, that is, to designate the polythetic class of all cultural systems that it seems reasonable to call religions. These are minor matters. It should be clear – and would be but for the confusions which plague the topic of definition – that how we should use words, and how we should conceptualise phenomena, are two quite distinct questions. I do think we should use words clearly and prudently. My main object, however, has been to argue, and to begin to show, how by building on the polythetic character of our concept of religion we can enhance our understanding of the phenomena.

NOTES

I am grateful to the Social Science Research Council which supported my fieldwork with a Research Grant (No. HR 2969/1); and also to the University of Manchester for a Hayter Travel Grant which enabled me to make a shorter preparatory visit to Sri Lanka in 1973. My gratitude to the many people, mainly Sinhalese, who helped me with my research, deserves fuller expression on another occasion.

1. Similar descriptions are given in *Webster's International Dictionary*, and in many technical accounts of definition, including Robinson (1954). It should be pointed out that some modern logicians – notably Hempel (1952) – use the terms 'Nominal' and 'Real Definition' to express a quite different contrast; failure to notice that different writers use the terms in quite different senses is a serious cause of confusion. The reader who wants a fuller account of the technicalities of definition than can be provided here should consult Robinson (1954) or Southwold (1978).
2. Among the advantages of using a polythetic concept is the fact that it is not crucial to state the relevant attributes completely and precisely from the outset. If a critic points out that other attributes should be added to the list, or that attributes should be specified more precisely (as, e.g. the 4th ('ritual practices') clearly must – cf. Skorupski 1976), we can incorporate his suggestions without invalidating what has already been done. We can refine our concept piecemeal.
3. Though Horton (1960) is a distinguished exception.
4. The facts outlined in this and the next two paragraphs are commonplaces of Sri Lankan studies. Among many sources, see Nicholas and Paranavitana(1961) for the historical period (and Basham 1971: 54, for a map of the Asokan empire); and for the colonial and modern periods, Phadnis 1976, and Malalgoda 1976.

5. In philosophical Buddhism there is an analysis, based on the *anatta* doctrine, and attributed to the Buddha himself, which does provide a rational basis for non-egotistical behaviour. But this is not an exception to what I have stated, since it is clear, and acknowledged, that the analysis could not appear thoroughly convincing to more than a very few in any human society.
6. These terms are suggested by Gluckman (1955: 293).

MELFORD E. SPIRO
'RELIGION: PROBLEMS OF DEFINITION AND EXPLANATION'

Melford E. Spiro was born in 1920 and graduated from Northwestern University (Chicago) in 1950. That same year he published his first work, which was evocatively entitled 'Psychotic personality in the South Seas'. In 1982 Spiro was elected to the National Academy of Sciences, an honour that he still holds along with a fellowship of the American Academy of Arts and Sciences. He is currently Emeritus Professor of Anthropology at the University of California, San Diego, where he is still research active and involved in both the Anthropology and Religion programmes.

Spiro's discussion of religion brings together both psychological and functionalist elements. The specific definition has an essentialist basis arising from a Freudian presupposition about the role of religion and the place of god(s) within religion. Since religion ultimately arises from the Oedipus complex and the projection of the father on to a transcendent level, it must include god(s). Alongside this essentialist argument, which explains the origin and persistence of religion, Spiro adds a sophisticated functionalist analysis. Interestingly, this aspect of his discussion shares many similarities with aspects of Geertz's discussion of the functions of religion.

THE PROBLEM OF DEFINITION IN RELIGION

An examination of the endemic definitional controversies concerning religion leads to the conclusion that they are not so much controversies over the meaning either of the term 'religion' or of the concept which it expresses, as they are jurisdictional disputes over the phenomenon or range of phenomena which are considered to constitute legitimately the empirical referent of the term. In short, definitional controversies in religion have generally involved differences in what are technically termed ostensive definitions. To define a word ostensively is to point to the object which that word designates. In any language community, the fiery ball in the sky, for example, evokes a univocal verbal response from all perceivers; and a stranger arriving in an English-speaking community can easily learn the ostensive definition of the word 'sun' by asking any native to point to the object for which 'sun' is the name. Similarly the empirical referent of 'table' can be designated unequivocally, if not efficiently, by pointing to examples of each sub-set of the set of objects to which the word applies.

The community of anthropologists, however, is not a natural language community – more important, perhaps, it does not share a common culture – and although there is little disagreement among anthropologists concerning the class of objects to which such words as 'sister', 'chief', 'string

Melford E. Spiro (1966), 'Religion: problems of definition and explanation', in Michael Banton (ed.), *Anthropological Approaches to the Study of Religion*, London: Tavistock.

figure' – and many others – properly do apply, there is considerable disagreement concerning the phenomena to which the word 'religion' *ought* to apply. Hence the interminable (and fruitless) controversies concerning the religious status of coercive ritual or an ethical code or supernatural beings, and so on. From the affect which characterizes many of these discussions one cannot help but suspect that much of this controversy stems, consciously or unconsciously, from extra-scientific considerations – such as the personal attitudes to religion which scholars bring to its study. Since I am concerned with the logic of inquiry, I must resist a tempting excursion into the social psychology of science.

The scientific grounds for disagreement are almost always based on comparative considerations. Thus Durkheim rejects the belief in supernatural beings as a legitimate referent of 'religion' on the grounds that this would deny religion to primitive peoples who, allegedly, do not distinguish between the natural and the supernatural. Similarly, he rejects the belief in gods as a distinguishing characteristic of 'religion' because Buddhism, as he interprets it, contains no such belief (1954: 24–36). Such objections raise two questions; one factual, the other methodological. I shall return to the factual question in a later section, and confine my present remarks to the methodological question. Even if it were the case that Theravada Buddhism contained no belief in gods or supernatural beings, from what methodological principle does it follow that religion – or, for that matter, anything else– must be universal if it is to be studied comparatively? The fact that hunting economies, unilateral descent groups, or string figures do not have a universal distribution has not prevented us from studying *them* comparatively. Does the study of religion become any the less significant or fascinating – indeed, it would be even more fascinating – if in terms of a consensual ostensive definition it were discovered that one or seven or sixteen societies did not possess religion? If it indeed be the case that Theravada Buddhism is atheistic and that, by a theistic definition of religion, it is not therefore a religion, why can we not face, rather than shrink from, this consequence? Having combatted the notion that 'we' have religion (which is 'good') and 'they' have supersitition (which is 'bad'), why should we be dismayed if it be discovered that society x does not have 'religion', as we have defined that term? For the premise 'no religion' does not entail the conclusion 'therefore superstition' – nor, incidentally, does it entail the conclusion 'therefore no social integration', unless of course religion is defined as anything which makes for integration. It may rather entail the conclusion 'therefore science' or 'therefore philosophy'. Or it may entail no conclusion and, instead, stimulate some research. In short, once we free the word 'religion' from all value judgements, there is reason neither for dismay nor for elation concerning the empirical distribution of religion attendant upon our definition. With respect to Theravada Buddhism, then, what loss to science would have ensued if Durkheim had decided that, as he interpreted it, it was atheistic, and therefore not a religion? I can see only gain. First, it would have stimulated fieldwork in these apparently anomalous Buddhist societies and, second, we would have been spared the confusion created by the consequent real and functional definitions of religion which were substituted for the earlier substantive or structural definitions.

[. . .]

In sum, any comparative study of religion requires, as an operation antecedent to inquiry, an ostensive or substantive definition that stipulates unambiguously those phenomenal variables which are designated by the term. This ostensive definition will, at the same time, be a nominal definition in that some of its designata will, to other scholars, appear to be arbitrary. This, then, does not remove 'religion' from the arena of definitional controversy; but it does remove it from the context of fruitless controversy over what religion 'really is' to the context of the formulation of empirically testable hypotheses which, in anthropology, means hypotheses susceptible to cross-cultural testing.

But this criterion of cross-cultural applicability does not entail, as I have argued above, universality. Since 'religion' is a term with historically rooted meanings, a definition must satisfy not only the criterion of cross-cultural applicability but also the criterion of intra-cultural intuitivity; at the least, it should not be counter-intuitive. For me, therefore, any definition of 'religion' which does not include, as a key variable, the belief in superhuman – I won't muddy the metaphysical waters with 'supernatural' – beings who have power to help or harm man is counter-intuitive. Indeed, if anthropological consensus were to exclude such beliefs from the set of variables which is necessarily designated by 'religion', an explanation for these beliefs would surely continue to elicit our research energies.

[. . .]

To summarize, I would argue that the belief in superhuman beings and in their power to assist or to harm man approaches universal distribution, and this belief – I would insist – is the core variable which ought to be designated by any definition of religion. Recently Horton (1960) and Goody (1961) have reached the same conclusion.

Although the belief in the existence of superhuman beings is the core religious variable, it does not follow – as some scholars have argued – that religious, in contrast to magical, behavior is necessarily other-worldly in orientation, or that, if it is other-worldly, its orientation is 'spiritual'. The beliefs in superhuman beings, other-worldliness, and spiritual values vary independently. Thus, ancient Judaism, despite its obsession with God's will, was essentially this-worldly in orientation. Catholicism, with all its other-worldly orientation is, with certain kinds of Hinduism, the most 'materialistic' of the higher religions. Confucianism, intensely this-worldly, is yet concerned almost exclusively with such 'spiritual' values as filial piety, etc. In short, superhuman beings may be conceived as primarily means or as ends. Where values are worldly, these beings may be viewed as important agents for the attainment and/or frustration of worldly goals, either 'material' or 'spiritual'. Where values are materialistic, superhuman beings may be viewed as important agents for the attainment of material goals, either in this or in an after life. Where values are other-worldly, mystical union with superhuman beings may be viewed as an all-consuming goal; and so on.

Although the differentiating characteristic of religion is the belief in superhuman beings, it does not follow, moreover, that these beings are necessarily objects of ultimate concern. Again, it depends on whether they are viewed as means or as ends. For those individuals whom Weber has termed 'religiously musical' (Gerth and Mills 1946: 287), or whom Radin (1957: 9) has termed 'the truly religious', superhuman beings are of ultimate concern. For the rest, however, superhuman beings are rarely of ultimate concern, although the ends for which their assistance is sought may be. Hence, though their benevolent ancestral spirits are not of great concern to the Ifaluk, restoration of health – for which these spirits are instrumental – most certainly is. Similarly, while the Buddha may not be of ultimate concern to a typical Burmese peasant, the escape from suffering – for which He is instrumental – can certainly be so designated.

Conversely, while religious beliefs are not always of ultimate concern, non-religious beliefs sometimes are. This raises a final unwarranted conclusion, viz. that religion uniquely refers to the 'sacred', while secular concerns are necessarily 'profane'. Thus, if 'sacred' refers to objects and beliefs of ultimate concern, and 'profane' to those of ordinary concern, religious and secular beliefs alike may have reference either to sacred or to profane phenomena. For the members of Kiryat Yedidim, an Israeli *kibbutz*, the triumph of the proletariat, following social revolution, and the ultimate classless society in which universal brotherhood, based on loving kindness, will replace parochial otherhood, based on competitive hostility, constitutes their sacred belief system. But, by definition, it is not a religious belief system, since it has no reference to – indeed, it denies the existence of – superhuman beings.

Similarly, if communism, or baseball, or the stockmarket are of ultimate concern to some society, or to one of its constituent social groups, they are, by definition, sacred. But beliefs concerning communism, baseball, or the stockmarket are not, by definition, religious beliefs, because they have no reference to superhuman beings. They may, of course, serve many of the functions served by religious beliefs; and they are, therefore, members of the same functional class. Since, however, they are substantively dissimilar, it would be as misleading to designate them by the same term as it would be to designate music and sex by the same term because they both provide sensual pleasure. (Modern American society presents an excellent example of the competition of sports, patriotism, sex, and God for the title, perhaps not exclusively, of 'the sacred'. Indeed, if the dictum of Miss Jane Russell is taken seriously – God, she informs us, is a 'livin' doll' – I would guess that, whichever wins, God is bound to lose).

A DEFINITION OF 'RELIGION'

On the assumption that religion is a cultural institution, and on the further assumption that all institutions – though not all of their features – are instrumental means for the satisfaction of needs, I shall define 'religion' as 'an institution consisting of culturally patterned interaction with culturally postulated superhuman beings'. I should like to examine these variables separately.

Institution. This term implies, of course, that whatever phenomena we might wish to designate by 'religion', religion is an attribute of social groups, comprising a component part of their cultural heritage; and that its component features are acquired by means of the same enculturation processes as the other variables of a cultural heritage are acquired. This means that the variables constituting a religious system have the same ontological status as those of other cultural systems: its beliefs are normative, its rituals collective, its values prescriptive. This, I take it, is what Durkheim (1954: 44) had in mind in insisting that there can be no religion without a church. (It means, too, as I shall observe in a later section, that religion has the same methodological status as other cultural systems; i.e. religious variables are to be explained by the same explanatory schemata – historical, structural, functional, and causal – as those by which other cultural variables are explained.)

Interaction. This term refers to two distinct, though related, types of activity. First, it refers to activities which are believed to carry out, embody, or to be consistent with the will or desire of superhuman beings or powers. These activities reflect the putative *value system* of these superhuman beings and, presumably, they constitute part – but only part – of the actors' value system. These activities may be viewed as desirable in themselves and/or as means for obtaining the assistance of superhuman beings or for protection against their wrath. Second, it refers to activities which are believed to influence superhuman beings to satisfy the needs of the actors. These two types of activity may overlap, but their range is never coterminous. Where they do overlap, the action in the overlapping sphere is, in large measure, symbolic; that is, it consists in behavior whose meaning, cross-culturally viewed, is obscure and/or arbitrary; and whose efficacy, scientifically viewed, is not susceptible of ordinary scientific 'proof'. These symbolic, but definitely instrumental, activities constitute, of course, a *ritual*, or symbolic *action system*. Unlike private rituals, such as those found in an obsessive-compulsive neurosis, religious rituals are culturally patterned; i.e. both the activities and their meaning are shared by the members of a social group by virtue of their acquisition from a shared cultural heritage.

Superhuman beings. These refer to any beings believed to possess power greater than man, who can work good and/or evil on man, and whose relationships with man can, to some degree, be influenced by the two types of activity described in the previous section. The belief of any religious actor in the existence of these beings and his knowledge concerning their attributes are derived from and sanctioned by the cultural heritage of his social group. To that extent – and regardless of the objective existence of these beings, or of personal experiences which are interpreted as encounters with them – their existence is culturally postulated. Beliefs concerning the existence and attributes of these beings, and of the efficacy of certain types of behavior (ritual, for example) in influencing their relations with man, constitute a *belief system*.

This brief explication of our definition of 'religion' indicates that, viewed systemically, religion can be differentiated from other culturally constituted institutions by virtue only of its reference to superhuman beings. All institutions consist of *belief systems*, i.e. an enduring organization of cognitions about one or more aspects of the universe; *action systems*, an enduring organization of behavior patterns designed to attain ends for the satisfaction of needs; and *value systems*, an enduring organization of principles by which behavior can be judged on some scale of merit. Religion differs from other institutions in that its three component systems have reference to superhuman beings.

[. . .]

CONCLUSION

It would appear from the foregoing discussion that an adequate explanation for the persistence of religion requires both psychological and sociological variables. If the cognitive bases for religious belief have their roots in childhood experience, their explanation must be found in social structural and, more specifically, family structure variables. Here religion is the dependent variable, and family structure is the independent sociological variable which effects religious belief by means of such intervening psychological variables as fantasies, projections, perceptions, and the like.

If religion persists because of its gratification of desires, explanations for the bases of religious behavior must be found in psychological and, specifically, motivational variables. Here, again, religion is the dependent, and motivation is the independent, variable. Since, however, motivation consists in the intention of gratifying desires, and since desires are rooted either in organic or in acquired drives, the motivational roots of religious behavior can, ultimately, be found in those biological and social structural variables, respectively, by which they are produced and/or canalized. Again, it is the family which emerges as the crucial sociological variable. Religion, then, is to be explained in terms of society and personality.

Many studies of religion, however, are concerned not with the explanation of religion, but with the role of religion in the explanation of society. Here, the explanatory task is to discover the contributions which religion, taken as the independent variable, makes to societal integration, by its satisfaction of sociological wants. This is an important task, central to the main concern of anthropology, as the science of social systems. We seriously err, however, in mistaking an explanation of society for an explanation of religion which, in effect, means confusing the sociological functions of religion with the bases for its performance.

In this paper, I have been concerned almost exclusively with the latter aspect of religion. I have not, except incidentally, dealt with its sociological functions or, what is perhaps more important, with how these are to be measured. I have not dealt, moreover, with the problem of religious origins because – despite the fact that numerous speculations have been proposed (and I have my own, as well) – these are not testable. Nor have I dealt with the problem of the cross-cultural variability in religion, except to suggest some motivational bases for the persistence of different types of belief and ritual. But the crucial problems – to which Max Weber has most importantly contributed – I have not even touched upon. If, for example, religion is centrally concerned with the problem of 'suffering' why is it that explanations for suffering run such a wide gamut: violation of ethical norms, sin of ancestors, misconduct in a previous incarnation, etc.? Or, if religion promises redemption from suffering, how are the different types of redemption to be explained? And, moreover, what is the explanation for the different means by which the redemptive promise is to be achieved? These are but a few of the central problems in the study of religion with which this paper, with its limited focus, has not been concerned.

NOTE

Work on this paper is part of a cross-cultural study of religion supported by research grant M-2255 from the National Institutes of Health, U.S. Public Health Service.

4

SOCIOLOGICAL APPROACHES

Introduction

Sociological approaches are influenced by many of the figures touched on in the opening chapter of this book, particularly Marx, Weber and Durkheim. They have also been influenced by trends in anthropological theory. Among the theorists included here, perhaps the two strongest threads are the influence of Weber and Durkheim. Weber's influence can be seen in those theorists focusing on the institutional aspects of religion and the interrelationship between religion and society – it is developed here in a subtle way in the work of Bruce (pages 330–47). Durkheim's model of functionalism, with some aspects developed by Malinowski (pages 229–52) and Radcliffe-Brown (pages 253–64) in anthropology, was highly influential and is illustrated in the work of Parsons (pages 365–77). A slightly different aspect of both Durkheim and Weber is developed in the work of Berger (pages 317–29). These thinkers focus on the relationship between religion and worldview, or more precisely the role of religion in creating totalising systems of meaning and validation.

The sociological approaches share a number of common themes and trajectories. Perhaps the most theoretically significant of these is the focus on social institutions as the locus of analysis. This aspect of the approaches is closely related to the institutional focus of many strands of functionalism, particularly those influenced by Radcliffe-Brown. Due to the nature of sociological research, which has often been large scale and quantitative, sociologists have tended to look at societies, with institutions as the primary constituent elements rather than individuals. This institutional tendency is particularly apparent in discussions relating to secularisation. These discussions often use participation or membership in religious institutions as markers for the progress of secularisation rather than individual beliefs or practices.

An additional underlying theme found in many of the sociological approaches is an implicit or indeed explicit form of evolutionism. This aspect is explicitly found in the work of Bellah (pages 299–316). He employs a form of unilinear evolutionism highly reminiscent of the nineteenth-century anthropological theorists. Evolutionism, however, is also an underlying theme of many other modern sociological approaches, particularly secularisation theory – see particularly the work of Bruce (pages 330–47). Many secularisation theorists argue for an almost inexorable movement towards rationalism and the steady decline of religion as both an institution and by implication a set of beliefs. The theorists implicitly view societies that are less secularised as being either lower down the thread of development or as explainable temporary exceptions. While it is perhaps arguable that institutional secularisation is a feature of Western society, it remains to be demonstrated that it is the necessary path of development for all societies.

A final thematic thread that links many sociological approaches is that of 'methodological atheism'. In many senses this element is the opposite of the bracketing in of internal understandings found in phenomenology. Bracketing in privileges the theological internal explanation. Methodological atheism brackets this internal view out. The approach suggests that any supernatural or theological explanation should be excluded as an explanation for religion in favour of a humanistic or social explanation. While this aspect of the sociological approach is also shared by many anthropologists, increasingly ethnographers and theorists also emphasise the need to understand the internal point of view both as data and as a form of explanation.

ROBERT N. BELLAH
'RELIGIOUS EVOLUTION' [1]

Robert Bellah was educated at Harvard University, receiving a PhD in 1955. His teaching career began at Harvard, where he remained until 1967, after which he moved to the University of California, Berkeley, serving there for thirty years as Professor of Sociology as well as chairing the Center for Japanese and Korean Studies. Bellah has published widely, with Habits of the Heart *(1985) being particularly influential both inside and outside sociology.*

The material we have included here presents an evolutionary model of religion, tracing five stages of development from so-called 'primitive religions' to 'modern religions'. His evolutionary model focuses on the increase of complexity and cultural specialisation as markers for the different stages. These elements are also present in the implicitly evolutionary models developed by secularisation theorists.

Evolution in the sphere of religion is traced on three levels. First and most central is the evolution of religious symbol systems which are described as moving from 'compact' to 'differentiated'. In close conjunction with this evolution religious collectivities become more differentiated from other social structures and there is an increasing consciousness of the self as a religious subject. Five ideal typical stages of development are posited but it is recognized that these stages are not inevitable, that there is a wide variety of types within each stage, and that actual cases present many important features which cannot be neatly characterized in terms of any one stage. The close connection between religious evolution and other aspects of socio-cultural evolution is assumed but not explored.

'Time in its aging course teaches all things.'
—Aeschylus: *Prometheus Bound*

Though one can name precursors as far back as Herodotus, the systematically scientific study of religion begins only in the second half of the 19th century. According to Chantepie de la Saussaye, the two preconditions for this emergence were that religion had become by the time of Hegel the object of comprehensive philosophical speculation and that history by the time of Buckle had been enlarged to include the history of civilization and culture in general.[2] In its early phases, partly under the influence of Darwinism, the science of religion was dominated by an evolutionary tendency already implicit in Hegelian philosophy and early 19th century historiography. The

Robert N. Bellah (1995), 'Religious evolution', *American Sociological Review* 29(3).

grandfathers of modern sociology, Comte and Spencer, contributed to the strongly evolutionary approach to the study of religion as, with many reservations, did Durkheim and Weber.

But by the third decade of the 20th century the evolutionary wave was in full retreat both in the general field of science of religion and in the sociology of religion in particular. Of course, this was only one aspect of the general retreat of evolutionary thought in social science, but nowhere did the retreat go further nor the intensity of the opposition to evolution go deeper than in the field of religion. An attempt to explain the vicissitudes of evolutionary conceptions in the field of religion would be an interesting study in the sociology of knowledge but beyond the scope of this brief paper. Here I can only say that I hope that the present attempt to apply the evolutionary idea to religion evidences a serious appreciation of both 19th century evolutionary theories and 20th century criticisms of them.

Evolution at any system level I define as a process of increasing differentiation and complexity of organization which endows the organism, social system or whatever the unit in question may be, with greater capacity to adapt to its environment so that it is in some sense more autonomous relative to its environment than were its less complex ancestors. I do not assume that evolution is inevitable, irreversible or must follow any single particular course. Nor do I assume that simpler forms cannot prosper and survive alongside more complex forms. What I mean by evolution, then, is nothing metaphysical but the simple empirical generalization that more complex forms develop from less complex forms and that the properties and possibilities of more complex forms differ from those of less complex forms.

A brief handy definition of religion is considerably more difficult than a definition of evolution. An attempt at an adequate definition would, as Clifford Geertz has recently demonstrated, take a paper in itself for adequate explanation.[3] So, for limited purposes only, let me define religion as a set of symbolic forms and acts which relate man to the ultimate conditions of his existence. The purpose of this definition is to indicate exactly what I claim has evolved. It is not the ultimate conditions, nor, in traditional language, God that has evolved, nor is it man in the broadest sense of *homo religiosus*. I am inclined to agree with Eliade when he holds that primitive man is as fully religious as man at any stage of existence, though I am not ready to go along with him when he implies *more* fully.[4]

Neither religious man nor the structure of man's ultimate religious situation evolves, then, but rather religion as symbol system. Erich Voegelin, who I suspect shares Eliade's basic philosophical position, speaks of a development from compact to differentiated symbolization.[5] Everything already exists in some sense in the religious symbol system of the most primitive man; it would be hard to find anything later that is not 'foreshadowed' there, as for example, the monotheistic God is foreshadowed in the high gods of some primitive peoples. Yet just as obviously the two cannot be equated. Not only in their idea of God but in many other ways the monotheistic religions of Judaism, Christianity and Islam involve a much more differentiated symbolization of, and produce a much more complex relation to, the ultimate conditions of human existence than do primitive religions. At least the existence of that kind of difference is the thesis I wish to develop. I hope it is clear that there are a number of other possible meanings of the term 'religious evolution' with which I am not concerned. I hope it is also clear that a complex and differentiated religious symbolization is not therefore a better or a truer or a more beautiful one than a compact religious symbolization. I am not a relativist and I do think judgments of value can reasonably be made between religions, societies or personalities. But the axis of that judgment is not provided by social evolution and if progress is used in an essentially ethical sense, then I for one will not speak of religious progress.

Having defined the ground rules under which I am operating let me now step back from the subject of religious evolution and look first at a few of the massive facts of human religious history. The first of these facts is the emergence in the first millennium B.C all across the Old World, at least in centers of high culture, of the phenomenon of religious rejection of the world characterized by an extremely negative evaluation of man and society and the exaltation of another realm of reality as alone true and infinitely valuable. This theme emerges in Greece through a long development into Plato's classic formulation in the *Phaedo* that the body is the tomb or prison of the soul and that only by disentanglement from the body and all things worldly can the soul unify itself with the unimaginably different world of the divine. A very different formulation is found in Israel, but there too the world is profoundly devalued in the face of the transcendent God with whom alone is there any refuge or comfort. In India we find perhaps the most radical of all versions of world rejection, culminating in the great image of the Buddha, that the world is a burning house and man's urgent need is a way to escape from it. In China, Taoist ascetics urged the transvaluation of all the accepted values and withdrawal from human society, which they condemned as unnatural and perverse.

Nor was this a brief or passing phenomenon. For over 2,000 years great pulses of world rejection spread over the civilized world. The *Qur'an* compares this present world to vegetation after rain, whose growth rejoices the unbeliever, but it quickly withers away and becomes as straw.[6] Men prefer life in the present world but the life to come is infinitely superior – it alone is everlasting.[7] Even in Japan, usually so innocently world accepting, Shōtoku Taishi declared that the world is a lie and only the Buddha is true, and in the Kamakura period the conviction that the world is hell led to orgies of religious suicide by seekers after Amida's paradise.[8] And it is hardly necessary to quote Revelations or Augustine for comparable Christian sentiments. I do not deny that there are profound differences among these various rejections of the world; Max Weber has written a great essay on the different directions of world rejection and their consequences for human action.[9] But for the moment I want to concentrate on the fact that they were all in some sense rejections and that world rejection is characteristic of a long and important period of religious history. I want to insist on this fact because I want to contrast it with an equally striking fact – namely the virtual absence of world rejection in primitive religions, in religion prior to the first millennium B.C., and in the modern world.[10]

Primitive religions are on the whole oriented to a single cosmos – they know nothing of a wholly different world relative to which the actual world is utterly devoid of value. They are concerned with the maintenance of personal, social and cosmic harmony and with attaining specific goods – rain, harvest, children, health – as men have always been. But the overriding goal of salvation that dominates the world rejecting religions is almost absent in primitive religion, and life after death tends to be a shadowy semi-existence in some vaguely designated place in the single world.

World rejection is no more characteristic of the modern world than it is of primitive religion. Not only in the United States but through much of Asia there is at the moment something of a religious revival, but nowhere is this associated with a great new outburst of world rejection. In Asia apologists, even for religions with a long tradition of world rejection, are much more interested in showing the compatibility of their religions with the developing modern world than in totally rejecting it. And it is hardly necessary to point out that the American religious revival stems from motives quite opposite to world rejection.

One could attempt to account for this sequence of presence and absence of world rejection as a dominant religious theme without ever raising the issue of religious evolution, but I think I can account for these and many other facts of the historical development of religion in terms of a scheme of religious evolution. An extended rationale for the scheme and its broad empirical application must await publication in book form. Here all I can attempt is a very condensed overview.

The scheme is based on several presuppositions, the most basic of which I have already referred to: namely, that religious symbolization of what Geertz calls 'the general order of existence'[11] tends to change over time, at least in some instances, in the direction of more differentiated, comprehensive, and in Weber's sense, more rationalized formulations. A second assumption is that conceptions of religious action, of the nature of the religious actor, of religious organization and of the place of religion in the society tend to change in ways systematically related to the changes in symbolization. A third assumption is that these several changes in the sphere of religion, which constitute what I mean by religious evolution, are related to a variety of other dimensions of change in other social spheres which define the general process of sociocultural evolution.

Now, for heuristic purposes at least, it is also useful to assume a series of stages which may be regarded as relatively stable crystallizations of roughly the same order of complexity along a number of different dimensions. I shall use five stages which, for want of better terminology, I shall call primitive, archaic, historic, early modern and modern.[12] These stages are ideal types derived from a theoretical formulation of the most generally observable historical regularities; they are meant to have a temporal reference but only in a very general sense.

Of course the scheme itself is not intended as an adequate description of historical reality. Particular lines of religious development cannot simply be forced into the terms of the scheme. In reality there may be compromise formations involving elements from two stages which I have for theoretical reasons discriminated; earlier stages may, as I have already suggested, strikingly foreshadow later developments; and more developed may regress to less developed stages. And of course no stage is ever completely abandoned; all earlier stages continue to coexist with and often within later ones. So what I shall present is not intended as a procrustean bed into which the facts of history are to be forced but a theoretical construction against which historical facts may be illuminated. The logic is much the same as that involved in conceptualizing stages of the life cycle in personality development.

Primitive Religion

Before turning to the specific features of primitive religion let us go back to the definition of religion as a set of symbolic forms and acts relating man to the ultimate conditions of his existence. Lienhardt, in his book on Dinka religion spells out this process of symbolization in a most interesting way:

> I have suggested that the Powers may be understood as images corresponding to complex and various combinations of Dinka experience which are contingent upon their particular social and physical environment. For the Dinka they are the grounds of those experiences; in our analysis we have shown them to be grounded in them, for to a European the experiences are more readily understood than the Powers, and the existence of the latter cannot be posited as a condition of the former. Without these Powers or images or an alternative to them there would be for the Dinka no differentiation between experience of the self and of the world which acts upon it. Suffering, for example, could be merely 'lived' or endured. With the imaging of the grounds of suffering in a particular Power, the Dinka can grasp its nature intellectually in a way which satisfies them, and thus to some extent transcend and dominate it in this act of knowledge. With this knowledge, this separation of a subject and an object in experience, there arises for

them also the possibility of creating a form of experience they desire, and of freeing themselves symbolically from what they must otherwise passively endure.[13]

If we take this as a description of religious symbolization in general, and I think we can, then it is clear that in terms of the conception of evolution used here the existence of even the simplest religion is an evolutionary advance. Animals or pre-religious men could only 'passively endure' suffering or other limitations imposed by the conditions of their existence, but religious man can to some extent 'transcend and dominate' them through his capacity for symbolization and thus attain a degree of freedom relative to his environment that was not previously possible.[14]

Now though Lienhardt points out that the Dinka religious images make possible a 'differentiation between experience of the self and of the world which acts upon it' he also points out earlier that the Dinka lack anything closely resembling our conception of the 'mind', as mediating and, as it were, storing up the experiences of the self.'[15] In fact, aspects of what we would attribute to the self are 'imaged' among the divine Powers. Again if Lienhardt is describing something rather general, and I think there is every reason to believe he is, then religious symbolization relating man to the ultimate conditions of his existence is also involved in relating him to himself and in symbolizing his own identity.[16]

Granted then that religious symbolization is concerned with imaging the ultimate conditions of existence, whether external or internal, we should examine at each stage the kind of symbol system involved, the kind of religious action it stimulates, the kind of social organization in which this religious action occurs and the implications for social action in general that the religious action contains.

Marcel Mauss, criticizing the heterogeneous sources from which Lévy-Bruhl had constructed the notion of primitive thought, suggested that the word primitive be restricted to Australia, which was the only major culture area largely unaffected by the neolithic.[17] That was in 1923. In 1935 Lévy-Bruhl, heeding Mauss's stricture, published a book called *La Mythologie primitive* in which the data are drawn almost exclusively from Australia and immediately adjacent islands.[18] While Lévy-Bruhl finds material similar to his Australian data in all parts of the world, nowhere else does he find it in as pure a form. The differences between the Australian material and that of other areas are so great that Lévy-Bruhl is tempted to disagree with Durkheim that Australian religion is an elementary form of religion and term it rather 'pre-religion',[19] a temptation which for reasons already indicated I would firmly reject. At any rate, W. E. H. Stanner, by far the most brilliant interpreter of Australian religion in recent years, goes far to confirm the main lines of Lévy-Bruhl's position, without committing himself on the more broadly controversial aspects of the assertions of either Mauss or

Lévy-Bruhl (indeed without so much as mentioning them). My description of a primitive stage of religion is a theoretical abstraction, but it is heavily indebted to the work of Lévy-Bruhl and Stanner for its main features.[20]

The *religious symbol system* at the primitive level is characterized by Lévy-Bruhl as '*le monde mythique*', and Stanner directly translates the Australians' own word for it as 'the Dreaming'. The Dreaming is a time out of time, or in Stanner's words, 'everywhen', inhabited by ancestral figures, some human, some animal.[21] Though they are often of heroic proportions and have capacities beyond those of ordinary men as well as being the progenitors and creators of many particular things in the world, they are not gods, for they do not control the world and are not worshipped.[22]

Two main features of this mythical world of primitive religion are important for the purposes of the present theoretical scheme. The first is the very high degree to which the mythical world is related to the detailed features of the actual world. Not only is every clan and local group defined in terms of the ancestral progenitors and the mythical events of settlement, but virtually every mountain, rock and tree is explained in terms of the actions of mythical beings. All human action is prefigured in the Dreaming, including crimes and folly, so that actual existence and the paradigmatic myths are related in the most intimate possible way. The second main feature, not unrelated to the extreme particularity of the mythical material, is the fluidity of its organization. Lienhardt, though describing a religion of a somewhat different type, catches the essentially free-associational nature of primitive myth when he says,

> We meet here the typical lack of precise definition of the Dinka when they speak of divinities. As Garang, which is the name of the first man, is sometimes associated with the first man and sometimes said to be quite different, so Deng may in some sense be associated with anyone called Deng, and the Dinka connect or do not connect usages of the same name in different contexts according to their individual lights and to what they consider appropriate at any given moment.[23]

The fluid structure of the myth is almost consciously indicated by the Australians in their use of the word Dreaming: this is not purely metaphorical, for as Ronald Berndt has shown in a careful study, men do actually have a propensity to dream during the periods of cult performance. Through the dreams they reshape the cult symbolism for private psychic ends and what is even more interesting, dreams may actually lead to a reinterpretation in myth which in turn causes a ritual innovation.[24] Both the particularity and the fluidity, then, help account for the hovering closeness of the world of myth to the actual world. A sense of gap, that things are not all they might be, is there but it is hardly experienced as tragic and is indeed on the verge of being comic.[25]

Primitive *religious action* is characterized not, as we have said, by worship, nor, as we shall see, by sacrifice, but by identification, 'participation', acting-out. Just as the primitive symbol system is myth *par excellence*, so primitive religious action is ritual *par excellence*. In the ritual the participants become identified with the mythical beings they represent. The mythical beings are not addressed or propitiated or beseeched. The distance between man and mythical being, which was at best slight, disappears altogether in the moment of ritual when everywhen becomes now. There are no priests and no congregation, no mediating representative roles and no spectators. All present are involved in the ritual action itself and have become one with the myth.

The underlying structure of ritual, which in Australia always has themes related to initiation, is remarkably similar to that of sacrifice. The four basic movements of the ritual as analyzed by Stanner are offering, destruction, transformation, and return-communion.[26] Through acting out the mistakes and sufferings of the paradigmatic mythical hero, the new initiates come to terms symbolically with, again in Stanner's words, the 'immemorial misdirection' of human life. Their former innocence is destroyed and they are transformed into new identities now more able to 'assent to life, as it is, without morbidity'.[27] In a sense the whole gamut of the spiritual life is already visible in the Australian ritual. Yet the symbolism is so compact that there is almost no element of choice, will or responsibility. The religious life is as given and as fixed as the routines of daily living.

At the primitive level *religious organization* as a separate social structure does not exist. Church and society are one. Religious roles tend to be fused with other roles, and differentiations along lines of age, sex and kin group are important. While women are not as excluded from the religious life as male ethnographers once believed, their ritual life is to some degree separate and focused on particularly feminine life crises.[28] In most primitive societies age is an important criterion for leadership in the ceremonial life. Ceremonies are often handed down in particular moieties and clans, as is only natural when the myths are so largely concerned with ancestors. Specialized shamans or medicine men are found in some tribes but are not a necessary feature of primitive religion.

As for the *social implications* of primitive religion, Durkheim's analysis seems still to be largely acceptable.[29] The ritual life does reinforce the solidarity of the society and serves to induct the young into the norms of tribal behavior. We should not forget the innovative aspects of primitive religion, that particular myths and ceremonies are in a process of constant revision and alteration, and that in the face of severe historic crisis rather remarkable reformulations of primitive material can be made.[30] Yet on the whole the religious life is the strongest reinforcement of the basic tenet of Australian philosophy, namely that life, as Stanner puts it, is a 'one possibility thing'. The very fluidity and flexibility of primitive religion is a barrier to radical innovation. Primitive religion gives little leverage from which to change the world.

ARCHAIC RELIGION

For purposes of the present conceptual scheme, as I have indicated, I am using primitive religion in an unusually restricted sense. Much that is usually classified as primitive religion would fall in my second category, archaic religion, which includes the religious systems of much of Africa and Polynesia and some of the New World, as well as the earliest religious systems of the ancient Middle East, India and China. The characteristic feature of archaic religion is the emergence of true cult with the complex of gods, priests, worship, sacrifice and in some cases divine or priestly kingship. The myth and ritual complex characteristic of primitive religion continues within the structure of archaic religion, but it is systematized and elaborated in new ways.

In the archaic *religious symbol system* mythical beings are much more definitely characterized. Instead of being great paradigmatic figures with whom men in ritual identify but with whom they do not really interact, the mythical beings are more objectified, conceived as actively and sometimes willfully controlling the natural and human world, and as beings with whom men must deal in a definite and purposive way – in a word they have become gods. Relations among the gods are a matter of considerable speculation and systematization, so that definite principles of organization, especially hierarchies of control, are established. The basic world view is still, like the primitives', monistic. There is still only one world with gods dominating particular parts of it, especially important being the high gods of the heavenly regions whose vision, knowledge and power may be conceived as very extensive indeed.[31] But though the world is one it is far more differentiated, especially in a hierarchical way, than was the monistic world view of the primitives: archaic religions tend to elaborate a vast cosmology in which all things divine and natural have a place. Much of the particularity and fluidity characteristic of primitive myth is still to be found in archaic religious thinking. But where priestly roles have become well established a relatively stable symbolic structure may be worked out and transmitted over an extended period of time. Especially where at least craft literacy[32] has been attained, the mythical tradition may become the object of critical reflection and innovative speculation which can lead to new developments beyond the nature of archaic religion.

Archaic *religious action* takes the form of cult in which the distinction between men as subjects and gods as objects is much more definite than in primitive religion. Because the division is sharper the need for a communication system through which gods and men can interact is much more acute. Worship and especially sacrifice are precisely such communication systems, as Henri Hubert and Marcel Mauss so brilliantly established in their great essay on sacrifice.[33] There is no space here for a technical analysis of the sacrificial process;[34] suffice it to say that a double identification of priest and victim with both gods and men effects a transformation of motives comparable to that referred to in the discussion of primitive religious action. The main difference is that instead of a relatively passive identification in an all-encompassing ritual action, the sacrificial process, no matter how stereotyped, permits the human communicants a greater element of intentionality and entails more uncertainty relative to the divine response. Through this more differentiated form of religious action a new degree of freedom as well, perhaps, as an increased burden of anxiety enters the relations between man and the ultimate conditions of his existence.

Archaic *religious organization* is still by and large merged with other social structures, but the proliferation of functionally and hierarchically differentiated groups leads to a multiplication of cults, since every group in archaic society tends to have its cultic aspect. The emergence of a two-class system, itself related to the increasing density of population made possible by agriculture, has its religious aspect. The upper-status group, which tends to monopolize political and military power, usually claims a superior religious status as well. Noble families are proud of their divine descent and often have special priestly functions. The divine king who is the chief link between his people and the gods is only the extreme case of the general tendency of archaic societies. Specialized priesthoods attached to cult centers may differentiate out but are usually kept subordinate to the political elite, which at this stage never completely divests itself of religious leadership. Occasionally priesthoods at cult centers located interstitially relative to political units – for example, Delphi in ancient Greece – may come to exercise a certain independence.

The most significant limitation on archaic religious organization is the failure to develop differentiated religious collectivities including adherents as well as priests. The cult centers provide facilities for sacrifice and worship to an essentially transient clientele which is not itself organized as a collectivity, even though the priesthood itself may be rather tightly organized. The appearance of mystery cults and related religious confraternities in the ancient world is usually related to a reorganization of the religious symbol and action systems which indicates a transition to the next main type of religious structure.

The *social implications* of archaic religion are to some extent similar to those of primitive religion. The individual and his society are seen as merged in a natural-divine cosmos. Traditional social structures and social practices are considered to be grounded in the divinely instituted cosmic order and there is little tension between religious demand and social conformity. Indeed, social conformity is at every point reinforced with religious sanction. Nevertheless the very notion of well characterized gods acting over against men with a certain freedom introduces an element of openness that is less apparent at the primitive level. The struggle between rival groups may be interpreted as the struggle between rival deities or as a deity's change of favor from one group to another. Through the problems posed by religious rationalization of political change new modes of religious thinking may open up. This is clearly an important aspect of the early history of Israel, and it occurred in many other cases as well. The Greek preoccupation with the relation of the gods to the events of the Trojan War gave rise to a continuous deepening of religious thought from Homer to Euripides. In ancient China the attempt of the Chou to rationalize their conquest of the Shang led to an entirely new conception of the relation between human merit and divine favor. The breakdown of internal order led to messianic expectations of the coming of a savior king in such distant areas as Egypt on the one hand and Chou-period China on the other. These are but a few of the ways in which the problems of maintaining archaic religious symbolization in increasingly complex societies drove toward solutions that began to place the archaic pattern itself in jeopardy.

[. . .]

MODERN RELIGION

I am not sure whether in the long run what I call early modern religion will appear as a stage with the same degree of distinctness as the others I have distinguished or whether it will appear only as a transitional phase, but I am reasonably sure that, even though we must speak from the midst of it, the modern situation represents a stage of religious development in many ways profoundly different from that of historic religion. The central feature of the change is the collapse of the dualism that was so crucial to all the historic religions.

It is difficult to speak of a *modern religious symbol system*. It is indeed an open question whether there can be a religious symbol system analogous to any of the preceding ones in the modern situation, which is characterized by a deepening analysis of the very nature of symbolization itself. At the highest intellectual level I would trace the fundamental break with traditional historic symbolization to the work of Kant. By revealing the problematic nature of the traditional metaphysical basis of all the religions and by indicating that it is not so much a question of two worlds as it is of as many worlds as there are modes of apprehending them, he placed the whole religious problem in a new light. However simple the immediate result of his grounding religion in the structure of ethical life rather than in a metaphysics claiming cognitive adequacy, it nonetheless pointed decisively in the direction that modern religion would go. The entire modern analysis of religion, including much of the most important recent theology, though rejecting Kant's narrowly rational ethics, has been forced to ground religion in the structure of the human situation itself. In this respect the present paper is a symptom of the modern religious situation as well as an analysis of it. In the world view that has emerged from the tremendous intellectual advances of the last two centuries there is simply no room for a hierarchic dualistic religious symbol system of the classical historic type. This is not to be interpreted as a return to primitive monism: it is not that a single world has replaced a double one but that an infinitely multiplex one has replaced the simple duplex structure. It is not that life has become again a 'one possibility thing' but that it has become an infinite possibility thing. The analysis of modern man as secular, materialistic, dehumanized and in the deepest sense areligious seems to me fundamentally misguided, for such a judgment is based on standards that cannot adequately gauge the modern temper.

Though it is central to the problems of modern religion, space forbids a review of the development of the modern analysis of religion on its scholarly and scientific side. I shall confine myself to some brief comments on directions of development within Protestant theology. In many respects Schleiermacher is the key figure in early 19th century theology who saw the deeper implications of the Kantian breakthrough. The development of 'liberal theology' in the later 19th century, partly on the basis of Schleiermacher's beginnings, tended to fall back into Kant's overly rational limitations. Against this, Barth's reassertion of the power of the traditional symbolism was bound to produce a vigorous response, but unfortunately, due to Barth's own profound ambiguity on the ultimate status of dogma, the consequences were in part simply a regressive reassertion of the adequacy of the early modern theological formulation. By the middle of the 20th century, however, the deeper implications of Schleiermacher's attempt were being developed in various ways by such diverse figures as Tillich, Bultmann and Bonhoeffer.[35] Tillich's assertion of 'ecstatic naturalism', Bultmann's program of 'demythologization' and Bonhoeffer's search for a 'religionless Christianity', though they cannot be simply equated with each other are efforts to come to terms with the modern situation. Even on the Catholic side the situation is beginning to be recognized.

Interestingly enough, indications of the same general search for an entirely new mode of religious symbolization, though mostly confined to the Protestant West, also appear in that most developed of the non-Western countries, Japan. Uchimura Kanzō's non-church Christianity was a relatively early indication of a search for new directions and is being developed even further today. Even more interesting perhaps is the emergence of a similar development out of the Jōdo Shinshū tradition, at least in the person of Ienaga Saburo.[36] This example indeed suggests that highly 'modern' implications exist in more than one strand of Mahayana Buddhism and perhaps several of the other great traditions as well. Although in my opinion

these implications were never developed sufficiently to dominate a historical epoch as they did in the West in the last two centuries, they may well
prove decisive in the future of these religions.

So far what I have been saying applies mainly to intellectuals, but at least
some evidence indicates that changes are also occurring at the level of mass
religiosity.[37] Behind the 96 per cent of Americans who claim to believe in
God[38] there are many instances of a massive reinterpretation that leaves
Tillich, Bultmann and Bonhoeffer far behind. In fact, for many churchgoers
the obligation of doctrinal orthodoxy sits lightly indeed, and the idea that
all creedal statements must receive a personal reinterpretation is widely
accepted. The dualistic world view certainly persists in the minds of many
of the devout, but just as surely many others have developed elaborate and
often psuedo-scientific rationalizations to bring their faith in its experienced
validity into some kind of cognitive harmony with the 20th century world.
The wave of popular response that some of the newer theology seems to be
eliciting is another indication that not only the intellectuals find themselves
in a new religious situation.[39]

To concentrate on the church in a discussion of the modern religious
situation is already misleading, for it is precisely the characteristic of the
new situation that the great problem of religion as I have defined it, the
symbolization of man's relation to the ultimate conditions of his existence, is
no longer the monopoly of any groups explicitly labeled religious. However
much the development of Western Christianity may have led up to and in a
sense created the modern religious situation, it just as obviously is no longer
in control of it. Not only has any obligation of doctrinal orthodoxy been
abandoned by the leading edge of modern culture, but every fixed position
has become open to question in the process of making sense out of man and
his situation. This involves a profounder commitment to the process I have
been calling religious symbolization than ever before. The historic religions
discovered the self; the early modern religion found a doctrinal basis on
which to accept the self in all its empirical ambiguity; modern religion is
beginning to understand the laws of the self's own existence and so to help
man take responsibility for his own fate.

This statement is not intended to imply a simple liberal optimism, for
the modern analysis of man has also disclosed the depths of the limitations
imposed by man's situation. Nevertheless, the fundamental symbolization
of modern man and his situation is that of a dynamic multi-dimensional
self capable, within limits, of continual self-transformation and capable,
again within limits, of remaking the world including the very symbolic
forms with which he deals with it, even the forms that state the unalterable
conditions of his own existence. Such a statement should not be taken to
mean that I expect, even less that I advocate, some ghastly religion of social
science. Rather I expect traditional religious symbolism to be maintained
and developed in new directions, but with growing awareness that it is

symbolism and that man in the last analysis is responsible for the choice of his symbolism. Naturally, continuation of the symbolization characteristic of earlier stages without any reinterpretation is to be expected among many in the modern world, just as it has occurred in every previous period.

Religious action in the modern period is, I think, clearly a continuation of tendencies already evident in the early modern stage. Now less than ever can man's search for meaning be confined to the church. But with the collapse of a clearly defined doctrinal orthodoxy and a religiously supported objective system of moral standards, religious action in the world becomes more demanding than ever. The search for adequate standards of action, which is at the same time a search for personal maturity and social relevance, is in itself the heart of the modern quest for salvation, if I may divest that word of its dualistic associations. How the specifically religious bodies are to adjust their time honored practices of worship and devotion to modern conditions is of growing concern in religious circles. Such diverse movements as the liturgical revival, pastoral psychology and renewed emphasis on social action are all efforts to meet the present need. Few of these trends have gotten much beyond the experimental but we can expect the experiments to continue.

In the modern situation as I have defined it, one might almost be tempted to see in Thomas Paine's 'My mind is my church', or Thomas Jefferson's 'I am a sect myself' the typical expression of *religious organization* in the near future. Nonetheless it seems unlikely that collective symbolization of the great inescapabilities of life will soon disappear. Of course the 'free intellectual' will continue to exist as he has for millennia but such a solution can hardly be very general. Private voluntary religious association in the West achieved full legitimation for the first time in the early modern situation, but in the early stages especially, discipline and control within these groups was very intense. The tendency in more recent periods has been to continue the basic pattern but with a much more open and flexible pattern of membership. In accord with general trends I have already discussed, standards of doctrinal orthodoxy and attempts to enforce moral purity have largely been dropped. The assumption in most of the major Protestant denominations is that the church member can be considered responsible for himself. This trend seems likely to continue, with an increasingly fluid type of organization in which many special purpose sub-groups form and disband. Rather than interpreting these trends as significant of indifference and secularization, I see in them the increasing acceptance of the notion that each individual must work out his own ultimate solutions and that the most the church can do is provide him a favorable environment for doing so, without imposing on him a prefabricated set of answers.[40] And it will be increasingly realized that answers to religious questions can validly be sought in various spheres of 'secular' art and thought.

Here I can only suggest what I take to be the main *social implication* of the modern religious situation. Early modern society, to a considerable degree under religious pressure, developed, as we have seen, the notion of a self-revising social system in the form of a democratic society. But at least in the early phase of that development social flexibility was balanced against doctrinal (Protestant orthodoxy) and characterological (Puritan personality) rigidities. In a sense those rigidities were necessary to allow the flexibility to emerge in the social system, but it is the chief characteristic of the more recent modern phase that culture and personality themselves have come to be viewed as endlessly revisable. This has been characterized as a collapse of meaning and a failure of moral standards. No doubt the possibilities for pathological distortion in the modern situation are enormous. It remains to be seen whether the freedom modern society implies at the cultural and personality as well as the social level can be stably institutionalized in large-scale societies. Yet the very situation that has been characterized as one of the collapse of meaning and the failure of moral standards can also, and I would argue more fruitfully, be viewed as one offering unprecedented opportunities for creative innovation in every sphere of human action.

Conclusion

The schematic presentation of the stages of religious evolution just concluded is based on the proposition that at each stage the freedom of personality and society has increased relative to the environing conditions. Freedom has increased because at each successive stage the relation of man to the conditions of his existence has been conceived as more complex, more open and more subject to change and development. The distinction between conditions that are really ultimate and those that are alterable becomes increasingly clear though never complete. Of course this scheme of religious evolution has implied at almost every point a general theory of social evolution, which has had to remain largely implicit.

Let me suggest in closing, as a modest effort at empirical testing, how the evolutionary scheme may help to explain the facts of alternating world acceptance and rejection which were noted near the beginning of the paper. I have argued that the world acceptance of the primitive and archaic levels is largely to be explained as the only possible response to a reality that invades the self to such an extent that the symbolizations of self and world are only very partially separate.[...] Only by withdrawing cathexis from the myriad objects of empirical reality could consciousness of a centered self in relation to an encompassing reality emerge. Early modern religion made it possible to maintain the centered self without denying the multifold empirical reality and so made world rejection in the classical sense unnecessary. In the modern phase knowledge of the laws of the formation of the self, as well as much more about the structure of the world, has opened up almost unlimited new directions of exploration and development. World rejection marks the beginning of a clear objectification of the social order and sharp criticism of it. In the earlier world-accepting phases religious conceptions and social order were so fused that it was almost impossible to criticize the latter from the point of view of the former. In the later phases the possibility of remaking the world to conform to value demands has served in a very different way to mute the extremes of world rejection. The world acceptance of the last two stages is shown in this analysis to have a profoundly different significance from that of the first two.

Construction of a wide-ranging evolutionary scheme like the one presented in this paper is an extremely risky enterprise. Nevertheless such efforts are justifiable if, by throwing light on perplexing developmental problems they contribute to modern man's efforts at self interpretation.

NOTES

1. Part of this paper was given as an open lecture at the University of Chicago on October 16, 1963. Many of the ideas in the paper were worked out in presentations to a seminar on social evolution which I gave together with Talcott Parsons and S. N. Eisenstadt at Harvard University in the spring of 1963. I wish to acknowledge the criticisms received from Professors Parsons and Eisenstadt and the students in the seminar as well as the comments of Parsons on this manuscript.
2. Chantepie de la Saussaye, *Manuel d'Histoire des Religions*, French translation directed by H. Hubert and I. Levy, Paris: Colin, 1904, author's introduction.
3. Clifford Geertz, 'Religion as a Cultural System', unpublished, 1963.
4. Mircea Eliade, *Patterns in Comparative Religion*, New York: Sheed and Ward, 1958, pp. 459–65.
5. Erich Voegelin, *Order and History*, vol. I: *Israel and Revelation*, Baton Rouge: Louisiana State University Press, 1956, p. 5.
6. *Qur'an* 57, 19–20.
7. *Qur'an* 87, 16–17.
8. On these developments see Ienaga Saburo, *Nihon Shisōshi ni okeru Hitei no Ronri no Hattatsu* (The Development of the Logic of Negation in the History of Japanese Thought), Tokyo: 1940.
9. Max Weber, 'Religious Rejections of the World and Their Directions', in Hans H. Gerth and C. Wright Mills (eds.), *From Max Weber*, New York: Oxford University Press, 1946.
10. One might argue that the much discussed modern phenomenon of alienation is the same as world rejection. The concept of alienation has too many uses to receive full discussion here, but it usually implies estrangement from or rejection of only selected aspects of the empirical world. In the contemporary world a really radical alienation from the whole of empirical reality would be discussed more in terms of psychosis than religion.
11. Geertz, *op. cit.*
12. These stages are actually derived from an attempt to develop a general schema of sociocultural evolution during the seminar in which I participated, together with Talcott Parsons and S. N. Eisenstadt. This paper must, however, be strictly limited to religious evolution, which is in itself sufficiently complex without going into still broader issues.

13. Godfrey Lienhardt, *Divinity and Experience*, London: Oxford University Press, 1961, p. 170.
14. One might argue that it was language and not religion that gave man the capacity to dominate his environment symbolically, but this seems to be a false distinction. It is very unlikely that language came into existence 'first' and that men then 'thought up' religion. Rather we would suppose that religion in the sense of this paper was from the beginning a major element in the *content* of linguistic symbolization. Clearly the relations between language and religion are very important and require much more systematic investigation.
15. Lienhardt, *op. cit.*, p. 149.
16. This notion was first clearly expressed to me in conversation and in unpublished writings by Eli Sagan.
17. In his discussion of Lévy-Bruhl's thesis on primitive mentality, reported in *Bulletin de la Société française de Philosophie*, Séance du 15 Febrier 1923, 23e année (1923), p. 26.
18. Lucien Lévy-Bruhl, *La Mythologie primitive*, Paris: Alcan, 1935. This volume and Lévy-Bruhl's last volume, *L'Experience mystique et les symboles chez les primitifs*, Paris: Alcan, 1938, were recently praised by Evans-Pritchard as unsurpassed in 'depth and insight' among studies of the structure of primitive thought, in his introduction to the English translation of Robert Hertz, *Death and the Right Hand*, New York: Free Press, 1960, p. 24. These are the only two volumes of Lévy-Bruhl on primitive thought that have not been translated into English.
19. *La Mythologie primitive*, p. 217.
20. Of Stanner's publications the most relevant are a series of articles published under the general title 'On Aboriginal Religion' in *Oceania*, 30 to 33 (1959–63), and 'The Dreaming' in T. A. G. Hungerford (ed.), *Australian Signpost*, Melbourne: Cheshire, 1956, and reprinted in William Lessa and Evon Z. Vogt, editors, *Reader in Comparative Religion*, Evanston, Ill.: Row, Peterson, 1958. (References to 'The Dreaming' are to the Lessa and Vogt volume.) Outside the Australian culture area, the new world provides the most examples of the type of religion I call primitive. Navaho religion, for example, conforms closely to the type.
21. 'The Dreaming', p. 514.
22. This is a controversial point. For extensive bibliography see Eliade, *op. cit.*, p. 112. Eliade tends to accept the notion of high gods in Australia but Stanner says of the two figures most often cited as high gods: 'Not even by straining can one see in such culture heroes as Baiame and Darumulum the true hint of a Yahveh, jealous, omniscient and omnipotent.' 'The Dreaming', p. 518.
23. *Op. cit.*, p. 91.
24. Ronald Berndt, *Kunapipi*, Melbourne: Cheshire, 1951, pp. 71–84.
25. Stanner: 'On Aboriginal Religion I', *Oceania*, 30 (December, 1959), p. 126; Lienhardt, *op. cit.*, p. 53.
26. 'On Aboriginal Religion I', p. 118. The Navaho ritual system is based on the same principles and also stresses the initiation theme. See Katherine Spencer, *Mythology and Values: An Analysis of Navaho Chantway Myths*, Philadelphia: American Folklore Society, 1957. A very similar four act structure has been discerned in the Christian eucharist by Dom Gregory Dix in *The Shape of the Liturgy*, Westminster: Dacre Press, 1943.
27. 'On Aboriginal Religion II', *Oceania*, 30 (June, 1960), p. 278. Of ritual Stanner says, 'Personality may almost be seen to change under one's eyes.' 'On Aboriginal Religion I', *op. cit.*, p. 126.
28. Catherine Berndt, *Women's Changing Ceremonies in Northern Australia*, Paris: Herman, 1950.
29. Emile Durkheim, *The Elementary Forms of the Religious Life*, Glencoe, Ill.: The Free Press, 1947.

30. Anthony Wallace, 'Revitalization Movements', *American Anthropologist*, 58 (April, 1956), pp. 264–79.
31. Raffaele Pettazzoni, *The All-Knowing God*, London: Methuen, 1956.
32. By 'craft literacy' I mean the situation in which literacy is limited to specially trained scribes and is not a capacity generally shared by the upper-status group. For an interesting discussion of the development of literacy in ancient Greece see Eric Havelock, *Preface to Plato*, Cambridge: Harvard University Press, 1963.
33. Henri Hubert and Marcel Mauss, 'Essai sur la nature et la fonction du Sacrifice', *L'Année Sociologique*, 2 (1899).
34. Two outstanding recent empirical studies are E. E. Evans-Pritchard, *Nuer Religion*, London: Oxford, 1956, esp. chs. 8 through 11, and Godfrey Lienhardt, *op. cit.*, esp. chs. 7 and 8.
35. Paul Tillich, *The Courage to Be*, New Haven: Yale, 1952; Karl Jaspers and Rudolf Bultmann, *Myth and Christianity*, New York: Noonday, 1958; Dietrich Bonhoeffer, *Letters and Papers from Prison*, London: SCM Press, 1954. Numerous other works of these three theologians could be cited.
36. Robert N. Bellah, 'Ienaga Saburo and the Search for Meaning in Modern Japan', in Marius Jansen (ed.), *Changing Japanese Attitudes toward Modernization*, Princeton: Princeton University Press, [1965].
37. There are a few scattered studies such as Gordon Allport, James Gillespie and Jacqueline Young, 'The Religion of the Post-War College Student', *The Journal of Psychology*, 25 (January, 1948), pp. 3–33, but the subject does not lend itself well to investigation via questionnaires and brief interviews. Richard V. McCann in his Harvard doctoral dissertation, 'The Nature and Varieties of Religious Change', 1955, utilized a much subtler approach involving depth interviewing and discovered a great deal of innovative reinterpretation in people from all walks of life. Unfortunately lack of control of sampling makes it impossible to generalize his results.
38. Will Herberg, *Protestant, Catholic, Jew*, Garden City: Doubleday, 1955, p. 72.
39. Bishop J. A. T. Robinson's *Honest to God*, Philadelphia: Westminster, 1963, which states in straightforward language the positions of some of the recent Protestant theologians mentioned above, has sold (by November, 1963) over 300,000 copies in England and over 71,000 in the United States with another 50,000 on order, and this in the first few months after publication. (Reported in *Christianity and Crisis*, 23 (November 11, 1963), p. 201).
40. The great Protestant stress on thinking for oneself in matters of religion is documented in Gerhard Lenski, *The Religious Factor*, Garden City: Doubleday, 1961, pp. 270–3.

PETER BERGER
'THE SACRED CANOPY'

Peter Ludwig Berger was born in Vienna in 1929; however, at the age of seventeen, shortly after the end of the Second World War, he emigrated to America, where he received a higher education, first at Wagner College, New York, and later from the New School for Social Research (NSSR), also in New York. He graduated with a PhD from the NSSR in 1952 and in 1955 went to work at the Evangelische Akademie in Bad Boll, Germany. He subsequently taught at the University of North Carolina, Hartford Theological Seminary, the NSSR, Rutgers University and finally Boston University, where he still works as Professor of Sociology and Theology. Since 1985 he has held this position simultaneously with the post of Director of the University's Institute for the Study of Economic Culture. In 1992 he was awarded the Mannes Sperber Prize, which is presented by the Austrian government to individuals who have made significant contributions to culture.

Peter Berger's work has spanned the divide regarding secularisation theory; he initially supported arguments in favour of the theory and subsequently has argued against it. The material included here, however, is more closely related to the work of Thomas Luckmann, focusing on religion's relation to worldview, that is, as a system of meaning and of meaning construction.

RELIGION AND WORLD-CONSTRUCTION

[. . .]

Religion is the human enterprise by which a sacred cosmos is established.[1] Put differently, religion is cosmization in a sacred mode. By sacred is meant here a quality of mysterious and awesome power, other than man and yet related to him, which is believed to reside in certain objects of experience.[2] This quality may be attributed to natural or artificial objects, to animals, or to men, or to the objectivations of human culture. There are sacred rocks, sacred tools, sacred cows. The chieftain may be sacred, as may be a particular custom or institution. Space and time may be assigned the same quality, as in sacred localities and sacred seasons. The quality may finally be embodied in sacred beings, from highly localized spirits to the great cosmic divinities. The latter, in turn, may be transformed into ultimate forces or principles ruling the cosmos, no longer conceived of in personal terms but still endowed with the status of sacredness. The historical manifestations of the sacred vary widely, though there are certain uniformities to be observed cross-culturally (no matter here whether these are to be interpreted

Peter Berger (1967), *The Sacred Canopy*, New York: Anchor.

as resulting from cultural diffusion or from an inner logic of man's religious imagination). The sacred is apprehended as 'sticking out' from the normal routines of everyday life, as something extraordinary and potentially dangerous, though its dangers can be domesticated and its potency harnessed to the needs of everyday life. Although the sacred is apprehended as other than man, yet it refers to man, relating to him in a way in which other non-human phenomena (specifically, the phenomena of non-sacred nature) do not. The cosmos posited by religion thus both transcends and includes man. The sacred cosmos is confronted by man as an immensely powerful reality other than himself. Yet this reality addresses itself to him and locates his life in an ultimately meaningful order.

On one level, the antonym to the sacred is the profane, to be defined simply as the absence of sacred status. All phenomena are profane that do not 'stick out' as sacred. The routines of everyday life are profane unless, so to speak, proven otherwise, in which latter case they are conceived of as being infused in one way or another with sacred power (as in sacred work, for instance). Even in such cases, however, the sacred quality attributed to the ordinary events of life *itself* retains its extraordinary character, a character that is typically reaffirmed through a variety of rituals and the loss of which is tantamount to secularization, that is, to a conception of the events in question as *nothing but* profane. The dichotomization of reality into sacred and profane spheres, however related, is intrinsic to the religious enterprise. As such, it is obviously important for any analysis of the religious phenomenon.

On a deeper level, however, the sacred has another opposed category, that of chaos.[3] The sacred cosmos emerges out of chaos and continues to confront the latter as its terrible contrary. This opposition of cosmos and chaos is frequently expressed in a variety of cosmogonic myths. The sacred cosmos, which transcends and includes man in its ordering of reality, thus provides man's ultimate shield against the terror of anomy. To be in a 'right' relationship with the sacred cosmos is to be protected against the nightmare threats of chaos. To fall out of such a 'right' relationship is to be abandoned on the edge of the abyss of meaninglessness. It is not irrelevant to observe here that the English 'chaos' derives from a Greek word meaning 'yawning' and 'religion' from a Latin one meaning 'to be careful'. To be sure, what the religious man is 'careful' about is above all the dangerous power inherent in the manifestations of the sacred themselves. But behind this danger is the other, much more horrible one, namely that one may lose all connection with the sacred and be swallowed up by chaos. All the nomic constructions, as we have seen, are designed to keep this terror at bay. In the sacred cosmos, however, these constructions achieve their ultimate culmination – literally, their apotheosis.

Human existence is essentially and inevitably externalizing activity. In the course of externalization men pour out meaning into reality. Every human society is an edifice of externalized and objectivated meanings, always intending a meaningful totality. Every society is engaged in the never completed enterprise of building a humanly meaningful world. Cosmization implies the identification of this humanly meaningful world with the world as such, the former now being grounded in the latter, reflecting it or being derived from it in its fundamental structures. Such a cosmos, as the ultimate ground and validation of human nomoi, need not necessarily be sacred. Particularly in modern times there have been thoroughly secular attempts at cosmization, among which modern science is by far the most important. It is safe to say, however, that originally *all* cosmization had a sacred character. This remained true through most of human history, and not only through the millennia of human existence on earth preceding what we now call civilization. Viewed historically, most of man's worlds have been sacred worlds. Indeed, it appears likely that only by way of the sacred was it possible for man to conceive of a cosmos in the first place.[4]

It can thus be said that religion has played a strategic part in the human enterprise of world-building. Religion implies the farthest reach of man's self-externalization, of his infusion of reality with his own meanings. Religion implies that human order is projected into the totality of being. Put differently, religion is the audacious attempt to conceive of the entire universe as being humanly significant.

RELIGION AND WORLD-MAINTENANCE

[. . .]

It will readily be seen that the area of legitimation is far broader than that of religion, as these two terms have been defined here. Yet there exists an important relationship between the two. It can be described simply by saying that religion has been the historically most widespread and effective instrumentality of legitimation. All legitimation maintains socially defined reality. Religion legitimates so effectively because it relates the precarious reality constructions of empirical societies with ultimate reality. The tenuous realities of the social world are grounded in the sacred *realissimum*, which by definition is beyond the contingencies of human meanings and human activity.

The efficacy of religious legitimation can be brought home by asking an, as it were, recipe question on the construction of worlds. If one imagines oneself as a fully aware founder of a society, a kind of combination of Moses and Machiavelli, one could ask oneself the following question: how can the future continuation of the institutional order, now established *ex nihilo*, be best ensured? There is an obvious answer to the question in terms of power. But let it be assumed that all the means of power have been effectively employed – all opponents have been destroyed, all means of coercion are in one's own hands, reasonably safe provisions have been made for the transmission of power to one's designated successors. There still remains the problem of legitimation, all the more urgent because of the novelty and thus highly conscious precariousness of the new order. The problem would best be solved by applying the following recipe: let the institutional order be so interpreted as to hide, as much as possible, its *constructed* character. Let that which has been stamped out of the ground *ex nihilo* appear as the manifestation of something that has been existent from the beginning of time, or at least from the beginning of this group. Let the people forget that this order was established by men and continues to be dependent upon the consent of men. Let them believe that, in acting out the institutional programs that have been imposed upon them, they are but realizing the deepest aspirations of their own being and putting themselves in harmony with the fundamental order of the universe. In sum: set up religious legitimations. There are, of course, wide historical variations in the manner in which this has been done. In one way or another, the basic recipe was followed throughout most of human history. And, actually, the example of Moses-Machiavelli figuring the whole thing out with cool deliberation may not be as fanciful as all that. There have been very cool minds indeed in the history of religion.

Religion legitimates social institutions by bestowing upon them an ultimately valid ontological status, that is, by *locating* them within a sacred and cosmic frame of reference. The historical constructions of human activity are viewed from a vantage point that, in its own self-definition, transcends both history and man. This can be done in different ways. Probably the most ancient form of this legitimation is the conception of the institutional order as directly reflecting or manifesting the divine structure of the cosmos, that is, the conception of the relationship between society and cosmos as one between microcosm and macrocosm.[5] Everything 'here below' has its analogue 'up above'. By participating in the institutional order men, *ipso facto*, participate in the divine cosmos. The kinship structure, for example, extends beyond the human realm, with all being (including the being of the gods) conceived of in the structures of kinship as given in the society.[6] Thus there may be not only a totemic 'sociology' but a totemic 'cosmology' as well. The social institutions of kinship then merely reflect the great 'family' of all being, in which the gods participate on a higher level. Human sexuality reflects divine creativity. Every human family reflects the structure of the cosmos, not only in the sense of representing but of embodying it. Or, for another crucial case, the political structure simply extends into the human sphere the power of the divine cosmos. The political authority is conceived of as the agent of the gods, or ideally even as a divine incarnation. Human power, government, and punishment thus become sacramental phenomena, that is, channels by which divine forces are made to impinge upon the lives of men. The ruler speaks for the gods, or *is* a god, and to obey him is to be in a right relationship with the world of the gods.

The microcosm/macrocosm scheme of legitimating the social order, while typical of primitive and archaic societies, has been transformed in the major civilizations.[7] Such transformations are probably inevitable with a certain development of human thought beyond a strictly mythological worldview, that is, a worldview in which sacred forces are continuously permeating human experience. In the civilizations of eastern Asia the mythological legitimations were transformed into highly abstract philosophical and theological categories, though the essential features of the microcosm/macrocosm scheme remained intact.[8] In China, for instance, even the very rational, virtually secularizing, demythologization of the concept of *tao* (the 'right order' or 'right way' of things) permitted the continuing conception of the institutional structure as reflective of cosmic order. In India, on the other hand, the notion of *dharma* (social duty, particularly caste duty) as relating the individual to the universal order of the universe survived most of the radical reinterpretations of the latter's meaning. In Israel the scheme was broken through by the faith in a radically transcendent God of history, and in Greece by the positing of the human soul as the ground for the rational ordering of the world.[9] The latter two transformations had profound consequences for religious legitimation, in the Israelite case leading to the interpretation of institutions in terms of revealed divine imperatives, in the Greek case to interpretations based on rationally conceived assumptions about the nature of man. Both the Israelite and the Greek transformations carried within them the seeds of a secularized view of the social order. The resulting historical developments need not concern us at the moment, nor the fact that large masses of people continue to conceive of society in essentially archaic terms down to our own time and regardless of the transformations in the 'official' definitions of reality. What is important to stress is that, even where the microcosm/macrocosm scheme was broken through, religion continued for many centuries to be the central legitimating agency. Israel legitimated its institutions in terms of the divinely revealed law throughout its existence as an autonomous society.[10] The Greek city, and its subsidiary institutions, continued to be legitimated in religious terms, and these legitimations could even be expanded to apply to the Roman empire in a later era.[11]

To repeat, the historically crucial part of religion in the process of legitimation is explicable in terms of the unique capacity of religion to 'locate' human phenomena within a cosmic frame of reference. All legitimation serves to maintain reality – reality, that is, as defined in a particular human collectivity. Religious legitimation purports to relate the humanly defined reality to ultimate, universal and sacred reality. The inherently precarious and transitory constructions of human activity are thus given the semblance of ultimate security and permanence. Put differently, the humanly constructed nomoi are given a cosmic status.

This cosmization, of course, refers not only to the over-all nomic structures, but to specific institutions and roles within a given society. The cosmic status assigned to these is objectivated, that is, it becomes part of the objectively available reality of the institutions and roles in question. For example, the institution of divine kingship, and the several roles representing it, is apprehended *as* a decisive link between the world of men and the world of the gods. The religious legitimation of power involved in this institution does not appear as an *ex post facto* justification of a few theoreticians, it is objectively present as the institution is encountered by the man in the street in the course of his everyday life. Insofar as the man in the street is adequately socialized into the reality of his society, he cannot conceive of the king *except as* the bearer of a role that represents the fundamental order of the universe – and, indeed, the same assumption may be made for the king himself. In this manner, the cosmic status of the institution is 'experienced' whenever men come into contact with it in the ordinary course of events.[12]

The 'gains' of this kind of legitimation are readily evident, whether one looks at it from the viewpoint of institutional objectivity or from that of individual subjective consciousness. All institutions possess the character of objectivity and their legitimations, whatever content these may have, must continuously undergird this objectivity. The religious legitimations, however, ground the socially defined reality of the institutions in the ultimate reality of the universe, in reality 'as such'. The institutions are thus given a semblance of inevitability, firmness and durability that is analogous to these qualities as ascribed to the gods themselves. Empirically, institutions are always changing as the exigencies of human activity upon which they are based change. Institutions are always threatened not only by the ravages of time, but by those of conflict and discrepancies between the groups whose activities they are intended to regulate. In terms of the cosmic legitimations, on the other hand, the institutions are magically lifted above these human, historical contingencies. They become inevitable, because they are taken for granted not only by men but by the gods. Their empirical tenuousness is transformed into an overpowering stability as they are understood as but manifestations of the underlying structure of the universe. They transcend the death of individuals and the decay of entire collectivities, because they are now grounded in a sacred time within which merely human history is but an episode. In a sense, then, they become immortal.

Looked at from the viewpoint of individual subjective consciousness, the cosmization of the institutions permits the individual to have an ultimate sense of rightness, both cognitively and normatively, in the roles he is expected to play in society. Human role-playing is always dependent upon the recognition of others. The individual can identify himself with a role only insofar as others have identified him with it. When roles, and the institutions to which they belong, are endowed with cosmic significance, the individual's self-identification with them attains a further dimension. For now it is not only human others who recognize him in the manner appropriate to the role, but those suprahuman others with which the cosmic legitimations populate the universe. His self-identification with the role becomes correspondingly deeper and more stable. He *is* whatever society has identified him as by virtue of a cosmic truth, as it were, and his social being becomes rooted in the sacred reality of the universe. Once more, the transcendence of erosive time is of paramount importance here. An Arabic proverb puts it succinctly: 'Men forget, God remembers.' What men forget, among other things, is their reciprocal identifications in the game of playing society. Social identities and their corresponding roles are assigned to the individual by others, but others are also quite liable to change or withdraw the assignments. They 'forget' who the individual was and, because of the inherent dialectic of recognition and self-recognition, thus powerfully threaten his own recollections of identity. If he can assume that, at any rate, God remembers, his tenuous self-identifications are given a foundation seemingly secure from the shifting reactions of other men. God then becomes the most reliable and ultimately significant other.[13]

Where the microcosm/macrocosm understanding of the relationship between society and cosmos prevails, the parallelism between the two spheres typically extends to specific roles. These are then understood as mimetic reiterations of the cosmic realities for which they are supposed to stand. All social roles are representations of larger complexes of objectivated meanings.[14] For example, the role of father represents a wide variety of meanings ascribed to the institution of the family and, more generally, to the institutionalization of sexuality and interpersonal relationships. When this role is legitimated in mimetic terms – the father reiterating 'here below' the actions of creation, sovereignty, or love that have their sacred prototypes 'up above' – then its representative character becomes vastly enhanced. Representation of human meanings becomes mimesis of divine mysteries. Sexual intercourse mimes the creation of the universe. Paternal authority mimes the authority of the gods, paternal solicitude the solicitude of the gods. Like the institutions, then, roles become endowed with a quality of immortality. Also, their objectivity, over and beyond the foibles of the individuals who are their 'temporal' bearers, becomes immensely strengthened. The role of fatherhood confronts the individual as a divinely given facticity, ultimately untouchable not only by his own conceivable transgressions against it but also by all the conceivable vicissitudes of history. The point need hardly be belabored that legitimation of this kind carries with it extremely powerful and built-in sanctions against individual deviance from the prescribed role performances.

But even where religious legitimation falls short of cosmization and does not permit the transformation of human acts into mimetic representations, it still permits the individual to play his roles with a greater assurance that they are more than ephemeral human productions. At any rate those roles that have been specially circumscribed with religious mandates and sanctions will 'gain' in this way. Even in our own society, for example, where sexuality, the family, and marriage are hardly legitimated in mimetic terms, the roles pertaining to these institutional spheres are effectively maintained by religious legitimations. The contingent formations of a particular historical society, the particular institutions produced out of the polymorphic and pliant material of human sexuality, are legitimated in terms of divine commandment, 'natural law', and sacrament. Even today, then, the role of fatherhood not only has a certain quality of impersonality (that is, detachability from the particular person who performs it – a quality attaching to all social roles), but in its religious legitimation this becomes a quality of suprapersonality by virtue of its relationship to the heavenly father who instituted on earth the order to which the role belongs.

Just as religious legitimation interprets the order of society in terms of an all-embracing, sacred order of the universe, so it relates the disorder that is the antithesis of all socially constructed nomoi to that yawning abyss of chaos that is the oldest antagonist of the sacred. To go against the order of society is always to risk plunging into anomy. To go against the order of society as religiously legitimated, however, is to make a compact with the primeval forces of darkness. To deny reality as it has been socially defined is to risk falling into irreality, because it is well-nigh impossible in the long run to keep up alone and without social support one's own counterdefinitions of the world. When the socially defined reality has come to be identified with the ultimate reality of the universe, then its denial takes on the quality of evil as well as madness. The denier then risks moving into what may be called a negative reality – if one wishes, the reality of the devil. This is well expressed in those archaic mythologies that confront the divine order of the world (such as *tao* in China, *rta* in India, *ma'at* in Egypt) with an underworld or anti-world that has a reality of its own – negative, chaotic, ultimately destructive of all who inhabit it, the realm of demonic monstrosities. As particular religious traditions move away from mythology, this imagery will, of course, change. This happened, for instance, in the highly sophisticated ways in which later Hindu thought developed the original dichotomy of *rta* and *an-rta*. But the fundamental confrontation between light and darkness, nomic security and anomic abandonment, remains operative. Thus the violation of one's *dharma* is not just a moral offense against society, but an outrage against the ultimate order that embraces both gods and men and, indeed, all beings.

Men forget. They must, therefore, be reminded over and over again. Indeed, it may be argued that one of the oldest and most important prerequisites for the establishment of culture is the institution of such 'reminders', the terribleness of which for many centuries is perfectly logical in view of the 'forgetfulness' that they were designed to combat.[15] Religious ritual has been a crucial instrument of this process of 'reminding'. Again and again it 'makes present' to those who participate in it the fundamental reality-definitions and their appropriate legitimations. The farther back one goes historically, the more does one find religious ideation (typically in mythological form) embedded in ritual activity – to use more modern terms, theology embedded in worship. A good case can be made that the oldest religious expressions were always ritual in character.[16] The 'action' of a ritual (the Greeks called this its *ergon* or 'work' – from which, incidentally, our word 'orgy' is derived) typically consists of two parts – the things that have to be done (*dromena*) and the things that have to be said (*legoumena*). The performances of the ritual are closely linked to the reiteration of the sacred formulas that 'make present' once more the names and deeds of the gods. Another way of putting this is to say that religious ideation is grounded in religious activity, relating to it in a dialectical manner analogous to the dialectic between human activity and its products discussed earlier in a broader context. Both religious acts and religious legitimations, ritual and mythology, *dromena* and *legoumena, together* serve to 'recall' the traditional meanings embodied in the culture and its major institutions. They restore ever again the continuity between the present moment and the societal tradition, placing the experiences of the individual and the various groups of the society in the context of a history (fictitious or not) that transcends them all. It has been rightly said that society, in its essence, is a memory.[17] It may be added that, through most of human history, this memory has been a religious one.

The dialecticity between religious activity and religious ideation points to another important fact – the rootedness of religion in the practical concerns of everyday life.[18] The religious legitimations, or at least most of them, make little sense if one conceives of them as productions of theoreticians that are then applied *ex post facto* to particular complexes of activity. The need for legitimation arises in the course of activity. Typically, this is in the consciousness of the actors before that of the theoreticians. And, of course, while all members of a society are actors within it, only very few are theoreticians (mystagogues, theologians, and the like). The degree of theoretical elaboration of the religious legitimations will vary with a large number of historical factors, but it would lead to grave misunderstanding if only the more sophisticated legitimations were taken into consideration. To put it simply, most men in history have felt the need for religious legitimation – only very few have been interested in the development of religious 'ideas'.

This does *not* mean, however, that where there exists more complex religious ideation it is to be understood as nothing but a 'reflection' (that is, a dependent variable) of the everyday, practical interests from which it derives. The term 'dialectic' is useful precisely in avoiding this misinterpretation. Religious legitimations arise from human activity, but once crystallized into complexes of meaning that become part of a religious tradition they can attain a measure of autonomy as against this activity. Indeed, they may then *act back upon* actions in everyday life, transforming the latter, sometimes radically. It is probable that this autonomy from practical concerns increases with the degree of theoretical sophistication. For example, the thought of a tribal shaman is likely to be more directly linked to the practical concerns of society than the thought of a professor of systematic theology. In any case, one cannot properly assume *a priori* that to understand the social roots of a particular religious idea is *ipso facto* to understand its later meaning or to be able to predict its later social consequences. 'Intellectuals' (religious or otherwise) sometimes spin out very strange ideas – and very strange ideas sometimes have important historical effects.

Religion thus serves to maintain the reality of that socially constructed world within which men exist in their everyday lives. Its legitimating power, however, has another important dimension – the integration into a comprehensive nomos of precisely those marginal situations in which the reality of everyday life is put in question.[19] It would be erroneous to think of these situations as being rare. On the contrary, every individual passes through such a situation every twenty hours or so – in the experience of sleep and, very importantly, in the transition stages between sleep and wakefulness. In the world of dreams the reality of everyday life is definitely left behind. In the transition stages of falling asleep and waking up again the contours of everyday reality are, at the least, less firm than in the state of fully awake consciousness. The reality of everyday life, therefore, is continuously surrounded by a penumbra of vastly different realities. These, to be sure, are segregated in consciousness as having a special cognitive status (in the consciousness of modern man, a lesser one) and thus generally prevented from massively threatening the primary reality of fully awake existence. Even then, however, the 'dikes' of everyday reality are not always impermeable to the invasion of those other realities that insinuate themselves into consciousness during sleep. There are always the 'nightmares' that continue to haunt in the daytime – specifically, with the 'nightmarish' thought that daytime reality may not be what it purports to be, that behind it lurks a totally different reality that may have as much validity, that indeed world and self may ultimately be something quite different from what they are defined to be by the society in which one lives one's daytime existence. Throughout the greater part of human history these other realities of the nightside of consciousness were taken quite seriously *as* realities, albeit of a different kind. Religion served to integrate these realities with the reality of everyday life, sometimes (in contrast to our modern approach) by ascribing to them a *higher* cognitive status. Dreams and nocturnal visions were related to everyday life in a variety of ways – as warnings, prophecies, or decisive encounters with the sacred, having specific consequences for everyday conduct in society. Within a modern ('scientific') frame of reference, of course, religion is less capable of performing this integration. Other legitimating conceptualizations, such as those of modern psychology, have taken the place of religion. All the same, where religion continues to be meaningful as an interpretation of existence, its definitions of reality must somehow be able to account for the fact that there are different spheres of reality in the ongoing experience of everyone.[20]

Marginal situations are characterized by the experience of 'ecstasy' (in the literal sense of *ek-stasis* – standing, or stepping, *outside* reality as commonly defined). The world of dreams is ecstatic with regard to the world of everyday life, and the latter can only retain its primary status in consciousness if some way is found of legitimating the ecstasies within a frame of reference that includes *both* reality spheres. Other bodily states also produce ecstasies of a similar kind, particularly those arising from disease and acute emotional disturbance. The confrontation with death (be it through actually witnessing the death of others or anticipating one's own death in the imagination) constitutes what is probably the most important marginal situation.[21] Death radically challenges *all* socially objectivated definitions of reality – of the world, of others, and of self. Death radically puts in question the taken-for-granted, 'business-as-usual' attitude in which one exists in everyday life. Here, everything in the daytime world of existence in society is massively threatened with 'irreality' – that is, everything in that world becomes dubious, eventually unreal, other than one had used to think. Insofar as the knowledge of death cannot be avoided in any society, legitimations of the reality of the social world *in the face of death* are decisive requirements in any society. The importance of religion in such legitimations is obvious.

Religion, then, maintains the socially defined reality by legitimating marginal situations in terms of an all-encompassing sacred reality. This permits the individual who goes through these situations to continue to exist in the world of his society – not 'as if nothing had happened', which is psychologically difficult in the more extreme marginal situations, but in the 'knowledge' that even these events or experiences have a place within a universe that makes sense. It is thus even possible to have 'a good death', that is, to die while retaining to the end a meaningful relationship with the nomos of one's society – subjectively meaningful to oneself and objectively meaningful in the minds of others.

NOTES

1. This definition is derived from Rudolf Otto and Mircea Eliade. [...] Religion is defined here as a human enterprise because this is how it manifests itself as an empirical phenomenon. Within this definition the question as to whether religion may also be something more than that remains bracketed, as, of course, it must be in any attempt at scientific understanding.
2. For a clarification of the concept of the sacred, *cf.* Rudolf Otto, *Das Heilige* (Munich, Beck, 1963); Gerardus van der Leeuw, *Religion in Essence and Manifestation* (London, George Allen & Unwin, 1938); Mircea Eliade, *Das Heilige und das Profane* (Hamburg, Rowohlt, 1957). The dichotomy of the sacred and the profane is used by Durkheim in his *The Elementary Forms of the Religious Life* (New York, Collier Books, 1961).
3. *Cf.* Eliade, *Cosmos and History* (New York, Harper, 1959), *passim*.

4. *Cf.* Eliade, *Das Heilige und das Profane*, p. 38: 'Die Welt laesst sich als 'Welt', als 'Kosmos' insofern fassen, als sie sich als heilige Welt offenbart.'

5. On the microcosm/macrocosm scheme, *cf.* Eliade, *Cosmos and History*, and Eric Voegelin, *Order and History*, Vol. I (Baton Rouge, Louisiana State University Press, 1956). Voegelin's conception of 'cosmological civilizations' and their rupture through what he calls 'leaps in being' is of great importance for the present argument.

6. On the 'cosmic' implications of kinship structure, *cf.* Durkheim's *Elementary Forms of the Religious Life*. Also, *cf.* Claude Lévi-Strauss, *Les structures élémentaires de la parenté* (Paris, Presses Universitaires de France, 1949), and *La pensée sauvage* (Paris, Plon, 1962).

7. On transformations of the microcosm/macrocosm scheme, *cf.* Voegelin, *op. cit.*, especially the introductory chapter.

8. On the sociological implications of the microcosm/macrocosm scheme, *cf.* Weber's works on the sociology of the religions of India and China. Also, *cf.* Marcel Granet, *La pensée chinoise* (Paris, Albin Michel, 1934).

9. For a detailed analysis of the break through the microcosm/macrocosm scheme in Israel and in Greece, *cf.* Voegelin, *op. cit.*, Vol. I and Vols. II – III, respectively.

10. On religious legitimation in Israel, *cf.* R. de Vaux, *Les institutions de l'Ancien Testament* (Paris, Editions du Cerf, 1961). This important work is now available in an English translation.

11. On religious legitimation in Greece and Rome, the classic work for the sociology of religion is still Fustel de Coulanges' *The Ancient City*. This work is particularly interesting because of its influence on Durkheim's thinking about religion.

12. On divine kingship, *cf.* Henri Frankfort, *Kingship and the Gods* (Chicago, University of Chicago Press, 1948).

13. This discussion, of course, applies some important concepts of George Herbert Mead to the social psychology of religion.

14. This discussion of roles as 'representations' is indebted both to Durkheim and to Mead, with the Durkheimian term being placed in the context of a Meadian approach to social psychology.

15. '"How does one create a memory for the human animal? How does one go about to impress anything on that partly dull, partly flighty human intelligence – that incarnation of forgetfulness – so as to make it stick?" As we might well imagine, the means used in solving this age-old problem have been far from delicate: in fact, there is perhaps nothing more terrible in man's earliest history than his mnemotechnics. 'A thing is branded on the memory to make it stay there; only what goes on hurting will stick' – this is one of the oldest and, unfortunately, one of the most enduring psychological axioms. . . . Whenever man has thought it necessary to create a memory for himself, his effort has been attended with torture, blood, sacrifice.' *Vide* Friedrich Nietzsche, *The Genealogy of Morals* (Garden City, N. Y., Doubleday-Anchor, 1956), pp. 192 f.

16. The conception of religion as embedded in ritual was strongly emphasized by Durkheim, who influenced Robert Will in the latter's important work *Le culte*. Also, *cf.* S. Mowinckel, *Religion und Kultus* (1953), and H. J. Kraus, *Gottesdienst in Israel* (1954).

17. The sharpest formulation of this point in sociological literature is by Maurice Halbwachs: 'La pensée sociale est essentiellement une mémoire.' *Vide* Halbwachs, *Les cadres sociaux de la mémoire* (Paris, Presses Universitaires de France, 1952), p. 296.

18. This discussion is strongly indebted to the Marxian conception of the dialectical relationship between sub- and superstructure (*Unterbau* and *Ueberbau*), the former to be identified *not* with an economic 'base' but with *praxis* in general. How far this conception is in logical contradiction with Weber's understanding of the 'elective

affinity' (*Wahlverwandschaft*) between certain religious ideas and their social 'carriers' (*Traeger*)) is an interesting question. Weber, of course, thought so. But we would contend that this conviction of his is not unrelated to the fact that his work antedated by more than a decade the reinterpretation of Marx stimulated by the rediscovery, in 1932, of the *Economic and Philosophical Manuscripts of 1844*. For a very interesting discussion of religion (specifically, religion in seventeenth-century France) in terms of a Marxian sociology of religion, *cf.* Lucien Goldmann, *Le Dieu caché* (Paris, Gallimard, 1956).

19. The term 'marginal situation' is derived from Jaspers, but its use in this discussion is strongly influenced by Schutz, particularly by the latter's analysis of the relationship between the 'paramount reality' of everyday life and what he called 'finite provinces of meaning'. *Cf.* Schutz, *Collected Papers*, Vol. I (The Hague, Nijhoff, 1962), pp. 207 ff.

20. Even today, of course, religion has to cope with such 'marginal' realities. The current efforts to integrate religion with the 'findings' of 'depth psychology' may serve as an important illustration. These efforts, it may be added, presuppose that the reality-definitions of the psychologists have become more plausible than the ones of traditional religion.

21. The conception of death as the most important marginal situation is derived from Heidegger, but Schutz's analysis of the 'fundamental anxiety' developed this within his over-all theory of the reality of everyday life.

STEVE BRUCE
'THE SECULARIZATION PARADIGM'

Steve Bruce was educated at the University of Stirling, where he studied sociology, being awarded a BA in 1976. After graduating from Stirling he became a lecturer at Queen's University, Belfast and while undertaking these duties Stirling awarded him a PhD. In 1991 he was offered the chair of the University of Aberdeen, which he accepted, serving as Head of the Department of Sociology and currently as Head of the School of Social Sciences. In 2003 he was elected a fellow of the British Academy. He currently holds a chair in sociology at the University of Aberdeen, where he is involved in research on religious discrimination in Scotland.

Steve Bruce has been a highly influential figure in the sociology of religion. While his work on sectarianism is particularly important he has also been a leading advocate of secularisation theory. The material included here, taken from God Is Dead, *develops some aspects of this theoretical perspective.*

INTRODUCTION

If argument in the social sciences is to be useful rather than merely entertaining, it must treat competing positions in their own terms and as fairly as possible. Sadly many contemporary debates about the fate of religion in the modern world are mulched in layers of caricature. One generation's misrepresentations are taken as authoritative and accurate by a younger generation that lacks the time or inclination to read the work of those they are inclined to disdain. In 1985, when Rodney Stark and William S. Bainbridge (1985: 430) wanted to represent the secularization paradigm (in order to show it false), they ignored the sociologists who had developed those ideas and instead cited a 1960s undergraduate textbook written by an anthropologist. Despite others pointing out that Anthony Wallace's view – 'the evolutionary future of religion is extinction' – might not be representative, Stark used this quotation repeatedly for the next fifteen years (see Stark and Finke 2000: 58). It became so firmly established that others (for example, Buckser 1996) saved themselves the trouble of reading old sociology by repeating it. The waters then became further clouded when scholars sympathetic to the secularization approach took such caricatures as an accurate account of what the paradigm entailed. They devised responses that they presented as 'neo-secularization theory', despite them differing little from the forgotten originals. In so doing, they made respectable the caricatures of what they sought to defend (Yamane 1997).

The point of this chapter is to clear the way for sensible debate about secularization. It presents little evidence [...]. What I want to do here is lay

Steve Bruce (2002), *God Is Dead*, Oxford: Blackwell.

out as clearly and as briefly as possible just what modern sociologists mean by secularization. Of course, this is a personal selection and interpretation, but I believe I am sufficiently well acquainted with the work I summarize for it to be representative and reasonable. As will become clear, there is no one secularization theory. Rather, there are clusters of descriptions and explanations that cohere reasonably well. I take my remit as summarizing *sociological* contributions from Max Weber onwards. Interesting though they are, I have no brief for defending the views of psychiatrists such as Sigmund Freud or the overambitious evolutionary models of social development popular with such nineteenth-centuary thinkers as Auguste Comte and Karl Marx.[...]

The basic proposition is that modernization creates problems for religion. Modernization is itself a multifaceted notion, which encompasses the industrialization of work; the shift from villages to towns and cities; the replacement of the small community by the society; the rise of individualism; the rise of egalitarianism; and the rationalization both of thought and of social organization. It is not necessary to spend a lot of time at this point on the meanings of these terms; they will become clear as we proceed. Nor is it necessary to agonize over the meaning of 'religion' [...]. I follow common usage in defining religion substantively as *beliefs, actions and institutions predicated on the existence of entities with powers of agency (that is, gods) or impersonal powers or processes possessed of moral purpose (the Hindu notion of karma, for example), which can set the conditions of, or intervene in, human affairs.* Although rather long-winded, this seems to cover most of what we mean when we talk about religion and offers a reasonable starting place.

Defining secularization in advance of offering explanations of it is less easy because scholars often conflate their definitions and explanations, but two quotations will suffice to begin the account. Berger and Luckmann (1966: 74) point to the declining social power of religion in their definition of secularization as 'the progressive autonomization of societal sectors from the domination of religious meaning and institutions'. Wilson made the same point in more detail and added explicit references to the thinking and behaviour of individuals when he said of secularization:

> Its application covers such things as the sequestration by political powers of the property and facilities of religious agencies; the shift from religious to secular control of various of the erstwhile activities and functions of religion; the decline in the proportion of their time, energy and resources which men devote to supra-empirical concerns; the decay of religious institutions; the supplanting, in matters of behaviour, of religious precepts by demands that accord with strictly technical criteria; and the gradual replacement of a specifically religious consciousness (which might range from dependence on charms,

rites, spells or prayers, to a broadly spiritually-inspired ethical concern) by an empirical, rational, instrumental orientation; the abandonment of mythical, poetic, and artistic interpretations of nature and
society in favour of matter-of-fact description and, with it, the rigorous separation of evaluative and emotive dispositions from cognitive
and positivistic orientations. (1982: 149)

This depiction is complex because it involves the place of religion in the
social system, the social standing of religious institutions, and individual
beliefs and behaviour. Although they are here presented as a package and
Wilson believes them to be related, it is obvious that the societies we hope to
encompass with our generalizations differ sufficiently within and between
themselves that not all elements will develop in exactly the same way in
every setting. Nonetheless, a degree of generalization does seem possible.

Wilson is careful to distinguish between the social significance of religion
and religion as such. We should not foreclose on the possibility that religion
may cease to be of any great social importance while remaining a matter
of great import for those who have some. However, as I will argue, there
is a very clear implication that three things are causally related: the social
importance of religion, the number of people who take it seriously, and
how seriously anyone takes it. It is possible that a country that is formally
and publicly secular may nonetheless contain among its populace a large
number of people who are deeply religious. But [...] I will show ways in
which the declining social significance of religion causes a decline in the
number of religious people and the extent to which people are religious.[1]

In brief, I see secularization as a social condition manifest in (a) the
declining importance of religion for the operation of non-religious roles
and institutions such as those of the state and the economy; (b) a decline
in the social standing of religious roles and institutions; and (c) a decline
in the extent to which people engage in religious practices, display beliefs
of a religious kind, and conduct other aspects of their lives in a manner
informed by such beliefs.

As a final preliminary we may note that the secularization paradigm is
very largely concerned with what it is now popular to call the 'demand'
for religion. It supposes that changes in religious belief and behaviour are
best explained by changes in social structure and culture that make religion
more or less plausible and more or less desirable. [...] Some of the criticisms
of secularization are less challenges to specific propositions and more a
blanket rejection of the focus of study. Rodney Stark and his associates
argue that the main determinants of religious vitality lie not in causes of
varying demand but in features of the religious marketplace that affect the
'supply' of religious goods (Stark and Finke 2000). I have considered their
rational-choice approach to religion at considerable length elsewhere (Bruce
1999) [...].

THE PARADIGM

Figure 1 is a diagrammatic representation of the key elements and connections in the secularization paradigm. As each is well known and has its own extensive literature, in working my way through them, I will confine myself to brief elaborations.

I should stress two points about the status of the causal connections being identified. First, I am not suggesting that these causes are by themselves *sufficient* to produce their purported effects. Many other conditions, themselves

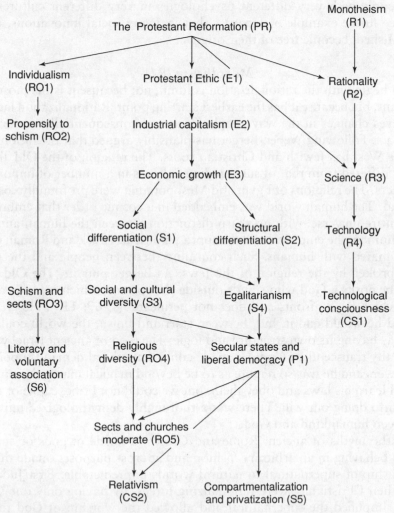

Figure 1 The secularization paradigm

deserving book-length treatment, are required. For example, the E1 to E2 link describes a change in ways of thinking about work that stimulated material changes already underway. In identifying the role of the Protestant ethic in the rise of modern capitalism, Weber is not suggesting that a Protestant culture could produce capitalism in any circumstance: the material conditions had to be right. Where they were not, Puritans simply experienced the frustration of their intentions (as in the Scottish case; see Marshall 1980). Secondly, I am not suggesting that any of these causes were enduringly *necessary*. To continue with the Weber example, once rational capitalism was well established and its virtues obvious, it could be adopted by people with very different psychologies in very different cultures (as we see in the example of Japan) – that is, many social innovations, once established, become free of their origins.

Monotheism (R1)

I will begin with the rationalization column, not because it is the most important, but because it has the earliest starting point. Rationalization largely involves changes in the way people think and consequentially in the way they act. Following Weber, Berger has plausibly argued that the rationality of the West has Jewish and Christian roots. The religion of the Old Testament differed from that of surrounding cultures in a number of important respects. The religions of Egypt and Mesopotamia were profoundly cosmological. The human world was embedded in a cosmic order that embraced the entire universe, with no sharp distinction between the human and the non-human, the empirical and the supra-empirical. Greek and Roman gods even mated with humans. Such continuity between people and the gods was broken by the religion of the Jews. As Berger puts it: 'The Old Testament posits a God who stands outside the cosmos, which is his creation but which he confronts and does not permeate' (1969: 115). He created it and he would end it, but, between start and finish, the world could be seen as having its own structure and logic. The God of ancient Israel was a radically transcendent God. He made consistent ethical demands upon his followers and he was so remote as to be beyond magical manipulation. We could learn his laws and obey them, but we could not bribe, cajole or trick him into doing our will. There was a thoroughly demythologized universe between humankind and God.

In the myths of ancient Rome and Greece, a horde of gods or spirits, often behaving in an arbitrary fashion and at cross purposes, made the relationship of supernatural to natural worlds unpredictable. First Judaism and then Christianity were rationalizing forces. By having only one God, they simplified the supernatural and allowed the worship of God to become systematized. Pleasing God became less a matter of trying to anticipate the whims of an erratic despot and more a matter of correct ethical behaviour.

As the Christian Church evolved, the cosmos was remythologized with angels and semi-divine saints. The Virgin Mary was elevated as a mediator and co-redeemer with Jesus. The idea that God could be manipulated through ritual, confession and penance undermined the tendency to regulate behaviour with a standardized and rational ethical code. No matter how awful one's life, redemption could be bought by funding the Church. However, this trend was reversed as the Protestant Reformation in the sixteenth and seventeenth centuries again demythologized the world, eliminated the ritual and sacramental manipulation of God, and restored the process of ethical rationalization.

Making formal what was pleasing to God made it possible for morality and ethics to become detached from beliefs about the supernatural. The codes could be followed for their own sake and could even attract alternative justifications. For example, 'Do unto others as you would be done by' could be given an entirely utilitarian justification in a way that 'Placate this God or suffer' could not. In that sense, the rationalizing tendency of Christianity created space for secular alternatives.

So we can summarize these points with the links R1 to R2 (monotheism encourages rationality) and PR to R2 (the Reformation further stimulates rationality). A common red herring can be eliminated if we appreciate that no particular virtue is implied in the use of the term 'rational'. We may also note that Weber and Berger are not concerned primarily with the structure of individual thought in the sense of philosophizing. Rather, the supposed variable is the extent to which means–ends rationality is embedded in social organizations (of which the modern rule-governed bureaucracy is the clearest embodiment). As Wilson puts it: 'Men may have become more rational, and their thinking may have become more matter-of-fact, as Veblen expressed it, but perhaps even more important is their sustained involvement in rational organizations, which impose rational behaviour upon them' (1966: 7).

The Protestant Ethic (E1)

Max Weber argued that the Reformation had the unintended consequence of creating a new attitude to work. In attacking the narrow priestly notion of vocation, Martin Luther elevated all work (excluding, of course, the servicing of vanities and vices) to the status of a *calling* that glorified God. By arguing against confession, penance and absolution, the Reformers deprived people of a way of periodically wiping away their sins. They thus increased the psychological strain of trying to live a Christian life and made it all the more important to avoid temptation; hence the additional premium on work. By insisting that God had already divided all people into the saved and the unsaved, the chosen and the rejected (that is, our fate is *predestined*), John Calvin and his followers inadvertently created a climate in which the Puritans could see worldly success, provided it was achieved honestly and diligently by pious people, as proof of divine favour. These elements combined to produce a new 'ethic'. Whereas previously especially religious people had cut themselves off from the world in monasteries and in hermitages (or, in the case of Simon Stylites, on top of a column), the Puritans exemplified what Weber called 'this-worldly asceticism'.

The link E2 to E3 represents the simple fact that those countries that first adopted industrial capitalism prospered ahead of their rivals and, as we will see below, prosperity itself has contributed to the weakening of religious commitments.

Structural differentiation (S2)

Modernization entails structural and functional differentiation, by which I mean the fragmentation of social life as specialized roles and institutions are created to handle specific features or functions previously embodied in or carried out by one role or institution (Parsons 1964).[2] The family was once a unit of production as well as the social institution through which society was reproduced. With industrialization, economic activity became divorced from the home. It also became increasingly informed by its own values (that is, S2 is informed by R2). At work we are supposed to be rational, instrumental and pragmatic. We are also supposed to be universalistic: to treat customers alike, paying attention only to the matter in hand. We are not supposed to vary our prices according to the race or religion of the purchaser. The private sphere, by contrast, is taken to be expressive, indulgent and emotional.

In addition to the indirect effects described shortly, increased specialization has the direct effect of secularizing many social functions that in the Middle Ages either were the exclusive preserve of the Christian Church or were dominated by the clergy.[3] Education, health care, welfare and social control were once all in the domain of religious institutions; now we have specialist institutions for each. The shift of control was gradual and proceeded at various speeds in different settings, but religious professionals were replaced as specialist professionals were trained and new bodies of knowledge or skill were generated. Where religious institutions retain what we would now regard as secular functions, those functions are performed by lay professionals trained and accredited by secular bodies, and are exercised within an essential secular value frame. For example, the Church of England provides various forms of residential social care, but its social workers are tested in secular expertise, not piety, and they are answerable to state- rather than church-determined standards. Spiritual values may inspire the Church's involvement in social work but there is very little in the expression of that inspiration that distinguishes it from secular provision.

Social differentiation (S1)

As Marx noted in his theory of class formation (Giddens 1971: 35–45), as the functions of society become increasingly differentiated, so the people also become divided and separated from each other – that is, structural differentiation was accompanied by social differentiation. The economic growth implicit in modernization led to the emergence of an ever-greater range of occupation and life situation. The creation of new social classes often led to class conflict; it was certainly accompanied by class avoidance. In feudal societies, masters and servants lived cheek by jowl. The master might ride while the servant walked, but they travelled together. The straw given to the master might be clean, but master and servant often slept in the same room. In medieval Edinburgh all manner of people occupied the same tenements and threw their excrement into the same street. Such mixing was possible because everyone knew his or her place in the social order. 'Stations' were so firmly fixed that the gentry need not fear that allowing the lower orders to occupy the same space would give them ideas 'above their station'. As the social structure became more fluid, those who could afford to do so replaced the previously effective social distance with literal space. When Edinburgh's Georgian New Town was constructed, the bourgeoisie moved out of the old city.

The plausibility of a single moral universe in which all people have a place depends on the social structure being relatively stable. With the proliferation of new social roles and increasing social mobility, traditional integrated organic or communal conceptions of the moral and supernatural order began to fragment. When the community broke into competing social groups, the religiously sanctified vision of that community, united under its God, also broke up. As classes and social fragments became more distinctive, so they generated metaphysical and salvational systems along lines more suited to their interests (MacIntyre 1967). People came to see the supernatural world as they saw the material world. Thus feudal agricultural societies tended to have a hierarchically structured religion where the great pyramid of pope, bishops, priests and laity reflected the social pyramid of king, nobles, gentry and peasants. Independent small farmers or the rising business class preferred a more democratic religion; hence their attraction to such early Protestant sects as the Presbyterians, Baptists and Quakers.

However, modernization was not simply a matter of the religious culture responding to changes in the social, economic and political structures. Religion itself had a considerable effect on social and cultural diversity (S3). To explain this I must go back a stage to the link between the Reformation, the rise of individualism and the propensity to schism.

Individualism (RO1)

David Martin neatly summarized a major unintended consequence of the Reformation when he wrote that 'the logic of Protestantism is clearly in favour of the voluntary principle, to a degree that eventually makes it sociologically unrealistic' (1978: 9). Belief systems differ greatly in their propensity to fragment (Wallis 1979; Bruce 1985). Much of the variation can be explained by the assumptions about the availability of authoritative knowledge that lie at the heart of the beliefs. To simplify the possibilities in two polar types, some religions claim a unique grasp of the truth while others allow that there are many ways to salvation. The Catholic Church claims that Christ's authority was passed to Peter, the first bishop of Rome, and was then institutionalized in the office of pope. The Church claims ultimate control of the means to salvation and the right finally to arbitrate all disputes about God's will. So long as that central assertion is not disputed, the Catholic Church is relatively immune to fission and schism. As the beliefs that one needs to abandon in order to depart from Rome go right to the heart of what one believed when one was a Catholic, such departures are difficult and are associated with extreme social upheavals, such as the French Revolution. Thus in Catholic countries the fragmentation of the religious culture that follows from structural and social differentiation tends to take the form of a sharp divide between those who remain within the religious tradition and those who openly oppose it. So Italy and Spain have conservative Catholic traditions and powerful Communist parties.

In contrast, the religion created by the Protestant Reformation was extremely vulnerable to fragmentation because it removed the institution of the church as a source of authority between God and man. Although Catholics sometimes use this as a stick with which to beat Protestants, it is a sociological, not a theological, observation. If, by reading the Scriptures, we are all able to discern God's will, then how do we settle disputes between the various discernings that are produced? Being theists who believed in one God, one Holy Spirit that dwelt in all of God's creation, and one Bible, the Reformers could hope that the righteous would readily and naturally agree, but history proved that hope false. Tradition, habit, respect for learning, or admiration for personal piety all restrained the tendency to split, but they did not prevent schism. The consequence of the Reformation was not one Christian church purified and strengthened but a large number of competing perspectives and institutions. In Protestant countries, social differentiation took the form not of a radical divide between clerical and secular elements but of a series of schisms from the dominant traditions. Rising social classes were able to express their new aspirations and ambitions by reworking the familiar religion into shapes that accorded with their self-image.

We might add a secular version of RO1. The notion of individualism, although crucially stimulated by the Reformation, gradually developed an autonomous dynamic as the egalitarianism I have located in the diagram as S4. It is placed there because I want to stress that the idea of individualism and the closely associated social reality of diversity (S3) could develop only in propitious circumstances and those where provided by structural differentiation (S2) and economic growth (E3).

The link between modernization and inequality is paradoxical. We need not explore the many differences between modern and traditional sources of power to note that, at the same time as creating classes shaped by what Marx called the forces of production, industrialization brought a basic egalitarianism. We should recognize the contribution that religious innovation made here. Although the Protestant Reformers were far from being democrats, one major unintended consequence of their religious revolution was a profound change in the relative importance of the community and the individual. By denying the special status of the priesthood and by removing the possibility that religious merit could be transferred from one person to another (by, for example, saying masses for the souls of the dead), Luther and Calvin reasserted what was implicit in early Christianity: that we are all severally (rather than jointly) equal in the eyes of God. For the Reformers, that equality lay in our sinfulness and in our obligations, but the idea could not indefinitely be confined to duty. Equality in the eyes of God laid the foundations for equality in the eyes of man and before the law. Equal obligations eventually became equal rights.

Though the details of case need not concern us here, Gellner has plausibly argued that egalitarianism is a requirement for industrialization; a society sharply divided between high and low cultures could not develop a modern economy (1983, 1991). The spread of a shared national culture required the replacement of a fixed hierarchy of stations and estates by more flexible class divisions. Economic development brought change and the expectation of further change. And it brought occupational mobility. People no longer did the job they always did because their family always did that job. As it became more common for people to better themselves, it also become more common for them to think better of themselves. However badly paid, the industrial worker did not see himself as a serf.

The medieval serf occupied just one role in a single all-embracing hierarchy and that role shaped his entire life. A tin-miner in Cornwall in 1800 might have been sore oppressed at work, but in the late evening and on Sunday he could change his clothes and his persona to become a Baptist lay preacher. As such he was a man of prestige and standing. The possibility of such alternation marks a crucial change. Once occupation became freed from an entire all-embracing hierarchy and became task specific, it was possible for people to occupy different positions in different hierarchies. In turn, that made it possible to distinguish between the role and the person who played it. Roles could still be ranked and accorded very different degrees of respect, power or status, but the people behind the roles could be seen as in some sense equal. To put it the other way round, so long as people were seen in terms of just one identity in one hierarchy, the powerful had a strong incentive to resist egalitarianism: treating alike a peasant and his feudal superior threatened to turn the world upside down. But once an occupational position could be judged apart from the person who filled it, it became possible to maintain a necessary order in the factory, for example, while operating a different system of judgements outside the work context.

The mine-owner could rule his workforce but sit alongside (or even under) his foreman in the local church. Of course, power and status are often transferable. Being a force in one sphere increases the chances of influence in another. The factory-owner who built the church could expect to dominate the congregation, but he would do so only if his wealth was matched by manifest piety. If it was not, his fellow churchgoers could respond to any attempt to impose his will by defecting to a neighbouring congregation.

Societalization

A number of important themes combine to produce a major change in the nature of societies that has a profound impact on the social roles and plausibility of religious belief systems. Societalization is the term given by Wilson to the way in which 'life is increasingly enmeshed and organized, not locally but societally (that society being most evidently, but not uniquely, the nation state)' (1982: 154). If social differentiation (S1) and individualism (RO1) can be seen as a blow to small-scale communities from below, societalization was the corresponding attack from above. Close-knit, integrated, communities gradually lost power and presence to large-scale industrial and commercial enterprises, to modern states coordinated through massive, impersonal bureaucracies, and to cities. This is the classic community-to-society transition delineated by Ferdinand Tönnies (1955).

Following Durkheim, Wilson argues that religion has its source in, and draws its strength from, the community. As the society rather than the community has increasingly become the locus of the individual's life, so religion has been shorn of its functions. The church of the Middle Ages baptized, christened and confirmed children, married young adults, and buried the dead. Its calendar of services mapped onto the temporal order of the seasons. It celebrated and legitimated local life. In turn, it drew considerable plausibility from being frequently reaffirmed through the participation of the local community in its activities. In 1898 almost the entire population of my local village celebrated the successful end of the harvest by bringing tokens of their produce into the church. In 1998 a very small number of people in my village (only one of them a farmer) celebrated the Harvest festival by bringing to the church vegetables and tinned goods (many of foreign provenance) bought in the local branch of an international supermarket chain. In the first case the church provided a religious interpretation of an event of vital significance to the entire community. In the second, a small self-selecting group of Christians engaged in an act of dubious symbolic value. Instead of celebrating the harvest, the service thanked God for all his creation. In listing things for which we should be grateful, one hymn mentioned 'jet planes refuelling in the sky'! By broadening the symbolism, the service solved the problem of relevance but at the cost of losing direct connection with the lives of those involved. When the total, all-embracing community of like-situated people working and playing together gives way to the dormitory town or suburb, there is little held in common left to celebrate.

The consequence of differentiation and societalization is that the plausibility of any single overarching moral and religious system declined, to be displaced by competing conceptions that, while they may have had much to say to privatized, individual experience, could have little connection to the performance of social roles or the operation of social systems. Religion retained subjective plausibility for some people, but lost its objective taken-for-grantedness. It was no longer a matter of necessity; it was a preference.

Again it is worth stressing the interaction of social and cultural forces. The fragmentation of the religious tradition (RO3) that resulted from the Reformation hastened the development of the religiously neutral state (P1). The development of a successful economy required a high degree of integration: effective communication, a shared legal code to enforce contracts, a climate of trust, and so on (Gellner 1991). And this required an integrated national culture. Where there was religious consensus, a national 'high culture' could be provided through the dominant religious tradition. The clergy could continue to be the schoolteachers, historians, propagandists, public administrators and military strategists. Where there was little consensus, the growth of the state tended to be secular. In Ireland and the Scandinavian countries, a national education system was created through the Catholic and Lutheran churches respectively. In Britain and the United States it was largely created by the state directly. However, even where a dominant church retained formal ownership of areas of activity, those still came to be informed primarily by secular values. Church schools may 'top and tail' their product with their distinctive religious traditions, but the mathematics, chemistry and economics lessons are the same in Ireland's church schools as in England's state schools.

After summarizing this case, James Beckford warned that 'the connection between religion, obligatory beliefs and community may be an historical contingency. Religion has, in the past, been primarily associated with local communities for sound sociological reasons, but it does not follow that this is the only modality in which religion can operate' (1989: 110). This is correct. I am certainly not assuming that, because religion used to be closely woven into the social life of stable communities, the decline of community must, as in a mathematical proof, logically entail the eclipse of religion. Instead I will argue for an empirical connection.

[. . .]

Compartmentalization and privatization (S5)
A key element of the secularization paradigm is the individual response to differentiation, societalization and pluralism. One way for believers to reconcile their faith with the fact of variety is to seek reintegration at a higher

level of abstraction by supposing that all religions are, in some sense, the same. [...] Another possibility (and they are not incompatible) is to confine one's faith to a particular compartment of social life. Indeed, a powerful observation about modernity introduced to the English-reading world by Berger and Luckmann's *The Social Construction of Reality* (1973) was that differentiation required us to live, not in a single world, but in a number of worlds, each informed by its own values and logics. With compartmentalization comes privatization – the sense that the reach of religion is shortened to just those who accept the teachings of this or that faith. As Luckmann puts it:

> This development reflects the dissolution of *one* hierarchy of significance in the world view. Based on the complex institutional structure and social stratification of industrial societies different 'versions' of the world view emerge.... With the pervasiveness of the consumer orientation and the sense of autonomy, the individual is more likely to confront the culture and the sacred cosmos as a 'buyer'. Once religion is defined as a 'private affair', the individual may choose from the assortment of 'ultimate' meanings as he sees fit. (1967: 98–9)

Daniel Bell has taken issue with Wilson's linking of privatization and a decline in the significance or popularity of religion. After agreeing that modernization has brought 'the shrinkage of institutional authority over the spheres of public life, the retreat to a private world where religions have authority only over their followers', he adds, 'there is no necessary, determinate shrinkage in the character and extent of beliefs' (1977: 427). This neatly presents us with a summary of a crucial element in the debate over the secularization paradigm. I will argue in subsequent chapters the point I have made in various places above: the privatization of religion removes much of the social support that is vital to reinforcing beliefs, makes the maintenance of distinct lifestyles very difficult, weakens the impetus to evangelize and encourages a *de facto* relativism that is fatal to shared beliefs. Of course, this is an empirical issue that must be settled by evidence. On that point it is worth noting that, although Bell's essay is entitled 'The return of the Gods', he provides almost no evidence for his anti-Wilsonian case that privatization does not weaken religion.

Jose Casanova (1994) has made an important contribution to the debate by arguing that differentiation (which he fully accepts) has not caused privatization. His case is that the major churches, having now accepted the rules of liberal democracy and the basic principles of individual rights, are able to regain a public role. They have achieved this not by returning to the old model of a compact between a dominant church and the state, but by acting as pressure groups in civil society. This may well be true, but to present it as a counter to the secularization paradigm is to miss a number of important points. First, it is clear from the recent fate of the 'new Christian right' in the United States (on which see Garvey 1993 and Bruce 1998) that religious interest groups have been effective in the public arena only when they have presented their case in secular terms. Hence creationism has to be presented as 'creation science', apparently every bit as compatible with the scientific record as any evolutionary model of the origins of species and open to testing in the same way. The case against abortion is made in terms of the inalienable rights of the individual. Divorce and homosexuality are damned as socially dysfunctional. That is, religious interest groups can be effective in civil society only when they accept the privatization of their distinctive religious beliefs and move on to secular ground. Secondly, even if Casanova does not exaggerate the influence of religious groups in modern societies, he does not address the social-psychological consequences of privatization.

[. . .]

Science (R3) and technology (R4)

[. . .] I have left the secularizing effects of science until this point. Various critics of the secularization paradigm misrepresent it by following popular misconceptions and elevating science to a central position. Quite erroneously, Stark says: 'Implicit in all versions, and explicit in most, is the claim that of all aspects of modernization, it is science that has the most deadly implications for religion' (Stark and Finke 2000: 61). Put briefly, I assume that a starting assumption of modern sociology is that reality is socially constructed (Berger and Luckmann 1973). By this slogan we draw attention to the role of social relationships and social interests in making ideas more or less persuasive. I have already mentioned various ways in which people can seek to preserve their beliefs against what disinterested outsiders might see as overwhelming refutation. It is a mistake to assume that ideas and observations are of themselves persuasive or that, while we need to explain why people hold false beliefs, somehow the 'truth' stands in no need of explanation.

The Enlightenment zero-sum view of knowledge (with rational thought and scientific knowledge gradually conquering territory from superstition) was carried into sociology by Comte and Marx among others, but it is not part of the modern secularization paradigm. Wilson stated the position very clearly when he followed observations about the increasing influence of science and technology with: 'All of this is not to suggest . . . that the confrontation of science and religion was in itself harmful to religion. Indeed religion and science can co-exist as alternative orientations to the world' (1966: 43). The crucial connections are far more subtle and complex than those implied in some zero-sum knowledge competition.

The secularizing effects of science as seen by modern sociologists are not primarily those of a direct clash of factual claims. Rather they are the more nebulous consequences of assumptions about the orderliness of the world and our mastery over it.

One of the most powerful connections was drawn by Robert Merton (1970) in his work on Puritan scientists. Merton argues that many seventeenth-century Protestant scientists were inspired to natural science by a desire to demonstrate the glory of God's creation, by the rationalizing attitude of the Protestant ethic and by an interest in controlling the corrupt world.[4] The end result was the same irony that followed from the general rationalization of ethics. Because the Puritan scientists were able to demonstrate the fundamental rule-governed nature of the material world, they made it possible for subsequent generations to do science without topping and tailing their work with the assertion that 'this shows God's glory'. At any stage in the growth of knowledge, God could be summoned to fill a gap. Newton, for example, believed God periodically took a hand in the movement of the planets to rectify a slight irregularity. Later improved models managed without the divine corrections. Science became autonomous and generated explanatory models of the world that did not require the divine.

We can also draw causal connections between the RO line and the rise of science. The fissiparousness of Protestantism enhanced the autonomy of science by weakening the power of the Church to dominate all fields of intellectual endeavour.

More important than science was the development of effective technologies. We should not forget that in the Middle Ages (and to this day in pre-technological societies) religion was often practical. Holy water cured ailments and prayers improved crop quality. Wilson among others has argued that technology has a powerful secularizing effect by reducing the occasions on which people have recourse to religion. Again, rather than see a direct conflict, we should see the change as a matter of 'bypass'. The farmers of Buchan did not stop praying to God to save their sheep from maggots because the invention of an agri-chemical sheep dip persuaded them that God was not very well informed. The gradual accumulation of scientific knowledge gave people insight into, and mastery over, an area that had once been a mystery; the need and opportunity for recourse to the religious gradually declined. Science and technology do not create atheists; they just reduce the frequency and seriousness with which people attend to religion.

More generally, as David Martin puts it, with the growth of science and technology 'the general sense of human power is increased, the play of contingency is restricted, and the overwhelming sense of divine limits which afflicted previous generations is much diminished' (1969: 116).

Technology (R4) and technological consciousness (CS1)

Although Berger's early writings are widely associated with the secularization approach, one particular strand of his thought has been neglected. In an exploration of the social psychological effects of certain styles of modern work, Berger, Berger and Kellner (1974) argue that, irrespective of the extent to which we are aware of it, modern technology brings with it a 'technological consciousness', a certain style of thought that is difficult to reconcile with a sense of the sacred.[5] An example is 'componentiality'. The application of modern machines to production involves the assumption that the most complex entities can be broken down into their components, which are infinitely replaceable. Any 1990 Volkswagen Golf radiator will fit any 1990 Golf. The relationship between the engine and one radiator is expected to be exactly the same as that between the engine and any other matching radiator. There is nothing sacred about any particular bond. Another fundamental assumption is 'reproducibility'. Technological production takes it for granted that any creative complex of actions can be subdivided into simple acts that can be repeated infinitely and always with the same consequence. This attitude is carried over from manufacture to the management of people in manufacture (a style known after its heroic promoter as 'Fordism') and to bureaucracy generally. While there is no obvious clash between these assumptions and the teachings of most religions, there are serious incompatibilities of approach. There is little space for the eruption of the divine.

To summarize the R line, I am suggesting that the effects of science and technology on the plausibility of religious belief are often misunderstood. The clash of ideas between science and religion is less significant than the more subtle impact of naturalistic ways of thinking about the world. Science and technology have not made us atheists. Rather, the fundamental assumptions that underlie them, which we can summarily describe as 'rationality' – the material world as an amoral series of invariant relationships of cause and effect, the componentiality of objects, the reproducibility of actions, the expectation of constant change in our exploitation of the material world, the insistence on innovation – make us less likely than our forebears to entertain the notion of the divine. As Weber put it:

> The increasing intellectualization and rationalization do *not* ... indicate an increased general knowledge of the conditions under which one lives. It means something else namely, the knowledge, or the belief, that if one but wished one *could* learn it at any time. Hence, it means that principally there are no mysterious incalculable forces that come into play, but rather that one can, in principle, master all things by calculation. This means that the world is disenchanted. One need no longer have recourse to magical means in order to master or implore the spirits, as did the savage, for whom such mysterious powers existed. Technical means and calculations perform the service. (1948: 139)

Relativism (CS2)

Relativism is perhaps the most potent and the most neglected part of the secularization paradigm. [...]

Finding precisely the right term is not easy; 'relativism' is perhaps misleading if it suggests an articulate philosophical attitude. I mean something closer to an operating principle or a cognitive style. I am concerned with the pragmatic concerns of what standing and what reach we accord our own ideas and how we view those who disagree with us. The Christian Church of the Middle Ages was firmly authoritarian and exclusive in its attitude to knowledge. There was a single truth and it knew what it was. Increasingly social and cultural diversity combines with egalitarianism to undermine all claims to authoritative knowledge. While compartmentalization can serve as a holding operation, it is difficult to live in a world that treats as equally valid a large number of incompatible beliefs, and that shies away from authoritative assertions, without coming to suppose that there is no one truth. While we may retain a certain preference for our worldview, we find it hard to insist that what is true for us must also be true for everyone else. The tolerance that is necessary for harmony in diverse egalitarian societies weakens religion (as it weakens most forms of knowledge and codes of behaviour) by forcing us to live as if there were no possibility of knowing the will of God.

First summary

[. . .]

I will very briefly summarize the case so far. In figure 1, I try to show the connections between a variety of changes in the industrial democracies of the West that for brevity we call 'modernization'. In different ways, elements of that package cause religion to mutate so that it loses social significance. I have gone further than some of those associated with the paradigm (though, in the case of Wilson, for example, I see that extension as merely making explicit what is already implicit) in adding that the decline of social significance and communal support causes a decline in the plausibility of religious beliefs. Changes at the structural and cultural level bring about changes in religious vitality that we see in the declining proportion of people who hold conventional religious beliefs and the commitment they bring to those beliefs. The bottom line is this: individualism, diversity and egalitarianism in the context of liberal democracy undermine the authority of religious beliefs.

NOTES

1. Although Wilson usually confines his definition of secularization to the declining social significance of religion, it is clear from the frequent use he makes of data on individual religious beliefs and behaviour (e.g. 1966: 21) that he regards personal religiosity as both an index of the social significance of religion and an effect of it.
2. Parsons (1960) himself thought secularization in the largest sense impossible because societies needed the integration that shared values provided. Although he identi-

fied the increasing separation of church and state as a distinctive feature of modern societies, he believed that it was possible only because Christian values had been generalized to the wider society.

3. It should be noted that I am concerned with the consequences of differentiation for the plausibility and salience of religious beliefs and institutions. Though the problem of social control and social integration fascinated most of those who originally wrote on the subject, the effect of differentiation on social regulation is not my interest.

4. Later historians of science have challenged some of Merton's work, but the general link between Puritanism and science has been sustained; see Klaaren (1977).

5. This is mainly a problem for theistic belief systems. It is easier for the more philosophical strands of Buddhism and Hinduism to effect a reconciliation by arguing that the natural and spiritual worlds all obey the same 'higher' laws. Transcendental Meditation's Natural Law Party frequently borrows language from subatomic physics to describe its beliefs.

DANIÈLE HERVIEU-LÉGER
'RELIGION AS A CHAIN OF MEMORY'

Danièle Hervieu-Léger is a French sociologist. She is the Director of Studies in Sociology at the Ecole des Hautes Etudes en Sciences Sociales (EHESS), Paris and is also the main researcher for the project on Secularity as a European and International Phenomenon at the University of Boston. This project is co-directed by Peter Berger (Boston University, CURA). The project involves a comparative, interdisciplinary investigation of the nature and manifestations of secularity, with contributions from scholars working on case studies on Europe, the United States, Turkey and Israel. Her best-known book is Religion as a Chain of Memory, *which was translated into English in 2000. Her chief area of interest is in the sociology of religion.*

Hervieu-Léger is an example of a trend in sociological theory that seeks to redefine religion without recourse to the usual oppositions of religion/modernity or religion/rationality that underlie many other sociological approaches. Her definition refocuses the discussion onto the religious practice of believing – emphasising the practice rather than the content of belief. Her definition also attempts to differentiate religious belief by emphasising the need for a concept of tradition.

SOCIOLOGY IN OPPOSITION TO RELIGION? PRELIMINARY CONSIDERATIONS

Determining the subject matter, as everyone knows, constitutes the initial operation in any sociological endeavour. Yet when it has to do with religion, a presentiment of uncertainty is pardonable. What if there was nothing to define? Or if the sociology of religion simply lacked a subject? On the face of it such questions may appear absurd. After all, research institutions, international gatherings, symposiums, teaching and publications provide sufficient evidence that this branch of sociology is thriving. Religion is the subject matter of sociological investigation, treated as a social phenomenon and explained in terms of other social phenomena. What more can be asked?

From religious sociology to the sociology of religion
However, things are not that straightforward. And the debate which, not so long ago, marked the designation of the discipline – should it be religious sociology, sociology of religion, sociology of religions? – was already proof of this.

It is more than thirty years now since French and French-speaking sociologists gradually gave up using the term religious sociology, suspected of

Danièle Hervieu-Léger (2000), *Religion as a Chain of Memory*, Cambridge: Polity Press.

implicitly invoking Christian – even Catholic – sociology which the ecclesiastical establishment could use as a pastoral instrument and consider to be a branch of moral theology. Current demarcation disputes between pure and applied sociology, settled as each occasion arises without threat to the discipline as a whole, render such issues even further outdated. Retrospectively, one may wonder whether terminological nicety has not been overdone in this context. After all, rural sociology was never suspected of being angled towards farmers nor political sociology of being partisan. How come then that the sociology of religious phenomena makes of its terminology an academic issue in itself?

Manifestly, historical and political circumstances peculiar to France serve to account for such scruples. The climate of conflict – or, at least, of suspicion – which hung for so long over relations between the universities, the intelligentsia and the world of research on the one hand, and the Catholic Church, its hierarchy and its theologians, on the other, played a part here.[1] One would merely add that the choice of words to some extent still symbolically echoed an affirmation of independence on the part of a university discipline breaking free from the various enterprises in self-interpretation which the Church, however much it claims to revere science, invariably maintains to be the last word in knowledge about religion. Evoking the need for collaboration between the different specialities – sociology, history, cultural anthropology, and so on – that together form the 'unique caravan of scientific discovery', Gabriel Le Bras in the first number of *Archives de Sciences Sociales des Religions* in 1956 celebrated a non-religious approach to religious phenomena, as the necessary condition of research independence, whatever the personal commitments of those involved. 'Let belief and unbelief go side by side in the enterprise, private feelings have no relevance here. This journal serves no doctrine, sectarian or non-sectarian, its single concern being to serve science.'[2]

Sociologists of religion have dwelt at length upon the difficulties of this emancipation,[3] which led to the abandonment of the term religious sociology. The introduction of the reference not to religion in general but to the plurality of religions received briefer comment, though it merits equal attention. The scientific study of religious phenomena was established as an academic discipline in France in the mid-1950s, under the aegis of the Centre National de la Recherche Scientifique; and by placing emphasis on the plural, those who founded the French sociology of religion explicitly recognized how fragmented, how confused, was their field of investigation. The same recognition of the plurality of territory and of approach prompted Henri Desroche to insist on the title *Sociologies religieuses* for his book published in 1968, prior notice of which had had the title in the singular. The diversification of research projects and the high probability of an ever-widening research field, in the view of Gabriel Le Bras, virtually ruled out a unified discipline, in the foreseeable future at least; how could one thus talk of a sociology of religion in the singular? 'To suppose that all sociologists embarked on the study of religions should ever see eye to eye as to the field, the aims and the methods of their research', he noted in the same programme, 'suggests naive optimism or else senile resignation.'[4]

After all, was it not sufficient for there to be near-unanimity among researchers for a minimal designation of the subject matter? In the absence of finding it possible to identify a common subject, sociologists of religion could – in Le Bras's opinion still – identify a common aim, 'the structure and nature of organized groups for whom the sacred provides both the principle and the purpose'.[5] That the social nature of such an enterprise might in fact pose too many problems for a consensus to emerge among those involved did not worry him unduly. To the extent that sociology should, in his view, restrict its scope to the community and refrain from exploring 'the mysteries of the supernatural or the *maquis* of the terrestrial city', the difficulties inherent in a definition of religion in terms of the sacred could easily be avoided. The question of the definition of religion as such was in fact left to others, to philosophers, for instance, who were properly concerned with general theories. Sociologists, Le Bras recommended, should be modest and make do with the observation of social groups, in the most ordinary expression of their rapport with the sacred, so as to construct the 'pyramid whose base is at the level of tribes and of parishes, of legend and the boundaries of magic'.

> The sociologist should move forward prudently, by degrees, applying himself to the most humble tasks – collecting accounts, conversing with elders, consulting treaties, interpreting ceremonials; then observing reality – a methodical count of buildings and documents, cartography and monographs, semiology and psychology among representative samples of the faithful. Study of the community will reveal the place of the religious group within it – confusion in Islam, intimacy in Christian countries, diaspora among secularized people. The relationship between the two visible communities, and the pull of the invisible will suggest a typology, an aetiology and a discreet nomology whose perfection will form the apex of the intrepid pyramid.[6]

This plea, inimitable for a descriptive sociology of the assemblies of disciples, gave considerable momentum to the empirical sociology of religious phenomena, setting it clearly apart from the social philosophy which French sociology was slowly distancing itself from. In proposing so vast yet modest a programme for sociologists of religion, Gabriel Le Bras without question succeeded in circumventing the problem he confronted, as a practising Catholic, of engaging in an enterprise which could well have struck at the very roots of Christian belief. In fact, he signified elsewhere his refusal to take as the subject matter of sociology the substance of faith and Christian dogma. But, however equivocal, the proposal met with the determination of sociologists engaged in research into religious phenomena to mark a distance, both with regard to phenomenological attempts to arrive at the essence of religion by way of manifestations of the religious and with regard to enterprises which, in order to make of sociology a general science of societies, reduced religion either to the materiality of its emergence or to a collective consciousness through which society affirms itself.

In constructing an empirical sociology at the level of groups and institutions, which were thereby observed in the specificity of their structures and modes of functioning, sociologists ran the risk of giving unique significance to the manifold expressions of religious experience.[7] At the same time, they enabled a notion to be formed of what constitutes religion, which in itself could not entirely undermine the positivist critique of religious ideologies. There one encounters – they said, in effect – a concrete body of reality which is not an optical illusion. It is made up of human groups, social actors and power systems that need to be studied in their specificity. Certainly, the cognitive, cultural, social, economic and political issues of religious phenomena need to be constantly stressed; there being no doubt that, in specific historical contexts, they serve to express views about the world, collective aspirations or social concerns which have no other outlet or else choose this one. Yet there are no grounds for maintaining that this task of elucidation explains away the significance of religious manifestations; except insofar as they are considered uniquely as representing an inchoate form of politics or an invalid form of science, a reductive point of view, which the more positivistic sociologists would now hardly find tenable.

In adopting the empirical study of the diversity of groups, beliefs and practices, and in developing a (plural) sociology of the plurality of religion, French sociologists of religion avoided the pitfalls of a philosophical debate on the nature of religion, at the same time steering clear of any ideological controversy as to the 'reality' of religious phenomena. This perhaps explains, in part at least, their long-held dislike of the grander theories, for which many of their colleagues – in particular, British and American – showed a fondness. Such reservations about theory, somewhat surprising given the mainstream of classical sociology in France, was perhaps a means of preserving their discipline from the ideological contagion which was especially threatening in a culture indelibly marked by the conflict between Church and state. Furthermore, it enabled them, to a degree at least, to hold off suspicions of connivance with the subject matter which inevitably attached itself to their interest in religion as a dimension of social reality.

Science opposed to religion

Until recently, the sociology of religion met with some misgivings on the part of colleagues working in the field of the social sciences, as if the will to objectify religion was in itself a contradictory aspiration, revealing the personal concerns of those who exercised it. Even now it is quite normal for a sociologist of religion on declaring his or her identity to evoke the response 'Oh, so you're Catholic' or 'Yes, of course, you're Protestant.' Almost invariably, in the course of conversation, the remark occurs, 'But are you yourself a believer?' And most of the time such conjectures are right. Those who choose research in the social sciences of religion have seldom done so by chance or by a purely intellectual choice unaffected by any non-academic consideration. But a degree of personal investment in choosing an area of research is common to all who work in the social sciences, whether or not they admit to it. Yet it would not occur to anyone, in assessing the output of a sociologist of the family, to enquire whether he or she were married, or how they related to their father. How come that the critical detachment characteristic of a scientific attitude in the social sciences is thought to be more difficult, if not impossible, to attain when the subject matter is religion?

Pierre Bourdieu has given a vigorous, indeed conclusive, reply to the question. For him the problem has to do with the nature of the subject studied, and the association with belief compounds it. 'The field of religion, like all fields, is a realm of belief, but one in which belief has the active role. The belief that is systematized by the institution (belief in God, in dogma and so on) tends to mask belief in the institution, the *obsequium*, and every concern associated with the reproduction of the institution.'[8]

The explanation is valid, but only on condition that religious belief is allowed to have a far stronger force of penetration than beliefs which apply in other social fields. Following Bourdieu's line of thought, there is no need to know whether or not the sociologist believes in God. What frustrates the task of objectification is belief in the institution, belief which lives on even after it is openly repudiated. The sociologist who belongs to the institution is clearly disqualified; the sociologist who once belonged, who is 'unfrocked', even more so, since the dishonesty 'with which the science of religion is instantly tarred' is aggravated. Since anyone who has never belonged has little chance of ever becoming interested in the subject matter of religion and/or a good chance of missing out on useful information, there are few let-outs for a sociology of religion. The fact that the text quoted above is reproduced from a speech given by Pierre Bourdieu at the Association Française de Sociologie Religieuse very probably accounts for its bluntness. Assuming his awareness of the doctrinal origins of this body and of the 'unfrocked' condition of a majority of its members (a condition applying to anyone exchanging adherence for analysis), Bourdieu struck a note familiar to his audience in order to exhort them not to 'save themselves the suffering implicit in renouncing membership'. The demonstration is nonetheless strange in allowing it to be supposed that belief in the institution contains less of a threat to a scientific attitude (or else is more plausibly brought under control) when dealing with the central institutions of secularized society –

schools, political institutions, universities and so on – than when dealing with religious institutions. In fact, the presumption of compromising with the subject matter is only given such aggressive expression here because religion is implicated. What this text is saying is not that the sociology of religion is (a) very difficult, so difficult as to be virtually impossible, or (b) condemned to be no more than an 'edifying science, destined to serve as a foundation for scholarly religiosity, enabling the advantages both of scientific lucidity and of religious loyalty to be combined',[9] but that religion as such is the obstacle that continues to stand in the way of the process of unimpeded critical rationalization which, in Bourdieu's mind, is the aim of sociology.

In order to understand the issues which are presented with particular intensity in this text, one needs to recall the debates surrounding the birth of sociology which make it clear that the question of religion is historically inseparable from the subject matter of the social sciences. As such it was an essential feature in the minds of the founding fathers of sociology and a major element in their attempts to determine to what extent a science of society was possible. As we are reminded by Raymond Boudon, sociology was conceived by its founders as a 'general nomothetic science of societies'. On the basis of very different paradigms – the search for evolutionary laws of society, with Comte, Marx, Spencer and the early Durkheim; the search for functional relations between social phenomena in the later Durkheim; the establishment of historical patterns in Weber; the rationale of non-rational action in Pareto; the recognition of social forms that originate in the interaction of individuals, with Tönnies and Simmel – on the basis of all this, the quest common to all is that of establishing the laws and conventions which rule society.[10]

The enterprise of imposing order on a social entity which by common experience is perceived as inextricably chaotic comes up against the aspiration present in every religion, considered as a system of meanings, namely to make complete sense of the world and to condense the infinite multiplicity of human experience. The clash between the unifying venture of emergent social sciences and the unifying vision of religious systems took the form in the field of sociology of rationally deconstructing the attempt by religion to embrace the whole of reality, which in turn consigned religion to the multiplicity of religious phenomena it embodies. And by so doing, sociology met with the resistance of religious systems to an interpretation from outside which emptied them of their substance and undermined from within the scheme nurtured by such as Burnouf to constitute a pre-eminent unified science of religion, which could be set up against self-interpreting systems of religion: 'Before the century ends we shall see a unified science established which is as yet fragmentary, a science unknown to previous centuries, which is still undefined and which perhaps for the first time we name the science of religion.'[11]

The whole debate seems to belong to the prehistory of the discipline. The programme, which Henri Desroche sees as an ambition of the nineteenth century, to 'define and fully account for the fact of religion in terms of society', considering it as a unique and quite specific order of social phenomena, gave way before the advance of a science of society which on principle rejected any specific treatment of religious phenomena. The majestic initial paradigms of this science of society in turn collapsed, giving way to a descriptive sociology that was built up gradually on the basis of empirically identified subject matter. In France the sociology of religion tried to rid itself of its associations with religious society by energetically embracing the empirical method. With the meticulous enumeration of the faithful and with the scrupulous attention given to the social history of institutions, the intellectual probity of those undertaking research seemed assured. But this empirical, descriptive façade afforded them no protection from the ever-insistent question of whether sociology can, with the conceptual tools available to it, recognize the essentially religious ingredient in the social manifestations it appropriates.

In order to appreciate what is at stake here, one needs to look further into the thought given to the subject matter of sociology. Sociology is defined less by its content than by the critique it implies, itself defined by Alain Touraine as 'a refusal to give credence to all interpretations, from the rationalization with which an actor accompanies an action to the meaning embodied in administrative categories which seem furthest removed from expressing intention'.[12] The generalized wariness which underlies every aspect of what social praxis has to say about itself is no more than a systemization of the first requirement advanced by Durkheim in *The Rules of Sociological Method*, around the notion according to which life in society must be explained 'not by the conception which those who participate in it have, but by profound causation which eludes consciousness'.[13] It is necessary to dissipate the smokescreen of the terminology commonly used, rescue the subject matter from its social demonstration, extricate it from inhibiting preconceptions, continually reconstruct it by updating presuppositions to accommodate the discourse as it changes.[14]

This ongoing critique which confers legitimacy on the comprehension of society by way of social phenomena, according to procedures and methods which are those of science, defines the task of sociology. The critique of spontaneous, naive experiences and expressions in the realm of society is inseparable from the close examination of the metasocial conceptions of society, and especially those which allow and invoke some sort of extra-human intervention in history.

In these two areas, inevitably, sociology, being an analytical enterprise, collides with religion. The initial impact occurs inasmuch as religion is a mode of imposing a social construction on reality, a system of references to which actors spontaneously have recourse in order to conceive the universe in which they live. As such, the critique of religion is an integral part of the scrutiny of the data of social experience in which sociological phenomena are embedded. It was – and it remains – the obligatory passageway in the process of their objectivization. But sociology also meets religion inasmuch as religion itself is a formalized explanation of the social world which, however far it may go in recognizing the freedom of human action, can only conceive autonomy within limits set by the divine purpose. Protestant, and more specifically Calvinist, theology of salvation constitutes the exemplary religious formalization of this dependent autonomy. The encounter between sociology and theology thus – and irrespective of the occasional ecumenicism attempted between one and the other – cannot but give rise to altercation, to conflict even.

What is at issue for sociology is whether it is able to conceive itself. Recognition of this state of conflict between sociology and theology – and first and foremost Christian theology, of course – does not mean that the conflict in itself is inescapable. Or rather, it is inescapable only on account of the path which has led to the conflict and which developed historically in the course of the relationship between science and religion in the west. One hardly needs to be reminded that at the birth of modern science, at any rate until the seventeenth century, the conflict did not exist, nor did it occur to those such as Pascal, Newton or Descartes who initiated the scientific revolution. Descartes, in fact, did not so much as imagine that an atheist could be a geometrist. The altered perspective occurred as a result of confrontation between the Church, fighting to preserve its social ascendancy on the pretext of defending Aristotelian authority, and the scientists wresting scientific experimentation from the control of religious institutions. The struggle continued over several centuries, whilst scientific investigation, which began at the extremities of the universe with astronomy and the Copernican revolution (anticipated by the school of Pythagoras), grew closer to humankind and to its physical and psychic functioning.

The story is familiar enough,[15] but one cannot help but call to mind the initial conflict once mention is made of the circumstances in which science took possession of religion. Because, before becoming one subject among others, religion was the adversary; and in the struggle for the secular autonomy of knowledge the common consciousness of the scientific community took shape across the differences, particularly with regard to social theory, which divide scientists. And it is by reference to this struggle that the legitimacy of the scientific quest is still secured. A scientist who is a believer is tolerated provided he never mentions his belief unless it be that the weight of honours and of years gives him *carte blanche* for confidences. The sociologist engaged in research must avoid communion with his subject, however self-denying the cost; so much at least is accepted by a conception of professionalism in sociology that is dominant and indeed legitimate. How much more then will this rigour apply to those who choose as their field the systems of religious belief and observance against which such legitimacy was established in the first place! Western science defines itself in terms of its historical rift with religion, and this is the abiding context in which the sociology of religion is obliged to define its own aspirations. In asserting its separateness from pastoral sociology, the sociology of religion in France has at times appeared trapped in an empirical positivism which other branches of sociology, and in particular the sociology of knowledge, have long ago left behind. Among other reasons, this is probably because the risk of connivance with the subject, which must mobilize the epistemological vigilance of any researcher in the social sciences, is doubly present in this field. For if complaisance towards social actors continues to disqualify sociological effort, it contains the further risk, in the case of the sociology of religion, that it may suggest an avenue to religious belief which is presumed to invalidate sociology itself.

Undermining the subject?

However, the project of the sociology of religion can be put quite simply – to treat religious phenomena in the way that sociology treats any social phenomena, by collating them, classifying and comparing them, and treating them in terms of relationship and conflict. The status of the sociology of religion can admit of no more exceptions than can that of sociology in general.

At the same time, one wonders – taking things to their extreme – whether the sociologist of religion can escape the destruction of his or her subject matter by the very act of exposing it to the process of analysis required by the discipline. To say as much is blunt and deliberately provocative, and it hardly represents the conscious objective of the sociology of religion. No professional would be so presumptuous as to claim to be able, with working tools alone, to grasp religious phenomena (any more than any other social phenomena) *as they are*, in all their complexity. Still less would he or she dare claim that they can be explained out or away. What sociology acquired, above all from the school of Simmel and of Weber, was the stamina to renounce the claim to restore reality as such or empirically to actualize the universal laws of history and society. Its claim to be scientific is based on its appreciation of the abstract, relative and revisable nature of the conceptual tools – forms, ideal types or models – with which it sets about ordering the boundless profusion of reality.

Even so, in the very act of recognizing its limits, indeed because of doing so, the objective of a unified, all-inclusive explanation continues to shape a vision (or fantasy), which is constantly rejected only to reappear, of a process of illumination which by its nature cannot accept self-limitation. The more exacting and rigorous the sociological quest looks to be, the more it has *both* to relativize its immediate project and broaden its driving objective. In the latter case, it is bound to assume that its subject matter can and must, in principle, be reduced to the elements to which it relates. The proposition brings about a methodical reductionism, a necessary phase in critical initiative, which applies to sociology as a whole. But in the context of the historical rift between science and religion, it takes on both theoretical and normative meaning. It implies first that religion is inseparable from the social, political, cultural and symbolic meanings and functions that it has in any given society. It further suggests that actualizing these meanings and functions corresponds to the dynamics of scientific knowledge, prevailing day by day over the illusions of the primitive or spontaneous, in other words over religion itself. Hence it is not a case simply of repressing the illusions of spontaneous self-explanation, by relating, for instance, messianic expectations to real, extant misery, or the force of mysticism to the social and political frustration of *déclassé* intellectuals, but a case of breaking up the subject matter itself, insofar as it is of its nature illusory.

What remains of such fervour when subjected to the critique proposed by sociology but subjective forms of resistance to exogenous explanation which can be decoded in the same terms? How can the sociologist of religion take the claim to be scientific for granted, the field of sociology and its historical context being what they are? He or she can only do so, if at the same time making the assumption – as does the psychologist or the linguist in their respective disciplines – that the explanation of religious phenomena in the social context is one where there is nothing left to explain, any element unaccounted for now being incapable of withstanding whatever future refinement sociology will bring to its equipment.

There is no point in rushing to say that, so put, the problem is grossly oversimplified, that the plurality of the scientific approach is a safeguard against the temptation to explain everything on the part of one single discipline, or again that such a view is a product of a now outdated positivism. It may well offer little insight for the routine social history of institutions, but the matter is one of urgency when one moves into the field of belief and systems of meaning and symbolic constructs. The question of the sociological reduction of religion can still create a storm. One only has to think of the bitter controversy set off early in the 1970s in the United States by propositions made by Robert Bellah questioning the reductionism of those who sought to account for religious symbols by tracing their origin to empirically apprehensible events, thus giving them greater authenticity. According to Bellah, who invoked Durkheim as a witness, the reality of these spiritual symbols is thereby lost:

> The canons of empirical science apply primarily to symbols that attempt to express the nature of objects, but there are non-objective symbols that express the feelings, values and hopes of subjects, or that organise and regulate the flow of interaction between subjects and objects, or that attempt to sum up the whole subject-object complex, or

even point to the context or ground of that whole. The symbols, too, express reality and are not reducible to empirical propositions. This is the position of symbolic realism.[16]

Such symbolic realism has been vigorously contested by those who, like Anthony and Robbins, straightway saw in it a theological plot at work in the social sciences.[17] The point here is not to discuss in detail the issues in a theoretical argument in which, as it happens, French sociologists took no part, but merely to note the discussion which the understanding of the critical function of sociology applied to religion gave rise to in the sociological community itself.

Let it be clear, however, that the need to destroy religion in order to clear a space for a scientific explanation of society (as well as for nature, history, the human psyche and so on) has seldom been formulated within the discipline itself as an explicit requirement for the practice of science in general, and for the social sciences in particular. Nor was it necessary, given the general view that religion was in terminal decline, a decline which the founding fathers of sociology all made use of as the fulcrum of their analysis of modernity. Their assessment of the significance of this process of decline for the future of humanity might differ, just as did the explanations they offered, without the assertion so clearly expressed by Émile Durkheim in *The Division of Labour in Society* being challenged, namely that religion encompasses an ever-decreasing portion of social time:

> Originally, it extended to everything; everything social was religious – the two words were synonymous. Then gradually political, economic and scientific functions broke free from the religious function, becoming separate entities and taking on more and more a markedly temporal character. God, if we may express it in such a way, from being at first present in every human relationship, has progressively withdrawn. He leaves the world to men and their quarrels. At least, if he continues to rule it, it is from on high and afar off.[18]

The developing social contraction of religion, which, according to Durkheim, coalesces with human history, is the exact counterpart of the process of expansion in science, with science annexing even the development of the scientific intelligence of religious phenomena. Even so, the manner of comprehending the historical path taken by humanity varies greatly with the cultural context of study. The divergence between American and French research tradition in this respect is glaring. Arthur Vidich and Stanford Lyman have clearly shown (even if the somewhat systematic character of their approach has been criticized) what social science in America owed to the Puritan tradition in which it is rooted. For the early American sociologists, religion was so fundamental a source of inspiration that for a long time they abstained from taking it as a research subject. Only by degrees in the early years of the twentieth century did American sociology distance itself from its early religious leanings. During this process of secularization, social science, in a novel departure, took over the Protestant ambition of social improvement through rational management. 'Sociodicy' took the place of theodicy, thanks to the special affinity existing between puritanical Protestantism and sociological positivism in their common belief in the perfectibility of society.[19] This course of action went naturally with the social and cultural attitudes of American democracy, in which religion is given a decisive role.

In the case of France, a tradition of confrontation between the world of religion and the world of political and cultural modernity very soon gave substance to the conviction – accepted as a hypothesis by the social sciences – of the inevitable eclipse of religion in the modern world. Moreover, it is clear that surveys conducted in the 1930s into the state of Catholicism in France strongly endorsed this hypothesis with its evidence of the collapse of religious practice and observance, the startling drop in the numbers of those entering the priesthood or choosing the monastic life, and the break-up of traditional communities with the movement to cities and into industry. The gradual reduction of religion, seen as the likely intellectual and cultural outcome of modernity, acquired observable and quantifiable substance across these surveys. This meant that sociologists of religion were spared having to engage in a philosophical and/or epistemological debate on the cultural significance of the equivalence, established by western scientific modernity, between the contracting space occupied by religion in society and the expansion of their discipline. Analysis of the reduction of the field occupied by religion eliminated the need to examine sociological reductionism as such. The matter of the 'fight against religion' was thus consigned to the area of outdated scientist notions. Progress required independence in exercising one's profession as a sociologist.

For sociologists of Catholicism such independence in the first place implied keeping out of the way of ecclesiastical influence. Nowhere else but in France was there so rigorous an insistence on the need to 'establish a barrier between the *condominium* [of the sciences of religion] and the applied sciences which exploit it'.[20] A determination to avoid pressure from the Catholic hierarchy or being taken over by pastors and theologians constituted the preliminary and initial requirement for all sociology of religious phenomena. And its reiteration, quite out of proportion – or so it seems retrospectively – to any concrete threat to the intellectual autonomy of scholars who enjoyed full academic status, can be interpreted (but the point clearly merits discussion) as a way of being seen to possess academic respectability, this time *vis-à-vis* the sociological community for whom religion remains – or remained until recently – suspect as subject matter. Was such highlighting of the relations between scientists and religious institutions a means of deflecting attention from the subject itself? Was it for those concerned a way of exhibiting their scientific credentials before their peers during a period, the 1960s and 1970s, when any attempt to question sociological reductionism might well have been received by their colleagues (and even in their own ranks) as an unacceptable concession to the illusion of religion and/or their personal involvement? One cannot be certain. One can do no more than suggest that the pressures that come from science were (and are) no less of a problem in the matter of constituting the field of a sociology of religion than those that come from religion. However that may be, it remains the case that the community of sociologists of religion has been deeply marked by the contradiction variously experienced by each of its members: that of having to assume the rationalist tradition linking the end of religion with the advance of science and the scientific attitude, and the properly scientific need to treat the subject matter seriously and in all its irreducible complexity.

[. . .]

Back to the question of definition

The insistence on the process whereby religious belief is based on appeal to a line of witnesses (for all that the line may be dreamt up) again raises the question of the limits of religion. One of the aims of the task of definition carried out so far has been to maintain a clear distance from inclusive approaches to religion which are inclined to dissolve it into the totality of ultimate meanings. But would not making tradition the fulcrum of religious believing in the end produce the same result by incorporating anything society claims to be a heritage from the past into the sphere of religion?

It would certainly be a misunderstanding to conclude [. . .] that whatever has been socially transmitted must be included in the concept of religion. The definition we are proposing is much more precise, given that its three elements are closely adhered to – the expression of believing, the memory of continuity, and the legitimizing reference to an authorized version of such memory, that is to say to a tradition. In modern society, freed from the constraint of continuity which is characteristic of so-called traditional societies, tradition no longer constitutes an order constricting the life of the individual and society. Hence it no longer represents the unique matrix of expressions of believing that result from the uncertainties of living, which themselves are as characteristic of the human condition now as they were when human beings were defenceless and nature was hostile and mysterious. Hence there is no automatic overlapping of the fragmented world of believing and the equally fragmented world of tradition. This point need hardly be dwelt on further. On the other hand, before putting the proposed definition of religion to the test, two further implications must be considered.

The first implication can be expressed as follows: everything in modernity that has to do with tradition is not necessarily an integral part of believing, and therefore does not necessarily fall within the sphere of religion. Thus, for instance, all the know-how and expertise acquired through experience is vindicated because it stands the test of time. This is best illustrated by an example. Makers of string instruments who continue to apply ancestral techniques of treating wood do what they do, not in the name of a belief but of a practice that has been verified, that of the special quality these time-honoured methods bring to the sound of the instrument. Upholding the tradition is not valued in itself, or if it is, only secondarily, as is the special sense of complicity created between members of a guild who possess a secret in common, or else as is the cultural heritage such knowledge represents, and which is worth while preserving along with other equally esoteric knowledge. But what above all counts is the result obtained, in the absence of proof that more modern techniques are capable of producing at least comparable results. There is no occasion here for adding to the vast assortment of so-called implicit religions the case of the instrument-maker who says of himself: 'I've tried other ways, but this way has not been bettered.' Étienne Vatelot, with a world reputation as a string instrument-maker, shows no sign of an inclination to develop string instrument-making into a religious practice. Questioned recently about the mystery of the varnishes used by Stradivari, he had this to say:

> What secret? The varnish used by Stradivari was produced by a Cremona apothecary, proof of which is that all the varnishes used by string instrument-makers in Cremona have the same quality. If you go to Naples, they are quite different, the reason being that the humidity of the air is different; with the result that a violin needed the protection of harder varnishes. In Venice too, you'll find a more or less similar varnish used by all string instrument-makers, but different again from the one used in the other cities.[21]

The advice Vatelot is giving to young string instrument-makers is not to rediscover and copy the lost secret of the Stradivarius, but to perfect new products so that they can be as effective as possible in protecting and enhancing violins. The past does not furnish a model for reproduction, which as such would be unsurpassable. It merely affords proof that it is possible to achieve success with the means available at any given moment, and that is quite a different thing.

On the other hand, once the act of conforming to a recognized lineage becomes a passionately felt obligation and finds concrete expression in observance as a believer, the possibility arises that one is dealing with religion. Thus one would need to look closely at the case of a string instrument-maker who might say: 'For me this method is special because, when I apply it, I take on the gestures and even the spirit that enabled Stradivari or Guarneri or Amati to give life to violins whose perfection has never been equalled.' Confirming or denying the religious nature of whatever traditional practice can only come from a highly refined empirical exploration of each case to establish whether it shows signs of ideal-typically embodying religion. It is very likely that such an approach will only exceptionally produce a clear answer, so in most cases leaving one to conclude that religious features are there in a more or less marked degree. Clearly, an approach which consists in measuring the religious ingredient in terms of its degree of conformity to an ideal type removes us decisively from classifying religion into what is implicit or analogical on the one hand, and what is fully religious on the other, according to the substance of the beliefs conveyed.

The second implication can be put in the following way. Anything in our society which relates to believing does not necessarily relate to tradition, and hence cannot be attributed to what is implicitly or potentially religious. One can believe in progress, in science, in revolution, in a better tomorrow or in impending disaster. In each of these cases (and in that of any other referents), the work of the imagination can merge with the task of projection in extrapolating on the basis of known and established facts or of analysing change that has occurred or is currently occurring. But the evidence of past historical experience serves to justify rational projection of the future, it does not constitute, in principle at least, the invoking of a tradition that is validated by its own continuity.

The scientist who believes in the science he practises certainly recognizes himself as continuing a line. He sees himself as heir to Galileo, Newton, Pasteur, Einstein and so on, the heroic figures of modern science. But, aside from a mythological anomaly which would take him outside the sphere of science, it is not his belonging to this lineage that justifies his conviction that he will obtain a result; rather it is the proven certainty of the efficacy of the experimental and control methods which are those of his discipline and which enable him to innovate and to invent, just as they enabled his predecessors to do in the course of making their own discoveries. It could indeed be shown that belief in the inherent value of scientific method has sometimes been taken to the point of making it the condition of the authenticity of any discourse or action. This scientism which triumphed in the second half of the nineteenth century, in the writing of Ernest Renan and Marcellin Berthelot and others, has acquired in our own time, with someone like Jacques Monod, a new – but no less lyrical – formulation of the dream of scientific method reaching into all aspects of human behaviour and conditions.[22]

The unrestricted validity of the model of scientific knowledge has sometimes been presented as conferring a sacred quality on science, whereby scientism is equated with religion. We have already given our opinion about a too great readiness to establish correspondence between processes of conferring sanctity and processes of constituting a religion. It need only be remarked here that the scientist's recognition of what he owes to his predecessors and the will to preserve the memory of their work, as a legacy that is precious and valuable for his own endeavour, cannot constitute ends in themselves. If they did, and only then, could one speak of science having a religious extension (in which case we should be outside the sphere of science). But the scientific attitude in fact imposes the need to go beyond the kind of fidelity to forerunners that is self-justifying. It implies the need at any moment to break such fidelity should it contradict the rationality which is proper to the scientific process.

According to Gaston Bachelard, scientific thought requires constant conversion which calls into question the very principles of knowledge.[23] The dynamic nature of scientific knowledge, which even so implies belief in the values and potential of knowledge as such, is at bottom radically incompatible with the need to put an exclusive value on tradition, even on intellectual tradition. One knows the extent to which the inertia of the academic attitude in science has in the past worked – and can still work – against this dynamic. One knows also what established interests can, knowingly or unknowingly, be served by the religious anomaly of paying the respect due to the recognized authorities in science. Yet there are no grounds for applying the term 'religious' to the aspect of believing which attaches itself uncompromisingly to the exercise of scientific activity, inasmuch as it invariably looks beyond the present state of knowledge. The modern differentiation of social fields and institutions, each of which functions according to its own set of rules, also produces a differentiation in ways of believing proper to each of the fields, and in particular the ways in which, within such believing, the imaginary link with the past and projection into the future are joined. In our view, religion is only one of the figures in this pluralized world of believing, a figure characterized by the legitimizing exclusiveness of reference to tradition.

NOTES

1. See Poulat (1987) and Béguin et al. (1987).
2. Le Bras (1956: 6).
3. Desroche (1968: ch. 1); Desroche and Séguy (1970); Poulat (1986, 1990).
4. Le Bras (1956: 6).
5. Ibid.
6. Ibid., p. 7.
7. François-André Isambert gives a penetrating analysis of this essentialist deviation in phenomenology in his comments on Roger Caillois's interpretation of festivals (1966: 291–308), which he returns to in Desroche and Séguy (1970: 217–57); see also Isambert (1982: 125ff.).
8. Bourdieu (1987: 155–61).
9. Ibid., p. 160.
10. Boudon (1988: 73–6).
11. Burnouf, *La Science des religions* (Paris, 3rd edn, 1870), quoted in Desroche and Séguy (1970: 175).

12. Touraine (1974: 26).
13. Durkheim (1982: preface to 2nd edn).
14. Bourdieu (1968: introduction).
15. See Bertrand Russell's graphic summary in *Science and Religion* (1999).
16. Bellah: 'Christianity and Symbolic Realism', *Journal for the Scientific Study of Religions*, 9 (1970), p. 93, included in Bellah (1970); also see Bellah: 'Comments on the Limits of Symbolic Realism', *Journal for the Scientific Study of Religions*, 13 (1974), pp. 487–9.
17. Robbins et al., 'The Limits of Symbolic Realism', *Journal for the Scientific Study of Religions*, 12 (1973), pp. 259–71; 'Reply to Bellah', ibid., 13 (1974), pp. 491–5; and Anthony and Robbins, 'From Symbolic Realism to Structuralism', ibid., 14 (1975), pp. 403–13.
18. Durkheim (1984: 119).
19. Vidich and Lyman (1985).
20. Le Bras (1956: 15).
21. *Le Monde*, 28 March 1991, p. 28: 'Les Mystères Stradivarius'.
22. See Jacques Monod, *Le Hasard et la nécessité* (Paris: Éd. du Seuil, 1970), pp. 190ff.
23. See Gaston Bachelard, *La Philosophie du non* (Paris, PUF, 1940), p. 7.

TALCOTT PARSONS
'THE THEORETICAL DEVELOPMENT OF THE SOCIOLOGY
OF RELIGION: A CHAPTER IN THE HISTORY OF MODERN
SOCIAL SCIENCE'

Talcott Parsons can be considered to be one of the fathers of American sociology. Parsons was born in Colorado in 1902. He received his doctorate from the University of Heidelberg in 1927. He taught sociology at Harvard from 1931 until his death in 1979. Parsons was strongly influenced by the work of Max Weber and, following in Weber's footsteps, he attempted to develop a general theory of social action. His work was also significantly influenced by the theory of structural functionalism that was being developed in social anthropology.

The material taken from Parsons's work illustrates the influence of structural functionalism. Parsons draws from the two approaches to functionalism developed by Malinowski (pages 229–52) and Radcliffe-Brown (pages 253–64). This is seen by his dual emphasis on the individual and society as the basis of the needs to which religion relates.

The present paper will attempt to present in broad outline what seems to the writer one of the most significant chapters in the recent history of sociological theory, that dealing with the broader structure of the conceptual scheme for the analysis of religious phenomena as part of a social system. Its principal significance would seem to lie on two levels. In the first place, the development to be outlined represents a notable advance in the adequacy of our theoretical equipment to deal with a critically important range of scientific problems. Secondly, however, it is at the same time a particularly good illustration of the kind of process by which major theoretical developments in the field of social theory can be expected to take place.

Every important tradition of scientific thought involves a broad framework of theoretical propositions at any given stage of its development. Generally speaking, differences will be found only in the degree to which this framework is logically integrated and to which it is explicitly and self-consciously acknowledged and analyzed. About the middle of the last century or shortly thereafter, it is perhaps fair to say, generalized thinking about the significance of religion to human life tended to fall into one of two main categories. The first is the body of thought anchored in the doctrinal positions of one or another specific religious group, predominantly of course the various Christian denominations. For understandable reasons, the main tenor of such thought tended to be normative rather than empirical and analytical, to assure its own religious position and to expose the

Talcott Parsons (1954), *Essays in Sociological Theory*, rev. edn., Glencoe, IL: Free Press.

errors of opponents. It is difficult to see that in any direct sense important contributions to the sociology of religion as an empirical science could come from this source.[1] The other main category may be broadly referred to as that of positivistic thinking. The great stream of thought which culminated in the various branches of utilitarianism, had, of course, long been much concerned with some of the problems of religion. In its concern with contemporary society, however, the strong tendency had been to minimize the importance of religion, to treat it as a matter of 'superstition' which had no place in the enlightened thinking of modern civilized man. The result of this tendency was, in the search for the important forces activating human behavior, to direct attention to other fields, such as the economic and the political. In certain phases the same tendency may be observed in the trend of positivistic thought toward emphasis on biology and psychology, which gathered force in the latter part of the nineteenth century and has continued well into our own.

Perhaps the first important change in this definition of problems, which was highly unfavorable to a serious scientific interest in the phenomena of religion, came with the application of the idea of evolution to human society. Once evidence from non-literate societies, not to speak of many others, was at all carefully studied, the observation was inescapable that the life of these so-called 'primitive' men was to an enormous degree dominated by beliefs and practices which would ordinarily be classified according to the common-sense thinking of our time as magical and religious. Contemporary non-literate peoples, however, were in that generation predominantly interpreted as the living prototypes of our own prehistorical ancestors, and hence it was only natural that these striking phenomena should have been treated as 'primitive' in a strictly evolutionary sense, as belonging to the early stages of the process of social development. This is the broad situation of the first really serious treatment of comparative religion in a sociological context, especially in the work of the founder of modern social-anthropology, Tylor,[2] and of Spencer,[3] perhaps the most penetrating theorist of this movement of thought. Though there was here a basis for serious scientific interest, the positivistic scheme of thought imposed severe limitations on the kind of significance which could be attributed to the observed phenomena. Within the positivistic schema, the most obvious directions of theoretical interpretation were two. On the one hand, religious phenomena could be treated as the manifestations of underlying biological or psychological factors beyond the reach of rational control, or interpretations in terms of subjective categories. Most generally this pattern led to some version of the instinct theory, which has suffered, however, some very serious scientific handicaps in that it has never proved possible to relate the detailed variations in the behavioral phenomena to any corresponding variations in the structure of instinctual drives. The whole scheme has on the level of social theory never successfully avoided the pitfalls of reasoning in a circle.

The other principal alternative was what may be called the 'rationalistic' variation of positivism,[4] the tendency to treat the actor as if he were a rational, scientific investigator, acting 'reasonably' in the light of the knowledge available to him. This was the path taken by Tylor and Spencer with the general thesis that primitive magical and religious ideas were ideas which in the situation of primitive men, considering the lack of accumulated knowledge and the limitations of the technique and opportunities of observation, it would reasonably be expected they would arrive at. With beliefs like that in a soul separable from the body, ritual practices in turn are held to be readily understandable. It is, however, a basic assumption of this pattern of thinking that the only critical standards to which religious ideas can be referred are those of empirical validity. It almost goes without saying that no enlightened modern could entertain such beliefs, that hence what we think of as distinctively religious and magical beliefs, and hence also the accompanying practices, will naturally disappear as an automatic consequence of the advance in scientific knowledge.

Inadequate as it is in the light of modern knowledge, this schema has proved to be the fruitful starting-point for the development of the field, for it makes possible the analysis of action in terms of the subjective point of view of the actor in his orientation to specific features of the situation in which he acts. Broadly speaking, to attempt to deal with the empirical inadequacies of this view by jumping directly, through the medium of anti-intellectualistic psychology, to the more fundamental forces activating human behavior, has not proved fruitful. The fruitful path has rather been the introduction of specific refinements and distinctions within the basic structural scheme with which 'rationalistic positivism' started. The body of this paper will be concerned with a review of several of the most important of these steps in analytical refinement, showing how, taken together, they have led up to a far more comprehensive analytical scheme. This can perhaps most conveniently be done in terms of the contributions of four important theorists, Pareto, Malinowski, Durkheim, and Max Weber, none of whom had any important direct influence on any of the others.

It is of primary significance that Pareto's[5] analytical scheme for the treatment of a social system started precisely with this fundamental frame of reference. Like the earlier positivists, he took as his starting-point the cognitive patterns in terms which the actor is oriented to his situation of action. Again like them, he based his classification on the relation of these patterns to the standards of empirical scientific validity – in his terms, to 'logico-experimental' standards. At this point, however, he broke decisively with the main positivistic tradition. He found it necessary, on grounds which in view of Pareto's general intellectual character most certainly were primarily empirical rather than philosophical, to distinguish two modes of deviance from conformity with logico-experimental standards. There were, on the one hand, the modes of deviance familiar to the older positivists, namely the failure to attain a logico-experimental solution of problems intrinsically capable of such solution. This may be attributable either to ignorance, the sheer absence of logically necessary knowledge of fact, or possibly of inference, or to error, to allegations of fact which observation can disprove or to logical fallacy in inference. In so far as cognitive patterns were deviant in this respect, Pareto summed them up as 'pseudo-scientific' theories. Failure to conform with logico-experimental standards was not, however, confined to this mode of deviance, but included another, 'the theories which surpass experience'. These involved propositions, especially major premises, which are intrinsically incapable of being tested by scientific procedures. The attributes of God, for instance, are not entities capable of empirical observation; hence propositions involving them can by logico-experimental methods neither be proved nor disproved. In this connection, Pareto's primary service lay in the clarity with which the distinction was worked out and applied, and his demonstration of the essentially prominent role in systems of human action of the latter class of cognitive elements. It is precisely in the field of religious ideas and of theological and metaphysical doctrines that its prominence has been greatest.

Pareto, however, did not stop here. From the very first, he treated the cognitive aspects of action in terms of their functional interdependence with the other elements of the social system, notably with what he called the 'sentiments'. He thereby broke through the 'rationalistic bias' of earlier positivism and demonstrated by an immense weight of evidence that it was not possible to deal adequately with the significance of religious and magical ideas solely on the hypothesis that men entertaining them as beliefs drew the logical conclusions and acted accordingly. In this connection, Pareto's position has been widely interpreted as essentially a psychological one, as a reduction of non-logical ideas to the status of mere manifestations of instinct. Critical analysis of his work[6] shows, however, that this interpretation is not justified, but that he left the question of the more ultimate nature of non-cognitive factors open. It can be shown that the way in which he treated the sentiments is incompatible in certain critical respects with the hypothesis that they are biologically inherited instinctual drives alone. This would involve a determinacy irrespective of cultural variation, which he explicitly repudiated.

It is perhaps best to state that, as Pareto left the subject, there were factors particularly prominent in the field of religious behavior which involved the expression of sentiments or attitudes other than those important to action in a rationally utilitarian context. He did not, however, go far in analyzing the nature of these factors. It should, however, be clear that with the introduction, as a functionally necessary category, of the non-empirical effective elements which cannot be fitted into the pattern of rational techniques, Pareto brought about a fundamental break in the neatly closed system of positivistic interpretation of the phenomena of religion. He enormously broadened the analytical perspective which needed to be taken into account before a new theoretical integration could be achieved.

The earlier positivistic theory started with the attempt to analyze the relation of the actor to particular types of situations common to all human social life, such as death and the experience of dreams. This starting-point was undoubtedly sound. The difficulty lay in interpreting such situations and the actor's relations to them too narrowly, essentially as a matter of the solution of empirical problems, of the actor's resorting to a 'reasonable' course of action in the light of beliefs which he took for granted. Pareto provided much evidence that this exclusively cognitive approach was not adequate, but it remained for Malinowski[7] to return to detailed analysis of action in relation to particular situations in a broader perspective. Malinowski maintained continuity with the 'classical' approach in that he took men's adaptation to practical situations by rational knowledge and technique as his initial point of reference. Instead of attempting to fit all the obvious facts positively into this framework, however, he showed a variety of reasons why in many circumstances rational knowledge and technique could not provide adequate mechanisms of adjustment to the total situation.

This approach threw into high relief a fundamental empirical observation, namely that instead of there being one single set of ideas and practices involved, for instance in gardening, canoe-building, or deep-sea fishing in the Trobriand Islands, there were in fact two distinct systems. On the one hand, the native was clearly possessed of an impressive amount of sound empirical knowledge of the proper uses of the soil and the processes of plant growth. He acted quite rationally in terms of his knowledge and above all was quite clear about the connection between intelligent and energetic work and a favorable outcome. There is no tendency to excuse failure on supernatural grounds when it could be clearly attributed to failure to attain adequate current standards of technical procedure. Side by side with this system of rational knowledge and technique, however, and specifically not confused with it, was a system of magical beliefs and practices. These beliefs concerned the possible intervention in the situation of forces and entities which are 'supernatural' in the sense that they are not from our point of view objects of empirical observation and experience, but rather what Pareto would call 'imaginary' entities, and on the other hand, entities with a specifically sacred character. Correspondingly, the practices were not rational techniques but rituals involving specific orientation to this world of supernatural forces and entities. It is true that the Trobriander believes that a proper performance of magic is indispensable to a successful outcome of the enterprise; but it is one of Malinowski's most important insights that this attribution applies only to the range of uncertainty in the outcome of rational technique, to those factors in the situation which are beyond rational understanding and control on the part of the actor.

the disposal of the corpse and other practical adjustments. There is always specifically ritual observance of some kind which, as Malinowski shows, cannot adequately be interpreted as merely acting out the bizarre ideas which primitive man in his ignorance develops about the nature of death.

Malinowski shows quite clearly that neither ritual practices, magical or religious, nor the beliefs about supernatural forces and entities integrated with them can be treated simply as a primitive and inadequate form of rational techniques or scientific knowledge; they are qualitatively distinct and have quite different functional significance in the system of action. Durkheim,[11] however, went farther than Malinowski in working out the specific character of this difference, as well as in bringing out certain fur-ther aspects of the functional problem. Whereas Malinowski tended to focus attention on functions in relation to action in a situation, Durkheim became particularly interested in the problem of the specific attitudes exhibited to-ward supernatural entities and ritual objects and actions. The results of this study he summed up in the fundamental distinction between the sacred and the profane. Directly contrasting the attitudes appropriate in a ritual con-text with those towards objects of utilitarian significance and their use in fields of rational technique, he found one fundamental feature of the sacred to be its radical dissociation from any utilitarian context. The sacred is to be treated with a certain specific attitude of respect, which Durkheim identified with the appropriate attitude toward moral obligations and authority. If the effect of the prominence which Durkheim gives to the conception of the sa-cred is strongly to reinforce the significance of Malinowski's observation that the two systems are not confused but are in fact treated as essentially separate, it also brings out even more sharply than did Malinowski the inadequacy of the older approach to this range of problems which treated them entirely as the outcome of intellectual processes in ways indistinguish-able from the solution of empirical problems. Such treatment could not but obscure the fundamental distinction upon which Durkheim insisted.

The central significance of the sacred in religion, however, served to raise in a peculiarly acute form the question of the source of the attitude of respect. Spencer, for instance, had derived it from the belief that the souls of the dead reappear to the living, and from ideas about the probable dangers of association with them. Max Müller and the naturalist school, on the other hand, had attempted to derive all sacred things in the last analysis from personification of certain phenomena of nature which were respected and feared because of their intrinsically imposing or terrifying character. Durkheim opened up an entirely new line of thought by suggesting that it was hopeless to look for a solution of the problem on this level at all. There was in fact no common intrinsic quality of things treated as sacred which could account for the attitude of respect.

In fact, almost everything from the sublime to the ridiculous has in some society been treated as sacred. Hence the source of sacredness is not intrinsic;

the problem is of a different character. Sacred objects and entities are symbols. The problem then becomes one of identifying the referents of such symbols. It is that which is symbolized and not the intrinsic quality of the symbol which becomes crucial.

At this point Durkheim became aware of the fundamental significance of his previous insight that the attitude of respect for sacred things was essentially identical with the attitude of respect for moral authority. If sacred things are symbols, the essential quality of that which they symbolize is that it is an entity which would command moral respect. It was by this path that Durkheim arrived at the famous proposition that society is always the real object of religious veneration. In this form the proposition is certainly unacceptable, but there is no doubt of the fundamental importance of Durkheim's insight into the exceedingly close integration of the system of religious symbols of a society and the patterns sanctioned by the common moral sentiments of the members of the community. In his earlier work,[12] Durkheim had progressed far in understanding the functional significance of an integrated system of morally sanctioned norms. Against this background the integration he demonstrated suggested a most important aspect of the functional significance of religion. For the problem arises, if moral norms and the sentiments supporting them are of such primary importance, what are the mechanisms by which they are maintained other than external processes of enforcement? It was Durkheim's view that religious ritual was of primary significance as a mechanism for expressing and reinforcing the sentiments most essential to the institutional integration of the society. It can readily be seen that this is closely linked to Malinowski's view of the significance of funeral ceremonies as a mechanism for reasserting the solidarity of the group on the occasion of severe emotional strain. Thus Durkheim worked out certain aspects of the specific relations between religion and social structure more sharply than did Malinowski, and in addition put the problem in a different functional perspective in that he applied it to the society as a whole in abstraction from particular situations of tension and strain for the individual.

One of the most notable features of the development under consideration lay in the fact that the cognitive patterns associated with religion were no longer, as in the older positivism, treated as essentially given points of reference, but were rather brought into functional relationship with a variety of other elements of [the] social system of action. Pareto in rather general terms showed their interdependence with the sentiments. Malinowski contributed the exceedingly important relation to particular types of human situation, such as those of uncertainty and death. He in no way contradicted the emphasis placed by Pareto on emotional factors or sentiments. These, however, acquire their significance for specifically structured patterns of action only through their relation to specific situations. Malinowski was well aware in turn of the relation of both these factors to the solidarity of the social group, but this aspect formed the center of Durkheim's analytical attention. Clearly, religious ideas could only be treated sociologically in terms of their interdependence with all four types of factors.

There were, however, still certain serious problems left unsolved. In particular, neither Malinowski nor Durkheim raised the problem of the relation of these factors to the variability of social structure from one society to another. Both were primarily concerned with analysis of the functioning of a given social system without either comparative or dynamic references. Furthermore, Durkheim's important insight into the role of symbolism in religious ideas might, without further analysis, suggest that the specific patterns, hence their variations, were of only secondary importance. Indeed, there is clearly discernible in Durkheim's thinking in this field a tendency to circular reasoning in that he tends to treat religious patterns as a symbolic manifestation of 'society', but at the same time to define the most fundamental aspect of society as a set of patterns of moral and religious sentiment.

Max Weber approached the whole field in very different terms. In his study of the relation between Protestantism and capitalism,[13] his primary concern was with those features of the institutional system of modern Western society which were most distinctive in differentiating it from the other great civilizations. Having established what he felt to be an adequate relation of congruence between the cognitive patterns of Calvinism and some of the principal institutionalized attitudes towards secular roles of our own society, he set about systematically to place this material in the broadest possible comparative perspective through studying especially the religion and social structure of China, India, and ancient Judea.[14] As a generalized result of these studies, he found it was not possible to reduce the striking variations of pattern on the level of religious ideas in these cases to any features of an independently existent social structure or economic situation, though he continually insisted on the very great importance of situational factors in a number of different connections.[15] These factors, however, served only to pose the problems with which great movements of religious thought have been concerned. But the distinctive cognitive patterns were only understandable as a result of a cumulative tradition of intellectual effort in grappling with the problems thus presented and formulated.

For present purposes, even more important than Weber's views about the independent causal significance of religious ideas is his clarification of their functional relation to the system of action. Following up the same general line of analysis which provides one of the major themes of Pareto's and Malinowski's work, Weber made clear above all that there is a fundamental distinction between the significance for human action of problems of empirical causation and what, on the other hand, he called the 'problem of meaning'. In such cases as premature death through accident, the problem of *how* it happened in the sense of an adequate explanation of empirical causes can readily be solved to the satisfaction of most minds and yet leave a sense not merely of emotional but of cognitive frustration with respect to the problem of *why* such things must happen. Correlative with the functional need for emotional adjustment to such experiences as death is a cognitive need for understanding, for trying to have it 'make sense'. Weber attempted to show that problems of this nature, concerning the discrepancy between normal human interest and expectations in any situation or society and what actually happens are inherent in the nature of human existence. They always pose problems of the order which on the most generalized line have come to be known as the problem of evil, of the meaning of suffering, and the like. In terms of his comparative material, however, Weber shows there are different directions of definition of human situations in which rationally integrated solutions of these problems may be sought. It is differentiation with respect to the treatment of precisely such problems which constitute the primary modes of variation between the great systems of religious thought.

Such differences as, for instance, that between the Hindu philosophy of Karma and transmigration and the Christian doctrine of Grace with their philosophical backgrounds are not of merely speculative significance. Weber is able to show, in ways which correlate directly with the work of Malinowski and Durkheim, how intimately such differences in doctrine are bound up with practical attitudes towards the most various aspects of everyday life. For if we can speak of a need to understand ultimate frustrations in order for them to 'make sense', it is equally urgent that the values and goals of everyday life should also 'make sense'. A tendency to integration of these two levels seems to be inherent in human action. Perhaps the most striking feature of Weber's analysis is the demonstration of the extent to which precisely the variations in socially sanctioned values and goals in secular life correspond to the variations in the dominant religious philosophy of the great civilizations.

It can be shown with little difficulty that those results of Weber's comparative and dynamic study integrate directly with the conceptual scheme developed as a result of the work of the other writers. Thus Weber's theory of the positive significance of religious ideas is in no way to be confused with the earlier naively rationalistic positivism. The influence of religious doctrine is not exerted through the actor's coming to a conviction and then acting upon it in a rational sense. It is rather, on the individual level, a matter of introducing a determinate structure at certain points in the system of action where, in relation to the situation men have to face, other elements, such as their emotional needs, do not suffice to determine specific orientations of behavior. In the theories of Malinowski and Durkheim, certain kinds of sentiments and emotional reactions were shown to be essential to a functioning social system. These cannot stand alone, however, but are necessarily integrated with cognitive patterns; for without them there could be no coordination of action in a coherently structured social system. This is because functional analysis of the structure of action shows that situations must be subjectively defined, and the goals and values to which action is oriented must be congruent with these definitions, must, that is, have 'meaning'.

It is of course never safe to say a scientific conceptual scheme has reached a definitive completion of its development. Continual change is in the nature of science. There are, however, relative degrees of conceptual integration, and it seems safe to say that the cumulative results of the work just reviewed constitute in broad outline a relatively well-integrated analytical scheme which covers most of the more important broader aspects of the role of religion in social systems. It is unlikely that in the near future this analytical scheme will give way to a radical structural change, though notable refinement and revision is to be expected. It is perhaps safe to say that it places the sociology of religion for the first time on a footing where it is possible to combine empirical study and theoretical analysis on a large scale on a level in conformity with the best current standards of social science and psychology

When we look back, the schemes of Tylor and Spencer seem hopelessly naive and inadequate to the modern sociologist, anthropologist, or psychologist. It is, however, notable that the development sketched did not take place by repudiating their work and attempting to appeal directly to the facts without benefit of theory. The process was quite different. It consisted in raising problems which were inherent in the earlier scheme and modifying the scheme as a result of the empirical observation suggested by these problems. Thus Malinowski did not abandon all attempt to relate magic to rational technique. Not being satisfied with its identification with primitive science and technology, he looked for specific modes of difference from and relation to them, retaining the established interpretation of the nature and functions of rational technique as his initial point of reference. It is notable again that in this process the newer developments of psychological theory in relation to the role of emotional factors have played an essential part. The most fruitful results have not, however, resulted from substituting a psychological 'theory of religion' for another type, but rather from incorporating the results of psychological investigation into a wider scheme.

In order for this development to take place it was essential that certain elements of philosophical dogmatism in the older positivism should be overcome. One reason for the limitations of Spencer's insight lay in the presumption that if a cognitive pattern was significant to human action, it must be assimilable to the pattern of science. Pareto, however, showed clearly that the 'pseudoscientific' did not exhaust significant patterns which deviated from scientific standards. Malinowski went further in showing the functional relation of certain non-scientific ideas to elements of uncertainty and frustration which were inherent in the situation of action. Durkheim called attention to the importance of the relation of symbolism as distinguished from that of intrinsic causality in cognitive patterns. Finally, Weber integrated the various aspects of the role of non-empirical cognitive patterns in social action in terms of his theory of the significance of the problems of meaning and the corresponding cognitive structures, in a way which precluded, for analytical purposes, their being assimilated to the patterns of science.[16] All of these distinctions by virtue of which the cognitive patterns of religion are treated separately from those of science have positive significance for empirical understanding of religious phenomena. Like any such scientific categories, they are to the scientist sanctioned by the fact that they can be shown to work. Failure to make these distinctions does not in the present state of knowledge and in terms of the relevant frame of reference[17] help us to understand certain critically important facts of human life. What the philosophical significance of this situation may be is not as such the task of the social scientist to determine. Only one safe prediction on this level can be made. Any new philosophical synthesis will need positively to take account of these distinctions rather than to attempt to reinstate for the scientific level the older positivistic conception of the homogeneity of all human thought and its problems. If these distinctions are to be transcended it cannot well be in the form of 'reducing' religious ideas to those of science – in the sense of Western intellectual history – or vice versa. The proved scientific utility of the distinctions is sufficient basis on which to eliminate this as a serious possibility.

NOTES

1. It was far less unfavorable to historical contributions than to those affecting the analytical framework of the subject.
2. *Primitive Culture.*
3. Esp. *Principles of Sociology*, vol. I.
4. See the author's *The Structure of Social Action*, Chaps. II and III.
5. *The Mind and Society.* See also the author's *The Structure of Social Action*, Chap. V – VII; and 'Pareto's Central Analytical Scheme', *Journal of Social Philosophy*, I, 1935, 244–62.
6. Cf. *The Structure of Social Action*, 200 ff., 241 ff.
7. See esp. *Magic, Science, and Religion*, by Bronisław Malinowski, edited by Robert Redfield, the Free Press, Glencoe, IL.
8. *Primitive Mentality.*
9. *The Golden Bough.*
10. For example, the field of health is, in spite of the achievements of modern medicine, even in our own society a classical example of this type of situation. Careful examination of our own treatment of health even through medical practice reveals that though magic in a strict sense is not prominent, there is an unstable succession of beliefs which overemphasize the therapeutic possibilities of certain diagnostic ideas and therapeutic practices. The effect is to create an optimistic bias in favor of successful treatment of disease which apparently has considerable functional significance.

11. *The Elementary Forms of the Religious Life*. See also *The Structure of Social Action*, Chapter XI.
12. Especially *De la division du travail* and *Le Suicide*. See also *The Structure of Social Action*, Chap. VIII, X.
13. *The Protestant Ethic and the Spirit of Capitalism*.
14. *Gesammelte Aufsätze zur Religionssoziologie*. See also *The Structure of Social Action*, Chaps. XIV, XV, and XVII.
15. See especially his treatment of the role of the balance of social power in the establishment of the ascendancy of the Brahmans in India, and of the international position of the people of Israel in the definition of religious problems for the prophetic movement.
16. See the writer's paper, 'The Role of Ideas in Social Action,' *American Sociological Review*, III, 1938, for a general analytical discussion of the problem included in the present volume.
17. Every treatment of questions of fact and every empirical investigation is 'in terms of a conceptual scheme'. Scientifically the sole sanction of such a conceptual scheme is its 'utility', the degree to which it 'works' in facilitating the attainment of the goals of scientific investigation. Hence the conceptual structure of any system of scientific theory is subject to the same kind of relativity with 'arbitrariness'. It is subject to the disciplining constraint both of verification in all questions of particular empirical fact, and of logical precision and consistency among the many different parts of a highly complex conceptual structure. The 'theory of social action' is by now a theoretical structure so highly developed and with so many ramifications in both these respects that elements structurally essential to it cannot be lightly dismissed as expressing only 'one point of view'.

Rodney Stark and W. S. Bainbridge
'Towards a theory of religion: religious commitment'

Rodney Stark (born 1934) began his academic career studying journalism at the University of Denver, where he graduated with a BA in 1959. In 1961 Stark returned to academia, embarking upon a series of graduate studies in sociology at the University of California, Berkeley, which awarded him an MA in 1965 and a PhD in 1971. After gaining his doctorate he was appointed Professor of Sociology and Comparative Religion at Washington University. It was while working at Washington that he collaborated with Bainbridge, publishing their famous theory of religion. Their collaborative publication 'The Future of Religion' received the Society for the Scientific Study of Reading (SSSR) Distinguished Book Award in 1986, an award that Stark was to receive again in 1993, the same year the Pacific Sociological Association presented him with an award for distinguished scholarship. In 2004, after thirty-two years of service, Rodney Stark left Washington University to become Professor of Social Sciences at the Texan Baptist University, Baylor. At Baylor he has been involved in the formation of a graduate programme in sociology of religion and he continues to be an active researcher.

William Sims Bainbridge was born in Connecticut in 1940. He studied sociology first at Boston University and later at Harvard, which awarded him a PhD in 1975. Before completing his PhD he became an instructor in anthropology at Wellesley College; however, after being awarded his doctorate he moved to the University of Washington, where he worked as assistant professor of sociology. Bainbridge subsequently taught at Harvard, Illinois State University, and Towson University before becoming director of the sociology programme at the National Science Foundation, based in Virginia. He is still active at the National Science Foundation where he currently works as Deputy Director for the Division of Information and Intelligent Systems.

The work of Stark and Bainbridge provides a highly original contribution to the study of religion, offering a complex analysis of the motivational factors leading individuals to make choices in relation to religious institutions and ideas. Their work is an important element within the secularisation debate and raises interesting questions in regard to the relationship between modern social theory and capitalism.

This paper presents the basic axioms and some initial definitions from which we are constructing a general theory of religion. Here we carry the deductive process only to the point where three testable and non-trivial propositions about religious commitment are obtained. These propositions explain and clarify the available empirical literature. In subsequent papers we shall deduce and test other results from this theoretical system.

We are launched on the immodest task of constructing a general theory of religion. We propose to deduce from a small set of axioms about what humans are like and how they behave, and from a larger number of definitions, a series of propositions explaining why religions exist, how they originate, how religious movements are transformed – indeed, answers to the whole list of classic questions.

In our judgment, this task is both necessary and possible. It is necessary because, while the past several decades have produced an amazing array of new and well-tested facts about religion, we lack theories to organize these facts and tell us which are relevant to what. Current theories are little more than glosses on the work of nineteenth century social theorists. The task seems possible because, while little theorizing has gone on in the social-scientific study of religion (and indeed in much of sociology), important progress has been made in micro-economics, social psychology, and anthropology. We propose to ransack these riches for a theory of religion.

This paper is the pivotal work in a series of papers, published and forthcoming, which present a new exchange paradigm for analyzing and explaining religious phenomena and which subject it to a variety of empirical tests. Eventually, the entire theory will appear in a book, expressed in the most detailed and complete manner, illustrated and supported by the empirical studies. Our object here is to present the basic set of axioms, key definitions, and the first of literally hundreds of propositions we have derived about religion and its social context. We only carry the deductive process to the point where some non-trivial, testable, and perhaps counter-intuitive propositions about *religious commitment* have been obtained.

The form of deductive theories requires selecting some small number of rules (axioms) governing the phenomena to be explained. If these are the correct axioms, then logical permutations will give rise to a number of propositions (derived statements) that will predict or prohibit certain relations within the domain addressed by the theory. Thus, if the axioms are correct and complete, the propositions must hold. The correspondence of such theories to the real world is tested by determining empirically whether or not propositions do hold. In the case of a theory, such as our own, that is still evolving and as yet incompletely formalized, empirical research can also be used to uncover faulty logic in the derivation of propositions and to establish appropriate means for operationalizing concepts.

Our primary reason for having some confidence in the theory thus far is that it has successfully confronted data at several points, as we report at length in other papers. Moreover, the deductive process has yielded a number of well-known middle-range propositions. Since our purpose is not to

Rodney Stark and William Sims Bainbridge (1980), 'Towards a theory of religion: religious commitment', *Journal for the Scientific Study of Religion* 19(2).

create a new field, but to advance this field, it is extremely encouraging to find that such classics as Malinowski's theory of magic, or Durkheim's argument about why religion produces stable organizations but magic cannot, derive from the deductive chain. Of this, more later.

The theory rests on six axioms (although we include a temporary seventh axiom to facilitate the presentation, since the deductive chain by which it can be deduced from the other six is quite long). *Axioms* are designated by the letter 'A'. The theory also contains a number of *definitions*. These link the axioms to the empirical world, and are designated by the abbreviation 'Def'. Finally, statements logically deduced from the axioms and definitions are *propositions*, designated by the letter 'P'.

We begin with an axiom that is so basic that standard social scientific theories seldom mention it. Yet it is essential before we can understand anything else. The first axiom places human existence in *time*.

> A1 Human perception and action take place through time, from the past into the future.
> > Def. 1 The *past* consists of the universe of conditions which can be known but not influenced.
> > Def. 2 The *future* consists of the universe of conditions which can be influenced but not known.

The second axiom is a restatement of the first proposition in exchange theory, operant learning theory, and micro-economics (Homans 1961, 1974).

> A2 Humans seek what they perceive to be rewards and avoid what they perceive to be costs.
> > Def. 3 *Rewards* are anything humans will incur costs to obtain.
> > Def. 4 *Costs* are whatever humans attempt to avoid.

We find it facilitates comprehension and discussion to use the most familiar words in our statements. Therefore we speak of rewards and costs rather than of positive and negative reinforcers.

Our first proposition derives directly from A2, Def. 3 and Def. 4.

> P1 Rewards and costs are complementary: a lost or foregone reward equals a cost, and an avoided cost equals a reward.

Proposition 1 extends A2 by expressing in another way the relationship between its terms. *Seeking* and *avoiding* are opposites. To obtain a reward, a person accepts costs. When a person attempts to avoid a cost, he *seeks* the *avoidance* of that cost, and this avoidance is by Def. 3 a reward. If rewards and costs were not complementary, there could be no human action. But human action is still not possible without a further principle:

A3 Rewards vary in kind, value, and generality.
   Def. 5 Reward A is more *valuable* than reward B if a person will usually exchange B for A.
   Def. 6 Rewards are *general* to the extent that they include other (less general) rewards.

All our experience supports the truth of this axiom. We know we desire some things more than others. Some desires are biologically conditioned, some by environment, others by culture, and some even depend upon an individual's unique history. Here this variation is not germane. All we assert is that for all individuals there are things they want more or less of. This also implies that for each individual there are rewards which the person does not possess at any given moment, while other rewards may already be in the person's possession.

The second proposition is derived from all the previous statements, and gives the condition under which human action is possible:

P2 Sometimes rewards can be obtained at costs less than the cost equivalent to foregoing the reward.

Stated another way, P2 says that sometimes human action can be profitable. This means that over time an individual may gain some desired rewards through the expenditure (as costs) of less desired rewards. If rewards did not differ in *kind*, then there would only be one reward, and it is difficult to see how one could make a profit through trading in it. If rewards did not differ in *value*, there would be no sense in giving up one to acquire another. The fact that rewards differ in *generality* is implied by the mathematical possibility of addition. When a person seeks a collection of rewards, by Def. 3 this collection constitutes a reward in itself, and yet it includes other lesser rewards. Thus, any collection of rewards is more general than any single reward in the collection. If reward A is more valuable than reward B, then they must differ in kind, generality, or both.

These axioms and propositions give us the context in which human action is possible, but they do not sufficiently specify the necessary characteristics of the human actor. Axiom 4 expresses the human capacity to perceive and act effectively in a complex environment:

A4 Human action is directed by a complex but finite information-processing system that functions to identify problems and attempt solutions to them.
   Def. 7 The *mind* is the set of human functions that directs the action of a person.

Def. 8 Human *problems* are recurrent situations that require investments (costs) of specific kinds to obtain rewards.

Def. 9 To *solve* a problem means to imagine possible means of achieving the desired reward, to select the one with the greatest likelihood of success in the light of available information, and to direct action along the chosen line until the reward has been achieved.

Definition 9 is a rather long statement of how the human mind must operate if it is to achieve its task in complex circumstances. This definition reminds us of what our minds actually do, while intentionally being quite nonspecific. We note that the mind performs certain functions, but we do not say very much about how it accomplishes this. To say that the mind is finite means that it is limited in the amount of information it can store and process.

Because rewards differ in many ways, problems also differ, and solutions must differ as well if complex human action is to be possible. Solutions often must be somewhat novel, since humans constantly encounter circumstances they have not previously experienced. Yet solutions are not the result of random experimentation. Efficiency requires that organisms attempt to deal with novel circumstances as variations on circumstances with which they are already familiar. Thus, humans attack new situations as mixtures of the familiar and the unfamiliar, and attempt conceptually to break down novelty into combinations of familiar elements. Conceptual simplifications of reality, models of reality designed to guide action, may be called *explanations*.

P3 In solving problems, the human mind must seek explanations.

Def. 10 *Explanations* are statements about how and why rewards may be obtained and costs are incurred.

Because humans *seek* explanations, and by Def. 3 whatever humans seek is a reward, it follows that:

P4 Explanations are rewards of some level of generality.

Explanations differ along all the dimensions that other rewards do. For example, they differ in generality. An explanation can guide action on more than one occasion, and therefore potentially can provide several lesser rewards. Thus, an explanation is relatively general. Explanations tell us what costs to expend under what circumstances and in what time sequence in order to obtain the desired reward. Given an effective explanation X_1, we can imagine another explanation X_2 identical to X_1 but with the addition of some costly action C which does not alter the value of the reward obtained. Thus we can deduce that:

P5 Explanations vary in the costs and time they require for the desired reward to be obtained.

Explanations should also vary according to the kind, value, and generality of the rewards to be obtained through them, but here we note that they vary even when the reward achieved is held constant. There is an infinite number of ways of *attempting* to accomplish anything, thus an unlimited number of competing explanations, and usually there are many routes to success, each of a distinctive length.

Often, it is fairly easy to find a successful explanation and solve the problem of obtaining a desired reward. But sometimes this is not the case. Axiom 5 introduces this tragic fact and is the turning point on which the crucial parts of our argument hinge:

A5 Some desired rewards are limited in supply, including some that simply do not exist.
    Def. 11 A *limited* supply means that persons cannot have as much of a reward as they desire.
    Def. 12 Rewards that do *not exist* cannot be obtained by any person or group.

People always tend to want more rewards than they can have. Put another way, aggregate demand tends always to exceed supply. While this may not be true of a given reward at a given time, it is true of the sum of rewards. Natural resources and human productive capacities tend to limit the supply of many rewards. For example, most societies have never possessed more food than their populations would have consumed. Obviously, the extent to which any given reward is in short supply varies from society to society and from time to time. But unsated appetites always remain and some, like the desire for honor, tend to be insatiable.

How do humans get those rewards that do exist? Much of what we desire can come only from someone else, whether the reward be affection or apples. When we seek a reward from someone else, that person usually must pay a cost for providing us with the reward. Thus, in order to induce another to supply us a reward, we must offer an inducement – some other reward – in return. Proposition 2 tells us that a deal is possible. Sometimes we can offer the other person a reward that he evaluates more highly than what he gives us, while we likewise value what we get over what we give. Thus, through seeking rewards people are forced into exchange relationships (Homans 1961, 1974).

P6 In pursuit of desired rewards, humans will exchange rewards with other humans.

People will not engage in these exchanges in an aimless way. All our discussion explains that they will tend to act rationally to maximize rewards and minimize costs. Thus, it follows that:

P7 Humans will seek high exchange ratios.
  Def. 13 *Exchange ratio* is a person's net rewards over costs in an exchange.

So far in this discussion we have been dealing with abstract 'persons' who are equally constrained by our propositions. But we know that real people do not possess equal rewards, nor are they treated equally by each other. There might be many ways of expressing the fact that some individuals have greater resources than others, but the way we find most convenient for our deductions is stated in Axiom 6.

A6 Individual and social attributes which determine power are unequally distributed among persons and groups in any society.
  Def. 14 *Power* is the degree of control over one's exchange ratio.

Power has proved elusive of definition in sociology. Usually it is defined as the capacity to get one's way even against the opposition of others. Such a definition fails to say what it means to get one's way. Obviously, getting one's way has to do with gaining rewards or avoiding costs and is lodged in exchange relationships. It proves fruitful to define power as controlling the exchange ratio with the consequence that the more powerful, the more favorable the exchange ratio.

With power defined thus, attention must turn to capacities or attributes that enable persons or groups *to be powerful*, to control exchange ratios with others. Some of these capacities are biological features of human organisms – height, weight, eyesight, reflexes, endurance, strength, beauty, health, agility, and intelligence, for examples. But it also will be obvious that many achieved and ascribed characteristics serve as power-giving capacities. Achieved skills, training, knowledge, and experience tend to give power. Ascribed statuses such as sex, race, family background, and the like also often serve to give power.

Among the important determinants of power are the outcomes of previous exchanges. That is, power may be used to accumulate resources that confer still more power. This tendency may have limits. For example, some rewards may be difficult to concentrate in great quantities, while any that are unlimited in supply cannot be concentrated at all. But rewards that exist only in limited supply are particularly susceptible to the exercise of power.

This approach to the analysis of primitive magic enabled Malinowski clearly to refute both the view of Lévy-Bruhl,[8] that primitive man confuses the realm of the supernatural and the sacred with the utilitarian and the rational, and also the view which had been classically put forward by Frazer[9] that magic was essentially primitive science, serving the same fundamental functions.

Malinowski, however, went beyond this in attempting to understand the functional necessity for such mechanisms as magic. In this connection, he laid stress on the importance of the emotional interests involved in the successful outcome of such enterprises. The combination of a strong emotional interest with important factors of uncertainty, which on the given technical level are inherent in the situation, produces a state of tension and exposes the actor to frustration. This, it should be noted, exists not only in cases where uncontrollable factors, such as bad weather or insect pests in gardening, result in 'undeserved' failure, but also in cases where success is out of proportion to reasonable expectations of the results of intelligence and effort. Unless there were mechanisms which had the psychological function of mitigating the sense of frustration, the consequences would be unfavorable to maintaining a high level of confidence or effort, and it is in this connection that magic may be seen to perform important positive functions. It should be clear that this is a very different level of interpretation from that which attributes it only to the primitive level of knowledge. It would follow that wherever such uncertainty elements enter into the pursuit of emotionally important goals, if not magic, at least functionally equivalent phenomena could be expected to appear.[10]

In the case of magic, orientation to supernatural entities enters into action which is directed to the achievement of practical, empirical goals, such as a good crop or a large catch of fish. Malinowski, however, calls attention to the fact that there are situations which are analogous in other respects but in which no practical goal can be pursued. The type case of this is death. From the practical point of view, the Trobrianders, like anyone else, are surely aware that 'nothing can be done about it'. No ritual observances will bring the deceased back to life. But precisely for this reason, the problem of emotional adjustment is all the greater in importance. The significance both practically and emotionally of a human individual is of such a magnitude that his death involves a major process of readjustment for the survivors. Malinowski shows that the death of another involves exposure to sharply conflicting emotional reactions, some of which, if given free range, would lead to action and attitudes detrimental to the social group. There is great need for patterns of action which provide occasion for the regulated expression of strong emotions, and which in such a situation of emotional conflict reinforce those reactions which are most favorable to the continued solidarity and functioning of the social group. One may suggest that in no society is action on the occasion of death confined to the utilitarian aspects of

Scarce rewards will tend to flow through exchanges into the hands of the powerful and away from the weak. In other words:

P8 Exchange ratios will vary among persons and groups in any society.

P9 Rewards that exist in limited supply will tend to be monopolized by powerful persons and groups, thereby becoming relatively unavailable to others.

When persons seek scarce but valuable rewards, they usually do not give up at the first sign of difficulty. Humans are persistent in pursuit of strongly desired rewards. This is another way of stating that they are willing to pay great costs for great rewards, a fact that follows from the definition of value. Some problems can be solved only through extended and costly effort, and among them are the satisfactions of several strong desires. Difficulty in obtaining strongly desired rewards not only produces the emotion we call *frustration*, but also leads to a knotty intellectual and logical quandary. How do people decide if they are on the right track? How do people evaluate the explanations on which they base their action?

P10 Explanations can be evaluated correctly only by reference to their known ability to facilitate the attainment of the desired reward.

Def. 15 *Evaluation* is the determination of the value of any reward, including explanations; value is equivalent to the maximum cost a person would pay to obtain the reward.

As noted in P5, explanations do vary in the costs and time required before they can give us the desired reward. As A4 pointed out, the human mind has to compare explanations to decide which is the cheapest way of getting what is wanted. If our current situation is very similar to past situations, we can simply repeat what worked for us before. That means that evaluations, in the terms of Axiom 1, are used to influence the *future* but must be based on knowledge of the *past*.

In A5 we noted that some desired rewards are scarce, and others do not even exist. In saying that some rewards do not exist, we are postulating a fact which we cannot prove. Certainly, human observation demonstrates that some rewards are *very scarce*. No one is reliably known to have survived death. Although some religions report evidence on outstanding cases, the other religions do not accept their claims. Logically, some rewards cannot exist because their terms are contradictory. As we usually interpret the words, we cannot have our cake and eat it too. It is a fact of life that some of the most desired, most general rewards have not been shown to exist, and we suspect that they do not in fact exist. If A5 is a little unsettling as it is stated, we could interpret it to say that some desired rewards are so scarce that they do not seem to exist *in this world*.

However, unless the definition of a given desired reward contains a logical contradiction, we cannot be absolutely sure that there is no solution to the problem of obtaining it. This follows from Axiom 1, because until the end of time – until we run out of *future* – we will not have complete information about all possible explanations, that is, we cannot evaluate the success of all possible courses of action. This is true in lesser degree for scarce rewards which can be obtained only through relatively costly action, including rewards that require lengthy sequences of exchange. Suppose we want to compare the values of two competing explanations for obtaining a scarce reward. We cannot honestly end the test until we have expended at least twice the cost required by the explanation that is in fact the cheaper of the two. We must have succeeded with one and have invested slightly more than an equal amount in the other before it is ideally justifiable to abandon the one that has not yet led to success. Until *some* course of action succeeds for us, we cannot completely reject any others that possibly could be followed under the given circumstances. It is not surprising that people often stick with explanations that seem to work, without ever testing others. Because explanations can only be evaluated through a process that actually invests the minimum cost required to obtain the desired reward, the following propositions hold:

> P11 It is impossible to know for certain that a given reward does not exist.
>
> P12 When a desired reward is relatively unavailable, explanations that promise to provide it are costly and difficult to evaluate correctly.
>
> P13 The more valued or general a reward, the more difficult will be evaluation of explanations about how to obtain it.

Taken together, these three propositions explain why people will often persist in following an incorrect explanation or one that has at least not proved fruitful, especially when strong desires are concerned. Some explanations will be invalidated, because they set specific terms for themselves. If they state the exact interval of time required for the reward to appear, then they will be discredited if the time passes and nothing happens. If people are determined to invest in seeking a reward, false explanations that *can* be discredited easily will drop by the wayside, leaving explanations (whether correct or not) which are not as vulnerable. Therefore:

> P14 In the absence of a desired reward, explanations often will be accepted which posit attainment of the reward in the distant future or in some other nonverifiable context.

Def. 16 *Compensators* are postulations of reward according to explanations that are not readily susceptible to unambiguous evaluation.

The concept of *compensators* is the key to the theory of religion which follows. When humans cannot quickly and easily obtain strongly desired rewards they persist in their efforts and often may accept explanations that provide only compensators – empirically unsubstantiated faith that the rewards *will be* obtained – not the rewards themselves. Such faith is quite distinct from actually obtaining the reward.

P15 Compensators are treated by humans as if they were rewards; compensators are intangible substitutes for a desired reward, having the character of I.O.U.s, the value of which must be taken on faith.

P16 For any reward or cluster of rewards, one or more compensators may be invented.

P17 Compensators vary according to the generality, value, and kind of the rewards for which they substitute.

Def. 17 Compensators which substitute for single, specific rewards are called *specific* compensators.

Def. 18 Compensators which substitute for a cluster of many rewards and for rewards of great scope and value are called *general* compensators.

These propositions hint at a major orphan generalization in social science analysis of the functions of religion. Malinowski's (1948) celebrated theory of magic – as an attempt to provide people with a compensatory sense of control over dangerous or vital events they cannot control – is pertinent here. So are Marx's ruminations about false consciousness and opium of the people, Durkheim's analysis of primitive religions, Freud's conjectures about religion as illusion, and much of church/sect theory. As it stands, however, these propositions *do not equate* compensators with religion. Many compensators have no connection with religion.

All societies utilize compensators. Perhaps the most universal is some promise of a triumph over death. If means were provided to evade death here and now, that would be a reward. But at present immortality is to be achieved somewhere (somewhen?) else, and the validity of the promise cannot be determined. Thus the desire for immortality is not satisfied with a reward, but with an intangible promise, a compensator. The validity of this promise cannot be determined empirically, but must be accepted or rejected on faith alone. If the promise turns out true, then at that point compensators are redeemed as rewards. If not, not.

It must be seen that some desired rewards are so general as to require explanations that also are so general that they can best be described as philosophies of life, theologies, or solutions to questions of ultimate meaning. As discussed more fully later in this paper, humans have a habit of asking why – a habit captured in our axioms. When human 'whys' are repeated along certain logical chains they lead eventually to questions about the fundamental meaning and purpose of the existence of humans and of the natural world. It will be evident that some of these desired explanations are not susceptible to unambiguous evaluation. That is, we cannot surely discover whether these explanations are correct. According to our definition, such untestable and extremely general explanations are compensators. This is not to suggest that they are untrue. But we cannot find out anytime soon. It is this, and *only* this, aspect of such explanations that leads us to identify them as compensators. Surely there is nothing controversial about distinguishing between statements that can be tested and those that must be taken on faith.

It will be evident that, insofar as the empirical world is concerned, at any given moment a more favorable exchange ratio is possible if one can obtain a reward in trade for a compensator. Unlike bonds and other financial I.O.U.s, compensators do not pay interest to the holder. On the contrary, they are often costly to keep and maintain. Any compensator entails the risk that it cannot be redeemed for the promised reward, and therefore must be judged less valuable than that reward.

> P18 Humans will prefer rewards to compensators and will attempt to exchange compensators for rewards.

This is merely to recognize that intangible I.O.U.s represent a low cost to the giver. If you demand a better deal, and I can keep things as they are by issuing promises, I can continue to enjoy a more favorable exchange ratio. Drawing together many pieces of the argument to this point, we can specify when people will succeed in obtaining rewards, and when they will be forced to accept compensators instead:

> P19 It will be impossible to obtain rewards rather than compensators when: (1) a reward does not exist; (2) a compensator is mistaken for a reward; (3) one lacks the power to obtain the desired reward.

Obviously, one can at best accept a compensator if the desired reward does not exist. Malinowski's Trobriand Islanders undoubtedly would have preferred ocean liners to outrigger canoes. But in their world liners did not exist. The best they could do was use magical compensators for the risk of sailing on the open sea. By the same token, humans would prefer not to die.

Lacking scientific means to achieve immortality, they can at best settle for compensators in the form of hopes for the life to come.

It is equally obvious that people often will fail to obtain a reward and will accept a compensator instead if they cannot distinguish the one from the other. One capacity influencing power – control over one's exchange ratio – is the ability or knowledge to make discriminations. This also reminds us of how compensators sometimes have been used to con the unsuspecting out of their treasure.

Finally, awareness is not enough if we are unable to control our exchange ratios. As Proposition 9 states, scarce rewards will tend to be monopolized by powerful persons and groups, leaving the powerless to content themselves with compensators. Here one thinks of the transvaluational character of religions of the poor and dispossessed. For example, folks who belong to fundamentalist sects in Apalachia know perfectly well that jewels, fancy clothes, and other material luxuries exist. They also know perfectly well they have little chance to get any. So they define these things as sinful and accept the compensatory belief that by doing without now, they will triumph in heaven, where the first shall be last, and the last, first. However, in keeping with Proposition 18, when the economic circumstances of such groups change, they tend quite rapidly to become worldly and materialistic – which is, of course, what church/sect theory partly is about.

We have now reached the point at which we can introduce the concept of *religion* itself. We do so in a *definition* appended to a proposition about compensators. Thus we show that religion must emerge in human society, and we derive its existence entirely from axioms and propositions in which religion is not an original term. In another paper delineating the concepts *church, sect,* and *cult* we show that the term religion is best reserved for systems of the most general compensators, while less general compensators may be found in many contexts (Stark and Bainbridge 1979). But the proposition itself is about the sources of faith in general compensators. It follows most immediately from Proposition 13, Proposition 14, Proposition 17, and Definition 18.

> P20 The most general compensators can be supported only by supernatural explanations.
>> Def. 19 *Supernatural* refers to forces beyond or outside nature which can suspend, alter, or ignore physical forces.
>> Def. 20 *Religion* refers to systems of general compensators based on supernatural assumptions.

Earlier in this paper we mentioned very general compensators that offer explanations for questions of ultimate meaning. It is evident that many humans often desire answers to such questions: Does life have purpose? Why are we here? What can we hope? Is death the end? Why do we suffer? Does justice exist? Why did *my* child die? Why am *I* a slave? Humans are bound to raise questions about how great rewards can be obtained and why great costs are sometimes incurred. Indeed, evidence that our rude Neanderthal ancestors performed burial rites indicates that the tendency to ask such questions and to fashion answers to them reaches far back into human evolution.

When we consider such questions it is self-evident that some of them *require* a supernatural answer. To seek the purpose of life is to demand that it have one. The word *purpose* is not compatible with blind chance, but assumes the existence of intentions or motives. These assume a consciousness. For the universe to have a purpose it must be directed by a conscious agent or agents – the capacity to form plans or have intentions is to be conscious.

Conscious agents on this scale are beyond the natural world. Their existence is not subject to empirical inspection. Thus, to answer certain common questions about ultimate meaning it is necessary to assume the existence of the supernatural.

Our decision to restrict the definition of religion to very general compensator systems that rest on *supernatural assumptions* is in keeping with a very long and fruitful tradition in social science (Tylor 1924: Parsons 1957; Swanson 1960; Goody 1961; Spiro 1966; Wallace 1966). A few scholars have dissented in order to apply the definition of religion to systems of thought that inspire devotion even when these are explicitly opposed to supernatural assumptions (Luckmann 1967; Bellah 1970; Yinger 1970). In so doing, however, as Swanson (1960) pointed out, they blur a vital theoretical question. If, for example, scientific rationalism, Roman Catholicism and Russian Communism are all declared to be religions we lose the conceptual tools to explore the constant and profound conflicts among them. Berger (1967: 177) has demonstrated the futility of this too-inclusive definition of religion. If we define all systems of very general compensators (Berger calls them self-transcendent symbolic universes) as religion then we are forced to define in what way science, for example, is '*different* from what has been called religion by everyone else ... which poses the definitional problem all over again'. For if we then adopt new terms to identify these differences we merely make superfluous the original definition of religion which classified all of them as the same. We prefer to honor the commonly understood meaning of the term religion, especially when we can anticipate increased theoretical utility from so doing.

The insistence on limiting the definition of religion to systems of *very general* compensators also permits us to distinguish between religion and magic, and, in turn, between magic and science. In accord with Durkheim (1915: 42), we identify magic as a set of relatively specific compensators. And, with Weber (1963: 2) we distinguish between magic and science on the basis of empirical verification. Thus *magic* is a set of *specific compensators* offered for quite specific rewards, which are offered as correct explanations *without regard* for empirical evaluations, and which, when evaluated, are *found wanting.* Note that we have not included a supernatural assumption in magic. Hence the definition applies to present-day pseudosciences (e.g., certain psychotherapies in the human potential tradition) which do not explicitly posit a supernatural. This permits us to recognize the potential for such groups to evolve into religious movements (cf. Bainbridge 1978).

In later papers we will examine the nature and sources of different forms of religion. But before we can discuss the contrasts between churches and other kinds of religious organization, we must show that such organizations can exist. Through a lengthy analysis of exchanges between persons in populous and economically developed societies it is possible to derive the statement which we present below as provisional Axiom 7. We offer it as an axiom here only because such a derivation lies beyond the scope of our current analysis. Observation of complex societies exhibiting advanced division of labor supports the following statement:

> A7 (Provisional) Social organizations tend to emerge in human society as social enterprises which specialize in providing some particular kinds of gratifications.

General compensators supported by supernatural explanations are very special merchandise. Even a fairly rudimentary division of labor leads to the establishment of independent enterprises primarily dedicated to providing this product. Competition with organizations dedicated to selling secular products will tend to limit the tendency of religious enterprises to expand very far beyond the scope of their primary business. Because the demand for general compensators is universal, we can conclude:

> P21 Religious organizations will tend to emerge in society.
> Def. 21 *Religious organizations* are social enterprises whose primary purpose is to create, maintain, and exchange supernaturally-based general compensators.

The role of religious organizations in producing and promulgating compensators will be obvious. A major emphasis in religious proselytization is that religion will provide a cure for pain and trouble. Indeed, because religions have recourse to a supernatural realm they have an unmatched capacity to create and sponsor compensators. But it also should be emphasized that religious organizations, like other organizations, also have the *capacity to provide rewards.*

Because compensators function *as if* they were rewards, humans are prepared to expend costs to obtain them. Religious organizations provide compensators through exchanges in which at least some measure of real rewards is collected. Proposition 18 should not be misinterpreted to mean that persons will *never* give up a reward to obtain a compensator. Just as they will exchange a lesser reward for a more valuable one, so they will readily exchange a reward of lower value for a compensator that promises to provide a reward of great value. Upon reflection it is obvious that, although religions usually cannot match the reward-generating capacity of some other societal institutions, they do in fact provide rewards. For example, through religious organizations one can gain leadership positions (with attendant status and power), human companionship, leisure and recreational activity, and the like. Any organization that provides a stage for human action and interaction will produce scenes in which all manner of rewards are created and exchanged.

> P22 As social enterprises, religious organizations will tend to provide some rewards as well as compensators.

This proposition permits us to introduce our derivations concerning *power* into the religious realm, in the three propositions that follow.

> P23 The power of an individual or group will be *positively* associated with control of religious organizations and with gaining the rewards available from religious organizations.
> P24 The power of an individual or group will be *negatively* associated with accepting religious compensators, when the desired reward exists.

Power means control of one's exchange ratio. Control of religious organizations facilitates control of one's exchange ratio by increasing one's ability to exchange compensators for rewards. Furthermore, those most able to gain rewards will tend to gain a bigger share of religious rewards too. Because the powerful are more able to gain rewards, they will find less need for compensators. But this does not mean that powerful persons and groups will have absolutely no use for compensators. Some rewards are so scarce – or nonexistent – that even the powerful will not be able to obtain them. Therefore:

> P25 Regardless of power, persons and groups will tend to accept religious compensators when desired rewards do not exist.

Some will interpret Propositions 23 and 24 in Marxist fashion – that the powerful will profit while the poor pray. If so, then by the same token the twenty-fifth proposition is unMarxist, and reflects basic functionalist assumptions: that all members of a society can have significant common interests, that they will tend to pursue these interests in a cooperative fashion, and that there will be considerable consensus on such matters (to say nothing of the integrative functions of such common interests). Of course, in a pluralist society competing religious organizations may exist, and there is always the competition offered by secular organizations in those areas where demonstrable rewards and less general compensators are offered.

P26 If multiple suppliers of general compensators exist, then the ability to exchange general compensators will depend upon their relative availability and perceived exchange ratios.

Religious organizations vary in terms of how well-developed and credible a set of compensators they offer. Furthermore, they vary in terms of their degree of formal organization, and the extent to which they are differentiated from other social institutions. Such variations are likely to matter.

Furthermore, in some societies other institutions and organizations offer serious competition to religion in offering both rewards and compensators. The quasi-religious character of some political movements has long been recognized. While there are substantial differences between, for example, the location and character of socialist and Christian utopias, the two nevertheless compete. By the same token, a scientific perspective may compete with religion in offering very general explanations, concerning the most important human rewards and costs. Proposition 26 is crucial for understanding the great complexity found in the real world, but in present form it is so general as to be a truism. We must plead that we can neither break it down into the needed subset of propositions nor derive all of them in a short space. This task we postpone to a later opportunity. Our final proposition is another truism, but a vital one.

P27 All patterns of human perception and action are conditioned by socialization.
    Def. 22 *Socialization* is the accumulation of explanations over time through exchanges with other persons.

Clearly it matters, for example, whether an American is raised by Baptists or Unitarians. Furthermore, regardless of the content of socialization, the effectiveness of socialization varies. Variations in socialization probably will account for much variation in religious behavior across individuals – and probably across groups as well. This is an area that deserves extensive exploration. But for present purposes it is best to end the exposition of our theory here.

CONCLUSION

Limiting ourselves for the moment to the topic of variations in religious commitment, what does this theory tell us that was not already well-known? First of all, it shows that the long tradition of deprivational theories of religious commitment was very incomplete. In Proposition 24 we do derive such a theory. However, Proposition 23 permits us to see that religious organizations are not merely 'otherworldly' purveyors of compensators. They also serve as a source of direct rewards. This permits us to explain forms of religious commitment not prompted by deprivation, but which are, instead, a *religious expression of privilege*. Finally, Proposition 25 allows us to take into account the fact that, vis-a-vis certain kinds of desired rewards, *everyone is potentially deprived*. Thus if Proposition 24 points towards a *sectlike* mode of religious commitment, and Proposition 23 points towards a *churchlike* mode, Proposition 25 points towards a *universal* dimension of commitment, variation in which is not the result of power differences, but of socialization and competition with competing sources of compensators (science and politics, for example).

The question is: do these predicted patterns of relationships hold? Briefly, yes. If we consider socio-economic status as a measure of power-giving attributes then studies ought to show SES is *positively* related to those aspects of religious commitment that can serve as direct rewards: church membership, church attendance, holding office in religious organizations and the like. Conversely, SES ought to be *negatively* related to aspects of commitment that can serve as compensators: belief, prayer, mystical experiences, and the like. However, SES ought *not be* related to accepting compensators when no reward is known to exist, such as life after death. This is the pattern found in the data (cf. Stark 1972). Moreover, when IQ replaces SES as the power-giving attribute, the same differential patterns are found empirically. Thus the theory clarifies and explains why different aspects of religious commitment have long been known to be differentially related to power characteristics such as SES.

However, these explanations of differential religious commitment are but the first small step in following out the implications of the theory. From these three propositions it can be deduced that an *internal contradiction* will exist within religious organizations. That is, within religious groups there will always be subgroups having a conflict of interest over whom the religious organization is to serve. Some will wish to maximize rewards. Some will wish to maximize compensators. It can be shown that these two goals tend to be contradictory. Therefore, the seeds of schism can be deduced to exist within religious organizations. From there it requires but a few additional steps to discover a fully-developed church/sect theory: the conditions under which schisms erupt as sect movements or church movements and the conditions under which religious bodies are transformed in a churchlike direction, or remain sects. Indeed, at the end of our long chain of deductions we will examine propositions that predict that the process of secularization is self-limiting – that it generates revivals and the formation of new religious groups. Laying out these conclusions and testing them will occupy us for the next several years. Here we have merely tried to make explicit some basic elements of the deductive system on which our work is based.

5

FEMINIST APPROACHES

INTRODUCTION

Feminist approaches have critiqued religion and the understanding of religion from both internal and external perspectives. One of the most significant trends is overtly theological. It attempts to reformulate theology to suit women's needs; this entails both a critique of previous theological models and the introduction of a new emphasis on women's voices. While this material falls outside the scope of this volume, as it usually focuses on the revisioning of specific theological traditions, the underlying critique of religion upon which it is based relies on a theory of both religion and society. At its simplest, this theory can be seen as a feminist version of the Marxist concept of false consciousness. Religion is seen as an expression of an ideology that arises from and justifies patriarchal dominance. Thus maintaining religious structures unchallenged is seen as perpetuating and validating these forms of exploitation. Religion must be challenged and transformed both by recovering women's voices from the past and by restructuring it, as it exists today, so as not to reflect patriarchal systems of power.

The underlying concept of false consciousness is also an overt feature of many feminist discussions of religion and theories of religion. This is particularly true of discussions of Judaism or Islam, in which the explanation/justification of the exclusion of women from public religious roles by both women and men (as for example 'a separate but equally important form of spirituality') were seen as patterns of false consciousness through which the paradigms of exploitation were perpetuated. Some more recent debates within the feminist approach have challenged this suggesting that the models of women's roles upon which it was based were a neo-colonialist imposition of Western models of gender. While many feminist discussions have taken this critique on board, the issue of false consciousness is not so easily laid to rest – the internal views underlying the neo-colonialist critique may themselves be the product of false consciousness.

The debate regarding false consciousness is closely related to that of essentialism. One of the themes of many feminist discussions relates to the problem of essentialism – either in respect of human beings (in which women's identities are submerged into those of men) or in an essentialised view of women set in opposition to that of men. Many feminists have implicitly or explicitly argued for a essentialised view of women that can serve as a basis for critique of religions within any cultural context. The challenge of womanist approaches has raised serious questions about the nature of this form of essentialisation – can one argue for a single essentialised view of women outside cultural context? Recent approaches have thus tended to emphasise the diversity within women's experience, and hence the identities, spiritualities and theologies that arise from them.

Although much of the above discussion relates specifically to the praxis of religion, and in the case of the womanist approaches to the effects of different feminist models on that praxis, feminist approaches have also challenged the basis of many aspects of the study of religion, often specifically raising the issue of essentialisation. This is specifically developed in Shaw's critique of Eliade (pages 425–33). She argues that while phenomenological analysis was positive in privileging the internal point of view, the problem was 'whose point of view'. The phenomenologists, due to their emphasis on canonical texts, tended to essentialise the experiences of men, ignoring the unspoken and unwritten experiences of women. Phenomenology thus is seen as perpetuating the entrenched power structures of patriarchal religion. Both Shaw and King (pages 411–24) argue for a new way of studying and conceptualising religion: one based on an 'experiential and personal' approach reflecting both women and men, rather than an institutional and textual approach that reflects and essentialises the experience of men.

SERENE JONES
'WOMEN'S EXPERIENCE BETWEEN A ROCK AND A HARD
PLACE: FEMINIST, WOMANIST, AND *MUJERISTA* THEOLOGIES
IN NORTH AMERICA'

Serene Jones received a BA from the University of Oklahoma, a MDiv from Yale Divinity School and a PhD from Yale University. She also studied at Tamil Nadu Theological Seminary in India. She has held a number of posts at Yale and is currently Associate Professor of Theology in Yale Divinity School. While much of her published work has related to feminist theology she has also written on Calvin and other issues within systematic theology.

One of the most significant trends in feminist theology is the rise of womanist approaches. Jones's paper highlights the nature of these challenges to feminist orthodoxy and presents a clearly developed outline of many of the faultlines and issues within modern feminism.

This essay is designed to map out the different conceptual frameworks within which a new generation of North American feminist, womanist, and *mujerista* theologians are situating their constructive projects. Although there are, no doubt, a number of ways to draw this map, I have chosen to chart these theologians' positions by looking at the methodological assumptions which have accumulated around their varied conceptions of women's experience. As an extremely open-ended category, *women's experience* serves as a useful starting place for mapping the theologies in question because it functions as a theological flash point where one can see clearly both the similarities and the differences which mark their emergent perspectives.

In terms of their similarities, this new generation of texts represents the exciting culmination of the long struggle to place constructivist, nonessentialized understandings of *woman* at the center of theological reflection; and, as each of these texts illustrates, the fruits of this struggle are quite remarkable, opening these theological projects onto a richly textured landscape where women's experiences are as multiple as their varied social locations, histories, and personal stories. At the same time, these theologians' shared affirmation of the nonessential nature of women is highly diversified with regard to the term *experience* – a notion which, in contrast to the term *woman*, remains methodologically essentialized by some while being radically historicized by others. On this score, there are thus significant philosophical differences between the texts, differences located in their disparate

Serene Jones (1997), 'Women's experience between a rock and a hard place: feminist, womanist and *mujerista* theologies in North America', in Rebecca S. Chopp and Sheila Greeve Davaney (eds), *Horizons in Feminist Theology: Identity, Tradition, and Norms*, Minneapolis: Augsburg Fortress.

understandings of how one measures and defines this thing they call experience. Although much more should be said about the similarities between these texts, particularly their shared rejection of gender essentialisms, this essay focuses primarily on their differences, namely, their different theories of experience.

The map I have drawn to identify their varied theoretical perspectives divides roughly into two sides, the rock and the hard place. On the *rock* side, I place those theologians who continue to employ universalizing and/or ahistorical frames of reference to structure their accounts of human experience – the rock here referring to their penchant for analytic measurements which are solid, foundational, comprehensive in scope, and generalizable in character. In this context, I further identify three types of universalizing frames of reference: the *phenomenological* frame found in the works of Elizabeth Johnson and Catherine LaCugna, the *process/psychoanalytic* frame developed in the writings of Rita Brock and Catherine Keller, and the *literary/textual* frame deployed in the analyses of Delores Williams and Sallie McFague. The advantages of these perspectives should be evident to those who engage their texts: the stability of their frameworks allows them to generate theological images which are resilient and visionary – no small accomplishment in a postmodern context. On the other hand, what they lose with this reliance on universalizing structures is, I will argue, a place for that which 'does not fit', for the incommensurable experience, and thus for the marginal theological voice which defies the general and subsequently resists the closure of universal categorizations.

On the *hard place* side of the map, I locate the work of those theologians who self-consciously avoid universalizing gestures and opt instead for descriptions of experience which are historically localized and culturally specific. Here, I divide the map into two subgroups: those theologians who use the tools of *cultural anthropology* to localize experience, namely, Kathryn Tanner and Ada María Isasi-Díaz, and those who deploy *poststructuralist* gestures to uncover the play of language and power in the construction of identity, as seen in the work of Rebecca Chopp. This side is solid enough to be a hard place but its formulations are less stable than those of the rock. The challenges confronting those standing on such shifting ground are numerous: the status of normative claims, the limits and value of immanent critique, the viability of deconstructive rhetoric, and the still undecided fate of 'truth' and its relation to doctrine.

As to which side of the map this essay favors, it will no doubt be obvious that my critiques of the rock are more forceful than my criticisms of the hard place. Let me say from the outset, however, that if this essay were focusing on the substance of the theological visions put forth by these texts, and not on their methodological appraisals of experience, my assessment would most likely be reversed, for it is clear that the six authors who fall on the rock side of the map take on substantive topics like embodiment and rework crucial doctrines like the Trinity with a theological boldness not yet found in the works of feminists located in the hard place. I therefore hope that my analysis and criticisms of these works will not be taken as a critique of their theologies as a whole, but rather as an attempt to map out the edges of a methodological chasm – between the rock and the hard place – which currently runs through our collective conversations, serving both as a divide that separates us and as a yawning gap which challenges us to daringly negotiate that still open space of 'between'.

THE ROCK
Phenomenological accounts of women's experience
Let me begin with the universalizing (rock) side of the map by turning to two texts which announce a new generation of voices in Roman Catholic feminist thought: Elizabeth Johnson's *She Who Is: The Mystery of God in Feminist Theological Discourse*, and Catherine Mowry LaCugna's *God for Us: The Trinity and Christian Life*. Given the theological complexity and richness of both texts, it is difficult to limit my review of them to a discussion of their definitions of women's experience, for such a focus over-looks the enormity of their contribution to the fields of historical theology and contemporary Roman Catholic systematics. However, the advantage of focusing on their definitions of experience is that it highlights an aspect of their common heritage which is often overlooked in strictly doctrinal assess-ments of their work, namely, their shared commitment to the philosophical tradition of *continental phenomenology*.

What is significant about the fact that they both work out of this particu-lar tradition? With regard to the question of experience, their commitment to engaging in phenomenological analysis points to their desire to describe women's experience by attaching it, at least partially, to a more general account of the basic structure of human experience. This attachment of women's experience to a broader phenomenology of the human is only par-tial, however, because both LaCugna and Johnson embrace a constructivist analysis of gender which rigorously avoids essentializing the term *women*. The same cannot be said for the term *experience*, which is described as having – in good phenomenological fashion – an 'essential structure' replete with 'universal features' and 'constitutive dynamics'.

When it comes to giving shape and contour to this essential structure, however, Johnson and LaCugna generate two very different descriptions: the former focuses on 'the hoping subject' and the latter on 'the radically relational self'. In *She Who Is*, Johnson presents an account of women's ex-perience that is not only theologically insightful but poetically compelling, written in a language which invites the reader into an inclusive and hope-filled textual drama where God and the creature meet in an empowering em-brace. Given that her feminist commitments are crafted into the very drama of this phenomenological account, her accomplishment in this regard is no small matter; she effectively writes a new script about personhood, history, and God, a script in which the insights of Paul Ricoeur, Karl Rahner, and Johann Baptist Metz are bound together and dramatically deepened by their encounter with feminism. This newly scripted theological anthropology also serves as the arena within which she introduces her readers to several major historical figures in Christian theology, bringing them as well into a reciprocally advantageous conversation with contemporary feminism. She further pulls into this drama of historical theology, continental philosophy, and feminist theory strands of the Sophia traditions in the Christian Scriptures. In the end, she leaves her reader with a complex and existentially compelling word about *She Who Is:* an 'elusive female metaphor' which discloses 'the mystery of Sophia-God as sheer, exuberant, relational aliveness in the midst of the history of suffering, inexhaustible source of new being in situations of death and destruction, ground of hope for the whole created universe...'.

In Johnson's case, identifying the universalizing gestures which support the infrastructure of this project is not difficult; as I stated earlier, they simply come with her commitment to writing her new script of personhood in the language of phenomenology. Although these gestures are scattered throughout the text, they are most clearly evidenced at two points: first in her discussion of symbolic language and, second, in her description of essential human nature. With regard to the first (her analysis of the symbolic character of God-talk), she invokes Ricoeur's account of the mediating and paradigmatic function of image in experience and, in doing so, she also invokes his ontologically grounded hermeneutical understanding of how language as symbol acquires meaning. With respect to the second (her discussions of the human subject), she describes the frame of universal anthropology, wherein lie 'essential features' and 'anthropological constraints', which include not only the usual existential suspects but also a Rahnerian reference to an 'orientation to hope and the pull of the future'.

What is interesting about Johnson's invocation of these and other phenomenological 'essentials' of human experience is that they stand side by side with her adamant refusal to essentialize woman and to eclipse thereby the multiple differences which structure the lives of women. In light of this refusal, one then wonders why the eclipses implicit in her structurally universal account of human experience and language are any less threatening to difference and particularity. In other words, why is her 'universal subject' any less theologically suspect than the 'universal woman' she so clearly rejects as essentialist? Given that feminist theorists have raised, in recent years, a number of critiques about the dangers inherent in this type of phenomenological universalizing – its resistance to racially historicizing identity, its idealist tendency toward expressive symbolism, and its potentially reductive drive to generate exhaustive accounts of experiential structures – Johnson's own use of feminist theory could be deepened by a response to such critiques. And with Johnson's facility for offering clear and accessible descriptions of theological problems, such a response would no doubt move us closer to understanding how one might deploy universalizing gestures or make generalizing statements without concomitantly invoking a conceptual apparatus which may be too restrictive and too totalizing to allow for the inclusiveness she so heartily applauds.

Within the category of phenomenological feminist theology, I also locate LaCugna's timely contribution to the unfolding renaissance of the doctrine of the Trinity in contemporary theology. Like Johnson, LaCugna falls into this category because she believes it is both possible and necessary to ground one's theological claims about the doctrine of God in a territory called 'the universal structure of existence'. Unlike Johnson, however, she finds the territory traditionally occupied by the Western 'subject' to be deeply problematic as well, both in terms of its investment in an individualized rhetoric of substance/being, and in its uncritical adherence to a notion of reflective consciousness. As a way of countering this view of the self, LaCugna positions her theological anthropology in another territory – one marked by a relational ontology in which 'persons', not 'subject', are conceived of in communal, nonsubstantive, dynamic, and agentic terms. She develops this relational ontology by borrowing from and reworking several sources: the Trinitarian metaphysics of the Cappadocians, the agentic philosophy of John Macmurray, the neopatristic synthesis of Jean Zizioulas, the relational sensibilities of feminist thought, and the social-political analysis of liberation theology. When combined, these varied perspectives form a philosophical edifice which both sustains and is sustained by a doctrine of the Trinity wherein the event of communion – described as the perichoretic dance of divine persons – marks God's own being as agentic being-in-relation, being-in-communion, and being-for-us.

When it comes to defending the philosophical universals embedded in this creative account of 'relational experience', LaCugna fends off prospective critics with a directness not found in Johnson. Her most decisive move in this regard is the assertion that her portrait of relational being reflects the dynamics of Trinitarian interrelatedness found in biblical and liturgical patterns of thought about salvation history. She thereby roots her analysis of being-in-relation in the language of historically particular communities of faith and not in the territory of an epistemically universal rendition of experience, a move which suggests that her philosophical commitments originate in communal narrative and are hence more pragmatic than philosophically foundational in character. As her description of being-in-relation unfolds, however, it often seems that it is a founding philosophical ontology and not a narrative scriptural drama which structures her analysis of both God-in-relation and persons-in-communion.

If this is the case, then LaCugna's text powerfully illustrates what is perhaps the most common universalizing tendency found in her generation of feminist theological writings: the tendency to critically dismantle the 'modern subject' by positing a counterdiscourse in which relationality serves as the central organizing principle of one's theological anthropology – and in doing so, to posit *relationality* as the locus of a *new essence*, a new point around which the structural coherence of the subject (albeit a new subject-self-person) is secured. As a counterdiscourse to the old 'essentialized subject', it is quite evident that this more relational framework works well as a means of conceptualizing women's experience in a more open-ended, historicized manner. There is, however, a double irony which attends this desire to open up the category *experience* by highlighting its essentially relational structure.

First, there is the ironic tension produced by the fact that, on the one hand, LaCugna remains committed to divesting the experiencing subject of its falsely inscribed borders and limits and to opening up theological anthropology to the coursing of history, difference, and community; and yet, on the other hand, she lifts these borders and removes these limits by positioning the experiencing self in an alternative structure called 'relational ontology'. As a universal structure, it thus continues to be a place where the chaotic tides of a thoroughgoing historicism are held at bay, where a new philosophical edifice called 'relationality' holds back the potential of generating radically localized conceptions of experience and identity. It is also a place where the 'unfitting' – the unmeasured, the marginal, and the silent – find a systematic home which ironically helps them 'fit' into an inclusive understanding of community.

A second irony lies in that now old but still unsettling question: if women have long been cast as the bearers of being-in-relation, will ontologically valorizing what has been a 'relational prison' really be liberating? With regard to this last question, LaCugna's discussion of 'perichoresis' – the dance in which there is permeation without confusion – may suggest a way out of this prison and perhaps a way beyond the present ontologizing of relational talk. It may also suggest one way of negotiating the space between the rock and the hard place by marking the point at which relational ontologies (the rock) and poststructuralist discourses (the hard place) begin to overlap and mingle with creative but uneasy grace.

Process/psychoanalytic accounts of women's experience
This interest in exploring a feminist version of the 'relational self', in both its ontological and historicist dimensions, also structures the reflections of feminist process theologians. As representative texts in this rapidly expanding field, Rita Brock's *Journeys by Heart* and Catherine Keller's *From a Broken Web* both offer influential accounts of this relation-seeking, 'connective' self, accounts which, like Johnson's and LaCugna's, emphasize the interactive character of identity formation, the embodied quality of human

experience, and the uniquely eschatological orientation of the self toward God. Insofar as they remain committed to describing such general features of human experience, they also share with Johnson and LaCugna universalizing structures which organize this relational self. As process thinkers, however, the conceptual resources which fund their depiction of the relational self are quite different from phenomenology. In the case of both Brock and Keller, these resources are of two basic sorts: *process metaphysics* and the conceptual world of *psychoanalytic discourse*.

[. . .]

Literary/textual constructions of women's experience
The third type of situating framework used by womanist and feminist theologies is one I refer to as a *textual* or *literary* framework. In contrast to the two previous groups of books, the texts which exemplify this dynamic, Delores Williams's *Sisters in the Wilderness* and Sallie McFague's *The Body of God*, clearly do not employ methodological strategies that tie the notion of experience to either an underlying set of philosophical principles or a founding ontology. These theologies are thus remarkably free of references to the subject, the self, consciousness, and ontic relationality. Having detached experience from a static conceptual edifice, however, these theologies neither abandon it altogether nor leave it floating free and ambiguous. To the contrary, both Williams and McFague remain committed to articulating thick accounts of the multiple experiences which presently provide contexts for North American theology. Where do they turn to generate the material necessary for such thick accounts? To literature, to language, to the multiple fields of cultural production which – in all their variety – form the linguistic contexts or paradigmatic frames within which experience occurs.

[. . .]

In *Sisters in the Wilderness*, Delores Williams offers her reader a deftly crafted and vividly painted account of the parallels between the biblical character of Hagar and modern 'African-American women's social identity'. As she moves between the biblical text and the modern context, she highlights a number of recurring themes which provide her with the basis for a compelling womanist critique of the servanthood/sacrifice images embedded in Anselmic strands of contemporary Christology. These resonating themes in African American women's experience – 'wilderness experiences', coerced surrogacy, survival strategies, and 'close personal relations with God' – are gleaned from several different textual sources which she combines to produce 'an historically realistic model of non-middle-class black womanhood'. It is a portrait which at once challenges the hegemony of cultural definitions of white, Victorian womanhood and gains critical leverage against persistent myths about black women's essential nature as mothers, workers, and believers.

Williams's contribution to contemporary theology, in this regard, cannot be overestimated, both with respect to the innovative method she offers and the doctrinal revisions she defends. In terms of method, Williams creatively demonstrates how diverse forms of African American women's literature (slave narratives, spirituals, novels, interviews, liturgies) can be used to reconstruct the lived experience of a community whose voice has seldom been figured into the dominant culture's assessment of 'Christian truth' and 'Christian faith experience'. In terms of doctrinal revisions, the powerful vision of faith that she pulls out of these materials is certain to leave its mark on contemporary discussions of 'the atonement' and 'servanthood' – just as her treatment of surrogacy is sure to inform present-day theological discussions of the connections between reproductive rights and race. It must also be said that because Williams's book is written in such accessible prose and addresses a number of currently pressing social questions, it promises to be one of those rare theological texts which is read not only outside the academy but in communities where it speaks directly to the audience it describes. For a work in liberation womanist theology, no single accomplishment could be more important.

As I suggest earlier, however, her use of textual materials is also not without its limitations. These limitations are of two basic sorts: first, Williams's tendency to make the meaning of the texts appear overly static, and second, her correlative tendency to then define the experience of 'black womanhood' in overly static – typologically rigid – terms. The first tendency is most apparent in the way she interprets the rich spectrum of literary materials which fund her descriptions of African American women's lived experience. Although Williams is sensitive to the context in which these various works were written, she often interprets these narratives as if they offer a transparent window onto a discursively stable reality, be it an antebellum tract describing 'black motherhood' or a modern study describing African American women's 'god-consciousness'. When she does so, the meaning of these particular texts appears to be unambiguous. Thus, Williams's own narrative overlooks questions about the texts' original social functions and multiple audiences; it misses questions about historical and geographic migrations of linguistic usage; and it never asks questions about textual play, indeterminacy, and silence. As recent literary-critical study on the slave narratives in particular has illustrated, asking these sorts of textual questions can serve to deepen and advance the emancipatory agenda of works such as those by Williams.

[. . .]

THE HARD PLACE

Thus far I have described three different conceptual rocks (universalizing frameworks) to which the term *experience* has been tied in recent feminist theologies. In the case of the phenomenologists and the process feminists, I have argued that although they free the concept of gender from weighty essentialisms, they nonetheless keep their concept of experience attached to what has become the new rock of feminist theology – relational ontology. In the case of the theologians who engage in literary analysis, I have argued that although they clearly intend their analysis to assist in historicizing the concepts of gender and experience, they nonetheless seek to excavate static meanings out of the texts they use – an undertaking which runs counter to their otherwise deeply constructivist sensibilities.

These three essentializing frameworks, however, do not exhaust the conceptual possibilities presently available for theorizing experience in feminist theology. In the past five years, several texts have appeared in which 'women's experience' remains a normative category of analysis but that emphasize the historical and cultural texture of identity and language. As I stated earlier, these texts can be roughly divided into two groups: those which use the tools of cultural anthropology to generate thick descriptions of communal experiences, and those which draw on the insights of post-structuralism to shape their analysis of identity, language, and power. Again, I refer to this side of the map as a hard place because the issues confronting those who stand here are numerous – establishing the status of normative claims, measuring the value of immanent critique, and assessing the political viability of localized descriptions and deconstructive rhetoric.

Cultural-anthropological accounts of women's experience

In the first group of texts, those which use the tools of cultural anthropology to analyze experience, I locate the recent work of Kathryn Tanner, *The Politics of God*, and the work of Ada María Isasi-Díaz, *En la lucha*. Although these texts represent two distinct genres of theological discourse, they share a commitment to opening up the emancipatory potential of Christianity by noting the shifting cultural functions religious beliefs serve in different Christian communities. This shared interest also signals their general agreement on two related points: that experience is best described by reference to culturally specific forms of life, and that language is best understood by reference to the work it does – in other words, by reference to its sociolinguistic function.

In *The Politics of God*, Tanner develops a sociocultural understanding of doctrine by offering her reader a tightly argued, metatheoretical, and metahistorical analysis of the relation between belief and practice. Her analysis of this relation is based on the observation that in the history of doctrinal developments, the relationship between faith claims and social practice is ever changing. She argues this point by considering, as just one example, the diverse political sensibilities articulated by Christian communities who assert the absolute transcendence of God, and points out that when an oppressed group uses this belief to contest the absolute authority of an earthly ruler, its political use is subversive, whereas the same belief, when used by an elite to sanction its power, elicits social practices which support the status quo.

Tanner further argues that once one begins to appreciate the complexity of this relation between belief and practice, one's understanding of the meaning and use of traditional doctrines begins to shift. Tanner hopes that when this shift occurs, liberal Christians might begin to reassess their relation to oppressive doctrines within the tradition. To this end, she suggests that it may be possible to use seemingly conservative doctrines to bolster, in surprising ways, a progressive Christian ethic. As an example of such a use, she shows how the hierarchical logics of divine sovereignty and providence can be used, when effectively situated, not to foster a politics of exclusionary hierarchy, but rather to garner support for a constructive, feminist politics of difference.

However, just as Tanner's analysis of doctrine shows the agility of a theology which is not tied to essentializing rocks, her discussion also offers a glimpse of some of the hard places which attend theology of this type. In Tanner's case, two specific difficulties emerge. The first concerns the 'meta' character of her postmodernist sensibilities. In reading Tanner's text, one cannot help but be impressed with her grasp of historic Christian doctrines and her subtle estimations of culture and language. But her facility for mapmaking keeps her strangely distanced from the beliefs and practices she charts. This postmodern version of a 'view from nowhere' is evidenced by the fact that her map never dips into the messy lived experience of the cultural actors she describes – an odd absence given her insistence that cultural specificity be considered in assessing the function of doctrine. By holding the specificity of particular voices at bay, she prevents one from hearing the imaginative insights that such voices bring to theology, insights that often do not 'fit' into the forms of traditional doctrines nor into her estimated calculus of belief and practice.

Second, Tanner's project provides an excellent model of how liberation theology might continue to profit from immanent critiques of the tradition using internally generated norms as the basis for a rigorous self-evaluation of belief and action. Alongside this view of tradition and critique, however, one might ask if there are other ways to understand cultural transformation. Is it possible to hold, as Tanner does, that the normative force of tradition/language can never be completely escaped, and yet simultaneously affirm the possibility of ruptures within the tradition, where fresh theological ground is broken – ground beyond the terrain of historical doctrines? Although Tanner herself would probably not reject this possibility, I use her text to make a point: namely, if the projects of feminist theologians who engage in internal critique cannot accommodate the new – the emergent voice – then they may well end up replacing the essentializing rocks of foundational philosophy with potentially rocklike descriptions of tradition and doctrine.

If Tanner provides an example of a theologian using a cultural-linguistic framework to chart grand maps, then Ada María Isasi-Díaz provides an example of a theologian using the same framework to opposite ends, using it to explore the particular, uneven, and conflicted terrain of a specific community's lived experience. In *En la lucha*, Isasi-Díaz continues the task of engaging in a liberation theological analysis that avoids essentializing or universalizing experience by its focus on the unique ways in which cultural practices and religious languages have served to constitute the richly textured identities of North American Hispanic women. Her commitment to avoiding universal claims about Latinas is evident in the mosaic quality of her text, pieced together from the diverse voices of Hispanic women she interviews and from the different social theories which she uses to situate their lives. It is also a mosaic whose coherence rests in Isasi-Díaz's stated goal: to reflect back theologically to the community a voice that will empower its speakers to be subjects of their own lives and agents of their own history.

Perhaps the most remarkable methodological feat of Isasi-Díaz's book is the degree to which she keeps a notion of 'women's experience' alive and working without anchoring it in any one analytic scheme or single textual meaning. This lively view of experience allows her to perform a difficult balancing act with regard to the relation between thick description and normative generalities. On the one hand, she adamantly refuses to eclipse substantive differences between Latinas. On the other hand, she acknowledges the pragmatic value of identifying shared 'generative themes' which serve as the basis for a common, liberatory vision. Among such themes are first, the conception of *proyecto histórica*, a strategic eschatology of liberation; and second, the lived experience of *mestizaje*, the embracing and celebrating of diversity. Both of these themes provide Isasi-Díaz with a hermeneutical key for reinterpreting theological themes such as moral agency, truth, and difference in a manner which accords with *mujerista* experiences.

What remains to be seen, however, is how this lively conception of Hispanic women's social experience will fare when Isasi-Díaz, in her future work, turns her attention from theological method to theological construction. At this point, she has set the stage for such work, but what it will actually look like remains unclear. Will she be able to glean from her interviews with Hispanic women all the material she needs for rethinking such topics as creation, salvation, and Christology? If she can, will she be able to maintain such a deeply communal understanding of truth and value when dealing with topics which have traditionally required one to make not only universal but also objective claims about God and the world? And finally, if and when she steps onto the terrain of normative claims, will she provisionally gesture toward the rocks of essentialism (maybe even a relational ontology), particularly if they are communally generated essentialisms which serve the strategic ends of liberation? For answers to these questions, we will have to wait and see where her project will move in the future and where this ethnographic-cultural trajectory as a whole will lead as it develops in the context of *mujerista*, womanist, and feminist agendas.

Poststructuralist accounts of women's experience

In addition to this sociocultural perspective, recent years have seen a flourishing of feminist and womanist texts which attempt to move beyond essentialized conceptions of experience by deploying the eclectic tools and insights of poststructuralist theory. I wish to highlight the term *eclectic* to emphasize that for the theologians I would locate here – Rebecca Chopp, Mary Fulkerson, Susan Thistlethwaite, and Emilie Townes – poststructuralism provides, in broad strokes, the dramatic plot line of their analysis, but it does not serve the explanatory or empirically invested function that the cultural-linguistic tools give Tanner and Isasi-Díaz. For this reason, the theologians I locate here quite freely employ an eclectic array of conceptual tools whose final coherence rests not on an analytic scheme but on the ability of the tools to illuminate the central theological drama of their texts. For the purposes of this review, I will look at only one of these projects as a way of introducing what is still a nascent conversation.

In Chopp's text, *The Power to Speak*, the theological vision stretches not only across a number of doctrinal loci, ranging from scriptural hermeneutic to sin and ecclesiology, but also into a number of modernity's favored themes: the subject, language, politics, history, and power. Chopp draws the basic insight which drives this vision from a gendered analysis of the structural drama of discourse. According to the French theorists from whom Chopp draws, the dramatic logic of Western conceptions of language is one in which linguistic definition and order are established by setting up margins and backgrounds which give 'meaning' its contour and edges, but only by virtue of the position these margins occupy as 'other' to the central term. Following the example of Hélène Cixous, Julia Kristeva, and to a lesser degree Luce Irigaray, Chopp attributes a distinctly gendered play to this dynamic, naming the ordered definition as masculine and the margin of otherness as feminine. She then makes the observation that in the discourse of 'theology proper', as in all the dominant discourses of our culture, there is a repressed margin which, standing on the edge of language, marks the space of women's eclipsed theological voice. The task Chopp takes up in this text lies in articulating the emancipatory possibilities this voice from the margin holds for theology. According to Chopp, this emerging voice disrupts theological order and meaning and celebrates difference as it moves and dances on the borders of time and space. It is thus a voice which speaks freedom and authors new communities of emancipatory practice.

One of the most powerful aspects of Chopp's account of this voice is the lively presence in the text of her own voice – a voice which plays with genre in order to capture a cadence and a rhythm which contrast well with the disinterested, well-ordered voice of academic theology. In this regard, she shares Isasi-Díaz's view that feminist theologians need to honor, as best they can, the unique discursive practices of the historically marginal voices they seek to empower, for both believe that it is in the play of these voices that feminist theologians will find their freshest and most imaginative resources for a deep reconstruction of Christian doctrine. In contrast to the more static interpretations of McFague and Williams, both Chopp and Isasi-Díaz try to honor these voices by celebrating their instabilities as well as their thematic generalities.

Chopp's attempt to generate creative insights from the 'other world' of marginal voices also stands as an interesting counterpoint to Tanner's strategic preference for critiquing the 'tradition' *not* by speaking from its borders, but by recalculating the logic of its shifting centers. It is in the face of this strategic difference that the fragility and ambiguity of Chopp's project most clearly surface – just as Chopp's project betrays the limits of Tanner's. From the perspective of immanent critique, there are at least two issues one must raise. First, although Chopp is not naive about the possibility of getting completely outside the constraints of the dominant discourse, there are points in her text where she seems to overestimate how far 'out' this speaking voice of women is actually able to travel in its resistance. It is when she invokes a space not unlike Cixous's *écriture féminine* that this overestimated leap appears most clearly. In that space beyond – where bones dance and difference is celebrated – the rhetoric of the possible, the new, and the subversive becomes so strong that the burdensome weight of our constitutive histories, our institutional forms, and our tedious traditions and languages seems to fade and then disappear. While it is obvious that Chopp does not intend to underestimate the power of this weight, the aesthetic quality of the text may tend in this direction nonetheless and, in doing so, cut against the more pragmatic, historical dimensions of her analysis.

Related to this issue is a second one concerning the practical ends of this type of poststructuralist project. Is Chopp's 'positionally marginal' voice capable of actually sustaining the strategic end to which it speaks, the goal of emancipatory transformation? Can this often ephemeral, fragmented, evocative – but slippery – rhetoric accomplish its tasks? Although there is obviously no one answer to this question, one must consider it carefully in light of two potential critiques of such endeavors. First, given the nature of her stated audience – postmodern, First World Christians – does she move too far beyond the strictures of tradition to speak to them intelligibly?

Does her project work best for poststructuralist converts? The answer is not clear, for the book has already been used to great effect in contexts where the term *poststructuralism* has never been spoken. Second, is a rhetoric which celebrates the fragmentation of the subject strategically well suited for persons who are struggling to claim a sense of wholeness and stability, having been oppressively fractured by their time on the margin? Again, there is no obvious answer to this question, and because Chopp is most likely aware of both critiques, she does us a great service by presenting a text where these issues can be directly engaged.

CONCLUSION

Having come to the end of my survey of the methodological differences which divide the present-day terrain of feminist, womanist, and *mujerista* theologies, what can be said in conclusion about its two sides, the rock and the hard place? First, it is clear that each side has its own strengths. For those theologians who build their projects on universal, foundational rocks, their constructive work in the area of Christian doctrine is refreshingly solid, strong, accessible, and steadily visionary. These works thus bespeak the confidence of a movement come of age; in doing so, they offer hope in a form of enduring wisdoms and sturdy graces. For theologians who stand in the hard place, their work remains restless and, as yet, lacking in constructive solidity, marking a place of healthy instability. Looking behind truths, testing the strength of goods, and pulling back edges in search of ever-retreating margins, these texts offer hope in the form of rupturing voices and more particularized graces.

Residing within the respective strengths of endurance and restlessness, however, one also finds, secondly, positions that warrant serious critique. For those who stand on universalizing rocks, the challenge of women's experiences which do not 'fit' into generalized categories of phenomenology, process metaphysics, psychoanalysis, or literary narrative will no doubt continue to make these foundationalists uneasy. Likewise, the pragmatic demand for sturdy visions and faith-filled truths will no doubt continue to keep those who stand in the hard places of cultural anthropology and poststructuralism wanting more substance than their methods seem able to deliver. In light of these tensions on both sides, it may well be that the still-uncharted chasm which stretches between the rock and hard place, a space which my map has only noted but not explored, will provide a space where our future conversations and struggles can unfold in as yet unexpected ways.

URSULA KING
'GENDER AND THE STUDY OF RELIGION'

Ursula King was born in Germany in 1938. She received her first degree, a licentiate in theology, from the Catholic University in Paris. She received an MA in philosophy from the University of Delhi and her PhD from the University of London. Since 1989 she has been a professor in the Department of Theology and Religious Studies at the University of Bristol. Her work has included theology, religious studies and feminist theory (in relation to religion and theology).

King's work included here is taken from a collection edited by her on feminist approaches to religion and gender. It presents a useful outline of the issues raised by feminism in relation to theories of religion and theology as well as a brief discussion of King's own definition of religion.

Gender issues are of great importance in contemporary society and culture. Although they concern both women and men, at present gender studies are still mainly focused on women because women have been voiceless for so long. Throughout most of human history there has existed an asymmetry in the relations of power, representation, knowledge and scholarship between men and women. Thus there exists a large agenda to be addressed in order to overcome women's invisibility, marginalization and subordination in history and society.

Gender has now become a critical category for the analysis of all data, including those of religion. At present most gender studies are almost identical with women's studies. Many current issues in the debates about women, their experience and self-understanding, status and role, are still influenced by or indirectly related to religious teachings and world-views, even when these are sharply criticized and rejected. At present there is often no recognition of women as agents and participants in their own right in most literature surveys in the field of religious studies. Frequently unexamined androcentric presuppositions underpinning the work of many male scholars cause serious deficiencies at the level of data gathering, model building and theorizing in religious studies. Despite this, many scholars continue to affirm their equally unexamined commitment to 'value neutrality' and 'objectivity'. Much of their sexism is not overt, but rather a 'sexism by omission'. They do not view their subject matter in relation to gender construction and traditional gender roles, both of which create uneven and unjust power structures.

Ursula King (1995), 'Introduction: gender and the study of religion', in Ursula King (ed.), *Religion and Gender*, Oxford: Blackwell.

In the past, women's religious roles and statuses have occasionally been an object of inquiry for male scholars but with the growth of critical feminist awareness and women's own scholarly development, women themselves are now both subjects as well as agents of scholarly analysis. The existence of women scholars and the critical transformation of their consciousness means that their research challenges the existing paradigms of religious studies because all phenomena are examined from the perspectives of gender and power. This has introduced an important paradigm shift in the contemporary study of religion, both in theology and in religious studies.

[. . .]

Gender and religion are closely interrelated as our perceptions of ourselves are shaped by and deeply rooted in our culturally shared religious and philosophical heritage, even when this is rejected. Religious traditions, beliefs and practices too are shaped by and perceived from the perspective of gender. Initially, this may be an unconscious process but with the contemporary growth of critical gender studies the transmission and perception of religious beliefs and the participation in religious activities have themselves become reflexive activities. Gender studies are beginning to make an impact on the contemporary study of religion and are setting new research agendas for religious studies. However, this is a slow process and the profoundly transformative effect of a basic paradigm shift has so far been less noticeable in religious studies than in other areas of the humanities.

[. . .]

Both religion and gender are widely ramified concepts which can be used in either a general or more specific sense. It is important that this multi-dimensionality is always kept in mind. The following discussion will look at religion [. . .], consider the impact of contemporary gender studies on religious studies, and examine the methodological and practical implications of the paradigm shift in religious studies brought about by the attention to gender.

RELIGION

What understanding of 'religion' is implicitly assumed or explicitly articulated when referring to 'religion and gender'? We are aware of the complexities attached to the definition of 'religion', the difficulties in using such a term cross-culturally, especially in the study of non-Western religions, and the dangers inherent in the reification of the concept 'religion' evident in recent Western history, as Cantwell Smith (1990) has so well demonstrated. But what new problems and difficulties or, alternatively, which new insights occur when the notion of 'religion' is linked to gender specific inquiries? Is the concept 'religion', then, used as traditionally defined by Western philosophy and theology, or is it arrived at by empirical induction? In other words, do we accept 'religion' as it has been historically and culturally evolved, as primarily a 'cumulative tradition', or is 'religion' rather understood as something experiential and personal, especially in relation to the personal experience of women and the different forms in which that experience finds its historical and contemporary expression? There is also the question of whether religion is mostly seen in terms of its institutional structures and historical-cultural embodiments which would require the investigation of gender-specific issues in very particular ways, or whether we can adopt in our research a much more open-ended, heuristic concept which enables us to investigate and explain particular activities of women (both past and present) as distinct from those of men. How far were women's religious experiences and activities important and meaningful without being recognized as such from the traditional point of view of the dominant religious institution(s)? It seems to me that different studies on women and religion adopt quite different understandings of the concept of 'religion' without necessarily discussing this: not all authors are methodologically critical and self-aware. I would like to underline the importance of the polysemic nature of the concept 'religion', especially in relation to gender issues. There is much talk today about the social, cultural and historical construction of gender, but such construction applies equally to the concept of 'religion'. Religion cannot be understood without its history and the multi-layered pluralism through which it has found complex social and cultural expression.

Religion is more than an object of study. It has been described as a core concern, as expressing and addressing the sacred, or as disclosing a transcendent focus linked to ultimate value. Religion has not only been the matrix of cultures and civilizations, but it structures reality – all reality, including that of gender – and encompasses the deepest level of what it means to be human. Thus the study of religion, as the study of all creative activities of human beings, involves one's own subjectivity and reflexivity. It therefore raises complex questions for methodology, i.e. *how* it can be most appropriately studied and known. From a perspective of critical gender analysis, established methodologies prove inadequate, as will be discussed below.

Both the deconstruction and reconstruction of religious studies as an established discipline and of 'religion' as a concept – a lived and shared reality, a humanly meaningful activity, associated with both very specific and also more general, universal meanings for women – are important intellectual goals to be arrived at in reflecting on the study of religion in relation to gender.

[. . .]

Gender and Religious Studies

In the area of religion more inclusive gender perspectives have been explored by several studies, as for example in Patricia Altenbernd Johnson's and Janet Kalven's (1988) edited volume *With Both Eyes Open: Seeing Beyond Gender*. More recently a substantial study of historical, cross-cultural and theological perspectives on gender relations has been produced as a team project edited by Mary Stewart Van Leeuwen et al. (1993) under the title *After Eden: Facing the Challenge of Gender Reconciliation*. Concerned with the 'decentring' of feminism, especially white, Western feminism, this project thoroughly explores the application of critical theory to gender relations and challenges the concepts of masculinity and femininity by laying bare the sources of gender brokenness in the Western world. Written from a Christian theological perspective the book examines ways of dealing with human difference by proposing a model of gender reconciliation grounded in a Christian feminist vision that embraces both women and men.

Caroline Walker Bynum, in her introduction to a volume on *Gender and Religion: The Complexity of Symbols* (Bynum et al. 1986) also argues for a comprehensive rather than an exclusively woman-centred approach in the study of gender by investigating how religious symbols relate to 'genderedness' – to people's experiences as females and males – rather than studying women's religious roles and behaviour only. It is no longer possible to study religious thought, language, practice and experience as well as religious symbols without taking gender into account, but it is still not enough to investigate the construction of gender and of gender-related symbols, which may function very differently in different religious traditions, by examining female experience alone. A larger agenda for the study of gender in religion is indicated by Bynum's statement:

> Gender-related symbols, in their full complexity, may refer to gender in ways that affirm or reverse it, support or question it; or they may, in their basic meaning, have little at all to do with male and female roles. Thus our analysis admits that gender-related symbols are sometimes 'about' values other than gender. But our analysis also assumes that all people are 'gendered'. It therefore suggests, at another level, that not only gender-related symbols but all symbols arise out of the experience of 'gendered' users. It is not possible ever to ask How does a symbol – *any* symbol – mean? without asking For whom does it mean? (Bynum et al. 1986: 2–3)

Put differently, many studies have demonstrated that while constructs of ultimate reality are conceived in a variety of ways and transcendence can be envisaged as male, female or androgynous, it is also seen as being beyond form and gender altogether. Yet at the empirical level world religions have 'maintained male social dominance in the prevailing social structure' (Young 1987: 7). Another important insight concerns the fact that while 'the transcendent may or may not have a gender component, the prominent soteriology of a world religion is always gender inclusive, even when the transcendent is a supreme male being' (Young 1987: 16). Most women scholars recognize the need to give priority to the female gender in their studies in order to invert the very asymmetrical treatment of women in the study of religion, but it must not be overlooked that the idea of genderedness has far wider ramifications than is often recognized at present.

The discussion so far has shown how the critical lens of gender can bring into view either a very specific or a more wide-ranging perspective. If the lens is one, it can yet centre on two different foci – the female or the male aspect of gender – or it can approach both together in their relational structure.

[. . .]

Theoretical developments have widened out from women's studies and feminist concerns to men's studies and more inclusive gender analyses. The significance of religion for gender formation and gender relations, and the impact of women's studies, feminism and gender studies on the study of religion, though relatively neglected in earlier discussions (Langland and Gove 1981; Spender 1981; Farnham 1987), is now much more widely acknowledged in general surveys on the cross-cultural study of women (Sinclair 1986) and in the social scientific analysis of gender (Briggs 1987). Yet in men's studies the area of religion seems to remain unexplored apart from the field of classical mythology where certain ideals of masculinity have their origin. However, I have yet to find a critical examination of the influence of religion on masculine gender construction. For this reason most of what follows is concerned with women.

In religious studies the scholarship on gender has so far been closely connected with developments in women's studies and contemporary feminist theories. In 1987 Constance H. Buchanan described women's studies in religion in an exemplary article in *The Encyclopedia of Religion* edited by Mircea Eliade (vol. 15, pp. 433–40); Rosemary Radford Ruether provided a similarly helpful entry on the presence of androcentrism in religion in the same work (vol. 1, pp. 272–6). These were the only two articles to explicitly examine the impact of feminism on the study of religion in this large contemporary reference work of sixteen volumes (for a feminist critique of *The Encyclopedia of Religion* see King 1990, 1995).

Buchanan succinctly summarized the magnitude of the critical and constructive tasks undertaken by women scholars in religion. The critical task implies a critique of both the religious and anthropological assumptions found in the different religions of the world. The task of reconstruction involves detailed historical research in order to uncover the voices, experiences and contributions of women in the religious history and life of humankind. It also implies a reconstruction of religious beliefs – 'the task of reweaving the sacred symbolic fabric of culture based on distinctive female experience' (Buchanan 1987: 437) – and the reconstruction of ethical thought as well as the creation of new religious worlds linked to women's spiritual quest and the celebration of the Goddess. Such critical reconstruction involves the deconstruction of false universalist claims relating to all women or all human beings. The development of feminist theory on gender, religion and culture is thoroughly cross-disciplinary: women scholars from different religious backgrounds are working on diverse religious traditions, drawing on methods and insights from several disciplines and gathering a new body of data which can form the starting point for further theoretical debates.

Also very helpful is the chapter on 'The scholarship of gender: women's studies and religious studies' in Anne E. Carr's (1990: 63–94) book *Transforming Grace: Christian Tradition and Women's Experience*. This demonstrates how the insights of feminist history and philosophy are applied to the study of religion. While emphasizing the need for a feminist perspective in teaching women's studies, the author warns against a false ghettoization of women's studies within the university curriculum. This leads on to a discussion of the concept of gender in terms of 'an implied, assumed or explicit *meaning* of sexual differentiation whenever the study of women (and men) is undertaken' (Carr 1990: 76).

Carr maintains that we have now reached a third stage of women's studies, which follows after a first stage of the deconstruction of error and a second stage of the reconstruction of reality from a feminist perspective. This third stage is devoted to the construction of general theories and seeks a unifying framework which may be developed around a more inclusive gender system. Carr also discusses some early examples of the critique of religious traditions and of the recovery of lost women's history in relation to Christianity. She argues for the development of an inclusive Western theology, not an exclusive feminist spirituality built on the new goddess movement.

The innovative research of women in religion means that:

> ... much of past scholarship is placed on a new map of religious reality. Less than half the story has been told. To begin to tell the other part is to acknowledge that women have always been involved (even when excluded or ignored) in everything human, in everything religious. As the distinct subject matter of women's studies is the experience of women, that of women's studies in religion is the religious experience, expression, and understanding of women. But the concept of gender reminds us that the experience of women has been and always is in relationship to men in the whole of human society. Thus women's studies affects the study of men (now seen as part of the whole), the

study of the human in its wholeness, and religious studies generally. That wider whole will not be fully understood, given the androcentric history of the disciplines, without women's studies as a subject matter in its own right and as a necessary transition to the transformation of scholarship and the university curriculum. (Carr 1990: 93)

Carr stresses the pluralism of questions and methods together with the feminist perspective or angle of vision which distinguish contemporary women's studies from any traditional study of women. To discover the experience of women some of the major questions in any period or area of study are:

What was/is happening to women, what were/are women doing and thinking, what was/is the relative status of women and men with regard to symbolization, valuation, creativity, participation, opportunity, power, institutional and informal support and constraint? What images of the female and the male are employed in any religious context, and how are these used? What are their practical effects? How is sexuality viewed? What issues of family and society, the public and the private, class and race, need to be taken into account? (Carr 1990: 93–4)

This quotation points implicity to the dual nature of gender: on the one hand it is only a partial factor in explaining reality, relating to other factors such as race, class, ethnicity, generation differences, etc., but on the other hand it is also all encompassing as far as social relations are concerned. We have two sexes, no more, and the complex aspects of engenderment affect all areas of human life, not least the complex worlds of religion.

[. . .]

FEMINIST METHODOLOGICAL DEBATES AND THE PARADIGM SHIFT IN RELIGIOUS STUDIES

Methodological debates among contemporary women scholars in religion are much influenced by current feminist theory which fundamentally calls into question the basic assumptions of the prevailing organization of knowledge, its claims to universality, objectivity and value-neutral detachment.

In the study of religion and gender two fundamental problems arise for feminist scholars. One has to do with the subject matter of the research, the other with the attitude of the researcher. As to the subject matter, most religious phenomena, even when studied by women, still remain set in the context of an androcentric framework which defines our intellectual task in the very effort of deconstruction and reconstruction. The sources, concepts, models and theories of religious studies are male-derived and male-centred; they operate with a generic masculine which implies that men have almost always spoken for and about women. Even when studying the history, literature and religious experience of women themselves, we have to rely to a great extent on the materials and data described by men. The sacred writings of the world religions are all thoroughly androcentric. However, women are not only readers of androcentric texts, they are also writers and creators of such texts when they are schooled in and express themselves through the dominant modes of thinking of their age. Dissenting voices can be heard in the past, but they are few. A fully articulated critical consciousness of women has only developed in our own time and contemporary feminist 'gynocritics' (Showalter 1986: 128), or what I prefer to call the gynocritical approach, is particularly interested in women as *writers*, that is women who as their own agents create their own structures of meaning. In religious studies such a gynocritical approach means that women scholars analyse and interpret religious phenomena specifically associated with, experienced, articulated and described by women.

As to the attitude of the researcher, there already exists a lively, wide-ranging methodological debate in contemporary religious studies in general. This is concerned with determining the most appropriate methods for studying religion. Many different approaches and positions are debated, such as that of insider and outsider, neutrality and commitment, for example. Many scholars criticize the over-intellectualist and heavily text-orientated approaches of traditional religious studies; many are beginning to recognize that the study of religion, especially of religious experience, involves one's own subjectivity and reflexivity. The religious position and commitment of the researcher can thus influence the subject matter that is being researched. However, the current general methodological debates in religious studies do not yet take into account the specific methodological insights and realignments found among feminist scholars.

Women's profoundly new experience of critical personal, social and religious transformation makes them ask challenging and uncomfortable questions. Critically aware of their own positioning in society, they question the existing structure of knowledge and their own place in it. The process of consciousness-raising has led women to the discovery of self autonomy and self agency, but also to that of solidarity and relationality. From the perspective of these experiences women criticize the suppression of personal, subjective human experience in general and of women's experience in particular in what traditionally counts as knowledge. Attention to gender is beginning to reshape both the perception of and the participation in knowledge. In the study of religion it is therefore no longer enough to ask *what* we know about religion, but equal attention must be paid to how we come to know what we know. Feminist research in religion has epistemological significance [...] Critical attention to gender variables not only affects the analysis of religious texts, but it also raises many questions about conceptual categories governing the gathering of data in fieldwork.

[. . .]

Women scholars are searching for a more experientially grounded, more gender balanced and more dialogical methodology. In doing so, they still have to argue for a feminist perspective of gender analysis which cannot yet be taken for granted. Debates about the challenge of feminist methodological insights for the transformation of religious studies have been going on since the early 1970s. Yet so far mainstream methodological works have simply ignored them. Could this perhaps have something to do with the fact that detailed textual work and revision appear to be less threatening and more acceptable to male scholars than theoretical and interpretative work which reflects women's original and independent thinking?

Without claiming to be comprehensive I shall list some significant discussions on methodology. Rosemary Radford Ruether (1981) published an early article on 'The feminist critique in religious studies'. It focuses largely on the Judeo-Christian tradition and on theology rather than the more inclusive concerns of religious studies. But unlike other writings on the same subject, it raises the important question of how women's studies in religion can be translated into educational praxis in institutions of higher learning in terms of both curriculum development and staff appointments.

Other publications on methodology, criticizing the prevalent androcentrism in the history of religions, came from Rita M. Gross (1974, 1977, 1983) who must be recognized as a lonely pioneer in calling so early for a fundamental reorientation of the whole field of religious studies. I discussed her earlier work in my paper 'Female identity and the history of religions' (King 1986), first delivered at the XIVth International Congress of the History of Religions in 1985. In it I emphasized that the feminist perspective is not yet part of the common horizon of religious studies and I argued 'that the development of a truly inclusive framework for the study of religion, of more differentiated conceptual tools as well as of different perspectives of analysis and synthesis requires that full space is given to the voices and perspectives of women' (King 1986: p. 91). Women scholars in religion work in relative isolation. They can experience crises of identity due to the absence of role models and of a well-established community of discourse in their field. There exists also a continuing silence about the contribution of women scholars to the study of religion in the past.

[. . .]

The importance of methodological clarifications and of a basic shift in orientation is highlighted by numerous articles which the *Journal of Feminist*

Studies in Religion has published since its foundation in 1985. Its second number included a roundtable discussion 'On feminist methodology' (Fiorenza et al. 1985) and a later volume presented another one on 'A vision of feminist religious scholarship' (Schechter 1987). Other articles worth singling out are those by Carol P. Christ on 'Embodied thinking: reflections on feminist theological method' (1989) and on 'Mircea Eliade and the feminist paradigm shift' (1991).

Such methodological articles are evidence of how feminist scholarship makes use of alternative, non-traditional sources and methods which in turn produce alternative contents and structures in scholarly knowledge. The feminist paradigm in religious studies is one of transformation. Its critique of the traditional sources and content of an established field involves an alternative vision which transforms both the subject matter and the scholar at the same time.

The methodological process can be summed up as starting with a hermeneutics of suspicion *vis-à-vis* traditional sources and methods, followed by a critical deconstruction and reconstruction of the key elements of the discipline, eventually resulting in its transformation. The close alliance between feminism as an academic method and social vision born out of a new experience and consciousness has been challengingly expressed by Rita Gross, especially in the two methodological appendices of her book *Buddhism after Patriarchy* (1993). Her scholarly self-understanding and commitment is deeply rooted in a feminist perspective which leads to a large increase in the data to be studied and also to an increase in the critical reflection on the nature of religion and on the most appropriate methods for its study. Gross argues that religion is not reducible to its cultural matrix, but that the religious impulse for world-construction, for seeking meaning and orientation, constitutes an inalienable part of human life.

From her stance as an engaged, committed woman scholar she also argues against the division of the study of religion into separate, narrow theological and historical subdisciplines. The attitude of the scholar must in her view be one of empathy and commitment while maintaining honesty and objectivity in the sense of declaring one's interests and methodologies. As a feminist engaged in the cross-cultural study of religion Gross speaks of a 'double assignment' which on one hand requires to explain the world-view of patriarchy with empathy, yet on the other hand refuses to undertake scholarship 'that extends, perpetuates, legitimates, or justifies patriarchy' which she considers as a destructive traditional religious value that must be exposed (Gross 1993: 315). Her feminist and scholarly experience and reflection converge in her conclusion that the 'engaged study of religion, with its combination of dispassionate de-absolutized understanding and passionate existential commitment to just and humane values, is the single most powerful lens through which one can view religion' (Gross 1993: 317).

Much important work based on critical gender analysis exists in the contemporary study of religion. Yet one can still argue over the question of whether a paradigm shift in religious studies has already occurred or whether we are only at the threshold of a new paradigm. Feminist scholarly commitment expressed in both women's studies and wider gender studies requires nothing less than the transformation of the author's world-view and scholarship. The process of this transformation becomes visible at different levels: at that of one's personal existential and spiritual quest, at the level of scholarly discourse and knowledge construction, and also in the critique of whole religious systems. Numerous examples for these different forms of transformation can be found in contemporary scholarship on different religious traditions.

Some years ago Randi R. Warne (1989), when assessing the impact of women's studies on religious studies, spoke of moving 'toward a brave new paradigm'. She saw this move as occurring in three different areas: (1) in women asking new questions of traditional materials; (2) in the move from universality to particularity, from abstraction to engagement; (3) in the critique of objectivity and the revisioning of all knowledge as morally significant, thus raising basic questions about the nature of all knowledge. Critical feminist and gender perspectives are certainly much debated and attest to a profound transformative potential in their effect on traditional forms of knowledge. How far these debates have made a real impact on the dominant practitioners of the field and changed the way religion is studied in universities is another matter, however. Carol Christ, who has written on the feminist paradigm shift in religious studies more than once (Christ 1987b, 1991), still describes the field of religious studies as highly patriarchal and speaks of feminist scholars in religion as 'sojourners for a long time to come' (Christ 1992: 87). Women's critical debates are set 'within an academic power structure which is not only male, but white, heterosexual, middle and upper class, for the most part Christian, and not particularly hospitable to feminism' (Christ 1992: 86). Thus she concludes that a great deal remains to be done if feminist scholarship is to transform the teaching and research of religious studies in universities, although research and reflection on women and religion are flourishing both inside and outside the academic world.

Feminist scholarship offers exciting critical perspectives and, as mentioned earlier, these critical perspectives are also foundational for contemporary men's studies and the development of more inclusive gender studies. To maintain this critical momentum and challenge, to put into practice the transformative potential of such critical insights, necessitates that neither women's nor men's studies are ghettoized, and that gender studies are not simply reduced to 'blender studies', as Mary Daly maintains. A successful development of inclusive, balanced critical gender studies requires also a balanced gender representation and the full participation of both genders in all areas of religious studies – in religion as studied, taught, and practised. This requirement raises many practical questions, not least about institutional power and teaching authority. As Randi Warne has pointed out, to meet the challenge of women's studies, religious studies 'must ensure that its departments are materially constructed in such a way that the presumption of male privilege is not maintained' (Warne 1989: 43). Will feminist scholars always remain sojourners in the field of religious studies or will they on the contrary soon become fully established citizens and inheritors of a whole field and its wide-ranging cluster of inquiries? This is a legitimate contemporary concern which invites further reflection.

[. . .]

CONCLUSION

As this essay has tried to show, critical attention to gender variables provides such a significant new orientation for the contemporary study of religion that one can justifiably speak of a paradigm shift in the entire field of religious studies. The important impact of gender on current theoretical and empirical work and on methodological debates provides us with critical tools for an alternative vision and different scholarly praxis which are beginning to transform and reconceptualize the study of religion.

Looking at religion through the sharp lenses of gender first developed by feminist theory produces a genuine advance in the intellectual processes, explanations and results of scholarship. Women's insights, academic inquiries and research efforts are currently at the cutting edge of contemporary scholarship. It is crucial that the knowledge gained is integrated into mainstream teaching and research without losing its critical edge and impact.

Considering the implications of the feminist paradigm for the contemporary study of religion, what are the possible directions for religious studies in the near future? It is impossible to prophesy, but it is clear that we need far more women scholars in the study of religion – ideally 50 per cent in all teaching and research positions – to effect not only a paradigm shift, but to get our new paradigm universally accepted and thereby transform our discipline more radically. In the view of some scholars, current studies on women and religion represent one of the liveliest, most creative and challenging developments in contemporary religious studies. Yet such studies are far from being given general academic recognition and acceptance. Some of the liveliest debates at present concern God-language, feminist ethics, feminist spirituality, religious attitudes to the body and sexuality, the relationship between feminism, religion and psychoanalysis. In feminist theology there is the additional significance of Third World theology which increasingly attracts attention (Russell et al. 1988; King 1994). There is also fascinating new work being developed on feminism, religion and ecology (Primavesi 1991; Ruether 1992; Adams 1993).

In looking for a future research agenda for religious studies we must also bear in mind that the feminist critical approach to the study of religion represents a paradigm shift *within* another paradigm shift which is larger still. This is the new discourse and consciousness about globality and globalization which has emerged over the last few years and which is of deep significance for religion as practised and studied, especially for spirituality. It is because of this global perspective that the theology of women from the Third World is of such great importance.

At present, the notion of difference and pluralistic diversity among women is widely discussed among feminists, but many of these discussions still remain too confined to local and regional boundaries. Women's studies are far from truly inclusive of all women, far from being comprehensive and global. This may be illustrated by just one example where others could be given. In a survey tracing the development of women's studies in religion Judith Plaskow (1993) strongly affirms that feminist work in religion belongs to a larger universe of feminist discourse, yet the universe surveyed by her is entirely restricted to North America (though it includes a few Asian women scholars teaching in the United States). North American studies on women and religion are leading in the field, but many of them suffer from their own parochialism by limiting their discussion only to other North American authors. Plaskow's (1993) article does not cite a single non-American publication and one may legitimately ask how representative her presentation of the development of women's studies in religion is. Such studies now have a truly global dimension and include publications from many countries, in many different languages, and on many different traditions.

It is impossible to develop thoughts on religion and gender in a global perspective further here, but globalization as a process whereby we become conscious of the whole world as a single place – a unity created by the bonds of one human family – has deep ramifications for feminism, gender and religion. In the future this may bring with it a further shift from woman-centred approaches to the study of religion – where religious thought, language, practice and structures are primarily examined with reference to women – to a wider focus on religion and gender where the field is enlarged to include critically reflected data about both sexes rather than about women alone.

Feminist critical analysis has called into question the false universalism of androcentric thinking. Women must not commit the mistake now of constructing a new, false universalism of a different sort on the basis of female experience alone. We are faced with the difficulty that the notion of gender, though applicable to both sexes, is currently mostly investigated with regard to women. Women scholars, for fairly obvious reasons, concentrate their research on women; it is not their main task to critically investigate gender issues as they arise for men. Men have to do this for themselves. The next step in further reconstruction will be an additional phase of integration where female and male gender issues are brought into fruitful relationship with each other. Only then can we fully understand the complex interconnections between gender and power; and only then can we develop the strength and wisdom needed to shape the human community in a more just and balanced way and thereby radically transform the social order at both a local and global level.

ROSALIND SHAW
'FEMINIST ANTHROPOLOGY AND THE GENDERING
OF RELIGIOUS STUDIES'

Rosalind Shaw received her BA and PhD from the University of London. She is currently Associate Professor of Anthropology at Tufts University. Shaw's monographs have dealt with syncretism in religion and more recently the issue of memory in relation to the slave trade.

The paper by Shaw included here presents a critique of the phenomenological study of religion, particularly in relation to the work of Eliade. She particularly challenges the phenomenologists' claims to universalism and the androcentric nature of their analyses due to the selection of sources and the acceptance of hierarchical claims to authority.

Feminist projects of disciplinary transformation may be caught up in contradictions arising from the histories of the disciplines in which change is sought. In the history and phenomenology of religions, problems of disciplinary transformation appear to extend far beyond the difficulties of eradicating 'male bias' or of including women's standpoints. Such transformation may entail nothing less than the dissolution and reconstruction of the discipline itself. In anthropology, attempts to effect a feminist metamorphosis in the 1970s and early 1980s were subject to contradictions whose identification and critique by Strathern (1981, 1987) assisted scholars in rethinking the relationship between feminism and anthropology. Strathern's characterization of the 'awkward relationship' between anthropology and feminism finds important parallels in the history of religions, and her critiques may usefully be applied to certain forms of feminist religious studies today.

Strathern (1987) characterizes feminism and anthropology as close neighbours, enmeshed in a relationship of mutual mockery. They do not so much contradict as 'mock' each other, she argues, because each so nearly attains the ideal which eludes the other. On the one hand, anthropologists have a comparative perspective which can give them a critical distance from dominant Euro-American understandings of gender and women's power – a distance which is highly valued in much of feminist thought. On the other hand, anthropologists are striving to reform anthropology from the conditions of its production, in which knowledge has been constituted within unequal power relationships between white Western anthropologists and colonized peoples of the Third World, among whom most anthropologists have worked. Anthropologists' struggles to effect a shift from a 'view from

Rosalind Shaw (1995), 'Feminist anthropology and the gendering of religious studies', in Ursula King (ed.), *Religion and Gender*, Oxford: Blackwell.

above' in order to reinvent anthropology contrast sharply with the apparent ease with which feminist scholars have assumed a 'view from below', in which relations of domination are analysed from a subordinate standpoint.

While anthropology 'mocks' feminism from its advantaged position for cultural critiques of Western social forms, then, feminism – from its own assumed standpoint of the subordinate's perspective – mocks anthropology. Anthropology can never really achieve its desired perspective of the 'view from below' until non-Western anthropologists have a stronger voice in its reinvention (see Moore 1989). Because of this mutual mockery, 'feminist anthropology' is, for Strathern, not quite an oxymoron, but a hybrid beast. The awkwardness between feminism and anthropology thus involves disjunctions which extend beyond the problems of introducing women's perspectives into a discipline with a history of 'male bias'. This is because other forms of domination – in particular those of colonialism and racism – are just as central as that of gender inequality to the relationship between feminist thought and anthropology.

The same could be said of those forms of domination implicit in the relationship between feminism and the history of religions, but the mockery here is one-sided. Like anthropology, the history of religions has a long tradition of a perspective which is valued highly in feminist scholarship. A hermeneutic approach which makes empathy with lived religious experience central to interpretation and comparison was developed in the history and phenomenology of religions when other disciplines were working through their positivist phases (see, for example, Dudley 1977; Allen 1978). Since critiques of positivism have been prominent in many strands of feminist epistemology, the history of religions could be said to have had at its core an interpretive standpoint which many have seen as central to feminist scholarship.

But in practice, the history/phenomenology of religions is an apt illustration that a hermeneutic of empathy and experience is far from being automatically feminist. The question of *whose* subjective experience is being empathized with is crucial. All too typically, it is not that of real persons but of a 'collective subject' whose supposedly authoritative experience is either undifferentiated by gender, race, class or age, or defined explicitly as male. In particular, the writings of Eliade and his followers are premised upon this collective subject, usually known as '*homo religiosus*':

> Eliade understood that religious man will take a wife, build a house, make love, raise children, eat, sleep, go to war, make peace, and prepare for death out of [a] felt relationship to the gods, and what he believes they expect of him. (Idinopulos 1994: 72)

What does 'lived religious experience' *mean* when it is located in a purportedly universal subject? And how universal can this impersonal subject be when represented through such unabashedly gender-specific depiction? In this totalizing but exclusionary empathy for a reified *homo religiosus*, the mockery of feminism by the history of religions – like the mockery of feminism by anthropology – falls flat.

This mockery, moreover, is not reciprocated. Those in mainstream history of religions have not typically striven for ideals represented by feminist scholarship. Allen, for example, draws attention to feminist critiques of Eliade (such as Saiving 1976), and observes that 'one would never guess from Eliade's treatment that androcentrism and a theologically misogynist tradition, that patriarchal structures of exploitation and oppression, were key notions in the interpretation of witchcraft' (Allen 1978: 117–18). Yet he does so merely to make a point about the perspectival nature of knowledge; he cites such critiques 'not...so much...to show that Eliade's scale is explicitly androcentric, but rather that his perspective emphasizes certain notions and overlooks or de-emphasizes other dimensions of the phenomena' (Allen 1978:118–19). But to argue that the standpoint of mainstream history and phenomenology of religions and the stand-point of feminist critiques are merely two perspectives among many misses the point of such critiques: it is not just that all knowledge is partial, but that some perspectives represent a 'view from above'. In the history of religion, a 'view from above' is entrenched through, first, the overwhelming emphasis given to religious texts and, second, the concept of the *sui generis* nature of religion, in which religion is treated as a discrete and irreducible phenomenon which exists 'in and of itself'. Feminist scholarship can only collide with, rather than mock, mainstream history of religions: not only has the latter had a very poor record of overhauling itself in terms of critiques 'from below', but its central *sui generis* argument is incompatible with the very basis of such critiques.

The 'Distinctively Religious' and the Distinctly Apolitical

Both the textual and the *sui generis* definitions emphasized in religious studies scholarship are, in practice, 'bracketing' devices which support each other in representing religion as socially decontextualized and ungendered. Understandings of 'religion as scripture' tend, for example, to privilege (a) religions with texts, and (b) scholarly elites within scriptural religious traditions who claim the authority to interpret texts (and from whom women are usually debarred). The religious understandings of those excluded from authorizing discourses of textual interpretation are implicitly discounted and relegated to a 'lower' level. To 'saby book', as the Nigerian participants in Hackett (1995) put it, has indeed been used to define the centre of religious traditions – as well as of the discipline concerned with their study – and to relegate women to the periphery. That strand of women's scholarship which simply presents accounts of 'women who wrote texts too' thus does little to recast this dominant focus. This orthodoxy has recently been challenged, however, by feminist studies which explore innovative ways of reading and critically interrogating scriptures and other texts (e.g. Fiorenza 1983; Atkinson et al. 1985).

Like the understanding of 'religion as text', the concept of the *sui generis* nature of religion also entails the decontextualization of religion. In mainstream history of religions, understandings of 'the uniquely religious' are usually constituted by excluding or peripheralizing social and political content in defining what really counts as 'religion'. Historians of religion who make the *sui generis* claim do not suggest 'pure religious' phenomena can exist empirically, but that

> certain experiences or phenomena exhibit a fundamental religious character and that our method must be commensurate with the nature of our subject-matter. From the perspective of the History of Religions, the sociological, economic, or anthropological dimensions of the phenomena are 'secondary'. (Allen 1978: 83–4)

Thus desocialized, 'the uniquely religious' is deemed interpretable only 'on its own terms': studies of religion which entail social or political analysis are typically dismissed as reductionist. Eliade, who more than anyone else has defined this dominant 'antireductionist' discourse in the history of religions, offers the following axiom:

> A religious phenomenon will only be recognized as such if it is grasped at its own level, that is to say, if it is studied *as* something religious. To try to grasp the essence of such a phenomenon by means of physiology, psychology, sociology, economics, linguistics, art or any other is false. (Eliade, 1963, p. xiii)

As some of the contributors to a recent volume on reductionism and religion (Idinopulos and Yonan 1994) point out, such essentializing assumptions close off the potentially awkward question of what 'the nature of religion' is:

> If I am right about the intellectual history of the notion of religion, it has shifted several times in the last hundred years already ... Eliade slams the door shut on possible competitors to his own 'spiritualist' position. Instead, he just insists on the identity of religious phenomena by appeal to 'what they are ...' But 'what they are' is or should be an open question; Eliade's anti-reductionist (by replacement) stance rejects alternatives out of hand. (Strenski, 1994, p. 101; see also Segal, 1989, 1994)

Since 'religion' as a category is not indigenous to most parts of the world, moreover, the *sui generis* concept often involves the imposition of 'the irreducibly religious' upon a landscape of human practices and understandings which do not divide up into the categories cherished by Western scholars.

As part of its discouragement of debates about 'the nature of religion', the discourse of irreducibility also deflects questions of power and inequality: the 'distinctively religious' is constituted as distinctly apolitical. Eliade writes, for example:

> Few religious phenomena are more directly and more obviously connected with socio-political circumstances than the modern messianic and millenarian movements among colonial people (cargo-cults, etc.). Yet identifying and analyzing the conditions that prepared and made possible such messianic movements form only a part of the work of the historian of religions. For these movements are equally creations of the human spirit, in the sense that they have become what they are – religious movements, and not merely gestures of protest and revolt – through a creative act of the spirit. (Eliade 1969: 6)

Eliade leaves us in no doubt that for him 'mere gestures of protest and revolt' are not part of the creative repertoire of 'the human spirit'. But for those within millenarian movements, politics and protest are *implicated in the very constitution* of their religious practice. Their experience of colonial power is 'interior' to – not somehow detachable from – their lived religious experience. Power, then, cannot simply be bracketed off as a 'dimension' or 'aspect' of religion (see Shaw and Stewart 1994).

To take another example, attempting to understand a woman's experience of religion in terms of (not just 'in the context of') her position within a male-dominated religious tradition is reductionist only if we have severed 'religion' from 'power' in the first place. On the contrary, it *would* be a 'reduction' – in the rather different sense of a diminished and distorted representation of her experience – to bracket off 'male dominance' and 'gender asymmetry' as a mere biographical backdrop to, but not really part of, experiences which she calls 'religious'. With power and social organization detached from the analysis of gender and religion, we are left either with meaningless accounts of 'religious gender roles' ('the men do this; the women do that'), or with disconnected descriptions of female deities ('add goddesses and stir').

The *sui generis* concept thus stands in a contradictory relationship to the premises of feminist scholarship. By making power irrelevant to 'the nature of religion', it denies the scholar of religion a language with which to make a critique 'from below', relegating the very basis of a distinction between a 'view from above' and a 'view from below' to the realm of crass reductionism. By making it central to their discourse, scholars in the history of religions are effectively insulated from uncomfortable questions about standpoint and privilege – questions upon which feminist scholarship is based. The relationship between feminism and mainstream history of religions is not merely awkward; it is mutually toxic.

INSTITUTIONAL EMBATTLEMENT AND THE POLITICS OF INTERPRETATION

The concept of the irreducibility of religion was not, of course, intentionally formulated as a bulwark against feminist critiques (even if this is, in fact, a consequence). Its hegemony has to be understood within the politics of disciplinary identity, in the embattled institutional position of the history of religions within the academy. Like feminist scholarship and women's studies, religious studies is ambiguously situated as both a distinct discipline and a multidisciplinary field analogous to American studies or science studies. As such, in many universities it has been in constant danger of being demoted from a department to a sub-department or an interdisciplinary programme. In other institutions it is perceived to be subsumed by – and hence institutionally indistinct from – theology: in British universities in particular, the era of cuts euphemistically described as 'rationalization' in the late 1970s and throughout the 1980s saw the closure of most departments of religious studies which were not sheltered within departments of theology. In public, secular American universities, on the other hand, religious studies is often attacked as an apparent anomaly. As Idinopulos writes:

> ... we who taught in the Department of Religion were faced with difficult questions from our colleagues about the appropriateness of such a department in a tax-supported, public university ... Why teach religion in a secular university? Does the study of religion really warrant a separate department? ... What are the special credentials which attach to a professor of religion that differ from the credentials of any social scientist who takes an interest in the study of religion and offers courses based on his research? (Idinopulos 1994: 65)

In addition to this institutional embattlement, mainstream history of religions has for several decades been intellectually marginalized, consistently out of phase with broader debates and paradigm-shifts which cut across disciplines, such as feminism, structuralism, postmodernism, reflexivity and cultural critique. It has been so ignored by scholars in other disciplines who are concerned with religion that any attention from the latter tends to bring forth a spate of published reactions – witness Dudley's (1977) response to an anthropologist's attack upon Eliade in a mere book review (Leach 1966). Up to the 1960s, the strong phenomenological strand of the history of religions placed it, in many ways, ahead of its time. This also placed it beyond the pale, however, during the positivist and scientific phase of anthropology and other social sciences during their structural-functionalist and structuralist eras. In the 1960s and 1970s, however, anthropological interests shifted towards a concern with meaning and interpretation which took the form of symbolic anthropology in the USA (e.g. Geertz 1966) and semantic anthropology in the UK (e.g. Crick 1976). These shifts entailed a reawakening of interest in religion and in phenomenology, but this took place for the most part as if the phenomenology of religion had never existed.

It has been in response to the double threat of institutional embattlement and intellectual marginalization that the boundary-defending argument of the *sui generis* nature of religion – and accompanying claims for the unique interpretive privilege of the history of religions – have been developed into a kind of disciplinary creed. 'Antireductionist' arguments, usually reiterated as a counter-critique of a structural-functionalist anthropology which has not existed for thirty years, are still part of the prevailing discourse of the history of religions today (when many anthropologists, ironically, can scarcely remember what structural-functionalism was).

The 'straw discipline' argument of antireductionism may sometimes be tactically useful in institutional battles over departmental autonomy and resources, but at the ultimately self-defeating cost of continued intellectual marginalization. 'By imagining a continuing struggle between religious studies and the social sciences', one scholar of religion observes sadly, 'we can be encouraged that someone is taking us seriously, even if that someone is mostly only we ourselves' (Elzey 1994: 94). The high disciplinary walls which scholars of religion have created have cut them off from many new intellectual directions, debates and discourses, thereby transforming mainstream history of religions from an exciting approach ahead of its time in the 1950s and 1960s to a broken record endlessly rehearsing thirty-year-old debates in the 1990s. Some scholars in religious studies, aware of the missed opportunities entailed by Eliade's exaggerated claims of autonomy, argue for an end to 'all those interminable arguments about the transcendental reality of religion' (Strenski 1994:107):

> ... despite the real risks of reconceptualization, we must resist looking on reduction like our cry-baby colleagues... Reconceptualization also promises renewal and revival. .... We have to begin accepting conceptual change as a normal part of trading in the world of knowledge. (Strenski 1994: 104–5)

THE GENDERING OF RELIGIOUS STUDIES

By reconceptualizing power as integral to – as opposed to a detachable 'dimension' of – religion, feminist religious studies has the potential to generate conceptual change and renewal. Yet its capacity for disciplinary transformation is currently cramped by hangovers from mainstream religious studies which some forms of feminist religious studies have carried with them. In this way, these (fairly dominant) strands of feminist religious studies are in a position analogous to that of feminist anthropology in the 1970s, which responded to the marginalizing of women in the discipline's mainstream by an essentializing discourse which placed it securely in a feminist 'ghetto'. Another article by Strathern (1981) consists of a critique of such writings, which eventually enabled feminist anthropology to reconceptualize itself, leave its ghetto and acquire a more audible voice in the discipline.

Particularly important here was Strathern's critique of the assumption of a unitary and essentialized category of 'woman' which unites the female researcher with the women in the (different) social and cultural context she is researching. Strathern's scepticism helped to sensitize white feminist anthropologists to criticisms of Western feminism by non-Western women and women of colour, who pointed out that their race and their history of colonization make a difference which makes it impossible to talk of a universal 'women's nature'. Currently, few feminist scholars in any discipline assume a universal 'female reality'. That many scholars in feminist religious studies are an exception to this derives, I believe, from the universalizing and essentializing tendencies of the discipline's mainstream.

In a recent critique of the 'transubstantiation' of women's experience into images of goddesses and cyborgs in some forms of feminist theory, Hewitt (1993) examines recent writings in feminist spirituality, best exemplified in the work of Carol Christ (e.g. Christ, 1985, 1987; Christ and Plaskow, 1979). As its alternative name of 'thealogy' suggests, feminist spirituality is directed against – yet implicitly shaped by – patriarchal traditions of Christian theology and practice. Thus God the Father is replaced by the Goddess as Mother, the embodiment of a cosmic femininity which 'refers back to a feminine ontology that is little more than the inverse of masculinist conceptualizations' (Hewitt 1993: 138).

Although Christ is highly critical of Eliade (Christ, 1991), moreover, her methodology is closer to his than her criticism would suggest. Where Eliade proposed a universalized (but male) *homo religiosus* as the true subject of religious experience, Christ proposes a universalized female spiritual essence in which all women participate. Eliade felt free to construct his version of this collective subject, unhampered by the self-representations of real religious participants:

> 'It does not matter in the least,' says Eliade beginning his dismissal of any Dilthey-like advocacy of the native's point of view, 'whether or not the "primitives" of today realize that immersion in water is the equivalent both of the deluge and of the submerging of a continent in the sea . . . '. . . Instead, Eliade proposes nothing less than a total theory

of religion, and thus one which *replaces* old meanings with (his) new ones. This 'totalizing' ambition explains why, in the end, Eliade does not care about what the 'natives' say or think ... (Strenski 1994: 102–3; see also Idinopulos 1994: 75–8)

Christ's approach – to use her own experiences of reconstructed goddess rituals as the basis for her interpretation of prehistoric goddess worship (e.g. Christ 1985:123) – is no less totalizing. With the aid of these experiences, she adapts Elisabeth Schüssler Fiorenza's method of 'imaginative reconstruction of reality'. Yet Fiorenza's method:

... is not easily adaptable to non-linguistic evidence from Neolithic times, which is where Christ ultimately wishes to apply it ... Without acknowledging the complexities involved, Christ uses Schüssler Fiorenza's method of 'imaginative reconstruction' as license for mythic and literary invention. By doing this, Christ hopes to avoid having to differentiate between the religious, symbolic meaning of the Goddess in her own spiritual life, and the public, historical claims that seek to establish the prevalence of Goddess worship, including the higher status of women, in prehistoric times. (Hewitt 1993: 147)

Through such appropriation of the experience of women in other times and places, a feminized *homo religiosus* lives on. A feminist religious studies which does not incorporate differences between women – in particular between the researcher and the women she writes about – will merely invoke the concept of power without applying it to its own colonizing discourse. That sensitivity to these differences does not, of course, mean 'objectivity' is clear in examples of feminist studies of women's religion which demonstrate such sensitivity (e.g. Boddy 1989; Brown, 1991). Quite the reverse: it requires more reflexivity rather than less; more attention to intersubjectivity; more attention to the voices of other women as personal actors that one cannot speak *for*; and more attention to the web of social relationships and cultural practices through which their power and experience are constituted.

6

PSYCHOLOGICAL APPROACHES

Introduction

Although we have chosen to include some of the most substantial psychological theories in Chapter 1, that is, James and Freud, they could equally be repeated in this chapter due to their significance and influence (both positively and negatively) on subsequent psychological approaches. The theorists included in this section are particularly chosen as they represent a range of alternative psychological explanations from those of the 'ancestors' and their followers in the twentieth century and beyond.

While the discipline of psychology has moved through a wide range of theoretical perspectives, including some that move towards sociological models of construction of reality and others taking a more strongly biological stance, as do some of the recent theorists who see religious experience as fully explainable via chemical processes within the brain, perhaps the most significant commonality is the focus on the individual. The focus on the individual as the locus of analysis is related to both psychological methodology and theory. One of the features that distinguishes the discipline of psychology from that of anthropology is that psychologists focus on individuals while anthropologists focus on groups. An additional feature that arises out of psychological methodology is that of abnormality – while neurosis and neurotics are not the only features and individuals studied by psychologists they make up a significant element of the data. This methodological focus may thus affect the nature of the theories that are made in relation to that data; this issue is specifically but not uniquely found in the work of Freud (pages 53–62). On a broader level the focus on the individual raises a significant problem in relation to religion. While religion may include a significant element of individual experience, explainable and analysable purely in individual psychological terms, much of religion is institutional and social and seems to operate on a very different level. This problem is indicated by the difference in use of private symbols and public symbols; while private symbols may reflect unconscious psychological states and feelings (and are indeed motivated by those states and feelings) public symbols are used conventionally and may not actually express anything about the psychological states of the individuals using them.

A second feature that is common to many psychological approaches is that of psychic universalism, that is, that all human beings share the same psychological structures. This universalism can be in a strong sense as in Freud (pages 53–62) or in a weaker sense as in Hill (pages 457–65). The underlying basis of this universalism is some form of essentialism. Unlike the theologians, who tend to place the essential and fundamental characteristic onto the transcendent plain, psychological approaches tend to place it within the human psyche. While the basic proposition that all human beings are essentially biologically identical is clearly correct and thus certain aspects of the psyche will be universal, it is not as demonstrably correct that the contents of the psyche (or even at some level the structures found in the psyche) are also shared by all human beings regardless of their social context. Those psychological theories that argue for strong forms of universalism, for example Jung in his theory of the collective unconscious and the archetypes, are more difficult to sustain on a broad ethnographic basis. Other essentialist theories that argue for more open-ended structures, as for example schema theory (pages 466–77), seem to be more defensible and cross-culturally applicable.

C. DANIEL BATSON AND W. LARRY VENTIS
'TOWARD A SOCIAL PSYCHOLOGY OF RELIGION'

C. Daniel Batson achieved his MA and PhD at Princeton University in 1971 and 1972 respectively. His current post is Professor of Social Psychology at the University of Kansas. His research interests include prosocial emotion, motivation and behaviour and he is currently investigating the empathy–altruism relationship and other forms of prosocial motivation. W. Larry Ventis achieved his BS, MA and PhD at the University of Tennessee in 1964, 1966 and 1970 respectively. He has held a professorship in psychology at William and Mary since 1985.

The text selected here comes from a book co-authored by Batson and Ventis on religious experience. In many senses the analysis can be seen as part of the approach established by William James. We have included material relating to their definition of religion, which includes both functionalist elements as well as conceptual links with the sociology represented by Berger.

Social commentators, viewing modern society from the ivory towers of academia and the arts, have long predicted the demise of religion. Yet religion persists. Public opinion polls reveal that the youth of today, like their parents and grandparents, place heavy importance on religion. Among American teenagers interviewed in 1978, 71 percent reported that religion was either the most important or one of the most important influences in their life; 68 percent reported feeling that they had been in the presence of God (Gallup 1978b). In another poll, approximately 95 percent of those interviewed said that they believed in God or a universal spirit (Gallup 1978a). This extremely high rate of reported belief was found for a range of ages, from thirteen to over thirty. Although percentages in such polls are probably inflated by respondents' desire to give socially 'right' responses (Demerath and Levinson 1971), it is clear that when one ventures out of the ivory towers into the mainstream of modern life, religion still occupies a central role.

And even within the academic and artistic communities, religious concerns persist. Although the answers given may not be those of traditional institutions and doctrines, religious questions are being asked: Is there any meaning and purpose to my life? How shall I deal with my death? How shall I relate to others? In fact, it is often to confront such questions more directly that the scholar, student, writer, and artist lay aside traditional religious

C. Daniel Batson and W. Larry Ventis (1982), *The Religious Experience: A Social-psychological Perspective*, New York: Oxford University Press.

answers. They strip themselves of the cloak of tradition to feel the chilling bite of the questions more sharply.

Religion not only persists; it has long had a dramatic impact on human life. It has given us some of our most memorable literature, lines that have provided comfort and challenge for centuries: 'Yea, though I walk through the valley of the shadow of death...' 'Blessed are the meek...' 'But I say unto you, love your enemies...' It has also given us celebrated acts of selfless concern for others. Albert Schweitzer's deep religious conviction led him to sacrifice prestige and comfort to go to Africa and provide medical care for thousands. Martin Luther King's dream of a society in which all people, black and white, would be free was essentially a religious vision. Religious conviction lay behind Mahatma Gandhi's life of asceticism and nonviolent protest. And for literally millions of less celebrated people, the most significant, the most joyful, the most meaningful moments of their lives have been religious.

But if many of humanity's highest and best moments have been religious, so have many of its lowest. The mass suicide and murder of 913 members of the People's Temple in Jonestown, Guyana, was but a recent reminder of the potential destructiveness of religious fervor. Wars and crusades have been waged in the name of religion, as have persecution and torture. Throughout known history, religion has motivated callousness, elitism, and hypocrisy. 'O Lord, I thank Thee that I am not as this poor beggar...' is an all too familiar prayer.

When we contemplate the powerful effects of religion on human life, both for good and for ill, it is easy to become confused. We may yearn for understanding, including any understanding that social psychology can provide. But even to propose a social-psychological analysis of religion raises several difficult questions: What do we mean by religion? Is a social-psychological analysis of religion really possible? If it is, what should it involve? [...]

WHAT DO WE MEAN BY RELIGION?

Our interest is in the religious experience, that is, in religion as experienced by individuals, not in religion as a self-contained set of beliefs or an institution in society. But what makes an individual's experience religious? In thinking about this question, it may help if we have some examples before us. Consider the following:

   a. A middle-aged woman hurries during her lunch hour to the nearby Catholic Church to light a candle and pray for her son, a soldier serving overseas.

b. After preparing carefully, a young Jewish boy reads from the Torah at his Bar Mitzvah. The experience makes a deep impression on him; he senses for the first time that he is an active member of God's chosen nation, Israel. Although he does not attend synagogue regularly during his adult life, this impression stays with him.

c. A prostitute responds to an altar call in a storefront church. Convinced of her sin and deeply repentant, she goes forward and accepts Jesus as her personal Lord and Savior.

d. Three times a day an Islamic businessman faces Mecca, kneels and prays. He tries to live all of his life according to the teachings of the Koran.

e. Put off by the hypocrisy of institutional religion and skeptical of traditional religious answers, a young woman comes to the conclusion that there is no God and no life after death. The only meaning in life is to be found in caring for others and living every day to the fullest.

f. A prosperous businessman and his wife attend church each Sunday because 'it's the thing to do' and 'good for business'. Neither takes the spiritual side of the service seriously.

g. A young man decides to spend two weeks alone hiking and camping in Yosemite National Park 'just to have a chance to think about things and try to sort out what's important in my life'.

Which of these are examples of religious experience? Most of us would probably agree that the first four qualify; but what about the last three? Whether we consider any of them to be religious will depend on our definition of religion.

As early as 1912, James Leuba was able to catalogue forty-eight different definitions of religion; doubtless one could list many more today. Given this range of possibilities, what definition should we adopt? In trying to decide, we are both chastened and comforted by the words of sociologist Milton Yinger: 'Any definition of religion is likely to be satisfactory only to its author' (1967: 18). We can only add that the definition we shall propose is not even fully satisfactory to us. It has the status of a working definition, nothing more.

Still, if a working definition is going to work, it must be chosen carefully. Specifically, we believe that ours should be responsive to two pressures: first, it should reflect the uniqueness, complexity, and diversity of the religious experience. Second, it should have heuristic value; that is, it should invite and encourage a social-psychological analysis by emphasizing the way that religion fits into, rather than stands apart from, the ongoing life of the individual.

Uniqueness, complexity, and diversity
of the religious experience

Uniqueness. It has frequently been noted that the religious experience is unique, that it is somehow different from everyday experience. Rudolph Otto (1923) described religious experience as 'wholly other'. William James (1902) spoke of religion in terms of a unique emotion, 'solemn joy'. Paul Pruyser (1968) suggested that religion involves 'serious' belief, behavior, feeling, and attitude. Yinger (1970) and, following him, Machalek and Martin (1976) considered religious concerns to be those that emerge when one is 'thinking beyond the immediate problems of the day – however important – beyond headlines, beyond the temporary . . . to the most important concern or concerns of life' (Machalek and Martin 1976: 314–15).

Let us try to be more explicit about how religious experience is unique. Religious concerns seem to differ from everyday concerns both in the *comprehensiveness* of their scope and in their personal *centrality*. Everyday concerns might include what you will have for dinner, what the right answer was to the third question on today's history exam, or whether you will get the job you applied for yesterday. Although any of these concerns may seem all-consuming, at least for the moment, each deals with only a limited aspect of your life and does not touch the core. How you answer is not likely to change the way you look at yourself in relation to life itself. You may discover a new dish you like; you may learn that you do not know as much about the reign of Louis XIV as you thought you did; you may find yourself embarking on a new career. But you are not likely to change your fundamental notions of who you are as a person or whether your life has any ultimate meaning and purpose. Religious concerns and experiences are unique in that they *do* affect central perceptions about oneself and life itself; they *are* likely to change your notions of who you are and whether your life has any ultimate meaning and purpose.

Complexity. Because of its comprehensiveness and centrality, the religious experience is psychologically complex. It involves a complex array of psychological categories – emotions, beliefs, attitudes, values, behaviors, and social environments. But it is complex in another way as well. Even if we were to catalogue religious individuals' beliefs and attitudes about God, an afterlife, and the Church, few people would feel that such a catalogue adequately described their religious experience. Nor would it be sufficient simply to extend the catalogue to include various emotions, such as a sense of awe and mystery, or various behaviors, such as attending church and praying.

Religion as experienced has a coherence that goes beyond a collection of beliefs, attitudes, emotions, and behaviors. The religious experience seems to combine and transcend these psychological categories, providing a sense of *integrity*. This integrity comes from the dynamic character of the

440

experience, which seems, at once, to emerge from and to transform an individual's life. To provide but one classic example, Saul was so changed that he adopted a new name, Paul, after his experience on the Damascus road. As he wrote later, 'Old things have passed away; behold, all things have become new' (II Cor. 5:17).

Diversity. It need hardly be said that the religious experience of different individuals can be very different. If one considers only recognized world religions, the range of experiences is immense. Indeed, it seems impossible to identify any one characteristic that they all have in common. For example, one might think that at least within recognized world religions all experiences would involve some notion of divinity, some God or gods. But they do not. There are well-established traditions within Buddhism and Confucianism that explicitly exclude such notions.

To compound the problem of diversity, it seems inappropriate to limit religion to experiences associated with recognized religious traditions. Some recent sociological research suggests that many people now pursue religious concerns outside the structure of the recognized traditions (Luckmann 1967; Machalek and Martin 1976; Yinger 1970). Personal growth groups like est, encounter groups, political movements, and even parapsychology have come to serve religious functions. Given this diversity, it would seem impossible to provide a definition that includes a description of all the forms that religious experience takes.

A functional definition of religion

Fortunately, it is possible to define religion by describing its *function* rather than all of its forms. We shall opt for a definition of this kind, one that we believe allows for the uniqueness, complexity, and diversity of the religious experience. We shall define religion as *whatever we as individuals do to come to grips personally with the questions that confront us because we are aware that we and others like us are alive and that we will die*. Such questions we shall call *existential questions*.

No other species has the same degree of awareness that we human beings have of personal existence, of the personal existence of others, of the possibility of other worlds, and of personal finitude. As social psychologist Brewster Smith pointed out in his presidential address to the American Psychological Association, this existential awareness provokes profound questions.

> Self-consciousness with forethought and afterthought gives rise to the human existential predicament. At least for the last 50,000 years, we and our forebears have faced the puzzle (which we have had the words to pose to ourselves) of whence we came into the world, why we are here, and what happens when we die. But as we know, this is no matter

of mere curiosity. Since reflective language made us persons, we have cared about ourselves and each other *as* persons. So the inevitability of the eventual death of self and loved ones and the arbitrary unpredictability of death from famine, disease, accident, predation, or human assault become the occasion not only for momentary animal terror, but also for a potentially unremitting human anguish. And the quest for meaning, for meanings compatible with a human life of self-conscious mortality, becomes a matter of life-and-death urgency. (Smith 1978: 1055)

Existential questions may be articulated in the language of philosophy, as has been done by existentialists Martin Heidegger and Jean-Paul Sartre, or the language of theology, as has been done by Paul Tillich. But they can also be stated in less sophisticated, more direct language. It is in such language that most of us confront them:

What is the meaning and purpose of my life?
How should I relate to others?
How do I deal with the fact that I am going to die?
What should I do about my shortcomings?

We believe that religion arises from our attempt to deal with such questions. As Brewster Smith says, 'Thus emerged the many worlds of myth, ritual, and religion that provide the traditional answers to the question of what it means to be human' (1978: 1055).[1]

Having stated our definition of religion, we hasten to add four points of elaboration.

1. The existential questions listed above are illustrative only. The questions that arise as a result of existential awareness, the relative importance of these questions, and the form the questions take will vary from individual to individual.

2. The way different individuals deal with the questions will also vary. Our definition is intended to include all those ways of coming to grips with existential concerns that are traditionally associated with the term religion – belief in God and an afterlife, dramatic mystical or conversion experiences, worship and other forms of religious ritual, devout adherence to a prescribed code of conduct, prayer, meditation, ascetic self-denial, and so on. But the definition also allows for non-traditional forms of religious experience – belief in some impersonal cosmic force, focus on self-actualization in this life, participation in self-help or social-action rituals, even the experience of being converted away from one's religious heritage into the sense of personal freedom and responsibility that can accompany living without any gods.

The definition also allows for diversity along another dimension, the degree of closure or finality in one's response. Many religious individuals sincerely believe that they have found the answer to one or more existential questions; they know the Truth. Others, like Hesse's *Siddhartha* (1951), may be intensely religious without ever reaching any clearly defined answers. For them, seeking but never finding is a way of coming to grips with existential concerns.

3. Our definition of religion is not without precedent. Similar functional definitions have been proposed by other social scientists, although usually by sociologists rather than psychologists. For example, Yinger has defined religion as 'a system of beliefs and practices by means of which a group of people struggle with the ultimate problems of human life' (1970: 7; see also Frank 1977; Machalek and Martin, 1976). Although clearly similar, our definition differs from Yinger's in two ways. First, we do not wish to limit religion to beliefs and practices. To respect the complexity of religion, we have tried to allow for many ways of coming to grips with issues of existence, not only through beliefs and practices, but also through attitudes, values, emotions, and the dynamic integration of all these into religious experience. Second, to respect the diversity of religion, we have tried to allow for individual as well as group responses.

In addition to respecting the complexity and diversity of religion, we have tried to reflect its uniqueness. We have done this by identifying religion with a specific set of questions or concerns, those arising from existential awareness. Many profound personal questions are not of this kind: Should I ask Sally to marry [me] or shall I wait? Should I go into law or medicine? Such questions may be extremely important, and the answers one gives may have lasting effects on one's life. But coming to grips with such questions is not religious, for they do not concern matters of existence. By our definition, only when a person is responding to those issues that transcend problems in one's life and concern the nature of life itself is that individual dealing with religious questions.

This means that not everyone is religious, at least not all the time. One can easily imagine the individual who, at a given period in life, has no interest in confronting any existential questions. By our definition, at that point in his or her life, such an individual is not religious.

4. Although existential questions are often the basis for philosophical discussions, there is a difference between dealing with these questions in a philosophical and in a religious manner. As philosophical questions the issues tend to be dealt with in the abstract. Answers are universal, not personal, and are not necessarily assumed to affect one's own subsequent life. As religious questions, the same issues are confronted on an intensely personal level; answers are expected to have dramatic effects on one's life (see Fowler 1977). Of course, the line between religion and philosophy, especially moral philosophy and metaphysics, is far from clearcut. One

can discuss religion philosophically, and one's response to philosophical questions can be deeply religious.

Who is and is not religious?

Equipped with this functional definition of religion, let us return to the seven examples presented at the beginning of this section. Which ones are examples of religious experience? According to our definition, all are except example *f*, in which a businessman and his wife attend church regularly for purely social reasons. In each of the other examples the individual involved appears to be dealing at some level with one or more existential concerns. The middle-aged woman finds meaning and comfort in knowing that her son is in God's hands; the young woman who opts for atheism finds meaning and purpose, bittersweet perhaps but nonetheless real, in trying to care for others and live every day to the fullest; the young hiker may come up with no answers, but he is addressing existential questions, and so on. In contrast, the businessman is not dealing with any issues of existence, even though he is frequenting a religious setting. Therefore, by our definition he is not religious.[2]

Of course, there are those who would disagree with our definition. Some would consider it too narrow. Gordon Allport (1950), for one, resists any attempt to specify the nature or function of religion at a general level. Rather, he says,

> the subjective religious attitude of every individual is, in both its essential and non-essential features, unlike that of any other individual. The roots of religion are so numerous, the weight of their influence in individual lives so varied, and the forms of rational interpretation so endless, that uniformity of product is impossible. (1950: 26).

Instead of attempting to develop a comprehensive definition as we have, Allport recommends that we 'refer the task of characterizing the religious consciousness to the only authorities capable of knowing what it is – namely individuals who experience it' 1950: 6). Clearly, if we did this, the businessman and his wife would be considered religious.

We find much merit in Allport's idea of listening with care to the way religious individuals characterize their own experience; indeed, we have tried to do this in our research. But we must reject Allport's highly individualistic approach to defining religion, because we fear that it would fail to give any clear direction or focus to our analysis. It would amount to having no definition at all.

At the other end of the spectrum, there are those who would consider our definition too broad. They would argue that some apprehension of or belief in a transcendent, divine reality is a necessary part of the religious experience. For example, William James defines religion as 'the feelings, acts, and experiences of individual men in their solitude, so far as they apprehend themselves to stand in relation to whatever they may consider the divine' (1902: 42). Similarly, sociologist Peter Berger favors what he calls substantive definitions over functional definitions:

> substantive definitions of religion generally include only such meanings and meaning-complexes as refer to transcendent entities in the conventional sense – God, gods, supernatural beings and worlds, or such metaempirical entities as, say, the *ma'at* of the ancient Egyptians or the Hindu law of *karma*. (Berger, 1974: 127–8).

According to either of these definitions, the young atheist in example *e* would not be religious.

Although we would readily accept that a divine or transcendent reality can be and often is a part of the religious experience, we have explicitly rejected the idea that it must be. We would agree that there is always a transcendent dimension to religion, but we have defined it in functional rather than metaphysical terms; the individual transcends everyday matters to deal with existential concerns. This functional rather than metaphysical approach to transcendence allows our definition to include greater diversity, including the young atheist. In addition, we believe that it has more heuristic value for a social-psychological analysis.

Heuristic value of our functional definition

While recognizing the uniqueness of religious experience relative to everyday experiences, our functional definition still emphasizes that religion is an integral and dynamic part of human life. It suggests that, by providing a new sense of reality and of one's own place within reality, an individual's religion is both a response to and a contributor to his personality and social experience.

This suggestion invites a number of important psychological questions: What leads an individual to become religious, to come to grips with one or more existential questions? What happens in a religious experience? What, psychologically, are the different ways of being religious? Is religion a source of personal freedom, of enslaving ideology, or both? In some lives religion seems constructive, in others it seems destructive; what accounts for this? We believe that questions like these are precisely the kind that a social psychology of religion should address. [...] But first, another preliminary question must be considered, for it casts doubt on our entire enterprise.

IS A SOCIAL PSYCHOLOGY OF RELIGION POSSIBLE?

The social psychologist interested in studying religion faces a problem. If the study is to provide insight into religious experience, then the subtlety, richness, and profundity of this experience must not be lost. If the experience is deformed or distorted through oversimplification, the under-standing achieved will suffer accordingly. At the same time, the psychologist must proceed scientifically, for psychology is a science. He or she must be ready to subject religious experience to careful, critical scrutiny, including detailed analysis of the nature and function of its components. To provide even tentative scientific answers to questions like the ones just listed, it is necessary to go beyond common sense to develop theories concerning the role of religion in human life and to test these theories by making careful empirical observations. Such testing is necessary if one is to find out whether the religious experience actually functions in human life as one's theories say it does. Now the problem is this: is there not a fundamental incompat-ibility between the requirements of respecting the integrity and complexity of the religious experience and of proceeding scientifically? If there is, a social psychology of religion seems impossible.

To provide some perspective, it is important to remember that this kind of problem is not unique to the social psychologist studying religion. It is quite common in science. Consider, for example, a botanist studying a delicate, beautiful rose. While still respecting the integrity and complexity of the rose, the botanist may find it necessary to dissect it, to measure its different parts carefully and dispassionately, to analyze their chemical make-up, to examine their cell structure under a microscope, to compare them with similar parts of other flowers, and to consider how they interact with their environment both inside and outside the bush from which the rose was taken. A rose thus scrutinized may lose its beauty; indeed, it may not be recognizable as a rose at all. But few would question the value of the botanist's work. Not only does it seem worthwhile to try to understand the nature and function of the rose blossom, but success in doing so has contributed much to our having more and prettier roses to enjoy. And if those of us who are not botanists find roses no more beautiful as a result of the increased understanding, we do not find them less so.

In some ways the task of the social psychologist studying religion is anal-ogous to that of the botanist studying roses, but in some important ways it is not. The goal of both is to understand the nature and function of a complex phenomenon. In pursuing this goal, both must go beyond the ev-eryday reaction of awe, wonder, and reverence at the phenomenon to look more critically at its structure and function. The scientist's more critical look often involves subjecting the phenomenon to analysis, measurement, and experimental manipulation. At the same time, both the botanist and the psychologist must take care not to create a distorted picture of the phenomenon in the process of trying to understand it.

The clear success that botanists and other life scientists have had in conducting scientific analysis of complex, living systems underscores the fact that this basic scientific problem is not inherently insoluble. Analysis and measurement – even dissection and chemical decomposition – are not inconsistent with treating a rose as a complex, integrated living system. Far from inhibiting understanding, these techniques allow the botanist to go beyond simple awareness and appreciation to an understanding of why a rose is the way it is.

But in spite of these similarities in their tasks, the social psychologist studying religion confronts three potential stumbling blocks that the botanist studying roses does not. First, people may object to the scientific study of religion. Second, the psychologist's preconceptions may lead him or her to approach religion with motives other than an honest desire to understand. Third, since religious experience is not observable in the same sense as a rose, many consider it impossible to apply the scientific method to its study. If we are to develop a social psychology of religion, we need to surmount each of these potential obstacles.

Concerns about a scientific study of religion

Religion is a part of people; roses are not. It is hardly surprising, then, that people are more concerned when a psychologist scrutinizes religion than when a botanist does the same to roses. One can imagine that a rosebush might take a very different view of the botanist's work; we may regret the loss of some beauty, but the bush has lost something potentially vital to survival. In a parallel manner, many people view religion as something vital to their survival, and they are naturally uneasy about having it subjected to analysis by a psychologist. They do not want their own or others' religion dissected, manipulated, or mutilated for any reason. Respecting this wish places severe constraints on the social psychologist studying religion. He or she must avoid using research techniques that involve a risk of damaging individuals' religion.

But even if the psychologist eschews research techniques that could do damage, a person whose religious beliefs are a matter of life and death still has reason to be concerned. This is because the person's beliefs are likely to include some ideas about the nature and function of his own religion, answers to questions such as: Why am I religious? What actually happened during this or that religious experience? What difference has my religion made in the way I act? As we noted earlier, the psychologist's task is to address these same questions, although in more general terms. The problem is that the psychologist's answers may provide plausible alternatives to the answers of the religious individual, thereby challenging the individual's beliefs.

It is important for the social psychologist to be honest at this point. Often, social psychologists bend over backward to emphasize the limited relevance and impact of their research. But our experience observing the reactions of religious individuals suggests that social psychological research on religion has so much potential for relevance and impact that the consumer should be warned. It is frequently said that science cannot prove the existence or nonexistence of God, and we would agree. But it is frequently also said that a scientific study of religion carries no implications for a person's religious beliefs; here we would disagree.

Consider, for example, a reader of this book whose religious faith includes a belief that Jesus came to live in his heart when, as a teenager, he was on a religious retreat with a group of friends, all of whom were saying that Jesus had come to live in their hearts. He is likely to have some doubts about this belief when [. . .] he encounters a social influence explanation for such experiences. He may, of course, reject this alternative explanation, or he may decide that he is an exception to the general rule of social influence, or he may reconcile social influence with his religious conviction by concluding that 'the Lord works in mysterious ways', one way being through peer pressure. Still, it seems both naive and misleading to suggest that the scientific study of religion has no relevance for and so cannot challenge personal beliefs. Exposure to research on religion may make it difficult ever again to look at one's own religion in the same way. Whether the religious individual is willing to face the questions that a social psychological analysis of religion may raise about cherished experiences and beliefs – or, ideally, is eager to face them – is something that he or she must decide personally.

Because of the potential impact of a social-psychological analysis of religion on individuals' beliefs, we need to be very careful about jumping to conclusions. As Donald Campbell (1975) observed in his presidential address to the American Psychological Association, probably one reason that religious beliefs and practices have survived for centuries is that they serve important functions for individuals and for society. Before we even consider challenging them, we need to count the cost carefully. If we proceed with a psychological study of religion, as we have, it is important that we proceed responsibly. This rather obvious requirement brings us to the second potential stumbling block.

Motives of psychologists studying religion

Although only a few social psychologists have studied religion, a number of other psychologists have. Indeed, there is a rather large literature in the psychology of religion. But even a cursory look at this literature underscores the fact that one can pursue a psychological study of religion for motives other than an honest attempt to understand the nature and consequences of religion. To be blunt, some psychologists have tried to conduct smear campaigns against religion in the guise of science; others have used the trappings of science to clothe the equally unscientific purpose of extolling the virtues of religion.

If a psychologist is to conduct a scientific analysis of religion, it seems essential that he or she remain open to a wide range of hypotheses, whether or not these hypotheses are flattering to religion. We believe that William James (1902) provided an ideal model in this regard, and we shall try to walk in his footsteps. He approached the varieties of religious experience carefully and critically, always looking both for potentially constructive and destructive aspects.

In part because ulterior motives have undermined concern for honest inquiry, the psychology of religion seems to have drifted into a rather stagnant backwater, far from the mainstream of modern psychology. As Bernard Spilka has noted, 'Connections between the psychology of religion and psychology in general are not well established. The former utilizes methods and techniques from the mainstream of psychology, but rarely the ideas' (1978: 97).

At an earlier point in the history of psychology, this lack of contact with mainstream psychology might have been justified. After all, there may have been little of relevance to religion in the myriad studies of rats and pigeons used in the 1930s and 1940s to develop the learning theories of Skinner and Hull. But psychology has come a long way since then. Theory and research into complex information processing and creativity, into the formation and change of perceptions of one's reality and one's place in that reality, into the behavioral consequences of one's attitudes, beliefs, and values, even into possible neurophysiological substrates for the way we make sense of our world – all of these seem potentially relevant to understanding the religious experience.

In criticizing the literature on psychology of religion, we do not mean to suggest that it contains nothing of value. There is much of value, both theoretical ideas and empirical research. Our points are simply that psychologists studying religion often appear to have ulterior motives, and they have not taken as much advantage of developments in mainstream psychology as they should. We believe that it is time for the psychology of religion to cast off these ulterior motives and return to the mainstream.

The scientific study of religion: phenomenological or empirical?

The first two stumbling blocks may be overcome, at least in part, if the psychologist sticks to his or her business as a scientist, conducting a careful, sensitive, honest, and scholarly inquiry. But when attention is turned to conducting such an inquiry, a further problem arises. As individuals come to grips with existential questions, they often claim contact with an otherworldly realm – with God, Allah, the One, etc. Does this otherworldliness not make it impossible to study religion scientifically? This is obviously a crucial and difficult question, one we must consider in some detail. It has proved to be the greatest hindrance to the development of a viable social psychology of religion.

Many people, including many psychologists of religion, believe that there is an irreconcilable incompatibility between the intensely personal, mysterious, otherworldly character of religious experience and the scientific demand for objective, empirical observations. Faced with this incompatibility, these people give us a choice: either insist on the irreducible character of the religious experience and deny that it is amenable to scientific analysis, or insist on objective, empirical observations and deny that religious experience (as opposed to religious behavior) can be included in a scientific study of religion.

Those who choose the first option are often called *phenomenologists* or *humanists*. They believe that religious experience must occupy a central role in any study of religion and that the only way to study religious experience is to use wholistic techniques such as in-depth clinical interviews with religious individuals. Those who choose the second option are often called *empiricists* or *positivists*. They contend that the research techniques proposed by the phenomenologists do not produce the empirical observations essential for scientific analysis. They further contend that if religious experience in its complexity and integrity does not yield such observations, then the psychologist cannot study religious experience. Instead, the psychological study of religion must be limited to observable behavior such as going to church, praying, or marking agreement or disagreement with questionnaire items concerning religious attitudes and beliefs. According to this empiricist view, one can have a science of religious *behavior* but not of religious *experience*. (See Hanford 1975, and Spilka 1977, for further elaboration of the phenomenology–empiricism controversy in the study of religion.)

Which option should we choose? Neither. For as is true in so many debates about underlying assumptions, both sides in this debate seem right in what they affirm but wrong in what they deny. The phenomenologist affirms that we must respect the integrity and complexity of religious experience; it cannot be reduced to observable, quantifiable behavior. The empiricist affirms that any social-psychological study of religion must be scientifically respectable; it must be based on empirical observations. Both sides deny the same thing, that one can use traditional scientific methods to study religious experience.

We believe that both sides are wrong in this denial and that their error stems from an inaccurate and outmoded view of science. This view, derived from logical positivism, has long been rejected by leading philosophers of science (e.g., Hanson 1958; Popper 1959; Kuhn 1962) and was never an accurate description of more than a very small percentage of scientific research. We further believe that a more contemporary and realistic view of science enables one to transcend the phenomenology–empiricism controversy. This more contemporary view rests on understanding the relationship between personal experience and publicly verifiable observations.

The relationship between experience and empirically observable behavior in a contemporary view of science. According to the contemporary view, religious experience, like other experience, leaves publicly observable 'tracks' in the life of the individual. The scientist can make much use of these tracks, so long as he or she is careful not to confuse the tracks with the experience that produced them. The observable fact that someone describes an experience that he has had as an encounter with God is part of a set of tracks that makes the experience, but not the experienced (i.e., God), amenable to scientific research.

To use another metaphor, one suggested by the philosopher Ludwig Wittgenstein, the behavioral consequences of religious experience function much like the symptoms of a disease. The symptoms are not the disease; instead, says Wittgenstein (1958), the symptoms serve as observable *criteria* for the disease. They are the observable tracks that allow the doctor to know when the disease is present. Similarly, for religious experience various descriptions of the experience, nonverbal cues, and changes in belief and behavior are all tracks or symptoms that serve as observable criteria. They provide clues both to the existence and to the character of the experience. The scientist can use these tracks or symptoms as publicly verifiable observations, making it possible to test explanatory theories concerning the nature and function of an individual's religious experience.

Of course, the scientist must be careful at this point. He or she cannot assume that a description is face-valid any more than the doctor can assume that a report of symptoms means that a particular disease is present. As a patient may be malingering, reporting symptoms that he is not really experiencing, a person can claim to have had a religious experience when he knows he has not. Or, as a hysterical patient can feel and honestly describe symptoms without having the underlying disease, a person may describe a religious experience, honestly believing that he has accurately described what he experienced, when what he actually experienced was quite different. The doctor must be sensitive to these possibilities when diagnosing illness; similarly, the scientist studying religious experience must approach the available observable criteria carefully and critically in order to determine what experience actually lies behind them.

Two strategies have been developed to help scientists decide what experience lies behind the observable criteria. One is *convergence*. This strategy involves collecting a range of relevant criteria and using them as checks on one another. To illustrate, if someone says, 'I met God yesterday' in a matter-of-fact tone as he might say, 'I met Fred yesterday', and then goes on talking about the weather, it would be very different from the person who haltingly and with deep emotion whispers, 'I met God yesterday.'

But even if all of the relevant criteria agree – verbal statements, nonverbal cues, and subsequent behavior – what should we conclude actually occurred? Should we accept at face value the claim to have met God yesterday? Or should we assume that what the person actually experienced was quite different? At this point a second strategy provides some guidance: *the rule of parsimony*. Simply put, this rule states that if different explanations can account equally well for some phenomenon, we should prefer the simplest one. To illustrate, it is possible that all inanimate objects are imbued with invisible little engines that propel them about in a manner that conforms perfectly to the patterns predicted by the laws of physics. But so long as the behavior of objects can be accounted for equally well in terms of an explanation that does not include the invisible-engine hypothesis, that explanation is preferable.

The rule of parsimony suggests that if the claim to have met God yesterday can be as adequately accounted for in terms of simpler, more commonplace processes such as socialized expectations, guilt, fatigue, and peer pressure, then this simpler explanation should be preferred. As a matter of strategy (not, of course, as a statement of reality), the social-psychological analysis of the experience should proceed at the simplest level that provides an adequate account of the observed criteria.

But having said this, we hasten to add that even though the rule of parsimony is rather straightforward in principle, it is less clearcut in practice. Which of two explanations is simplest is not always apparent. One may, for example, account for complex problem-solving in terms of a complex array of relatively simple processes, such as trial-and-error consideration of all possible solutions. Alternatively, one may account for the same behavior in terms of a simple array of relatively complex processes, such as implementation of a heuristic strategy like reasoning by analogy. Which explanation is most parsimonious? The former assumes simpler processes; the latter, a simpler, more elegant array. There is no ready answer. Insofar as possible, the scientist tries to preserve parsimony of both types. But often, especially when explaining religious experience, simplicity in terms of simple processes and simplicity in terms of elegance are in conflict. Was it an encounter with God, or was it a combination of more commonplace processes such as peer pressure, guilt, and fatigue? Often, the most parsimonious explanation is not obvious, so we cannot say which explanation is better.

If the scientist can only approach religious experience indirectly through its tracks or symptoms, and these cannot be taken at face value but must be interpreted using strategies like convergence and parsimony, strategies that often involve ambiguities, have we not lost the certainty and factual precision frequently claimed to be the hallmark of science? Yes, we have. In doing so, however, we have lost something that was never really there. This point lies at the heart of the contemporary view of science. As Polanyi (1958), Kuhn (1962), and others have pointed out, the scientist's facts and laws always involve subjective inference and interpretation. Scientists have long studied unobservable phenomena indirectly through reliance on publicly verifiable, but potentially distortable, criteria.

To provide some examples, psychologists and physiologists never capture depression or stress in a test tube; they must rely on tracks or symptoms that serve as criteria for the presence of these states. Yet much valuable scientific work has been done on each. Similarly, the physicist only observes criteria such as curved tracks in a cloud chamber for the presence or absence of protons, electrons, and the ever-thickening fog of subatomic particles. But this has by no means prohibited the development of scientific theories concerning these particles nor subjection of these theories to empirical test. And in astrophysics, black holes can by definition never be seen, for their immense gravitational force prevents any light from escaping them to reach other parts of the universe. Still, theories about their nature and function have been developed and are being tested through observation of their effects on other celestial bodies.

Transcending the phenomenology–empiricism debate. Having pointed out the distinction between an unobservable event or experience and the observable tracks or symptoms that can serve as empirical criteria for that experience, we can see that the phenomenology versus empiricism debate rests on a failure to recognize this distinction. Both sides in the debate implicitly assume that because scientists insist on using publicly verifiable observations to test their theories, scientists can study only observable events. But as we have seen, explanatory theories concerning the nature and function of unobservable phenomena can be developed and, by using the observable criteria, tested empirically. The criteria do not serve as an empirical equivalent of the phenomena as would be true in the empirical reduction proposed by positivism (see Carnap 1938); they serve as tracks or symptoms that permit us to make inferences about the unobservable event. So long as an event leaves observable tracks or symptoms (and it is not clear that we would even know about it if it did not), it is amenable to empirical analysis. Therefore, so long as religious experience in all its individuality, transcendence, and mystery leaves observable tracks or symptoms, it is amenable to empirical analysis. (For similar but more detailed discussions of the phenomenology versus empiricism debate in psychology in general, see Child 1973; Mandler and Mandler 1974; Rychlak 1977.)

When the distinction between unobservable experiential phenomena and the observable criteria for these phenomena is recognized and employed, the incompatibility between a phenomenological and an empirical approach to the study of religion disappears. It is possible to develop a social psychology of religion that is at once phenomenological *and* empirical: phenomenological in its focus on religious experience as the central aspect of religious life, empirical in its reliance on empirical observations to test one's theories. It is our goal to develop just such a social psychology of religion, one that is both phenomenological and empirical.

WHAT SHOULD A SOCIAL-PSYCHOLOGICAL ANALYSIS OF RELIGION INVOLVE?

A phenomenological and empirical social psychology of religion should involve application of the scientific method to the study of religious experience, while maintaining the unique orientation of social psychology. Although there is considerable overlap, each area of the social and behavioral sciences has its unique orientation. The unique orientation of social psychology is the study of psychological processes within the individual while at the same time recognizing that the individual is always subject to direct and indirect influence from his or her social environment. Consistent with this orientation, the theories making up our social-psychological perspective on religion involve attempts to explain the nature and consequences of religion in the individual's life, while at the same time keeping in mind the impact on the individual of his or her social environment.

As already suggested, our theories should address questions such as: What leads an individual to choose one religious stance over another? Psychologically, what happens during a religious experience? What are the consequences of various ways of dealing with religious questions? Does being religious make a person happier, more open, more caring? As we have also suggested, in developing theories to answer such questions, the social psychologist studying religion needs to take advantage of theories developed in other areas of mainstream psychology, both inside and outside social psychology. Specifically, recent attempts to understand complex psychological processes such as social influence, creativity, the development and change of one's view of reality, belief formation, and commitment would seem to hold much promise.

Theory development is an essential first step in a social psychology of religion, but it is only that. If our analysis is to be scientific, we must take a second step as well: our theories must be subjected to empirical test. [...]

SUMMARY AND CONCLUSION

We adopted a functional definition of religion: religion is whatever we do to come to grips with existential questions – the questions that confront us because we are aware that we and others like us are alive and that we will die. Such questions include: What is the meaning or purpose of my life? How should I relate to others? How do I deal with the fact that I am going to die? What should I do about my shortcomings? This definition of religion underscores the uniqueness, complexity, and diversity of the religious experience. Moreover, it suggests that religion is both a response and a contributor to the individual's total personality and social experience, and so it invites psychological questions about the nature and consequences of religious experience. Such questions are, we believe, precisely the sort that a social psychology of religion should address.

But can social psychologists address such questions scientifically without at the same time doing violence to what is being studied, the religious experience? We believe they can. The basic problem of respecting the integrity of complex phenomena while subjecting them to careful analysis is a common one in science, and the history of science provides ample evidence that it can be solved. Further, although several specific stumbling blocks stand in the way of the development of a social psychology of religion, none seem inherently insurmountable.

The social psychologist can deal with the concern of religious individuals about the implications of a scientific study of religion by warning them that there may be challenges to their beliefs, by leaving it to them to find personal relevance in a social-psychological analysis as they see fit, and by resisting quick pronouncements about the practical implications of a social-psychological analysis, whether such pronouncements are favorable or unfavorable to religion. The problem of ulterior motives on the part of psychologists studying religion can, we hope, be overcome by the adoption of an attitude of open inquiry and by better integration of the psychological study of religion into mainstream psychology.

What is usually considered to be the most serious stumbling block standing in the way of the development of a social psychology of religion is, we believe, actually the easiest to overcome. The phenomenology versus empiricism debate – the debate over whether one will focus on religious experience at the sacrifice of empirical observation (the phenomenological view) or will insist on empirical observation and so limit one's analysis to religious behavior rather than religious experience (the empiricist view) – seems to us to be based on a misunderstanding of what science is. In science, the phenomena being studied need not be observable so long as they leave observable tracks or symptoms. These tracks, rightly interpreted, can provide empirical criteria for the presence of an inherently mysterious, unobservable, deeply personal experience. Capitalizing on this approach, a social psychology of religion can, and we believe should, be both phenomenological and empirical: phenomenological, in that it focuses not only on religious behavior but also on religious experience; empirical, in that it employs the scientific method, including reliance on publicly verifiable observation.

With the way cleared of obstacles, it is time to take the humbling trip from possibility to reality, to consider what insights and information a social-psychological analysis of religion can provide. But as we do, it is important that we not forget our goal, a scientifically sound perspective that does not do violence to the diversity and mystery of the religious experience. Though at present far off, this is the Celestial City toward which we hope, like Bunyan's pilgrim, to make some progress.

NOTES

1. There is some, admittedly sketchy, evidence that questions of this type are not simply a reflection of Western values. First, archaeologists have uncovered flower-lined burial graves dating from 50,000 years ago, attesting to concern about death and afterlife among our ancient ancestors (Marshak, 1976). Second, Yinger (1977) asked 751 individuals from five different countries (Japan, Korea, Thailand, New Zealand, and Australia) to indicate in response to an open-ended question what they considered to be the basic and permanent question(s) for mankind. Responses from each country were quite similar. Across the entire sample, meaning and purpose in life was mentioned by 60 percent of the respondents; suffering was mentioned by 54 percent, and injustice was mentioned by 38 percent. Recent anecdotal evidence suggests that such questions are central even in China. In 1980 a young worker wrote in a letter to *China Youth* magazine: 'Life, is this the mystery you try to reveal? Is the ultimate end nothing more than a dead body?' Apparently, these questions struck a very resonant chord among Chinese youth, for they prompted 60,000 letters in response.

   There is also some evidence that people identify questions of this type with religion. In a survey of 2,509 American college students and adults, Braden (1947) found that the reason most frequently given for being religious was that 'religion gives meaning to life'. And in a large nationwide survey in Britain (ITA, 1970), it was found that 'death' was the word that evoked religious associations (e.g., 'God') for the largest percentage of respondents (64 percent).

2. This is not to say that the businessman and his wife will never consider existential questions. They may even be prompted by their attendance at church to do so, at least on occasion. And to the degree that they are, their experience becomes religious. Being religious by our definition is not an all-or-none phenomenon; it is more appropriately viewed as a matter of degree. Indeed, [...] we shall suggest that it is a matter of degree along at least three distinct continua, and one of these continua explicitly takes account of the type of religious involvement shown by the businessman and his wife.

Professor Peter C. Hill has held a chair in psychology at Grove City College, Pennsylvania. He has published numerous works, amongst the most recent being Measures of Religiosity, *which he co-authored with Ralph Hood.*

The material from Peter Hill included here applies cognitive theory to the area of religious experience. It focuses on the issue of attitudes, that is, judgements attached to an object, and their role in relation to conscious or unconscious control. These elements become a means of categorising different forms of religious experience on the basis of the presence or absence of conscious control.

The cognitive revolution has affected most areas of investigation that interest psychologists. To date, however, there has been little research on cognitive processes in the psychological study of religion. Neglect of this dimension is surprising, given that religious behavior is generally rooted in a belief system. Similarly, a void involving the general study of affect (Hill 1995) appears in the psychology of religion despite William James's insistence to be 'bent on rehabilitating the element of feeling in religion and subordinating its intellectual part' (1902: 492). This chapter addresses this dearth of research on cognition and affect by investigating the promising role that the attitude concept has for the psychology of religion.

I focus specifically on what has been dubbed the 'mediational' (Cooper and Croyle 1984) or 'process' (Chaiken and Stangor 1987; Fazio 1986) model. Of special interest is an adaptation of the process model offered by Fazio (1986, 1989). This perspective attempts to capture an interaction of cognitive and affective processes that underlie attitudes.

Religious Experience as Attitudes

Attitudes are central to religious experience. Hill and Bassett (1992) point out how the spiritual and mental aspects of humanity are incomplete unless the concept of attitude is included. Viewing religion in terms of attitudes generally does not conflict with extant models. Rather, an attitude approach may complement these other models by examining more precisely the underlying attitudes embedded within the models' major constructs, thus preserving and potentially expanding the truths found therein. For example, an attitudinal approach augments both Allport's (1950) conception

Peter C. Hill (1997), 'Toward an attitude process model of religious experience', in Bernard Spilka and Daniel N. McIntosh (eds), *The Psychology of Religion*, Boulder, CO: Westview Press.

of intrinsic–extrinsic religious orientation and Rokeach's (1960) theory of the open and closed mind. The attitude process model promoted suggests that the accessibility of a religious attitude at a given moment may have important implications for measuring religious experience, such as in determining how central or important religion is to a person.

One of the reasons the concept of attitude has not often been used is the considerable historical disarray found in attitudinal research. Abelson (1988) suggests that a primary reason for this disarray is that researchers may not have devoted 'enough attention to those attitudes that make a difference to people and society, attitudes that people hold with some degree of conviction' (p. 267). By arguing that the strong belief has much to offer, Abelson recommends religion as one of the most important, yet heretofore overlooked, domains for attitudinal research.

Abelson's (1988) use of the term 'conviction' is but one way of conceptualizing attitude importance. A relatively new and provocative attitude model (Fazio 1986, 1989) shares Abelson's view by stressing that the accessibility of an attitude should offer much to the psychology of religion.

Two Foundational Issues

Attitude accessibility

Social psychologists commonly agree that an attitude involves categorizing an object along some sort of good–bad evaluative dimension. This perspective led Fazio (1986) to the following definition: 'An attitude is essentially an association between a given object and a given evaluation' (p. 214). Both 'object' and 'evaluation' are to be understood in a broad sense: individuals may have attitudes on almost anything. Similarly, an evaluation is to be viewed on a broad continuum, from that which is strongly affectively based to that which is almost entirely cognitive.

The key construct in Fazio's (1986, 1989) model is *attitude accessibility*, which is conceptualized in terms of the strength of the association between an object and its evaluation. Fazio's associationist orientation suggests that strong attitudes are more readily available with surer applicability when an issue arises that calls for their expression.

Automatic and controlled processes

One particular element of the cognitive component of attitude is the distinction between automatic and controlled processes. Shiffrin and Dumais (1981) support this two-process view, suggesting that controlled processing 'requires attention and decreases the system capacity available for other processing. Automatic processing does not necessarily demand processing resources, freeing the system for higher level processing and alternative control processing' (p. 111). In reality, most cognitive processes contain some sort of mixture of automatic and controlled components.

Schneider and Shiffrin (1977) and Schneider and Fisk (1980) suggest that the two most distinguishing characteristics between automatic and controlled processing are *capacity* and *control*. With regard to capacity, controlled cognitions require active attention, thereby utilizing resources from the limited cognitive capacity of the individual. Shiffrin and Dumais (1981) not only support this claim but also imply that automatic processing does not decrease processing capacity. Thus, an individual may engage in automatic processes (and may be influenced by the object of such processes) without interfering with other cognitive activities.

The second distinguishing characteristic, control, is especially relevant in applying the attitude process model to the psychology of religion. Here, 'control' refers to the degree of regulation an individual may have over a given cognitive process. Again citing prior research, Schneider and Shiffrin (1977), Schneider and Fisk (1980), and Shiffrin and Dumais (1981) characterize as automatic any process that requires attention despite the efforts of the individual to prevent the attention system from being engaged, suggesting a lack of cognitive control. A key feature of automatism, then, is its inescapability.

AN ATTITUDE PROCESS MODEL: REPRESENTATION IN MEMORY

When we experience an object, any previously stored assessment toward it will highly influence our evaluation of that object. Among the factors involved in how memories are stored, those moderating variables that have been empirically established as contributors to attitude importance will be the focus here.

Moderating variables

Considerable research (Brent and Granberg 1982; Krosnick 1988) has compared important attitudes (i.e., attitudes that involve an issue or object about which the person cares deeply) and unimportant attitudes on a number of topics. The most relevant findings are that attitudes of greater importance are more accessible in memory (Krosnick 1989) and are characterized by stronger associations between an object and its evaluation. Krosnick has suggested that attitude accessibility and importance are functions of at least three important factors: *frequency of activation* (Yankelovich et al. 1981), *saliency* or *distinctiveness* (Krosnick 1986), and *linkage with other constructs* (Wood 1982). Therefore, more important attitudes are likely to be more frequently activated, relatively distinct, and highly linked to related constructs.

Object–evaluation association

Some attitudes are strong in the sense that they result from closely linked associations between an object and its accompanying evaluation, whereas the more divorced object-to-evaluation relationship defines a weak attitude. The attitude process model predicts that the associative strength of the evaluation to the object is a major determinant of whether the attitude is expressed automatically or as a controlled process. A strong object–evaluation relationship is necessary for the spontaneous automatic attitude that is relatively easy to access.

However, if the attitude results from controlled cognitive processing, then one has to either actively retrieve a previously stored assessment or create an entirely new evaluation. Such an attitude requires greater effort and is more difficult to access than an attitude that is automatically activated. Such processing occurs when there is a weak object–evaluation relationship (i.e., a weak attitude).

Whether an attitude is strong or weak, it will involve certain beliefs, affect, and values (BAVs). Gorsuch's (1986) extension of Fishbein and Ajzen's (1975) 'reasoned action' model of attitudes and behavior suggests that the relationship between attitudes and their guiding beliefs is mediated through both affect (understood as personal feelings engendered by perceived consequences) and values (defined as views of an ultimate end desirable for all people under all circumstances), thus making the model of particular relevance to the psychology of religion. Gorsuch's BAV model is somewhat limited, however, to BAVs, attitudes, and behavior that are construed as a product of 'reasoned action'. Gorsuch recognizes this limitation and recommends that unconscious decisionmaking models for the psychology of religion also be developed. Though not *explicitly* discussed in detail here, unconscious processes characterize automatic attitude activation far more than controlled activation (Shiffrin and Dumais 1981).

Associative networking

The associate network theory of memory and emotion is highly regarded and has been the focus of considerable research (see Anderson 1983; Bower 1981). A proposition (which links two or more concepts or images, e.g., 'Mary kissed me on the Ferris wheel') is processed by a 'spreading activation' to related concepts and propositions through associative linkages. Thus, remembering that Mary kissed me on the Ferris wheel (a proposition), which produces from memory various emotions (e.g., excitement), is an event that becomes affiliated with other events that produce the same emotion(s). Many aspects of the emotion (autonomic patterns, expressive behaviors, evoking appraisals, verbal labels, and so on) are collected together that help strengthen the linkage with the associated event from memory (Bower 1981).

Consistent with the notion of spreading activation, Judd, Drake, Downing, and Krosnick (an unpublished study reported in Tesser and Shaffer 1990) found that the response time of one's evaluation of an issue was faster when it had been primed by an attitude response to a related issue than by a response to an unrelated issue. These same authors also noted that responses on one issue tend to polarize subsequent attitudes, but only on related issues.

Associative networking may occur for both automatic and controlled attitudes. Under conditions of controlled processes, the individual may recognize additional (and potentially measurable) BAVs that further strengthen expressed attitudes as predicted by the reasoned action models. Of greater interest here is the spreading activation process from automatic attitudes. Such linkages should also increase the perceived importance of the attitude (Higgins and King 1981), enhancing the probability of its subsequent automatic processing and its associated network of related attitudes.

Perception, situation definition, and behavior

By approaching attitudes in terms of their functional significance, one can easily see how they influence perceptions. For example, Lynn and Williams (1990) found that attitudes toward labor unions influence how individuals perceive the validity and extremity of either pro-union or anti-union statements and create bias in causal interpretations of actions. The strength of religious attitudes may create a similar perception bias (Lynn 1987). Lord et al. (1979) discovered that people with strong attitudes on complex social issues are likely to examine empirical evidence in a biased manner by accepting confirming evidence at face value but subjecting disconfirming evidence to critical evaluation.

Certainly one's perceptions will influence how the situation is defined, which in turn will influence behavioral action (Fazio 1986). Latane and Darley (1968) demonstrated that of subjects who experienced smoke coming from under a door, only those who defined the event as a possible indicant of fire were willing to report it to the experimenter. Thus, perceptions and interpretations of encountered situations strongly influence behavioral actions.

APPLICATION TO THE PSYCHOLOGY OF RELIGION

The notion that an automatic attitude is immediately activated upon the mere presentation of a corresponding attitude object, regardless of any attempt to ignore it, may describe what a highly religious person experiences toward a religious attitude object. A person with a strong attitude toward a religious object or issue may activate that attitude spontaneously and without conscious control upon mere presentation of the object. In contrast, a less religious person, without a strong religious attitude, may require a more reflective effort to formulate an assessment of a religious object or issue. This effort may include retrieving a previously stored but difficult to access evaluation or may involve active construction of an attitude on the spot. In either case, more time and effort would be involved than for the more religious person using an automatic process (Fazio et al. 1986).

It is tempting to equate the distinction between automatic and controlled activation of religious attitudes with that between an affective and cognitive basis of religious belief. Given that automatic activation occurs spontaneously without conscious reflection, an automatic attitude, although strong, may actually be rather superficial. In a similar vein, Batson and Raynor-Prince (1983) reasoned that religious questers (who would more likely use controlled cognitive processes with regard to religious objects) should demonstrate greater cognitive complexity in the religious domain than those with an end (intrinsic) or means (extrinsic) orientation. Indeed, it may often be the case that an affectively based automatic activation of a religious attitude may not be well thought through.

Caution is, however, necessary. First, automatism in the process model reflects attitude strength, defined as the strength of the association between a given object and its evaluation. A strong attitude is not necessarily an attitude without prior thought. Indeed, the attitude may be subjected to considerable reflection before it becomes automated. Thus, mindlessness does not necessarily characterize automatic activation. Second, it is premature to label an automatically activated religious attitude as either immature or mature (or pathological or healthy). To do so confuses the *process structure* of the attitude with its *content*.

Measuring religious attitude strength

The importance of a religious attitude is understood in the process model in terms of the associative strength between a particular religious object (such as the Bible) and its evaluation. The strength of the association can be operationalized for empirical testing by a latency of response measure to an attitudinal inquiry (Fazio et al. 1982, 1986; Powell and Fazio 1984). A relatively fast response indicates a stronger (i.e., more accessible) attitude. Lending support to the validity of this idea, Fazio and Williams (1986) found that response time was inversely correlated with attitude–behavior correspondence.

An initial study investigating religious object–evaluation associations (Hill et al. 1992) supports the response latency technique as a way of measuring religious attitude strength. These associations predicted that although attitude strength of religious and nonreligious people toward religiously neutral objects would be similar, attitude strength toward religious objects should be greater for religious people. This was found. Although not designed to be a definitive test of the attitude process model, this initial empirical study not only suggests the validity of the latency response measure of religious attitude importance, but also provides promising preliminary data about the model itself.

What does the Process Model offer the Psychology of Religion?

Many potential benefits can be identified by applying the attitude process model to the study of religious experience. To begin with, it provides an alternative conceptualization of the importance and centrality of religion in the life of a religious believer. Kirkpatrick and Hood (1990) have questioned whether the domination of the intrinsic–extrinsic (I/E) religious orientation paradigm during the past few decades has been good for the psychology of religion. By proposing as central features such concepts as attitude importance, attitude accessibility, and the automatic/controlled attitude distinction, the process model is an attempt to provide a called-for alternative.

Relation to extant models

One of the virtues of an attitudinal approach to religion is that it need not conflict with current theoretical models and may increase the utility of such extant models by enhancing our understanding of underlying cognitive and motivational processes.

Religious orientation. After decades of research on Allport's (1950) conception of mature and immature religion, Kirkpatrick and Hood (1990) lament that there is little understanding of what such terms as *religious orientation, intrinsic*, and *extrinsic* actually mean. They ask, 'Is it [religious orientation] about motivation, personality, cognitive style, or something else?' and suggest that 'perhaps it is a little of each; but in any case, greater precision in definition is clearly called for from a scientific perspective' (p. 444). They are especially disappointed with the lack of both a conceptual and empirical underpinning of the intrinsic dimension, suggesting that 'in the end it seems to measure the important but theoretically impoverished construct of (something like) "religious commitment"' (p. 448).

Allport's I/E distinction can be traced back to his personality concept of *functional autonomy* of motives, suggesting that religious orientations are essentially motivational in nature (cf. Meadow and Kahoe 1984: 290–9). Nevertheless, the heuristic value of the religious commitment variable (whether conceptualized as intrinsic religion or not) needs further development. What, for example, are the cognitive and affective bases of such a commitment?

In response to Masters's (1991) concerns with their disappointment in I/E research, Kirkpatrick and Hood state that a good theory of religious commitment 'should try to show how religious experience crosscuts these various domains [i.e., motivation, cognition, and personality style] in a dynamic and interactive way' (1991: 320). An approach to religious experience stressing attitude importance may not only be useful in further conceptualizing religious commitment, but it may also help researchers elucidate some cognitive and affective processes underlying such commitment. As a case in point, rather than relying upon a rather simplistic descriptive typology of 'living' or 'using' religion, researchers could explore the conditions under which the religiously committed are more likely to use automatic cognitive processes. Such an investigation, in turn, may help explain the extent to which religious beliefs are used to comprehend everyday experiences. Kwilecki's (1991) view of religious development as a process through which perceived 'awareness of the supernatural becomes 'chronic' in a life, that is, broadly and consistently functional' (p. 65) is compatible with the religious commitment perspective promoted here. By measuring attitude importance, researchers may also begin to disentangle relations such as what components of religious experience (e.g., ritual, doctrinal, experiential, ethical, and so forth) are typically demanding of (or reflect) religious commitment.

Open- and closed-mindedness. Rokeach's (1960) theory of the open and closed mind distinguishes two types of cognitive systems: a highly centralized system with a small number of central 'authority beliefs' from which other beliefs emanate, and a relatively decentralized system where authority beliefs are more tentative and less controlling of related beliefs. Both centralized (i.e., closed-minded) and decentralized (i.e., open-minded) belief systems are inherent in disbelief systems as well. That is, central authority beliefs in the closed system say much more about what not to believe than do authority beliefs in the open system. Similarly, changes in authority beliefs in the closed mind (though less likely to occur) have, relative to the open mind, greater repercussions throughout the belief system. Rokeach (1960: 4) identified Eric Hoffer's *The True Believer* (1951), a book with a heavy focus on religious belief, as the single major stimulant of his thinking.

Again, the attitude process model may illuminate many of the cognitive and affective processes at work in both open and closed systems. For example, peripheral beliefs in Rokeach's theory (which are often *attitudes* as they are defined here) may be more automatically activated within the context of an authority belief in a closed rather than open system. The lack of reflective effort in accessing the peripheral belief may help explain why contradictory peripheral beliefs can coexist within the closed system, though Rokeach himself (1960: 36) explained such coexistence in terms of belief compartmentalization. It is clear that Rokeach has provided the psychology of religion with a helpful *descriptive* model of two general cognitive structures. The attitude process model may provide missing explanatory linkages within Rokeach's theory, thus making it more useful for the study of religious experience.

Other advantages

Other benefits of the attitude process model for the psychology of religion can be identified. First, it has introduced what may be a valuable unobtrusive measure of religious attitudes, namely, latency of response to an attitudinal inquiry. This may be a fairly good indicator of automatic activation of an attitude toward an object (Fazio et al. 1986). Such a measure may be useful as an adjunct to a number of self-report scales designed as measures of either substantive or functional aspects of religion. Attitude researchers are constantly searching for measures other than self-reports, with their well-documented social desirability confounds. Within the scientific study of religion, the social desirability issue has been one focus of many in the debate regarding the validity of measures of intrinsic religion (cf. Batson and Ventis 1982: 277–81). This approach provides a means for measuring attitudes without the accompanying social desirability bias.

Second, Fazio, Sanbonmatsu, Powell, and Kardes (1986) suggest that the degree to which an attitude is automatically activated predicts the resiliency of the attitude to counterinfluence. How one processes new information may differ, depending on whether or not the attitude is automatically activated at the presentation of an attitude object. Attitudes automatically activated may make the individual less vulnerable to counterattitudinal information (Wood 1982). People with religious attitudes that are automatically activated may make the individual less vulnerable to countermessages (such as other religious conversion appeals). Thus, the automatic–controlled distinction may be useful in investigating such phenomena as religious apostasy.

Finally, the process model may have important implications for the well–documented attitude–behavior inconsistency. Fazio, Sanbonmatsu, Powell, and Kardes (1986) suggest that automatically activated attitudes more reliably guide behavior than do attitudes governed by controlled processes. They reason that in the case of controlled processes, activation of an attitude may not always occur and behavior toward the object may proceed either without an evaluative consideration of the object or solely on the basis of whatever feature of the object happens to be salient in the immediate situation. Such factors may lead to behavior that is not congruent with one's true attitudes. This hypothesis, if supported, would also apply to the religious domain.

Social psychologists increasingly recognize the theoretical merits and apparent benefits of conceptualizing attitudes in terms of process. Given the central role that attitudes play in religious experience, an attitude process approach also appears worthy of further development by psychologists of religion.

DANIEL N. MCINTOSH
'RELIGION-AS-SCHEMA, WITH IMPLICATIONS FOR THE
RELATION BETWEEN RELIGION AND COPING

Daniel McIntosh achieved his PhD in social psychology from the University of Michigan in 1992. As an undergraduate at the University of Denver he was awarded a BA in psychology in 1987. He then moved to the University of Michigan, where he was awarded an MA in psychology in 1989 and was a Regents Fellow from 1987 to 1988. He then worked as a National Science Foundation Graduate Fellow between 1988 and 1991 before moving back to the University of Michigan, where he gained his PhD and was again a Regents Fellow from 1991 to 1992. He is currently an associate professor in the Department of Psychology at the University of Denver, Colorado. McIntosh has responsibilities as Director of the Emotion and Coping Lab in Denver's Psychology department. His current interests include the role of religion in low-control situations and the extent of social interaction involving non-verbal and affective processes. His latest work, published in 2004, is a co-authored paper, 'Prevalence of parents' perceptions of sensory processing disorders among kindergarten children'.

McIntosh's work on religion suggests that religion can be understood in a similar way to other cognitive phenomena, that is, as a schema (a mental model for establishing the relations and defining a particular area of knowledge). This model provides a very open-ended and cross-culturally applicable model for religion that has an essentialist basis without being prescriptive in terms of content or value. His approach shares many similarities with that of Berger.

Religion is more than an organization of beliefs. It is broader in that it exists in the form of texts, symbols, and traditions, and it is narrower in that it appears in the form of individuals' rites, habits, and other behaviors (Spilka et al. 1985; Spiro 1987a). However, at one level religion can be viewed as cognitive in that every religious system includes a set of propositions held to be true (Spiro 1987b). One way to conceptualize how these beliefs function and are organized is to consider religion to be a cognitive schema. Viewing religion as such has heuristic value and serves to explain some of the psychological reality of what religion is and how it functions in people's lives. Recently, Janoff-Bulman (1989) examined the relation between people's unquestioned assumptions about the world and the stress of traumatic events, with the view that these assumptions are schematic in nature. Her work made two important contributions. She used the notion of cognitive schema to understand how people's

Daniel N. McIntosh (1997), 'Religion-as-schema, with implications for the relation between religion and coping', in Bernard Spilka and Daniel N. McIntosh (eds), *The Psychology of Religion*, Boulder, CO: Westview Press.

assumptions function, and she addressed the relation between these assumptions and coping with aversive events. The present chapter expands this framework to include not just individual assumptions but also broader systems of beliefs – specifically, religion. Viewing religion as a cognitive schema has advantages for both the psychology of religion and coping research, because it connects these fields to the wealth of findings and perspectives about beliefs developed recently in social psychology (cf. Fiske and Taylor, 1991).

RELIGION-AS-SCHEMA

What is a schema?

Definition. A *schema* is a cognitive structure or mental representation containing organized knowledge about a particular domain, including a specification of the relations among its attributes (Fiske and Linville 1980; Taylor and Crocker 1981; Gardner 1985). Schemas are built via encounters with the environment and can be modified by experience (Bartlett 1932; Neisser 1976). People have schemas for many things, not only for objects (Neisser 1976) but also for events, roles, individuals, and the self (Markus 1977; Fiske and Linville 1980; Taylor and Crocker 1981). A God schema might include, for example, assumptions about the physical nature of God, God's will or purposes, God's methods of influence, and the interrelations among these beliefs.

Cognitive schemas operate at various levels of generality, with broad, abstract schemas usually having more specific ones embedded within them (Neisser 1976; Taylor and Crocker 1981). For example, a schema for God might be part of a larger, more abstract schema for religion – which might also include schemas for death, morals, and so forth. Work on schemas has not often dealt with the most abstract schemas that are least subject to reality testing (Janoff-Bulman 1989). However, because schematic processing appears to occur in approximately the same fashion at each level of abstraction (Taylor and Crocker 1981), knowledge about the functioning of lower-level schemas can help us understand more abstract-level schemas, such as religion.

One consistent finding about schemas is their propensity for stability. During the constant barrage of stimuli, the tendency is toward adapting data to an existing schema (assimilation) rather than the reverse (accommodation; Neisser 1976). Also, schemas constantly change, usually through small modifications (Bowlby 1969; Horowitz 1976). For example, people tend to persist in maintaining theories they have formed in the laboratory, even when this evidence is later described as false (Ross et al. 1975; Anderson et al. 1980; see also Parkes 1975; Bowlby 1980). Similarly, people may continue to believe 'theories' learned in a church or temple class even when later faced with contradictory or inconsistent information.

Function. The notion of schema is connected with how schemas are seen as functioning. Schema research was stimulated by findings that people bring to situations certain knowledge that influences how they perceive and understand the situation (see Fiske and Linville 1980, for a review, and Bartlett 1932, as an example).

To begin with, schemas influence what is perceived. Neisser (1976) wrote that people notice 'only what they have schemas for, and willy-nilly ignore the rest' (p. 80). Further, because relations among schema elements are imposed on the stimulus configuration, schemas influence how people understand what they perceive (Bartlett 1932; Bruner 1957b; Taylor and Crocker 1981). They arrange their environment to reflect the organization of relevant schemas. For example, subjects who possess a masculine self-schema (i.e., consider themselves highly masculine and view masculinity as very important to themselves) perceive a video of everyday behavior in terms of masculinity to a greater degree than those without such a masculine self-schema (Markus et al. 1985). Similarly, a religious schema can provide a framework for understanding events and, therefore, can influence how the perceiver evaluates the events. Generally, if a series of events is ambiguous, someone with a religious schema is more likely than a person without such a schema to impose a religious interpretation on the events. Further, those with a particular religious schema may understand events much differently than those without that schema. An example of how a specific religious schema causes different understandings of an event was reported by Gorer (1965). He noted that the Spiritualists and Christian Scientists in his sample denied completely the importance of death and, therefore, did not experience grief. To the Spiritualists and Christian Scientists, the situation does not call for grief. Put in more schematic terms, the datum of someone's death is assimilated into the Spiritualist or Christian Scientist religious schema, and with this schema, death is not viewed as important and worthy of grief.

Similarly, schemas allow people to go beyond the information given by providing elements to fill in missing pieces of what is perceived (Bruner 1957a; Rumelhart & Ortony 1977). On hearing a fellow bus passenger mention that she has just donated some clothes to Deseret Industries and is going home to read her 'triple combination', those having a Mormon schema will be able to infer that the speaker is Mormon. Note that if the perceiver's schema does not, in reality, match the situation, the perceiver may *in*correctly fill in missing information. Two passersby might make different inferences when seeing one person dunk another into a river (e.g., baptism or homicide); both schemas allow the observers to go beyond the information given (i.e., the actions of the people in the river), but only one of them can be correct.

Related to this, schematic conceptions of how the world works may help create the reality that people anticipate even in the absence of objective environmental bases (Taylor and Crocker 1981). To wit, if a person whose religious schema includes a belief in faith healing sees a once terminally ill person healthy, he or she may assume, even without further information, that someone had prayed for that person's healing. The datum of the person's cure is easily and quickly assimilated into the faith-healing schema. The cure is then connected to beliefs about healing in ways defined by the person's schema (e.g., prayer must have been involved). This person will thus have created an example of the power of prayer; someone with another schema may have understood the stimulus (the cured person) much differently – perhaps relating it to beliefs about 'doctors being quacks'. As another example, one person may incorrectly infer from his or her religious schema that a second person is religious, from cues such as hairstyle or dress. Based on this assumption, a theological discussion may take place. Even if the second person is not religious, the discussion may be politely continued. This will help confirm the first person's inference. In addition, the discussion itself may make the second person more religious. In this example, the first person's view of reality, based on his or her schema, created a situation that made that person more certain of the assumption (the second person discussed theology) and may potentially have changed reality (the second person's religiousness).

A benefit of conceptualizing religion as a schema is that research on the effects of schema on the processing of information can be applied to religion. Several of these functions are described later. Because schemas allow people to fill in gaps in input or knowledge, they allow individuals to employ heuristics or shortcuts that simplify and shorten the process of problem solving (Taylor and Crocker 1981). When a problem has cues that activate a schema, people can use that schema to assist in solving the problem. Taylor, Crocker, and D'Agostino (1978) found that problems with schema-relevant cues were solved faster than problems with schema-irrelevant cues. Perhaps individuals with religious schemas can employ heuristics to solve problems that are relevant to the religious domain (e.g., finding meaning in misfortune, explaining seemingly 'unnatural' occurrences).

Relatedly, Taylor and Crocker (1981) reported that a large number of studies show faster cognitive processing for schema-relevant versus schema-irrelevant material. For example, Markus (1977) found that students who had schemas about themselves for being either dependent or independent responded faster to schema-relevant information than students who did not possess schemas in these domains. Related to religion, individuals with religious schemas have significantly shorter response latencies than those without such schemas when asked to indicate if a religious adjective describes them (Spencer and McIntosh 1990). Taylor and Crocker (1981) pointed out, however, that some studies find *longer* processing times for schema-relevant stimuli. One reason for this may be the centrality of the stimuli. 'Information that is highly redundant and/or central to the schema might be processed faster than schema-irrelevant material, whereas information that has novel implications for the schema and/or is peripheral to the schema might be processed more slowly' (Taylor and Crocker 1981: 102). In the realm of religion, this suggests, for example, that an individual whose religious schema includes an explanation for why good things happen to bad people will be able to process information about the successes of a 'bad' person more quickly than a person for whom the instance would be novel or not included in the schema.

The complexity of a schema also has implications for the processing of information. Tesser (cited in Taylor and Crocker 1981) suggested that schemas provide criteria for evaluation and that people with highly developed schemas make confident and extreme evaluations more quickly than people without schemas. Similarly, people are faster and more confident in predicting the future if they have a schema for the stimulus domain (Markus 1977). Those who possess a complex religious schema should be able to evaluate the religious significance of stimuli more quickly and would be more confident when predicting future religious outcomes (e.g., what will happen to church–state relations if the Supreme Court makes this ruling?) than those without a complex religious schema.

In short, schemas enable people to identify stimuli quickly, fill in information missing from the stimulus array, and select a strategy for obtaining the information or solving a problem (Taylor and Crocker 1981). Schemas frame the way information is perceptually organized, stored, retrieved, and processed. Schemas sort the myriad stimuli, make them meaningful, and facilitate their processing.

How does the schema construct relate to previous work?

The idea that beliefs about the physical or metaphysical universe influence how one views events or novel information is not new to psychology in general or to the psychology of religion in particular. Previous scholars have discussed schemas and schemalike constructs. For example, Bowlby (1969, 1980) presented the idea that individuals have inner *working models* of the world. Hall (1986) discussed *cosmologies*, defined as belief systems based on viewing the universe as an orderly system involving complex interacting processes of energy or life force. Ball-Rokeach, Rokeach, and Grube (1984) suggested that a person's value-related attitudes toward objects and situations and organization of values and beliefs about the self form a comprehensive belief system that provides a cognitive framework, map, or theory. Glock and Piazza (1981) saw people as structuring reality in causal terms – such as what or who has power to influence events. What Parkes (1975) termed the *assumptive world* is a strongly held set of assumptions about the world and the self.

Schemalike functions for belief systems have also been discussed. Just as schemas are built through experience, so previous experience constructs systems of beliefs (e.g., Bowlby 1969; Parkes 1975). Ball-Rokeach et al. (1984)

saw belief systems as relatively enduring, yet able to undergo change as well. Harvey, Hunt, and Schroder (1961) proposed that they provide a network of relations that give people an orientation and ties to the world. This supplies people with linkages to the surrounding world through which reality is read (see also Luckmann 1967). The framework described by Ball-Rokeach et al. (1984) enables the person to engage in cognitive activity related to 'selective remembering and forgetting, information processing, decision-making, conflict resolution, ego defense, denial, withdrawal, judging, intending, trying, praising and condemning, exhorting, and persuading – and doing' (p. 27). Bowlby (1969) stated that people have maps of the environment that influence reactions to changes in the environment. Parkes (1975) indicated that a view of reality is 'maintained and used as a means of recognizing, planning, and acting' (p. 132).

More specific to the psychology of religion, the schema construct can be tied to Allport's conception of intrinsic religiosity (Allport 1966; Allport and Ross 1967). He indicated that for individuals with an intrinsic orientation, religion serves as the framework within which they live their lives; he conceived intrinsic religiousness as relating to all of life and as being integrative and meaning-endowing (Donahue 1985a). These attributes can be seen as functions of having and using a developed religious schema. Some part of being 'intrinsically religious' may be possessing such a schema.

How does the schema construct help the psychology of religion?

If previous scholars have worked with concepts similar to the schema construct, what reason is there to adopt the idea of religion-as-schema? There are several.

It is a virtue of the schema construct that it does not conflict with previous work. Whatever bit of reality the other frameworks have tapped may be shared by viewing religion as a schema. One advantage of adopting the schema notion is that it combines previous work into a unified framework. For example, Allport's (1966; Allport and Ross 1967) religious framework can be combined with Bowlby's (1969) idea that working models are built via experience and with the notion of Harvey et al. (1961) that belief systems affect how people structure their understanding of the world. Thinking of religion as a schema allows us to integrate much previous work into a consistent framework.

More important, adopting the schema concept links research by cognitive and social psychologists on thinking and information processing to work on systems of beliefs in general and religion in particular. It is more probable that the way people's minds function is consistent across content areas than that the way the mind works relative to religion is different from, say, how it works relative to astronomy.

The processing of religious information has already received attention. Lipson (1983) considered religious background as providing children with religious schemas. She gave Catholic and Jewish children neutral and religion-specific readings. Each group recalled more text-based propositions, generated more implicit recall, made fewer recall errors, and spent less time reading the schema-relevant passage than the schema-irrelevant passage. Religious knowledge strongly affected their perception or memory, or both. Using a cognitive psychology approach in examining memory for religious messages, Pargament and DeRosa (1985) evaluated the effects of students' beliefs about whether God or people control people's lives on memory for three sermonlike messages, each advocating a particular combination of God and personal control. Results supported the view that students' religious schemas affected their memory or perception of the speeches. This influence is likely to occur in other domains as well (e.g., news reports).

Lechner (1990) applied work on cognitive schemas to his study of people's God concepts. A well-delineated concept of God was associated with integration of religious beliefs into daily life. Being religious can thus be seen as involving, in part, more elaborate schemas in the religious domain and more overlap between that domain and others.

In his description of Christian evangelism, Ingram (1989) provided an example of how viewing religion as a schema integrates both psychological and sociological perspectives on religion. Using Goffman's (1974) notion of frames (a type of schema), Ingram (1989) indicated that proselytizers use an evangelical schema to interpret the events of a witnessing encounter and try to shift the potential convert's interpretation of the situation – and life – to an evangelical frame. Thus, religious schemas can both be introduced from the outside (by society, peers, missionaries, and so on) and, once possessed by an individual, can influence both perceptions of events and actual behavior.

One domain in which a cognitive-schematic understanding of religion has been constructive is in examining the relation between religion and coping.

RELIGION AND COPING

Treating religion as a cognitive schema is useful in investigating how religion can influence the coping process and outcome and also in exploring how traumatic events can affect faith. To explore these questions, we must first consider from a cognitive standpoint what happens when an individual experiences a stressful event. When a life change occurs (e.g., relocating to a new place, the death of a loved one), people must make the event, which has occurred in external reality, real inside the self (Parkes 1975; Horowitz 1976). This involves integrating the data of the occurrence with prior assumptions (Janoff-Bulman 1989). Hastie (1981) noted that any specific event can be evaluated as congruent, incongruent, or irrelevant with regard to a particular schema. How a particular event relates to one's religious schema is likely to have an impact on coping and adjustment. A major coping task of people experiencing potentially stressful life changes is assimilating their experiences into their extant cognitive schemas or changing their basic schemas about themselves and their world (accommodation), or both (Horowitz 1976; Janoff-Bulman 1989).

Many major life events (e.g., births, transitions to adulthood, marriages, deaths) have historically been linked to religion and are often given religious significance (Spilka et al. 1985). This may cause religious schemas to be cued when such events occur. In addition, people dealing with major life events often indicate that they use religion as part of coping (e.g., Friedman et al. 1963; Balk 1983; Koenig et al. 1988). Religious schemas are therefore likely to be activated when people are coping. Thus, attributes of individuals' religious schemas may have an impact on how they deal with such events. Of course, not everyone has a religious schema, and many people's religious schemas may be peripheral and undeveloped. Some probably have other schemas that fulfill the same functions that a religious schema can. These are individual-difference variables that can be examined in the religion-as-schema perspective.

How might a religious schema influence coping with an event? Two particular functions of schemas seem applicable here: (1) increased speed of processing domain-relevant information, and (2) assimilation of stimuli to a form congruent with an extant schema. The first function may expedite cognitive processing of the event, and the second may facilitate the finding of meaning in the event.

Cognitive processing

Recall that possessing a schema in a domain of interest enables the person to process schema-relevant information more quickly and efficiently and that the perceiver may be able to employ shortcuts or heuristics that simplify and shorten the process. If religious people do possess a cognitive structure that includes ways of thinking about traumatic events, such a schema should facilitate faster cognitive processing of such events.

Faster processing may also be related to better adjustment to aversive events. Recall that people must integrate data from traumatic events with extant beliefs. Being able to cognitively process a negative event quickly and efficiently could facilitate the integration of the event. Having a well-developed religious schema may be analogous to having a closer match between the event and one's schema. Instead of having to fumble around inventing or modifying a less developed schema after the event occurs, one can just plug the event into the extant schema and begin processing. Thus, processing is likely to occur more quickly and more smoothly. Parkes (1975) claimed that a successful transition from an old situation to a new one is more likely if the person has a relatively realistic model of the new situation. Processing 'on the fly' is likely to be more sloppy and hazardous than processing according to established plans. To the extent that religious beliefs promote the latter type of processing, religion should relate to better adjustment.

McIntosh, Silver, and Wortman (1993) evaluated the role of religion in parental coping with the loss of a child to sudden infant death syndrome (SIDS). SIDS death was studied because it provides a good arena in which to examine ideas about the impact of traumatic occurrences. The death of one's child is certainly one of the most traumatic events that can occur (Palmer and Noble 1986), and the nature of SIDS does not allow the bereaved time to cognitively prepare for the crisis. McIntosh et al. (1993) found that the more important religion was to respondents, the more cognitive processing (e.g., intentional and unintentional thinking about the baby and its death) was evident immediately after the loss. To the degree that those for whom religion is more important also possess a more developed religious schema, this is consistent with the notion that having a religious schema can facilitate thinking about the death of a loved one. More cognitive processing immediately after the loss is linked to greater well-being and potentially less distress eighteen months later. Thus, religion is associated with an important part of the coping process, and this was predicted by viewing religion as a cognitive schema.

Finding meaning

Taylor (1983) proposed that the search for meaning (i.e., finding a purpose for or an understanding of the event) is one of three important themes in the coping process (see also Silver and Wortman 1980; Rothbaum et al. 1982). A number of studies reported that meaning is often sought during crises (e.g., Glick et al. 1974; Bulman and Wortman 1977; Sanders 1980; Dollinger 1986) and that finding meaning in misfortune is associated with effective adjustment (Silver et al. 1983; Thompson 1991; but see Dollinger 1986 for evidence of an attribution–distress link).

Religion may well be able to provide this meaning (Allport 1950; Clark 1958; Wuthnow et al. 1980; Spilka et al. 1985). Sherrill and Larson (1987) maintain that among burn patients, the meaning supplied by religious commitment is an important and understudied part of coping. In fact, religion-as-schema does relate to this process. Recall that schemas influence how people understand what they perceive. A schema may shape the individual's reality to be in line with the schema, even without objective foundation (Taylor and Crocker 1981). For example, Bartlett (1932) found that subjects frequently added causal ties, ignored unusual information, and revised the plot of a non-Western-style Indian folktale until the story resembled a Western schema for folktales. In a similar fashion, a person whose religious schema already includes an understanding of traumatic events may better be able to fit such an event to an extant schema, perhaps imposing understanding and meaning (see Wuthnow et al. 1980). McIntosh et al.

(1993) found in their study of religion's role in parental coping after losing a child to SIDS that greater importance of religion was associated with parents finding more meaning. Having found meaning, a person may be more likely to experience better adjustment to the event. Indeed, McIntosh et al. (1993) reported that the finding of meaning is associated with less distress and more feelings of well-being immediately after the loss and less distress eighteen months later. Viewing religion as a schema allows us to understand *how* religion can impose meaning on traumatic events and *why* religious beliefs might be helpful when dealing with a crisis.

Schemas not only affect how people respond to incoming events and information (and thus how they cope with traumatic events), but schemas themselves are influenced by events and information. Thus, viewing religion as a schema also assists in making predictions about how religious beliefs will change in response to traumatic events.

Religious change from trauma

Trauma has been proposed as a cause of religious conversion (e.g., Ullman 1982) as well as a generator of religious doubts (e.g., Friedman et al. 1963). Traumatic events can challenge generally unquestioned and unchallenged fundamental beliefs (Parkes 1975; Janoff-Bulman and Frieze 1983; Janoff-Bulman 1989); sometimes radical changes occur in people's belief systems (Bowlby 1969). Janoff-Bulman and Frieze (1983: 7; Janoff-Bulman 1989) seemed to assume that everyone's basic beliefs will be 'shattered' by victimization. However, as reported by Janoff-Bulman (1989), multiple victimizations do not continue to generate change in a person's assumptive world or belief system. Thus, once one is victimized, further victimizations do not necessarily destroy one's beliefs and do not require the same reorganization as an initial victimization. This leaves the door open to the existence of those who do not experience a radical adjustment of beliefs as a result of the initial victimization. Janoff-Bulman and Frieze (1983) wrote that the number of assumptions affected depends on the individual. Perhaps some have developed schemas prior to any victimization that allows them to bypass any dramatic reorganization.

Considering differences in religiosity as differences in elaboration of a religious cognitive schema may allow us to predict who will experience religious change after a crisis. For example, because those who have an elaborated belief system that incorporates understandings of a particular event (e.g., death) should have less of a need to modify or reject their schema when confronted by such events, those people who are most religious at the time of the trauma may experience less religious change. This gains some support by Cook and Wimberley's (1983) findings that there is little evidence that adjustment to the death of one's child produces stronger adherence to religion for those having a religious commitment already – those who already have a framework do not appear to change.

Using a panel of parents who had lost a child to SIDS, McIntosh, Silver, and Wortman (1989) tested hypotheses about religious change derived from viewing religion as a cognitive schema. Because a more developed or elaborated religious schema might be able to assimilate the event better and thus obviate the need for change, McIntosh et al. (1989) predicted that the most religious respondents – those assumed to have the most complex schemas – would experience the least actual change in religion between three weeks after the loss and three months after the loss. Further, a comparison of absolute change supported the hypothesis; pairwise comparisons of differences between group means revealed that absolute change for those who indicated at three weeks after the loss that religion was 'not very important' through 'very important' did not differ from each other, but each was greater than the absolute change found in those who indicated religion was 'extremely important'. That this difference is not due to a ceiling effect is inferred from open-ended responses on the effect of the loss and the small number relative to the other groups of those originally in the 'extremely important' group who showed a decrement in importance of religion. These findings suggest that those who possess an elaborate or complex religious schema prior to a traumatic event change this schema less – perhaps because the power of the schema reshapes the event rather than vice versa.

FUTURE DIRECTIONS

Viewing religion as a cognitive schema is consistent with previous psychological investigations of beliefs and religion. Further, it has proven useful in understanding how people comprehend and remember religious messages, in the relation between religiousness and people's concept of God, in the process of public evangelism, and in how religion and coping with trauma are related.

These studies exemplify what can be done when viewing religion as a cognitive schema. One area that needs further work is the direct examination of religious schemas. How many people have them? What areas of perception or processing do they influence? What are [the] different ways in which they are formed and organized? Understanding how religious schemas function in general can provide insight into a number of questions.

Psychologists of religion long ago put aside the notion that religion was unidimensional, with people simply varying on how religious they were (Spilka et al. 1985). Thus, if the religion-as-schema view is to be helpful, it must be more than a way to describe 'religious' versus 'nonreligious' people or people with religious knowledge versus those without it; it must prove useful in dealing with individual differences among religious people. One potential distinction made apparent by viewing religion as a schema is differences in the organization of people's beliefs. Some cognitive organizations of religious beliefs might be highly structured and hierarchical, whereas others might be simple, abstract, and vague. What effect does this individual difference have on the functions of religion in people's lives? Another important difference among people may be in whether their religious schema is salient or central – or whether it is connected to the self (cf. Markus 1977; Spiro 1987a). Two people may have very complex religious schemas. If, for one of them, religion is an important part of the self, then the religious schema is likely to be activated often – perhaps chronically – and thus will have more influence in life than will the other person's schema (cf. Markus 1977).

Another domain in which viewing religion as a schema would be helpful is that of religious experience. For example, certain religious schemas may cause individuals to interpret ambiguous stimuli as religious or mystical in nature. Relatedly, knowing what stimuli or environmental cues activate religious schemas could be used to understand the structure and function of individuals' religious beliefs.

Finally, as suggested by both work on evangelism (Ingram 1989) and on the effect of trauma on religion (McIntosh et al. 1989), considering religion as a schema can be helpful in studying religious change and conversion.

Viewing religion as a cognitive schema is conceptually rich and empirically useful. Whenever an investigator is interested in not only the content of religious beliefs but also their organization, relation to other beliefs, role in problem solving, and effects on perceiving, evaluating, and remembering stimuli, the researcher could consider conceptualizing and applying what psychology knows about the structure and functions of a schema. Psychologists of religion have long known that religion can powerfully affect the way people perceive and understand the world. They have also long known that the world can influence religious beliefs. Religion is more than a cognitive schema, but thinking of it as such provides a useful way to analyze these relations and to understand religious beliefs themselves.

ABRAHAM MASLOW
'RELIGIONS, VALUES, AND PEAK-EXPERIENCES'

Abraham Harold Maslow was born in 1908 in New York; his parents were Jewish Russian immigrants to the United States. He enrolled at the City College of New York to study law; however, he was unhappy and after transferring back and forth between CCNY and Cornell, he finally moved to Wisconsin, where he transferred his studies to the discipline of psychology. He graduated from Wisconsin with a BA in 1930, a MA in 1931 and a PhD in 1934. After a period of further research at Columbia University he found employment there as a lecturer and eventually, in 1951, Professor of Psychology. He died in California at the relatively young age of sixty-two, in 1970.

Maslow's approach to religion is closely related to that of William James, focusing on the experience that leads to religion as opposed to religious beliefs or institutions. For Maslow all religion has the same experiential basis, that is, the peak experience. Maslow adds to this analysis a developmental model – the form, if not the content, of which was highly influential on subsequent psychological theories.

DICHOTOMIZED SCIENCE AND DICHOTOMIZED RELIGION

My thesis is, in general, that new developments in psychology are forcing a profound change in our philosophy of science, a change so extensive that we may be able to accept the basic religious questions as a proper part of the jurisdiction of science, once science is broadened and redefined.

It is because both science and religion have been too narrowly conceived, and have been too exclusively dichotomized and separated from each other, that they have been seen to be two mutually exclusive worlds. To put it briefly, this separation permitted nineteenth-century science to become too exclusively mechanistic, too positivistic, too reductionistic, too desperately attempting to be value-free. It mistakenly conceived of itself as having nothing to say about ends or ultimate values or spiritual values. This is the same as saying that these ends are entirely outside the range of natural human knowledge, that they can never be known in a confirmable, validated way, in a way that could satisfy intelligent men, as facts satisfy them.

Such an attitude dooms science to be nothing more than technology, amoral and non-ethical (as the Nazi doctors taught us). Such a science can be no more than a collection of instrumentalities, methods, techniques, nothing but a tool to be used by any man, good or evil, and for any ends, good or evil (Maslow 1970).

Abraham H. Maslow (1964), *Religions, Values, and Peak-experiences*, Columbus: Ohio State University Press.

This dichotomizing of knowledge and values has also pathologized the organized religions by cutting them off from facts, from knowledge, from science, even to the point of often making them the enemies of scientific knowledge. In effect, it tempts them to say that they have nothing more to learn.

But something is happening now to both science and religion, at least to their more intelligent and sophisticated representatives. These changes make possible a very different attitude by the less narrow scientist toward the religious questions, at least to the naturalistic, humanistic, religious questions. It might be said that this is simply one more instance of what has happened so often in the past, i.e., of snatching away another territory from the jurisdiction of organized religion.

Just as each science was once a part of the body of organized religion but then broke away to become independent, so also it can be said that the same thing may now be happening to the problems of values, ethics, spirituality, morals. They are being taken away from the exclusive jurisdiction of the institutionalized churches and are becoming the 'property', so to speak, of a new type of humanistic scientist who is vigorously denying the old claim of the established religions to be the sole arbiters of all questions of faith and morals.

This relation between religion and science could be stated in such a dichotomous, competitive way, but I think I can show that it need not be, and that the person who is deeply religious – in a particular sense that I shall discuss – must rather feel strengthened and encouraged by the prospect that his value questions may be more firmly answered than ever before.

Sooner or later, we shall have to redefine both religion and science.

As always, dichotomizing pathologizes (and pathology dichotomizes). Isolating two interrelated parts of a whole from each other, parts that need each other, parts that are truly 'parts' and not wholes distorts them both, sickens and contaminates them (Maslow 1963). Ultimately, it even makes them non-viable. An illustration of this point can be found in Philip Wylie's fascinating novel *The Disappearance*. When men and women disappear into two separated, isolated worlds, both sexes become corrupted and pathologized. The point is driven home fully that they need each other in order to be themselves.

When all that could be called 'religious' (naturalistically as well as supernaturalistically) was cut away from science, from knowledge, from further discovery, from the possibility of skeptical investigation, from confirming and disconfirming, and, therefore, from the possibility of purifying and improving, such a dichotomized religion was doomed. It tended to claim that the founding revelation was complete, perfect, final, and eternal. It had the truth, the whole truth, and had nothing more to learn, thereby being pushed into the position that has destroyed so many churches, of resisting change, of being *only* conservative, of being anti-intellectual and anti-scientific, of making piety and obedience exclusive of skeptical intellectuality – in effect, of contradicting naturalistic truth.

Such a split-off religion generates split-off and partial definition of all necessary concepts. For example, faith, which has perfectly respectable naturalistic meanings, as for example in Fromm's writings, tends in the hands of an anti-intellectual church to degenerate into blind belief, sometimes even 'belief in what you know ain't so'. It tends to become unquestioning obedience and last-ditch loyalty no matter what. It tends to produce sheep rather than men. It tends to become arbitrary and authoritarian (Maslow 1943).

The word 'sacred' is another instance of the pathologizing by isolation and by splitting-off. If the sacred becomes the exclusive jurisdiction of a priesthood, and if its supposed validity rests only upon supernatural foundations, then, in effect, it is taken out of the world of nature and of human nature. It is dichotomized sharply from the profane or secular and begins to have nothing to do with them, or even becomes their contradictory. It becomes associated with particular rites and ceremonies, with a particular day of the week, with a particular building, with a particular language, even with a particular musical instrument or certain foods. It does not infuse all of life but becomes compartmentalized. It is not the property then of all men, but only of some. It is no longer ever-present as a possibility in the everyday affairs of men but becomes instead a museum piece without daily usefulness; in effect, such a religion must separate the actual from the ideal and rupture the necessary dynamic interplay between them. The dialectic between them, the mutual effect and feedback, the constant shaping of each other, their usefulness to each other, even, I would say, their absolute need for each other is disrupted and made impossible of fulfillment. What happens then? We have seen often enough throughout history the church whose pieties are mouthed in the middle of human exploitation and degradation as if the one had nothing to do with the other ('Render unto Caesar that which is Caesar's'). This pie-in-the-sky kind of religion, which often enough has turned into an actual *support* of daily evil, is almost inevitable when the existent has no intrinsic and constant connection with the ideal, when heaven is off some place far away from the earth, when human improvement becomes impossible *in* the world but can be achieved only by renouncing the world. 'For endeavor for the better is moved by faith in what is possible, not by adherence to the actual,' as John Dewey pointed out. (Dewey 1934: 23).

And this brings us to the other half of the dichotomy, dichotomized science. Whatever we may say about split-off religion is very similar or complementary to what we may say of split-off science.

For instance, in the division of the ideal and the actual, dichotomized science claims that it deals only with the actual and the existent and that it has nothing to do with the ideal, that is to say, with the ends, the goals, the purposes of life, i.e., with end-values. Any criticism that could be made of half-religion can equally be made of half-science in a complementary way. For instance, corresponding to the blind religions' 'reduction to the abstract' (Maslow 1957) – its blindness to the raw fact, to the concrete, to living human experience itself – we find in non-aspiring science a 'reduction to the concrete', of the kind that Goldstein has described (1963a, 1963b), and to the tangible and immediately visible and audible. It becomes amoral, even sometimes anti-moral and even anti-human, merely technology which can be bought by anyone for any purpose, like the German 'scientists' who could work with equal zeal for Nazis, for Communists, or for Americans. We have been taught very amply in the last few decades that science can be dangerous to human ends and that scientists can become monsters as long as science is conceived to be akin to a chess game, an end in itself, with arbitrary rules, whose only purpose is to explore the existent, and which then makes the fatal blunder of excluding subjective experience from the realm of the existent or explorable.

So also for the exclusion of the sacred and the transcendent from the jurisdiction of science. This makes impossible in principle the study, for instance, of certain aspects of the abstract: psychotherapy, naturalistic religious experience, creativity, symbolism, play, the theory of love, mystical and peak-experiences, not to mention poetry, art, and a lot more (since these all involve an integration of the realm of Being with the realm of the concrete).

To mention only one example that has to do directly with education, it could be shown easily that the good teacher must have what I have called elsewhere B-love (unselfish love) for the child, what Rogers (1961) has called unconditional positive regard, and what others have called – meaningfully, I would maintain – the sacredness of each individual. To stigmatize these as 'normative' or value-laden and, therefore, as 'unscientific' concepts is to make impossible certain necessary researches into the nature of the good teacher.

And so it could go on and on almost indefinitely. I have already written much on scientistic, nineteenth-century, orthodox science, and intend to write more. Here I have been dealing with it from the point of view of the dichotomizing of science and religion, of facts (merely and solely) from values (merely and solely), and have tried to indicate that such a splitting-off of mutually exclusive jurisdictions must produce cripple-science and cripple-religion, cripple-facts and cripple-values.

Obviously such a conclusion concerns the spiritual and ethical values that I started with (as well as the needs and hungers for these values). *Very* obviously, such values and such hungers cannot be handed over to any church for safekeeping. They cannot be removed from the realm of human inquiry, of skeptical examination, of empirical investigation. But I have tried to demonstrate that orthodox science neither wants this job nor is able to carry it out. Clearly what is needed then is an expanded science, with larger powers and methods, a science which is able to study values and to teach mankind about them.

Such a science would and – insofar as it already exists – *does* include much that has been called religious. As a matter of fact, this expanded science includes among its concerns practically everything in religion that can bear naturalistic observation.

I think I may go so far as to say that if we were to make a list of the key words which have hitherto been considered to be the property of organized religion and which were considered to be entirely outside the jurisdiction of 'science' of the older sort, we would find that each and all of these words today are acquiring a perfectly naturalistic meaning, i.e., they are within the jurisdiction of scientific investigation.

Let me try to say it in still another way. One could say that the nineteenth-century atheist had burnt down the house instead of remodeling it. He had thrown out the religious questions with the religious answers, because he had to reject the religious answers. That is, he turned his back on the whole religious enterprise because organized religion presented him with a set of answers which he could not intellectually accept – which rested on no evidence which a self-respecting scientist could swallow. But what the more sophisticated scientist is now in the process of learning is that though he must disagree with most of the answers to the religious questions which have been given by organized religion, it is increasingly clear that the religious questions themselves – and religious quests, the religious yearnings, the religious needs themselves – are perfectly respectable scientifically, that they are rooted deep in human nature, that they can be studied, described, examined in a scientific way, and that the churches were trying to answer perfectly sound human questions. Though the answers were not acceptable, the questions themselves were and are perfectly acceptable, and perfectly legitimate.

As a matter of fact, contemporary existential and humanistic psychologists would probably consider a person sick or abnormal in an existential way if he were *not* concerned with these 'religious' questions.

THE 'CORE-RELIGIOUS,' OR 'TRANSCENDENT,' EXPERIENCE

The very beginning, the intrinsic core, the essence, the universal nucleus of every known high religion (unless Confucianism is also called a religion) has been the private, lonely, personal illumination, revelation, or ecstasy of some acutely sensitive prophet or seer. The high religions call themselves revealed religions and each of them tends to rest its validity, its function, and its right to exist on the codification and the communication of this original mystic experience or revelation from the lonely prophet to the mass of human beings in general.

But it has recently begun to appear that these 'revelations' or mystical illuminations can be subsumed under the head of the 'peak-experiences'[1] or 'ecstasies' or 'transcendent' experiences which are now being eagerly investigated by many psychologists. That is to say, it is very likely, indeed almost certain, that these older reports, phrased in terms of supernatural revelation, were, in fact, perfectly natural, human peak-experiences of the kind that can easily be examined today, which, however, were phrased in terms of whatever conceptual, cultural, and linguistic framework the particular seer had available in his time (Laski).

In a word, we can study today what happened in the past and was then explainable in supernatural terms only. By so doing, we are enabled to examine religion in all its facets and in all its meanings in a way that makes it a part of science rather than something outside and exclusive of it.

Also this kind of study leads us to another very plausible hypothesis: to the extent that all mystical or peak-experiences are the same in their essence and have always been the same, all religions are the same in their essence and always have been the same. They should, therefore, come to agree in principle on teaching that which is common to all of them, i.e., whatever it is that peak-experiences teach in common (whatever is *different* about these illuminations can fairly be taken to be localisms both in time and space, and are, therefore, peripheral, expendable, not essential). This something common, this something which is left over after we peel away all the localisms, all the accidents of particular languages or particular philosophies, all the ethnocentric phrasings, all those elements which are *not* common, we may call the 'core-religious experience' or the 'transcendent experience'.

To understand this better, we must differentiate the prophets in general from the organizers or legalists in general as (abstracted) types. (I admit that the use of pure, extreme types which do not really exist can come close to the edge of caricature; nevertheless, I think it will help all of us in thinking through the problem we are here concerned with.)[2] The characteristic prophet is a lonely man who has discovered his truth about the world, the cosmos, ethics, God, and his own identity from within, from his own personal experiences, from what he would consider to be a revelation. Usually, perhaps always, the prophets of the high religions have had these experiences when they were alone.

Characteristically the abstraction-type of the legalist-ecclesiastic is the conserving organization man, an officer and arm of the organization, who is loyal to the structure of the organization which has been built up on the basis of the prophet's original revelation in order to make the revelation available to the masses. From everything we know about organizations, we may very well expect that people will become loyal to it, as well as to the original prophet and to his vision; or at least they will become loyal to the organization's version of the prophet's vision. I may go so far as to say that characteristically (and I mean not only the religious organizations but also parallel organizations like the Communist Party or like revolutionary groups) these organizations can be seen as a kind of punch card or IBM version of an original revelation or mystical experience or peak-experience to make it suitable for group use and for administrative convenience.

It will be helpful here to talk about a pilot investigation, still in its beginnings, of the people I have called non-peakers. In my first investigations, in collaboration with Gene Nameche, I used this word because I thought some people had peak-experiences and others did not. But as I gathered information, and as I became more skillful in asking questions, I found that a higher and higher percentage of my subjects began to report peak-experiences. I finally fell into the habit of expecting everyone to have peak-experiences and of being rather surprised if I ran across somebody who could report none at all. Because of this experience, I finally began to use the word 'non-peaker' to describe, not the person who is unable to have peak-experiences, but rather the person who is afraid of them, who suppresses them, who denies them, who turns away from them, or who 'forgets' them. My preliminary investigations of the reasons for these negative reactions to peak-experiences have led me to some (unconfirmed) impressions about why certain kinds of people renounce their peak-experiences.

Any person whose character structure (or Weltanschauung, or way of life) forces him to try to be extremely or completely rational or 'materialistic' or mechanistic tends to become a non-peaker. That is, such a view of life tends to make the person regard his peak- and transcendent experiences as a kind of insanity, a complete loss of control, a sense of being overwhelmed by irrational emotions, etc. The person who is afraid of going insane and who is therefore, desperately hanging on to stability, control, reality, etc., seems to be frightened by peak-experiences and tends to fight them off. For the compulsive-obsessive person, who organizes his life around the denying and the controlling of emotion, the fear of being overwhelmed by an emotion (which is interpreted as a loss of control) is enough for him to mobilize all his stamping-out and defensive activities against the peak-experience. I have one instance of a very convinced Marxian who denied – that is, who turned away from – a legitimate peak-experience, finally classifying it as some kind of peculiar but unimportant thing that had happened but that had best be forgotten because this experience conflicted with her whole materialistic mechanistic philosophy of life. I have found a few non-peakers who were ultra-scientific, that is, who espoused the nineteenth-century conception of science as an unemotional or anti-emotional activity which was ruled entirely by logic and rationality and who thought anythig which was not logical and rational had no respectable place in life. (I suspect also that extremely 'practical', i.e., exclusively means-oriented, people will turn out to be non-peakers, since such experiences earn no money, bake no bread, and chop no wood. So also for extremely other-directed people, who scarcely know what is going on inside themselves. Perhaps also people who are reduced to the concrete à la Goldstein, etc. etc.) Finally, I should add that, in some cases, I could not come to any explanation for non-peaking.

If you will permit me to use this developing but not yet validated vocabulary, I may then say simply that the relationship between the prophet and the ecclesiastic, between the lonely mystic and the (perfectly extreme) religious-organization man may often be a relationship between peaker and non-peaker. Much theology, much verbal religion through history and throughout the world, can be considered to be the more or less vain efforts to put into communicable words and formulae, and into symbolic rituals and ceremonies, the original mystical experience of the original prophets. In a word, organized religion can be thought of as an effort to communicate peak-experiences to non-peakers, to teach them, to apply them, etc. Often, to make it more difficult, this job falls into the hands of non-peakers. On the whole we now would expect that this would be a vain effort, at least so far as much of mankind is concerned. The peak-experiences and their experiential reality ordinarily are not transmittable to non-peakers, at least not by words alone, and certainly not by non-peakers. What happens to many people, especially the ignorant, the uneducated, the naíve, is that they simply concretize all of the symbols, all of the words, all of the statues, all of the ceremonies, and by a process of functional autonomy make *them*, rather than the original revelation, into the sacred things and sacred activities. That is to say, this is simply a form of the idolatry (or fetishism) which has been the curse of every large religion. In idolatry the essential original meaning gets so lost in concretizations that these finally become hostile to the original mystical experiences, to mystics, and to prophets in general, that is, to the very people that we might call from our present point of view the truly religious people. Most religions have wound up denying and being antagonistic to the very ground upon which they were originally based.

If you look closely at the internal history of most of the world religions, you will find that each one very soon tends to divide into a left-wing and a right-wing, that is, into the peakers, the mystics, the transcenders, or the privately religious people, on the one hand, and, on the other, into those who concretize the religious symbols and metaphors, who worship little pieces of wood rather than what the objects stand for, those who take verbal formulas literally, forgetting the original meaning of these words, and, perhaps most important, those who take the organization, the church, as primary and as more important than the prophet and his original revelations. These men, like many organization men who tend to rise to the top in any complex bureaucracy, tend to be non-peakers rather than peakers. Dostoevski's famous Grand Inquisitor passage, in his *Brothers Karamazov*, says this in a classical way.

This cleavage between the mystics and the legalists, if I may call them that, remains at best a kind of mutual tolerance, but it has happened in some churches that the rulers of the organization actually made a heresy out of the mystic experiences and persecuted the mystics themselves. This may be an old story in the history of religion, but I must point out that it is also an old story in other fields. For instance, we can certainly say today that professional philosophers tend to divide themselves into the same kind of characterologically based left-wing and right-wing. Most official, orthodox philosophers today are the equivalent of legalists who reject the problems and the data of transcendence as 'meaningless'. That is, they are positivists, atomists, analysts, concerned with means rather than with ends. They sharpen tools rather than discover truths. These people contrast sharply with another group of contemporary philosophers, the existentialists and the phenomenologists. These are the people who tend to fall back on experiencing as the primary datum from which everything starts.

A similar split can be detected in psychology, in anthropology, and, I am quite sure, in other fields as well, perhaps in *all* human enterprises. I often suspect that we are dealing here with a profoundly characterological or constitutional difference in people which may persist far into the future, a human difference which may be universal and may continue to be so. The job then will be to get these two kinds of people to understand each other, to get along well with each other, even to love each other. This problem is paralleled by the relations between men and women who are so different from each other and yet who *have to* live with each other and even to love each other. (I must admit that it would be almost impossible to achieve this with poets and literary critics, composers and music critics, etc.)

To summarize, it looks quite probable that the peak-experience may be the model of the religious revelation or the religious illumination or conversion which has played so great a role in the history of religions. But, because peak-experiences are in the natural world and because we can research with them and investigate them, and because our knowledge of such experiences is growing and may be confidently expected to grow in the future, we may now fairly hope to understand more about the big revelations, conversions, and illuminations upon which the high religions were founded.

(Not only this, but I may add a new possibility for scientific investigation of transcendence. In the last few years it has become quite clear that certain drugs called 'psychedelic', especially LSD and psilocybin, give us some possibility of control in this realm of peak-experiences. It looks as if these drugs often produce peak-experiences in the right people under the right circumstances, so that perhaps we needn't wait for them to occur by good fortune. Perhaps we can actually produce a private personal peak-experience under observation and whenever we wish under religious or non-religious circumstances. We may then be able to study in its moment of birth the experience of illumination or revelation. Even more important, it may be that these drugs, and perhaps also hypnosis, could be used to produce a peak-experience, with core-religious revelation, in non-peakers, thus bridging the chasm between these two separated halves of mankind.)

To approach this whole discussion from another angle, in effect what I have been saying is that the evidence from the peak-experiences permits us to talk about the essential, the intrinsic, the basic, the most fundamental religious or transcendent experience as a totally private and personal one which can hardly be shared (except with other 'peakers'). As a consequence, all the paraphernalia of organized religion – buildings and specialized personnel, rituals, dogmas, ceremonials, and the like – are to the 'peaker' secondary, peripheral, and of doubtful value in relation to the intrinsic and essential religious or transcendent experience. Perhaps they may even be very harmful in various ways. From the point of view of the peak-experiencer, each person has his own private religion, which he develops out of his own private revelations in which are revealed to him his own private myths and symbols, rituals and ceremonials, which may be of the profoundest meaning to him personally and yet completely idiosyncratic, i.e., of no meaning to anyone else. But to say it even more simply, each 'peaker' discovers, develops, and retains his own religion (Warmoth 1965).

In addition, what seems to be emerging from this new source of data is that this essential core-religious experience may be embedded either in a theistic, supernatural context or in a non-theistic context. This private religious experience is shared by all the great world religions including the atheistic ones like Buddhism, Taoism, Humanism, or Confucianism. As a matter of fact, I can go so far as to say that this intrinsic core-experience is a meeting ground not only, let us say, for Christians and Jews and Mohammedans but also for priests and atheists, for communists and anti-communists, for conservatives and liberals, for artists and scientists, for men and for women, and for different constitutional types, that is to say, for athletes and for poets, for thinkers and for doers. I say this because our findings indicate that all or almost all people have or can have peak-experiences. Both men and women have peak-experiences, and all kinds of constitutional types have peak-experiences, but, although the content of the peak-experiences is approximately as I have described for all human beings, the situation or the trigger which sets off peak-experience, for instance in males and females, can be quite different. These experiences can come from different sources, but their content may be considered to be very similar. To sum it up, from this point of view, the two religions of mankind tend to be the peakers and the non-peakers, that is to say, those who have private, personal, transcendent, core-religious experiences easily and often and who accept them and make use of them, and, on the other hand, those who have never had them or who repress or suppress them and who, therefore, cannot make use of them for their personal therapy, personal growth, or personal fulfillment.

APPENDIX A: RELIGIOUS ASPECTS OF PEAK-EXPERIENCES

Practically everything that happens in the peak-experiences, naturalistic though they are, could be listed under the headings of religious happenings, or indeed have been in the past considered to be only religious experiences.

1. For instance, it is quite characteristic in peak-experiences that the whole universe is perceived as an integrated and unified whole. This is not as simple a happening as one might imagine from the bare words themselves. To have a clear perception (rather than a purely abstract and verbal philosophical acceptance) that the universe is all of a piece and that one has his place in it – one is a part of it, one belongs in it – can be so profound and shaking an experience that it can change the person's character and his Weltanschauung forever after. In my own experience I have two subjects who, because of such an experience, were totally, immediately, and permanently cured of (in one case) chronic anxiety neurosis and (in the other case) of strong obsessional thoughts of suicide.

This, of course, is a basic meaning of religious faith for many people. People who might otherwise lose their 'faith' will hang onto it because it gives a meaningfulness to the universe, a unity, a single philosophical explanation which makes it all hang together. Many orthodoxly religious people would be so frightened by giving up the notion that the universe has integration, unity, and, therefore, meaningfulness (which is given to it by the fact that it was all created by God or ruled by God or *is* God) that the only alternative for them would be to see the universe as a totally unintegrated chaos.

2. In the cognition that comes in peak-experiences, characteristically the percept is exclusively and fully attended to. That is, there is tremendous concentration of a kind which does not normally occur. There is the truest and most total kind of visual perceiving or listening or feeling. Part of what this involves is a peculiar change which can best be described as non-evaluating, non-comparing, or non-judging cognition. That is to say, figure and ground are less sharply differentiated. Important and unimportant are also less sharply differentiated, i.e., there is a tendency for things to become equally important rather than to be ranged in a hierarchy from very important to quite unimportant. For instance, the mother examining in loving ecstasy her new-born infant may be enthralled by every single part of him, one part as much as another one, one little toenail as much as another little toenail, and be struck into a kind of religious awe in this way. This same kind of total, non-comparing acceptance of everything, as if everything were equally important, holds also for the perception of people. Thus it comes about that in peak-experience cognition a person is most easily seen per se, in himself, by himself, uniquely and idiosyncratically as if he were the sole member of his class. Of course, this is a very common aspect not only of religious experience but of most theologies as well, i.e., the person is unique,

the person is sacred, one person in principle is worth as much as any other person, everyone is a child of God, etc.

3. The cognition of being (B-cognition) that occurs in peak-experiences tends to perceive external objects, the world, and individual people as more detached from human concerns. Normally we perceive everything as relevant to human concerns and more particularly to our own private selfish concerns. In the peak-experiences, we become more detached, more objective, and are more able to perceive the world as if it were independent not only of the perceiver but even of human beings in general. The perceiver can more readily look upon nature as if it were there in itself and for itself, not simply as if it were a human playground put there for human purposes. He can more easily refrain from projecting human purposes upon it. In a word, he can see it in its own Being (as an end in itself) rather than as something to be used or something to be afraid of or something to wish for or to be reacted to in some other personal, human, self-centered way. That is to say, B-cognition, because it makes human irrelevance more possible, enables us thereby to see more truly the nature of the object in itself. This is a little like talking about god-like perception, superhuman perception. The peak-experience seems to lift us to greater than normal heights so that we can see and perceive in a higher than usual way. We become larger, greater, stronger, bigger, taller people and tend to perceive accordingly.

4. To say this in a different way, perception in the peak-experiences can be relatively ego-transcending, self-forgetful, egoless, unselfish. It can come closer to being unmotivated, impersonal, desireless, detached, not needing or wishing. Which is to say, that it becomes more object-centered than ego-centered. The perceptual experience can be more organized around the object itself as a centering point rather than being based upon the selfish ego. This means in turn that objects and people are more readily perceived as having independent reality of their own.

5. The peak-experience is felt as a self-validating, self-justifying moment which carries its own intrinsic value with it. It is felt to be a highly valuable – even uniquely valuable – experience, so great an experience sometimes that even to attempt to justify it takes away from its dignity and worth. As a matter of fact, so many people find this so great and high an experience that it justifies not only itself but even living itself. Peak-experiences can make life worthwhile by their occasional occurrence. They give meaning to life itself. They prove it to be worthwhile. To say this in a negative way, I would guess that peak-experiences help to prevent suicide.

6. Recognizing these experiences as end-experiences rather than as means-experiences makes another point. For one thing, it proves to the experiencer that there are ends in the world, that there are things or objects or experiences to yearn for which are worthwhile in themselves. This in itself is a refutation of the proposition that life and living is meaningless. In other

words, peak-experiences are one part of the operational definition of the statement that 'life is worthwhile' or 'life is meaningful'.

7. In the peak-experience there is a very characteristic disorientation in time and space, or even the lack of consciousness of time and space. Phrased positively, this is like experiencing universality and eternity. Certainly we have here, in a very operational sense, a real and scientific meaning of 'under the aspect of eternity'. This kind of timelessness and spacelessness contrasts very sharply with normal experience. The person in the peak-experiences may feel a day passing as if it were minutes or also a minute so intensely lived that it might feel like a day or a year or an eternity even. He may also lose his consciousness of being located in a particular place.

8. The world seen in the peak-experiences is seen only as beautiful, good, desirable, worthwhile, etc. and is never experienced as evil or undesirable. The world is accepted. People will say that then they understand it. Most important of all for comparison with religious thinking is that somehow they become reconciled to evil. Evil itself is accepted and understood and seen in its proper place in the whole, as belonging there, as unavoidable, as necessary, and, therefore, as proper. Of course, the way in which I (and Laski also) gathered peak-experiences was by asking for reports of ecstasies and raptures, of the most blissful and perfect moments of life. Then, of course, life *would* look beautiful. And then all the foregoing might seem like discovering something that had been put in a priori. But observe that what I am talking about is the perception of evil, of pain, of disease, of death. In the peak-experiences, not only is the world seen as acceptable and beautiful, but, and this is what I am stressing, the bad things about life are accepted more totally than they are at other times. It is as if the peak-experience reconciled people to the presence of evil in the world.

9. Of course, this is another way of becoming 'god-like'. The gods who can contemplate and encompass the whole of being and who, therefore, understand it must see it as good, just, inevitable, and must see 'evil' as a product of limited or selfish vision and understanding. If we could be god-like in this sense, then we, too, out of universal understanding would never blame or condemn or be disappointed or shocked. Our only possible emotions would be pity, charity, kindliness, perhaps sadness or amusement. But this is precisely the way in which self-actualizing people do at times react to the world, and in which all of us react in our peak-experiences.

10. Perhaps my most important finding was the discovery of what I am calling B-values or the intrinsic values of Being. When I asked the question, 'How does the world look different in peak-experiences?', the hundreds of answers that I got could be boiled down to a quintessential list of characteristics which, though they overlap very much with one another can still be considered as separate for the sake of research. What is important for us in this context is that this list of the described characteristics of the world as it is perceived in our most perspicuous moments is about the same as what

people through the ages have called eternal verities, or the spiritual values, or the highest values, or the religious values. What this says is that facts and values are not totally different from each other; under certain circumstances, they fuse. Most religions have either explicitly or by implication affirmed some relationship or even an overlapping or fusion between facts and values. For instance, people not only existed but they were also sacred. The world was not only merely existent but it was also sacred (Maslow 1963).

11. B-cognition in the peak-experience is much more passive and receptive, much more humble, than normal perception is. It is much more ready to listen and much more able to hear.

12. In the peak-experience, such emotions as wonder, awe, reverence, humility, surrender, and even worship before the greatness of the experience are often reported. This may go so far as to involve thoughts of death in a peculiar way. Peak-experiences can be so wonderful that they can parallel the experience of dying, that is of an eager and happy dying. It is a kind of reconciliation and acceptance of death. Scientists have never considered as a scientific problem the question of the 'good death'; but here in these experiences we discover a parallel to what has been considered to be the religious attitude toward death, i.e., humility or dignity before it, willingness to accept it, possibly even a happiness with it.

13. In peak-experiences, the dichotomies, polarities, and conflicts of life tend to be transcended or resolved. That is to say, there tends to be a moving toward the perception of unity and integration in the world. The person himself tends to move toward fusion, integration, and unity and away from splitting, conflicts, and oppositions.

14. In the peak-experiences, there tends to be a loss, even though transient, of fear, anxiety, inhibition, of defense and control, of perplexity, confusion, conflict, of delay and restraint. The profound fear of disintegration, of insanity, of death, all tend to disappear for the moment. Perhaps this amounts to saying that fear disappears.

15. Peak-experiences sometimes have immediate effects or aftereffects upon the person. Sometimes their aftereffects are so profound and so great as to remind us of the profound religious conversions which forever after changed the person. Lesser effects could be called therapeutic. These can range from very great to minimal or even to no effects at all. This is an easy concept for religious people to accept, accustomed as they are to thinking in terms of conversions, of great illuminations, of great moments of insight, etc.

16. I have likened the peak-experience in a metaphor to a visit to a personally defined heaven from which the person then returns to earth. This is like giving a naturalistic meaning to the concept of heaven. Of course, it is quite different from the conception of heaven as a place somewhere into which one physically steps after life on this earth is over. The conception of

heaven that emerges from the peak-experiences is one which exists all the time all around us, always available to step into for a little while at least.

17. In peak-experiences, there is a tendency to move more closely to a perfect identity, or uniqueness, or to the idiosyncrasy of the person or to his real self, to have become more a real person.

18. The person feels himself more than at other times to be responsible, active, the creative center of his own activities and of his own perceptions, more self-determined, more a free agent, with more 'free will' than at other times.

19. But it has also been discovered that precisely those persons who have the clearest and strongest identity are exactly the ones who are most able to transcend the ego or the self and to become selfless, who are at least relatively selfless and relatively egoless.

20. The peak-experiencer becomes more loving and more accepting, and so he becomes more spontaneous and honest and innocent.

21. He becomes less an object, less a thing, less a thing of the world living under the laws of the physical world, and he becomes more a psyche, more a person, more subject to the psychological laws, especially the laws of what people have called the 'higher life'.

22. Because he becomes more unmotivated, that is to say, closer to non-striving, non-needing, non-wishing, he asks less for himself in such moments. He is less selfish. (We must remember that the gods have been considered generally to have no needs or wants, no deficiencies, no lacks, and to be gratified in all things. In this sense, the unmotivated human being becomes more god-like.)

23. People during and after peak-experiences characteristically feel lucky, fortunate, graced. A common reaction is 'I don't deserve this'. A common consequence is a feeling of gratitude, in religious persons, to their God, in others, to fate or to nature or to just good fortune. It is interesting in the present context that this can go over into worship, giving thanks, adoring, giving praise, oblation, and other reactions which fit very easily into orthodox religious frameworks. In that context we are accustomed to this sort of thing – that is, to the feeling of gratitude or all-embracing love for everybody and for everything, leading to an impulse to do something good for the world, an eagerness to repay, even a sense of obligation and dedication.

24. The dichotomy or polarity between humility and pride tends to be resolved in the peak-experiences and also in self-actualizing persons. Such people resolve the dichotomy between pride and humility by fusing them into a single complex superordinate unity, that is by being proud (in a certain sense) and also humble (in a certain sense). Pride (fused with humility) is not hubris nor is it paranoia; humility (fused with pride) is not masochism.

25. What has been called the 'unitive consciousness' is often given in peak-experiences, i.e., a sense of the sacred glimpsed *in* and *through* the particular instance of the momentary, the secular, the worldly.

[. . .]

APPENDIX F: RHAPSODIC, ISOMORPHIC COMMUNICATIONS

In trying to elicit reports of peak-experiences from reluctant subjects or from non-peakers, I evolved a different kind of interview procedure without being consciously aware that I had done so. The 'rhapsodic communication', as I have called it, consists of a kind of emotional contagion in isomorphic parallel. It may have considerable implications for both the theory of science and the philosophy of education.

Direct verbal description of peak-experiences in a sober, cool, analytic, 'scientific' way succeeds only with those who already know what you mean, i.e., people who have vivid peaks and who can, therefore, feel or intuit what you are trying to point to even when your words are quite inadequate in themselves.

As I went on interviewing, I 'learned', without realizing that I was learning, to shift over more and more to figures of speech, metaphors, similes, etc., and, in general, to use more and more poetic speech. It turns out that these are often more apt to 'click', to touch off an echoing experience, a parallel, isomorphic vibration than are sober, cool, carefully descriptive phrases.

We are taught here that the word 'ineffable' means 'not communicable by words that are analytic, abstract, linear, rational, exact, etc'. Poetic and metaphorical language, physiognomic and synesthetic language, primary process language of the kind found in dreams, reveries, free associations and fantasies, not to mention pre-words and non-words such as gestures, tone of voice, style of speaking, body tonus, facial expressions – all these are more efficacious in communicating certain aspects of the ineffable.

This procedure can wind up being a kind of continuing rhapsodic, emotional, eager throwing out of one example after another of peaks, described or rather reported, expressed, shared, 'celebrated', sung vividly with participation and with obvious approval and even joy. This kind of procedure can more often kindle into flame the latent or weak peak-experiences within the other person.

The problem here was not the usual one in teaching. It was not a labelling of something public that both could simultaneously see while the teacher pointed to it and named it. Rather it was trying to get the person to focus attention, to notice, to name an experience inside himself, which only he could feel, an experience, furthermore, which was not happening at the time. No pointing is possible here, no naming of something visible, no controlled and purposeful creation of the experience like turning on an electric current at will or probing at a painful spot.

In such an effort, one realizes vividly how isolated people's insides are from each other. It is as if two encapsulated privacies were trying to communicate with each other across the chasm between them. When the experience one is trying to communicate has no parallel in the other person, as in trying to describe color to the congenitally blind, then words fail almost (but not) entirely. If the other person turns out to be a literal non-peaker, then rhapsodic, isomorphic communication will not work.

In retrospect, I can see that I gradually began to assume that the non-peaker was a *weak* peaker rather than a person lacking the capacity altogether. I was, in effect, trying to fan his slumbering fire into open flame by my emotionally involved and approving accounts of other people's stronger experiences, as a tuning fork will set off a sympathetic piano wire across the room.

In effect, I proceeded 'as if' I was trying to make a non-peaker into a peaker, or, better said, to make the self-styled non-peaker realize that he really was a peaker after all. I couldn't teach him how to have a peak-experience; but I could teach that he had already had it.

Whatever sensitizes the non-peaker to his own peaks will thereby make him *fertile ground for the seeds which the great peakers will cast upon him.* The great seers, prophets, or peakers may then be used as we now use artists, i.e., as people who are more sensitive, more reactive, who get a profounder, fuller, deeper peak-experience which then they can pass on to other people who are at least peakers enough to be able to be a good audience. Trying to teach the general population how to paint will certainly not make them into great painters, but it can very well make them into a better audience for great artists. Just as it is necessary to be a bit of an artist oneself before one can understand a great artist, so it is apparently necessary to become a small seer oneself before one can understand the great seers.

This is a kind of I–thou communication of intimates, of friends, of sweethearts, or of brothers rather than the more usual kind of subject–object, perceiver–percept, investigator–subject relationship in which separation, distance, detachment are thought to be the only way to bring greater objectivity.

Something of the sort has been discovered in other situations. For instance, in using psychedelic drugs to produce peak-experiences, general experience has been that if the atmosphere is coldly clinical or investigatory, and if the subject is watched and studied as if with a microscope, like a bug on a pin, then peaks are less apt to occur and unhappy experiences are more apt to occur. When the atmosphere becomes one of brotherly communion, however, with perhaps one of the 'investigator-brothers' himself also taking the drug, then the experience is much more likely to be ecstatic and transcendent.

Something similar has been discovered by the Alcoholics Anonymous and by the Synanon groups for drug addicts. The person who has shared the experience can be brotherly and loving in a way that dispels the dominance hierarchy implied in the usual helping relationship. The reported reciprocal interdependence of performers and audiences could also serve as an example of this same kind of communication.

The existential and humanistic psychotherapists are also beginning to report that the 'I–Thou encounter' can bring certain results which cannot be brought about by the classical Freudian mirror-type psychoanalyst (although I feel sure that the reverse is also true for certain *other* therapeutic results). Even the classical psychoanalysts would now be willing to admit, I think, that care, concern, and agapean love for the patient are implied, and *must* be implied, by the analyst in order that therapy may take place.

The ethologists have learned that if you want to study ducks and to learn all that is possible to know about ducks, then you had better love ducks. And so also, I believe, for stars, or numbers, or chemicals. This kind of love or interest or fascination is not contradictory of objectivity or truthfulness but is rather a precondition of certain kinds of objectivity, perspicuity, and receptivity. B-love encourages B-cognition, i.e., unselfish, understanding love for the Being or intrinsic nature of the other, makes it possible to perceive and to enjoy the other as an end in himself (not as a selfish means or as an instrument), and, therefore, makes more possible the perception of the nature of the other in its own right.

All (?), or very many, people, including even young children, can in principle be taught in some such experiential way that peak-experiences exist, what they are like, when they are apt to come, to whom they are apt to come, what will make them more likely, what their connection is with a good life, with a good man, with good psychological health, etc. To some extent, this can be done even with words, with lectures, with books. My experience has been that whenever I have lectured approvingly about peak-experiences, it was as if I had given permission to the peak-experiences of *some* people, at least, in my audience to come into consciousness. That is, even mere words sometimes seem to be able to remove the inhibitions, the blocks, and the fears, the rejections which had kept the peak-experiences hidden and suppressed.

All of this implies another *kind* of education, i.e., experiential education. But not only this, it also implies another kind of communication, the communication between alonenesses, between encapsulated, isolated egos. What we are implying is that in the kind of experiential teaching which is being discussed here, what is necessary to do first is to change the person and to change his awareness of himself. That is, what we must do is to make him become aware of the fact that peak-experiences go on inside himself. Until he has become aware of such experience and has this experience as a basis for comparison, he is a non-peaker; and it is useless to try to communicate to him the feel and the nature of peak-experience. But if we can change him, in the sense of making him aware of what is going on inside himself, then he becomes a different kind of communicatee. It is now possible to communicate with him. He now knows what you are talking about when you speak of peak-experiences; and it is possible to teach him by reference to his own weak peak-experiences how to improve them, how to enrich them, how to enlarge them, and also how to draw the proper conclusions from these experiences.

It can be pointed out that something of this kind goes on normally in un-covering, insight psychotherapy. Part of the process here is an experiential-educational one in which we help the patient become aware of what he has been experiencing without having been aware of it. If we can teach him that such and such a constellation of preverbal subjective happenings has the label 'anxiety', then thereafter it is possible to communicate with him about anxiety and all the conditions that bring it about, how to increase it, how to decrease it, etc. Until that point is reached at which he has a conscious, objective, detached awareness of the relationship between a par-ticular name or label or word and a particular set of subjective, ineffable experiences, no communication and no teaching are possible; so also for passivity or hostility or yearning for love or whatever. In all of these, we may use the paradigm that the process of education (and of therapy) is helping the person to become aware of internal, subjective, subverbal experiences, so that these experiences can be brought into the world of abstraction, of conversation, of communication, of naming, etc., with the consequence that it immediately becomes possible for a certain amount of control to be exerted over these hitherto unconscious and uncontrollable processes.

One trouble with this kind of communication, for me at least, has been that I felt rhapsodizing to be artificial when I tried to do it deliberately and consciously. I became fully aware of what I had been doing only after trying to describe it in a conversation with Dr. David Nowlis. But since then I have not been able to communicate in the same way.

NOTES

1. If we were to go further with our analysis, we should find that, succeeding upon the discovery of the generality of all peak-experiences, there are also 'specific' factors in each of the peak-experiences which differentiate them from each other to some extent. This relationship of specific to general is as figure to ground. It is something like that described by Spearman for 'g' and 's' factors in intelligence.

    I do not discuss these 's' factors here because the 'g' factor is far more important for the problem at hand and at this stage in its development.
2. I have made no effort in this chapter [...] to balance accounts by detailing the virtues and even the unavoidable necessity of organizations and organizers. I have written about these elsewhere (Maslow 1965).

REFERENCES

Abelson, R. P. (1988), 'Conviction', *American Psychologist* 43: 267–75.

Adams, C. J. (ed.) (1993), *Ecofeminism and the Sacred*, New York: Continuum.

Allen, D. (1978), *Structure and Creativity in Religion*, The Hague: Mouton.

Allport, G. W. (1950), *The Individual and His Religion*, New York: Macmillan.

Allport, G. W. (1966), 'The religious context of prejudice', *Journal for the Scientific Study of Religion* 5: 447–57.

Allport, G. W. and Ross, J. M. (1967), 'Personal religious orientation and prejudice', *Journal of Personality and Social Psychology* 5: 432–43.

Alston, W. P. (1967), 'Religion', in P. Edwards (ed.), *The Encyclopedia of Philosophy*, New York: Macmillan/Free Press, vol. 7, pp. 140–5.

Anderson, J. R. (1983), *The Architecture of Cognition*, Cambridge, MA: Harvard University Press.

Atkinson, C. W., C. H. Buchanan and M. R. Miles (eds) (1985), *Immaculate and Powerful*, Boston: Beacon Press.

Atkinson, J. J. (1903), *Primal Law*, London: Longmans.

Bachofen, J. J. (1861), *Das Mutterrecht*, Stuttgart: Krais & Hoffmann.

Bainbridge, W. S. (1978), *Satan's Power*, Berkeley: University of California Press.

Balk, D. (1983), 'How teenagers cope with sibling death', *School Counselor* 31: 150–8.

Ball-Rokeach, S. J., M. Rokeach and J. W. Grube (1984), *The Great American Values Test*, New York: Free Press.

Bartlett, F. C. (1932), *Remembering*, Cambridge: Cambridge University Press.

Basham, A. L. (1971), *The Wonder That Was India*, London: Fontana.

Batson, C. D. and L. Raynor-Prince (1983), 'Religious orientation and complexity of thought about existential concerns', *Journal for the Scientific Study of Religion* 22: 38–50.

Batson, C. D. and W. L. Ventis (1982), *The Religious Experience*, New York: Oxford University Press.

Beckford, J. A. (1989), *Religion and Advanced Industrial Society*, London: Unwin Hyman.

Béguin, J., C. Tardits, J. Baubérot, F. Laplanche, E. Poulat and J.-P. Vernant (1987), *Cent ans de sciences religieuses en France à l'Ecole Pratique des Hautes Etudes*, Paris: Cerf.

Bell, C. (1914), *Art*, London: Chatto & Windus.

Bell, D. (1977), 'The return of the sacred?', *British Journal of Sociology* 28: 419–49.

Bellah, R. N. (1967), 'Civil religion in America', *Daedalus* 96(1): 1–21.

Bellah, R. N. (1970a), *Beyond Belief*, New York: Harper & Row.

Bellah, R. N. (1970b), 'Christianity and symbolic realism', *Journal for the Scientific Study of Religion* 9: 89–96.

Bellah, R. N. and P. E. Hammond (1980), *Varieties of Civil Religion*, San Francisco: Harper & Row.

Berger, P. L. (1967), *The Sacred Canopy*, Garden City, NY: Doubleday.

Berger, P. L. (1969), *The Social Reality of Religion*, London: Faber & Faber.

Berger, P. L. (1974), 'Some second thoughts on substantive versus functional divisions of religion', *Journal for the Scientific Study of Religion* 13: 125–33.

Berger, P. L. and T. Luckmann (1966), 'Secularization and pluralism', *International Yearbook for the Sociology of Religion* 2: 73–84.

Berger, P. L. and T. Luckmann (1973), *The Social Construction of Reality*, Harmondsworth: Penguin.

Berger, P. L., B. Berger and H. Kellner (1974), *The Homeless Mind*, Harmondsworth: Penguin.

Boddy, J. (1989), *Wombs and Alien Spirits*, Madison: University of Wisconsin Press.

Boudon, R. (1988), 'Sociologie: les développements', in *Encyclopædia Universalis*, Paris: Encyclopædia Universalis, vol. 21, pp. 211–14.

Bourdieu, P. (1968), *Le Métier de sociologie*, Paris: Mouton-Bordas.

Bourdieu, P. (1987), 'Sociologues de la croyance et croyances de sociologues', *Archives de Sciences Sociales des Religions* 63(1): 155–61.

Bower, G. H. (1981), 'Mood and memory', *American Psychologist* 36: 129–48.

Bowlby, J. (1969), *Attachment and Loss, vol. 1: Attachment*, New York: Basic Books.

Bowlby, J. (1980), *Attachment and Loss, vol. 3: Loss*, New York: Basic Books.

Braden, C. S. (1947), 'Why people are religious', *Journal of Bible and Religion* 15: 38–45.

Brent, E. E. and D. Granberg (1982), 'Subjective agreement and the presidential candidates of 1976 and 1980', *Journal of Personality and Social Psychology* 42: 393–403.

Briggs, S. (1987), 'Women and religion', in B. B. Hess and M. M. Ferree (eds), *Analyzing Gender*, Newbury Park, CA: Sage, pp. 408–41.

Brown, K. M. (1991), *Mama Lola*, Berkeley: University of California Press.

Bruce, S. (1985), 'Authority and fission', *British Journal of Sociology* 36: 592–603.

Bruce, S. (1998), *Conservative Protestant Politics*, Oxford: Oxford University Press.

Bruce, S. (1999), *Choice and Religion*, Oxford: Oxford University Press.

Bruner, J. S. (1957a), 'Going beyond the information given', in J. S, Bruner, H. E. Gruber, K. K. Hammond and R. Jessor (eds), *Contemporary Approaches to Cognitions*, Cambridge, MA: Harvard University Press, pp. 41–69.

Bruner, J. S. (1957b), 'On perceptual readiness', *Psychological Review* 64: 123–52.

Buchanan, C. H. (1987), 'Women's studies', in M. Eliade (ed.), *The Encyclopedia of Religion*, New York: Macmillan; London: Collier Macmillan, vol. 15, pp. 433–40.

Buckser, A. (1996), 'Religion, science and secularization theory', *Journal for the Scientific Study of Religion* 35: 432–41.

Bulman, R. J. and C. B. Wortman (1977), 'Attribution of blame and coping in the "real world"', *Journal of Personality and Social Psychology* 35: 351–63.

Burke, K. (1941), *The Philosophy of Literary Form*, Baton Rouge: Louisiana State University Press.

Bynum, C. W., S. Harrell and P. Richman (eds) (1986), *Gender and Religion*, Boston: Beacon Press.

Campbell, D. T. (1975), 'On the conflicts between biological and social evolution and between psychological and moral tradition', *American Psychologist* 30: 1103–26.

Campbell, J. (1949), *The Hero with a Thousand Faces*, New York: Pantheon.

Campbell, K. (1965), 'Family resemblance predicates', *American Philosophical Quarterly* 2(3): 238–44.

Cantwell Smith, W. ([1964] 1990), *The Meaning and End of Religion*, Minneapolis: Augsburg Fortress.

Carnap, R. (1938), 'Logical foundations of the unity of science', *International Encyclopedia of Unified Science* 1: 42–62.

Carr, A. E. (1990), *Transforming Grace*, San Francisco: Harper & Row.

Casanova, J. (1994), *Public Religions in the Modern World*, Chicago: University of Chicago Press.

Chaiken, S. and C. Stangor (1987), 'Attitudes and attitude change', *Annual Review of Psychology* 38: 575–630.

Child, I. L. (1973), *Humanistic Psychology and the Research Tradition*, New York: Wiley.

Christ, C. P. (1985), 'Discussion: what are the sources of my theology?', *Journal of Feminist Studies in Religion* 1: 120–3.

Christ, C. P. (1987a), *Laughter of Aphrodite*, San Francisco: Harper & Row.

Christ, C. P. (1987b), 'Toward a paradigm shift in the academy and in religious studies', in C. Farnham (ed.), *The Impact of Feminist Research in the Academy*, Bloomington: Indiana University Press, pp. 53–76.

Christ, C. P. (1989), 'Embodied thinking', *Journal of Feminist Studies in Religion* 5(1): 7–17.

Christ, C. P. (1991), 'Mircea Eliade and the feminist paradigm shift', *Journal of Feminist Studies in Religion* 7(2): 75–94.

Christ, C. P. (1992). 'Feminists – sojourners in the field of religious studies', in C. Kramarae and D. Spender (eds), *The Knowledge Explosion*, New York and London: Athene Press, pp. 82–8.

Christ, C. and J. Plaskow (eds) (1979), *Womanspirit Rising*, San Francisco: Harper & Row.

Clark, W. H. (1958), *The Psychology of Religion*, New York: Macmillan.

Coleman, L. and P. Kay (1981), 'Prototype semantics: the English word lie', *Language* 57: 26–44.

Craik, K. (1952), *The Nature of Explanation*, Cambridge: Cambridge University Press.

Crick, M. (1976), *Explorations in Language and Meaning*, London: Malaby Press.

Demerath, N. J. and R. M. Levinson (1971), 'Baiting the dissident hook', *Sociometry* 34: 346–59.

Desroche, H. (1968), *Sociologies religieuses*, Paris: Presses Universitaires de France.

Desroche, H. and J. Séguy (1970), *Introduction aux sciences humaines des religions*, Paris: Cujas.

Dewey, J. (1934), *A Common Faith*, New Haven: Yale University Press.

Dollinger, S. J. (1986), 'The need for meaning following disaster', *Personality and Social Psychology Bulletin* 12: 300–10.

Donahue, M. J. (1985), 'Intrinsic and extrinsic religiousness', *Journal for the Scientific Study of Religion* 24: 418–23.

Dudley, G. (1977), *Religion on Trial*, Philadelphia: Temple University Press.

Durkheim, E. (1912), *Les Formes élémentaires de la vie religieuse*, Paris: Alcan.

Durkheim, E. (1915), *The Elementary Forms of the Religious Life*, tr. J. W. Swain, London: Allen & Unwin.

Durkheim, E. ([1915] 1954), *The Elementary Forms of the Religious Life*, tr. J. W. Swain, Glencoe, IL: Free Press.

Durkheim, E. ([1895] 1982), *The Rules of Sociological Method*, tr. W. D. Hall, London: Macmillan.

Durkheim, E. ([1893] 1984), *The Division of Labour in Society*, tr. W. D. Hall, London: Macmillan.

Edwards, R. B. (1972), *Reason and Religion*, New York: Harcourt Brace Jovanovich.

REFERENCES

Eliade, M. (1963), *Patterns in Comparative Religion*, New York: Meridian.

Eliade, M. (1969), *The Quest*, Chicago: University of Chicago Press.

Elzey, W. (1994), 'Mircea Eliade and the battle against reductionism', in T. A. Idinopulos and E. A. Yonan (eds), *Religion and Reductionism*, Leiden: E. J. Brill.

Evans-Pritchard, E. E. (1937), *Witchcraft, Oracles and Magic among the Azande*, Oxford: Clarendon Press.

Evans-Pritchard, E. E. (1965), *Theories of Primitive Religion*, Oxford: Clarendon Press.

Farnham, C. (ed.) (1987), *The Impact of Feminist Research in the Academy*, Bloomington: Indiana University Press.

Fazio, R. H. (1986), 'How do attitudes guide behavior?', in R. M. Sorrentino and E. T. Higgins (eds), *The Handbook of Motivation and Cognition*, New York: Guilford Press, pp. 204–43.

Fazio, R. H. (1989), 'On the power and functionality of attitudes', in A. R. Pratkanis, S. J. Breckler and A. G. Greenwald (eds), *Attitude Structure and Function*, Hillsdale, NJ: Lawrence Erlbaum Associates, pp. 153–79.

Fazio, R. H. and C. J. Williams (1986), 'Attitude accessibility as a moderator of the attitude–perception and attitude–behavior relations', *Journal of Personality and Social Psychology* 51: 505–14.

Fazio, R. H., J. Chen, E. C. McDonel and S. J. Sherman (1982), 'Attitude accessibility, attitude–behavior consistency, and the strength of the object–evaluation association', *Journal of Experimental Social Psychology* 18: 339–57.

Fazio, R. H., D. M. Sanbonmatsu, M. C. Powell and F. R. Kardes (1986), 'On the automatic activation of attitudes', *Journal of Personality and Social Psychology* 50: 229–38.

Fiorenza, E. S. (1983), *In Memory of Her*, New York: Crossroad.

Firth, R. (1951), *Elements of Social Organization*, London: Watts; New York: Philosophical Library.

Fishbein, M. and I. Ajzen (1975), *Belief, Attitude, Intention, and Behavior*, Reading, MA: Addison-Wesley.

Fiske, S. T. and P. W. Linville (1980), 'What does the schema concept buy us?', *Personality and Social Psychology Bulletin* 6: 543–57.

Fiske, S. T. and S. E. Taylor (eds) (1991), *Social Cognition*, New York: McGraw-Hill.

Fortune, R. F. (1935), *Manus Religion*, Philadelphia: American Philosophical Society.

Fowler, J. W. (1977), 'Faith and the structure of meaning', paper presented at the annual convention of the American Psychological Association, San Francisco, August.

Frank, J. D. (1977), 'Nature and functions of belief systems', *American Psychologist* 32: 555–9.

Frazer, J. G. (1911), *The Golden Bough, part 1: The Magic Art and the Evolution of Kings* (2 vols), London: Macmillan.

Freud, S. ([1900] 1932), *The Interpretation of Dreams* (3rd edn), tr. A. A. Brill, London: Allen & Unwin.

Friedman, S. B., P. Chodoff, J. W. Mason and D. A. Hamburg (1963), 'Behavioral observations on parents anticipating the death of a child', *Pediatrics* 32: 610–25.

Frisch, K. von (1962), 'Dialects in the language of the bees', *Scientific American*, August.

Gallup, G. H. (1978a), *The Gallup Poll: Public Opinion 1972–1977*, Wilmington, DE: Scholarly Resources.

Gallup, G. H. (1978b), *Gallup Youth Survey 1978*, Princeton: Gallup Associates.

Gardner, H. (1985), *The Mind's New Science*, New York: Basic Books.

Garvey, J. H. (1993), 'Fundamentalism and American law', in M. E. Marty and R. S. Appleby (eds), *Fundamentalisms and the State*, Chicago: University of Chicago Press, pp. 28–48.

Geertz, C. (1958), 'Ethos, world-view and the analysis of sacred symbols', *Antioch Review*, Winter: 421–37.

Geertz, C. (1960), *The Religion of Java*, Glencoe, IL: Free Press.

Geertz, C. (1962), 'The growth of culture and the evolution of mind', in J. Scher (ed.), *Theories of the Mind*, New York: Free Press, pp. 713–40.

Geertz, C. (1964), 'Ideology as a cultural system', in D. Apter (ed.), *Ideology and Discontent*, New York: Free Press.

Geertz, C. (1966), 'Religion as a cultural system', in M. Banton (ed.), *Anthropological Approaches to the Study of Religion*, New York: Praeger.

Gellner, E. (1983), *Nations and Nationalism*, Oxford: Blackwell.

Gellner, E. (1991), *Plough, Sword and Book*, London: Paladin.

Gerth, H. H. and C. W. Mills (eds) (1946), *From Max Weber: Essays in Sociology*, New York: Oxford University Press.

Giddens, A. (1971), *Capitalism and Modern Social Theory*, Cambridge: Cambridge University Press.

Glick, I. O., R. S. Weiss and C. M. Parkes (1974), *The First Year of Bereavement*, New York: John Wiley.

Glock, C. Y. and T. Piazza (1981), 'Exploring reality structures', in T. Robbins and D. Anthony (eds), *In Gods We Trust*, New Brunswick, NJ: Transaction.

Gluckman, M. (1955), *The Judicial Process among the Barotse*, Manchester: Manchester University Press.

Goffman, E. (1974), *Stigma*, New York: Jason Aronson.

Goldstein, K. (1963a), *Human Nature*, New York: Schocken.

Goldstein, K. (1963b), *The Organism*, Boston: Beacon Press.

Goodenough, W. H. (1989), 'The nature of religion as a human phenomenon', *Institute on Religion in an Age of Science Newsletter* 37(3): 6–7.

Goody, J. (1961), 'Religion and ritual', *British Journal of Sociology* 12: 143–64.

Gorer, G. (1965), *Death, Grief, and Mourning in Contemporary Britain*, London: Cresset Press.

Gorsuch, R. L. (1986), 'Measuring attitudes, interests, sentiments, and values', in R. B. Cattell and R. C. Johnson (eds), *Functional Psychological Testing*, New York: Brunner/Mazel, pp. 316–33.

Gross, R. M. (1974), 'Methodological remarks on the study of women in religion', in J. Plaskow and J. Arnold Romero (eds), *Women and Religion* (rev. edn), Missoula, MT: Scholars Press, pp. 153–65.

Gross, R. M. (1977), 'Androcentrism and androgyny in the methodology of history of religions', in R. M. Gross (ed.), *Beyond Androcentrism*, Missoula, MT: Scholars Press, pp. 7–21.

Gross, R. M. (1983), 'Women's studies in religion', in P. Slater and D. Wiebe (eds), *Traditions in Contact and Change*, Waterloo, ON: Wilfred Laurier University Press, pp. 579–91.

Gross, R. M. (1993), *Buddhism after Patriarchy*, Albany: State University of New York Press.

Hackett, R. I. J. (1995), 'Women and new religious movements in Africa', in U. King (ed.), *Religion and Gender*, Oxford: Blackwell, pp. 257–90.

Hall, C. M. (1986), 'Crisis as opportunity for spiritual growth', *Journal of Religion and Health* 25: 8–17.

Hanford, J. T. (1975), 'A synoptic approach', *Journal for the Scientific Study of Religion* 14: 219–27.

Hanson, N. R. (1958), *Patterns of Discovery*, New York: Cambridge University Press.

Harris, M. (1968), *The Rise of Anthropological Theory*, New York: Harper & Row.

Harvey, O. J., D. E. Hunt and H. M. Schroder (1961), *Conceptual Systems and Personality Organization*, New York: John Wiley.

Hastie, R. (1981), 'Schematic principles in human memory', in E. T. Higgins, C. P. Herman and M. P. Zanna (eds), *Social Cognition*, Hillsdale, NJ: Lawrence Erlbaum Associates, vol. 1, pp. 39–88.

Hempel, C. G. (1952), *Fundamentals of Concept Formation in Empirical Science*, Chicago: Chicago University Press.

Hesse, H. (1951), *Siddhartha*, tr. H. Rosner, New York: New Directions.

Hewitt, M. A. (1993), 'Cyborgs, drag queens, and goddesses', *Method and Theory in the Study of Religion* 5: 135–54.

Higgins, E. T. and G. King (1981), 'Accessibility of social constructs', in N. Cantor and J. Kihlstrom (eds), *Personality, Cognition, and Social Interaction*, Hillsdale, NJ: Lawrence Erlbaum Associates, pp. 69–121.

Hill, P. C. (1995), 'Affective theory and religious experience', in R. W. Hood Jr (ed.), *Handbook of Religious Experience*, Birmingham, AL: Religious Education Press, pp. 253–377.

Hill, P. C. and R. L. Bassett (1992), 'Getting to the heart of the matter', in M. L. Lynn and D. O. Moberg (eds), *Research in the Social Scientific Study of Religion*, Greenwich, CT: JAI Press, vol. 4, pp. 159–82.

Hill, P. C., M. A. Jennings, D. D. Haas and K. S. Seybold (1992), 'Automatic and controlled activation of religious attitudes', paper presented at the meeting of the American Psychological Association, Washington, DC, August.

Hoffer, E. (1951), *The True Believer*, New York: Harper & Row.

Homans, G. C. (1961), *Social Behavior*, New York: Harcourt Brace & World.

Homans, G. C. (1974), *Social Behavior* (2nd edn), New York: Harcourt Brace Jovanovich.

Hope, D. (1987), 'The healing paradox of forgiveness', *Psychotherapy* 24: 240–4.

Horowitz, N. H. (1956), 'The gene', *Scientific American*, February.

Horton, R. (1960), 'A definition of religion and its uses', *Journal of the Royal Anthropological Institute* 90: 201–26.

Hudson, W. D. (1977), 'What makes religious beliefs religious?', *Religious Studies* 13: 221–42.

Idinopulos, T. A. (1994), 'Must professors of religion be religious?', in T. A. Idinopulos and E. A. Yonan (eds), *Religion and Reductionism*, Leiden: E. J. Brill.

Idinopulos, T. A. and E. A. Yonan (eds) (1994), *Religion and Reductionism*, Leiden: E. J. Brill.

Ingram, L. C. (1989), 'Evangelism as frame intrusion', *Journal for the Scientific Study of Religion* 28: 17–26.

Isambert, F.-A. (1966), 'La Fête et les fêtes', *Journal de Psychologie Normale et Pathologique*, July–December.

Isambert, F.-A. (1982), *Le Sens du Sacré*, Paris: Minuit.

ITA (1970), *Religion in Britain and Northern Ireland*, London: Independent Television Authority.

James, W. (1902), *The Varieties of Religious Experience*, New York: Longman.

James, W. (1904), *The Principles of Psychology* (2 vols), New York: Henry Holt.

Janoff-Bulman, R. (1989), 'Assumptive worlds and the stress of traumatic events', *Social Cognition* 7: 113–36.

Janoff-Bulman, R. and I. H. Frieze (1983), 'A theoretical principle for understanding reactions to victimization', *Journal of Social Issues* 39: 1–17.

Johnson, P. A. and J. Kalven (eds) (1988), *With Both Eyes Open*, New York: Pilgrim Press.

Jung, C. G. (1912), *Wandlungen und Symbole der Libido*, Leipzig and Vienna: Deuticke.

Kirkpatrick, L. A. and R. W. Hood Jr (1990), 'Intrinsic–extrinsic religious orientation', *Journal for the Scientific Study of Religion* 29: 442–62.

Kirkpatrick, L. A. and R. W. Hood Jr (1991), 'Rub-a-dub-dub: Who's in the tub?', *Journal for the Scientific Study of Religion* 30: 318–21.

King, U. (1986), 'Female identity and the history of religions', in V. C. Hayes (ed.), *Identity Issues and World Religions*, Bedford Park, SA: Australian Association for the Study of Religions, pp. 83–92.

504

King, U. (1990), 'Women scholars and the Encyclopedia of Religion', *Method and Theory in the Study of Religion* 2(1): 91–7.

King, U. (ed.) (1994), *Feminist Theology from the Third World*, London: SPCK; Maryknoll, NY: Orbis.

King, U. (1995), 'A question of identity', in U. King (ed.), *Religion and Gender*, Oxford: Blackwell, 219–44.

Klaaren, E. M. (1977), *Religious Origins of Modern Science*, Grand Rapids, MI: Eerdmans.

Kluckhohn, C. (1949), 'The philosophy of the Navaho Indians', in F. S. C. Northrop (ed.), *Ideological Differences and World Order*, New Haven: Yale University Press, pp. 356–84.

Kluckhohn, C. (1953), 'Universal categories of culture', in A. L. Kroeber (ed.), *Anthropology Today*, Chicago: University of Chicago Press, pp. 507–23.

Koenig, H. G., L. K. George and I. C. Siegler (1988), 'The use of religion and other emotion-regulating coping strategies among older adults', *Gerontologist* 28: 303–10.

Krosnick, J. A. (1986), 'Policy voting in American presidential elections', unpublished doctoral dissertation, University of Michigan, Ann Arbor.

Krosnick, J. A. (1988), 'Attitude importance and attitude change', *Journal of Experimental Social Psychology* 24: 240–55.

Krosnick, J. A. (1989), 'Attitude importance and attitude accessibility', *Personality and Social Psychology Bulletin* 15: 297–308.

Kuhn, T. S. (1962), *The Structure of Scientific Revolutions*, Chicago: Chicago University Press.

Kwilecki, S. (1991), 'The relationship between religious development and personality development', in M. L. Lynn and D. O. Moberg (eds), *Research in the Social Scientific Study of Religion*, Greenwich, CT: JAI Press, vol. 3, pp. 59–87.

Lakoff, G. (1987), *Women, Fire, and Dangerous Things*, Chicago: University of Chicago Press.

Langer, S. (1953), *Feeling and Form*, New York: Scribner's.

Langer, S. (1960), *Philosophy in a New Key* (4th edn), Cambridge, MA: Harvard University Press.

Langer, S. (1962), *Philosophical Sketches*, Baltimore: Johns Hopkins University Press.

Langland, E. and W. Gove (eds) (1981), *A Feminist Perspective in the Academy*, Chicago and London: University of Chicago Press.

Latane, B. and J. M. Darley (1968), 'Group inhibition of bystander intervention in emergencies', *Journal of Personality and Social Psychology* 10: 215–21.

Le Bras, G. (1956), 'Sociologie religieuse et science des religions', *Archives de Sociologie des Religions* 1.

Leach, E. R. (1954), *Political Systems of Highland Burma*, London: G. Bell; Cambridge, MA: Harvard University Press.

Leach, E. (1966), 'Sermons by a man on a ladder', *New York Review of Books*, 20 October, 28–31.

Lechner, P. L. (1990), 'Application of theory and research on cognitive schemata to the concept of God', *Dissertation Abstracts International* 50(11): 5298–9.

Lévy-Bruhl, L. (1926), *How Natives Think*, New York: Alfred A. Knopf.

Lienhardt, G. (1961), *Divinity and Experience*, Oxford: Clarendon Press.

Lipson, M. Y. (1983), 'The influence of religious affiliation on children's memory for text information', *Reading Research Quarterly* 18: 448–57.

Lord, C. G., L. Ross and M. R. Lepper (1979), 'Biased assimilation and attitude polarization', *Journal of Personality and Social Psychology* 37: 2098–2109.

Lorenz, K. (1952), *King Solomon's Ring*, London: Methuen.

Lowie, R. H. (1924), *Primitive Religion*, New York: Boni & Liveright.

Luckmann, T. (1967), *The Invisible Religion*, New York: Macmillan.

Lukes, S. (1973), *Emile Durkheim*, London: Allen Lane, The Penguin Press.

Lynn, M. L. and R. N. Williams (1990), 'Belief-bias and labor unions', *Journal of Organizational Behavior* 11: 335–43.

Machalek, R. and M. Martin (1976), '"Invisible" religions', *Journal for the Scientific Study of Religion* 15: 311–21.

MacIntyre, A. (1957), 'The logical status of religious belief', in A. MacIntyre (ed.), *Metaphysical Beliefs*, London: SCM Press, pp. 167–211.

MacIntyre, A. (1967), *Secularization and Moral Change*, London: Oxford University Press.

Malalgoda, K. (1976), *Buddhism in Sinhalese Society 1750–1900*, Berkeley: University of California Press.

Malinowski, B. (1948), *Magic, Science and Religion*, Boston: Beacon Press.

Mandler, J. M. and G. Mandler (1974), 'Good guys versus bad guys', *Journal of Humanistic Psychology* 14: 63–78.

Markus, H. (1977), 'Self-schemata and processing information about the self', *Journal of Personality and Social Psychology* 35: 63–78.

Markus, H., J. Smith and R. L. Moreland (1985), 'Role of the self-concept in the perception of others', *Journal of Personality and Social Psychology* 49: 1494–1512.

Marshak, A. (1976), 'Implications of the paleolithic symbolic evidence for the origin of language', *American Scientist* 64: 136–45.

Marshall, G. (1980), *Presbyteries and Profits*, Oxford: Clarendon Press.

Martin, D. (1969), *The Religious and the Secular*, London: Routledge & Kegan Paul.

Martin, D. (1978), *The Dilemmas of Contemporary Religion*, Oxford: Blackwell.

Maslow, A. H. (1943), 'The authoritarian character structure', *Journal of Social Psychology* 18: 401–11.

Maslow, A. H. (1957), 'Two kinds of cognition and their integration', *General Semantics Bulletin* 20–1: 17–22.

Maslow, A. H. (1962), 'Notes on being-psychology', *Journal of Humanistic Psychology* 2: 47–71.

Maslow, A. H. (1963), 'Fusions of facts and values', *American Journal of Psychoanalysis* 23: 117–31.

Maslow, A. H. (1965), *Eupsychian Management*, Homewood, IL: Irwin-Dorsey.

Maslow, A. H. (1970), *Motivation and Personality* (2nd edn), New York: Harper & Row.

Masters, K. S. (1991), 'Of boons, banes, babies and bath water', *Journal for the Scientific Study of Religion* 30: 312–17.

McIntosh, D. N., R. C. Silver and C. B. Wortman (1989), 'Parental religious change in response to their child's death', paper presented at the meeting of the Society for the Scientific Study of Religion, Salt Lake City, October.

McIntosh, D. N., R. C. Silver and C. B. Wortman (1993), 'Religion's role in adjustment to a negative life event', *Journal of Personality and Social Psychology* 65: 812–21.

Meadow, M. J and R. D. Kahoe (1984), *Psychology of Religion*, New York: Harper & Row.

Merton, R. K. (1970), *Science, Technology and Society in the 17th Century*, New York: Fettig.

Minksy, M. (1975), 'A framework for representing knowledge', in P. H. Winston (ed.), *The Psychology of Computer Vision*, New York: McGraw Hill, pp. 211–77.

Moore, H. (1989), *Feminism and Anthropology*, Cambridge: Polity Press.

Nadel, S. F. (1957), 'Malinowski on magic and religion', in R. Firth (ed.), *Man and Culture*, London: Routledge & Kegan Paul, pp. 189–208.

Needham, R. (1975), 'Polythetic classification: convergence and consequences', *Man* 10(3): 349–69.

Neisser, U. (1976), *Cognition and Reality*, San Francisco: Freeman.

Nicholas, C. W. and S. Paranavitana (1961), *A Concise History of Ceylon*, Colombo: Ceylon University Press.

Otto, R. (1923), *The Idea of the Holy*, New York: Oxford University Press.

Palmer, C. E. and D. N. Noble (1986), 'Premature death', *Social Casework* 67: 332–9.

Pargament, K. I. and D. V. DeRosa (1985), 'What was that sermon about?', *Journal for the Scientific Study of Religion* 24: 119–236.

Parkes, C. M. (1975), 'What becomes of redundant world models?', *British Journal of Medical Psychology* 48: 131–7.

Parsons, T. (1957), 'Motivation of religious belief and behavior', in J. M. Yinger (ed.), *Religion, Society and the Individual*, New York: Macmillan, pp. 380–5.

Parsons, T. (1960), *Structure and Process in Modern Society*, New York: Free Press.

Parsons, T. (1964), 'Evolutionary universals in society', *American Journal of Sociology* 29: 339–57.

Parsons, T. and E. A. Shils (1951), *Toward a General Theory of Action*, Cambridge, MA: Harvard University Press.

Percy, W. (1958), 'Symbol, consciousness and intersubjectivity', *Journal of Philosophy* 15: 631–41.

Percy, W. (1961), 'The symbolic structure of interpersonal process', *Psychiatry* 24: 39–52.

Phadnis, U. (1976), *Religion and Politics in Sri Lanka*, London: C. Hurst.

Pike, K. (1999), 'Etic and emic standpoints for the description of behaviour', in R. McCutcheon (ed.), *The Insider/Outsider Problem in the Study of Religion*, London: Cassell.

Plaskow, J. (1993), 'We are also your sisters', *Women's Studies Quarterly*, 21(1–2): 9–21.

Polanyi, M. (1958), *Personal Knowledge*, Chicago: University of Chicago Press.

Poole, F. J. P. (1986), 'Metaphors and maps', *Journal of the American Academy of Religion* 54(3): 411–57.

Popper, K. R. (1959), *The Logic of Scientific Discovery*, New York: Basic Books.

Poulat, E. (1986), 'Genèse', in M. Guillaume (ed.), *L'État des sciences sociales en France*, Paris: La Découverte.

Poulat, E. (1987), *Liberté, laïcité*, Paris: Cerf/Cujas.

Poulat, E. (1990), 'La CISR de la fondation à la mutation', *Social Compass* 37(1).

Powell, M. C. and R. H. Fazio (1984), 'Attitude accessibility as a function of repeated attitudinal expression', *Personality and Social Psychology Bulletin* 10: 139–48.

Primavesi, A. (1991), *From Apocalypse to Genesis*, Tunbridge Wells: Burns & Oates.

Pruyser, P. W. (1968), *A Dynamic Psychology of Religion*, New York: Harper & Row.

Pünjer, G. (ed.) (1879), *Friedrich Schleiermachers Reden über die Religion: Mit Zugrundelegung des Textes der ersten Auflage besorgt von G. C. B. Pünjer*, Brunswick: Schwetschke.

Radin, P. (1957), *Primitive Religion*, New York: Mayflower & Vision Press.

Robinson, R. (1954), *Definition*, Oxford: Clarendon Press.

Rogers, C. (1961), *On Becoming a Person*, Boston: Houghton Mifflin.

Rokeach, M. (1960), *The Open and Closed Mind*, New York: Basic Books.

Rosch, E. (1978), 'Principles of categorization', in E. Rosch and B. B. Lloyd (eds), *Cognition and Categorization*, Hillsdale, NJ: Lawrence Erlbaum Associates, pp. 27–48.

Rothbaum, F., J. R. Weisz and S. S. Snyder (1982), 'Changing the world and changing the self', *Journal of Personality and Social Psychology* 42: 5–37.

Ruether, R. R. (1981), 'The feminist critique in religious studies', in E. Langland and W. Gove (eds) (1981), *A Feminist Perspective in the Academy*, Chicago and London: University of Chicago Press, pp. 52–66.

Ruether, R. R. (1987), 'Androcentrism', in M. Eliade (ed.), *The Encyclopedia of Religion*, New York: Macmillan; London: Collier Macmillan, vol. 1, pp. 272–6.

REFERENCES

Ruether, R. R. (1992), *Gaia and God*, San Francisco: HarperSanFrancisco.

Rumelhart, D. E. and A. Ortony (1977), 'The representation of knowledge in memory', in R. C. Anderson, R. J. Spiro and W. E. Montague (eds), *Schooling and the Acquisition of Knowledge*, Hillsdale, NJ: Lawrence Erlbaum Associates.

Russell, B. ([1935] 1999), *Religion and Science*, Oxford: Oxford University Press.

Russell, L. M., P. Kwok, A. M. Isasi-Díaz and K. G. Cannon (eds) (1988), *Inheriting Our Mothers' Gardens*, Philadelphia: Westminster Press.

Rychlak, J. (1977), *The Psychology of Rigorous Humanism*, New York: John Wiley.

Ryle, G. (1949), *The Concept of Mind*, London: Hutchinson; New York: Barnes & Noble.

Saiving, V. (1976), 'Androcentrism in religious studies', *Journal of Religion* 56.

Sanders, C. M. (1980), 'A comparison of adult bereavement in the death of a spouse, child, and parent', *Omega* 10: 303–19.

Schneider, W. and A. D. Fisk (1980), *Visual Search Improves with Detection Searches, Declines with Nondetection Searches*, Urbana IL: Human Attention Research Laboratory, University of Illinois.

Schneider, W. and R. M. Schiffrin (1977), 'Controlled and automatic human information processing 1: Detection, search, and attention', *Psychological Review* 84: 1–66.

Schutz, A. (1962), *Collected Papers, vol. 1: The Problem of Social Reality*, The Hague: Martinus Nijhoff.

Segal, R. A. (1989), *Religion and the Social Sciences*, Atlanta: Scholars Press.

Segal, R. A. (1994), 'Reductionism in the study of religion', in T. A. Idinopulos and E. A. Yonan (eds), *Religion and Reductionism*, Leiden: E. J. Brill.

Shaw, R. and C. Stewart (1994), 'Introduction', in C. Stewart and R. Shaw (eds), *Syncretism/Anti-syncretism*, London and New York: Routledge.

Sherrill, K. A. and D. B. Larson (1987), 'Recovery in adult burn patients', paper presented at the Southern Medical Association meeting, Section of Neurosurgery and Psychiatry, November.

Shiffrin, R. M. and S. T. Dumais (1981), 'The development of automatism', in J. R. Anderson (ed.), *Cognitive Skills and Their Acquisition*, Hillsdale, NJ: Lawrence Erlbaum Associates, pp. 111–40.

Showalter, E. (ed.) (1986), *The New Feminist Criticism*, London: Virago.

Silberer, H. (1909), 'Bericht über eine Methode, gewisse symbolische Halluzinations-Erscheinungen hervorzurufen und zu beobachten', *Jahrbuch für Psychoanalytische und Psychopathologische Forschung* 1.

Silver, R. L. and C. B. Wortman (1980), 'Coping with undesirable life events', in J. Garber and M. E. P. Seligman (eds), *Human Helplessness*, New York: Academic Press, pp. 279–340.

Silver, R. L., C. Boon and M. H. Stones (1983), 'Searching for meaning in misfortune', *Journal of Social Issues* 39: 81–102.

Sinclair, K. (1986), 'Women and religion', in M. I. Dudley and M. I. Edwards (eds), *The Cross-cultural Study of Women*, New York: Feminist Press, pp. 107–24.

Singer, M. (1955), 'The cultural pattern of Indian civilization', *Far Eastern Quarterly* 15: 23–36.

Singer, M. (1958), 'The great tradition in a metropolitan center: Madras', in M. Singer (ed.), *Traditional India*, Philadelphia: American Folklore Society, pp. 140–82.

Skorupski, J. (1976), *Symbol and theory*, Cambridge: Cambridge University Press.

Smith, J. Z. ([1980] 1982), 'Fences and neighbors', in *Imagining Religion*, Chicago: University of Chicago Press, pp. 1–18.

Smith, M. B. (1978), 'Perspectives on selfhood', *American Psychologist* 33: 1053–63.

Smith, W. R. (1894), *Lectures on the Religion of the Semites, 1st series: The Fundamental Institutions* (2nd edn), London: A. & C. Black.

Smith, E. W. and A. M. Dale (1920), *The Ila-speaking Peoples of Northern Rhodesia*, London: Macmillan.

Smith, E. E. and D. L. Medin (1981), *Categories and Concepts*, Cambridge, MA: Harvard University Press.

Sokal, R. R. and P. H. A. Sneath (1963), *Principles of Numerical Taxonomy*, San Francisco: W. H. Freeman.

Southwold, M. (1978a), 'Buddhism and the definition of a religion', *Man* 13: 362–79.

Southwold, M. (1978b), 'Definition and its problems in social anthropology', in E. Schwimmer (ed.), *The Yearbook of Symbolic Anthropology 1*, London: C. Hurst.

Spencer, S. J. and D. N. McIntosh (1990), 'Extremity and importance in attitude structure', paper presented at the meeting of the American Psychological Association, Boston, August.

Spender, D. (ed.) (1981), *Men's Studies Modified*, Oxford: Pergamon Press.

Spilka, B. (1977), 'Theory and empirical research in the psychology of religion', paper presented at the annual convention of the American Psychological Association, San Francisco, August.

Spilka, B. (1978), 'The current state of the psychology of religion', *Council on the Study of Religion Bulletin* 9: 96–99.

Spilka, B., R. W. Hood Jr and R. L Gorsuch (1985), *The Psychology of Religion*, Englewood Cliffs, NJ: Prentice Hall.

Spiro, M. E. (1966), 'Religion: problems of definition and explanation', in M. Banton (ed.), *Anthropological Approaches to the Study of Religion*, London: Tavistock; New York: Praeger, pp. 85–126.

Spiro, M. E. (1987a), 'Collective representations and mental representations in religious symbol systems', in B. Kilborne and L. L. Langness (eds), *Culture and Human Nature*, Chicago: University of Chicago Press, pp. 161–84.

Spiro, M. E. (1987b), 'Religion: problems of definition and explanation', in B. Kilborne and L. L. Langness (eds), *Culture and Human Nature*, Chicago: University of Chicago Press, pp. 187–222.

Stanner, W. E. H. (1967), 'Reflections on Durkheim and aboriginal religion', in M. Freedman (ed.), *Social Organization*, London: Frank Cass.

Stark, R. (1972), 'The economics of piety', in G. Thielbar and S. Feldman (eds), *Issues in Social Inequality*, Boston: Little, Brown.

Stark, R. and W. S. Bainbridge (1979), 'Of churches, sects, and cults', *Journal for the Scientific Study of Religion* 18: 117–31.

Stark, R. and W. S. Bainbridge (1985), *The Future of Religion*, Berkeley and Los Angeles: University of California Press.

Stark, R. and R. Finke (2000), *Acts of Faith*, Berkeley and Los Angeles: University of California Press.

Strathern, M. (1981), 'Culture in a netbag', *Man* 16.

Strathern, M. (1987), 'An awkward relationship', *Signs* 12, 276–92.

Strenski, I. (1994), 'Reduction without tears', in T. A. Idinopulos and E. A. Yonan (eds), *Religion and Reductionism*, Leiden: E. J. Brill.

Tambiah, S. J. (1976), *World Conqueror and World Renouncer*, Cambridge: Cambridge University Press.

Taylor, S. E. (1983), 'Adjustment to threatening events', *American Psychologist* 38: 1161–73.

Taylor, S. E. and J. Crocker (1981), 'Schematic bases of social processing', in E. T. Higgins, C. P. Herman and M. P. Zanna (eds), *Social Cognition*, Hillsdale, NJ: Lawrence Erlbaum Associates, vol. 1, pp. 89–134.

Taylor, S. E., J. Crocker and J. D'Agostino (1978), 'Schematic bases of social problem solving', *Personality and Social Psychology Bulletin* 4: 447–51.

Tesser, A. and D. R. Shaffer (1990), 'Attitudes and attitude change', *Annual Review of Psychology* 41: 479–523.

Thompson, S. C. (1991), 'The search for meaning following a stroke', *Basic and Applied Social Psychology* 12: 81–96.

REFERENCES

Thrower, J. (1992), *Marxism-Leninism as the Civil Religion of Soviet Society*, Lewiston, NY: Edwin Mellon Press.

Thrower, J. (1999), *Religion: The Classical Theories*, Edinburgh: Edinburgh University Press.

Tönnies, F. (1955), *Community and Association*, London: Routledge & Kegan Paul.

Touraine, A. (1974), *Pour la sociologie*, Paris: Seuil.

Tylor, E. B. (1924), *Primitive Culture* (7th edn), New York: Brentano's.

Ullman, C. (1982), 'Cognitive and emotional antecedents of religious conversion', *Journal of Personality and Social Psychology* 43: 183–92.

Van Leeuwen, M. S., H. M. Sterk and A. Knoppers (1993), *After Eden*, Grand Rapids, MI: Eerdmans.

Vidich, A. J. and Lyman, S. M. (1985), *American Sociology*, New Haven: Yale University Press.

Wallace, A. F. C. (1966), *Religion*, New York: Random House.

Wallis, R. (1979), *Salvation and Protest*, London: Frances Pinter.

Warmoth, A. (1965), 'A note on the peak experience as a personal myth', *Journal of Humanistic Psychology* 5: 18–21.

Warne, R. R. (1989), 'Toward a brave new paradigm', *Religious Studies and Theology* 9(2–3): 35–46.

Watanabe, S. (1969), *Knowing and Guessing*, New York: John Wiley.

Weber, M. (1948), *From Max Weber*, tr. and ed. H. H. Gerth and C. Wright Mills, London: Routledge & Kegan Paul.

Weber, M. (1963), *The Sociology of Religion*, tr. Ephraim Fischoff, Boston: Beacon Press.

Wilson, B. R. (1966), *Religion in Secular Society*, London: C. A. Watts.

Wilson, B. R. (1982), *Religion in Sociological Perspective*, Oxford: Oxford University Press.

Wittgenstein, L. (1958), *The Blue and Brown Books*, New York: Harper & Row.

Wood, W. (1982), 'Retrieval of attitude-relevant information from memory', *Journal of Personality and Social Psychology* 42: 798–810.

Wuthnow, R., K. Christiano and J. Kuzlowski (1980), 'Religion and bereavement', *Journal for the Scientific Study of Religion* 19: 408–22.

Yamane, D. (1997), 'Secularization on trial', *Journal for the Scientific Study of Religion* 37: 109–22.

Yankelovich, D., F. Skelly and A. White (1981), *The Mushiness Index*, New York: Yankelovich Chalcey Shulman.

Yinger, J. M. (1967), 'Pluralism, religion, and secularism', *Journal for the Scientific Study of Religion* 6: 17–28.

Yinger, J. M. (1970), *The Scientific Study of Religion*, New York: Macmillan.

Yinger, J. M. (1977), 'A comparative study of the substructures of religion', *Journal for the Scientific Study of Religion* 16: 67–86.

Young, K. K. (1987), 'Introduction', in A. Sharma (ed.), *Women in World Religions*, Albany: State University of New York Press, pp. 1–36.

SOURCES FOR BIOGRAPHIES

Ackerman, Robert (1987), *J. G. Frazer: His Life and Work*, Cambridge: Cambridge University Press.

Alpert, Harry (1961), *Emile Durkheim and His Sociology*, New York: Russell & Russell.

Bendix, Reinhard (1960), *Max Weber: An Intellectual Portrait*, London: Heinemann.

Blumenberg, Werner (1972), *Karl Marx*, London: New Left.

Brandt, Richard B. (1941), *The Philosophy of Schleiermacher: The Development of His Theory of Scientific and Religious Knowledge*, London: Harper.

Cazeneuve, Jean (1972), *Lucien Lévy-Bruhl*, Oxford: Blackwell.

Chaudhuri, Nirad C. (1974), *Scholar Extraordinary: The Life of Professor the Rt Hon. Friedrich Max Müller, P.C.*, London: Chatto and Windus.

Craig, Edward (ed.) (1998), *Routledge Encyclopaedia of Philosophy*, London: Routledge.

Downie, R. Angus (1970), *Frazer and 'The Golden Bough'*, London: Victor Gollancz.

Eidelberg, Ludwig (1968), 'Freud', in Ludwig Eidelberg (ed.), *Encyclopaedia of Psychoanalysis*, London: Collier Macmillan.

Eliade, Mircea (1990), *Autobiography, vol. 1: 1907–1937, Journey East, Journey West*, Chicago: University of Chicago Press.

Eliade, Mircea (1977), *No Souvenirs: Journal 1957–1969*, New York: Harper & Row.

Fenton, Steve (ed.) (1984), *Durkheim and Modern Sociology*, Cambridge: Cambridge University Press.

Firth, Raymond (1970), 'Malinowski as Scientist and as Man', in Raymond Firth (ed.), *Man and Culture: An Evaluation of the Work of Bronisław Malinowski*, London: Routledge & Kegan Paul.

Gerrish, Brian (1987), 'Friedrich Schleiermacher', in Mircea Eliade (ed.), *Encyclopaedia of Religion*, New York: Macmillan.

Harris, H. S. (1995), *Hegel: Phenomenology and System*, Indianapolis: Hackett.

Honderich, Ted (1995), *Oxford Companion to Philosophy*, Oxford: Oxford University Press.

Hutchins, Robert (ed.) (1952), *Hegel*, vol. 46 in *Great Books of the Western World*, Chicago: Encyclopaedia Britannica.

Inglis, Fred (2000), *Clifford Geertz: Culture, Custom and Ethics*, Cambridge: Polity Press.

Kasler, Dirk (1988), *Max Weber: An Introduction to His Life and Work*, Chicago: University of Chicago Press.

Kitagawa, Joseph and Long, Charles (1969), *Myths and Symbols: Studies in Honor of Mircea Eliade*, Chicago: University of Chicago Press.

Knowles, Dudley (2002), *Hegel and the Philosophy of Right*, London: Routledge.

Kamenka, Eugene (1970), *The Philosophy of Ludwig Feuerbach*, London: Routledge & Kegan Paul.

Kuper, Adam (1973), *Anthropologists and Anthropology: The British School 1922–1972*, London: Allen Lane.

Nordby, Vernon J. and Hall, Calvin S. (1974), *A Guide to Psychologists and Their Concepts*, San Francisco: W. H. Freeman.

Poggi, Gianfranco (2000), *Durkheim*, Oxford: Oxford University Press.

Rennie, Bryan S. (1996), *Reconstructing Eliade: Making Sense of Religion*, Albany: State University of New York Press.

Riviere, C. (1987), 'Lucien Lévy-Bruhl', in Mircea Eliade (ed.), *Encyclopaedia of Religion*, New York: Macmillan.

Schultz, D. (1981), *A History of Modern Psychology*, (3rd edn), New York: Academic Press.

Temple, R. (ed.) (1996), *The Illustrated Golden Bough*, London: Labyrinth.

Van den Bosch, Lourens (2002), *Friedrich Max Müller: A Life Devoted to the Humanities*, Boston: Brill.

Weber, Max (1963), *Max Weber: Selections from His Work*, New York: Thomas Crowell.

Young, Michael (2004), *Malinowski: Odyssey of an Anthropologist 1884–1920*, New Haven: Yale University Press.

Zangwill, O. L. (1987), 'Freud', in Richard L. Gregory (ed.), *Oxford Companion to the Mind*, Oxford: Oxford University Press.

COPYRIGHT ACKNOWLEDGEMENTS

INDEX